Also by Armond D. Budish

Avoiding the Medicaid Trap:
How to Beat the Catastrophic Costs
of Nursing-Home Care

GOLDEN OPPORTUNITIES

*Hundreds of
Money-making, Money-saving Gems
for Anyone over Fifty*

❖ ❖ ❖

AMY BUDISH
and ARMOND BUDISH

HENRY HOLT AND COMPANY ✦ NEW YORK

Henry Holt and Company, Inc.
Publishers since 1866
115 West 18th Street
New York, New York 10011

Henry Holt® is a registered trademark
of Henry Holt and Company, Inc.

Published in Canada by Fitzhenry & Whiteside Ltd.,
91 Granton Drive, Richmond Hill, Ontario L4B 2N5.

Library of Congress Cataloging-in-Publication Data
Budish, Amy.
Golden opportunities : hundreds of money-making, money-saving gems
for anyone over fifty / Amy Budish and Armond Budish. — 1st ed.
p.   cm.
1. Aged—United States—Finance, Personal.   2. Middle-aged
persons—United States—Finance, Personal.   3. Retirement income—
United States—Planning.   4. Social Security—United States.
I. Budish, Armond D.   II. Title.
HG181.B86   1993
332.024'01—dc20   92-30815
                                                                          CIP

ISBN 0-8050-1290-7

First Edition—1992

Designed by Victoria Hartman

Printed in the United States of America
All first editions are printed on acid-free paper. ∞

1 3 5 7 9 10 8 6 4 2

To our beloved grandparents and parents
who gave us a past worth remembering
and a present worth living for.
And to our children who give us hope
for an even better tomorrow.

✦

Contents

Acknowledgments

This book would not have been possible without the tremendous contributions of many individuals.

Four very special people spent a great deal of time and energy providing their expertise to make known the very best gems available. Susan H. Starr, consultant for The Wyatt Company, was of invaluable help with the Social Security chapters. Diane Archer, Executive Director of the Medicare Beneficiaries Defense Fund, and Mike Klug, Senior Program Specialist for the Medicare/Medicaid Assistance Program of the American Association of Retired Persons, both nationally recognized for their knowledge and experience with Medicare, patiently and carefully worked us through the Medicare maze. Gary A. Zwick, Director of Tax for the public accounting firm of Cohen and Company, deserves tremendous thanks for the hundreds of hours he devoted to writing, developing, and shaping the many glittering Retirement Plan gems in Chapter 6.

Thanks to James M. Brown, past president of the National Organization of Social Security Claimants Representatives and an expert in handling Social Security disability claims; Douglas C. Carlson, tax partner at Hahn Loeser & Parks; Ken Scholen, founder and director of the National Center for Home Equity Conversion and the nation's leading authority on reverse mortgages; and Ronald B. Abrams, director of legal publications and training for the National Veterans Legal Services Project and editor of *The Veterans Advocate;* all of these experts in their fields helped us discover the keys to open the treasure chest of gems presented in the following pages.

We also want to acknowledge a number of other professionals who graciously shared their perspectives with us: Susan Axelrod, Director, City of Cleveland Department of Aging; Kathleen Hogue and Elaine Molis at Mediform, Inc.; Sue Biagianti, Tony Thomas, and Lynn Wasserman of Jewish Family Service Association; Janine Weisfeld, M.S.S.A., geriatric social worker at Mt. Sinai Medical Center; Ned Grossman, president of Grossman and Associates; and Susan Strippy,

President, Hospitalization Assistance. And, not to be forgotten, Carl Jones, for providing the encouragement and strong java that kept Amy going through the seemingly endless drafts of this book.

There even were people within the Government who helped. To make sure they don't lose their jobs, we won't thank them by name—but you know who you are. You are public servants in the truest sense.

Finally, we would like to thank Melanie Handlovic, April Funke, and Joyce Gordon, who helped transform our scrawl into type. And a very special thanks to Susan Kreps, who somehow managed to do a thousand jobs at the same time!

Introduction

The "golden years." We Americans spend our lives working and saving for the day when we will finally get the freedom to really start enjoying life. At least that's the dream.

But millions of older Americans have discovered that the gold in their golden years is of the "fool's" variety. The retirement they lived and planned for will never come to pass because they don't have sufficient cash. Forget about all those nice extras; we're talking basics—money to buy food, shelter, and health care.

The pot of gold that is supposed to be waiting at the end of the rainbow does not have to be as fictional as a leprechaun. Most seniors actually are missing out on money that is legally available to them. The treasure is out there—you just need to know where to dig. In the pages that follow, we'll help you find your way.

Sadly, thanks to our friends in Washington (the keepers of the keys), millions of tax-paying older citizens have suffered financial pressures that could have been avoided. *You* do not have to join the unhappy ranks. We have committed an act of piracy—we have broken into the Fort Knox of Government benefits and uncovered the best legal strategies available to you for claiming your share of the gold from the Government's treasure chest.

We'll explain how you can "strike gold" in the Social Security, Medicare, and Medicaid programs; how you can s-t-r-e-t-c-h your income from company pensions, IRAs and other retirement programs, Supplemental Security Income, Civil Service, and Railroad Retirement; how you can find hidden cash in your home; and how you can beat the tax man. Our proven techniques will empower you to change "old" to "gold."

With this book we are handing you the treasure map, deciphered from a mine of unintelligible government rules and regulations. Read on to discover the resource-stretching gems that can add lustre to your golden years.

Here's a sampling of what you are about to dig up:

- Retiring at age 62, and even at age 60, rather than waiting until 65 or 70, can add tens of thousands of dollars to your bank account; pages 12–15.

- A carefully timed divorce can add hundreds of dollars to your monthly income, and can also put extra cash into the pockets of your spouse and children. Don't worry; you may remarry your ex-spouse after you cash in (if you want to); pages 22–26.
- The Government charges a top secret tax on Social Security benefits. By spreading out the terms of investments, or making tax-free investments, you can cut this secret tax and save many hundreds of dollars; pages 30–33.
- Working after you retire can cost you plenty—Uncle Sam takes as much as 50 cents of every dollar you earn! We'll tell you about the legal loopholes that will let you keep a *lot more* of your money; pages 36–39.
- Take stock of your income—by changing salary into dividends, you can reap big profits; pages 39–42.
- Uncle Sam provides you with a lucrative life insurance policy—and it's free for the asking; Chapter 2.
- If your spouse dies, you could retire with benefits as early as age 50—if you know how! Pages 63–64.
- Strategically timed shifts from Social Security retirement to survivor benefits, or from survivor to retirement benefits, can add hundreds of dollars to your monthly checks; pages 67–73.
- Back pain, arthritis, headaches, and any other health problems that prevent you from working may qualify you for lucrative disability benefits under Social Security. We'll give you the buried tips on how to cash in! Pages 82–101.
- You can work and receive disability paychecks at the same time, but you need to know the hidden rules; pages 102–106.
- If you are denied Social Security benefits, you *can fight city hall and win!* Our "gems" will help; pages 116–120.
- Knowing your "real birthday" can gain you one extra month of Medicare benefits—a surprise present from Uncle Sam! Page 140.
- The Government doesn't tell you when to apply for Medicare, yet any delay can be *very* costly. We'll tell the secrets on how to time your application so you don't get caught naked; pages 136–140, 176–182.
- Get retroactive Medicare coverage for bills already incurred; page 139.
- Medicare will pay for nursing home services and at-home care in many cases, but the Government doesn't want you to know about it; pages 146–173.
- The Government unfairly denies *many* valid Medicare claims. But you can overcome! Chapter 5.
- You can get an interest-free and tax-free loan from your pension plan or IRA! Pages 299–303.
- Have you been told your pension is locked up until you reach 59½? Wrong! We'll tell you how to get your money early, without any penalty! Pages 289–293.

- Have you been told you have to start withdrawing retirement funds when you reach 70½? Wrong again! We'll explain how to increase income by delaying withdrawals until age 72; page 297.
- Should you take your pension money in a lump sum or in monthly installments? Or should you roll it over into an IRA? We'll tell you which strategy is best; pages 270–277.
- Instead of taking a monthly pension for your and your spouse's lifetimes, save money by combining a pension with private life insurance! Pages 275–276.
- If you are 50 or older, does it make sense to contribute to a pension or IRA? You bet! And we'll tell you how to maximize the benefits available; pages 308–320.
- A little-known program, called COBRA (Consolidated Omnibus Budget Reconciliation Act of 1985), provides *invaluable* medical insurance protection when you retire or leave your job for any reason; see Chapter 7.
- Would you like to add $400, $900, even $1,100 to your monthly income for life? Of course you would. We'll tell you about three programs—SSI (Chapter 10), CED (387–389), and EIC (389–394)—which can do just that!
- The Government makes SSI eligibility look impossible to meet. But just shuffling your assets may help you qualify; pages 452–458.
- If you or your spouse have high medical bills, filing separate tax returns can cut your income tax bill; page 406.
- We'll map out the little-known tips to help you claim a parent as a dependent—and get a nice tax deduction; pages 354–360.
- Our special tax tips can cut thousands of dollars off the cost of selling your home; pages 361–377.
- You can double your one-time $125,000 home sale tax exclusion—Uncle Sam won't tell you how, but we will! Pages 369, 372–373.
- You can turn your home into a treasure house of money—without having to sell or move out. Reverse mortgages and sale-and-leaseback arrangements will let you cash in on the value of your home; Chapter 9.
- For those who like black humor, we have unburied the facts you need to make death pay off in reduced taxes; pages 382–387.
- If taxes make you sick, our list of medical deductions is a good prescription for the tax–payment blues; pages 395–397.
- Nursing-home costs continue to strip older Americans and their families of their life savings. The "gems" we've uncovered can help you escape the "Medicaid Trap"; Chapter 11.

This is just a small sampling of the "gems" we've extracted from Uncle Sam's gold mine. The hundreds of tips that follow can add many thousands of dollars to your retirement coffers.

Armond Budish's book, *Avoiding the Medicaid Trap: How to Beat the Catastrophic Costs of Nursing-Home Care,* blew the shroud of secrecy off the Medicaid program; we hope that this book will end the secrecy that has been preventing older Americans from cashing in on all the "golden opportunities" they so richly deserve.

Ready to get started? Good! The gold is waiting.

GOLDEN OPPORTUNITIES

See golden days, fruitful of golden deeds,
With joy and love triumphing.
—Milton,
Paradise Lost

◆ 1 ◆

Get Real Security from Social Security Retirement Benefits

Over the years, you've paid taxes—*lots* of taxes—to fund your retirement. And now it's finally time to collect! Social Security offers a pot of gold at retirement, there just for the asking. Unfortunately, older Americans miss out on a *lot of money* that is *rightfully theirs,* just because they don't understand their rights. Don't feel bad—most lawyers, accountants, and other so-called experts don't have the foggiest idea how Social Security works, either.

In this chapter we explain the secrets of the Social Security retirement program and we'll give you dozens of "gems" to fill your retirement treasure chest. Get all you're due—don't settle for less.

ELIGIBILITY

How do you know whether you qualify for retirement benefits? If your answer is yes to both of these following questions, you are eligible.

- Did you work in jobs that were covered by Social Security?
- Did you work long enough to earn the required number of work credits?

What Jobs Are Covered?

Your job was covered if the employer paid Social Security taxes, or if you were self-employed and you paid Social Security taxes. Most older Americans are covered. But you may not be able to cash in if you worked for:

- The federal government before 1984. (You are probably covered by Civil Service retirement, discussed in Chapter 12.)

1

- A nonprofit organization before 1984. (You may be covered by a private pension plan instead of Social Security; see Chapter 6.)
- A state or local government agency. Some belong to the Social Security program and some do not. (Check with the agency.)
- Clergy. The clergy generally will be eligible only if they elected to be covered.
- A railroad. (You are probably covered by the Railroad Retirement pension program, discussed in Chapter 13.)
- Yourself. Before 1951, self-employment was not covered by Social Security. (We hope you created your own retirement fund!)
- A household employer. For example, if you cleaned houses or mowed lawns for 20 years, but your employer never paid Social Security taxes, your employment won't be covered.

How Much Work Time Gets You Qualified?

If you are 63 or younger in 1992, you will need a total of 10 years of work—40 credits—in all jobs that were covered by Social Security. You generally get one credit for each quarter-year (three months) worked—four credits in a year.

If you are 64 or older in 1992, you can get Social Security with fewer than 10 years of covered work. Table 1.1 shows the number of credits you'll need.

TABLE 1.1

Number of Credits Required for Retirement

Year Born	Age in 1992	Quarters Needed*
1929 or later	63 (or younger)	40 (10 years)
1928	64	39 (9¾ years)
1927	65	38 (9½ years)
1926	66	37 (9¼ years)
1925	67	36 (9 years)
1924	68	35 (8¾ years)
1923	69	34 (8½ years)
1922	70	33 (8¼ years)
1921	71	32 (8 years)
1920	72	31 (7¾ years)
1919	73	30 (7½ years)
1918	74	29 (7¼ years)

*Quarters do not have to be consecutive.

How Do You Earn Credit?

To receive a credit, you must have earned a minimum amount of money on the job. Until 1978, Social Security gave you one credit for each quarter-year

(January–March, April–June, July–September, or October–December) that you earned $50 or more. That shouldn't have been too tough to reach—it's only about 77 cents per day! Even very low-paying jobs or part-time work probably earned you credits from Social Security.

Since 1978, the rules have made it even simpler to qualify. Instead of looking at your earnings in a quarter-year, Uncle Sam now gives credits based on earnings over the whole year. The amount of earnings needed for each credit is listed in Table 1.2.

TABLE 1.2

Earnings Needed for Each Credit

Year	Amount Needed per Credit*
1978	$250
1979	260
1980	290
1981	310
1982	340
1983	370
1984	390
1985	410
1986	440
1987	460
1988	470
1989	500
1990	520
1991	540
1992	570

*No more than four credits can be earned in a year.

Four credits is still the most you can earn in a year. Example 1 shows how this works.

EXAMPLE 1

In 1978 you earned $1,000 in January and February, and then you stopped working. Your reward: four credits ($1,000 ÷ $250 = four credits). It makes no difference whether you earned the money in 1 month or 12 months. But if you had earned $1,000 in January and February of 1977, you would have received only one credit because all your earnings were in one quarter-year.

❖ GEM: Get "Extra Credits"

Do you have enough credits to qualify for Social Security retirement payments? Most people don't give any thought to this question until they're ready to retire—and by then it may be too late. If you check your Social Security credits before retirement is at hand, you may be able to earn enough "extra credits" to cash in.

EXAMPLE 2

You are age 60 and no longer working. You would like to start taking Social Security retirement benefits in two years. You've got your Personal Earnings and Benefit Estimate Statement from Social Security, and you have a total of 32 credits. Unfortunately, you need 40 credits, so you don't have quite enough to get any retirement checks.

Since you checked early, rather than waiting until the last minute, you should be able to earn eight extra credits so that you can start taking retirement checks as planned. It won't take much to earn the extra credits—a part-time job, working a couple of days per week, should be more than enough.

Checking your earnings record early and, if necessary, getting enough extra credits to qualify for retirement benefits could easily add thousands of dollars to your annual income. The sooner you check your record, the more time you'll have to fill in any gaps—now is not too soon!

You can check your earnings by sending for your Personal Earnings and Benefit Estimate Statement from Social Security. We will talk more about this statement in the next few pages.

♦ ♦ ♦

GET YOUR "CREDIT RATING" FROM UNCLE SAM

Now that you qualify for benefits, the next question is: How much will you receive (either now or in the future)? The Government will tell you an amount, but if there's a mistake, your failure to catch it now could cost you thousands of dollars every year of your retirement life!

Your monthly Social Security retirement checks will be based on the number of years you worked and on the amounts you earned during those years. The longer you worked and the more you earned, the higher your checks will be. The exact amount is calculated based on a complicated formula—did you expect anything else from the Government?

Most people just take what Social Security gives them—no fuss, no questions asked. If the Government says you're supposed to get $400 a month, that must be correct, right? If you agree, then we've got some swampland in Florida to sell you! Of course Washington makes mistakes.

Couldn't Social Security's records reflect the wrong amounts of your earnings? What if the Government's computer has a glitch and makes an error in computation? The result could be *disastrous!* By checking your file at Social Security and *promptly* correcting any errors, you might save yourself a lot of money and heartaches.

Jeepes, Creepes, Get Your "PEBES"

Your first step to verifying your Social Security account is to obtain a Personal Earnings and Benefit Estimate Statement (PEBES) from the Social Security Administration. The PEBES will provide you with important information, including:

1. A year-by-year list of all your earnings covered by Social Security
2. Estimated retirement benefits at age 62, 65, and 70
3. Estimated life insurance and disability benefits

You can get your PEBES by filling out the PEBES request form, available at your local Social Security office or by calling (800) 772-1213. The form is easy to fill out. Make sure you spell your name exactly as it appears on your Social Security card. Return it to the Social Security Administration at the address on the form. Several weeks later, you'll get your PEBES.

Even if you're already receiving Social Security retirement checks, get your PEBES. It will show your annual earnings in jobs covered by Social Security, which is *crucial* information in determining whether you are getting the right amount.

Check Your Earnings Record

You *know* you worked in 1963 and 1964, but no earnings are shown on your PEBES for that year. And your earnings are listed at $10,000 for 1970, but your total wages were at least three times that amount. Take a close look—do the earnings listed for you on your PEBES match your actual income?

Believe it or not, there really could be a mistake. Since the calculation of your benefits is based on the earnings listed for you in Social Security's files, mistakes in the listed earnings will mean mistakes in the amount you are paid.

What could go wrong? Check the Social Security number on the PEBES—maybe you were sent the wrong one. Or maybe your employer failed to accurately report your wages. Or maybe you were self-employed and earnings weren't reported under the right Social Security number. Or maybe one year you changed jobs and something got lost in the shift. Or maybe your employer didn't take out FICA (Federal Insurance Contributions Act) taxes and you never noticed. Or maybe, just maybe, Social Security screwed up!

Here's a real-life example of what could happen: For many years, Sally ran her own business, always mindful to pay her Social Security taxes. Her accountant—we'll call him Jack—sent in tax returns for Sally under the wrong Social Security number, and her earnings were posted to the wrong account. When Sally retired, she received much less than she was entitled to, until the problem was finally caught and straightened out.

Mistakes are often made when an employee works two jobs or makes a job change. Many employers are ignorant of the tax laws. Your employer, knowing that you have a second job, may assume that you will pay the maximum FICA (Social Security) tax on the other job, and decide not to take any FICA tax out of your earnings. Or when you switch jobs, one employer may assume FICA taxes on your earnings were fully paid by the other employer, and so again he'll decide not to take out FICA. In either case, you may find—much later—that at least some of your earnings for that year weren't counted by Social Security. Why? Because Uncle Sam only gives you credit for earnings on which FICA was paid.

Correct the Mistakes—Get Credit Where Credit Is Due!

A mistake in your earnings record, no matter the reason, can be *very costly!* *Immediately* report it to Social Security. There are three reasons for the urgency.

First: You generally only get 3 years, 3 months, and 15 days from the date of the error to submit a correction. For example, if your earnings for 1989 were reported incorrectly, you have only until April 15, 1993 to notify the Government of the error. The time limit is not iron-clad; there are a number of exceptions. For example, if you can produce a W-2 form to show a mistake was made or that an employer failed to report some or all of your earnings, there is no legal limit on how far back you can go. But you'll always have a far easier time getting mistakes corrected within the legal time period.

❖ GEM: Report Your Employer If He's Not Taking Out FICA

If you are still working and your employer isn't taking out FICA, call the IRS immediately—call anonymously so your employer won't know who squealed. The IRS will then launch an investigation. If you are right, the IRS will collect the FICA tax from the business, and you'll get your proper Social Security credits—and you may wind up never actually having to pay the FICA tax yourself!

✦ ✦ ✦

Second: The longer you wait, the harder it will be to get proof of your earnings. *You* have the burden of showing Uncle Sam that a mistake was made on your PEBES and to establish the proper amount of your earnings.

The best evidence of your earnings is your pay stubs or a W-2, which should always be kept. *Never* throw out W-2s! A W-2 can be used to correct your PEBES, even if the employer is out of business. And there's no limitation period—a W-2 can be used to prove your correct earnings at any time.

If you don't have your old W-2 forms from 10 and 20 years ago, good luck in trying to track them down. Employers are required to retain these employee records only for three years. While some larger businesses, like Ford or GM, might keep records for a longer period of time, smaller businesses almost surely will not. Your employer may not even be in business anymore, and then the records of your earnings are probably long gone. After the employer's records are destroyed and the statute of limitations is up, you've usually got big problems.

Your federal income tax returns may help you prove the amount of your earnings—but retrieving the tax forms is no picnic, and sometimes may be impossible. For tax returns filed within the last six years, request Form 4506 from your local IRS office. Older returns themselves are not available, but information from your returns—including earnings—may be available by writing to the IRS.

Third: Social Security may take from six months to as much as a year to correct your records. The sooner you find and take steps to correct a mistake, the sooner you'll get the added money in your checks.

If you are still working, check your PEBES regularly—every two to three years is wise. As we've said, mistakes are harder to correct the longer you wait.

❖ GEM: Get the Tax Man to Pay You!

When you check your PEBES, you may find that too much FICA tax was taken out. In that case, you're in for an added benefit—Uncle Sam will refund the overpayment.

Here's what to look for: Your PEBES lists the earnings on which FICA tax was paid. Now turn to Table A in Appendix 1. Compare the amounts you earned to the maximum amounts subject to FICA tax each year, listed in Column B. Earnings over these maximums should not have been subject to Social Security tax.

Your PEBES shows the earnings on which FICA was actually paid. For any year that your PEBES shows earnings higher than the maximum, you've overpaid the tax. For example, if you had more than one job in a particular year, you might find that you actually paid FICA tax on more than the maximum earnings.

EXAMPLE 3

In 1990 you worked for one company and earned $30,000 during the first half of the year. Then you switched jobs and earned $30,000 for the second half of the year from another company. Both employers withheld FICA tax on all of your earnings, because one employer didn't know how much the other withheld. You ended up paying FICA tax on $60,000 of earnings—well over the $53,400 maximum. If you catch this mistake, you can get yourself a refund!

By checking your W-2 forms, you will see exactly how much FICA tax has been withheld. If you see that you paid FICA on too much of your earnings, claim a credit when you file your next federal income tax return. Contact a professional tax preparer for assistance. Don't miss out—this is money in your pocket!

◆ ◆ ◆

Figure Your Benefits

Even if your earnings record on the PEBES is accurate, you're not clear yet. Again, it's possible that there's been some mistake in the Government's calculation of your benefits. The Social Security Administration does a good job of computing benefits (a lot better than the IRS does in figuring taxes), but mistakes do occur—and you don't want to be the one who loses out. Do yourself a favor by checking your benefits against Table 1.3.

TABLE 1.3

Monthly Benefits If You Retire at Age 65

Your Earnings in 1991

Your Age in 1992	Who Gets Benefits	15,000	20,000	25,000	30,000	35,000	40,000	45,000	50,000	55,500 or over
65	You	615	745	875	975	1010	1037	1061	1081	1088
	Your spouse	308	373	438	488	505	519	531	541	544
60	You	611	739	868	974	1015	1049	1079	1106	1123
	Your spouse	306	370	434	487	508	525	540	553	562
55	You	613	742	872	982	1032	1074	1114	1149	1176
	Your spouse	307	371	436	491	516	537	557	575	588

Table 1.3 gives you an estimate of what your payments should be if you begin taking benefits at age 65. The full age 65 retirement benefit is called the Primary Insurance Amount (PIA).

The figures in Table 1.3 are only estimates. They assume you have worked steadily throughout your career and have received average pay increases. You can get a much more accurate estimate of your benefits by using the tables in Appendix 1.

❖ GEM: Get the Maximum with the Special Minimum

All right. You've obtained your PEBES, checked the calculation, and—to your horror—the amount of your benefits is unbearably low.

Social Security retirement benefits are supposed to provide an income safety net for older Americans. But for many people, especially those who worked during the 1950s and earlier and were paid very low amounts by today's standards, the standard retirement program falls short. Since retirement benefits are based on prior earnings, many senior citizens risk falling through holes in the safety net.

Uncle Sam has taken steps to remedy this serious problem. Extra cash may be available to you under the Special Minimum Benefits Rule! Under this rule, the Government uses a special formula to calculate benefits for people who worked at low-paying jobs (covered by Social Security) for many years. Use Appendix 2 to see whether you are entitled to Special Minimum Benefits. Don't miss out on this Golden Opportunity.

EXAMPLE 4

You started working as a secretary in 1945 and stayed at lower-paying jobs until 1975. From 1945 through 1950, you earned a total of $4,500. From 1951 through 1975, each year you earned from $900 to about $3,500 (amounts listed in Appendix 2, Table A). After 1975, you stopped working.

Now you're 65 and looking forward to starting your Social Security retirement benefits. But when you hear from Social Security, you're horrified to learn the amount comes to only $357/month.

That's where most people stop. But that's not where *you* should stop. Under the Special Minimum Benefits Rule, you should be entitled to $478/month—a full $121/month over your regular benefits!

✦　✦　✦

❖ GEM: Special Benefits for Our Oldest Elders

Even if you have *no* Social Security credits, you have one last chance to get a Social Security retirement paycheck. A special benefit generally is available, regardless of need, if you are either:

- A male, age 92 or older in 1992
- A female, age 94 or older in 1992

(Some credits will be necessary if you were born between 1896 and 1900.)

The benefit can come in handy: $173.60/month—$347.20/month if both spouses qualify.

WHAT'S THE BEST TIME TO RETIRE?

The question we hear most often is: "When should I start taking retirement benefits? Am I better off taking lower monthly benefits starting at age 62, or should I wait until I reach age 65, or maybe even age 70?" For most older Americans, early retirement offers a Golden Opportunity—waiting can be a costly mistake. Here's the *Golden Rule: Take the money and run!*

First, let's give you a little background. At age 65 you can retire with "full" benefits. If you wait past age 65, you get "boosted benefits"—a higher monthly retirement check. You can start taking monthly retirement checks as early as age 62, but the amounts will be *permanently reduced*—and the reduction can be stiff. Benefits starting at age 62 will amount to only 80 percent of the sums you'd get by waiting until age 65. Table 1.4 shows the reductions for early retirement.

TABLE 1.4

Early Retirement Reductions

You Retire at	You Receive This Percentage of the Full Amount Available at Age 65
62	80%
63	86.67%
64	93.33%
65	100%

The closer to age 65 you retire, the more you'll get from Social Security; the closer to 62, the less you'll get. Table 1.5 shows how to figure the amount of money you lose when retiring early.

TABLE 1.5

Use this formula to determine how much you'll lose by retiring early:

1. Count the number of months between the date you intend to start benefits and your 65th birthday. Let's say you want to begin receiving retirement benefits at age 63; this is 24 months early.

2. Multiply the number of months in number (1) by .5555 percent—that will give you the percentage by which your benefits will be reduced. If you take benefits 24 months early, your benefits will be reduced by 13.33 percent (24 × .5555%).

3. Multiply the percentage in number (2) by your full age 65 retirement benefit—that will give you the amount you will lose by taking early retirement benefits. If your benefits at 65 would be $800 a month, you would lose $107 (13.33% of $800) each month, or $1,284 per year, by choosing early retirement benefits at age 63.

Although early retirement is "punished" now, wait until you see what's coming. Your friends in Congress have extended the "normal retirement age" for citizens who are now 54 or younger. In the future, retirement at age 62 will cost even more of your full retirement benefit, as shown in Table 1.6.

TABLE 1.6

Penalty for Early Retirement in the Future

If You Were Born in	Normal Retirement Age Will Be	If You Retire at Age 62, You Will Receive This % of Full Benefits
1938	65/2 months	79.2%
1939	65/4 months	78.3%
1940	65/6 months	77.5%
1941	65/8 months	76.7%
1942	65/10 months	75.8%
1943–1954	66/0 months	75.0%
1955	66/2 months	74.2%
1956	66/4 months	73.3%
1957	66/6 months	72.5%
1958	66/8 months	71.7%
1959	66/10 months	70.8%
1960 and after	67/0 months	70.0%

You may also delay retirement past age 65, all the way to age 70. Each year you delay boosts your eventual retirement benefits. If you reached age 65 in 1992, your retirement benefits would get a 4.0 percent boost for every year past age 65 that you delay taking benefits. The delayed benefit boost is scheduled to go up, as Table 1.7 shows.

TABLE 1.7

Increases for Delayed Retirement

You Reach Age 65 in	For Every Year Past Age 65 You Delay, Your Retirement Benefit Increases by
Years prior to 1982	1.0%
1982–1989	3.0%
1990–1991	3.5%
1992–1993	4.0%
1994–1995	4.5%
1996–1997	5.0%
1998–1999	5.5%
2000–2001	6.0%
2002–2003	6.5%
2004–2005	7.0%
2006–2007	7.5%
2008 or later	8.0%

Let's summarize: your benefits are lowest at age 62 and highest at 70. If you start taking Social Security retirement checks before reaching 65, your payments will be reduced *forever*—they don't go up when you reach 65 or 70. Why, then, would we recommend starting your benefits as early as possible? Our recommendation makes perfect "cents"—by putting you dollars ahead.

❖ GEM: Take Early Retirement Money and Run

Let's say your full retirement paycheck at age 65 would be $800 a month; if you waited until age 70, you'd get $960 a month (20% higher). So why are we telling you to lock in retirement benefits of $640 a month at age 62—33.3 percent less than you'd get at age 70?

Looking at figures like these, it's not surprising so many older Americans fail to take advantage of the Golden Opportunity to cash in on early retirement. You can almost always do better by taking your money early. Examples 5 and 6 show why.

EXAMPLE 5

You decide to start your monthly $640 benefits at age 62, rather than waiting. Each month, you put the check into a mutual fund earning an average yield of 8 percent. By your 65th birthday, you've given yourself quite a present: an account worth $25,000.

At 65 you start pulling out the 8 percent yield—$167 each month. (Interest and dividend income do *not* reduce Social Security benefits.) Added to your $640 Social Security check, you're getting $807/month—$7 *more* than you'd be getting had you waited until 65 for your full benefits.

And don't forget, you've got $25,000 in cash that you didn't have before. That's the Golden Opportunity of taking early retirement; it's a gem that many older Americans miss.

When you get those ads in the mail telling you that you may have already won cash and prizes worth $25,000, don't you get excited? Well, get excited by early benefits because Uncle Sam has a valuable prize for you. Even if you invest the money in CDs or some other investment earning 6 percent, you still come out ahead taking the money early. At 65, you'd have a pot of $24,500. Add the $123/month in interest to your $640/month Social Security check and you have a total of $763/month—just under the $800/month if you had waited.

EXAMPLE 6

Take a look at how early retirement compares to late retirement at age 70.

Let's take the same facts as in Example 5. You start taking $640 checks at age 62, and deposit them in CDs (at 6%) until you reach age 70. At that time, your account has reached a whopping $76,000. If you withdraw the interest (at 6%), $380 per month, and add that to your $640/month benefits, your income will total $1,020—compare that to the $960 monthly benefit you would be entitled to receive by waiting to age 70. Early retirement has even *more* luster when compared to delayed retirement.

If you need (or want) to keep working past age 62, then starting retirement benefits at 62 won't be an option. (We'll explain why combining work and retirement doesn't pay off on pages 34–36.) But many older Americans are not working full time past age 62, yet they're holding off taking their retirement benefits because they know their benefits will go up over time. That's usually a bad idea.

Even if you don't *need* the money at 62, take it and put it into CDs, stocks, bonds, or some other safe investment. Better yet, use a tax-deferred retirement plan like an IRA (see pages 270–272). That requires some self-discipline. We suggest setting up an account whereby your retirement checks are deposited directly, so as to reduce any temptation to use the money early.

Taking the money early is important for another reason. Not only will it give you a cash bonus, but you'll be assured of getting something from all your years of paying Social Security taxes. Too many people, waiting until 65 or 70 to start their benefits, die and get *nothing*. Let's look back at Example 5: If you died at age 65, your family would get the $25,000 from your early retirement checks. If you had waited to collect full benefits, your entire Social Security benefits would be lost (though a surviving spouse might get a slightly increased future benefit).

Aren't we ignoring the impact that added years of earnings will have on your retirement benefits? Don't higher earnings increase future benefits? The answers are yes and yes. We are ignoring the impact of earnings on future benefits—for a good reason: For people who have worked most of their lives, a few years of added earnings don't add much to retirement benefits.

EXAMPLE 7

You turned 62 in 1987. You worked throughout your adult life receiving average pay increases and your 1986 pay was $25,000. Your monthly benefit at age 65 would be $879 (including cost-of-living increases). Let's say you worked another three years, still receiving average pay increases. At age 65, your benefits would have "skyrocketed" to about $892/month—an increase of only $13/month. You can see that a few additional years of toil doesn't increase benefits much. And over the three years, you will have paid thousands of dollars extra in FICA taxes on your earnings.

Remember hearing your elected officials say that Social Security is like a private pension—the more you put in, the more you will take out? You should know by now that if the news comes from your elected officials, chances are you're not getting the whole story. As Example 7 demonstrates, your added benefits probably will not be enough to cover the additional taxes you pay into the system.

Now, this is not to say that you shouldn't work past age 62. If you need the earnings, or if you love your job, by all means continue. But don't be misled by your public officials: added work will not, in the long run, mean more retirement money in your pocket!

"ALL IN THE FAMILY" RETIREMENT BENEFITS

So far, we've been talking only about the worker's getting retirement benefits. But others may also be eligible, during the worker's lifetime, based on the worker's earnings. These lucky people include the worker's:

- Wife or husband who is 62 or older
- Wife or husband, under 62, if caring for a child under 16 or disabled
- Divorced spouse at least 62
- Unmarried children under 18 (19 if full-time elementary or high school student)
- Unmarried children 18 or over who were severely disabled before 22 and continue to be disabled (only children who have never married are eligible; once a disabled child has married, he or she is never again eligible)
- Stepchildren and grandchildren under certain conditions

Family members' benefits will be subject to the Maximum Family Benefit, discussed on page 25.

Spouse Retirement Benefits

Not only can you collect Social Security retirement benefits based on your own work record, but you can also cash in on your spouse's record. Spouse benefits are available if you can answer yes to all three of the following questions:

- Is your spouse collecting Social Security retirement or disability benefits?
- Are you at least 62, or are you caring for a child who is: (1) under 16 or disabled and (2) entitled to benefits on your spouse's record?
- Have you and your spouse: (1) been married to each other for at least a year, or (2) had a child together?

Spouse retirement benefits can provide a healthy boost for your income. At age 65, you can get half of your spouse's full age 65 retirement benefit (PIA). If you (the spouse of the worker) retire earlier, your spouse retirement benefits will be reduced. If you qualify because you are caring for a young or disabled child, you will be entitled to 50 percent of your spouse's PIA, regardless of your age. Spouse retirement benefits are listed in Table 1.8. If you retire early and start getting reduced spouse benefits, they will stay reduced for life—you don't get a raise when you reach 65.

TABLE 1.8

Spouse Retirement Benefit

If You Retire at Age	Your Benefits Will Be This Percent* of Your Spouse's Full Age 65 Retirement Benefit
62	37.5
63	41.7
64	45.8
65	50.0
Any age, caring for a child who is under 16 or disabled	50.0

*Your spouse retirement benefits are reduced .694 percent for each month before age 65 you retire.

EXAMPLE 8

Your husband just turned 62 and has retired. You are 53 and your daughter, still living with you, is 15.

You, too, are eligible for benefits—not based on your age, but because of your daughter's age. Since she is only 15, you get 50 percent of your husband's full age 65 retirement benefit for one year (assuming you and your spouse have been married at least a year, or your spouse is a parent of the child).

Once your daughter reaches 16, your benefits end. But you can pick them up again when you reach 62—without any reduction for the amount you already received. At 62 you'd get 37.5 percent of your husband's full age 65 retirement benefit.

When Is the Best Time to Retire If Eligible for Spouse Retirement Benefits?

You may have three options for Social Security retirement benefits: They may be based on your spouse's work record only; your work record only; or both work records. Each option presents different issues. We've already talked about the best time to start taking benefits based on your own record alone (see pages 12–15). Now we'll take each of the other two situations.

1. *You're eligible for spouse benefits only.* Let's start by looking at a situation in which you don't qualify for Social Security retirement benefits based on your own work record, but you can get spouse retirement benefits. This is the situation many older women, in particular, find themselves in today. When should you start taking benefits?

❖ GEM: Both Spouses Should Take the Money Early and Run

If you are married, both you and your spouse should take the money and run as soon as possible. Examples 9, 10, and 11 show how you will be better off:

EXAMPLE 9

You and your husband are both 62. Your husband's full retirement benefit at 65 would be $800/month; you don't have any retirement benefits based on your own record. If both of you had waited to take your benefits until age 65, your husband would have received $800/month and you would have received $400/month (50% of his benefit), for a total of $1,200/month.

But you both started taking benefits at age 62: your husband receives $640/month (80% of $800) and you get $300/month (37.5% of $800), for a total of $940/month. You put the $940 monthly benefits into an investment paying 6%, and in three years the investment account has grown to more than $36,000. At age 65, you and your spouse begin taking the income (6%), which is $180 each month. Added to your continuing benefits, you'd receive $1,120, just slightly below the $1,200 you would have received if you both had waited to age 65.

But now you've got a bank account with more than $36,000! You are *way ahead* by taking the money early. Plus, if you or your spouse died, you'd have a pot of money that would *not* be there had you waited to collect full benefits. If you can earn 8 percent in your investment, you'll be even better off—your total monthly income would increase to $1,180.

EXAMPLE 10

Your husband is 62 and you are 59. Your husband starts taking benefits immediately, so he gets $640/month (80% of $800, which would be his full benefits at age 65). You get nothing because you're not yet 62. When your husband hits 65, you will have $24,500 extra (assuming 6% interest) sitting in the bank, accumulated from his benefits. The interest, $123 a month, added to his continuing $640 benefit, yields $763/month. You now become eligible for $300/month (37.5% of your husband's $800 benefit), for a total income of $1,063 month.

Compare that to what your husband would have received if he had delayed taking any of Uncle Sam's money until he reached 65. At that time, he would get $800 and you would get $300 each month—only $37 more. But without taking your benefits early, there would be $24,500 *less* sitting in a bank account with your names on it!

EXAMPLE 11

In 1986, your husband was 62 and you were 54. He took early benefits of $640/month at age 62, which he saved; when he reaches age 70 in 1994, he'll have a whopping $76,000 in the bank (at 6% interest). The monthly interest that will throw off, at 6 percent, is $380. Added to his $640 continuing benefits and your $300 benefits (37.5% of your husband's $800 age 65 benefit), your total combined income will be $1,320/month.

Now compare that to your income if your husband delays benefits until 70. His monthly benefit will be $920, and your benefit will be $300—total $1,220. That's $100/month *less* than you have by starting early, and you won't have that nice pot of gold worth $76,000 waiting for a rainy day.

2. *You're eligible for both spouse benefits and your own benefits.* What happens when you are eligible both for spouse retirement benefits (based on your spouse's work record) and your own retirement benefits (based on your work record)? Do you:

- Add the benefits together?
- Choose the higher?
- Apply some complicated formula that only public officials could create?

Remember, we're dealing with the federal government here—the same government that created the Income Tax Code. So, obviously, the answer is 3. Generally you get no choice when you are eligible for both; Social Security applies a complicated formula that takes into account both your spouse and your own retirement benefits. Appendix 3 explains how to calculate your benefit when you're eligible for both.

But there is a loophole that may open a Golden Opportunity to put added dough in your pocket. If you first become eligible for your own retirement benefits, and only later become eligible for spouse retirement benefits, you may choose either to: (1) start with your own retirement benefits and later switch to spouse benefits; (2) start with your own benefits and stay with them; or (3) forget your own benefits and wait to start spouse benefits. What should you do? The choice is clear-cut.

❖ GEM: Start with Your Own Retirement Benefits, and Then Switch to Spouse Retirement Benefits ASAP!

When you qualify for your own retirement benefits, but you can't yet get spouse benefits, start taking your own benefits as early as possible. Remember the *Golden Rule:* When it comes to Social Security, take the money early and run.

Then when you become eligible for spouse benefits, switch ASAP. You can never lose that way. Examples 12, 13, and 14 show how this works.

EXAMPLE 12

You are 62 and your husband is 61; your full age 65 retirement benefit is $200 and his is $800. You are not yet eligible for spouse retirement benefits, since your husband has not retired. Remember, he must actually retire and be 62 or older before you can take spouse benefits. But you can—and should—start taking your own benefits of $160/month (80% of $200).

The following year, your husband retires at 62 and gets $640/month (80% of $800). You may now choose to switch to spouse benefits, which would be $327/month.

Clearly, you'd switch from your own retirement checks of $160/month to $327/month—that's easy. But if you had waited to start any benefits until your husband retired, you'd start at age 63 with spouse benefits of $333/month—higher than the $327/month you'll now get. Should you have waited? NO!

By taking your own retirement benefits at age 62 (which were the only benefits you could get at that time), you got 12 paychecks of $160 each. If you put those aside, you'd have $2000 in the bank in a year. Interest on that account at 6 percent would add another $10 each month to your spouse benefits of $327, for a total of $337. Had you delayed, your spouse benefit would have been almost the same—but you wouldn't have $2000 sitting in your bank account!

EXAMPLE 13

Let's say you are older than your husband—you're 62 and he's 59. Your full age 65 retirement benefit is $300 and his is $900. But you're not eligible for a spouse retirement benefit because your husband hasn't retired. So you take your own retirement benefit, which is $240/month (80% of $300). For the next three years, that's what you get. Since you put your checks in the bank, you have $9,200 (assuming 6% interest) by the time your husband hits 62 (and you are 65).

When your husband hits 62, he takes his retirement benefit, $720/month (80% of $900). And you immediately make the switch to your spouse benefit—$390/month. Add to that $46/month of interest from your $9,200 account, and that brings your total income to $436/month.

If you had waited to take any benefits until your spouse reached 62, you'd start receiving spouse retirement benefits of $450/month (50% of $900—almost the same as you're receiving anyway—but you'd have $9,200 less in your savings!

EXAMPLE 14

You and your husband are both turning 62 this year. Your full age 65 retirement benefit is $200 and his is $800. You reach that special age first and start taking your retirement benefits, based on your own work record, of $160/month; you can't start taking spouse retirement benefits yet because your husband hasn't retired. The next month, your spouse retires. You could—and *should*—immediately switch to spouse benefits, which would be $310/month (your husband's full retirement benefit is $800/month).

What if you wait to switch to spouse retirement benefits to when you reach age 65? Until then, you would continue to receive your own

$160/month retirement benefits. At 65, your spouse retirement benefits would be $360/month—$50/month *higher* than the $310/month you are receiving. Wouldn't you have been better off taking your own lower retirement amount and waiting to switch until 65? NO!

Don't forget—for the three years, from age 62 to 65, you will be getting $310/month, which is $150/month more than the $160/month benefits you otherwise would receive on your own. If you save those added funds until age 65, your bank account will be $5,700 fatter. That $5,700 would provide $29/month interest (at 6%) which, added to your continuing $310 spouse benefit, gives you total income of $339/month—and your bank account is $5,700 richer!

If you qualify for your own retirement benefits before you can get spouse benefits, *start with your own.* But then *switch to your spouse retirement benefit as early as possible.* Don't forget to *reapply* for spouse retirement benefits as soon as your spouse becomes eligible—Uncle Sam won't start them for you automatically, and waiting may prove very costly!

The only time switching from your own retirement benefits to spouse retirement benefits doesn't add cash to your pocketbook is when your own full age 65 retirement benefit is at least half of your spouse's full age 65 benefit. In that case, switching to spouse benefits won't increase your benefits. But because of the way benefits are calculated, you *never lose* by switching. See Example 15.

EXAMPLE 15

You are 62 and your wife is 59. Your full retirement benefit at 65 would be $400/month; hers would be $800/month. At age 62 you start taking your own checks of $320/month. You can't take spouse retirement benefits because your wife isn't yet eligible.

Three years later, your wife retires. Does switching to spouse retirement benefits add to your checks? The answer is no. But it doesn't hurt, either. Your spouse retirement benefit would be the same $320/month under the Government's formula.

You don't have to be a mathematician to figure out how to take Social Security retirement benefits. Here's the *Golden Rule:* If you first become eligible for your own retirement benefits, take them as soon as possible; then if you become eligible for spouse retirement benefits, switch at the first chance. You'll come out dollars ahead!

When Spouse Benefits End

Your spouse retirement benefits end when:

- Your spouse dies. (You may then qualify for survivor benefits—see pages 54–55.)
- You are divorced.
- Your child reaches 16 (if benefits were based on the child's age).
- You die.

While you can't do much about timing death or a child's growth, you might schedule your divorce to maximize benefits.

❖ GEM: "Split Decisions"—Time Divorce to Maximize Benefits

You don't get spouse retirement benefits for the entire month in which the divorce occurs. So if you are divorced on April 30, you lose spouse retirement benefits for the entire month of April (unless you qualify for divorced spouse benefits—see below). A one-day delay, to May 1, could save you several hundred dollars (probably enough to pay for about ten minutes of the divorce lawyer's time).

❖ ❖ ❖

Divorced Spouse Retirement Benefits

When you get divorced, your relationship with your ex-spouse is ended for almost all purposes. Thank heaven for that, right? But a divorce does *not* end your right to cash in on your ex-spouse's work record when you're ready to retire. Thank Uncle Sam for that! You can qualify for spouse retirement benefits based on your *ex*-spouse's work record if you can say yes to these four questions:

- Are you at least 62?
- Is your ex-spouse entitled to benefits (he's reached age 62 or is disabled)?
- Are you unmarried at the time you apply?
- Were you and your ex-spouse married for at least 10 years?

In fact, you may be much better off divorced than married when it comes to Social Security. If you were married, you could only get spouse retirement benefits if your spouse had retired and started taking his own benefits. But you can collect on your *ex-*spouse's record, *even if he has not actually retired,* as long as you meet the requirements listed above *and* the two of you have been divorced for at least two years.

If you qualify, you receive the same retirement benefits as you would if you had remained married (see pages 15–16). And here's more good news: you don't reduce your benefits by deducting your former spouse's current earnings (see pages 34–36 for the impact of a spouse's earnings on benefits). Although *his* benefits may be reduced by his earnings until he's 70, *your* ex-spouse retirement benefits will be figured as if he were *not* working.

Note: If you are remarried at the time you apply, you will not qualify for divorced spouse retirement benefits. But your ex-spouse's remarriage will have *no* effect on your right to collect.

❖ GEM: Getting a Divorce May Put Money in Your Pocket

While divorce is not something most people look forward to, it can sometimes provide a means of maximizing Social Security retirement benefits. If you are having trouble making ends meet, consider Examples 16 and 17:

EXAMPLE 16

You have remarried, and your new spouse, George, is working and earning a regular paycheck. You have no Social Security work record of your own, so even though you're 62, you get no benefits. And you can't qualify for divorced spouse benefits based on your first husband's (Harry's) work record since you've remarried. How about divorcing George? You might continue to live together and share your lives together. But by getting a divorce, you could fatten your pocketbook.

Let's say Harry's full age 65 retirement benefit is $1,000. By divorcing George, you would make yourself eligible for monthly divorced spouse retirement payments of $375 (37.5% of Harry's full benefits) based on Harry's work record. (You don't even have to wait two years before starting to collect ex-spouse benefits if Harry is retired and not working.)

You don't have to stay divorced long! As soon as you qualify for divorced spouse benefits, you can remarry George *and keep your ex-spouse retirement benefits* based on Harry's work record. You only have to be unmarried at the time you apply for ex-spouse retirement benefits— there's no rule against remarrying after you qualify for those benefits.

EXAMPLE 17

You and your husband are both 60, and he plans to work until he's at least 65. You never worked, so you will get no Social Security retirement on your own. And since your husband will continue working until he reaches age 65, you won't be able to get any spouse retirement benefits on his record until then. Divorcing him might be financially beneficial.

Two years after you divorce, you are both 62 and eligible for Social Security retirement benefits. You can now qualify for divorced spouse retirement benefits. Since your ex-husband's full age 65 retirement benefit is $1,100/month, your monthly ex-spouse benefit becomes $412.50—that's $412.50 *more* than you would receive without the divorce! Because you are divorced, your ex-husband's continued earnings don't reduce your benefits. Had you stayed married, you would have received flowers on your anniversary but nothing from Uncle Sam.

Don't get so excited by the idea of cashing in on your ex-spouse's record that you forget your own earnings record, however. If your own full retirement benefit is half (or more than half) of your ex-spouse's full retirement benefit, then you will be better off on your own record. (See page 21.)

❖ GEM: Delaying a Divorce May Also Add to Income

As we've explained, getting a divorce can add glitter to your golden years. But in some cases, delaying a divorce is wise. See Example 18.

EXAMPLE 18

You were remarried at age 50, after your first husband died. Almost 10 years later, things just weren't working and so you got divorced. Now you are 65 and looking to Social Security for benefits. Your ex-husband worked all his life and has a nice full age 65 retirement benefit of $1,000/month. Can you cash in and collect monthly divorced spouse retirement payments of $500?

The answer is no! You were only married a little over nine years to him, so you don't qualify. Instead, you're stuck with a much lower amount based on your own or your late husband's work record.

If you had delayed the divorce just a few more months, you could have qualified for divorced spouse retirement benefits. Because you didn't know the Social Security retirement rules, you lost out on thousands of dollars that could have been yours for the rest of your life. So, if you've made it through almost 10 years of marriage, try to stick it out just a little longer. Uncle Sam will reward your tenacity.

✦　✦　✦

Children's and Grandchildren's Benefits

Children of older Americans are rarely eligible for retirement benefits on a parent's work record, since eligibility requires a child (including an adopted child or stepchild) to be unmarried and either:

- Under age 18 (19 if still in high school)
- Any age if disabled before age 22 (and still disabled)

The same requirements apply to grandchildren, but they must also be dependent on the grandparents, and their parents must be deceased or disabled.

Each eligible child or grandchild is entitled to 50% of the parent's or grandparent's full retirement benefit while alive (75% after he/she dies).

Maximum Family Benefits (MFB)

Assorted family members may collect Social Security retirement benefits based on one worker's earnings record. These lucky folks are listed on page 15. The total amount of all retirement benefits *can* go beyond the worker's full age 65 retirement benefits, but there are limits. Family members collecting benefits based on a worker's benefits cannot exceed limits by the MFB. The only exception is a divorced spouse: his or her benefits are completely independent of the MFB, whether the worker is alive or dead. Table 1.9 shows the MFB limits, and Appendix 4 explains how the MFB is calculated.

TABLE 1.9

Limits on Family Benefits

Worker's Full Age 65 Retirement Benefit	MFB
$ 300	$ 450
400	600
500	756
600	1,028
700	1,300
800	1,453
900	1,587
1,000	1,750

The MFB is the most the family can receive based on the worker's earnings. The worker's retirement benefit is first subtracted from the MFB; it is not reduced. Then the remaining family members' benefits are reduced proportionately to bring total benefits down to the MFB limit.

❖ GEM: A Divorce May Be Good for the Family

We've already explained how the Government encourages divorces. Well, here we go again: MFB = Means Family Break-ups. Compare Examples 19 and 20.

EXAMPLE 19

Your full age 65 retirement benefit is $900/month. At 62, you start receiving checks of $720/month. Other members of your family can also cash in. Your wife is 52 and is caring for your disabled child, so they each are entitled to $450/month (50% of your full benefit). Total family benefits are $1,620/month ($720 + $450 + $450).

But your family can't collect $1,620/month. The Maximum Family Benefit is $1,587/month—see Table 1.9. Your wife and child together lose $33/month ($1,620 – $1,587).

EXAMPLE 20

Take the same facts as in Example 19, except you and your wife get divorced. You remain entitled to $720/month, and your ex-wife and child each remain entitled to $450/month. But now your ex-spouse's benefits *don't count* in the Maximum Family Benefit. The three of you can collect the full $1,620/month—a raise of $396 each and every year!

The politicians who write the Social Security laws are saying that, if you're smart, you'll divorce and live together. Staying married becomes a liability. Isn't that sad?

◆   ◆   ◆

THE GOVERNMENT'S SECRET
TAX ON SOCIAL SECURITY BENEFITS

What Uncle Sam giveth, he can taketh away. Since 1984, the Government has been taxing the Social Security retirement benefits of many older Americans. Why would the same Government that provides these benefits with one hand take them back with the other? Only your congressman knows for sure!

Benefits are taxed as income, supposedly at the standard income tax rates of 15 and 28 percent. But in fact, the tax on retirement benefits can secretly push your income tax rate well *above* the published brackets. Even though you may think you're in the 15 percent tax bracket, the hidden tax on Social Security benefits can push your actual tax rate *much higher.*

Let us tell you how the Secret Social Security tax trap works and, more important, how you can avoid a secret tax trap that unfairly burdens older Americans. The first step is to figure what portion of your Social Security retirement benefits will be taxed. Uncle Sam has decided that you have to pay tax on as much as half of your Social Security retirement benefits if your income exceeds the limits in Table 1.10.

TABLE 1.10

You Must Pay Tax on Social Security Benefits If Your Income* Goes Above:

- $25,000 if you are single
- $25,000 if you are married filing separate returns, and you did not live with your spouse at any time during the year
- $32,000 if you are married and file a joint return (you and your spouse must combine your incomes, even if your spouse didn't receive any benefits)
- $0 if you are married filing separate returns, and you lived with your spouse at any time during the year

*Income includes (1) half your annual Social Security benefits (before any deductions for Medicare Part B premiums), and (2) *all* your other income (including your pension, wages, dividends, interest—even tax-exempt interest, such as from mutual funds or bonds). From this, you can subtract the amount of any IRA deduction you are entitled to take and alimony you paid.

If your income is above the Social Security limits in Table 1.10, you can expect to pay tax on whichever is less:

- Half your Social Security retirement benefits (subtracting any repayment of overpaid benefits, but adding any workers' compensation benefits)
- Half the amount by which your income exceeds the applicable limit

Table 1.11 demonstrates how to calculate the taxable portion of your benefits.

TABLE 1.11

---

1. Your (and your spouse's, if applicable) annual Social Security benefits are $_____.

2. Half of line 1 is $_____.

3. Your (and your spouse's) additional income for the year, taxable and nontaxable, is $_____.

4. Adding lines 2 and 3 equals $_____.

5. The applicable limit from Table 1.10 is $_____.

6. Subtracting line 5 from line 4 equals $_____. (Do not enter less than $0.)

7. Half of line 6 equals $_____.

8. The lesser of lines 2 and 7 is $_____, your taxable benefits.

Example 21 shows how you use Table 1.11 to calculate the amount of benefits that are taxable.

EXAMPLE 21

You are widowed, and your Social Security benefits are $600/month ($7,200/year). You also receive a private pension of $400/month ($4,800/year). Your interest and dividends total $24,000/year.

1. Social Security benefits are *$7,200.*
2. Half of your benefits is *$3,600.*
3. Your additional income is *$28,800.*
4. Adding $3,600 and $28,800 equals *$32,400.*
5. The applicable limit from Table 1.10 is *$25,000.*
6. Subtracting $25,000 from $32,400 equals *$7,400.*
7. Half of $7,400 is *$3,700.*
8. The lesser of line 2 and 7 is *$3,600,* your taxable benefits.

Therefore, fully half of your Social Security retirement benefits are taxable.

How much does the taxation of benefits really cost you? Much too much! See the sinister effect of the secret tax trap by comparing Examples 22 and 23.

EXAMPLE 22

You are married (filing a joint return), and you and your spouse annually receive Social Security benefits of $10,000, pensions of $15,000, and interest and dividends of $16,000. First, figure how much of your Social Security benefits are taxable, using Table 1.11.

1. Social Security benefits are *$10,000.*
2. Half the benefits is *$5,000.*
3. Your and your spouse's additional income (pension, interest and dividends) is *$31,000.*
4. Adding lines 2 and 3 equals *$36,000.*
5. The applicable limit from Table 1.10 is *$32,000.*
6. Subtracting lines 5 from 4 equals *$4,000.*
7. Half of line 6 is *$2,000.*
8. The lesser of lines 2 and 7 is *$2,000.*

The taxable portion of your and your spouse's Social Security benefits is $2,000.

Now, let's calculate your income tax. First, take all taxable income together: $15,000 (pension), $16,000 (interest and dividends), and $2,000 (Social Security)—that equals $33,000. Then subtract the standard deduction, which we'll say is $7,400 ($6,000 basic deduction plus $700 for each of you since you're both 65 or older) and personal exemptions of $4,600 ($2,300 for each of you), which leaves you with net taxable income of $21,000 ($33,000 – $7,400 – $4,600). The tax you pay on $21,000 is $3,150.

EXAMPLE 23

Now we'll change Example 22 just slightly, adding $5,000 more in interest income. In the 15 percent bracket, you should expect to pay $750 in taxes on the added income. But because of the Government's secret tax trap, you'll pay a lot more.

Let's first calculate taxable benefits:

1. Social Security benefits are *$10,000.*
2. Half the benefits is *$5,000.*
3. Additional income is *$36,000.*
4. Adding lines 2 and 3 equals *$41,000.*
5. The applicable limit from Table 1.10 is *$32,000.*

6. Subtracting line 5 from line 4 equals *$9,000.*
7. Half of line 6 is *$4,500.*
8. The lesser of lines 2 and 7 is *$4,500.*

By adding $5,000 of interest, your Social Security taxable benefits increase by $2,500. Now let's recalculate the tax. Adding all your taxable income gives you $40,500 ($15,000 pension, $21,000 interest and dividends, and $4,500 Social Security). Subtracting the same deductions and exemptions leaves you net a total taxable income of $28,500 ($40,500 – $7,400 – $4,600). In other words, by increasing interest and income by $5,000, you add *$7,500* of taxable income. The tax you pay is $4,275, an increase of $1,125.

Okay, what's all this mean? It means you're paying a lot of tax on your income—more than the Government is telling you. Although at your income level you are supposedly in the 15 percent bracket, you *actually* pay 22½ percent on the additional $5,000 of income—7½% *more* than the highest published rate. The Government says you're paying 15 percent tax, *when the real tax is 50 percent higher!* Talk about taxation without truthful representation! That's the Secret Social Security tax trap that's hurting older Americans.

❖ GEM: Sidestep the Secret Tax Trap with Tax-free Investments

If you can avoid the hidden tax trap, you will save yourself money that can surely be put to better use than paying off the federal deficit. Tax-free investments such as municipal bonds may do the trick. See Example 24.

EXAMPLE 24

Let's change Example 23 a little. Instead of putting all your funds into taxable investments, suppose you put a portion into *tax-free* instruments. The $5,000 of added income that we included in Example 23 is now tax-free rather than taxable. Watch what happens:

Your taxable Social Security benefits remain exactly the same—$4,500. But your net total taxable income is reduced by the $5,000 of tax-free income. The tax you pay is $3,525—$750 *less* than the tax you paid in Example 23, when the $5,000 income was *taxable*.

Even tax-free investments don't completely avoid the Government's secret tax trap. In this example you still wind up paying about 7½ percent on the $5,000 investment income which is supposedly "tax free." But that's a lot better than paying 22½ percent on the same *taxable* income, right?

Tax-free investments often don't pay as much interest as do taxable investments, and you must examine the actual impact different investments will have on your bottom line. But tax-free investments, even with lower returns, may put more money in your pocket because you're avoiding the Government's secret tax trap, as Example 25 shows.

EXAMPLE 25

Let's go back to Example 23 once more. Remember, that's the situation where you made investments yielding $5,000 of *taxable* income. If the principal invested was $55,500, and the rate of return was 9 percent, that would yield $5,000 taxable income. In Example 23, your net after-tax income was $41,725 ($46,000 − $4,275 tax). Now take the same $55,000 and invest it in tax-free bonds, which yield $4,400—$560 *less* than the $5,000 from taxable investments. How can you be better off? Take a look:

First, figure your taxable Social Security benefits:

1. Social Security benefits are *$10,000.*
2. Half of line 1 is *$5,000.*
3. Additional income is *$35,440.*
4. Adding lines 2 and 3 equals *$40,440.*
5. The limit from Table 1.10 is *$32,000.*
6. Subtracting line 5 from line 4 equals *$8,440.*
7. Half of line 6 is *$4,220.*
8. The lesser of line 2 and 7 is *$4,220.*

Adding all your taxable income gives you $35,220 ($15,000 pension, $16,000 interest and dividends, and $4,220 Social Security); subtracting the same deductions and exemptions as in Example 23 gives you a net taxable income of $23,220. The tax on that amount is $3,483.

Your net after-tax income is $41,957 ($45,440 − $3,483). Although the tax-free investments earned you $560 *less,* you wind up with $232 *more* in your pocket ($41,957 − $41,725, which was your net after-tax income in Example 23). The extra benefit comes from beating the secret Social Security tax trap.

❖ GEM: Stagger or Defer Income to Avoid the Secret Social Security Tax Trap

Deferring or staggering your income is another way to cut the hidden tax on your Social Security retirement benefits. Compare Examples 26 and 27 to see how this can have a staggering effect on your income:

EXAMPLE 26

You are a widow, your annual Social Security retirement benefits are $8,500, and your pension pays $25,000 per year. In addition, you have 12-month Treasury Bills (or CDs or other investments) yielding $5,000 income per year.

Your taxable Social Security benefits, using Table 1.10, are $4,250:

1. Social Security is *$8,500.*
2. Half of line 1 is *$4,250.*
3. Additional income is *$30,000.*
4. Adding lines 2 and 3 equals *$34,250.*
5. The applicable limit is *$25,000.*
6. Subtracting line 5 from line 4 equals *$9,250.*
7. Half of line 6 equals *$4,625.*
8. The lesser of lines 2 and 7 is *$4,250.*

All taxable income is $34,250 ($25,000 pension, $5,000 interest, plus $4,250 taxable Social Security). Now subtract the standard deduction ($4,300) and the personal exemption ($2,300); this gives you a net taxable income of $27,650. The income tax to be paid on that amount is $4,954 (using the IRS tax tables).

EXAMPLE 27

Let's change Example 26 just a little. Instead of collecting $5,000 interest each year, suppose you collect $10,000 every other year. One way this can be done is by purchasing two-year Treasury Notes (instead of one-year Treasury Bills).

In the year the Treasury Notes come due, your taxable benefits remain at $4,250:

1. Social Security is *$8,500.*
2. Half of line 1 is *$4,250.*

    3. Additional income is *$35,000.*
    4. Adding lines 2 and 3 equals *$39,250.*
    5. The applicable limit is *$25,000.*
    6. Subtracting line 5 from line 4 equals *$14,250.*
    7. Half of line 6 equals *$7,125.*
    8. The lesser of lines 2 and 7 is *$4,250.*

Taxable income goes up to $39,250, less the same standard deduction and exemption. You end up with a net taxable income of $32,650. The income tax you pay on that amount is $6,354 (using IRS tax tables).

    In the off-year, when the notes don't come due, your taxable benefits drop to $2,125:

    1. Social Security is *$8,500.*
    2. Half of line 1 is *$4,250.*
    3. Additional income is *$25,000.*
    4. Adding lines 2 and 3 equals *$29,250.*
    5. The applicable limit is *$25,000.*
    6. Subtracting line 5 from line 4 equals *$4,250.*
    7. Half of line 6 equals *$2,125.*
    8. The lesser of lines 2 and 7 is *$2,125.*

Taxable income drops to $27,125, less the same deduction and exemption, for a net taxable income of $20,525. The tax on that amount is $3,079.

    So what have you accomplished? Had you gone along as you were in Example 26, the tax you would have paid over two years would have been $9,908 ($4,954 each year). But by deferring income as in Example 27, you pay tax of only $9,433 over the two years ($6,354 and $3,079). That's a tax savings of $475! And it cost you *nothing* (except the cost of this book). You receive the same total income (maybe even a little more by purchasing longer-term notes instead of one-year instruments), and you pay much less tax.

    As you can see, staggering or deferring income can reduce the secret Social Security tax bite. Example 27 showed one way to stagger or defer income, but there are many other ways to accomplish the same thing. Investing in EE bonds or single premium deferred annuities and stretching out withdrawals from IRAs are three other methods. Talk to your financial advisor about how to avoid the secret Social Security tax trap—you'll be putting more dollars into your own pocket!

WORKING TO SUPPLEMENT BENEFITS

You're 65 and you'd like to supplement your income from your Social Security, pension, and investments. Does it pay to work? For Uncle Sam, the answer is clearly yes. Uncle Sam may easily get more from your efforts than you do!

Triple Working Whammy

Our elected officials have put a triple whammy on working to supplement Social Security retirement: (1) they reduce your benefits; (2) they tax your benefits; and, to make sure they've gotten you, (3) they tax (twice) your supplemental income. This triple whammy, described in Table 1.12, can cost you 50 cents of every dollar you earn!

TABLE 1.12

Triple Working Whammy

Whammy One: Reduction in Benefits

You may earn up to $10,200 (in 1992) if you are between 65 and 69 years old, and still receive *all* your Social Security benefits; if you are 62 to 65, you may earn $7,440 without losing any benefits. But if you earn more than the allowed amounts, your Social Security benefits (your own retirement, spouse retirement or survivor benefits) will be reduced: $1 for every $3 over the limits, for workers 65–69; $1 for every $2 over the limits for workers under 65. For example, if you are 63 and earn $9,440, you'll lose $1,000 in benefits (because you earned $2,000 over the $7,440 limit). Once you reach age 70, you can earn any amount without losing benefits.

Whammy Two: Taxation of Benefits

Your added income may make your Social Security benefits taxable by boosting your income over the limits in Table 1.10. This penalty applies at any age—even after you reach age 70.

Whammy Three: Taxation of Income

You pay both income tax and Social Security (FICA) tax on your added income, as is true at any age.

❖ GEM: Watch Out for the Triple Working Whammy!

A job that pays $10 an hour may sound pretty good, but would you still be interested if you actually take home less than $5 an hour? Well, that's exactly the potential impact of the Triple Working Whammy. Before interrupting the serenity of retirement by getting a job, make sure you understand how much you'll actually be increasing your spending power. You may change your mind. Consider Example 28.

EXAMPLE 28

You and your spouse are 65. Together you receive $13,000 in Social Security benefits, $10,000 in pension benefits, and $15,000 in interest and dividends. Plugging into Table 1.11, you find that none of your Social Security benefits are taxable:

1. Social Security benefits are *$13,000.*
2. Half of line 1 is *$6,500.*
3. Your combined additional income is *$25,000.*
4. Adding lines 2 and 3 equals *$31,500.*
5. The applicable limit from Table 1.10 is *$32,000.*
6. Since total income in line 4 is less than the limit in line 5, no benefits are taxable.

Since no Social Security benefits are taxable, your taxable income is $25,000 (pension, interest, and dividends). Subtracting your deductions and exemptions of $12,000 gives you a net taxable income of $13,000. The income tax is $1,950, which is less than 8 percent of your taxable income and only 5 percent of your total income. Your real, spendable, after-tax income is $36,050.

Now $36,050 isn't bad, but you'd like to supplement that amount by working. You take a job paying about $2,000/month—not a fortune, but enough to make a difference. How much of that added money do you think you'll get to keep? Since the top tax bracket is 31 percent, you surely will get to keep at least 69 percent of your added income, right? Wrong!

First, let's figure the amount of your Social Security benefits that you get to keep. Say your job earnings are $25,200. That's $15,000 over the limit of $10,200 which you may earn and retain all your benefits. You lose $1 for every $3 earned over the limit, so $15,000 "excess" earnings will cost you $5,000 in benefits. That's Working Whammy No. 1.

Second, your taxable Social Security benefits are now $4,000:

1. Social Security benefits are *$8,000* (remember, your benefits are reduced owing to earnings).
2. Half of line 1 is *$4,000.*

3. Your combined additional income is *$50,200* (pension, interest, dividends, and wages).
4. Adding lines 2 and 3 equals *$54,200.*
5. The applicable limit from Table 1.10 is *$32,000.*
6. Subtracting line 5 from line 4 equals *$22,200.*
7. Half of line 6 equals *$11,100.*
8. The lesser of lines 2 and 7 is *$4,000.*

Your taxable Social Security benefits went from $0 to $4,000—that's Working Whammy No. 2.

Working Whammy No. 3 is the added income tax and Social Security tax on the earnings. First let's figure the income tax. Taxable income is $54,200 (including $4,000 of benefits). Assuming the same deductions and exemptions, net taxable income is $41,720. The income tax on that amount is $7,028. Social Security (FICA) tax is paid only on the earnings. The tax is 7.65 percent of $25,200, or $1,928. So total tax (income and Social Security) is $8,956.

Ready to see the combined effect of the Triple Working Whammy? Although you earned an additional $25,200, you paid an additional $7,006 in taxes, plus you lost $5,000 in Social Security benefits, leaving you with a gain of just $13,194. In other words, the effective "tax" on the added income was not 15 percent, or even 28 percent—*the tax was 48 percent!* Uncle Sam received almost as much of your additional earnings as you did (and we haven't even figured in state and local income taxes on the earnings yet). Not exactly what we call a work incentive!

Retirement-Year Loopholes to Minimize the Triple Working Whammy

We have already explained that, after you retire, annual earnings over the limits ($10,200 if 65–69; $7,440 if 62–65) will reduce your benefits. But two special rules apply *for the year in which you retire:*

- *Retirement year loophole 1:* Earnings during the part of the year before retirement do not count against you.
- *Retirement year loophole 2:* For each month after retirement that you do not earn ¹⁄₁₂ of the applicable limit ($850 a month if 65–69; $620 a month if 62–65), you will not lose any benefits.

The following examples show how these retirement year loopholes work.

EXAMPLE 29

Suppose during the first three months of 1992 you were still working. Your earnings were $6,400/month, for a total of $19,200. Starting in April, you retired (at 65) and started taking Social Security benefits of $700/month. For the year of 1992, you had earnings of $19,200 and Social Security benefits of $6,300.

Your $19,200 of earnings exceeded the $10,200 limit by $9,000. Under the normal retirement rules, you'd lose $3,000 of benefits ($1 for every $3 over the limit). But the retirement-year loophole—for your retirement year only—allows you to keep all your Social Security benefits, without any reduction. Earnings during the part of the year before you retired don't count against you.

EXAMPLE 30

Let's take the same facts as in Example 29, except that you continued working part time after you retired. For each month, April through December, you earned $700/month to supplement your benefits.

You still don't lose a penny of your retirement checks. For each month that you earned less than $850 (if 65–69), you receive all your Social Security retirement benefits too.

❖ GEM: Don't Lose Benefits Because of Income Earned Before Retirement but Received After

Earnings before retirement don't count against you in your retirement year, even if you don't receive the income until later.

EXAMPLE 31

Let's go back to Example 29. You are a gardener-landscaper, and you earned $19,200 during the first three months of 1992. Starting on April 1, you retired. As we all know, people don't pay their bills the moment they get them. So let's say $12,000 of the $19,200 didn't come in until the months *after* you retired. Does that money reduce your Social Security retirement benefits?

No! Not if you make sure the Government understands that the money was earned *before* you retired. That way, you get to keep all of your benefits.

❖ GEM: Shift Income to Take Advantage of the Retirement Year Loophole

In some jobs, particularly if you are self-employed, you may have the ability to control the timing of income. By moving income into the months before retirement, and by carefully shifting around income during the months after retirement, you can save yourself hundreds—maybe thousands—of dollars during your first retirement year. See Examples 32 and 33.

EXAMPLE 32

You have operated your own gardening business for many years. On March 31, when you turn 65, you plan to retire and start taking Social Security retirement benefits. You'll still continue to take some gardening jobs, but you'll be cutting way back.

Get as much of the income as you can *before* you officially retire. For example, if you've already got some jobs under way in March, bill in March; don't wait to bill until the job is done in May or June. Why?

The Government usually counts income as earnings in the month you receive it. Now, we did say that money earned before you retired, but received after, shouldn't reduce your retirement benefits. But if you're still working after retirement, it may be hard to prove how much of your income was actually earned before retirement. Reduce your headaches by shifting as much income into preretirement months as possible.

EXAMPLE 33

Let's continue with the facts of Example 32. After you retire on March 31, you are due to receive monthly Social Security retirement payments of $600. To supplement your income, and to keep busy, you continue to work your gardening business part time. Your income comes in at $900/month. Unfortunately, since that's over the earnings limit, your income each month will reduce your benefits. Depending on how much you earned from January through March before retirement, you might lose all $5,400 of your benefits ($600/month for nine months).

But let's say you can slide income around a little. Instead of getting $900 income every month, you take in $1,800 every other month. During the four or five months in which you received no income, your benefits are protected. In other words, by carefully shifting income during your retirement year, you are able to save $2,000 to $3,000 in benefits (four or five months at $600 a month)!

✦　✦　✦

70th Year Loophole to Minimize the Triple Working Whammy

Earnings after you reach age 70 will not reduce your Social Security retirement benefits. That opens up another Golden Opportunity to increase income.

❖ GEM: During Your 70th Year, Postpone Income

Example 32 shows how you can benefit by moving income up into the months before you retire. During the year you reach age 70, do the reverse—*postpone* income until after your birth date. That should allow you to avoid a reduction of benefits for the portion of the year before you reach 70. Have a happy 70th birthday—thanks to Uncle Sam!

✦　✦　✦

INVESTMENTS TO SUPPLEMENT BENEFITS

Uncle Sam must work part time on Wall Street because, while he discourages work after retirement by penalizing earnings with a triple whammy, he encourages investments by treating them more favorably. Investment returns, no matter how large, will *not* trigger Whammy No. 1, a reduction in Social Security benefits. Table 1.13 lists the do's and don'ts of income calculations. When you calculate your income to see if any of your Social Security retirement benefits must be reduced, make sure you include *only* income that counts.

❖ GEM: Change Salary into Dividends

Investment income avoids the reduction in Social Security benefits based on earnings from work. For older Americans who are self-employed, changing salary into dividends can be an "interesting" way to save money. Examples 34 and 35 show how.

TABLE 1.13

Income That Reduces Social Security Benefits

When calculating your income to decide whether any of your Social Security benefits will be reduced:

Do Count

- Salary and wages
- Earnings from self-employment (net of business costs)
- Bonuses and commissions

Do Not Count

- Interest from CDs, bank accounts, etc.
- Dividends
- Pensions
- Income from IRAs and other retirement funds
- Inheritance
- Payments from certain trust funds or annuities that are exempt from income tax, such as profit-sharing
- Capital gains
- Rental income
- Damages (other than back wages) awarded in a court judgment
- Contest winnings
- Tips under $20 a month or not paid in cash
- Sick pay, if received more than six months after you last worked
- Worker's and Unemployment Compensation benefits
- Reimbursements or allowances for travel or money expenses to the extent not counted as wages by the IRS
- Self-employment earnings from work performed before you retired

EXAMPLE 34

You own your own small business, which you have been running for a number of years. You've been drawing a decent salary for your efforts and pouring the rest of the profits back into the business. Now that you and your spouse have reached 65, you are ready to retire. Your daughter will continue to run the business, and she'll continue to pay you a $24,000-a-year salary. How do you come out?

Not very well! Assuming the same facts as in Example 28 (Social Security benefits of $13,000, and $50,200 in other income, including the $25,200 of income from the business), you are left with approximately half of the $25,200 salary thanks to the Triple Working Whammy. Uncle Sam gets the rest. But if you take the $25,200 as *dividends* on your ownership of the company, rather than as salary, you are far better off, as Example 35 shows.

EXAMPLE 35

You and your spouse's Social Security benefits are $13,000, and your additional income is $50,200 ($25,200 from the business and $25,000 other income). But *none* of the $25,200 is earnings, because you take the $25,200 from your business as dividends rather than wages and you get to keep $18,424 after taxes. Thus *you put $6,424 more in your pocket every year just by calling the business income "dividends" rather than "salary."*

Here's how it is figured: First, dividends "do not count" to reduce Social Security benefits (Table 1.13); you keep all your retirement benefits. Second, your taxable Social Security benefits, plugging into Table 1.11, are figured as follows:

1. Social Security benefits are *$13,000.*
2. Half of line 1 is *$6,500.*
3. Your combined additional income is *$50,200.*
4. Adding lines 2 and 3 equals *$56,700.*
5. The applicable limit from Table 1.10 is *$32,000.*
6. Subtracting line 5 from line 4 is *$24,700.*
7. Half of line 6 equals *$12,350.*
8. The lesser of lines 2 and 7 is *$6,500.*

Your taxable Social Security benefits are $6,500, making your total taxable income $56,700 ($50,200 plus $6,500 in benefits). Assuming the same deductions and exemptions, your net taxable income is $44,700 ($56,700 − $12,000). The income tax on that amount is $7,862.

Third, there is no Social Security (FICA) tax on dividends. So the total tax is $7,862.

Income tax on your net taxable income without considering the business income would have been $1,950 (see Example 28). So the tax resulting from the business income, considered as dividends, is $5,912. After taxes, you keep $18,088 of the $24,000 business dividends.

But make sure your business income really is dividends. Uncle Sam won't let you profit by playing name games. For instance, you can't continue to run a business (after you have supposedly "retired") and just call your earnings "dividends." The money you receive cannot be wages for work performed; you've got to really be retired, or your income is likely to be counted as earnings.

Now that doesn't mean you can never step foot in the business. You can stay involved a little, but you cannot perform "significant services" for the income. Just what are "significant services"? This depends on the particular situation. The Social Security Administration says that you are *not* performing "significant services" by:

- Hiring a manager to run the business
- Looking at the financial records to evaluate the company's performance
- Personally contacting an old and valued customer to maintain goodwill, as long as the contact has no more than minimal effect on the business
- Occasionally filling in for an employee in an emergency

Be careful! The Government has been known to watch a business to see if an individual has really retired. For example, in one actual case an older man owned a small grocery store. At 65, he retired, claiming the continuing payments from the business were dividends. But he continued to come in to work regularly. The government sent a spy to take a look, and discovered he was still operating the business. Although he called his income dividends, the Government called it a four-letter word—*wage*.

❖ GEM: Make Sure You Look Retired

Here are four don'ts to help show the Government you have actually retired from a business you own:

- Don't sign business checks
- Don't sign company correspondence
- Don't sign purchase orders
- Don't suddenly add your spouse or children to the payroll as senior management

IMPACT OF WORK ON EARLY RETIREMENT

Remember that we said you are usually better off financially starting retirement benefits at age 62, rather than waiting until age 65 or later? Even though you get reduced benefits for life, investments from the checks you receive from age 62 to 65 more than make up the difference (see pages 12–15).

But if you go back to work, you can end up in the worst possible situation. You then have locked yourself into lower Social Security benefits for life by taking early benefits, but because your earnings exceed the allowable amount they wipe out your benefit checks. The financial benefits of early retirement are wasted.

EXAMPLE 36

You retire at 62 and start taking your retirement benefits. But after several months you start to go crazy staying at home; even the daily soap operas can't hold your interest. You begin working again, part time at first, but soon the hours creep up and after a while you're earning too much to receive your reduced Social Security retirement benefits thanks to Working Whammy No. 1.

While you're happier working, the decision to take early benefits is costing you a lot of money. Is going back to the soaps your only option?

❖ GEM: Get Increased Benefits at Age 65!

If you go back to work after taking early retirement, and your earnings are reducing your benefits, make sure your benefits are increased when you reach 65—under the Retirement Earnings Break. Take a look at Example 37.

EXAMPLE 37

You retired at 62, expecting retirement benefits of $600/month. But you continued to work, earning $10,640 each year ($3,200 over the limit of $7,440). Since the government penalizes your continued toil by taking $1 of benefits for every $2 earned over the limit, you lose $1,600 of benefits every year. So this working retirement is becoming too costly. You are locked into lower lifetime benefits owing to early retirement, but your benefits are being slashed by your extra work. Then Uncle Sam cuts a bargain: the Retirement Earnings Break. Although early retirement generally locks you into lower benefits for life, you are entitled to have your early retirement benefits increased at age 65 if they were reduced owing to earnings.

Figure that the $1,600 of lost benefits is nearly equal to three of your monthly $600 Social Security retirement checks ($600 + $600 + $400 = $1,600). If you lost $1,600 in benefits each of the three years from age

62 to 65, you lost most of nine checks (three checks for each of three years). When you reach 65, the Retirement Earnings Break entitles you to have your retirement benefits recalculated as if you retired at age 62 *plus nine months* (you regain one month for each lost check). You are then entitled to a 5 percent increase in your monthly benefits—a $30 raise, up to $630/month—for the rest of your life!

Under the Retirement Earnings Break, the Government should *automatically* recalculate your benefits at age 65. But if it messes up, contact the Social Security Administration to make sure you don't lose out. Example 37 showed how you can have your benefits recalculated at age 65. Example 38 shows another way to accomplish the same result.

EXAMPLE 38

At age 62 you decide to retire and take your reduced $600 a month Social Security benefits. Then six months later, you change your mind and get a job that earns you $21,840 per year. The earnings from your job exceed the $7,440 limit by $14,400. Since you lose $1 benefit for every $2 of earnings, your benefits are entirely wiped out (you lose $7,200 of benefits per year, or $600/month).

You may withdraw your application for retirement benefits, even after you have already started receiving benefits, if you repay any benefits received and if all individuals whose entitlement to benefits would be nullified agree in writing to the withdrawal. (Remember, when you start receiving benefits, others such as your spouse may also become entitled to benefits.)

If you withdraw your application and repay your benefits (and all benefits paid to others on your work record are also repaid), you can reapply later. Uncle Sam gives you the "benefit of a doubt." At age 65 you then get full benefits for life, with no reduction even though you initially applied at age 62.

GOVERNMENT PENSION OFFSET PENALTY

Let's say you have worked hard and have earned yourself a nice little pension. That combined with Social Security retirement benefits to be paid to your spouse and to you should give you a secure retirement income, right?

Don't be too sure! If your pension is from work in federal, state, or local government, you might find your Social Security benefits cut or even eliminated! (Note: the Government Pension Offset applies only to *public* pensions; you retain private pensions and *all* of your Social Security benefits.)

We cannot overemphasize the importance of knowing how much retirement benefits you and your spouse will be eligible to receive. For example, if you are expecting Social Security and a pension to pay $2,000 per month, and you make plans based on that assumption, you could find yourself in big trouble if your benefits turn out to be only $1,500 monthly. Retired government employees can find themselves in this exact situation if they don't understand the Government Pension Offset.

For example, as the spouse of a retired worker, normally you are able to claim as much as one-half the benefits for which your spouse (or divorced spouse or late spouse) is eligible (or will be eligible). But if you worked for federal, state or local government, surprise. Your spouse benefits may be slashed.

EXAMPLE 39

Your spouse's monthly retirement benefits are $900; at age 65, you would normally be entitled to $450 (one half) monthly spouse benefits based on his earnings record. But if your pension pays $300 per month, your monthly spouse retirement benefits are cut to $250/month (a loss of $200/month) because Uncle Sam says you are entitled to receive only spouse retirement benefits that exceed two-thirds the amount of your pension. Two-thirds of your $300 pension is $200, and $450 exceeds $200 by $250, so that is the limit of your Social Security spouse retirement benefit. The Government Pension Offset Penalty costs you $200/month.

The Government Pension Offset is a mean-spirited rule that harms our public servants, but that's the law. Fortunately, there are a few exceptions to the Government Pension Offset which we've listed in Table 1.14.

❖ GEM: Government Pensions Won't Penalize Medicare Coverage

At age 65, you can get Medicare on your spouse's Social Security work record, even if your own Social Security benefits are reduced or eliminated by the Government Pension Offset.

✦ ✦ ✦

TABLE 1.14

Exceptions to the Government Pension Offset

Your Social Security spouse retirement benefits will *not* be reduced by your Government pension benefits if:

- Your government work was covered by Social Security on the last day of your employment. If your government job was not initially covered by Social Security but later became covered, then the Government Pension Offset will not apply to you.

- You applied for (and were entitled to) Social Security benefits before December 1977.

- You received or were eligible for (based on age and length of service requirements) a government pension at any time from December 1977 to December 1982. If you are male, you must also have been dependent on your wife for at least one-half of your support in the 12 months before she became entitled to Social Security benefits. If you are a divorced woman, your marriage must have lasted 20 years.

- You were entitled to Social Security benefits after November 1982, *and* you received or were eligible for a government pension before July 1, 1983, *and* you were receiving at least one-half support from your spouse (male or female) at the time he or she became entitled to benefits, became disabled or died.

- You are a federal employee who switched from Civil Service to Federal Employees' Retirement System (FERS) before January 1988. If you made the switch after that time, you will need five years of federal employment under FERS to be exempt from the Government Pension Offset.

So far, we've explained how the Government Pension Offset can affect your Social Security spouse retirement benefits. But even your *own* Social Security retirement benefits, based on your own work record, may be reduced by this rule. For instance, if you get a pension from the Government (or from private work *not* covered by Social Security), and you also have enough credits under the Social Security system to get Social Security retirement, your Social Security retirement benefits are reduced under a complicated formula, from 5 to as much as 55 percent!

But again there's hope. Your benefits will *not* be reduced if:

- You reached age 62 or became disabled before 1986.
- You first became eligible for a pension before 1986.
- You were a federal worker hired after December 31, 1983.
- You were employed on January 1, 1984, by a nonprofit organization that was not covered by Social Security before that time.
- You have 30 or more years of substantial earnings (as defined by law) under Social Security.

- Your only pension is from railroad work.
- Your only work not under Social Security was before 1957.

On page 5, we advised you to get your PEBES and figure your Social Security benefits when planning for retirement. But don't stop there. Contact Social Security and ask whether those amounts will be reduced owing to a pension. Otherwise, you may find out—when it's too late—that you're not getting the full amount you were expecting.

OVERPAYMENTS

Suppose you have been receiving Social Security benefits for a few years. As you check your mail one day, you are horrified to find a letter from Uncle Sam claiming you've been paid too much in Social Security benefits, and demanding that you immediately repay $15,000! What can you do? Immediately contact the local Social Security office and ask for an explanation. If there's been a mistake, tell them.

But what if there's been no mistake and you really were overpaid? You should be able to keep the money if you weren't at fault in getting the money, *and* if you can show that making you repay would either:

- Be against "equity and good conscience"
- "Defeat the purpose" of the Social Security program

Your Fault

You will be considered "at fault," and so will be required to repay the extra money, if you:

- Lied to or misled the Government
- Failed to provide information to the Government that you should have known would reduce your payments
- Accepted a payment from the Government that you *should have known* was not correct

Here are a few examples of when you should *not* be considered "at fault" for an overpayment:

1. You mistakenly reported only net take-home pay, rather than gross earnings, when figuring how much of your Social Security benefits would be reduced by earnings.
2. You received more earnings than expected, in excess of the earnings limit.

3. You underreported income because you didn't know that bonuses and vacation pay are earnings.
4. You simply didn't understand the rules despite making a good-faith effort to get complete information.
5. You relied on incorrect information from the Social Security Administration.
6. You told Social Security of an error, and they failed to recalculate benefits.
7. Your reading or educational level is extremely low.

❖ GEM: Keep Records of Calls to the Social Security Administration

When you have a question about the Social Security rules, call the Social Security Administration (800-772-1213) or stop in at your local office. Take notes of your conversation and keep them. Get the name of the Government employee whom you talk to. Write down the time you begin and end your conversation. And make notes of the Government's answers to your questions. If you do all this, and the Government gives you wrong information which results in an overpayment, you should be able to show you were not at fault—and that can help you keep the money.

◆ ◆ ◆

Repayment Would Be Against Equity and Good Conscience
You should not be made to repay an overpayment if you honestly believed that the money was yours and you:

- Relied on the overpayment and changed your position for the worse
- Gave up a valuable right in reliance on the benefits
- Were not living with the person who actually received the overpayment (and you didn't receive any of the money)

Your financial circumstances should *not* be considered when deciding whether repayment is against equity and good conscience. These tests apply whether you are rich or poor. Example 40 shows a situation in which repayment is not required since it would be against equity and good conscience:

EXAMPLE 40

Suppose you applied for early retirement and were approved. You quit your job and started receiving benefits. Two years later, the Government says, "Sorry, we were wrong. You didn't have enough work credits." And now they want their money back.

> Tell them to forget it. You gave up a valuable right—your job—in reliance on the Government's benefits. Just try to get another job now at your age! You should be able to keep the money.

Repayment Would Defeat the Purpose of the Law
Social Security is supposed to provide basic financial security for older Americans. If forcing you to repay overpayments will destroy that security, you shouldn't have to come up with the funds.

Your financial status will have an impact on this argument. If you can show that you need your current income to make ends meet, and you can't afford to use part of your income to repay the Government for an overpayment, you should be allowed to keep the money. The Government will want to see bills and receipts for expenses, including food and clothing, rent, mortgage payments, utilities, insurance, taxes, medical costs, and payments to support others.

❖ GEM: Keep Proof Positive— Don't Toss Bills and Receipts

The Government may claim an overpayment years after you started receiving benefits. As a general rule, keep bills and receipts for five years. These supporting papers can prove your point and save you lots of money in the future!

❖ GEM: Spread Out the Repayments

Even if you can't convince the Government to drop its claim to the money, at least try to spread the repayments over time. The law allows the Government to accept as little as $10 a month. If you have to repay, spread the burden!

◆   ◆   ◆

DO YOU APPLY FOR SOCIAL SECURITY RETIREMENT BENEFITS?

Yes! You can't collect if you don't apply. But applying for benefits is a little more involved than just signing your name on an application form. Here are our five steps to filing a successful application:

1. Figure Out What Benefits Are Best
You may have several benefit options: your own retirement benefits, spouse retirement benefits, survivor benefits (which we will discuss in the next chapter), and so on. You must first figure out which benefits to apply for.

2. Decide When to Apply

If you are retiring before age 65, apply *no later* than the last day of the month in which you want benefits to begin. For example, if you turn 62 on December 15, 1992, and would like to retire then, you should apply *no later* than December 31, 1992. If you file your initial application after that date, you'll lose out on benefits for the month of December. In general, benefits payable for any months before age 65 can begin no earlier than the month you apply.

If you apply for retirement benefits after age 65, the rules aren't quite so strict. Back payments can be made for as many as six months preceding the month you apply. So if you apply for retirement benefits on June 30, 1993 (and you are 65 or older), you may receive benefits dating back to the first of the year.

Even though the Government may go back six months to make payments for persons 65 or older, don't delay your application. Delays in applying can sometimes mean a loss of benefits. You can apply up to three months before you want benefits to start; the earlier you apply, the better.

3. Gather Necessary Information

Appendix 6 provides a checklist of information that will help speed your application to approval. The more of this information you can provide with your application, the easier and faster will be the Government's review. (Don't delay your application just because you don't yet have all the information listed in Appendix 6. Once you apply, the folks at Social Security will tell you about other evidence that can be used to support your application if these materials aren't available.)

4. File for Benefits

An application can be obtained at, and generally must be submitted to, your local Social Security office. Find the nearest office in the telephone white pages directory under U.S. Government, Social Security Administration.

Apply in writing. Don't rely on a telephone call. And above all, don't be discouraged just because someone in the Social Security office tells you not to apply since you don't qualify. The Government bureaucrat could be wrong (believe it or not), but you lose your right to appeal if you haven't applied in writing.

5. Keep Track of Your Documents

Don't send important documents through the mail. Take them to the Social Security office in person, if at all possible. That way, no one can say they got "lost in the mail." Keep copies for yourself, too.

Write your claim number on something attached to your original papers. With millions of pieces of paper to be processed, the local office sometimes loses or mixes up documents—providing your claim number will help avoid that problem.

GETTING APPROVAL

If your claim is approved, the Government will notify you in writing. You should hear within two months. And once you are approved, those wonderful checks will start coming.

❖ GEM: Have Checks Deposited Directly into a Bank Account

You can choose how to receive your benefits: through the mail to you or directly deposited into an account. Many people like the idea of actually seeing their check, but getting your checks through the mail can be a costly mistake. Instead, direct deposit almost always saves time. If your check is mailed to you, you don't start earning interest until you've deposited it. If you're too busy to get to the bank, or you become ill, the check may not be deposited right away—and the delay costs you.

And sometimes checks sent through the mail are lost or stolen. On a number of occasions, thieves have been caught robbing mailboxes of Social Security recipients. If that were to happen to you, expect headaches and delays in getting a substitute check. It may take another month before you see your money.

Stop in to your bank and ask about direct deposits. Someone there will explain how this can be arranged. (And while you're at it, why not also arrange for the bank to make direct payments for your standard, recurring bills, like gas and electric? Make your life a little easier!)

REPRESENTATIVE PAYEE

As people age, they sometimes decide to turn over management of their finances to someone else. The reasons vary; for some, they are tired of paying bills and reconciling bank statements; for others, illness or injury may require them to give up control.

You (or someone on your behalf) can ask Social Security to have a person appointed as a "representative payee." Your Social Security checks then go to the representative payee, and that person must use the funds for your benefit. For example, the representative payee can use your funds to pay bills for food, shelter, clothing, and other personal needs. Anything left over must be saved for you; the representative payee can't take the money for himself or herself.

The representative payee must keep track of where your money goes, and must account for all the funds by preparing and filing a Representative Payee Report (Form SSA-623) with the Social Security Administration. The form should be mailed automatically to the representative payee each year. For more information about representative payees, get the free brochure, "A Guide for Representative Payees," from your local Social Security office.

❖ GEM: Don't Let the Government Assign a Representative Payee If You Don't Need One

If the Government decides you need help handling your funds, it may assign a representative payee on its own. Once appointed, it is extremely tough to get rid of this person. Since a representative payee takes control of your Social Security income, object immediately if you don't think you need one.

APPEALS

The Government does a pretty good job reviewing and deciding on applications for Social Security retirement benefits, but it still makes mistakes. And that often means pursuing appeals. When it comes to correcting Uncle Sam's mistakes, perseverance pays!

If your application is denied, or if you disagree with the amount of benefits or some other Government decision, you can and *should* appeal. You get not one, not two, but *five* bites at the apple—your original application and four appeals. Many older Americans get the benefits rightfully due them only after going through one or more appeals. The appeals process is described in Chapter 3 because it is disability benefits that generate the most errors, the most appeals, and the most reversals of denials. But the process is the same for Social Security retirement and survivor benefits. Look to Chapter 3 for our gems on how to handle the appeals process.

HELP! WHERE CAN YOU GO FOR ASSISTANCE?

Surprise! Uncle Sam can be your ally.

Although we criticize the Government when necessary, we also gladly point to the positives. Social Security generally has very well trained personnel answering their hotline—(800)772-1213—and they are happy to try to answer your questions.

There are no ideal times to call. Try to wait until mid-week and mid-month. The first week of the month is usually busiest, as are Mondays and Tuesdays of each week. With respect to times of day to call, very early or very late are best. Try to get in first thing when the office opens or during the hour before closing.

The Government also puts out a number of useful, easy-to-read brochures and fact sheets covering Social Security retirement benefits. These include:

- *Understanding Social Security,* SSA Publication No. 05-10024.
- *Retirement,* SSA Publication No. 05-10035.
- *When You Get Social Security Retirement or Survivors Benefits . . . What You Need to Know,* SSA Publication No. 05-10077.
- *How Your Retirement Benefit Is Figured,* SSA Publication No. 05-10070.
- *The Appeals Process,* SSA Publication No. 05-10041.

You can also get help from senior centers, the AARP, and your local office on aging. Don't be shy; take advantage of all available assistance.

For most older Americans, Social Security retirement benefits are crucial to their secure retirement. Make sure you get all that you're entitled to receive. Don't miss out on any of the Golden Opportunities available from Uncle Sam.

·2·

Social Security Survivor Benefits:
A Security Blanket to Protect the Family

When you think of Social Security, you probably think of retirement benefits. But you may be surprised to learn that Social Security also provides family "life insurance" benefits to survivors. The Government calls these survivor benefits.

If your spouse, parent, or child has died, Uncle Sam may have money for you. By knowing your rights, you can make sure you receive the benefits you're entitled to, going a long way toward easing your financial burdens.

ELIGIBILITY

To qualify for Social Security survivor benefits, your deceased relative must have worked a minimum time period in jobs covered by Social Security, and you must be one of the survivors considered eligible by the Government. Table 2.1 lists the survivors eligible for benefits.

Survivors can collect Social Security benefits if the deceased earned enough credits. But the minimum credits needed for survivor benefits is much lower than for retirement benefits. Depending on the age of the person when he or she died, a survivor may qualify even if the deceased worked for as little as 1½ years, earning only six credits!

Table 2.2 shows how to figure the number of credits needed to qualify.

Examples 1 and 2 show how to use Table 2.2 to calculate the credits needed to qualify for Social Security survivor benefits.

TABLE 2.1

Individuals Eligible for Social Security Survivor Benefits

- *A spouse,*[1] if one of the following:
  1. At least 60
  2. At least 50 and disabled[2]
  3. Any age, and caring for a child under 16 or disabled before age 22[3]
- *A child,*[4] if unmarried and one of the following:
  1. Under age 18
  2. Under age 19 and in high school
  3. Any age, and disabled before age 22
- *A parent,*[5] if dependent and age 62 or over

[1]A spouse generally must have been married to the deceased for at least nine months (although there are many exceptions to this requirement). Also, a spouse must be unmarried at the time of application for benefits, or must not have remarried until after reaching age 60 (50 if disabled). A spouse includes a divorced spouse if married to the deceased for at least 10 years.

[2]You will be considered disabled if you have a serious mental or physical impairment that has lasted at least five months. The impairment must make you unable to work (see Chapter 3 discussing Social Security disability). You generally must also have become disabled either before or within seven years after your spouse died.

[3]A spouse caring for a young or disabled child includes a divorced spouse regardless of length of marriage to deceased. Your remarriage will cut off this survivor benefit.

[4]Children include illegitimate children, adopted children, stepchildren, and dependent grandchildren with both parents deceased or disabled.

[5]A parent will be considered dependent if he or she received more than half of his or her support from the deceased.

TABLE 2.2

How to Figure Credits Needed for Social Security Survivor Benefits

1. What year did the deceased turn age 21? _____ (year).

2. If the year in line 1 is after 1950, write that year here; if 1950 is later, write 1950 here: _____ .

3. The year before the deceased died was _____ (year).

4. The year the deceased turned 61 was _____ (if applicable).

5. The earlier of lines 3 and 4 is _____ .

6. Subtracting line 2 from line 5 equals _____ .

7. If the number in line 6 is less than 6, write 6 here; if line 6 is 6 or more, then write the number in line 6 here: _____ . This is the number of credits (one credit per quarter-year) that the deceased would need to have earned in employment covered by Social Security for survivors to collect benefits.

EXAMPLE 1

Your husband died in 1990 at age 65. Using Table 2.2:

1. Your husband was born in 1925, so he turned age 21 in *1946*.
2. Since 1950 is later than 1946, write in *1950*.
3. Your husband died in 1990; the year before his death was *1989*.
4. Your husband turned age 61 in *1986*.
5. *1986* is earlier than 1989.
6. 1986 minus 1950 equals *36*.
7. Since 36 is more than 6, your husband would have needed to have earned *36* credits for you to get survivor benefits from Social Security.

EXAMPLE 2

Your husband died in 1962 at age 28. Using Table 2.2:

1. He turned 21 in *1955*.
2. *1955* is later than 1950.
3. *1961* was the year before the deceased died.
4. Your late husband never turned 61.
5. *1961*.
6. 1961 minus 1955 equals *6*.
7. *6* is the number of credits needed to qualify you for survivor benefits.

As Example 2 shows, even a worker who died extremely young may have enough work credits to qualify the survivors for Social Security survivor benefits. In Example 2, 1½ years of work (6 quarters) would have been enough!

Some people may find Tables 2.3 and 2.4 simpler to use when figuring the number of work credits for survivor benefits.

If your spouse died, leaving you to care for a young or disabled child, you may qualify for Social Security survivor benefits even if the deceased did *not* have enough credits. As long as the deceased worked 1½ years (6 credits) during the three years immediately before he or she died, you should be eligible.

TABLE 2.3

**Number of Credits Needed When
Deceased Was Born After January 1, 1930**

Deceased Died at Age	Credits Needed
28 or younger	6
30	8
32	10
34	12
36	14
38	16
40	18
42	20
44	22
46	24
48	26
50	28
52	30
53	31
54	32
55	33
56	34
57	35
58	36
59	37
60	38
61	39
62	40

AMOUNT OF MONEY YOU SHOULD GET

Once you determine that you qualify for survivor benefits, the next question is how much you will receive. Social Security survivors benefits are different from most private life insurance policies. Private life insurance is usually paid to survivors in one lump sum; Social Security survivor payments are paid monthly. Table 2.5 provides an estimate of Social Security survivor benefits, based on national averages.

The amounts in Table 2.5 are just averages. Actual amounts are based on the deceased's work record, your status (widow or widower, parent or child), your age, and whether the deceased was retired.

TABLE 2.4

Number of Credits Needed When Deceased Was Born Before January 2, 1930

Deceased Died in*	Credits Needed
1992 or later	40
1991	40
1990	39
1989	38
1988	37
1987	36
1986	35
1985	34
1984	33
1983	32
1982	31
1981	30
1980	29
1979	28
1978	27
1977	26
1976	25
1975	24
1974	23
1973	22
1972	21
1971	20
1970	19
1969	18
1968	17
1967	16
1966	15
1965	14
1964	13
1963	12
1962	11
1961	10
1960	9
1959	8
1958	7
1957 or earlier	6

* Compare the year in which the deceased reached age 62. If earlier than the year in which the deceased died, use that year instead.

TABLE 2.5

Approximate Monthly Benefits If Insured Died in 1992[1]

Deceased Worker's Earnings in 1991

Deceased Worker's Age at Death	Who Receives Benefits	20,000	25,000	30,000	35,000	40,000	45,000	50,000	53,400 or over
65	Spouse at age 65	745	875	975	1,010	1,037	1,061	1,081	1,088
	Spouse at age 60 (or disabled spouse 50–59)	532	625	697	722	741	758	772	778
	Child (or spouse caring for child)[2]	558	656	731	757	777	795	810	816
	Maximum for whole family[3]	1,379	1,553	1,705	1,767	1,814	1,856	1,897	1,903
55	Spouse at age 65	736	865	973	1,012	1,043	1,071	1,093	1,101
	Spouse at age 60 (or disabled spouse 50–59)	526	618	695	723	745	765	781	787
	Child (or spouse caring for child)	552	648	729	759	782	803	819	825
	Maximum for whole family	1,367	1,540	1,702	1,770	1,824	1,873	1,912	1,926
45	Spouse at age 65	737	865	981	1,041	1,089	1,132	1,166	1,180
	Spouse at age 60 (or disabled spouse 50–59)	526	618	701	744	778	809	833	843
	Child (or spouse caring for child)	552	648	735	780	816	849	874	885
	Maximum for whole family	1,369	1,540	1,716	1,821	1,905	1,980	2,040	2,064

[1]This table assumes that the deceased worker had worked steadily since entering the work force at about age 22 and had received regular, average pay increases. These are the estimated amounts payable in 1992. Benefits increase in later years.

[2]Double the amounts for child and spouse caring for child, or for 2 children (no spouse).

[3]Maximum family benefits are discussed on page 25.

(*Continued*)

TABLE 2.5 (Continued)

Deceased Worker's Age at Death	Who Receives Benefits	20,000	25,000	30,000	35,000	40,000	45,000	50,000	53,400 or over
35	Spouse at age 65	738	867	982	1,043	1,103	1,163	1,223	1,252
	Spouse at age 60 (or disabled spouse 50–59)	527	619	702	745	788	831	874	895
	Child (or spouse caring for child)	553	650	736	782	827	872	917	939
	Maximum for whole family	1,370	1,543	1,718	1,824	1,929	2,034	2,139	2,190

Your Social Security survivor benefits are calculated as a percentage of the deceased worker's full age 65 retirement benefits, based on his work record. Just as with retirement benefits, you should obtain the deceased's PEBES (page 5), check the earnings record (page 5), correct any mistakes (page 6), and double-check the Government's calculations. The tables in Appendix 1 give you the deceased's full retirement benefit at age 65; from that, you can figure your monthly survivor benefits, which are a percentage of the deceased's full retirement benefits.

WIDOW OR WIDOWER BENEFITS

Social Security survivor benefits most commonly are paid to widows or widowers. Don't underestimate the value of these benefits; they can be more important than private life insurance policies or pensions. You will find that Social Security survivor benefits can be a real asset.

The amount of your monthly survivor payment from Uncle Sam is based on your late spouse's full retirement benefit. Table 2.6 shows the portion you can expect to receive.

Here's how to read Table 2.6. You could start taking Social Security survivor benefits as early as age 60 (50 if disabled), but you'd receive only 71.5 percent of your late spouse's full age 65 retirement benefit.

The first and fifth columns in Table 2.6 are identical—these show how much you would receive if your late spouse had retired at age 65 or had not yet retired

TABLE 2.6

Surviving Spouse Survivor Benefits

You Become Eligible for Survivor Benefits at Age	Your Benefits Are the Following Percentage of Late Spouse's Full Retirement Benefits				
	1 Deceased Spouse Was *Not* Taking Retirement Benefits at Time of His Death	2 Deceased Spouse Took Retirement at 62	3 Deceased Spouse Took Retirement at 63	4 Deceased Spouse Took Retirement at 64	5 Deceased Spouse Took Retirement at 65*
50–59 (and disabled)	71.5%	71.5%	71.5%	71.5%	71.5%
60	71.5	71.5	71.5	71.5	71.5
61	77.2	77.2	77.2	77.2	77.2
62	82.9	82.5	82.9	82.9	82.9
63	88.6	82.5	86.7	88.6	88.6
64	94.3	82.5	86.7	93.3	94.3
65	100	82.5	86.7	93.3	100

*If your late spouse had delayed taking his retirement past age 65, increasing his retirement benefits beyond the full retirement age 65 amount, then you as surviving spouse would get the same increase. You get this increase even if your late spouse had not yet retired at his death.

at the time of his death. If your late spouse had taken early retirement before age 65, your survivor benefits would be reduced, as shown in Columns 2 through 4.

Example 3 shows how Table 2.6 works.

EXAMPLE 3

Your husband's full age 65 retirement benefits were $800/month. He retired at age 62, taking $640 monthly payments. He died last year.

You are 63. If your late husband had not taken early retirement, you would have been entitled to $708/month (88.6% of $800; see Column 1). But because he retired at 62, you only get monthly survivor benefits of $660 (82.5% of $800; see Column 2).

Can You Collect Survivor Benefits If You Remarry?

To get Social Security survivor benefits, you either:

- Must be unmarried at the time you apply
- If remarried, you must not have remarried until after reaching age 60 (50 if disabled)

You can collect survivor benefits upon the death of a divorced spouse as long as you were married to the person at least 10 years and you satisfy these same limits on remarriage. These rules can make remarriage hazardous to your financial health if you're not careful about the timing.

❖ GEM: Watch Out for the Wedding Bell Blues

Although the laws of this country are supposed to be pro-family and pro-marriage, putting off a wedding—and even getting a divorce—may be financially rewarded by the Government! See Examples 4 and 5.

EXAMPLE 4

You have been widowed for several years. Now you are 59 and about to be remarried. Your late husband's full age 65 retirement benefit was $800/month. As soon as you turn 60, you'd be entitled to monthly survivor benefits of $572/month forever (71.5% of $800). By remarrying before your 60th birthday, you will lose the right to that money. You must be *unmarried* when you apply for widow benefits. When you kiss your new husband after the marriage vows, you kiss good-bye $572/month ($6,864 per year) for life.

But let's say you wait a few months to marry, until just after you turn 60. Now you can have your wedding cake and eat it too: remarriage *after* age 60 does *not* affect your survivor benefits. You'll be able to start taking your $572 monthly payments at age 60, and you'll continue to receive them after the marriage. And even if your new spouse is still working, your survivor benefit will *not* be reduced. Unlike spouse retirement benefits, survivor benefits are not affected by a later spouse's earnings.

EXAMPLE 5

Your first husband, Ralph, died a number of years ago, and you later remarried. You are now approaching age 60 and wondering about Social Security benefits. Unfortunately, you don't qualify for survivor benefits based on Ralph's earnings, since you are remarried and not yet age 60. If Ralph's full retirement benefit was $800/month, your remarriage is costing you $572/month.

What happens if you divorce your current husband, Tom? You then *would* qualify for Ralph's survivor benefits of $572/month. Once you reach age 60, you could then remarry Tom if you want to and have an extra $6,864/year in your pocket!

❖ GEM: Your Ex-Spouse May Be Worth More Dead Than Alive

Now don't misinterpret our point; we are not advocating murder. But in some cases, the death of an ex-spouse can put money in your pocket. Example 6 shows how.

EXAMPLE 6

You are divorced from Sam, and you married Phil at age 61. You are now 62 and ready to apply for Social Security. Based on Phil's work record, you can get spouse retirement benefits of $200/month. Sam has a full age 65 retirement benefit of $1,000/month, but you can't get any ex-spouse retirement benefits because you remarried before you became eligible for retirement. Sam isn't worth anything to you alive.

Three years later Sam dies, and now you can cash in! Since you remarried after age 60, you qualify for Social Security survivor benefits even though you couldn't get ex-spouse retirement benefits. If Sam had not retired at the time of his death, you would suddenly be entitled to get $1,000/month benefits (100% of $1,000)—not a bad increase over the $200 monthly checks you had been getting! All you have to do is apply to Social Security.

Survivor Disability

If you are disabled, Uncle Sam gives you a special break. You can start Social Security survivor benefits as soon as you turn 50. But, sadly, while the Government tantalizingly holds out this benefit, it makes qualification rough. To qualify, you generally must answer yes to these questions:

- Did you become disabled within seven years after your spouse's death?
- Has the disability lasted at least five months?
- Are you unable to do any substantial gainful work (earning $500 a month or more) due to a serious mental or physical impairment?

The test for Social Security survivor disability is the same as for standard Social Security disability benefits, discussed in Chapter 3. This test requires proof that you can't undertake any "substantial gainful work." Nonmedical factors, such as your age, education, and work experience, may be used to show that there's no substantial work (paying at least $500 a month) that you could do.

Why then would anyone ever seek Social Security disability survivor payments rather than standard disability benefits? To get standard Social Security disability benefits, you've got to have your own work record. Many people, particularly older women, can't qualify because they never worked. The big advantage of survivor benefits is that *you don't need any work record* under Social Security; you qualify based on your late spouse's work.

When Is the Best Time to Take Survivor Benefits?

Uncle Sam gives you a financial break when your spouse dies. While you can't start your normal retirement benefits until age 62, you can begin taking Social Security survivor benefits as early as age 60 (50 if disabled). But the earlier you begin, the less you'll receive (see Table 2.6). When is the best time to start? The answer depends on your circumstances.

1. *You're eligible for survivor benefits only.* Let's start with the situation in which many older Americans, particularly older women, find themselves. You haven't worked enough under Social Security–covered jobs to have your own right to retirement benefits, so your only income will be survivor benefits from your late spouse's work record.

❖ GEM: Start Taking Survivor Benefits as Soon as Possible

Take the money as early as you can. This is the same gem we gave you for retirement benefits. The longer you wait, the more you'll lose. You can bank on it (and you should!). See Example 7.

EXAMPLE 7

Your spouse died years ago, and you have just reached 60. His full age 65 benefit would have been $800/month. He had enough work credits to qualify you for benefits. Should you start taking $572/month now, wait two years and take $663/month at age 62, or wait until you reach 65 and get his entire $800/month?

If you start benefits at age 60 and put them aside, you'll have more than $14,000 (assuming 6% interest) sitting in the bank at age 62. If you then start taking the interest of $70/month, your total income would rise to $642/month ($572 plus $70). Compare that to the $663/month you'd be entitled to by delaying survivor benefits until 62 (82.9% of $800). You're way ahead by taking the money early, because your income is about the same *and* you've got a $14,000 pot of gold that you wouldn't otherwise have.

If you wait until age 65 to take the benefits, you'd be making an even more costly mistake. Starting benefits at 60 and putting them into CDs, you'd have $40,000 in five years. That would yield $200/month in interest (at 6%). Adding that to the $572/month continuing benefits gives you $772/month—only $28 less than the $800 benefit you'd get by waiting, but you've now got a rainy day fund of more than $40,000.

Let's say your spouse dies when you're already 62. Are you better off immediately starting to take survivor benefits, or should you wait until you reach age 65? You guessed it—take the benefits, as Example 8 shows.

EXAMPLE 8

You are 62 when your husband dies. His age 65 benefits would have been $800/month. As his widow, you opt to start receiving $663 in monthly benefits (82.9% of $800). When you reach 65, you will have accumulated more than $25,000 (at 6% interest). If you then add the $125/month interest produced by your little pot of gold to your $663/month continuing benefits, you'll have $788/month income—only $12 less than the $800 you would receive by waiting to 65. But don't forget; you'd also have a much larger bank balance!

✦   ✦   ✦

2. *You're eligible for survivor and retirement benefits.* When your spouse dies, you'll often have not one but *two* options for Social Security benefits: survivor benefits based on your late spouse's work record *or* retirement benefits based on your own work record. That raises two questions: Which benefits should you start? Can (and should) you switch?

❖ GEM: Start with Your Higher Benefits

Compare your survivor and retirement benefits; in most cases you should take the higher amount. (Our gem on page 70 tells you when to take the lower benefit first.) Table 2.7 compares these benefits.

TABLE 2.7

Survivor Benefits vs. Retirement Benefits

| You Become Eligible for Benefits at Age | SURVIVOR (BASED ON LATE SPOUSE'S WORK RECORD) Your Benefits Are the Following Percentage of Late Spouse's Full Retirement Benefits | | | | | Retirement (Based on Your Work Record) Your Benefits Would Be the Following % of Your Own Full Retirement Benefits[1] |
	1 Deceased Spouse Was *Not* Taking Retirement Benefits[2]	2 Deceased Spouse Took Retirement at 62	3 Deceased Spouse Took Retirement at 63	4 Deceased Spouse Took Retirement at 64	5 Deceased Spouse Took Retirement at 65[1]	
50–59 (and disabled)	71.5%	71.5%	71.5%	71.5%	71.5%	0
60	71.5	71.5	71.5	71.5	71.5	0
61	77.2	77.2	77.2	77.2	77.2	0
62	82.9	82.5	82.9	82.9	82.9	80%
63	88.6	82.5	86.7	88.6	88.6	86.7
64	94.3	82.5	86.7	93.3	94.3	93.3
65	100	82.5	86.7	93.3	100	100

[1]Add .555 percent for each additional month.
[2]Add .475 percent for each additional month, up to the highest percent in the list.

In essence, if you are younger than 62 when your spouse dies, you'll *always* want to start taking survivor benefits. If your spouse dies when you are 62 or older, you'll have to compare the amounts you would get for retirement and survivor benefits; in most cases pick the one that pays more.

EXAMPLE 9

You are 62 and would like to start Social Security benefits. Should you take retirement or survivor benefits?

Your full age 65 retirement benefit would be $500/month; at 62 you'd be entitled to retirement checks of $400/month (80% of $500; see last column of Table 2.7). Your late husband's full age 65 retirement benefit would have been $800/month. Since he had not retired at the time of his death, your survivor payment would be $663/month (82.9% of $800; see Column 1 of Table 2.7).

Take the survivor benefit to put more money in your pocket.

Once you take survivor benefits, the amount of that benefit is fixed *for life:* when you get older, it won't go up (except for small cost-of-living increases). The same holds for your own retirement benefit; once you take it, it's locked in. But you may switch from your survivor benefit to your own retirement benefit, or from your own retirement to a survivor benefit. And that's where a little-known Golden Opportunity comes in.

❖ GEM: Switch Benefits to Increase Income

Whether you start taking survivor or retirement benefits, there may come a time when it pays to switch to the other. Each year, make a comparison to see if change should be on your agenda. Examples 10 to 15 show how switching benefits can help you.

EXAMPLE 10

You are 60 and a widow. Your full age 65 retirement benefit would be $600/month; your late spouse's full age 65 retirement benefit would have been $800/month. You should start immediately to take your survivor benefit of $572/month (71.5% of $800; see Columns 1–5 of Table 2.7).

When you reach age 62, you become eligible for your own retirement benefits. If you switch then, you'd only get $480/month (80% of $600)—obviously not a good idea. At age 63, you'd be entitled to $520 monthly, and at age 64 you'd be entitled to $560/month—still less than your $572/month survivor benefit.

But by 65, you should switch to your own retirement benefits. You'll be entitled to 100 percent of your full $600/month benefit (see last column of Table 2.7), $28/month *more* than the survivor benefit you've been receiving as a widow.

EXAMPLE 11

Your husband died and you just turned 60. His full age 65 retirement would have been $1,000/month, so you are entitled to $715/month survivor benefits (71.5% of $1,000; see Columns 1–5 of Table 2.7). Since you can't yet get any retirement benefits, you clearly start with the survivor payments.

Your full age 65 retirement benefits are $600/month. That's what you'd get at age 65. Even at age 70, you'd get less than $705/month if you were born before 1927. So it never makes sense to switch to retirement benefits.

EXAMPLE 12

Your late spouse's full age 65 retirement benefit would be $800/month; your full age 65 retirement benefit would be $700/month. At age 60, you start survivor benefits of $572/month (71.5% of $800; see Columns 1–5 of Table 2.7).

At age 62, you can take retirement benefits of $560/month (80% of $700; see last column of Table 2.7), so of course you do not switch. But at 63, your retirement benefit will be $607/month (86.7% of $700; see last column of Table 2.7). Switching benefits at 63 adds $35/month to your pocketbook!

EXAMPLE 13

You are 61 when your husband dies, so you immediately begin survivor benefits of $617/month (77.2% of $800). Remember—take the money from Uncle Sam as soon as possible.

At 62, you'd be able to switch to retirement benefits. Since your full age 65 retirement benefit is $700/month, you'd get $560/month (80% of $700; see last column of Table 2.7) at 62. Clearly, no switch should be made yet.

At 63, you'd be entitled to retirement payments of $607/month (86.7% of $700; see last column of Table 2.7)—still less than you're already getting.

But at 64, the time for a change will come. You can get $653/month (93.3% of $700; see last column of Table 2.7)—a raise of $36/month for life!

EXAMPLE 14

You are 62 and your husband has just died. Your full age 65 retirement benefit would be $800; his full age 65 retirement benefit would have been $700.

At 62, you could start with retirement benefits of $640/month (80% of $800; see last column of Table 2.7) or survivor benefits of $580/month (82.9% of $700; see column 1 of Table 2.7). Naturally, you take the higher retirement benefits.

At 63, you'd be entitled to survivor benefits of $620 a month (88.6% of $700; see Column 1 of Table 2.7)—no change yet. At 64, you could get survivor payments of $660 a month—$20 a month *more* than you'll have been getting. Do we have to spell it out? SWITCH!

EXAMPLE 15

Your late husband took early retirement at age 62. His full age 65 retirement benefit was $800 a month. You just reached age 60, and your full age 65 retirement benefit is $600/month. Table 2.7 shows that you could get survivor benefits of $572/month (71.5% of $800), and no retirement benefit yet. Obviously, you start taking survivor checks.

But you also can figure that at some point you'll switch to retirement benefits. That's clear because, at least when you're 65 and entitled to your full retirement benefit of $600/month, that will be more than the $572/month survivor benefits.

At 64 you'd be entitled to retirement benefits of 93.3 percent of your $600 benefit, or $560 a month—less than the $572 survivor benefit. So you won't switch to retirement benefits until you reach 65, and then you get a $28/month raise ($600 retirement checks are $28 more than your $572 survivor benefit).

NOTE

In most cases you can switch benefits without any reduction or penalty. There's one exception: If you were born before January 2, 1928, and you start receiving survivor benefits between age 60 and 62, your benefits will be reduced somewhat if you switch to retirement benefits.

❖ GEM: If Your Full Retirement Benefit Is More Than Your Late Spouse's, Start with Lower Survivor Benefits

Up until now, we've told you to compare retirement and survivor benefits, start with the higher amount, and then switch later to increase income. That usually is the best policy. But as with every rule, there's an exception.

If your age 65 full retirement benefit is more than your late spouse's full retirement benefit, take the lower survivor benefits to start. In Examples 10 to 15, the surviving spouse had a significantly lower full age 65 retirement benefit than the deceased spouse. That's fairly typical—the husband dies, the wife survives, and her full age 65 retirement benefit usually is much lower than the late husband's. But Example 16 shows how taking *lower* starting benefits can sometimes pay big dividends.

EXAMPLE 16

Your husband, who retired at age 63, has died; you have just reached 62. Your late husband's full retirement benefit was $800; yours is $850/month. Here's your immediate choice: take survivor payments of $663/month (82.9% of $800; see column 3 of Table 2.7) or choose retirement payments of $680/month (80% of $850; see last column of Table 2.7).

Most people would jump at the higher retirement payments, which would normally be the best plan. But since your late husband's full retirement benefit ($800) is lower than yours, you should opt for the lower survivor benefits.

From age 62 to 65 you would continue to get $663/month; if you save those checks, you'd have over $25,000 by age 65. Then you can switch to your retirement benefits of $850/month. Add the $125/month interest (at 6%) from your fat account, and your total income will rise to $975/month.

Now compare where you would be if you had jumped at the larger retirement benefits first. Putting aside $680/month until age 65 would give you a bank account of about $26,000—slightly more than if you took survivor benefits. When you reach age 65, you could switch to survivor benefits. But your survivor benefits would be limited to $693/month (see Column 3 of Table 2.7). Adding interest of $130/month from your bank account would bring your monthly income up only to $823—far less than the $975 you'd get by starting with the lower survivor benefits and then switching to retirement benefits.

In most cases, you are better off starting with the *higher* benefits. But if your full age 65 retirement benefit is higher than your late spouse's, opt for the lower survivor amount to start.

WARNING: YOU CAN'T SWITCH BACK AND FORTH

You can't jump from benefit to benefit and back again. You can switch from survivor to retirement benefits, or from retirement to survivor benefits—but that's it. You can't go from retirement to survivor and then back to retirement.

As with all rules, there's an exception. If you are receiving spouse retirement benefits when your spouse dies, you *must* switch, you can't keep spouse benefits with no living spouse. Your choice is to switch to either your own retirement benefits or to survivor payments. But when your spouse dies, you *can* go from spouse retirement benefits to survivor benefits, and then switch back to your own retirement benefits; or you can go from spouse retirement benefits to your own retirement, and then switch to survivor benefits.

---

3. *You're eligible for survivor, retirement, and spouse retirement benefits.* So far, we've discussed situations in which you are eligible just for survivor benefits, and those in which you are eligible for both survivor and retirement benefits. As if comparing survivor and retirement benefits weren't complicated enough, remarriage sometimes opens a third option: spouse retirement benefits based on your new spouse's work record. To get the most from Uncle Sam's treasure chest, you must consider and compare *all* potential benefits. Let's start with a situation involving only survivor benefits and spouse retirement benefits.

❖ GEM: Tie the Knot to Secure Spouse Retirement Benefits

EXAMPLE 17

You are 64, and for the last four years you have been receiving Social Security survivor benefits of $375/month. You didn't work, so you have no retirement benefits of your own. You've been dating a man who is tall, dark, and handsome, which isn't too bad. But his best attribute is that he's got a great retirement benefit—$1,000/month at age 65. Marriage may be bliss—at least for your pocketbook!

Marriage won't help immediately; you must be married a year before you can get spouse retirement. But after a year, you can switch to spouse retirement benefits of $500/month (50% of $1,000; see Table 1.8 in Chapter 1), based on your new spouse's work record. The extra $125/month in your checks can pay for some honeymoon!

❖ GEM: After Remarriage, Compare All of Your Social Security Options

Remarriage will sometimes create three options: survivor benefits, your own retirement benefits, and spouse retirement benefits. Example 18 shows how choosing wisely can add glitter to your golden years.

EXAMPLE 18

You are 62 and have been widowed for some time. Your late husband's full age 65 retirement benefit was $550/month; at age 60 you started taking survivor benefits of $393/month (71.5% of $550). Your own full age 65 retirement benefit is $500/month. The man you've been dating has just asked you to marry him, and you've agreed. Since you are over 60, your remarriage won't stop your survivor payments. His full age 65 retirement benefit is $1,100/month. Now let's take a look at your possible money strategies:

1. Switch now—before the marriage—to your own retirement benefits of $400/month (80% of $500), and then switch again at age 65 to new spouse retirement benefits of $450/month (see page 62).
2. Switch to new spouse retirement benefits at age 63 (after you've been married a year), amounting to $477/month (see Appendix 3 for calculation). That gives you a raise of $84/month over your survivor benefits (and the amount would be higher than the retirement benefits you'd get under strategy 1).
3. Stay with the $393/month survivor benefits until you reach age 65, then switch to spouse retirement benefits of $550/month (50% of $1,100).

Option 3 is the best if you figure you'll live past age 68. Even though you'll be taking $84/month less for two years than you'd get by taking new spouse retirement benefits at age 63 (strategy 2), the payoff at age 65 should more than make up for it. Why? At 65, your monthly benefits jump up to $550/month, $73/month more than you would get under strategy 2. Within three years, the extra $73 should cover the loss you suffered by taking $84 less for two years.

❖ GEM: Apply for More Benefits!

When you decide to switch from one type of benefit to another, you must apply to Social Security for the change. Uncle Sam doesn't sit there with a calculator figuring when it will pay for you to switch benefits. If you don't take the initiative, you'll lose some very important Golden Opportunities.

◆ ◆ ◆

How Do You Take Your Lumps?

So far, we've been talking about *monthly* survivor benefits. Uncle Sam also has a one-time lump-sum $255 check available for many widows or widowers just for the asking. Unfortunately, many older Americans fail to ask. Here's one time when you *should* take your lumps from the Government.

If you were receiving spouse retirement benefits at the time of your spouse's death, then the Government should send your $255 check *automatically*. But in all other situations, you must apply.

You are eligible for this special benefit if you are also eligible for monthly survivor payments. Even if you can't get the monthly survivor benefits, you can still get this one-time $255 check (regardless of age) if both:

- Your late spouse had worked at least one-and-a-half of the three years before he died.
- You were living together.

Don't delay in applying. You have only two years after your spouse's death to ask Social Security for the money. Exceptions are made only in rare circumstances; after the time is up, the Government keeps your money. So if you think you can use the $255 more than Uncle Sam can, go get it!

SURVIVOR BENEFITS FOR OTHER SURVIVORS

A spouse is not the only survivor entitled to Social Security survivor benefits. As shown in Table 2.1, parents and children may also have a claim. Table 2.8 sets out the amount that these other family members can get. Here we discuss the most important of these other survivor benefits: parent survivor benefits.

TABLE 2.8

Survivor Benefits for Surviving Family (Other Than Spouse)

You Are	Percentage of Deceased's Retirement Benefits
Dependent parent of deceased	82½
Two dependent parents of deceased	Each receives 75
Surviving spouse caring for young or disabled child	75
Young or disabled child of deceased	75

Benefits for Parents

The wonders of modern science have made it possible for Americans to live ever-longer. Unfortunately, older citizens sometimes outlast their pocketbooks, leaving parents reliant on children for financial assistance. Children usually are happy to help when they can—and that's as it should be. But what if tragedy strikes and the child dies before the parent? How will the parent continue to survive?

Uncle Sam may lend a hand. If you were dependent on a child who died before you, you may be entitled to survivor benefits based on your child's work record. (Parents are not entitled to Social Security benefits based on a child's work record while the supportive child is still living.)

The benefit for one parent is 82½ percent of the late child's full age 65 retirement benefit; if there are two surviving parents, each can get 75 percent. These benefits can put a nice sum in your pocket *if* you claim them. Tragically, many older Americans lose out on millions of dollars just because they don't understand their rights.

You are entitled to parent survivor benefits if your child had the required number of Social Security work credits (see Tables 2.2, 2.3, and 2.4), and you can answer yes to these five questions:

- Are you at least age 62?
- Were you receiving at least half your support from your child before his death?
- Can you provide proof of support within two years of your child's death?
- Have you not married since the child died?
- Were you the child's parent?

Each of these requirements is discussed below.

Age. You cannot receive survivor benefits as a parent until you reach age 62. But this doesn't mean you must be 62 when your child dies. Even if you were, say, 50 when your child died, you can collect once you reach 62, as long as you meet the other requirements.

You get the same parent survivor benefits whether you start them at 62, 65, or older. There is no sliding scale based on age. So start as soon as possible, or you'll lose funds that should be yours.

Support. Your child will be considered to have provided at least half of your support if he or she paid at least half of your ordinary living expenses (such as food, clothing, shelter, medical care). Your child must have paid these costs for a reasonable time (usually a year) just prior to either his death or his becoming disabled, if the disability continued until his death. Support may be provided in goods or services, as well as in cash.

EXAMPLE 19

You were living with your son, in his home, for several years before his death. Your son did not charge any rent, and he paid for much of the food (though you periodically did the shopping).

Your total income is $500/month (pension and interest from some accounts). You figure that, based on rental costs in the neighborhood, the value of your room was about $500/month. In addition, your son paid at least $30/month for your food, and he paid for the telephone and utilities that you used, maybe worth another $30/month to you.

Based on these figures, your son provided more than half your support—*even though he didn't actually give you a penny in cash!* He paid approximately $560/month for your support, and your income totaled only $500/month; clearly, you pass the support test.

Your income is considered as used for your support even if it actually was not. You can't qualify for survivor benefits by letting your child pay for your needs while you put your own money in the bank.

Your child's personal services, which you may have taken for granted, can be considered in figuring the amount of support. For instance, if your child did repairs around the house, cooked meals, or filled out your Medicare forms, you can give a value to these services, and that amount can be considered as a contribution by your child to your support.

❖ GEM: Support Your Support Claim with Proof!

You can't just guess at the value of room, board, and other noncash contributions to your support. The Government wants proof. For example, check the rentals in your newspaper to determine the market value of the room provided by your child. Call a bookkeeper and get a written estimate for the services (bill paying, Medicare form filing, and so on) provided by your child. These objective proofs from third parties can enable you to cash in on survivor benefits.

◆　◆　◆

Proof of support within two years. Here's where most people get tripped up. There are important time limits. You must file your proof of support with the Social Security Administration within two years of your child's death. If you were receiving support from your child at the time your child began suffering from a disability, you must provide proof of support within two years of your child's application for Social Security disability benefits.

You have to file evidence of support within these time limits, *even if you won't qualify for survivor benefits until much later.* For example, if your child dies when you are 50, you probably aren't thinking much about Social Security benefits, and nobody in the Government will tell you that you'd better file proof of your child's support before you reach age 52. By the time you focus on retirement at age 62, it's too late.

The two-year limit for filing can be extended if you've got a good excuse for missing the deadline. Good excuses include:

1. Circumstances beyond your control, such as an extended illness or mental or physical incapacity
2. Language barrier
3. Incorrect information from the Social Security Administration

Ignorance of the law, by itself, is no excuse. However, if there were unusual or unavoidable circumstances that show you couldn't reasonably have known about the time limit, then you should be exempt.

Even if you can't provide complete proof of support within the two-year limit, try to give some evidence to the Social Security Administration. The Government is much more likely to let you prove support later if you've made some good-faith effort to give evidence within the time limit.

Remarriage: when you say yes, Uncle Sam says no! A crazy (and outrageous) provision in the law says that if you marry after your child's death, you lose your right to survivor benefits (age makes no difference). If you marry before you apply for benefits, you won't qualify; if you marry after you've qualified, your benefits will end.

❖ GEM: Living Together May Be Better

Uncle Sam doesn't penalize you if you're just living together. So if you've lost a child and you otherwise qualify for survivor benefits, consider living together without a marriage license.

If you were married at the time of your child's death, your existing marriage won't prevent you from receiving survivor benefits. But if your child dies while you're married and then your spouse dies, don't remarry without considering the impact on your Social Security survivor benefits.

❖ ❖ ❖

Parent of deceased. Survivor benefits are not limited to natural parents. You may be eligible if you adopted a child or became the child's stepparent before the child turned 16 years old.

Which Benefits Should You Take?

If you qualify for Social Security survivor benefits on your child's work record *and* for Social Security retirement benefits on your own work record, compare the two to see which would be better.

❖ GEM: Start with Survivor, Then Retire to Retirement Benefits

If you opt for retirement benefits, you can *never* switch to the survivor payments, but if you start with survivor benefits, you can switch to retirement benefits at age 65. For many older Americans, this little known opportunity is a hidden treasure. See Example 20.

EXAMPLE 20

You just turned 62, and you are eligible for both Social Security survivor benefits based on your late child's work record and your own retirement benefits. Your full age 65 retirement benefit is $700/month, so you are entitled to take retirement benefits of $560/month (80% of $700). Your late child's full age 65 retirement benefit was $600/month, so you are entitled to $495/month survivor benefits as a parent (82½% of $600; see Table 2.8).

Your first instinct is to opt for the higher retirement benefit of $560/ month. If you set aside the retirement payments until you reached age 65, you'd have about $21,400 in the bank at that time. You could then draw interest of $107/month (at 6%) which, added to your continuing retirement benefit of $560/month, would give you a total monthly paycheck of $667/month.

Now let's see where you'd be if you started with the *lower* survivor benefit of $495 a month. At age 65, you'd have about $19,000 in the bank. Then at 65 you could switch to your full retirement benefit of $700/ month—that amount is *not* reduced by previous parent survivor payments. Add $95/month interest (6% on the $19,000 bank account), and your total monthly paycheck is $795—$128/month *more*. Starting with the lower life survivor payments and switching to your own retirement benefits pays big dividends. By waiting until 65, you can then lock into the highest retirement benefit rates.

◆　◆　◆

When choosing between Social Security retirement and survivor benefits, it isn't always the best policy to focus only on your own best interest; there's another important consideration. If you opt for parent benefits, you may be cheating your child's spouse and children out of benefits due them, owing to the Maximum Family Benefits Rule discussed next.

Maximum Family Benefits (MFB)

In the last chapter, we told you about the cap on total Social Security benefits for the family (page 25). The same Maximum Family Benefits (MFB) rule applies to survivor payments. Table 1.9 shows the limits on family Social Security retirement *and* survivor benefits, and Example 21 shows how this works.

EXAMPLE 21

Your husband died, leaving you, a dependent parent and a dependent disabled child. You are 65, and your late husband's full age 65 retirement benefit is $650. You are entitled to $650/month survivor benefits (100% of $650), his parent is entitled to $536/month (82½% of $650; see Table 2.8), and your child is entitled to $487/month (75% of $650; see Table 2.8). Total benefits would be $1,673/month—but that's not what everyone receives, because the MFB is only $1,164/month. Each family member gets a proportionately reduced benefit: you get $452/month, the parent gets $372/month, and the child collects $338/month.

❖ GEM: Work Can Avoid the Harmful Effects of the MFB

We explained the Triple Working Whammy in Chapter 1: Uncle Sam can claim more of your post-retirement earnings than you can. But when a widow or widower and dependents have had their benefits limited by the MFB, working may pay big dividends, as Example 22 shows.

EXAMPLE 22

Your husband died, leaving you, a dependent parent, and a dependent disabled child. You are 65, and your late husband's full age 65 retirement benefit is $650. As we explained in Example 21, *without* the MFB the three of you would be entitled to total benefits of $1,673/month. But the MFB reduces the total monthly benefits to $1,164. Now you go to work to supplement your income. Your earnings are $20,480/year; that's $10,280 more than you are allowed to earn without any benefit cut. Since you lose $1 of benefits for each $3 of excess earnings, your annual benefits of $5,424 ($452/month) are reduced by $3,426, leaving you with $1,996 per year, or $166/month.

But the three of you together won't lose a penny of benefits, because the MFB reduced the total benefits for the three of you to $1,164/month. If your benefits are cut to $166/month, then the dependent parent's and child's benefits can go *up* to bring the three of you back to $1,164/month. Their benefits increase to $523/month (parent) and $475/month (child); when added to your $166/month, the total is back to $1,164/month. In other words, when the Maximum Family Benefit has worked its evil reduction, the damaging impact of post-retirement earnings is significantly reduced.

TAXES AND EARNINGS

In Chapter 1, we revealed the Government's secret tax trap that eats away at your Social Security retirement benefits. The same tax trap can wipe out much of your survivor benefits. But the gems that protect retirement benefits (pages 30–33) can also cut the taxes on your Social Security survivor benefits.

We also told you about the Triple Working Whammy, which slashes post-retirement earnings. If you are hoping to supplement your Social Security survivor benefits, you will have to watch out for that same Triple Working Whammy. Review our gems on pages 34–45 before you start working.

OVERPAYMENTS

Wouldn't it be nice if the Government sent you too much money? Maybe not! Because if the Government later discovers its mistake, you might be held responsible for paying the funds back with interest.

In Chapter 1, we described the rules covering Government overpayments of retirement benefits. The same rules apply to survivor benefits. You might be able to keep the extra funds if repayment is "against equity and good conscience" or would "defeat the purpose" of the Social Security program. Knowing your rights means you might benefit from Uncle Sam's mistake.

EXAMPLE 23

You were awarded survivor benefits following the death of your husband. The benefits made it possible for you to sign up for art school, something you always wanted to do. After you collect benefits for a year, the Government tells you that your late husband really didn't have enough work credits, and the benefits shouldn't have been paid.

You are in a panic. You used the funds for tuition and books, which you would not have done if you had never been given any benefits, and now you don't have extra money. Don't worry, you don't have to repay the benefits. You changed your position for the worse (financially) in reliance on the benefits.

EXAMPLE 24

Your husband divorced you and married Lucy. After he died, you applied and collected Social Security survivor benefits.

Lucy was overpaid benefits of $5,000. The Government has tried to get the money from her, but can't. Of course, you've always known she was after your ex-spouse's money! But now the Government is trying to get the funds from you, since you also are collecting benefits on your late husband's record (even though *you* were not overpaid).

Don't worry. Since you were living separate from your ex-husband at the time of the overpayments and didn't get that money, you're in the clear. Stand firm.

APPLICATION AND APPEALS

For Social Security survivor benefits, there are the same rules for applying and appeals as for retirement benefits. If you don't apply, you don't collect. And if you are turned down, appeal. We won't repeat the rules and gems here, since they are described on pages 49–53.

The loss of a loved one, particularly a husband or wife, can be emotionally devastating. But it shouldn't have to be financially devastating, too. The Government offers valuable Golden Opportunities under the Social Security survivor program.

·3·

Social Security Disability Benefits:
A Treasure That Really Has Been Buried!

During your working years when you paid into the Social Security system, did you know that you also bought a disability insurance policy? If you or a loved one suffers a disabling illness or accident, don't forget the benefits due you!

And don't skip this chapter just because you haven't had a *sudden* illness or accident. Many disabled older Americans retire from work because their health won't let them continue, but they don't consider themselves "disabled" because their health problems have slowly worsened over time rather than occurred suddenly.

Let's explode that dangerous myth right now: If your health prevents you from holding a job, you are disabled. Disabilities aren't limited to sudden accidents or illnesses. You may be disabled by a condition that you've lived and worked with for years. Many people who retire from work do so for health reasons, and many of them should be able to cash in on Social Security disability benefits.

Why is this so important? Because Social Security disability benefits for many older Americans will be *much higher* than Social Security retirement payments. And these benefits are not only for a disabled worker; the entire family can benefit.

Even if you aren't 62 and yet eligible for retirement checks, you may be able to collect substantial disability dollars; they are available at *any* age! If you qualify, you can receive the same monthly check that you would have received by retiring at age 65—100 percent of all retirement benefits.

EXAMPLE 1

You worked on a factory assembly line for as long as you care to remember. The job required you to be on your feet all day, and your arthritis finally got so bad that you just couldn't handle the work anymore. So last year, at age 60, you retired.

> Your full Social Security retirement benefit at 65 would be $800/ month; at age 62 you'll become eligible to receive $640/month (80%; see Table 1.4) from Social Security retirement. There's no way you'd be eligible for Social Security retirement any earlier than 62. But you can start collecting Social Security *disability* checks *now* for the full $800/ month!

As you can see from Example 1, Social Security disability benefits provide a Golden Opportunity to enhance your income. Unfortunately, every year millions of people who are eligible never apply, losing out on millions of dollars due them. Why? Most older Americans don't understand the program. Don't fall into the disability trap. Read on to learn if you are entitled to disability benefits; if you are, apply for them.

ELIGIBILITY

Our friends in Congress have created a complicated set of rules governing eligibility. Let's start with a few facts about what is *not* required for Social Security disability benefits.

- You do *not* have to have been working. You may qualify even if you have been retired for a long time.
- You do *not* have to be 62, or any specific age for that matter.
- You do *not* have to be destitute. Wealth is not considered when looking at eligibility.
- You do *not* have to be disabled as a result of your work. This is not Worker's Compensation—the disability does *not* have to be work related.

Now that we've told you what is not required, let's look at what *is* required.

- You must have earned sufficient *work credits* under Social Security.
- You must be *disabled*.

That seems simple enough, right? Let's take a closer look at these two requirements.

How Many Work Credits Do You Need for Disability Benefits?

In Chapter 1, we talked about work credits for Social Security retirement benefits. The same general rules apply to disability coverage. You must have earned a minimum amount on the job to earn a "credit," and you must have the required number of credits. You should have no trouble with work credits for disability benefits if you worked for a total of 10 years at jobs paying into Social Security, and you worked during 5 of the last 10 years.

Even if you haven't worked a total of 10 years (40 quarters), you may still qualify, as shown in Table 3.1.

TABLE 3.1

Number of Credits Required for Disability Benefits

If You Were Born Before 1930 and Became Disabled Before Reaching Age 62, in	OR	If You Were Born After 1929 and Became Disabled at Age	You Need This Number of Credits
1992 (or later)		63 (or older)	40 (10 years)
1991		62	40 (10 years)
1990		61	39 (9¾ years)
1989		60	38 (9½ years)
1988		59	37 (9¼ years)
1987		58	36
1986		57	35
1985		56	34
1984		55	33
1983		54	32
1982		53	31
1981		52	30
1980		51	29
1979		50	28
1978		49	27
1977		48	26
1976		47	25
1975		46	24
1974		45	23
1973		44	22
1972		43	21
1971		31–42	20

Special Note: If you become disabled before age 31, special rules apply. For people disabled between age 24 and 31, you need only to have worked half the time from age 21 to the disability. For example, if you become disabled at age 25, you need two years (eight credits) of work (half of the four years) between 21 and 25. If you became disabled before age 24, you need only 1½ years of work (six credits) in the three years before the disability.

❖ GEM: Part-time Work Can Pay Big-time Dividends

The requirement that you work for 5 of the 10 years prior to a disability can be an expensive trap. There's an easy way around this, as you can see by comparing Examples 2 and 3.

EXAMPLE 2

You worked hard all your life, paying into the Social Security system for 30 years. You quit at 55 to enjoy your golden years. Unfortunately, at age 61 you suffer a disabling illness. Though you have far more than 10 years of work (40 credits), you won't qualify for Social Security disability insurance because you have not worked during 5 of the last 10 years.

EXAMPLE 3

Let's take the same facts as in Example 2. After you retire at age 55 from your full-time job, you continue to work part time. Your annual earnings barely exceed $2,280.

Why keep working? Those minimal earnings are enough to keep your Social Security disability insurance in force during your retirement. Earnings of $2,280 in 1992 get you four Social Security credits, the maximum number of credits you can get in a year. When the illness strikes at age 61, you become entitled to your full age 65 retirement benefits of $800/month.

Without the disability insurance, you would have received *no* benefits until age 62, and then only $640/month (80% of $800) for retirement benefits after that. By working part time during retirement, you saved yourself many thousands of dollars over the rest of your life.

As Example 3 demonstrates, a little part-time work after retirement can keep your disability insurance protection in force, and that can mean thousands of dollars to you in the event you become ill or injured.

✦   ✦   ✦

What Is the Definition of Disability?

There is no easy, clear definition of a disability. The Government will say that you are disabled if you have a physical or mental impairment which both:

- Is expected to last (or has lasted) for at least one year or to result in death
- Prevents you from doing any "substantial gainful work"

How long must you be disabled to qualify? Uncle Sam expects you to be disabled for at least 12 months. Optimism about your recovery may cost you.

EXAMPLE 4

You fall down the stairs and do serious damage to your body, breaking a hip, both legs, and both arms. The doctor tells you that you should be back on your feet within nine months. In this case, you *won't* qualify for disability benefits. Remember, the disability must be projected to last at least one year.

❖ GEM: Pessimism Creates Optimism

A gloomy forecast about your health can help you get disability benefits, as Example 5 shows.

EXAMPLE 5

Let's take the same facts as in Example 4, but your doctor predicts your disability will last over a year. With that dire prediction, you qualify for disability.

But forecasting disability is an inexact science; if it turns out the doctor was overly pessimistic, and you fully heal after nine months, the Government will come after you to get its money back.

✦ ✦ ✦

What is substantial gainful work? To determine whether you can do "substantial gainful work," the Government looks at whether you could earn at least $500/month doing some type of work. Even if you can't still do your former job, you won't be considered disabled if you can earn $500/month doing any other job. Here's the catch: the type of job you could do must exist in reasonable numbers in the region where you live, but there need not be any actual openings. This means that if your training and condition allow you to work as a bookkeeper, the Government will say you can do "substantial gainful work" even if you can't find a bookkeeping job. Because you can do substantial gainful work, you won't qualify for benefits. It's not fair, but it's the law.

If you are already working at a job that pays $500/month, you won't be considered disabled—even if you are earning far less than you were before the disability.

❖ GEM: Uncle Sam Is Crafty
When It Comes to Hobbies

If you do volunteer work or spend time on a hobby or in classes at school, the Government may take these activities into consideration when determining your *ability* to do profitable work. You may want to put these nonprofit activities on hold for a while as you go through the disability application process.

❖ GEM: Don't Make a Gross Error—
Use Net Earnings to Get Benefits

You can cheat yourself out of benefits by counting gross earnings rather than net income. You may qualify for disability benefits by reducing your earnings below $500/month. How can you do that? Subtract work-related expenses!

EXAMPLE 6

Suppose you are working as a bookkeeper, earning $525/month. That would probably make you ineligible for Social Security disability payments.

But you are confined to a wheelchair, for which you paid $360 ($30 a month if the cost is averaged over 12 months), and you pay $25 a month for prescribed medications that allow you to work. Deducting these amounts from your gross earnings reduces your net earnings to $470/month—*below* the $500 threshold. Now you should be able to pick up Social Security disability benefits.

Golden Rule: You can subtract from gross earnings the cost of items and services that enable you to work. Costs can be deducted even if you use the items in your daily living. Deductible items include:

• Wheelchair
• Cane

- Crutches
- Inhalator
- Pacemaker
- Prosthetic devices
- Respirator
- Braces
- Artificial limbs
- Special telephone amplifiers and readers for persons with hearing or seeing impairments
- Wheelchair ramps or railings at home if you work at home
- Drugs to control your impairment, reduce symptoms, or slow down the impairment's progression
- Modifications to your vehicle
- Attendant care services, such as assistance in going to and from work, or an interpreter for the deaf
- One-handed typewriters
- Braille devices
- Expendable medical supplies (such as bandages)
- Costs for keeping a guide dog

When you make monthly payments for a deductible item (such as rental payments, installment payments, payments for services), you can subtract the monthly costs from your monthly income. If you pay a one-time cost, you may either deduct the whole amount that month or deduct $\frac{1}{12}$ each month for a year.

◆ ◆ ◆

Listed disabilities. Deciding whether an individual can do "substantial gainful work" is not an easy task. To simplify the job, Uncle Sam has created a list of disabling conditions that he says are so bad anyone with one of these *must* be unable to do substantial gainful work. In other words, if your disability is included in the Government's List of Disabling Conditions, you should be considered disabled (unable to work) for purposes of getting Social Security disability benefits. Table 3.2 lists some of the more common of these. A much more detailed listing is available in Appendix 1 to Subpart P, Volume 20, of the Code of Federal Regulations, Part 404, available in your library.

Even if your specific impairment is not listed in Table 3.2, you should be considered disabled if the severity of your health problems, taken together, equals or passes the severity of these listed impairments. In measuring the severity of your conditions, and comparing them to the listed impairments, the Government looks at your ability to:

TABLE 3.2

List of Disabling Conditions

1. Diseases of the heart, lungs, or blood vessels that have resulted in serious loss of function as shown by medical tests and that produce a severe limitation (like breathlessness, pain, tiredness) in spite of medical treatment
2. Severe arthritis causing recurring inflammation, pain, swelling, and deformity in major joints so that the ability to get about or use your hands is severely limited
3. Mental illness resulting in marked constriction of activities and interests, deterioration in personal habits or work-related behavior, and seriously impaired ability to get along with other people
4. Brain abnormality or damage that has resulted in severe loss of judgment, intellect, orientation, or memory
5. Cancer that is progressive and has not been controlled or cured
6. Digestive system diseases resulting in malnutrition, weight loss, weakness, and anemia
7. Disorders that have resulted in the loss of a leg or that have caused the limb to become useless
8. Loss of major functions of both arms, both legs, or a leg and an arm
9. Serious loss of function of the kidneys
10. Total inability to speak

- Do physical activities, such as walking, standing, sitting, lifting, bending, pushing, or pulling
- See, hear, or speak
- Understand, remember, and respond to instructions
- Exercise judgment
- Deal with changes in a routine work setting

Is blindness a disability? Although blindness is not included in the list of disabilities in Table 3.2, it surely can be a disability that prevents you from doing "substantial gainful employment." And qualifying for disability benefits based on blindness is made a little easier under some special rules.

You may be considered blind if your vision can't be corrected to at least 20/200 in your better eye, or if your visual field is 20 degrees or less, even with glasses or contacts. A person who is blind may qualify for benefits with earnings (or potential earnings) of as much as $850 a month (in 1992).

❖ GEM: Uncle Sam Has a Blind Spot— Apply for Disability Even with Higher Earnings

If you are earning more than $850 a month, you will not qualify for Social Security disability benefits even if you are blind. But *apply anyhow!* You're not wasting your time. In Chapter 1 we explained that the amount of Social Security retirement benefits is based on an average of your earnings over the years. If you had higher earnings before becoming blind, and lower earnings after, the lower earnings (though more than $850 a month) would drag down your overall average, and so cause a reduction in your retirement benefits. But if you apply for Social Security disability benefits based on blindness, you can increase your future Social Security *retirement* benefits; blindness triggers an exception to the normal averaging rules so that your average earnings should *not* be reduced because of lower earnings in years when you are blind.

✦ ✦ ✦

We have explained that in most cases you will not be considered disabled if you can perform *any* substantial work, even if you can no longer continue your prior job. The test for disability if you are blind is a little more relaxed. If you are blind and 55 or older, you are considered disabled if you are unable to work in a job requiring skills or abilities similar to those involved in your prior employment. The Government will *not* look to see if you could get a job in a different line of work.

Age, education, and work experience. If your impairment is listed in Table 3.2, or if it is as severe as those listed in the table, then you should be considered disabled. That's it—the Government won't have to get involved in evaluating nonmedical factors that may further limit your ability to work.

But if your condition is not listed in Table 3.2 or is not as bad as those listed impairments, you're not out of luck. You may be able to prove you are disabled by showing that your physical or mental impairment *and* your age, education, and past work experience together render you unable to work. The Government must consider the combined effect of *all* your physical and mental impairments; though any one condition may not be enough, the total impact might be disabling.

EXAMPLE 7

You had been assembling electronic products in a factory. You handled tiny transistors and wires, and the work required great dexterity.

Working with a saw at home one day, you accidently sliced three of your fingers, losing most use of them. You no longer could continue your job. Though your impairment is not listed in Table 3.2, you may still qualify as disabled, based on your age, education, and past work experience. For instance, if you are 50 and otherwise in good health, the Government will probably deny disability coverage and require you to train for other work. But if you are 62, you should be able to convince the Government that you are too old to start retraining for a completely new field, and so you should get disability benefits.

What Are the Grids?

To provide some consistency in decision making, the Government adopted Medical-Vocational Guidelines, also known as "Grids." If you can't do heavy work—lifting or carrying objects of up to 50 pounds—and you can't return to your former job, then the Government probably will use the Grids to decide whether your disability makes you unable to do substantial gainful work.

The Grids are made up of three tables, excerpted in Appendix 7 as Tables A, B, and C. As you can see from the tables, the less physical ability you have to work (carry and lift), the older you are, the less education you have, and the less skilled you are, the more likely you will be considered disabled.

The three tables are divided by physical ability. Table A is for people who can do, at most, only sedentary work, which generally involves sitting for as much as six hours a day, though it may involve occasional walking or standing. No lifting of more than 10 pounds at a time is usually required.

Table B is for people who can do light work, which generally requires a good deal of walking or standing, or sitting and pushing or pulling arm or leg controls. The type of work often involves lifting or carrying up to 10 pounds, with occasional lifting up to 20 pounds, but not more. Someone capable of light work will usually be considered capable of sedentary work too, unless there is some reason why not (like an inability to sit for long periods).

Table C is for people who can do medium work, which generally involves frequent lifting or carrying of objects weighing up to 25 pounds, and occasional lifting up to 50 pounds. Work may include grasping, holding and turning objects, and also bending or stooping.

To determine whether you are disabled based on the Grids, first find the table that describes the type of work you can do (sedentary, light, or medium). Then find the line that best describes your age, education, and previous work experience. Once you have located your place in the table, you can determine whether or not you are disabled.

❖ GEM: Go "Lite"—Pick the Table Requiring the Least Physical Activity

The less physical work you can do, the more likely you'll be considered disabled. Table A, limited to sedentary work, has eight opportunities to be disabled; Table B, for people who can do light work, has only five chances; and Table C, for people with the capacity for greater physical activity, contains only three situations in which a person would be called disabled. See Example 8.

EXAMPLE 8

You worked as a crate loader in a warehouse for your entire working career. Your education was limited to the 10th grade. Now that you are 53, the heavy lifting has taken its toll and you can no longer continue the job. Can you cash in on disability benefits?

If you can no longer lift objects of more than 10 pounds without terrible pain, you find in Table A that you would be considered disabled (based on your age, education, and work experience). But if you can lift up to 50 pounds, you're into Table C, and that table says you are *not* disabled.

❖ GEM: S-Age Advice—Avoid Disqualification Due to Age

Age is important when determining disability. The older you are, the more likely you'll be considered disabled. The Grids are split into four general age categories: 49 and under; 50–54; 55–59; and 60 and over. If you are within a few months of the next age category listed in the Grids, and using the next category would help you qualify for disability benefits, the Government should give you the "benefits of the doubt." See Example 9.

EXAMPLE 9

You are capable of doing light work; your education stopped at the 10th grade; and your prior work experience was in a semiskilled job, but the job skills aren't transferable. You are only a couple months short of your 55th birthday.

Looking at Table B, you would *not* be considered disabled as a 54-year-old, but you would at age 55. Since you are so close, the Government should let you qualify now.

The purpose of the age differences in the Grids makes some sense: the Government assumes that the older you get, the more difficult it is to adapt to a new type of job. But even if you are too "young" to qualify for benefits under the Grids, you can still get benefits by presenting to the Government other evidence of the difficulty you would have in learning a new position. Such evidence includes occupational tests showing unusual physical deterioration (reflexes, senses, etc.) and I.Q. testing that shows less ability to adapt than others your age would have.

❖ GEM: Transferability Means No Disability

If your prior work experience gave you skills that *are transferable* (usable in other types of work), you will not be considered disabled. Tables A, B, and C all disallow disability benefits for someone with transferable skills, regardless of age or education.

To qualify for benefits, you want to provide evidence that your skills from former employment were so unique or specialized that they aren't useful in other types of work. For example, skills you picked up in mining, farming, fishing, music, dancing, professional athletics, or space exploration are usually not transferable to other types of jobs.

Note, however, when looking at your prior work experience, the Government can only go back 15 years; work experience *before* that time should not be considered.

❖ GEM: Talents Aren't the Same as Skills

The greater your skills, the less likely you'll be able to get disability benefits. But just because you have a talent or aptitude doesn't mean you have a skill. Skills must be learned; talents are innate. And talents should not be considered in disability decisions.

For example, courts have said that skills include the ability to do clerical work, prepare reports, read blueprints, operate a cash register, and supervise workers; all these can be learned. But manual dexterity and independent judgment, by themselves, cannot be billed as skills.

❖ ❖ ❖

Getting Around the Grids

Let's say that the Grids show you can work, though you really are disabled. The key to receiving benefits is to convince the Government that the Grids don't fairly apply to you and that other factors should be considered. How can you get out of the Grids? Here are a couple of gems.

❖ GEM: Escape Grid-Lock and Show That the Grids Shouldn't Apply to Your Disability

The Grids are based primarily on how much you can lift or carry; your goal is to show that in your case Grids are unfair because the nature of your disability doesn't affect your physical capacity to lift or carry. For example, mental problems, sensory or skin problems, speech, hearing or sight impairments, limitations on hands or fingers for fine activities, alcoholism, side effects of medication, postural problems, pain, allergies or intolerance to things in the environment, and limits on your ability to balance, stoop, climb, kneel, crouch, crawl or reach all can make you unable to work, though you may still be able to lift or carry heavy objects. For that reason, all of these impairments can get you out of the Grids. But you must take special care to provide as much evidence as possible of these disabilities. See Example 10.

EXAMPLE 10

Your back is strong, and you can lift 50 pounds without much trouble. But you've got constant, severe headaches that prevent you from holding any job. The pain makes it impossible for you to concentrate, remember, and respond to problems. Even though the Grids say you are able to work, you should be considered disabled.

❖ GEM: Years of Hard Labor Pay Off!

You must be considered disabled if you've put in 35 years or more of hard, unskilled labor and can no longer continue. This is true even if you can still do less strenuous work. Don't worry about the Grids—this one is automatic (unless you have an education that allows you to get a job that has little physical exertion).

◆　◆　◆

Family Disability Benefits

The family of a worker who is disabled may also collect from Social Security. When a breadwinner is disabled, the following family members become eligible for Social Security benefits:

- Spouse age 62 or older
- Spouse, any age, caring for child under 16 or disabled
- Unmarried child under 18 (19 if in high school full time)
- Unmarried child, any age, if disabled since before becoming 18

HOW MUCH SHOULD YOU GET?

If you qualify for Social Security disability payments, how much should you get? The Government will tell you an amount. But as we warned in regard to Social

Security retirement benefits, there could be a mistake—and your failure to catch it could cost you a pot of money.

Check Earnings Record and Correct Mistakes

Your first step is to get your Personal Earnings and Benefit Statement (PEBES) from the Social Security Administration. The form will explain your disability benefits. You can get your PEBES request forms by calling the Social Security Hotline, (800) 772-1213. Fill out the form and send it to the address given.

Once you get your PEBES, check your earnings record (page 5) and correct any mistakes (page 6). Social Security disability benefits, like retirement and survivor benefits, are based on your earnings over the years. A mistake in your earnings record could cut your benefits drastically.

Figure Your Benefits

Even if the earnings record appears accurate, you're not done. The Government may have miscalculated benefits. Table 3.3 lists estimated disability benefits.

TABLE 3.3

**Approximate Monthly Disability Benefits
If You Became Disabled in 1992**

Your Present Age	Who Receives Benefits	Your Earnings in 1991					
		$10,000	$20,000	$30,000	$40,000	$50,000	$53,400 or more
64	You	$484	743	973	1,033	1,075	1,082
	Spouse age 65 or child[1]	242	371	486	516	537	541
	Maximum for whole family[2]	726	1,114	1,459	1,549	1,612	1,623
55	You	480	736	973	1,043	1,093	1,101
	Spouse age 65 or child	240	368	486	521	546	550
	Maximum for whole family	720	1,104	1,459	1,564	1,639	1,651

[1]Spouse or eligible child is entitled to 50 percent of disabled worker's full age 65 retirement benefit.
[2]Maximum for the entire family is 1½ times the disabled worker's full age 65 retirement benefit.

(*Continued*)

TABLE 3.3 (Continued)

Your Present Age	Who Receives Benefits	Your Earnings in 1991					
		$10,000	$20,000	$30,000	$40,000	$50,000	$53,400 or more
45	You	480	737	981	1,084	1,157	1,170
	Spouse age 65 or child	240	368	490	542	578	585
	Maximum for whole family	720	1,105	1,471	1,626	1,735	1,755

Check your benefits against the estimates in this table.

The figures in Table 3.3 are only estimates. They assume you have worked steadily until becoming disabled, and that you have received average pay increases. Disability benefits are figured as a percentage of your full retirement benefits at age 65. The percentages are listed in Table 3.4. For a more accurate estimate of your actual benefits, turn to Appendix 8. Note also that the total benefits a family can receive is limited under the Maximum Family Benefits (MFB) rule, described on page 25.

TABLE 3.4

Family Disability Benefits

Who Gets Benefits	% of Your Full Age 65 Retirement Benefit
You[1] at any age	100 %
Your spouse age 65	50
Your spouse age 64	45.8
Your spouse age 63	41.7
Your spouse age 62	37.5
Your child[2]	50
Your spouse, any age, caring for young or disabled child[3]	150

[1]This assumes you are the disabled individual.
[2]A child will be eligible for benefits if unmarried and under 18 (19 if in high school full time). An unmarried adult child may be eligible at any age if disabled since before becoming 18.
[3]The child must be under 16 or disabled.

HOW DO DIFFERENT GOVERNMENT "BENIES" FIT TOGETHER?

How do Social Security disability benefits fit together with Medicare? Supplemental Security Income (SSI) disability benefits? Early retirement benefits? Worker's Compensation benefits? Veterans' benefits? Private disability insurance? Since you generally can receive only one of these benefits, which should you take? The answers can reveal some hidden treasures.

Social Security Disability and Medicare

Most people think Medicare is only for those 65 years and up. But one important—often critical, and overlooked—disability benefit is that you can also get Medicare, *regardless* of your age. The value of the Medicare coverage may be worth more to you than the disability cash payments!

You can get Medicare hospital insurance protection (Part A) after you've been entitled to Social Security disability for 24 months (shorter if you have end-stage renal disease). Those months don't have to be in a row; they don't even have to be for the same disability. You may also enroll in Medicare medical insurance (Part B); you must pay for Part B, as does everyone else, but that's another Golden Opportunity you shouldn't miss. (Medicare is discussed in detail in Chapter 4.)

Disability vs. SSI Benefits

Supplemental Security Income (SSI), a program designed to provide a safety net for low-income people (discussed in Chapter 10), also pays disability benefits. Sometimes the SSI benefits are higher than Social Security disability payments, sometimes not. You can't double up, so go with the most you can get.

EXAMPLE 11

Suppose that, based on your work record, your Social Security disability checks would amount to $300/month. Not bad, but let's see how you'd do under SSI.

SSI payments are not dependent on your work record. Instead, you are entitled to a standard amount based on your other sources of income (see page 433). If your SSI checks would be higher than $300/month, opt for SSI; otherwise, take Social Security disability.

When comparing amounts available under Social Security disability and SSI, remember to consider reductions. SSI payments will be reduced by all sorts of income; Social Security disability will be reduced only by certain benefit payments, such as Worker's Compensation (page 101).

EXAMPLE 12

Your SSI benefits would be $422/month; Social Security disability would pay $300/month. But the interest income you receive reduces the amount of your SSI to $200/month, while the extra income has no impact on Social Security disability. So the decision is clear: you'll take Social Security disability.

Golden Rule: When you have no outside income to reduce SSI benefits, choose SSI; when your extra income reduces SSI benefits, choose Social Security disability.

When comparing Social Security disability and SSI, also keep in mind that with Social Security disability benefits your dependents may be entitled to some money. Under SSI, *you* are the only one entitled to benefits. So lower Social Security disability payments for you might mean more for your family.

Social Security disability may get you Medicare, but SSI is tied directly into Medicaid eligibility in many states. Medicaid (discussed in Chapter 11) provides very important medical coverage—even broader than Medicare. If you qualify for SSI, you will probably get Medicaid, too.

SSI imposes income and wealth limits on eligibility. You can qualify only if you meet those requirements. Social Security disability imposes no similar requirements. But for Social Security disability, you must have worked for a specified period to qualify (not the case for SSI).

❖ GEM: Instant SSI Coverage for Certain Impairments—Apply Immediately!

If you have one of the following impairments, apply for SSI right now:

- Amputation of two limbs
- Amputation of a leg at the hip
- Total deafness
- Total blindness
- Bed confinement, or immobility without a wheelchair, walker, or crutches due to a long-standing condition
- Stroke more than three months ago, which has caused continued difficulty in walking or using a hand or arm

- Cerebral palsy, muscular dystrophy, or muscle atrophy, which has caused difficulty in walking, speaking, or coordination
- Diabetes, which has caused amputation of a foot
- Down's syndrome
- Mental deficiency that causes the individual to require some special care and/or supervision
- AIDS

Why? The Government will start your SSI benefits immediately—even before making any final decision on your application. Payments for these impairments can be made for three months. If the Government later decides that you were not disabled, you keep the payments—the Government can't ask for its money back! See Example 13.

EXAMPLE 13

You have become totally deaf. Following our suggestion, you immediately apply for and begin receiving SSI benefits of $300 a month. After looking closely at your health, the Government decides you're not disabled. You get to keep the SSI payments already received.

❖ GEM: Apply for SSI Now Even If Social Security Disability Will Pay More

Even if your benefits under Social Security disability will be higher than SSI, apply for both at the same time. Why? Social Security disability won't cover the first five months from onset of the disability, while SSI will. After the five months expire, your Social Security disability should then begin.

◆ ◆ ◆

Social Security Disability vs. Early Retirement Benefits

Let's say you are 62 and could qualify for either Social Security disability or retirement benefits. Since you can't take both, which is better? In almost all cases, you'll put more dough in your pocket under the disability program than with early retirement benefits. Here's why: At age 62, you'll get Social Security retirement checks only equal to 80 percent of your full age 65 retirement benefits, but you'll get 100 percent of your age 65 retirement benefits with Social Security disability. *Plus*—and this is a huge plus—two years after starting disability you get Medicare. Otherwise, you wouldn't get Medicare until age 65!

EXAMPLE 14

At age 62, you have the option of taking early retirement or disability payments under Social Security. Your full age 65 retirement (benefit) is $800/month.

Early retirement will pay you $640; disability pays you the full $800. At age 64, you also get Medicare—if you take disability. There's no Medicare until age 65 otherwise. Tough decision? No way!

❖ GEM: At 62, Apply for Both Disability and Retirement

Even though Social Security disability pays more than early retirement, apply for both at 62. Why? Because Social Security disability won't pay for the first five months, while early retirement will. So start with Social Security early retirement for five months and then get the higher disability payments.

If you already started taking early retirement benefits, can you switch to disability payments? The answer is yes. Would it make sense to do that? Yes!

❖ GEM: Make the Switch to Disability Even After Starting Early Retirement Benefits

If you are disabled, normally you are entitled to 100 percent of your full age 65 retirement benefits (Table 3.4). But if you had already started taking early retirement benefits, your disability payments will be reduced by .556% for each month you received early retirement benefits. But even reduced Social Security disability payments will be higher than early retirement benefits. Example 15 shows how this works.

EXAMPLE 15

You retired at 62, taking early retirement benefits of $640/month (80% of $800). One year goes by, and then you suffer a disabling illness. If you switch to disability benefits, you'll receive 93 percent of your full age 65 retirement amount (the 7% reduction is due to the 12 monthly retirement benefit checks you received: $12 \times .556\%$).

Should you switch? Yes. The $744/month (93% of $800) is a lot better than $640/month! Switching to Social Security disability will put money in your pocket.

❖ ❖ ❖

**Social Security Disability and Worker's Compensation Benefits—
Both for the Asking!**

If your disability is work related, you may qualify for both Worker's Compensation and Social Security disability benefits. If so, you may be allowed to double up benefits, at least partially.

The Worker's Compensation benefits—paid under a federal, state, or local public law—will probably offset at least a portion of your Social Security disability payments. Total benefits from these two sources cannot exceed the higher of:

- 80 percent of your earnings before the disability
- Your Social Security disability benefit

When figuring your earnings before the disability, you would usually use the higher of either:

- The average earnings from employment on which you paid Social Security taxes during the five highest paid consecutive years after 1950
- The highest single year of earnings during the five years before you became disabled

---

EXAMPLE 16

Your Social Security disability benefit is $600/month, and Worker's Compensation will pay $500/month. Your earnings before the disability were $1,300/month. Do you get to keep both checks?

The answer is no, but you will get to keep all of the Worker's Compensation and most of the Social Security disability payments. With earnings before the disability of $1,300/month, 80% is $1,040—that's the total you can collect. Worker's Compensation pays $500/month, leaving you to keep $540/month of your Social Security disability payments.

❖ GEM: Get Full Benefits from Both at 65, and Maybe 62

If you first became disabled after February 1981, the offset we just described continues until you reach age 65. After you reach 65, you get to keep *all* of your Worker's Compensation and *all* of your Social Security benefits. If you first became disabled in February 1981 or before, you can get full benefits even sooner—at age 62!

✦ ✦ ✦

Social Security Disability, as Well as
Veterans' or Private Disability Benefits

You can keep your full Social Security disability benefits *plus* your entire disability payments from veterans' benefits; private pension or insurance; and federal, state, and local government employment benefits. Unlike Worker's Compensation, these benefits will not reduce your Social Security disability payments.

TAXES AND EARNINGS

In Chapter 1, we told you about the Government's secret tax trap, which eats away at your Social Security retirement and survivor benefits. The same tax trap can "disable" your disability benefits. However, our gems to protect retirement benefits also can cut the taxes on your disability payments.

Earnings will reduce your Social Security retirement and survivor benefits. Supposedly, earnings will *not* reduce Social Security disability payments—at least that's what they tell you. In truth, you must be careful; working may be hazardous to your health.

Earnings May Cut Your Income

If you get a job paying less than $300/month, the added income won't affect your Social Security disability payments. If your job pays over $500/month, you almost surely *will* lose all of your benefits—not because of any reduction but because you will no longer be considered disabled. With earnings between $300 and $500/month, the Government may look closely at your impairment, age, education, and work experience to determine whether you should continue receiving benefits.

EXAMPLE 17

Your days of loading boxes in the warehouse are over; your back just couldn't take it any longer. The Government has been sending you $800 a month in Social Security disability benefits.

But $800 doesn't go very far, so you got yourself a part-time job fixing bicycles in the local hardware store. The job pays $50 a week, keeps you busy, and lets you enjoy life a little more too. Don't worry—your Social Security disability checks are safe.

❖ GEM: Never Take a Job Paying More Than $300 a Month, as Long as It Pays Less Than Your Benefits

If you take a job paying more than about $300 a month, the job could cost you a lot of money, as Example 18 shows.

EXAMPLE 18

You get a job paying $550/month. Since that's over the $500/month benchmark, the Government will say you are no longer disabled and will cut off your benefits.

You were receiving Social Security disability payments of $900/month—$350/month more than your wages. By finding a job and getting off the Government rolls, you suffer a $350/month income loss!

The system is crazy. Uncle Sam should provide an incentive for people to go back to work. Yet the system works just the opposite, as Example 18 shows. Don't take a job for less than the amount of your Social Security disability benefits, or you may be in for a big cut in your income.

❖ GEM: Spouse's Earnings Can Provide Big Boost

Your husband or wife can work and earn as much as possible, without reducing your benefits at all! As long as you are getting disability payments based on your own work record, your spouse's earnings won't affect your benefits.

◆ ◆ ◆

Trial Work Period

You may want to try going back to work, but are afraid that you might not be able to continue for long. If you start work, and earn more than $500 a month, will you immediately lose your benefits? The answer is no. Uncle Sam provides a nine-month trial work period. This is a free trial offer—nine months on Uncle Sam, with no money down. During that trial period, you get your disability benefits *and* your wages (even if over $500 a month).

EXAMPLE 19

You are getting itchy to return to the working world, and you found a job doing filing in a local doctor's office. You're not sure how long you'll be able to stand on your feet before your back starts aching, but you'd like to give it a try. If it works, you could make $700/month (a lot more than your current disability payments of $500/month). Since you don't know if you'll be able to sustain the job, though, you don't want to lose your Social Security disability benefits. Should you sit home? No.

Contact your local Social Security office and tell them you are starting a trial work period. You will continue to receive full benefits for nine months, *plus* your wages. If you make it for that long, your benefits will terminate. But you don't have to repay benefits received during the trial period.

To qualify for a trial work period, you must tell the Social Security office. You have a right to a trial work period, but only if you notify them in writing that you're taking it. You get only one trial work period per disability (if you recover and later suffer a different disability, you get another trial period). So use it wisely!

❖ GEM: Trial and Errors: Months Need Not Be Consecutive

The nine months that you try your hand at working, while keeping your Social Security disability benefits, do not have to be consecutive and do not have to be for the same employer. You can work for a couple of months, take some time off, and work for a few more months. Only the months you actually work and earn more than $200 a month count against your trial period.

EXAMPLE 20

In January 1993, you take a job in a department store. You earn $500 the first month and $500 the second month. But you then must quit because it's too hard on you.

For the next three months, from March through May, you look around for another job you might be able to handle. On June 1 you start work in a music store, earning $350/month; you continue that job through September. But again, you can no longer take the pain and must quit at the end of September. After one month off, you get a job making purchases for a day care center. The job pays only $100/month, but at least you can do it. You work there in October, November, and December.

All this time, you've been receiving your Social Security disability benefits. You've used only six months of your trial work period: January, February, June, July, August, and September. The months you were off and the months you earned less than $200 don't count and are not subtracted from your nine trial months.

❖ GEM: Multiply Trial Months

When figuring your trial months, count only trial work months during the last five years. Months worked more than five years earlier won't count against you. See Example 21.

EXAMPLE 21

Let's take the same facts as in Example 20. You had six trial work months in 1993. If you had worked five months in 1992 as well, you'd be in trouble. You would have exhausted your trial work period in July 1993. But if you had worked five months in 1987, those months would not count against you.

❖ GEM: Put Yourself on Trial at the Start of a Month

You will use up one of your nine trial months each month you work and earn $200, even if you work only a few days of the month. As Example 22 shows, a short delay in starting work could provide you with some extra income.

EXAMPLE 22

You start work the last week of January, and you earn $250. The next eight months, February through September, you earn $1,000/month. During each of these months, you receive your Social Security disability benefits of $500/month.

Starting in October, your benefits are cut off because your nine trial months have expired. In October, you receive $1,000 earnings, but no more disability payments. The total—benefits and earnings—from January through October is $13,750.

What if you had waited a week to start your job? You would have received your $500 benefit check in January, but no earnings. For the next nine months, February through October, you'd collect $1,500/month ($1,000 earnings and $500 benefits).

Let's compare: During the same 10 months, you would have received $14,000, even though you waited a week to start your job. In other words, the one-week delay would have saved you $250. So when working trial months, always start at the beginning of a month. You'll come out ahead.

❖ GEM: If There's Pain You Can Regain Benefits

Let's say you return to work and you complete your nine-month trial period, earning more than $500 a month. Disability benefits will then end. But work soon gets the better of you, your condition worsens, and you've got to stop working. Do you have to go through the whole Social Security disability qualification process again?

Thankfully, no! For 36 months following the end of your trial work period you get special treatment. You are entitled to disability benefits for each and every month in which you fail to work and earn $500—and all you have to do is ask! You do *not* have to reapply or go through a five-month waiting period. Just notify the local Social Security office, in writing, that you're not working, and the checks should start flowing.

❖ GEM: Get Three Extra Months of Benefits

At the end of your trial work period, your work will be looked at by Uncle Sam to see if you should stay on disability benefits. If you are earning less than $500 a month, you should be allowed to continue your benefits. If your earnings are more than $500 a month, benefits will be shut off. But you should get *three more months* of benefit checks (following the end of the nine-month trial period). If Uncle Sam "forgets," remind him!

APPLICATION

If you believe you may be entitled to Social Security disability insurance benefits, reading this chapter isn't enough—you must *apply*. Social Security disability benefits are not automatic.

The application process for disability benefits is much more complicated than it is for retirement or survivor benefits. Your application must be in writing on an official form provided by the Social Security Administration. You can get a form by calling or stopping in to your local Social Security office. Personnel in the Social Security office are usually quite willing to help you fill out the application, and you should take advantage of their assistance. In some cases, Social Security personnel may even come to your home or hospital room.

You will need the information listed in our Checklist, Appendix 6. In addition, prepare a list and description of:

1. All physical and mental problems that cause you to be disabled. (Don't omit "hidden" impairments, like alcoholism and depression.)
2. Names, addresses, and telephone numbers of all doctors, psychologists, caseworkers, hospitals, clinics, and other institutions that treated you, and the approximate dates of treatment. Even better, get your medical records!
3. Current medications, noting side effects, and any devices needed to assist you (wheelchairs, cane, etc.).
4. Names and addresses of people who know of your disability and might be witnesses, if necessary (*i.e.,* spouse or roommates who live with you; friends who help with transportation and shopping).
5. Names and addresses of your employers during the last 15 years.
6. The tasks you performed in each prior job.
7. Dates of any military service.
8. Dates of marriages.
9. Any other benefits you receive (or expect to receive) because of your disability. Include claim numbers.
10. Educational background.
11. Typical daily activities.

The Government will usually require an interview as part of the application process. Bring the information listed above and in Appendix 6. To help you organize your thoughts and prepare the application properly, first fill out our Disability Planning Questionnaire in Appendix 9. If you decide to consult an attorney, it will also help the lawyer focus his or her efforts and to prepare your best claim or appeal. (See page 119 to decide when you need a lawyer.)

When you are preparing the information for your disability claim, don't be overly shy or proud. While it is sometimes very hard to describe your health problems to a stranger—particularly federal bureaucrats—you shouldn't hold back. Failing fully to describe your impairments may cause the Government to say you are not disabled.

As you describe your disability, don't just focus on "exertional" impairments, such as problems you may have lifting or carrying. Consider postural limitations, mental illness, seizures, loss of feeling in a hand, depression, and anything else that prevents you from working.

❖ GEM: Don't Exaggerate Prior Work Experience

If you were a janitor, don't describe your position as a "sanitation engineer"; if you were a secretary, don't call yourself an executive assistant. While those descriptions might help when you're applying for a new job, they can only hurt your chances for disability benefits. Remember, the Government will consider your transferable skills when deciding whether there is any substantial work you can do. The more experience you appear to have, the less likely you'll be considered disabled.

✦ ✦ ✦

Do your homework before applying. By making life as easy as possible for the Government bureaucrats, you also help yourself. The more facts you can bring to the interview, the better off you'll usually be. For example, rather than just identify the hospital at which you were treated, get the medical records. Without medical substantiation, your impairments will not be considered.

❖ GEM: Get a Letter from Your Doctor

Very often, a good, descriptive letter from someone who treated you (doctor, psychologist, nurse, caseworker) can be *very* useful. Unfortunately, if you simply ask "Could you please write a letter about my disability?" you may not get a very helpful response. Give your physician a specific prescription for what to include in the letter:

1. A detailed description of all of your ailments.
2. A statement of how long the ailments have lasted and are expected to continue.
3. A prognosis as to whether your ailments are stable or worsening.
4. His/her view of how your ailments affect daily activities and work ability.
5. An explanation of the tests and examinations upon which these conclusions are based.
6. A list of dates when examinations or tests occurred.
7. A description of your symptoms, including places, degree, and regularity of pain.

8. A list of the medications you are and have been taking, including the reason for the medication, the dates prescribed, the frequency they are taken, and any side effects.

In addition, ask your doctor to address the elements in the Grids, such as: how much you can carry or lift, how long you can sit, and whether you can handle fine motor activities.

EXAMPLE 23

Your doctor's letter should not focus only on the back pain that prevents you from working. Have your doctor also describe your hypertension and ulcer, which prevent you from taking pain medication and which therefore contribute to your disability.

The doctor should provide as much support for his conclusions as possible. He or she should attach and refer specifically to medical records, test results, and clinical evaluations. The more detail your doctor provides, the more persuasive will be his report.

❖ GEM: Get a Letter from Your Former Employer

A letter from your former employer(s) might also help your application. The letter should conclude that you can't return to your former position owing to your disability. In addition, your former employer should:

1. Describe your former duties and responsibilities (tell him or her not to exaggerate).
2. Talk about the physical requirements (lifting, carrying, walking, standing, stooping) of your job.
3. Describe the limited nature of skills gained on the job and explain why they are not transferable (if that's in fact true).
4. Explain the impact the disability had on your performance.

❖ ❖ ❖

A lot of people have lost out on a lot of money because they failed to provide enough evidence with their application. Uncle Sam is not psychic. Don't expect him to know what you didn't say; he won't go hunting for evidence you don't offer.

When your application is complete, it will be forwarded to a federal Disability Determination Service (DDS) office located in your state. Personnel in that office, normally including a physician, decide whether you are disabled. The DDS may ask you, your physicians, hospitals, or other institutions for more information. The better you are prepared in advance, the faster this evaluation will go (and the more likely you will be approved). If the DDS doesn't feel it can adequately evaluate your claim based on existing medical records, you may be asked to take a medical exam by physicians of the government's choice. Don't give the DDS folks a hard time—your application can be denied if you refuse to cooperate. The Government will pay for any costs involved (including travel).

What can happen at a Government-required medical exam? Take a look at Example 24.

EXAMPLE 24

The Government-hired doctor gives you a very cursory examination. You spend more time in the waiting room than in the exam. Yet, when you hear back about your disability application, it's been denied—and the denial was based on the Government doctor's report!

Unfortunately, the situation described in Example 24 is not so unusual. Here's a gem to reduce the risk.

❖ GEM: Take Notes About the Government's Exam

You can undercut the Government doctor's report by showing the cursory nature of the exam. Immediately after the exam, take notes that show:

- The exact time the doctor began and ended his exam.
- What parts of your body he checked.
- All the questions he asked you and the subjects discussed (related to your disability or not).
- Any tests taken by the doctor.

If your application is denied based on a Government doctor's report, these notes may help you on appeal. They can establish that the report by the Government's doctor shouldn't be given much weight, since his or her exam was not thorough.

❖ GEM: Have Tests Done by Your Doctor

While the Government has the right to have one of its doctors look you over, you have the right to ask that any required tests (EKGs, stress tests, etc.) be done by *your* doctor, at the Government's expense.

❖ GEM: Apply ASAP—There Are Deadlines to Meet!

Waiting to file an application will cost you money. If you delay longer than 17 months after the beginning of the disability, you lose money. This is because Social Security disability benefits can be paid retroactively for up to 12 months from the date you *apply*. There is a five-month waiting period from the onset of the disability, during which you can't get benefits. So if you apply for benefits within 17 months of the onset of the disability, you won't lose out; but waiting more than 17 months will cost you—as Example 25 demonstrates.

EXAMPLE 25

You suffered a debilitating stroke on May 31, 1991. It is now seventeen months later, October 1992. If you apply for disability benefits right away, you won't lose a penny of the benefits due to you. That's because no benefits can be paid for the first five months (June–October 1991), and the benefits, once approved, can be paid back through November 1991.

But if you wait until March 1993 to apply, you'll have permanently lost four months (November and December 1991, January and February 1992) of retroactive benefits—that's hundreds, maybe thousands, of dollars that were rightfully yours.

Finally, the Government usually takes a long time to decide disability applications—three to six months is not uncommon. If appeals are necessary, plan on a year or longer. So don't delay. The longer you take to apply, the longer the wait until the checks will start to come in.

CAN YOUR BENEFITS BE CUT OFF?

Okay, your application for Social Security disability benefits has been approved and you have been cashing in. Can the Government later take your benefits away?

The answer, of course, is yes. You didn't really think we would say no, did you? But the better you understand your rights, the better able you'll be to protect your pocketbook!

Periodic Review—Big Brother Is Watching

Uncle Sam is going to check up on you. He is hoping your condition has improved enough to allow you to work and earn $500 a month. Then, the Government can cut off your benefits if you are no longer disabled.

Even if your health has not improved, you may no longer be considered disabled, and your benefits may be terminated, if:

- Advances in medical or vocational therapy or technology make it possible for you to work and earn $500 a month or more.
- You underwent vocational therapy or training, which now allows you to earn at least $500 a month.
- New or improved diagnostic techniques reveal that your impairment is not as severe as previously believed.

Table 3.5 shows how often you can expect to hear from Uncle Sam.

TABLE 3.5

Review of Conditions of Disabled Americans

If Medical Improvement Is	Expect a Disability Review
Never expected	Every 7 years
Possible, though not expected (most people fall into this category)	Every 3 years
Expected	Every 18 months

The review is usually routine. The Government can cut off your benefits only if it decides you are no longer disabled based on *new evidence;* it cannot change its mind based on the information from your original application.

❖ GEM: You Can Run, but You Can't Hide, from a Disability Review

Some people are too smart for their own good. When they find out the Government is reviewing their disability, they hide or refuse to cooperate. This is not wise.

The Government may ask you to provide additional information, such as updated medical evidence from your doctor, as part of the review. In fact, you may even be told to go for a medical exam. Do it! Your failure to cooperate will allow the Government to terminate your benefits *for that reason alone!*

If you can't get the information to the Government within the time requested, or you are unable to go to an exam, let the Government know *in writing* and ask for more time. Don't just ignore deadlines set by the Government.

If the additional information required by the Government suggests that your health has improved, and you don't feel that's correct, insist on your right to respond by providing additional information, such as a statement from your doctor or therapist. Don't just try to bury it; if you do, your benefits are likely to get buried, too.

❖ GEM: Avoid Cut-off for Refusing Treatment

When reviewing your case, the Government can stop benefits if you failed to follow a reasonable treatment prescribed (not just suggested) by a doctor, which may have restored your ability to work. But if the prescribed treatment was not "reasonable," then your benefits can't be cut for refusing to try it. For example, if the doctor wanted to do surgery on your leg because it might allow you to stand and walk more easily, but the surgery poses a serious risk like the loss of the leg, you could refuse—*without* losing benefits.

And if a doctor prescribed treatment that you couldn't afford, don't let the Government stop your benefits. A treatment you can't afford is not reasonable for you.

❖ GEM: Don't Accept a Cut in Benefits If Health Improvement Is Not Related to Work

Even if your health has improved, your benefits cannot be stopped unless the improvement allows you to work.

EXAMPLE 26

You were just over 5 feet tall and weighed 220 pounds at the time you qualified for Social Security disability benefits. You had persistent edema (fluid causing swelling) in your legs, limiting your ability to stand or walk more than occasionally.

Since then you had a vein stripping operation and lost 35 pounds. The edema has been reduced, which is a medical improvement. But though you now have less discomfort than you did before, you still suffer enough so that you can stand or walk only for short periods of time.

Although your health has improved, the improvement is not related to your ability to work, because your capacity to do basic work activities (*i.e.,* stand and walk) has not increased. The Government can't strip your benefits.

❖ GEM: Use Your Age to Your Advantage

The older you are and the longer you've been receiving disability benefits, the better chance you should have to protect your benefits. Even if your health has improved, or if some other positive change has occurred (like improved technology or diagnostic techniques), it may not be fair to make you go back to work. The Government's own regulations state: "[T]he longer an individual is away from the workplace and is inactive, the more difficult it becomes to return to ongoing employment. In addition, a gradual change occurs in most jobs," so that skill acquired years ago will not "continue to apply to the current workplace." In case you need to tell the Government where you got this information, tell them it's in the Code of Federal Regulations, Vol. 20, Section 404.1594(b)(4)(iii).

In other words, don't let some young bureaucrat tell you that, even though you are 60 and have been out of work for a number of years, your health has improved, so he's cutting off your benefits.

❖   ❖   ❖

Benefits After Disability Has Ended

If the Government decides that you are able to work, it will cut off your disability benefits. Do they stop immediately? The answer is yes, *unless* you take steps to have them continued.

❖ GEM: Demand Special Payments After Termination

You have a right to Social Security disability payments for three additional months after the decision is made that you are no longer disabled. But these benefits are not automatic. You *must demand* these benefits, in writing, from the local Social Security office.

❖ GEM: Retain Medicare Coverage

Even if you have recovered enough to return to work, you generally can continue Medicare coverage for 39 months after your disability benefits end. Again, Medicare won't continue automatically; you must demand continued coverage from the Government in writing.

❖ GEM: Appeal Quickly to Preserve Benefits

If your disability benefits are terminated and you don't agree, you can appeal. (The appeal process after a termination of benefits is the same as for initial denials—see pages 116–120.) You get 60 days to file an appeal, but waiting that long to appeal a termination of benefits can be *very* costly.

File your written appeal with the local Social Security office within *15 days* from the date written on the termination notice received from the Government. By filing promptly, your benefits will continue during the first two appeal stages (Reconsideration and Administrative Hearing, pages 116–118). You must file a written request for continuation of benefits *in addition to your appeal* at each stage of appeal.

What happens if you've continued receiving disability checks for months during these appeals, and the termination is finally upheld? Can the Government demand that you return the amounts paid since the termination notice? The answer is yes—but don't give up hope. If repayment would cause you serious hardship, depriving you of money needed for ordinary living expenses (like food and medical costs), you should be able to obtain a waiver from the Government.

❖   ❖   ❖

Renewed Disability

If you received Social Security disability benefits, lost the benefits (for any reason), and then again become disabled, you can reapply for disability benefits. And if the renewed disability occurred within five years (seven years if you are a disabled widow or widower) after the benefits had been cut off, the checks should start again after you are approved—*without another five-month waiting period.*

What about the 24-month waiting period for Medicare? If you had been receiving Medicare with your previous disability, your coverage will resume with the first monthly disability check; no more waiting is required. And if you had not yet completed the 24-month waiting period, you pick up where you left off.

EXAMPLE 27

Your first period of disability lasted 15 months; during that time, you had not yet qualified for Medicare. You will have to wait only nine more months now (24 minus 15), not the full 24 months, to receive Medicare coverage.

APPEALS: YOU CAN FIGHT CITY HALL!

What happens if your application for Social Security disability is denied (or your benefits are wrongfully terminated)? *Don't be discouraged!* You're in good company; two of every three applicants are rejected. Unfortunately, the federal government denies *many* applications that should be approved. And, in fact, lots of people denied the first time—one in two—*are* finally approved as a result of appeals!

To get the benefits you deserve, you've got to be persistent. You've got to climb a very steep cliff to succeed. Don't give up; your tenacity will be rewarded! We'll help you reach the summit by providing an Appeals Ladder.

There are four steps on the Appeals Ladder, and if necessary you should climb them all. Let's take a look at each one.

Appeal Step 1: Request Reconsideration

You can ask the Government to reconsider its denial of your application within 60 days from the day you receive the rejection notice. (You actually will be given 65 days from the date stamped on the denial.) Your appeal must be in writing, either in a letter or on Government Form SSA-561-U2, available at your local Social Security office. A copy is included as Appendix 10. It's free.

Make sure your request for reconsideration includes your name, address, Social Security number, and disability claim number. If you have any new or additional information to support your claim, attach that, too. The Government may ask you for more information, and may also schedule a face-to-face meeting with one of its representatives. There is no formal hearing, and you can't bring in witnesses.

Your claim will not be reviewed by the same person who denied your application originally. But that probably won't make any difference. Your application likely will be rejected again. Fewer than one in seven reconsideration requests result in a change.

But don't give up! Your next step may be crucial.

Appeal Step 2: Administrative Hearing

This appeal may be your best chance to get benefits. Disabled Americans win more than half of all administrative hearings! (Disabled individuals won 60% of administrative hearings in 1990.)

After you receive written notice that the Government has denied your request for reconsideration (Appeal Step 1), you've again got 60 days to appeal. File your appeal in writing, either by letter or on Government Form HA-501-U5, a copy of which is in Appendix 11. The appeal must include your name and Social Security number, the reason why you think the denial is wrong, a summary of additional evidence you plan to provide, and the name of your lawyer, if applicable. The only cost is postage.

A hearing will take place from six weeks to 10 months after you file your appeal, depending upon where you live. Start to prepare immediately; don't wait until you get the notice scheduling the hearing, because that may only be two or three weeks before the scheduled date.

What should you do to prepare? Get and review the entire disability file the Government has put together for your claim. You are entitled to see it by law. Make sure that all your health records (doctors, hospitals, clinics, etc.) and employment records are included. Find any negative information and prepare to overcome it. For example, if there is a harmful doctor's statement, take it to your own doctor and have him write a rebuttal.

You may also decide to bring witnesses to the hearing. If so, you'll again have to prepare in advance. To get a doctor, former employer, counselor, or vocational expert to testify for you, you'll have to get on their schedule as soon as possible. You'll need time to work with them so they understand what's necessary for you to win. And you'll probably have to pay them.

If you need more time to get all this information together, you may call the Social Security office and reschedule, but that may delay the hearing another few months. You may be wiser to go ahead with the hearing and ask the judge for permission to provide supplemental materials within a week or two after the hearing.

The hearing will be held by the Social Security Office of Hearings and Appeals, which is different from the office that previously considered your application. An Administrative Law Judge, who is an attorney employed by the Social Security Administration, will preside and decide the appeal.

The hearing generally will be pretty informal. You tell your story in your own words, and you may present any written materials you believe will be useful. This is generally the last time you can present new evidence. Although two other appeals remain, they are based on information already provided.

You may present witnesses to support your claim. Who might you bring?

- Friends or relatives who can describe your condition, talk about your daily activities and your limitations, and maybe even indicate how they must help you.
- Doctor, nurse, therapist, or others who can explain your disability.
- Former employer(s) who will testify about how the disability prevents you from working.

If your witnesses won't appear voluntarily, you may subpoena (force) them. The Social Security office may help you with this, but you must let the office know that you want their help *no later* than five days before the hearing. However, think twice about forcing a witness to come to the hearing. An unhappy witness might cause you more harm than good.

The judge will probably ask you a lot of questions. Stay cool; don't assume he's the enemy; answer honestly; don't try to be funny or flip.

The judge may also ask a "vocational expert" to present his views at the hearing as to whether there are jobs you could perform, considering your impairment, age, education, and work experience. Ask about the person's qualifications; if you don't like what he's saying, you may challenge his expertise. If you fit into the Grids, no vocational expert should be involved.

You don't have to attend the hearing; you may have someone attend for you, or you may waive it. But you're almost always better off being there if possible.

Appeal Step 3: Appeals Council

If you lose the first two appeals, you're still not done. You've again got 60 days to take another step up the Appeals Ladder to the Social Security Appeals Council. Your appeal must be in writing, in a letter or on Government Form HA-520-U6, a copy of which is in Appendix 12. Your appeal may be filed with your local Social Security office, or sent by certified mail to the Appeals Council, P.O. Box 3200, Arlington, VA 22203.

The Appeals Council does not have to consider your appeal. And even if it does, no new evidence can be presented. You may present written arguments explaining why the denials of your application have been wrong, and you may appear in Washington, D.C. (at your expense) to argue your appeal. Chances are that you'll lose this appeal, but file it anyhow. You've still got one step left after this, but this step is available only if you go through with an appeal to the Appeals Council.

Appeal Step 4: Federal Court

If all else fails, you may make a "federal case" out of the denial of your disability claim. Although the burden is on you to show that your claim has been wrongfully denied, a *lot* of denials are reversed by federal judges.

You've got 60 days after the Appeals Council's negative decision to file your case in the local U.S. District (trial) Court. You will not be allowed to bring up any new evidence during this appeal; the court will base its decision only on the existing evidence.

❖ GEM: Get a Lawyer

Take one step yourself: file the application without hiring an attorney. We've explained the facts you need to present. If you win, you've saved a lawyer's fee.

But if you lose, get professional help for the climb up the Appeals Ladder. Don't be penny wise and pound foolish.

The most important function of the lawyer is to help organize and prepare your appeals. Among other things, the lawyer will help:

- Collect your medical records and organize them to support your claim.
- Prepare a description of your disability and prior work experience that best fits the Government's guidelines.
- Explain to your doctors and former employers the nature of the Government's disability rules that apply to your case, so they can write reports designed to qualify you for benefits.
- Make sure the physicians' reports are supported by appropriate medical records.
- Refer you to additional doctors who regularly work with disability applicants.
- Identify witnesses for the hearing, and prepare legal papers to require them to come if they won't attend voluntarily.
- Make sure you understand what facts to emphasize and which facts might be better left unsaid when you testify at the Administrative Hearing.
- Cross-examine Government witnesses, including doctors and vocational experts, at the Administrative Hearing.
- File appeals on time.
- Follow legal procedures that sometimes can be complicated, particularly in federal court.

Preparing for the appeals takes time. Don't tie your lawyer's hands by waiting too long to call him or her. As soon as your application is denied, get on the phone.

As we're sure you know, lawyers don't work for free. But you should *only* hire a lawyer on a contingency basis, which means that he or she gets paid only if you win. If you lose, the lawyer loses too. That gives the attorney a real incentive to do his best, and it guarantees that you won't be any worse off financially if the appeals are not successful.

Although you don't pay lawyer fees if you lose, you will probably be obligated to pay out-of-pocket costs. These may include copying charges and payments to medical doctors. Don't let these get out of hand. Before you hire a lawyer, get a written estimate of costs. And before the lawyer starts to hire a bunch of his doctor friends, require him (in writing) to explain the need and to obtain your advance approval.

The attorney generally will get 25 percent of past-due benefits if you win. He does *NOT* get a quarter of each monthly disability check forever. The fee must be approved by the Social Security Administration. If they decide that the attorney didn't do much, they can reduce the fee. Where else can you get such a bargain?

The toughest task may be to find the right lawyer—one that is experienced with disability cases. This is a highly specialized area of the law. *Don't* hire your divorce or real estate lawyer for a disability claim; you could probably do almost as well yourself.

Get referrals, preferably from relatives, friends, or co-workers who have used a lawyer for a disability claim and were satisfied. Ask other attorneys you trust; your real estate or divorce lawyer might have recommendations. You may also get names of experienced lawyers from a trade union.

Ask the attorney how many claims he or she handles each week or year. If the attorney handles fewer than about 100 claims a year, keep looking. The National Organization of Social Security Claimants' Representatives (NOSSCR) is the professional organization for lawyers in this specialty. You may call (800) 431-2804, and ask for the names of lawyers who handle disability claims in your geographic area. Then interview several, check their references, and decide which one is appropriate.

Social Security disability benefits are worth a lot to you. Make sure you get what is due you. A skilled attorney can steer you through the brush to the gold mine of benefits. And most important, don't give up. Two of every three claimants who appeal win. The Government has made the quest for Social Security disability into a real battle, but to those who persevere go the spoils!

·4·

Getting Uncle Sam to Play Fair with Medicare

Health care is the prime concern for most Americans in their prime of life. An illness or injury requiring medical attention can easily wipe out a life's savings. Health insurance is an absolute must. But the cost of basic private coverage is out of reach for most older Americans. The Government's answer is Medicare—federal health insurance available at age 65, which offers truly invaluable Golden Opportunities.

Unfortunately, your "friends" in Washington don't play fair; they have transformed your Medicare program into a complex game and have stacked the deck against you. The rules are so confusing that even Uncle Sam doesn't always understand them. And if that weren't bad enough, the politicians keep reshuffling the playing cards to create "new and improved" versions of the game. Then they bury the rules you need to successfully compete.

Enough is enough. In the pages that follow we explain why the Medicare Monopoly Game was created; what the *real* Golden Rules are; and how you can *WIN!* The secrecy and mystery surrounding Medicare is about to come to an end!

THE TRUTH (ALMOST) BEHIND WHY MEDICARE DOESN'T CARE ABOUT YOU

One of the best-kept secrets of all time is the "real" reason why our Government created Medicare. In 1965, when President Lyndon B. Johnson signed the legislation for this program, Americans were told that the purpose of Medicare was to provide basic national health insurance for seniors. Phooey. That story was simply a cover-up. What you are about to read has never before been revealed to the public: the secret goal of the Medicare program. Be forewarned, the truth might shock you.

In the late 1950s, census studies showed that the American population was rapidly graying. The implications were grave. Too many seniors with too much leisure time spelled trouble. What if all these competent retirees decided to become political activists? Congress panicked. The prospect of being monitored by thousands of seniors was frightening.

A solution was needed that would keep America's seniors so busy they wouldn't have any energy left to pester Congress. In a flash of skin-saving genius, our legislators found the perfect answer: Congress gave America Medicare. We were told the program was designed with our best interests at heart. But Congress never intended to create a workable health-care safety net. What our legislators wanted was a time-consuming national "hobby" for seniors. Now you know the "truth."

When President Johnson signed on the dotted line, what our citizens actually received was the rule book for the largest group activity ever created—the great Medicare Monopoly Game. (If you doubt the credibility of this theory, consider the following: Had Medicare truly been intended to provide you with health-care protection, don't you think it would work just a *little* better?)

The concept behind Medicare Monopoly is brilliant. Here are some of the game's key features:

1. Portable components—No matter where you travel in the United States, you will always be able to find playing pieces (stop in at any friendly Social Security office).
2. Socialization benefits—Swap Medicare war stories with others in any doctor's waiting room. A common rapport is immediate.
3. All-season use—So, outside it's too cold? Too hot? No sweat. You will never be at a loss for something to do. Interpreting and sorting denied claims is good for hours of activity.
4. Promotes family ties—If you are at a loss for ideas that will bring your relatives together, you can always invite them to Medicare Monopoly parties to develop new strategies for getting claims paid.

And you thought Medicare was a health insurance program!

WHEEL OF MISFORTUNE:
LEARNING HOW TO PLAY MEDICARE MONOPOLY

Now that you know the "why" behind Medicare, you need to develop a fresh strategy for dealing with the system. You must learn how to play the game.

To win any game of chance, a player needs a combination of luck, nerve, and timing. Playing Medicare Monopoly is no different in this regard. Some aspects of the game you will have control over, like making sure information on a claim is accurate; some you won't, like choosing the date and severity of an illness. But the key is *knowledge*. You would never think of going to Las Vegas, plunking down hundreds of dollars at the blackjack table, and playing, without ever bothering to learn the rules of the game. Yet when it comes to Medicare, that's exactly what most people do. They toss the dice, shut their eyes, and hope the right numbers come up so the medical bills can get paid. People keep playing until their pockets are empty and there is nothing left to lose.

This is a tragedy, but it doesn't have to happen to you. When you play Medicare Monopoly, don't just keep picking the "Take a Chance" cards. There are rules of the game; if you know them, and turn them to your favor, you can improve your odds of opening the Community Chest of valuable benefits.

As you prepare to play, keep two important principles in mind:

- *Medicare is not charity.* You have *earned* your right to Medicare through the Social Security taxes that were deducted from your or your spouse's salary. Remember when you looked at your paycheck and saw that big gap between gross and net income? Well, some of that hard-earned money should finally reappear in the form of Medicare benefits. When you play Medicare Monopoly, you're playing to win your own funds.
- *Medicare is confusing.* No, you are not senile or stupid because you can't understand all the ins and outs of the program. Medicare is a red-tape nightmare. (What did you expect when politicians, government bureaucrats, hospitals, doctors, and insurance companies all have a say in spending over $100 billion in taxpayer money!) Take heart—there is nothing wrong with *your* mind. To ask for help in battling the bureaucracy is *not* an admission of stupidity. Whether you have a high school diploma or three Ph.D.s, you will find dealing with Medicare exasperating because it often defies logic. Perseverance (not brains) is key for a successful game of Medicare Monopoly.

Preparing to Play

The official rules for playing Medicare Monopoly can be found in *The Medicare Handbook,* published annually by the U.S. Department of Health and Human Services. But as anyone who has used this guide knows, the instructions for playing are unclear at best. (Let's face it, Uncle Sam wants to win the game, so he's not anxious to reveal where the aces are hidden.) Don't despair, this chapter will help even the odds.

The Medicare Handbook, despite its flaws, is still an *essential* game piece. Since the *Handbook* is updated every year to reflect changes in the program, make sure you have the latest edition. Medicare automatically provides the first copy when you enroll, but after that, staying current is up to *you*. If you have misplaced your

Handbook, or if it's outdated, get another. Call or visit your Social Security Office or local Office on Aging.

The Medicare Handbook should always be your starting point for explanations about Medicare coverage. Before wasting any time on the phone with Medicare personnel, refer to this guide. Uncle Sam just might have something to say on the subject. Scan the Table of Contents and the Medicare Ready Reference Chart at the very beginning of the guide. If you have a simple question, such as "What is the phone number to call when reporting Medicare fraud?" chances are you will find the answer.

It's dealing with any issue beyond the realm of the most simple that can cause problems. The fine print of Medicare coverage, supposedly provided in the *Handbook,* can be so fine that it's nonexistent. If you want to find out the Government's "secret rules," this chapter is just what the doctor ordered.

Armed with the newest *Medicare Handbook* in one hand and this book in the other, you will be ready to play Medicare Monopoly, set to pass go, and collect the treasure you are entitled to receive under Medicare law.

Begin at the Beginning

"Begin at the beginning . . . and go on till you come to the end" is the wise advice the King of Hearts offers Alice during her journey through Wonderland. Since we are not ones to tamper with sound suggestions, that's exactly where we will begin our discussion of the Medicare Monopoly Game: at the beginning.

When we talk about Medicare, we're referring to the federal health insurance program for people 65 or older and certain disabled people. It is run by the Health Care Financing Administration of the U.S. Department of Health and Human Services. Your local Social Security Administration office has the job of taking applications and answering questions about eligibility and basic benefits of the program. (Medicare carriers and intermediaries are responsible for handling your specific questions about claims.)

Health Insurance Card

Uncle Sam will give you a card identifying you as an official Medicare Monopoly player. Everyone calls this card the "Medicare Card." It makes sense. The name is clear and simple. Even *The Medicare Handbook* refers to this document as the "Medicare Card." Nevertheless, Uncle Sam actually has chosen another name as the official title: the "Health Insurance Card." So don't be surprised when the card you receive has "Health Insurance," not "Medicare," written in bold letters.

Your Medicare card is as unique as your fingerprint. You are assigned a health insurance claim number (Medicare number) that has nine digits (your Social

Security number) and one letter (sometimes two letters), and it belongs to you alone. The only way the bureaucracy recognizes your existence as legitimate is by the identification information on the card. For this reason, always:

- Carry your Medicare card with you.
- Write your health insurance claim number on any documents or forms you send to Medicare.
- Replace a lost card immediately (call Social Security).
- Use your own card. *Never* use anyone else's claim number, even your spouse's. You are asking for a paperwork nightmare if you do.

The Medicare program has two parts: Hospital Insurance (Part A) and Medical Insurance (Part B). The highlights of both are summarized in Table 4.1. Table 4.2 shows the costs of health care services that will be shared between you and Medicare.

Medicare hospital (Part A) and medical (Part B) insurance are wonderful benefits—the rich rewards for winning Medicare Monopoly. But as we've said, Uncle Sam doesn't want to make it too easy for you. So he's written the rule book in Medicarese.

Medicarese

Medicarese is the mode of communication used by the folks at Medicare. It looks like English, but it's not. The unique feature of this language is that it was created for the sole purpose of promoting secrecy and misunderstanding. (You've heard of legalese—well this is worse!)

Obviously, you can't play a winning game of anything when the rules are not written in plain English. You've got to learn at least the basics of Medicarese vocabulary. The Government's *Medicare Handbook* provides a Glossary of Medicare Related Terms (written, of course, in Medicarese). You will find it buried at the back of the *Handbook*. We have taken the liberty of translating the key Medicarese terms from this list into people-friendly language. Mr. Webster might not approve of our style, but he probably never had to read a Medicare document, either!

Defined here are certain words and phrases central to understanding both Parts A and B of the Medicare program. These VIPs (Very Important Phrases) deserve VIP attention because you can't play Medicare Monopoly without them.

Medicare VIP Glossary

Approved Charge. This is the dollar amount that Medicare has decided is an appropriate fee for a provider's service. Medicare uses a complex formula to arrive at this figure. The approved charge is like a price ceiling. Medicare gener-

TABLE 4.1

Basics of the Medicare Program

Hospital Insurance—Part A

What Is Covered?

As you will see, Medicare's use of the term "covered" is a gross overstatement. There are lots of limitations, but here is the basic list:

1. Inpatient hospital care
2. Inpatient Skilled Nursing Facility (SNF) Care
3. Home health care
4. Hospice care

Who Is Eligible?

At 65, you are entitled to receive Part A benefits based on your (or your spouse's) employment record. Most people are covered.

What Are the Costs?

Part A is "free" (no premiums are required), but you must pay all deductibles ($652 in 1992) and co-insurance (a percentage of the bill for the care or service received—no small potatoes).

Medical Insurance—Part B

What Is Covered?

The following kinds of care and services fall under the Medicare Part B umbrella of coverage:

1. Doctor care
2. Outpatient hospital care
3. Diagnostic testing
4. Durable Medical Equipment (DME)
5. Ambulance travel
6. Various other services and supplies not included under Part A

See the *Medicare Handbook* under Medicare Medical Insurance (Part B) for an official summary.

At first glance, the range of care and services covered looks impressive. Don't be fooled. When your first rainy day arrives, you will discover many leaks in your Part B umbrella of coverage.

Who Is Eligible?

Basically, anyone (65 or older) who wants to pay.

What Are the Costs?

You pay a monthly premium, plus deductibles and co-insurance. In 1992, the Part B premium is $31.80 a month and the annual deductible is $100.

TABLE 4.2

Health Care Payments Under Medicare

Services	Medicare Pays	You Pay*
MEDICARE PART A		
Inpatient Hospital Care	All but $652 deductible for first 60 days	$652 deductible for first 60 days
	All but $163/day for days 61–90	$163/day for days 61–90
	All but $326/day for 60 reserve days	$326/day for 60 reserve days
Blood	All but cost of first three pints	Cost of first three pints
Inpatient Skilled Nursing Facility Care	All for first 20 days	Nothing for first 20 days
	All but $81.50/day for days 21–100	$81.50/day for days 21–100
Home Health Care	All costs of care; 80% of approved amount for durable medical equipment	Nothing but 20% of approved amount for durable medical equipment
Hospice Care	For up to 210 days (with unlimited extensions available), all but limited amount for outpatient drugs (lesser of 5% or $5 toward cost of prescription) and respite care (5% of allowable daily rate)	Nothing but limited amount for outpatient drugs and respite care for up to 210 days (with unlimited extensions available)
MEDICARE PART B		
Medical Services Provided by Doctors and Most Other Health Care Providers, Services and Supplies	80% of approved amount after $100 deductible	$100 deductible and 20% of approved amount (plus additional costs if provider does not accept assignment)
Psychologists Services	50% of approved charges	50% of approved charges

*There is no premium for Part A. You pay $31.80 a month for Part B.
Source: The Medicare Handbook, 1991. U.S. Department of Health and Human Services, Health Care Financing Administration, page i. All figures have been updated for 1992.

ally won't pay more than 80 percent of its approved charge for a service, no matter what the provider bills you. Don't be confused—just because Medicare "approves a charge" does *not* mean Uncle Sam will pay 100 percent of the bill.

Assignment. This is perhaps the most misunderstood term in the Medicare VIP Glossary; it applies to Part B medical insurance. Understanding *assignment* is essential for playing the Medicare Monopoly game.

Assignment is a three-way agreement among you, Medicare, and a service provider (*e.g.,* a doctor) to *share* the costs of your medical treatment. Here's how the deal works:

- The *provider* agrees to accept the Medicare approved charge as total payment for a service.
- *Medicare* then pays its share (usually *80%*) of that approved amount (less any unmet deductible) directly to the provider.
- To complete the triangle, *you* must pay your share (20% co-insurance for most services) of the approved charge to the provider (plus any unmet deductible).

Assignment Triangle

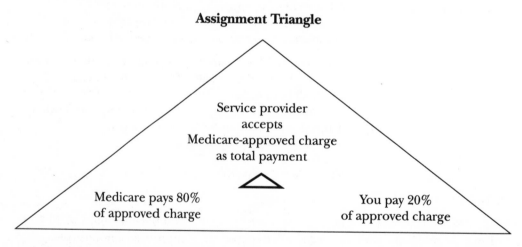

A provider who *accepts* assignment accepts as payment in full the amount Medicare has approved as a reasonable charge for this service, even if his normal fee would be higher. The provider is *not* agreeing to accept Medicare's check for 80 percent of the bill as payment in full. When a doctor accepts assignment *you still must pay* your 20 percent co-insurance; you *don't* get off the hook. Unfortunately, a sign in a doctor's office that reads "I accept assignment" is *not* a ticket to free medical care!

Benefit Period. This is Medicare's way of measuring your use of Part A covered services. It is the period of time during a spell of illness when the care you receive is eligible for Medicare reimbursement. Maximum benefit periods are listed in Table 4.2; a *spell of illness* is defined below.

Co-insurance (or Co-payment). This is the amount *you* must pay after Medicare pays its share of the bill for Medicare approved services and supplies. Both Parts A and B can require you to pay co-insurance.

Under Part A, you get 60 days in a hospital or 20 days in a skilled nursing home absolutely free (after paying your deductible). Once you have exceeded the free day limit, you and Medicare will share the costs. Your portion is called co-insurance.

Under Part B, if the provider accepts assignment, Medicare pays 80 percent of the cost and you (or your private supplemental insurance) pay 20 percent (your co-insurance). Remember, assignment means you will not have to pay more than the Medicare approved charge for a service; it does *not* mean Medicare picks up the entire bill.

When a provider does *not* accept assignment, expect to pay more. Since the provider is *not* agreeing to use Medicare's price lid on his fee, you will owe the 20 percent co-insurance (based on Medicare's approved charge) *plus* all of the "unreasonable" charges for a service (any amount the doctor bills above Medicare's approved charge) up to 120 percent of the Medicare approved amount. (Some states limit fees charged by providers even more.)

Deductible. This is a fee you must pay before Medicare will begin to pay for any of your hospital or medical expenses. In 1992, the Part A deductible (for each benefit period) is $652 and the Part B annual deductible is the first $100 in approved charges (see Table 4.2) and can be met by any Medicare-covered expenses over the course of a year. You must meet your Part A deductible each time you are admitted to the hospital or skilled nursing facility (SNF) if more than 60 days has passed since your last hospital or SNF stay. Medicare will keep a running tally and will deny payment until you hit the mark. It's a good idea for you to keep track of your expenses too, so you can make sure you aren't wrongfully denied benefits once the deductible is satisfied.

Reasonable and medically necessary. Medicare pays for "covered" services, but only if the services are also "reasonable and medically necessary." Unfortunately, this vague language allows the Government to unfairly deny all sorts of claims.

It's probably safe to say that no one really knows for sure what this term means, and Medicare likes it that way. What appears perfectly "reasonable" to you or us may not look that way to the Medicare claim processor who just happened to wake up on the wrong side of the bed the day your claim passed through. However, here's a "reasonable" way of applying this slippery standard: Had a panel of doctors been convened to review your case, would the majority agree that your doctor's plan for care:

- Was based on sound medical practice?
- Was a safe and effective choice of treatment?
- Gave consideration to your entire physical and mental condition?

If so, the service in question should be considered "reasonable and medically necessary."

❖ GEM: When You Choose, You Lose

In the vague world of "reasonable and necessary," there is a very important, clear-cut no-no. When you exercise your freedom of choice and opt for nonessential care, Uncle Sam will exercise his veto power.

❖ GEM: Be an Exception to the Rule

Your claim may be unfairly denied because the treatment you received is *usually* considered unreasonable and unnecessary. But the circumstances of *your* case might make you "exceptional" and, by law, Medicare must evaluate your claim based on the unique aspects of *your* total condition. If your claim is denied and you believe it's unfair because Medicare didn't notice that you were special, ask for a review. Have your doctor write and explain why the service was reasonable and necessary, and refile the claim. There's a good chance Medicare will see it your way this time. (For details on how to file an appeal, see Chapter 5.)

EXAMPLE 1

Your doctor tells you that a cyst must be removed. He says he can fix you up in the office. But you'd feel better if the treatment is done in a hospital, so you ask to have it done there.

Get out your checkbook. If necessary treatment can be done on an outpatient basis but you opt to check into the hospital, you'll have to pay yourself.

EXAMPLE 2

You might think a face-lift is essential to your well-being, but don't expect Uncle Sam to agree. You will pay the price for beauty, as well as for any other procedure that is not essential for preserving your health.

✦   ✦   ✦

Spell of Illness. You may receive Medicare benefits only during a spell of illness. A spell of illness begins when a patient is admitted to a hospital or skilled nursing facility and ends when the patient has not received hospital or skilled care for 60 consecutive days.

The Medicare Timer

When you play Medicare Monopoly, you'll play Part A against a Medicare timer. Uncle Sam sets the timer when you go into the hospital or skilled nursing facility, and when your timer runs out—buzzzz, you lose. You can start the timer again for each new spell of illness.

The Medicare timer starts running when you start a benefit period, which is the time during which you can get Medicare Part A coverage. For example, for each Medicare hospital insurance benefit period, after meeting your deductible, you are eligible for 60 "free days" of coverage (you actually pay the deductible on the first day and then you pay no co-insurance for the next 59 days) plus 30 "shared" cost days (you must pay co-insurance—see Table 4.2 for amounts). These 90 days (free and shared) are "renewable"; when you begin a new spell of illness, the timer is reset for 90 days. You also have 60 "reserve days" you can draw on over your life, but these are *not* renewable. You still must pay co-insurance for each day, and once lifetime reserve days are used up, they are gone forever. Example 3 shows how this works:

EXAMPLE 3

Your husband first enters a hospital on April 15. He is there three days, and pays his deductible. When he reenters on May 1, all costs are paid by Medicare right from the start. The Medicare timer began running from the day he paid his deductible.

After 60 days in the hospital (combining both visits), you start sharing the costs. The sharing continues for 30 days. Then the timer runs out. Now you have a choice: you start using your 60 reserve days or you pay out of your own pocket.

EXAMPLE 4

Same facts as Example 3, except your husband's prior hospitalization was February 15 to 18. When he reenters on May 1, he must pay his deductible ($652) again, even though he paid the deductible once already this year, because he is in a new spell of illness—he has been out of the hospital for more than 60 consecutive days. But the good news is he gets a new benefit period—60 new free days and 30 new shared-cost days.

How Does Medicare Calculate a Benefit Period?

The Medicare payment timer starts ticking on the first day you enter a hospital. Each free day is like one second on a stopwatch, and when the hands on the Medicare stopwatch reach 60, your full coverage days are over. You must begin paying co-insurance for the next 30 days of care.

How Do You Get a New Benefit Period?

Again, the stopwatch analogy applies. You can begin a new benefit period with each new spell of illness, after you have been *out* of the hospital (or SNF) for 60 days *in a row*. The day of discharge will count as your first day out.

There is no limit to the total number of benefit periods you can have, either in a year or in your life. If you are out of the hospital for 60 consecutive days, the timer goes back to zero and you are given a new benefit period (60 free days followed by 30 shared cost days). At the start of *each* new benefit period, you pay a deductible.

❖ GEM: Play the Numbers

As you can see, you are playing a "60s" number game: You want to stay out of a hospital for 60 consecutive days, and because Medicare limits the number of free hospital days to 60 for each benefit period, your other goal is to avoid exceeding that magic number. Obviously, you don't always have a choice, but sometimes you do. See Examples 5 and 6.

EXAMPLE 5

You require two complex nonemergency surgical procedures and extended hospitalization will be needed. Speak to your doctor about separating the treatments. By reentering the hospital after 60 days back home, you will be entitled to reset the Medicare timer for 60 more free days. Although you must pay a deductible again, it will still cost you less than the daily co-payments that you would have paid beginning on Day 61 of your long hospitalization. You and your doctor will need to consider all the medical and financial circumstances.

EXAMPLE 6

You are being treated for a chronic illness. You are hospitalized for 10 days, home for 20, then rehospitalized for 3 days and home for 15. If you keep this up, you will soon deplete your free days. So do whatever you can, without jeopardizing your health, to stay home for 60 days (e.g., arrange for home health care services). Then you can enter a new benefit period and gain new free days.

✦ ✦ ✦

How Does Medicare Calculate a Day?

Sounds like a dumb question. A day is a day, right? Wrong. Medicare views a day in a different way from how you or we would. Since your coverage is based on calculating inpatient service days, it's essential that you know how Uncle Sam defines a day. A Medicare day begins at midnight. (Not surprisingly, those bureaucrats chose the darkest hour as the starting point for a Medicare day!)

Any part of a day you are in a hospital or skilled nursing facility (including the day of admission) counts as one inpatient day. Your day of discharge does *not* count as an inpatient service day and will *not* be counted against you. To remember which days count, a quote from Shakespeare comes in handy (is it possible he had trouble with Medicare too?), "Life's but a walking shadow, a *poor* [emphasis added] player that struts and frets his hour upon the stage, and then is heard no more; it is a tale told by an idiot, full of sound and fury, signifying nothing." (*Macbeth,* Act V).

The day you depart does not count—it "signifies nothing."

❖ GEM: Avoid Late Charges

If you choose to stay in your room after normal checkout time for reasons of comfort or convenience, *you* will be responsible for any late charges, and the day will count even if you depart later that day. But if the delay is due to circumstances beyond your control (*e.g.,* a morning treatment you were scheduled for was delayed, or the ambulance service does not to pick you up on time), then Medicare should cover any late charges, and your late departure should not be counted against you as another inpatient day.

❖ GEM: Count Medicare Days

Double-check the dates of your admission and release on the hospital bill to make sure they are correct. When you are mistakenly billed for extra days, not only does it cost big bucks but it will also cause your Medicare game timer to run out early!

Also, keep watch on your Medicare timer to avoid unpleasant billing surprises later. You can't count on Medicare or the hospital to watch out for you.

❖ GEM: Watch Out for Unpaid Deductibles

Uncle Sam doesn't play fair in starting the Medicare timer. Let's say you are admitted to the hospital and this is your first illness. You have not yet met your Part A deductible. Even though you will be footing the bill until you have paid off your deductible, the Medicare timer does not go on hold. It will still begin ticking on the day you entered and will count toward your 60 free days.

✦　✦　✦

When Should You Use Reserve Days?

You, or someone acting for you, can decide at any time during a hospital stay whether or not to dip into your 60 nonrenewable reserve days. You can use these only once, and when they're gone—that's it! So use them wisely.

A hospital should notify you, at least five days before you have used up your 90 days of coverage, that you have the option to begin drawing on reserve days for the remainder of your stay. You will receive a form to sign to start taking reserve days. The reserve-day withdrawals will begin the day *after* your signed notice is filed and will remain in effect unless it is revoked.

❖ GEM: Recapture Lost Reserve Days

Your decision to use reserve days is not cut in stone—at least not immediately. If you change your mind after leaving the hospital, you can recapture reserve days if both:

- You notify the hospital within 90 days of discharge that you will pay back all costs for services not covered by insurance.
- The hospital agrees.

You can even recapture lost reserve days *after* 90 days if your expenses will be paid by a third party (insurance company) and the hospital agrees. See Example 7.

EXAMPLE 7

More than three months after leaving the hospital, you decide that you've made a mistake by using reserve days. You've discovered that your supplemental insurance will cover your hospital care after the first 90 days. Now you would like to recapture your reserve days.

Even though it's been longer than 90 days since your discharge, don't give up. Contact the hospital's billing department and ask if you can file a retroactive request not to use reserve days. If the hospital agrees, Medicare will be reimbursed and your private health insurance company will be billed for the additional care.

❖ GEM: Deal Yourself into the Game

Uncle Sam stacks the cards against you. Thanks to a "Joker" in the deck, the Medicare Monopoly Game may prevent you from getting necessary treatment. Why? Providers can only find out whether a service is covered by Medicare *after* they've given you the care. So if it's not a sure bet that Medicare will foot the bill, then chances are they won't take a gamble on treating you.

The trick is to convince the hospital, skilled nursing facility, or home health agency to provide service. How? If you can afford to pay in case Medicare denies the claim, say so. If you can't afford the cost, become a squeaky wheel: badger the provider to take a chance. A provider who hasn't filed many wrong claims may still get paid by Medicare even if it turns out that the service isn't really eligible for coverage.

MEDICARE HOSPITAL INSURANCE (PART A)

Now that you know the general rules of Medicare Monopoly, you're almost ready to play. We first look at Hospital Coverage (Part A), and then discuss Medical Coverage (Part B). By the time you're through, you should be able to give Uncle Sam a good run for your money.

Medicare Part A is the hospital, skilled nursing facility, and home health insurance that Uncle Sam provides when you turn 65. You can get Medicare Part A premium-free if you are *eligible to receive* Social Security retirement or survivor benefits (Chapters 1 and 2) or Railroad Retirement benefits (Chapter 13).

❖ GEM: Take Medicare
Even If You Delay Other Benefits

If you are eligible but choose *not* to file for retirement or survivor benefits yet, you are still entitled to receive Medicare at age 65. Don't pass up this freebie—delaying Medicare serves *no* purpose.

❖ GEM: Get Medicare Even If You Are Not Eligible for Free Coverage

At age 65, if you are a U.S. citizen or have been a permanent resident for five years, you can still enroll in Part A, even if you are not eligible for Medicare based on Social Security or Railroad eligibility. You will pay a monthly premium ($192 a month in 1992), but it is often worth the price. Contact your local Social Security office for enrollment information and an application.

❖ GEM: Get Medicare Before Age 65!

You can start taking Part A Medicare if you have received Social Security or Railroad *disability* benefits for at least 24 months (see pages 97, 518–520). Don't miss out on this valuable gem!

❖ GEM: Government Employees Can Now Cash In

Until recently, federal, state, and local government employees were not eligible to receive Medicare benefits. State and local government employees hired *before* April 1, 1986, are probably still *not* Medicare qualified. But the rules have been broadened, and if you are now paying for Medicare hospital insurance (Part A) as part of your FICA tax, you should be considered Medicare qualified at age 65.

The rules covering government employees are very confusing. Have the folks at Social Security check your and your spouse's employment record to determine if you are eligible. If you are told you are not qualified, request a specific explanation so you can double-check with a Medicare lawyer or someone familiar with the employee benefits where you work. Don't take one person's word as gospel. Mistakes are made.

❖ ❖ ❖

Enrollment

Application for Medicare Part A can be a hassle. Thankfully, most people don't have to apply. If you are 65 and will be receiving Social Security or Railroad Retirement benefits, you can escape the filing process. You are automatically enrolled as soon as you start taking these other government benefits.

EXAMPLE 8

You are turning 65 and starting to collect Social Security. Don't worry about Medicare application forms—you are automatically enrolled in Part A (you will also get Part B unless you choose to decline the opportunity and opt out).

EXAMPLE 9

At age 65, you were still working and didn't apply for Social Security at that time. Now, at age 67, you are retiring. Your Social Security application automatically triggers your Medicare enrollment.

Individuals who take early Social Security retirement benefits will be enrolled automatically at age 65. If you opt to continue working after age 65, and delay receiving Social Security benefits, you can still start Medicare at 65, but you'll have to apply—it won't come automatically. You'll also have to apply (at any age) to get Medicare benefits after receiving Social Security disability benefits for 24 months. Table 4.3 shows how this works.

If you qualify for automatic enrollment, your Medicare card should arrive in the mail. (If a card doesn't appear in your mailbox by two weeks before your birthday, contact Social Security.) When you are Medicare eligible because of dis-

TABLE 4.3

Work Status and Enrollment

Age	Work Status	Social Security/Railroad Retirement Benefit Status	Medicare Enrollment Automatic?
65	Retiring	You apply for Social Security or Railroad Retirement benefits.	Yes, at 65.
62–65	Retiring	You apply for Social Security or Railroad Retirement benefits.	Yes, when you reach 65.
65+	Working	No Social Security or Railroad Retirement benefits yet.	No. You must apply to get Medicare before you start taking your Social Security or Railroad Retirement benefits.
65+	Retiring	You apply for Social Security or Railroad Retirement benefits.	Yes; for Part A at time of Social Security or Railroad Retirement application; for Part B at time of Social Security or Railroad Retirement application or next general enrollment period (see pages 180–181).
Any age	Disabled	You have been receiving Social Security disability benefits for 24 months.	No. You must apply.

ability, your card will also come automatically. If you qualify at age 65, your card will be good for both Parts A and B. If you *don't* want Part B, you will need to follow the instructions and notify Uncle Sam.

If you do *not* meet the automatic enrollment requirements, paperwork unfortunately will be necessary. Call or visit your local Social Security office to obtain an application. Be prepared to provide the following information:

1. *Age.* Don't try fooling Uncle Sam; you need to submit proof—a birth certificate, hospital records, or some other documentation.
2. *Social Security Number.* If it's lost, Uncle Sam has ways to track it down.
3. *Income for the Previous Year.* A W-2 form or copy of income tax return. Don't worry, you won't be audited.
4. *Government Benefits.* A list of any benefits you are entitled to receive (*e.g.,* Federal Civil Service, Railroad Retirement).

❖ GEM: Timing Is Everything

If you don't qualify for automatic enrollment, sign up for Medicare Part A three months *before* your 65th birthday. Don't procrastinate; delays could cost you. If you become ill and incur expenses before obtaining coverage, you may get stuck for all the medical bills. In addition, if you don't apply promptly for Part B, you will pay a *higher* premium as a penalty for late enrollment, *and* your Part B coverage may be delayed a year or longer. Table 4.4 shows when to apply for Medicare.

TABLE 4.4

When to Apply for Medicare

If Your Birthday Is	Apply for Medicare in
January 2*–February 1	October
February 2–March 1	November
March 2–April 1	December
April 2–May 1	January
May 2–June 1	February
June 2–July 1	March
July 2–August 1	April
August 2–September 1	May
September 2–October 1	June
October 2–November 1	July
November 2–December 1	August
December 2–January 1	September

*Note: We will explain why we start with the second day of each month on page 140.

EXAMPLE 10

You have just turned 65. Although you are eligible to retire and to receive Social Security retirement payments, you have decided to continue working. You will wait to start Social Security, but you still expect to pick up Medicare now.

Your birthday came and went. You received cards from all your friends, but not the health insurance card from Uncle Sam. Should you be irate at the government bureaucracy for messing up again?

No. Here is one case where you can't blame Uncle Sam. You don't have to retire to receive Medicare Part A, but if you choose *not* to receive Social Security benefits at 65, your enrollment in Medicare Part A will *not* be automatic at that age. You must apply (contact your local Social Security office for an application).

EXAMPLE 11

You are retired and will begin receiving your Social Security benefits when you turn age 65 next month. You assume you don't have to do anything to get Medicare.

Right! You are automatically enrolled in Medicare Part A when you *receive* Social Security benefits.

❖ GEM: Get Medicare Part A Retroactively

You can change your mind and get Part A benefits retroactively! This is an extremely important tip to know when fate deals you an unlucky blow.

Let's say you were eligible for Social Security but chose to postpone receiving those benefits. You forgot to apply for Medicare. Unfortunately, two months after your 65th birthday, you have a bad fall and fracture your hip. You are hospitalized and upon your release will require skilled physical therapy. If you sign up to receive Social Security (as soon as you can get back on your feet, so to speak), the Medicare Part A benefits you will receive can pay for any covered hospital and health care expenses even though they occurred *before* you applied.

However, there are time limits to Medicare's patience. Here are the *Golden Rules:* You can pick up coverage dating back to the first day of your 65th birthday month, but not more than six months before the month you filed your application. (The deadline is 12 months if you are receiving Social Security survivor benefits.) You'll be stuck paying any expenses incurred more than six months before you applied.

◆ ◆ ◆

The date of your birthday can put money in your pocket. Our next three gems are Happy Birthday presents from your Uncle Sam.

❖ GEM: Get Coverage for Your Full Birthday Month

You turn 65 on September 27. Surprise! Uncle Sam will give you Medicare coverage starting on September 1—the first day of your birthday *month*. Those extra days of coverage can mean a lot of dough to you.

❖ GEM: Get an Extra Month Free If Your Birthday Falls on the First of the Month

Growing old is no laughing matter. Or is it? Consider this riddle: When is your birthday not your birthday? Answer: When you are dealing with Medicare!

Hard as it is to believe, Uncle Sam even had to stick his nose into this basic fact of life. For 65 years, you might have thought you knew your date of birth, but guess what? You were wrong. According to the folks at Social Security (who know better), you officially turn one year older on the day *before* your actual date of birth. Why do they do this? Who knows. Why does it matter? Because you can get an extra *month* of benefits, as Example 12 shows.

EXAMPLE 12

You turned 65 on February 1. Medicare says your birthday is really January 31. That means you can get Medicare benefits for the *whole month of January!*

Don't forget that this crazy birthday rule will also affect the month in which you should enroll for Medicare. We've taken this into account when setting up Table 4.4.

MEDICARE PART A: INPATIENT HOSPITAL CARE

As we mentioned earlier, Medicare Hospital Insurance Part A is not exactly the most fitting title Uncle Sam could have picked to describe this entire program, because Part A actually covers more than just hospital-based services. Also included are inpatient skilled nursing facility care, home health care, and hospice care.*

*Rehabilitation hospitals are also covered when a patient's condition requires multiple services or more intensive therapies than a general hospital can provide (*e.g.,* recuperation from strokes, hip and knee replacements). These facilities are not available in all communities. Your hospital discharge planner and physician should know if this option can be used.

We'll first tell you about inpatient hospital care, giving you a treasure chest of gems to help you extend your coverage. Then we'll uncover the secrets of the other Part A benefits.

How Do You Get in the Hospital Door?

Before the gates of Medicare Part A coverage are even opened to you, you need to meet Medicare's four Hospital Entry Conditions, as stated in *The Medicare Handbook* (page 12).

- Has a doctor (not you) decided that your medical condition requires inpatient care?
- Is the type of care you need only available in a hospital?
- Is the hospital participating in Medicare?
- Has the hospital's Utilization Review Committee (URC) or Uncle Sam's Peer Review Organization (PRO) not disapproved your stay?

If you answered yes to all four questions, then go knock on the hospital's doors. You should be allowed in, as Medicare's guest.

What Medical Services Does Part A Inpatient Hospital Care Actually Include?

A good understanding of the inpatient hospital services you are entitled to under Medicare Part A should help assure you get what you deserve and avoid wrongful charges (which often occur). We have listed the most important covered services in Table 4.5.

TABLE 4.5

Covered Hospital Services

- *Use of hospital facilities ordinarily provided to treat inpatients* (isn't that generous; there's no extra charge for walls and floors).
- *Semiprivate hospital room* (2–4 beds).
- *All your meals,* special diets too (of course, we know they should be paying you to eat the food).
- *Special care units,* such as coronary care and intensive care, are thrown in at no extra charge.
- *Medical social services,* which can include:
  1. Assessments of your social and emotional status to determine their impact on treatment and recovery
  2. Evaluations of your medical and nursing needs to determine what community and personal resources will be needed upon discharge
  3. Any social services ordinarily provided by the hospital that can contribute to the treatment of your illness

(Continued)

TABLE 4.5 (Continued)

Covered Hospital Services

- *Drugs ordinarily provided to hospital patients.* Drug must be FDA approved as safe and effective for treating your illness. Experimental drugs or drugs that have not received final FDA marketing approval are not covered, unless *specific* permission has been given by Medicare.

- *Blood transfusions.* Although blood *processing* fees, starting with the first pint of blood, are covered, you are expected to either pay for, or find donors willing to replace, the first three pints you used. Don't worry—Medicare does not intend to "bleed you dry." During a calendar year, if you satisfy the blood deductible under Part B, you won't be required to give another three pints for your Part A deductible. Isn't that comforting?

- *X-rays and other radiology services,* including radiation therapy. These services must be billed *by the hospital.* Medicare bureaucrats with "x-rated" vision can see through any claims submitted from unapproved facilities and will deny coverage.

- *Operating and recovery room costs,* including hospital fees for anesthesia services. You can put your mind at rest. You won't "go under" paying the hospital's fees for surgery. The surgeon's and anesthesiologist's fees, though not covered by Part A, should be covered by Part B (page 126).

- *Lab tests and diagnostic services performed by the hospital.*

- *Medical supplies and equipment.* Medicare will pay for items a hospital ordinarily provides for the care and treatment of its inpatients—casts, splints, wheelchairs. However, you generally can't take these items with you and expect Medicare Part A to pay (although Part B can cover these items; see page 126).

- *Routine nursing care.* You're in luck: the nurse who wakes you at 6:00 A.M. to take your temperature is included at no extra charge!

- *Specialists (e.g.,* nurses, anesthetists, psychologists). When the specialist works for the hospital, Medicare will pay.

- *Rehabilitation services,* such as speech therapy, occupational therapy, and speech pathology.

- *Hospitalization due to dental-related disorders.* Getting Medicare to pay for dental costs is, pardon the expression, like pulling teeth. But under certain circumstances, you will be covered for the hospital's charges. For example, Medicare should pay hospital expenses for a noncovered dental service if your stay is required because of either the severity of the procedure or your physical condition (*e.g.,* you have a history of heart trouble, and the dental surgery you're having requires anesthesia). Your dental surgeon or physician must certify that hospitalization is necessary.

- *Alcoholism treatment.* Inpatient hospital care for alcoholism and detoxification should be covered (usually two to three days), if medical complications are likely to occur. A stay for rehabilitation will not be covered unless specific reasons can be given for a hospital setting rather than using a less costly outpatient treatment program.

- *Inpatient psychiatric hospital care.* You generally are entitled to a lifetime total of 190 days of coverage at a Medicare-approved psychiatric hospital.

Source: The Medicare Handbook, page 13.

The following gems can help you cash in on the covered services listed in Table 4.5.

❖ GEM: Get Special Drug Coverage

If you can get the hospital to agree to specially order a drug for you because it is not routinely stocked, Medicare should cover the cost, even though it is not ordinarily provided to hospital patients. In addition, for a limited period of time, Medicare will pay the costs of drugs *after* you leave a hospital, if using that medication on an outpatient basis will speed your departure. Why? By treating you at home, Medicare saves money.

❖ GEM: Get Special Coverage for Off-site Lab or Diagnostic Tests

If an off-site location must be used to perform diagnostic procedures because the hospital is unable to provide this care, Medicare should cover the cost.

EXAMPLE 13

In order to diagnose your hearing disorder, complex testing is necessary. The hospital does not have an audiologist on staff so you are sent to a hearing and speech center. This off-site service should be covered.

Part A should pay for any off-site lab and diagnostic service if the hospital has an agreement with a Medicare-approved provider and the services will be billed directly to the hospital. Ask your doctor or the hospital to make sure Medicare is covering. If you receive a bill for the service, DO *NOT* PAY! Call the service provider and explain why.

❖ GEM: You Can Take It with You: Keep Your Pacemaker!

As Table 4.5 shows, Medicare generally won't pay for supplies and equipment you take with you. But when it would be medically unreasonable to demand their return, you should be allowed to "carry out" items you are "wearing," such as cardiac valves, pacemakers, drainage tubes, replaced body organs, and so on—

at Medicare's cost! Although equipment provided to use outside the hospital will not be paid under Inpatient Hospital coverage, you might be eligible for additional benefits under Medicare's Part A Home Health Care Insurance (page 127) or under Medicare Part B (page 127).

❖ GEM: Get Special Coverage for Nonstaff Members

While Medicare says it only pays for services by persons on the hospital staff, you should also be covered if hospital service is provided by a nonstaff member (such as a psychologist or therapist) under a contract with the hospital. (Any private agreements *you* work out don't count!)

❖ GEM: Pass the Rehabilitation Services Coverage Test

Although *The Medicare Handbook* states that rehabilitation services are covered, getting coverage is not as easy as it sounds. Medicare will pay *only* when you can prove the rehabilitation is "reasonable and necessary" for treating your illness. To meet these requirements, make sure the therapy is:

- Prescribed in writing by your doctor or physical therapist.
- Performed by a qualified therapist or done under his supervision. (Even health maintenance and routine services performed by nurses' aides or other support staff to promote fitness or flexibility can sometimes be covered; check with your doctor or hospital's representative who handles Medicare services.)
- Restorative. No matter who provides the service, Medicare won't pay a penny for therapy if you are not going to improve "significantly" after a "reasonable" period of time. When you and the Government don't see eye-to-eye on your progress, have your doctor or therapist write a letter explaining why the therapy is still justifiable to maintain or restore your health.

❖ GEM: A Hospital Can't Stick You Twice

If a service you receive at a hospital is eligible for Medicare coverage, the hospital is *not allowed* to charge you at all for that service, even if its actual cost for providing you with the care is more than the Medicare reimbursement. The hospital must pay any additional cost—so don't let them "needle" you for the money.

✦　✦　✦

What Hospital Services Will You Pay for?

Medicare will *not* pay for your "comfort and convenience" in the hospital. It is best to operate on the assumption that any care or service used to make your hospital visit more pleasant will *not* be paid for by Medicare. Therefore, according to *The Medicare Handbook* (page 13), you will be billed for:

1. Telephone, television (and any other personal conveniences).
2. Private-duty nurses. Even if this care was ordered by your doctor because the hospital was unable to provide the needed service, *you* must still pay.
3. Any extra charges for a private room, unless your condition required isolation or no semiprivate rooms were available.

What If You Go to a Non-Medicare Hospital?

Although most do, not every hospital participates in the Medicare program. If the hospital you go to has not signed a participation agreement with Medicare, Medicare will not pay even for covered services. Medicare does not pay for services performed at a nonparticipating hospital.

There's an important exception to this rule: Medical services provided by a nonparticipating hospital in life threatening situations *can* be covered.

EXAMPLE 14

You are involved in a car accident and are very seriously injured. The emergency medical squad takes you to the closest hospital that is qualified to handle such emergencies. The bad news is that you were unconscious and couldn't ask if it was a Medicare participating facility, and it isn't. The good news is that Medicare may still pay.

To qualify for emergency Medicare coverage, you must meet all of the following requirements.

1. Your medical condition, if not treated immediately, would have resulted in death or serious impairment.
2. The hospital chosen was significantly easier to reach or closer than the nearest participating facility. (Caution: Medicare has denied claims when a participating hospital was available 15 miles away.)
3. The hospital meets Medicare's standards for providing the needed emergency services.

The regional Health Care Financing Administration (HCFA) office is responsible for deciding if all criteria for coverage have been met. A physician's statement supporting the claim of a medical emergency will also be required.

❖ GEM: Get Out When the Emergency Is Over

Medicare will pay for your care at a non-Medicare facility for only as long as the emergency condition exists. When Medicare decides you are well enough to be transferred or released, coverage will stop.

✦　✦　✦

Will you be covered if a medical emergency arises while you are vacationing in a foreign country? *Non, Nein, Lo*—the answer in any language is *no,* with one exception: If you were in Canada or Mexico and you can prove that the foreign (non-Medicare) hospital was closer than the nearest participating U.S. hospital, Medicare might pay.

MEDICARE PART A: SKILLED NURSING FACILITY (SNF) CARE

Nursing-home costs can be catastrophic. In limited cases, your Part A insurance can continue to pay for care at an SNF after you leave the hospital. But, as you probably have guessed, Medicare does not make it easy to qualify; very specific conditions must be met. You are eligible for this type of extended care coverage if you can check yes to *all* of these statements, according to *The Medicare Handbook* (page 15).

	Yes	No
• An SNF is the only place that can provide the skilled services I need for my condition.	❏	❏
• I was hospitalized for at least three days in a row (don't count the day of discharge) before being transferred to an SNF.	❏	❏
• An illness or condition that I was treated for in the hospital is the same one I will be treated for at the SNF.	❏	❏
• I have been out of the hospital less than 30 days (discharge day counts as Day 1).	❏	❏
• My doctor has certified that I need skilled nursing or skilled rehabilitation at least five days each week.	❏	❏

Yes   No

- The Medicare Intermediary (insurance company chosen
by Medicare to process claims) has *not* told me my stay
does not meet their approval.   ❏   ❏

Medicare does not like paying for skilled nursing care. Nationally, only about 2 percent of all nursing-home costs are paid by Medicare. That is *far* too little. By understanding Medicarese and vigorously pursuing your rights, however, you should be able to get better results from Medicare. (If you can't cash in on Medicare, Medicaid may provide a Golden Opportunity for funding; see Chapter 11).

What Is a Skilled Nursing Facility?

According to *The Medicare Handbook,* an SNF is "a specially qualified facility with the staff and equipment to provide *skilled nursing care or rehabilitation services* and other related services." Some nursing homes provide only skilled care and participate entirely in Medicare. In others, only certain portions of the facility might participate in Medicare as an SNF, and some SNFs don't participate in Medicare at all. Make sure you are in a Medicare-qualified bed in a Medicare-qualified facility.

The key question is, Is this facility a Medicare-qualified SNF for the services I need? Have your doctor give you a complete list of the services you need. That way you will have an accurate record to work with when you are playing caregiver matchmaker.

How do you find out if the facility qualifies for Medicare coverage for your service? Here is a list of likely sources for help:

- Hospital Discharge Planners. These folks are familiar with the services available at local SNFs and can usually provide an answer, or they can call and inquire for you.
- Nursing Home Admissions Offices and their Utilization Review Committee (URC). Every facility that participates in Medicare has a URC, and it is their job to decide whether the services you need will be covered by Medicare.
- The Medicare Intermediary for Your Area. Each state chooses which insurance company will act as an intermediary and process its Medicare Part A claims. The toll-free numbers of the Medicare Intermediaries for every state can be found in Appendix 17.
- Social Security. If you are lucky enough to get through on the toll-free number, tell the representative that it is printed in *The Medicare Handbook* that Social Security can "check with the HCFA" to determine whether your specific needs will be covered. (See the *Handbook* section titled Skilled Nursing Facility Care.) Then read the list of services you require.

❖ GEM: Get Help to Help You Get Help

When we say "you," you don't need to take us literally. If you are not feeling up to taking action (and obviously if you were feeling terrific, you wouldn't be needing SNF care services), don't make yourself sicker trying to do all this alone. Get some help.

Whom should you ask? Consider all sources for assistance:

- Family
- Friends
- Hospital social worker or discharge planner
- Office on Aging (check the blue pages of your phone book under County Government)
- Senior citizen centers in your community
- State or county nursing home ombudsman (these individuals are paid by the state or county to act as advocates for nursing home residents)

❖ GEM: Don't Let the SNF's Goof Cost You

You shouldn't have to pay for someone else's mistake. If you are incorrectly placed in the *non*participating section of an SNF, Medicare will deny coverage. But since it is the facility's fault, not yours, you shouldn't be liable. Hold on to your wallet; let the facility fight it out with Uncle Sam.

✦　✦　✦

What Is the Difference Between Routine (Custodial) and Skilled Care?

When it comes to extended care coverage, Medicare makes it perfectly clear that there is a major distinction between *routine* (custodial) and *skilled* care. You'd better know the difference too, because how your care is defined will determine who is paying—Uncle Sam or you. *Medicare* pays for *skilled* nursing-home care provided on a daily basis; *you* pay for routine or custodial care (unless you have purchased private nursing-home insurance or can qualify for Medicaid—see Chapter 11).

Custodial Care. Could any Tom, Dick or Harry perform the job safely? A service that does not require the medical expertise of a skilled professional is considered routine or custodial (*e.g.,* help with bathing, feeding, dressing, eating, or walking). In practical terms, if Medicare defines your care as *custodial care,* you will pay the bill.

Table 4.6 provides a sampling of services which are "routinely" considered routine and custodial.

TABLE 4.6

Sampling of Custodial and Personal Care Services

- Assistance with routine application of eye drops, ointments, and other medications
- Maintenance of colostomy, ileostomy, bladder catheters
- Changes of dressings for noninfected postoperative or chronic conditions
- Baths or care for minor skin problems
- Routine care of incontinence (*e.g.,* diaper and linen changes)
- Routine help with braces, casts
- Heat treatments for comfort (*e.g.,* whirlpool)
- Assistance with medical gases, once a regimen has been established
- Help with dressing, eating, personal hygiene
- Supervision and assistance with exercise programs that have already been taught (*e.g.,* repetitive exercises to maintain or improve strength and endurance) and do not require skilled supervision

Source: 42 C.F.R. §409.33(d).

Skilled Care. As you probably can guess, skilled care is just the opposite of routine care. A service is skilled when only someone with special training can perform safely and effectively the tasks of care, observation, or assessment. At least on paper, the difference between routine and skilled care seems clear. But as you will see, determining what care requires skilled services is not at all clear. Shades of gray appear because each person's psychological, physical, and environmental circumstances are unique, and by law, Medicare is supposed to base its care decisions on your *total* situation [42 C.F.R. §409.33(a)(1)].

Medicare can barely handle black and white, so do you actually believe some bureaucrat buried in paperwork has the time to examine the "gray"? You can expect "differences of opinion" (read that denial of claims). In fact, the Government unfairly avoids paying claims by *strictly* interpreting "skilled" care. We have had clients who were connected to so many tubes they looked like something out of a science fiction movie, and yet Uncle Sam refused to pay, claiming their care was not skilled! The Government will trample your rights unless you (or a loved one) insist on coverage.

Here is an example that illustrates the gray variations that can arise over routine and skilled care.

EXAMPLE 15

After a complex surgery, you were admitted to an SNF for care. Why was an SNF appropriate? In addition to needing physical therapy three times a week, a nurse had to take your temperature hourly each day. When the claim for your care is submitted, the Medicare bureaucrat who reviews it says, "Aha—do they take us for fools? Obviously, SNF level care isn't needed for this person because reading a thermometer is an unskilled duty. The claim must be denied," she says with glee.

Now here comes the gray. What she failed to notice (or could not know because the claim form was not specific enough in its explanation) was this key fact: You had recently been placed on a potent, potentially lethal medication, and the first sign of toxicity is a slight fever. The services of a skilled nurse to read a thermometer were truly medically justified to evaluate and manage your condition. In this situation, although the care itself is unskilled, only an LPN had the level of expertise to interpret symptoms and make recommendations for adjusting the treatment. Your care should be considered skilled—and covered!

The best way to get an idea of which type of care is skilled is to look at actual situations. In Table 4.7, we list some real-life circumstances that should qualify for skilled nursing service coverage.

TABLE 4.7

Sampling of Skilled Nursing Services

- *Tube feedings and other related services.* Gastrostomy feedings, and nasopharyngeal and tracheostomy maintenance and replacement, are complex activities requiring skilled nursing and should be covered when needed to treat your illness.

- *Catheters.* Insertion, cleaning, and replacement of catheters should be covered skilled services.

- *Wound care.* Don't expect Medicare to pay for a skilled nurse to bandage your little nicks and scratches. But when the size and nature of a wound, burn, tube site, sore or tumor require application of medicated dressings or other special care and monitoring, the care should be considered skilled. Your doctor will need to document the reasons and provide specific instructions in your plan for care (your doctor's written prescription for the services and treatment you will need to stabilize or cure your condition); otherwise, you might be denied coverage.

- *Ostomy care.* Immediately following surgery, or where complications occur, care for an ostomy can be covered.

(Continued)

TABLE 4.7 (Continued)

Sampling of Skilled Nursing Services

- *Heat treatments (e.g.,* hot packs, whirlpool baths, infrared treatments). You'll take the heat for this care unless the treatments have been ordered by a physician and require observation by nurses to evaluate your progress.

- *Intravenous, intramuscular, or subcutaneous injections.* Diabetics take note: insulin injections fall into this category and so can be covered as a skilled service. This has often been a bone of contention for SNF eligibility.

- *Medical gases.* Administration of medical gases can be covered in an SNF. Teaching you or your caregivers how to administer treatment and also monitoring your response to the gases until your condition stabilizes also can be qualified as skilled service.

- *Treatment of serious skin disorders.* Serious skin problems, such as decubitus ulcers, often require skilled care.

- *Bowel and bladder training.* Helping a patient regain bowel and bladder control can qualify for coverage as skilled care.

Source: 42 C.F.R. §409.33(b).

What Are Skilled Rehabilitation Services?

You are entitled to coverage under Part A for skilled rehabilitation services—such as physical, speech, and occupational therapy—at an SNF. Speech therapy includes procedures necessary to diagnose and treat speech and language disorders. Occupational therapy includes treatment to improve or restore a patient's ability to handle daily activities.

EXAMPLE 16

You had a hip replacement, and after the operation you have difficulty regaining your balance. Your doctor prescribes physical therapy. Working with a qualified therapist at an SNF, you learn standing and walking techniques to improve your balance. The cost for these services should be covered by Uncle Sam.

EXAMPLE 17

You suffer a stroke and lose partial use of your right arm. An occupational therapist teaches you new ways to hold eating utensils so that you can feed yourself and regain independence. The SNF costs should be covered.

Table 4.8 lists some examples of rehabilitation services that should qualify as skilled care in an SNF.

TABLE 4.8

Sampling of Skilled Rehabilitation Services

- *Assessment of rehabilitation needs.* These include tests and measurements of range of motion, strength, balance, coordination, endurance and functional abilities.
- *Therapeutic exercises or activities.* If the type of exercises or your condition requires supervision to ensure your safety or the effectiveness of the treatment, it should be covered.
- *Walking evaluation and training.* If your ability to walk has been impaired, evaluation and training should be covered.
- *Exercises in response to loss or restriction of range of motion.*
- *Maintenance therapy.* Let's say you have Parkinson's disease. Exercises to maintain your present level of functioning, under the supervision of a qualified therapist, should be covered.
- *Ultrasound, short-wave, and microwave therapy.*
- *Hot pack, hydrocollator, infrared treatments, paraffin baths, and whirlpool.* These should be covered if warranted to treat your specific condition and the skills, knowledge and judgement of a qualified therapist are required.
- *Services of a speech pathologist or audiologist.*

Source: 42 C.F.R. §409.33(c).

The Government often catches you in one of two traps: your claim for SNF coverage will be denied if you can't show that the treatment or therapy is essential to improve or maintain your physical condition; and coverage will be denied if skilled care is not required on a daily basis.

Uncle Sam generally expects improvement over a "reasonable" and "predictable" time period.

EXAMPLE 18

As a result of a stroke, your speech is impaired. A skilled speech pathologist assesses your rehabilitation potential and determines that, with therapy, a measurable improvement in your communicative skills can be achieved. A plan of care is devised with specific goals for speech production. Medicare will pay for the skilled speech therapy because you have "rehabilitation potential" and it is hoped significant improvement can be achieved in a predictable time. Keep in mind that coverage will last *only* as long as you can continue to "pass" the tests. Once the benefit of therapy stops, Medicare coverage will, too.

❖ GEM: Maintenance Is Enough to Get Coverage

The Government has a tendency to overlook the fact that rehabilitation service should be covered as long as the treatment is necessary to *maintain* your condition. Don't let them!

EXAMPLE 19

Your father suffered a stroke and is having trouble walking. A therapist in the SNF has been helping him learn to walk with a walker, but now the Government says he's not making further progress.

Although he may not be making further progress, he is likely to regress if therapy is stopped. Without continued therapy, he will go back to the wheelchair. In this case, you can fight the Government's decision to cut off benefits.

To qualify for coverage in an SNF, the skilled care must be provided on a daily basis. This means that the skilled nursing or rehabilitation service you receive must be needed seven days a week. Uncle Sam does allow one important exception: if skilled rehabilitation services are not available every day, you can still qualify for coverage if you receive the service at least five days a week.

✦   ✦   ✦

❖ GEM: A Short Break in Rehabilitation Should Not End Coverage

Let's say your doctor suspends your rehabilitation program for a couple of days because you are exhausted and need a rest. Or maybe you get sick and miss three days. The short break should not cause you to lose Medicare coverage, but a break in skilled nursing care can terminate your benefits.

❖ GEM: Try Part B Coverage

Therapy at an SNF can also be covered under Medicare Part B insurance (pages 175–177). If you have used up, or aren't eligible for, Part A coverage, check out this option with the SNF. Note: under Part B, the services of an independent therapist are limited to $750 a year and you must pay co-insurance, too.

❖ GEM: Make Sure the Provider Uses the Right Claim Form

We have seen rehabilitation claims unfairly denied simply because the wrong claim form was used. You can't use a Part B claim form to get Part A services, and vice versa. If you are denied, check to see if the right form was used and ask the provider to refile. Your denial may have just been from incorrect paper work.

❖ GEM: Make Sure Doctor Certifies Need for Skilled Care

Your doctor *must certify* in writing that skilled-level care is required as an inpatient or on a daily basis (at least five days a week). If your doctor doesn't routinely attend to Medicare patients, make sure he works with the hospital's discharge planner to assure all the certification paperwork is done.

◆ ◆ ◆

What Are the Time Requirements?

To get Medicare to cover SNF services, you must have been hospitalized at least three consecutive days before entering an SNF. That three-day requirement is a hidden trap that can cost you plenty.

EXAMPLE 20

Dan entered the hospital on January 1 and was transferred to a Medicare-approved SNF on January 3. Will Medicare pay? *No.* Even though Dan went to an approved facility and was receiving skilled nursing care, he did not meet the three-consecutive-day hospitalization requirement. Medicare counts the day of admission as one day, but does *not* count the day of discharge. If Dan had stayed in the hospital one more day and transferred on January 4, he would have been eligible for Medicare coverage. Instead, he will be paying thousands of dollars to the nursing home out of his own pocket.

EXAMPLE 21

Dan spent three days in a psychiatric hospital before being transferred to an SNF. Will he be covered? *Yes.* Treatment in a psychiatric hospital should be considered equivalent to a "general hospital," so the three-day inpatient care requirement is met.

What if the three days prior to SNF admission were spent at a Christian Science Sanitorium? *No.* Medicare doesn't consider these facilities hospitals, so time spent there is *not counted.*

Medicare applies the three-day requirement strictly. It won't waive the three-day requirement even if you are forced out of a hospital because of a lack of beds.

EXAMPLE 22

You were treated in the hospital emergency room and required immediate hospitalization. Unfortunately no beds were available, so you were admitted to the SNF unit of the hospital. Medicare will *not* pay even though the unit was a participating SNF. Why? To receive benefits at an SNF, you must first be hospitalized for three days.

❖ GEM: Beat the Three-Day Requirement!

Don't let the hospital or doctor discharge you or a loved one to an SNF before you've spent three days in a hospital. Talk to your hospital discharge planner or doctor to see if an extra day can somehow be justified. That extra day can save you thousands of dollars in nursing costs.

If the hospital (through its Utilization Review Committee) or Peer Review Organization (PRO) tells you to leave, challenge their decision—*don't go!* Insist on staying another day. If the PRO told you to leave, and you lose the appeal, you will have to pay the extra day of hospital care, but the cost will be worth it if the extra day helps you meet the three-day hospitalization requirement for SNF coverage! And if the notice to leave came from the hospital, you won't have to pay while the PRO reviews your case (even if the PRO agrees with the hospital).

✦   ✦   ✦

In addition to the three-day requirement, Medicare imposes another time requirement: You must enter the SNF within 30 days after leaving the hospital, and your care at the SNF must be necessitated by the same condition that first sent you to the hospital. *Continuity of care* is the key phrase here.

EXAMPLE 23

Dan was hospitalized for a severe foot infection; he stabilized and four days later was discharged. Twenty-two days later his doctor admitted him to a Medicare-approved nursing home, where he received skilled nursing care for a *different* condition. Will Medicare pay? *No.*

But Dan met the 30-day limit and 3-day hospitalization requirements, right? Yes and no. Remember, for the stay to be covered, the need for extended care services must either be due to the condition that necessitated hospitalization or be an ailment that arose during that stay.

❖ GEM: Get Proof of Continuity of Care

Make sure your doctor's statement certifying your need for care clearly establishes a link between your hospital stay and the skilled nursing care you will need.

✦   ✦   ✦

Medicare expects you to enter an SNF within 30 days *after the day you left the hospital.* For example, if your date of discharge from the hospital is July 1, and you enter an SNF on July 31, you will be covered because the Medicare meter starts ticking on July 2, the day *after* discharge. But if you enter the SNF one day later on August 1, you will be out of luck. You will have exceeded the 30-day limit.

Will Medicare Pay?

Will Medicare pay if you:

- Enter an SNF for custodial care within 30 days after leaving the hospital but after 30 days you then need skilled care? *NO.* You must start skilled services within 30 days.
- Require skilled care for the first 10 days, only custodial care for the next twenty days, then on Day 31 skilled care again? *NO.* Medicare will pay for those first 10 days, but will *not* resume payment for the subsequent skilled care because 30 days have elapsed since your hospital discharge.
- Leave an SNF and are readmitted (to the same or a different SNF) within 30 days of your hospital discharge owing to the same illness? *YES.* You can go home again, so to speak, as long as it's within Medicare's time limits.
- Leave an SNF, then suffer a relapse within 30 days after discharge that requires a hospitalization? *YES.* If the hospitalization occurs within 30 days after your discharge from the SNF, Medicare will treat your hospital stay as if it's a return to an SNF.

❖ GEM: Extend the 30-Day Limit

Medicare—in its great wisdom—recognizes that, with certain health conditions, transfer to an SNF within 30 days to continue treatment is not always "medically appropriate." In that case, you may be able to get an extension. To qualify, at the time you leave the hospital, your doctor must have a specific timetable for continuing skilled treatment at an SNF, and you must really follow through.

Medicare won't accept any vague promises; Uncle Sam wants predictability. To illustrate this point, Examples 24 and 25 show two very different outcomes.

EXAMPLE 24

You fall and break a hip. After leaving the hospital you will still need physical therapy. Appropriate medical procedure requires a four- to six-week wait before treatment can begin. Your doctor prepares a written plan of care that states you will enter an SNF five weeks after hospitalization to begin rehabilitation therapy. Under Medicare rules, you shall be able to get an extension because the delay was "medically appropriate" and predictable.

EXAMPLE 25

You were hospitalized to treat a severe stomach disorder. It is very likely that you will require treatment again in the near future, but your doctor can't give an exact time frame or estimate the level of care that will be needed. After 30 days, if you do need skilled care, tough luck! Although the delay in care might be medically appropriate, it is *not predictable*. That means no money.

❖ GEM: If You Can't Get in Within 30 Days, Try to Delay to 60

If you don't need an SNF for 30 days, and you can't get an extension, try to stay at home for 60 days, so that you can enter a new benefit period. If you then return as a hospital inpatient for three days, you will be entitled to a new chance to qualify for SNF benefits. Example 26 shows how this happens.

EXAMPLE 26

Let's start with the same situation as Example 25. Just 59 days after your discharge from the hospital your stomach problems start to reappear. You immediately rush to the hospital, where you are treated for four days. You are then discharged to an SNF.

Unfortunately, since 60 days had not passed from the prior hospitalization, no new benefit period starts, so you don't get coverage for the SNF. Had you been able to wait one more day at home before entering the hospital, your SNF bills would have been covered.

◆ ◆ ◆

What Will Medicare Pay?

Once you qualify for SNF coverage, the questions are what Medicare will pay for, and what services are covered. Table 4.9 shows what Medicare pays.

TABLE 4.9

Who Pays for Skilled Nursing Facility Care Coverage?

If	Medicare Part A Pays	You Pay
You weren't hospitalized for at least 3 consecutive days prior to entering SNF	0	Entire amount
You didn't enter an SNF within 30 days of leaving the hospital	0	Entire amount
Your SNF is not participating in Medicare	0	Entire amount
You need skilled care less than 5 days a week	0	Entire amount
Your doctor didn't order the skilled care	0	Entire amount
You are at a Medicare approved SNF but services received are *not* performed or supervised by licensed medical personnel	0	Entire amount
You meet all conditions for SNF coverage	All for first 20 days All but $81.50/day for 21–100 Nothing after 100 days	0 for first 20 days $81.50/day for days 21–100 Entire amount after 100 days

As Table 4.9 shows, Medicare pays for all or part of your covered services for up to 100 days *each benefit period*. Keep in mind that once you are out of an SNF for 60 days in a row, the Medicare timer goes back to zero, and you are entitled to a new 100 days of SNF coverage. Of course, you must still meet all the same conditions (three-day hospital stay, etc.) before Medicare will pay.

What Services Do You Get?

Assuming you are in a participating SNF, you need skilled care, and you meet the time requirements, Medicare will pay for the services listed in Table 4.10. Table 4.11 lists services that Medicare will *not* pay for.

TABLE 4.10

SNF Services Paid by Medicare Part A

- Skilled nursing care.
- Semiprivate room (two to four beds in a room). If one isn't available at time of admission, Medicare will pay for a private room, but when a semiprivate is ready, you must switch or pay.
- All meals and special diets (unfortunately, pizza doesn't count as a special dietary need, so delivery charges for a pie aren't covered!).
- Regular nursing services provided by SNF staff (*e.g.*, taking your temperature or blood pressure).
- Rehabilitation services, including physical, speech, and occupational therapy.
- Drugs, medical supplies and therapeutic equipment (*e.g.*, splints and wheelchairs).
- Blood transfusions (after meeting your three-pint deductible).
- Medical social services and diagnostic services, including a social worker's assessment of your adjustment to treatment and help in responding to emotional issues resulting from the illness.
- Other services necessary to maintain your health that can only be provided by an SNF.

Source: The Medicare Handbook, pages 15–16.

TABLE 4.11

SNF Costs You Pay

- TVs, telephones, and any other personal luxuries
- Private-duty nurses
- Additional charges for a private room, unless medically necessary
- Custodial nursing home-care services (*e.g.*, haircuts), other than daily personal care needs like bathing, feeding, and dressing
- Doctors' bills (Medicare Part B insurance will help pay these fees—see page 175)

Source: The Medicare Handbook, page 16.

When Medicare is paying, don't expect a room with a view and privacy, too. You are entitled to a semiprivate room (two to four beds in a room). That is it, period. This rule applies to both hospitals and SNFs.

❖ GEM: Get a Private Room, at Uncle Sam's Expense

Here are two ways you might get a private room.

First, if your condition *requires* isolation to protect your health or others, a private room should be considered "medically necessary." Get Medicare to pay.

Second, if at the time you are admitted no semiprivate or ward rooms are available, you should be entitled to "fly first class for the price of coach." You can have a private room at no extra charge. But don't get too comfortable; as soon as a semiprivate room opens up, out you go (unless you're willing to pay the difference).

If your admission could have been delayed until a semiprivate room was available, but you still *chose* to enter the facility, *you* will foot the bill for the price difference between the two types of accommodation.

❖ GEM: Don't Get a Private Room by Mistake—at Your Cost

State your room preference to your doctor; otherwise, if he has first-class taste, you could end up paying for his decision.

❖   ❖   ❖

Extended care services that are custodial and not skilled are covered only if they are routinely provided by an SNF. Items and services that wouldn't be covered if you were a hospital inpatient won't be covered when you're at an SNF, either. For example, expect to pay for personal laundry (does it strike you as odd that although you are sick enough to require skilled care, the folks at Medicare expect you to wash clothes?). When it comes to personal services, Medicare will hang you out to dry.

Plan Now to Avoid Pain Later

As much as we don't like to think about needing nursing-home care, we should. Before a crisis arises, it makes sense for you (or a family member) to visit a few SNF facilities.

Where to Look. Ask friends who might have experience; call a local hospital's discharge planning department for names; check the yellow pages and look for nursing-home listings that say "Medicare Certified."

What to Look for. Call the chosen SNFs and request a tour and time to meet with the admissions director, then do some homework. There are many good books that deal with how to select an SNF. Checklists of questions to ask and what to look for are usually included. Take one with you when you visit.

How to Plan. After making the rounds, prepare a list of the facilities, noting any reasons why a particular SNF would not be acceptable to you.

When to Act. If you are hospitalized, begin your discharge planning ASAP! Don't wait to be told. Ask your doctor what kind of posthospital care you might need. If he feels an SNF is appropriate, pull out your list.

By taking the initiative, you will feel less like a helpless victim. Your decisions can be based on information *you* obtained rather than relying solely on someone else's advice (who might be under pressure to get you out of that hospital bed!). Of course, timing and luck are helpful because bed availability is an unknown variable. But by preplanning you can improve the odds of arriving at an acceptable SNF choice. And since seeking SNF care is far from fun, by making an informed choice at least you can transform a situation from nightmarish to tolerable. You and your family will sleep better knowing you have tried to do your best.

WARNING

When the hospital is ready to discharge you, you generally will have to accept the first SNF bed available, or pay for your extended hospital stay until a bed opens up in a facility of your choice. If you go home to wait for that bed to open, it may never become available because SNFs usually give preference to hospital patients.

❖ GEM: Don't Go to a Poor or Inconvenient SNF

You don't have to accept the first available bed if the SNF is unsuitable—either not up to quality standards or not in a location reasonably close to your family. In these cases, Medicare should pay for the extended hospital stay while you wait. Unfortunately, Medicare often mistakenly denies coverage in these cases, and you might have to battle with a Medicare appeal. When you can justify your disapproval of an SNF, hang on to your hospital bed—you are right to stay and fight.

MEDICARE PART A: HOME HEALTH CARE

Rather than enter a nursing home, wouldn't you prefer to be cared for in the warmth and comfort of your own home? Of course you would! In some circumstances, Uncle Sam may give you that option.

When it comes to home health care, there is good news and bad news. The good news is that Medicare does provide a wide range of benefits for this type of care. The bad news is that Uncle Sam does not make it very easy to qualify for the coverage. Even when you *are* entitled to home health care, unfair denials are common. To keep Uncle Sam honest, you must stay on your toes. (Now that's good incentive to stick with physical therapy!) Here are the rules for playing— and winning—this part of the Medicare Monopoly Game.

Medicare will pay for home health visits only when you can answer yes to these four eligibility statements:

- I need skilled nursing care provided on a part-time or intermittent basis or physical therapy, speech therapy, or medical social services in order to remain at home.
- I am receiving care from a doctor, and he or she set up a specific home health plan for care that will be reviewed periodically (every two months).
- I am confined to my home (an occasional walk around the block, if you are able, will not be held against you).
- The home health agency I use participates in Medicare.

If you meet these four requirements, Medicare should cover all medically necessary home health services for as long as you need skilled care, therapy (physical, speech, or occupational), or medical social services. There are *no* deductibles, *no* co-insurance (except for medical equipment), and *no* limits on how long the services may continue.

As you can see, Medicare coverage for home care does not carry all of the same requirements as does SNF coverage. The care must still be "skilled," but no prior three-day hospitalization is required, and no connection to hospital care need be shown.

Home health care carries some additional requirements, though. Most important, the care must be provided by a Medicare-approved home-health-care agency, skilled nursing care you receive must be provided only on an intermittent or part-time basis, and you must be confined to home.

What Is a Certified Home-Health-Care Agency?

To qualify for Medicare coverage, the home care you receive must be from a Medicare-approved home-health-care agency. The agency will make an initial evaluation visit to determine whether your medical needs can be satisfied in the home environment. Factors considered are your overall health, your surroundings, and the family support system.

❖ GEM: Don't Pay for the Initial Visit

Who pays for an initial evaluation visit? You don't! Medicare considers the cost of this first evaluation an operating expense for a home health agency. But don't let anyone provide skilled services for you at this first visit, unless you first have an agreement with the home-health-care agency in your hands! Otherwise, you could be stuck with a bill no one wants to pay.

❖ GEM: Shop Around for a Home-Health-Care Agency

Not all home-health-care agencies are alike. Some agencies bury a clause in their agreements stating you must foot the bill if Medicare disallows. Some offer more care than others, too. Read the fine print!

✦ ✦ ✦

There are many agencies out there, but not all participate in Medicare. You will need to do some detective work. Possible sources for help are:

- *Your Doctor.* Chances are he/she has been asked before and has referrals.
- *Friends.* Perhaps you know people who have had to research home-health-care agencies. If you can benefit from someone else's experience, that's great.
- *Hospital Discharge Planners.* It's their job to know the appropriate community resources and they probably have a list. (Oftentimes, hospitals are affiliated with home-health-care agencies and an assessment can be made without even leaving the comfort of your hospital bed!)
- *Yellow Pages.* The Home Health Service section will list numerous agencies. Some ads will state "Medicare/Medicaid Certified." Obviously, call those first.

If you do call a nonparticipating agency, chances are they, too, can offer names of agencies that are Medicare qualified.

❖ GEM: Plan Ahead

Don't wait until you are ready to leave the hospital before starting to plan for posthospital care. Formulate a plan of action *before* an emergency arises. Ask your doctor "what if?" Line up a family friend willing to be "on call" just in case you need help with organizing posthospital care plans. And have someone start exploring home health care as early as possible.

✦ ✦ ✦

What Is Intermittent or Part-time Skilled Care?

Uncle Sam expects you to know just what he means when he talks about "intermittent" or "part-time" skilled care. His insurance intermediaries obviously have no difficulty with the term, because they routinely deny claims that don't meet his standards. But guess what? Until 1988, no published federal regulations existed that clearly defined intermittent or part-time care! It was only when a brave soul sued HCFA over the unfairness of this "minor" omission, and the courts agreed, that Medicare rewrote the guidelines more specifically. If Medicare won't put the rules for Medicare Monopoly on paper, how can we be expected to follow them? Yet we are.

Meeting the requirement for part-time or intermittent skilled nursing care can be as easy as building a house in quicksand—the ground keeps shifting! But that won't stop us from providing some cement for building a solid case to receive benefits.

Part-time or intermittent care is care that is *not* required indefinitely on a full-time basis, seven days a week. For example, if you only need care at home for a few hours a day for several days a week, you should have no problem.

Part-time care means care provided less than eight hours per day. It can be any number of days per week, but no more than 35 hours total in a week. For example, Medicare should pay for three hours a day, seven days a week. This can go on indefinitely.

Intermittent care means care provided on a regular basis that is needed less than seven days per week. It can be any number of hours per day, up to 35 hours total in a week. For example, Medicare should pay for six hours a day, five days a week. This care also can go on indefinitely.

EXAMPLE 27

Your dad just had surgery, and the incision became infected. He needs a skilled nurse to come in for a short time every day to clean and monitor the skin. Because she will only be there a couple of hours each day, the care should be covered.

❖ GEM: Get Full-time Daily Care

Uncle Sam offers a bonus: you can get care seven days per week, eight hours per day (56 hours in a week) if the care is finite and predictable, meaning it won't last for more than about 21 days. In certain cases, this full-time daily care can be extended for up to six months. Don't assume you are the exception to the rule; make sure you get official approval for an extension. See Example 28.

EXAMPLE 28

Your mother has just had a severe heart attack. Although she was released from the hospital, she needs daily full-time skilled observation. She needs the skilled care for two weeks. Since it's only for a limited and predictable time, these services should be covered.

❖ GEM: Get Coverage for Services Required Only Once Every Three Months

Let's look at the other extreme. Generally Uncle Sam wants you to get home care on a regular, predictable schedule, which means at least once every 60 days. But if you need skilled care only once in 90 days, can that qualify as part-time or intermittent care? If your doctor shows that you have a *medically predictable need* for skilled services, we "predict" you should get coverage. See Example 29.

EXAMPLE 29

Mr. Roth, age 88, is a diabetic with limited vision. He self-injects insulin. Medicare will pay for skilled nursing visits once every 90 days because a professional is needed to assess any changes in his health and to assure that he's receiving the proper level of care. The care is medically predictable.

❖ GEM: Long-term Conditions Can Qualify

Part-time or *intermittent care* does not have to mean short term. Care for long-term conditions can still be covered if the care required is part time or intermittent, as we've explained. But don't expect Medicare to tell you that. As a matter of fact, Uncle Sam's insurance intermediaries want you to believe that "exceeding limitations on duration" is a valid reason for denial. They don't want to be shelling out thousands of dollars for long-term care. Yet the fact is, you are entitled to an unlimited number of visits as long as the care is medically necessary!

❖ ❖ ❖

When Are You Considered "Confined to Home"?

You are considered "confined to home" if you can leave on your own only with the help of a wheelchair, a walker, or another person, and only for limited periods of time. This should not be too tough a standard to meet; if you can't get around on your own, you should pass.

What Will You Pay for?

Before focusing on what Medicare will pay for, it's helpful to look at what Medicare *won't* pay for. In general, any care that is not *skilled* will be your responsibility, not the Government's. Everyday tasks that can be done by anyone are not covered. The "comfort and convenience" rule applies to home health care, too: services provided solely for your comfort, but which are not medically necessary, are not covered.

An important exception is home health aides. If you are receiving skilled care, you may get coverage for home health aides providing personal unskilled services (page 170).

Here is a list of services *not* covered by Medicare when you are at home. According to *The Medicare Handbook* (page 16), you will pay for these:

1. Meals delivered to your house (*e.g.,* meals-on-wheels).
2. Housekeeping and any other homemaker services not related to your illness.
3. Transportation services, even if necessary to enable you to receive medical services at an outpatient facility!
4. Drugs and the administration of drugs. (In certain cases, drugs that can only be administered by your doctor can be covered under Part B.)
5. 20 percent co-payment for durable medical equipment purchases.
6. Blood transfusions. (Dracula will be disappointed, but for most of us, this exclusion is no great loss.)
7. 24-hour-a-day nursing care on a permanent basis.

❖ GEM: Don't Let Medicare Just Say No to Drugs

Medicare specifically *excludes* the administration of drugs from coverage. But here is one small dose of good news. If a drug necessary for your treatment can only be administered safely by a licensed nurse, Medicare should pay for the service (*e.g.,* intravenous, intramuscular, or subcutaneous injections should be covered).

This fact might be hard to swallow, but Medicare does *not* think giving you oral medicine requires a skilled nurse's expertise, and so Uncle Sam won't generally pay for administering oral medicine. How can you get around this? If you can show that an unstable condition, or the quantity of drugs you must take, requires careful observation for side effects, a skilled nurse can be justified.

Uncle Sam really rubs it in when it comes to body ointments or eyedrops. Medicare generally won't agree to the need for a skilled nurse to deposit a few eyedrops or to apply a cream on your back, even when you can't do it yourself. But again, if observation by a skilled nurse is needed to monitor your condition, Medicare should pay. See Example 30.

EXAMPLE 30

Mr. Cotten is diabetic and needs an insulin shot once a day. He also has muscular dystrophy. Poor muscle control prevents him from filling the syringes and injecting the insulin he needs. Medicare *should* pay for a skilled nurse to perform the service for him.

If Mr. Cotten only needed help with prefilling the syringes, Medicare would *not* pay. Why? This service is routine and supposedly does not require *skilled* nursing. Anyone can do the job, according to the decision makers at Medicare.

Note: By law, some states require a licensed nurse to prefill syringes. In this situation, Medicare *will* pay (but only if you are also receiving some other skilled nursing care or therapy).

✦ ✦ ✦

What Will Medicare Actually Pay for?

You *must* understand the golden rules for home-health-care coverage. Otherwise you are sure to lose out on valuable benefits that are rightfully yours.

Skilled Nursing Care. Medicare covers skilled care provided by a nurse in your home, if the care is reasonable and necessary to treat an illness or injury. Our discussion of skilled care on pages 146–153 generally applies here, too. A nurse who is providing unskilled service must be paid by you.

EXAMPLE 31

Mr. Jones has a colostomy and needs help changing the colostomy bag. Although he has no one to assist him, Medicare won't pay for a nurse to help because the care is considered routine and could be performed by anyone.

But services that may not be skilled in one situation may be skilled in another.

EXAMPLE 32

Let's continue Example 31. Because Mr. Jones couldn't maintain the colostomy adequately on his own, he developed an infection. Now he requires special skilled treatment to clean and monitor the colostomy. Guess what? Medicare should now pay for these services.

Services that *generally* would be considered unskilled should be covered by Medicare when the nature of your condition requires a skilled professional to monitor or perform the task. Medicare should pick up the tab for the periodic visits of a skilled nurse, when ordered by your doctor, to assess your progress and to determine if changes in treatment are needed.

EXAMPLE 33

Bess Tyler, age 83, broke her leg. She is now wearing a cast. Normally, a leg cast involves no skilled supervision. But because she suffers from circulatory problems, her condition must be monitored by *skilled* rehabilitation personnel who can teach her correct movement techniques. The unique aspects of Ms. Tyler's situation make this level of care appropriate. Medicare should pay.

But don't expect Medicare bureaucrats to take the time to look closely at each case. Chances are, claims for care that look routine will be routinely denied. Your doctor's job is to prove why this care is reasonable for *you* (*e.g.,* supplying a detailed plan of care or letters of explanation from the home health agency), and your job is to make sure the doctor does his.

❖ GEM: Get Compensation for a Supervisor

Medicare may pay a skilled professional to manage and oversee unskilled help when the nature or complexity of your condition requires it. If your doctor can prove medical necessity, Medicare should accept the claim that necessary unskilled services you are receiving need skilled supervision. Example 34 shows how.

EXAMPLE 34

Mr. Carlisle is a 72-year-old diabetic who also suffers with angina. He has been hospitalized for a severe leg infection. His home-care plan will require several nonskilled treatments: exercise to restore muscle tone, careful skin-care treatments, and administration of oral medications.

Although these services normally could be performed by an unskilled health-care aide without supervision, the patient's condition creates a serious risk of complications. Until Mr. Carlisle's condition stabilizes, a skilled professional's expertise is necessary to assure the treatment plan is correctly coordinated—and that should be covered by Medicare.

❖ GEM: Get Medicare to Pay for Teaching Old Dogs New Tricks

If you or family members will be providing unskilled care, you generally can't get compensated by Medicare. But if you need a skilled professional to provide training, the education services of a skilled nurse to teach you or your caregivers how to manage your care program *can* be covered.

For example, according to the federal regulations (42 C.F.R. §409.33(a)(3)), Medicare should consider it reasonable to hire a skilled licensed nurse to teach:

1. Self-administration of injections or medical gases
2. New diabetics all facets of health management (*e.g.,* diet, foot care, etc.)
3. Wound care when severity or patient's overall condition requires
4. Care for an ostomy
5. Self-catheterization
6. Prosthesis care; use of braces and splints
7. Care and application of dressings to treat *severe* skin disorders
8. Correct administration of oral medications when side effects and interactions with other drugs and foods might occur

EXAMPLE 35

Sixty-eight-year-old Mr. Block has just been placed on insulin to treat his diabetic condition. His doctor has ordered a skilled nurse to teach him how to manage self-injection, recognize signs of insulin shock, and take emergency procedures. Medicare should pay because these skilled services are reasonable and necessary for his treatment.

EXAMPLE 36

Let's say Mr. Block has been self-injecting insulin for five years. He recently changed doctors. His new physician orders skilled nursing visits every two weeks to monitor his self-injection procedures. Since there's been no deterioration in Mr. Block's physical and mental status, skilled care is not reasonable or medically necessary, and Medicare won't pay.

EXAMPLE 37

Now, let's say Mr. Block suffers a mild stroke. As a result, the use of his right hand is limited. His doctor orders a skilled nurse to retrain him in the self-administration of insulin. Because there has been a change in Mr. Block's health status, reteaching is reasonable and necessary, and Medicare *should* pay.

✦ ✦ ✦

When it comes to skilled teaching, the *Golden Rule* for coverage is: Medicare will do unto others for only as long as they can't do for themselves. When Medicare decides you have learned your lesson and your condition is stable, coverage will end. If you disagree, be prepared to appeal and prove your point. You may have to agree to pay for the home-health-care agency privately to continue the service while you are fighting with Medicare.

Additional Therapies and Services. We have said that Medicare will cover skilled nursing care, physical therapy, or speech therapy at home. But that's not all you can get. You know the old song about love and marriage going "together like a horse and carriage . . . you can't have one without the other"? Well, it's true for Medicare home-health-care coverage, too.

If you are receiving part-time or intermittent skilled nursing care, physical therapy, or speech therapy at home, Medicare will *also* pay for:

- Occupational therapy
- Home health aides
- Medical social services
- Medical supplies
- Durable medical equipment (80% of approved amount)

We have already talked about occupational therapy in our discussion of SNF coverage; the same rules for coverage apply for home health care too. Durable medical equipment is discussed on pages 201–210. Home health aides and medical social services deserve special attention here, because these resources offer a true Golden Opportunity for important care.

Home Health Aides. A home health aide can provide any service, even *unskilled* service, but the aide must be from a Medicare-certified home-health-care agency. Medicare will cover personal-care services that are a "reasonable and necessary" part of your treatment, and the doctor must say so. The care provided by the aide need not be skilled, although you must *also* be receiving skilled care.

"Hands-on" care needed to recover or maintain your health can be covered. The doctor's written plan of care must specify how often the home health services are needed. For a better feel for Medicare's "rules of the game" for home health aides, here is a list of five common services that are covered.

PERSONAL CARE SERVICES. For example, bathing, dressing, feeding.

EXAMPLE 38

Mrs. Sax has a colostomy. Owing to complications, an LPN visits twice a month to monitor her condition. Because of arthritis, Mrs. Sax also has difficulty changing the colostomy bag. Her doctor orders home-health-aide services to perform this task. Because the care is reasonable and necessary to maintain Mrs. Sax's health, and she is also receiving skilled care, Medicare should pay for the home health aides.

SKIN TREATMENTS. These are treatments not requiring skilled care (*e.g.,* applications of ointments, simple bandaging tasks).

EXAMPLE 39

Mr. George recently had surgery. The incision is healing, but requires regular cleaning and rebandaging. Because of the location he can't do the job himself. If he also needs skilled services, Medicare should cover a home health aide to care for the incision.

ASSISTANCE WITH MEDICATIONS. These are usually self-administered, or are medications that don't require a skilled nurse to be given safely.

EXAMPLE 40

Mr. Fried is diabetic, and his vision is also impaired. A home health aide is needed to prefill his insulin syringes. (Note: Some state laws require a skilled nurse for this task.) This service should be covered.

ASSISTANCE WITH ROUTINE THERAPEUTIC EXERCISES. These exercises must enhance skilled therapy services.

EXAMPLE 41

As a result of a stroke, Mrs. Southers has suffered a loss of speech and arm mobility. Although she receives skilled therapy, she also needs to practice routine, repetitive exercises twice a day. Assistance is necessary, but she lives alone. A home health aide is called in to help. Guess what? It should be covered!

OTHER INCIDENTAL NONHEALTH-RELATED SERVICES. So far we've been talking about a home health aide providing health-related services. But can you get coverage if the aide also helps with nonhealth-related activities (*e.g.,* meal preparation, light cleaning, etc.)? The answer is yes! Incidental nonhealth services can be provided and covered as long as this type of assistance is not the *sole* reason for the visit—the aide must also have a health-related task.

WARNING: DON'T GET GREEDY

The need for a home health aide must be linked in some way to your medical treatment, and the frequency of visits must be reasonable. If you are using a qualified home health aide, Medicare will not pay for more than 35 hours of total home-health-care services (skilled and unskilled) per week. We all would like household help seven days a week, but unless you can prove it's essential for your condition don't expect Medicare to clean up after you!

Medical Social Services. Medicare should cover services needed to help you respond to the social and emotional problems that arise from an illness. A medical social service professional will assess your situation and develop a plan of care to address your specific needs. If the professionals you deal with are Medicare-certified, your care should be covered.

EXAMPLE 42

Seventy-eight-year-old Mr. Epton has heart disease and hypertension. His doctor is concerned because Mr. Epton is not eating properly. He also can't afford the medications needed to maintain his health. A medical social service worker is called; she assesses Mr. Epton's situation and develops a plan of action that links him with available community resources for food and medical assistance. Medicare will pay because the doctor could document that the medical social services provided were "reasonable and necessary."

❖ GEM: Get the Care Provider to Confirm That Social Services Are Medically Appropriate for You

Medical social services are a prime target for denials. It's not enough to know that a service generally is "covered." Try to get the care provider to verify that the specific services that you are or will be receiving are "medically appropriate" for *you.* It's always better to know ahead of time whether Medicare will pay for the service; you may decide that a particular social service isn't worth the cost if it will be coming out of your pocket!

MEDICARE PART A: HOSPICE CARE

Thankfully, Uncle Sam comes through by subsidizing hospice care, which involves specialized services for terminally ill patients and their families. The focus of this care is pain relief, symptom management, and supportive services. Hospice programs can be operated by public or private agencies.

Uncle Sam has recognized that standard Medicare benefits are not adequate for the special types of care needed for a terminal illness. In this situation—comfort and convenience must also be considered. Costs for pain medications and a variety of support services not usually paid for by Medicare will be covered if, according to *The Medicare Handbook* (page 17):

- A doctor certifies that the person is terminally ill.
- The person chooses to receive hospice coverage *instead* of regular Medicare coverage.
- The care is being provided by a Medicare-participating hospice program.
- An oral plan of care is developed within two days of entering the hospice and a written care plan is signed within eight days of entering the hospice. The plan will need to be created by an interdisciplinary group that includes a doctor and other health professionals (nurses, social workers, counselors). The care will be based on this plan and reviewed regularly.

When you choose hospice care, Medicare requires that you waive your rights to services other than hospice care. What does this mean for you? It sounds worse than it really is. While generally you would be denied medical care when receiving hospice benefits, you may switch from hospice to standard Medicare coverage if you require treatment for another ailment (unrelated to your terminal illness). The intent of this distinction in coverage is to limit the treatments you receive under hospice benefits to those appropriate to hospice care—pain and symptom management. Invasive, cure-oriented treatments are not included under hospice coverage, but will still be paid under your standard Medicare coverage.

Why Choose Hospice Coverage?

As you will see, when you elect hospice coverage a broader range of services for your terminal illness are paid for by Medicare than under standard Part A benefits. Table 4.12 lists hospice benefits.

TABLE 4.12

Hospice Services Covered by Medicare

- Nursing services (care does *not* have to be skilled).
- Doctors' services (related to the terminal illness).
- Drugs (when used mainly for pain relief and symptom management).
- Medical appliances and supplies needed to promote self-help or comfort when specified in the care plan.
- Therapies (physical, occupational, and speech pathology) when needed to help maintain basic functions or daily living activities.
- Home health aide and homemaker services to provide personal care (*e.g.*, bathing, grooming) and other services needed to keep a patient's environment safe and clean (*e.g.*, light cleaning, linen changing, laundering).
- Around the clock care by nurses or aides during a medical crisis when needed to keep the patient at home.
- Respite care and short-term inpatient care. To provide time off for a caregiver, the patient can be admitted for up to five consecutive days (day of discharge does not count as a day) to a participating hospital, hospice, inpatient unit, or SNF that meets Medicare's hospice requirements.
- Counseling for the patient, his or her family or other caregivers for a variety of purposes, including psychological counseling (to help with the emotional and physical issues related to terminal illness) and nutritional counseling (to provide dietary guidance and training). Although bereavement counseling after a patient's death is not covered by Medicare, many hospices do offer this help.

Source: The Medicare Handbook, page 17.

❖ GEM: Get More Than One Respite Stay

Table 4.12 shows that Medicare will pay up to five days in a hospital, hospice, or nursing home in order to give a caregiver a break. Five days isn't much time, but there's a loophole. Although the Medicare law states that you can only receive Medicare respite benefits for up to five days, the law does not specifically limit how many five-day respite visits you can have. The question of whether you get one or 10 respite breaks is left to the Medicare Intermediary. Check this out, and challenge anyone who tells you that you don't "deserve a break today."

❖   ❖   ❖

What Will Medicare Pay for?

You are entitled to receive hospice benefits for 210 days (two 90-day periods followed by a 30-day period), but you can be "recertified" for an unlimited extension. In other words, you should be able to continue hospice coverage as long as necessary. You don't need three days of hospitalization, and you don't have to meet a 60-day waiting period in order to be eligible.

Unlike the standard Medicare program, you won't need to pay any deductibles before hospice coverage begins. You will only have to pay:

- Drugs—5 percent of the cost of each outpatient drug or $5 (whichever is less).
- Inpatient respite care—5 percent of the Medicare allowed rate (about $4.53 a day in 1992).

How Do You Enroll?

To begin receiving hospice care, you (or a representative) must file an election form. Each hospice has its own form, so you will need to obtain and return it to the hospice you have chosen.

You can decide what date you want your coverage to start on (the first day you enter or any date after), but once you turn the meter on, it will run continuously from one benefit period to the next (and you won't get Medicare coverage for any services unrelated to your terminal illness) unless you say stop.

How Do You Revoke Coverage?

You can change your mind at any time, stop hospice benefits, and return to regular Medicare Part A coverage. Again, you will need to file a form (ask the hospice) that states the date you want your coverage to end. You can reenroll at a later time.

EXAMPLE 43

Mr. Thompson had received hospice care for 60 days when he was hospitalized for treatment of a condition unrelated to his terminal illness. Because of the level of care needed, his family decided to return to his standard Part A coverage. Upon discharge from the hospital, he resumed hospice care.

MEDICARE MEDICAL INSURANCE (PART B)

Just in case Medicare Part A didn't totally confuse you, Uncle Sam created Medicare Part B to have a second chance at completing the job.

Medicare Part B is a voluntary supplemental medical insurance program. Unlike Part A, which you get for free at age 65 when you start receiving Social Security benefits, you must pay for Part B coverage. If you have trouble remembering which is which, think "B is for BUCKS"!

The basic design of Medicare Part B is like any private health insurance policy. You, the beneficiary, must share the costs for the services you receive by paying *premiums, deductibles,* and *co-insurance.* The difference is that your partner is the Government. And with Uncle Sam, rest assured there is no free lunch. Medicare will buy you the basic no-frills sandwich (hold the lettuce and mayonnaise), and any extras will come out of your own pocket.

In a nutshell, Part B covers the "leftovers" from Part A. The three main categories of Part B coverage are:

- Doctors' care
- Outpatient hospital care
- Other medically necessary services and supplies

Table 4.13 lists the common Part B covered services. To simplify the chart's use, we have divided it into three coverage categories: persons, places, or things.

Eligibility

The eligibility requirements are very basic. You can buy Part B coverage if you are a 65-year-old American citizen. You do *not* have to be healthy to be accepted. Uncle Sam is an "equal opportunity insurer."

❖ GEM: Get Part B Even Without Part A

You can and should enroll in Part B even if you are not eligible to receive Social Security or Part A benefits. Although there are many gaps in the coverage, for the price you pay Part B is still a wise investment. (Of course, you won't need Part B if you are already covered under other insurance—for example, through your employer.)

❖ GEM: Get Part B to Get Medigap Coverage

Medigap or Medifil policies, as the names imply, are private insurance policies created to fill the many gaps in your Medicare coverage. If you haven't signed up for Medicare Parts A and B, you aren't eligible to purchase a Medicare supplement policy because you have a giant hole in your basic health insurance that can't be filled by a Medigap policy.

❖　❖　❖

Enrollment

Enrollment in Part B is similar to enrollment in Part A. If you will be receiving Social Security or Railroad benefits starting at age 65, you will automatically be

TABLE 4.13

Medicare Part B Covered Services*

Person Providing Service	Place of Service	Thing (Service or Supply)
Certified registered nurse anesthetist	Ambulatory surgical center	Ambulance (for medical emergencies)
Clinical psychologist (at mental health center or rural health clinic)	Comprehensive outpatient rehabilitation facility (CORF)	Ambulatory surgical center services
Medical social service workers (when prescribed in physician's plan for care)	Outpatient Hospital (for: care related to your doctor's treatment, diagnostic tests, partial hospitalization psychiatric programs)	Antigens and blood clotting factors
		Artificial limbs and eyes
Occupational and physical therapists (in independent practice reimbursement limited to $750)	Outpatient facilities providing physical or occupational therapies and speech pathology (by contract with a hospital)	Braces for back, limb, or neck
		Clinical diagnostic laboratory tests (no deductible or co-insurance)
Physicians	Rural health clinic	CORF services
Physician assistants		Diagnostic X-ray tests and other diagnostic tests
Psychologists		Drugs for immunosuppressive therapy
Speech therapists and speech pathologists (when providing outpatient care under contract with a hospital)		Durable medical equipment
		Hepatitis B vaccine
		Mammography screening
		Pneumococcal vaccine (no deductible or co-insurance)
		Prosthetic devices
		Radiation therapy
		Rural health clinic services
		Surgical dressings, splints, casts

*Unless otherwise noted, you must still meet your $100 deductible and 20 percent co-insurance for these services.

enrolled in Medicare Parts A and B. Your Medicare card will come and will show that you have Part A benefits and you will be billed for Part B premiums. Your coverage will begin on the first day of your birthday month (*e.g.,* if your birthday is February 27, coverage will begin February 1). If for some reason you don't want Part B benefits, follow the instructions that come with the card.

If you take early retirement Social Security or Railroad benefits, you won't be entitled to Medicare until age 65. But again you don't have to worry about applying; you should be enrolled automatically in both Parts A and B at age 65.

If you start receiving Social Security or Railroad benefits after age 65, and you elect to delay Medicare until that same time, your Social Security or Railroad benefits application will automatically trigger your application for Medicare Parts A and B at that later date.

If you delay Social Security or Railroad Retirement, but want to start taking Medicare at age 65, you *must apply* for both Medicare Parts A and B. And whenever you apply on your own, *you must act early;* delay will increase your premiums and leave you without coverage.

EXAMPLE 44

You are turning 65 and don't plan to retire until 70, but you want to begin Medicare Parts A and B as soon as possible. Don't assume that you automatically get Medicare at 65; that would be a costly mistake. When you delay Social Security past age 65, you must apply for Medicare if you want coverage to start at 65.

You can enroll for Medicare as early as three months before your birthday month (*e.g.,* if you were born on July 20, April 1 will be the first day you will be eligible to apply). Don't include your birthday month when counting back three months. Refer to Table 4.4 to see the earliest date you can apply.

❖ GEM: Enroll at the Earliest Possible Time So That You Don't Lose Coverage

If you apply for Medicare three months before your birthday month, your benefits will start promptly on the first day of your birthday month. In fact, if you apply one or two months before your birthday month—or even in your birthday month—Medicare benefits *should* start in your birthday month. But that's not guaranteed; processing delays might cause your benefits to start one to three months late. See Example 45.

EXAMPLE 45

Your birthday is June 15, so you could apply for Medicare as early as March 1. When you apply then, Medicare (Parts A and B) can start promptly on June 1. But "if you snooze, you may lose."

Let's say, you wait until May 15 to apply. Owing to processing delays, your Medicare Part B coverage may not go into effect until July 1. Oh well, can a few weeks really matter? You bet! On June 10 you become very ill and incur medical bills of thousands of dollars. Your delay will cost you a bundle!

◆ ◆ ◆

If you wait until your birthday month or after to apply, you will *definitely* lose coverage. Your Part B insurance will *not* start at the earliest date you became eligible. Table 4.14 shows the delays based on the date you apply, and Example 46 shows how to use the table.

TABLE 4.14

Starting Dates for Medicare Part B Coverage

If You Apply	Medicare Part B Coverage Will Begin*
3 months before your Month of Birth (MOB)	1st day of MOB
MOB	1 month after MOB
1 month after MOB	3 months after MOB
2 months after MOB	5 months after MOB
3 months after MOB	6 months after MOB
4 or more months after MOB	Much later

*Part A coverage works on a different, "no penalty," time schedule and coverage will not be delayed.

EXAMPLE 46

Your birthday is April 15, so your MOB is April.

If You Apply in:	Coverage Will Begin:
January, February, or March	April 1 (unless delayed by Medicare bureaucracy)
April	May 1
May	July 1

If You Apply in:	Coverage Will Begin:
June	September 1
July	October 1
After July	Much later

If you apply late, you are asking for disaster.

EXAMPLE 47

Your 65th birthday is April 29, but you don't apply for Medicare Part B until May 15. Why sweat over a few weeks? Unfortunately, you become ill on April 20. Your medical bills, totaling hundreds of dollars, are *not* covered. Start sweating—because your Medicare Part B coverage doesn't start until May 1.

The period starting three months before your birthday month, and ending three months after your birthday month, is called your "initial enrollment period"; that's the best time to apply. By missing this initial enrollment period, you will not be allowed to enroll in Part B until the next "general enrollment period," which runs from January 1 through March 31 each year. General enrollment is for people who either never applied or for those who dropped out and want to reenroll. (You can reenroll an unlimited number of times.)

When you apply in a general enrollment period, your Part B coverage will not begin immediately; you must wait until the following July 1. As you can see, by delaying you are risking financial disaster.

EXAMPLE 48

Your 65th birthday is April 29, but you don't apply for Social Security, and you forget to apply separately for Medicare until September. Since you missed your initial enrollment period, you can't enroll in Part B until the following January, when the next general enrollment period begins. You'll need to make a second visit or call to Social Security then. And your Part B coverage won't start until the following July. Better stay healthy!

We previously told you that if you wait until after age 65 to retire, your Social Security application at that time will automatically sign you up for both Medicare

Parts A and B. Your Part A coverage begins promptly (as soon as your papers are processed). But because you missed your initial enrollment period (3 months before and after your 65th birthday month), your Part B enrollment will be considered to occur on the following January 1, during the next general enrollment period. And that will delay your coverage.

EXAMPLE 49

Alice Green became entitled to Social Security when she turned 65 in April. But because she was still working in a small family business and had medical insurance through her job, she didn't apply for Social Security until the following September, when she left her job.

Ms. Green's Social Security application enrolled her in Medicare Parts A and B. But because she missed her 7-month initial enrollment period (which ended on July 31, three months after her birthday month), her application now falls under the general enrollment rules, and her Part B coverage won't begin until the following July 1.

She'd better not need expensive medical treatment before July. If she does, she may kiss her retirement nest egg goodbye.

❖ GEM: Make Medicare Work for You: Apply for Medicare at 65, Even When You Don't Retire

You can avoid disasters due to Medicare coverage gaps by applying for Medicare at the time or before you reach 65, even if you plan to keep working and you've got medical insurance at work. Otherwise, you could wind up without Medicare Part B for months after you retire.

❖ GEM: Avoid Late Enrollment Disasters With Special Enrollment Protection

Take a look back at Example 49. If Alice Green had worked for an employer with at least 25 employees, and she had been covered by the company's group plan, she should get "special enrollment protection" to avoid late filing disasters. This special protection allows a retiree to pick up Medicare Part B coverage immediately after leaving a job. Check with the company benefits supervisor about how and when to file for this special benefit.

❖ GEM: Enroll at the Earliest Possible Time to Save on Premium Costs

Loss of coverage isn't the only price you'll pay for late enrollment in Medicare Part B. In addition, after age 65, for each full year (from your birthday month) you could have enrolled but didn't, your monthly premium will be increased by 10 percent. For example, if you turned 65 in April 1991 but waited until June 1992 to enroll, your premium will be $34.98. Medicare math calculates as follows: $31.80 (1992 premium) + $3.18 (10% penalty for one-year delay) = $34.98. To put it simply, time is money—don't wait!

✦ ✦ ✦

Application Process

Three months before your 65th birthday, visit or call any Social Security office. (Look in the blue pages of your phone book. You will find the number listed under the U.S. Government heading.) If you are phoning, state that you want to apply for Medicare Part B. You might be able to complete most of the process over the phone. Whichever way you choose to apply, be prepared to provide the following information:

1. *What is your age?* Now is definitely *not* the time for coyness! You will need to submit proof; find a birth certificate or hospital birth record. Other documents are also okay, but ask.
2. *What is your Social Security number?* Don't panic if you've lost your card or can't remember the number. A replacement can be obtained from Social Security, and there are also ways to track down a number (*e.g.,* old income tax or payroll forms).
3. *What was your income for the past year?* Dig out your W–2 form or copy of income tax return.
4. *What other benefits are you entitled to?* (*e.g.,* Military, Railroad Retirement, Federal Civil Service). This information is used in order to coordinate coverage.

The Application for Hospital Insurance is Form SSA-18F5, which you can get from your local Social Security office. Look it over and if you have any questions, call your community's Office on Aging or a local senior citizen center. It might be faster than trying to reach someone at Social Security. (To locate, look in the blue pages of your phone book under City or County Government.)

End of Coverage

Your Part B coverage will continue uninterrupted unless one of the following happens:

- You file a form with Medicare stating you no longer want to participate. This can be done at any time. Your coverage will be cancelled on the last day of the month *after* the month you filed. This means if you notified Medicare in May, the last day of your coverage will be June 30.
- You don't pay your premium. If your payment isn't received on time, you are out of luck and insurance. (This is a good reason to have premium payments deducted from your SSA check.)
- You die. (If you really want to terminate coverage, the first option is a less drastic choice!)

❖ GEM: Try Not to Miss a Premium

Failing to pay premiums within the grace period can be *very* costly. After your Medicare Part B is cancelled, you can reenroll. But you'll have to wait until a new general enrollment period. Your coverage won't begin again until July 1. And you'll have to pay a higher premium. If there's any way to get the funds to pay the premium (*e.g.,* borrowing from a child, taking a loan against a retirement fund), do it. Try not to let your insurance lapse.

✦ ✦ ✦

What You Pay When You Have Part B Coverage
Part B "ain't" free. Your basic Part B costs will always be:

- Monthly premium. In 1992, the monthly charge was $31.80.
- Annual deductible. At the start of each year, you must pay the first $100 in approved charges before Medicare Part B coverage will begin.
- Co-insurance. Medicare usually requires that you pay 20 percent of the approved cost of any covered service.
- If the doctor does not accept assignment, you can be required to pay the difference between your doctor's actual charge and Medicare's approved charge, up to 20 percent of the Medicare-approved amount.

❖ GEM: Deduct the Costs

Just like other purchased medical insurance, costs of Part B are tax deductible.

✦ ✦ ✦

Under Part B, it's not enough to know the price of the supply or service. To determine your expenses, you must also know whether or not the provider accepts *assignment.* Not understanding the difference could cost you big bucks!

What Is Assignment?

When a doctor or supplier "takes assignment," it means he has agreed to accept Medicare's approved charge as full payment, even if his usual fee for that service or supply is higher. (See page 128 for a more detailed explanation.)

How Does Assignment Work?

Accepting assignment is *voluntary:*

- Some providers always accept assignment
- Some providers don't usually accept assignment but will make exceptions
- Some providers never accept assignment

Doctors and suppliers who always accept assignment are called *participating providers.* Participating providers have signed an agreement in advance with Medicare that requires them to accept assignment on *all* claims for Medicare-approved services. If a doctor says he's a participating provider, that's good financial news for you.

❖ GEM: Get "A Directory of Participating Doctors in Your Area"

This *free* annual directory lists all participating Medicare providers. For a copy call the Medicare carrier in your state. (To find the phone number of the carrier, see Appendix 17.)

❖   ❖   ❖

Some providers have not signed a contract with Medicare, but will accept assignment on a case-by-case basis. Since providers are *not* required by any law to work with Medicare, the decision is solely up to them. However, there is nothing illegal about trying to influence their choice. In this situation, your job is to take time out from Medicare Monopoly to play "Let's Make a Deal." If you like your doctor and have had a good working relationship, it is well worth your time to discuss assignment with him or her.

❖ GEM: Negotiate Before the Bills Pile Up

You will be in the best position to ask the doctor or supplier to accept assignment *before* you incur some big bills. Don't wait.

Successful negotiating requires:

- Knowing what you want.
- Stating these needs clearly.
- Leaving room for discussion to avoid creating a "win-lose" situation.

Ideally, your first choice is to have the physician agree to accept assignment for all Medicare-covered services provided. If the doctor turns down this opportunity, move on to your second choice: request that he accept assignment for specific treatments, especially high-cost procedures.

If this, too, is unacceptable, you must decide whether you want to continue as a patient or find a doctor who is a Medicare participating provider. Only you can decide what is best. Stay calm and shift to your third option: requesting his advice. Perhaps your doctor can recommend someone who does accept assignment. Bring along a copy of "A Directory of Participating Doctors in Your Area" and show it to your physician. He or she might recognize some peers—and maybe even feel guilty! At the very least, once you have found a new physician, it would be nice to have your doctor's support in paving the way for a smooth transition (*e.g.,* sending your records promptly, discussing your case history with the new provider) before an emergency arises. Ask.

There are very good reasons why *you* want the doctor to accept assignment, but what's in it for him? Would you call being given the opportunity to deal with Medicare an "offer too good to refuse?" So, what enticements can you offer a doctor to get him or her to accept less money? The advantage of direct and electronic payment from Medicare might be appealing since it reduces paperwork and billing costs. But there are no pat answers. The following five strategies should help.

Game Strategies for Negotiating with Your Doctor
1. *Be positive.* Now is the perfect time to become a "stroke patient"—let your doctor know how much you have appreciated his or her care and service. Doctors enjoy having their egos stroked as much as the next guy.
2. *Offer to be a responsible patient.* Acknowledge that you understand the assignment process. Let the doctor know he can count on you to keep your part of the bargain. In exchange for his agreement, you promise to:

- Pay your Part B 20 percent co-insurance *promptly* for all services.
- Show flexibility. Perhaps the doctor has suggestions to cut costs, or ways you can work more efficiently together.

3. *Choose the right time to talk.* Timing can be everything. Catching your doctor at the end of a long day probably reduces the odds of having a receptive audience.

If your physician has an office manager, try soliciting his or her support. Explain the purpose of your meeting and ask what time would be most convenient and what suggestions the person might have—perhaps she or he even knows what reasoning would be most persuasive. Try to arrange a personal meeting rather than a phone call.

4. *Be a good listener.* The bottom line is, the final decision rests with the doctor. You need to use common sense. If it is clear that your doctor is unmoved and unwilling to cooperate, there's no point in creating ill will by pushing the issue. Thank him, ask for his suggestions, and leave. If, however, he seems to be against the idea but "swayable," hang in there. Many doctors have a knee-jerk negative reaction; they automatically assume Medicare reimbursement is far too low. Perhaps he may conclude that accepting assignment for some services will not lead to financial ruin. (After all, the doctors who do accept assignment are maintaining practices.) Use the fine art of gentle persuasion to help him feel good about "doing the right thing" by accepting assignment.

5. *Take the informed patient's pledge.* To help you scout out the important answers you need from your doctor, we offer an "informed patient's pledge for action." By following the guidelines listed below, you will improve the odds for success (at the very least, you'll earn a merit badge from us!).

I promise to:

- Be prepared.
- Be polite.
- Be brief.
- Believe in the rightness of my request.

This means that you must do your homework. If you are discussing a specific treatment, find out beforehand what Medicare's "approved charge" is and what your doctor's fee will be. Perhaps the doctor is just not aware of the difference it can mean to you in out-of-pocket expenses.

You have the right to strive for the best quality care at the best price. Seeking a health care partnership with your doctor is not unreasonable. You don't need to apologize for being a good consumer.

If you are a female with a male physician, this last point is especially important to keep in mind. Many women feel uncomfortable being assertive. If you are widowed, and your late husband used to take care of all the "big" decisions, it can be especially difficult, because speaking up for yourself is a new role. But if you expect your doctor to step in and play the part of "Doctor Knows Best," you gain a false sense of security. In exchange for being "taken care of," you will be treated like a "good little girl" who should be seen and not heard. You lose control over your health care because you have a parent-child relationship and *not* a partnership.

If the idea of speaking up makes you nervous, it will help if you practice your presentation before you visit the doctor. Ask a friend to role-play with you: she gets to "play doctor" and raise possible responses to your request. When you are comfortable with the "script" before "opening night," it is easier to focus on the issues rather than your anxiety. It's perfectly okay to admit to your doctor that this is new for you, but extremely important. You are likely to gain a physician's respect, not disdain. The more often you take "the lead," the easier this type of discussion will become.

❖ GEM: There's a Good Chance Your Doctor Is Overcharging You!

Lots has been said about excessive health-care costs and the need for cost containment. Yet there's already a law on the books limiting health care costs, and the Government has kept it a secret.

Even if your doctor does *not* accept assignment, he or she cannot bill you (assuming you are a Medicare beneficiary) more than 20 percent over the approved Medicare fee. In 1993, the limit drops to 15 percent, reducing doctors' charges even more.

The Explanation of Medicare Benefits (EOMB) you receive shows the Medicare-approved amount for the service. Then add 20 percent (15% in 1993) to figure the maximum allowable charge.

EXAMPLE 50

The doctor bills you $200, but the EOMB shows the approved fee is only $100. The doctor legally can only charge $120—20 percent above the Medicare approved fee. Medicare will pay $80 (80% of its approved fee), and you pay $40 ($120 minus $80). If you have Medigap or Medi-fil insurance, the insurance should pay $20 (20% of the approved amount), leaving you a bill of only $20 to pay.

Many doctors are charging too much, often because they don't understand the law. To make matters worse, the Government has not been enforcing the law vigorously or educating the public. In many cases, in fact, personnel in the federal Health Care Financing Administration (HCFA), which oversees the Medicare program, have mistakenly told Medicare recipients to pay their entire bills—even when the fees charged exceed legal limits!

But this is beginning to change. Thanks to publicity by various public interest groups, including the American Association of Retired Persons (AARP), HCFA is starting to clamp down. If you are overcharged, contact the carrier. If you don't get your bill reduced, try the state attorney general next.

❖ GEM: Collect for Past Overcharges

Medicare recipients have been charged millions of dollars over the legal limits we've just described. Are you entitled to a refund if you've overpaid your doctor?

This question has not yet been answered. As we read the law, Medicare beneficiaries should have a right to reimbursement. But so far the Government has not taken any steps to make sure prior overcharges are repaid to patients.

Until the Government does something, you will only be able to collect through private action. Contact an attorney experienced in Medicare claims for assistance.

◆   ◆   ◆

Now it's time to look at services covered under Medicare Part B. These services—offered at a reasonable premium (at least as far as insurance goes)—provide a Golden Opportunity to secure basic health care for older Americans.

MEDICARE PART B: COVERED DOCTORS' SERVICES

What Services Does Part B Cover?

The Medicare Handbook provides a summary of the major covered doctors' services under Part B. For convenience, we have reproduced the list in Table 4.15. However, don't assume that just because the service you receive is listed in the table it is automatically covered. Remember, before Medicare will pay a penny, Uncle Sam will also look to see if, given the circumstances of *your* case, the service was all of the following:

- A covered service (it's on Medicare list as an acceptable treatment for your condition)
- Medically reasonable and necessary for you
- Provided by a medical professional who was the "right man for the job" (someone qualified to perform that treatment)

Whenever a provider files a claim for Part B insurance, Medicare will send you a notice called the Explanation of Medicare Benefits (EOMB). The EOMB will

TABLE 4.15

Services Covered by Medicare Part B

- Medical and surgical services, including anesthesia
- Diagnostic tests and procedures that are part of your treatment
- Radiology and pathology services by doctors while you are a hospital inpatient or outpatient
- Treatment for mental illness (Medicare payments for outpatient treatment are limited)
- Other services which are ordinarily furnished in the doctor's office and included in his or her bill, such as:
  1. X-rays
  2. Services of your doctor's office nurse
  3. Drugs and biologicals that cannot be self-administered
  4. Transfusions of blood and blood components
  5. Medical supplies
  6. Physical and occupational therapy and speech pathology services

Source: The Medicare Handbook, page 20.

tell you a number of things, including whether the claim meets Medicare's rules for coverage and how much Uncle Sam plans to pay.

Table 4.16 lists services Medicare Part B will *not* cover.

TABLE 4.16

Services Not Covered by Medicare Part B

- Routine physical examinations and tests directly related to such examinations (except some pap smears)
- Most routine foot care
- Examinations for prescribing or fitting eyeglasses (except after cataract surgery) or hearing aids
- Immunizations (except pneumococcal vaccinations or immunizations required because of an injury or immediate risk of infection, and hepatitis B for certain persons at risk)
- Cosmetic surgery, unless it is needed because of accidental injury or to improve the function of a malformed part of the body

Source: The Medicare Handbook, page 20.

❖ GEM: Playing the Name Game, or an Illness by Any Other Name Could Cost You Money

Although Tables 4.15 and 4.16 seem fairly straightforward, nothing is easy in the game of Medicare Monopoly. The way a doctor describes your illness and treatment to Medicare can mean the difference between reimbursement or denial of your claim.

Why? Medicare reviews your claim based on a complex coding system. Every illness and treatment in the book has been assigned a corresponding code. The codes are made up of three- to five-digit number combinations. Your doctor must play the name game and select the code that most closely matches your condition and the service provided. If he makes a careless mistake or doesn't choose the most specific code available, *you* end up being penalized. Your claim might be denied because the illness doesn't match the treatment. At the very least, reimbursement can be less than you are entitled to because Medicare will pay less for a less serious procedure.

Talk to your doctor about the name game—don't be shy. Make sure he or she describes your care in the best way to maximize your coverage.

EXAMPLE 51

You have been experiencing stomach pains and your doctor determines that you have an ulcer. The general code for a gastric ulcer is 531; when writing up the diagnosis, your doctor must use those three numbers. But that's not enough. Is there a hemorrhage or perforation? The answer must be represented by a fourth digit. Was there an obstruction? "Inquiring minds want to know" and so does Medicare; a fifth digit will tell all.

If your doctor ignores these details, Medicare will ignore you, too. Your claim can be denied simply because an inaccurate code was used. But don't assume Medicare is going to inform you about the source of the trouble. Keep this in mind when you are denied payment for a service that should be covered. Check with your doctor's office to make sure an accurate diagnosis code was used. A claim can always be refiled, and a wrongful denial can be appealed.

❖ GEM: Diagnostic Procedures Must Be Provided Directly to You

To be reimbursed for diagnostic procedures, your doctor must provide the service directly to you, the patient. That means he or she must examine your warm body or be looking at a direct visualization of you (*e.g.*, X-rays, tissue samples, electrocardiogram). A doctor can't take credit for a service if anyone else does the work for him.

EXAMPLE 52

A hospital cardiologist interprets your X-ray, bills Medicare, and sends your doctor a report. Your doctor then reads the information, scans the X-ray, and bills you for his review. Sound familiar? Unfortunately, Medicare won't pay. Medicare thinks that analysis should be included as part of the doctor's service fee and will not allow a separate charge.

❖ GEM: Before Surgery, Get a Second Opinion

When your doctor is recommending surgery, Medicare will pay for a second look. And in certain nonemergency cases, Medicare *requires* a second opinion. If you don't obtain this and go ahead with the surgery, you can't cut a deal with Medicare; you pay. Check with your doctor or hospital to see if the procedure in question requires a second look.

Your doctor can give you the name of another physician who is "second opinionated." Or if you prefer, you can call your Medicare Part B carrier for names. Toll-free numbers are listed in Appendix 17. If you get a second opinion and the recommendations of the two doctors differ, and if Medicare thinks it's essential, the costs for a third look will be covered. Any services necessary to make an informed evaluation are included. You won't have to pay a deductible or co-insurance, either.

❖ GEM: Watch Out for Concurrent Care Coverage (Otherwise Known as Multiple Doctor Disorder)

A complex medical condition often requires the expertise of several different specialists. There is no limit to the number of doctors you can use. But Medicare will only pay if your doctors can document that the extra care given was necessary and not duplicative. Claims for the same services provided by different doctors will be denied.

❖ GEM: Who Cares Where You Get the Care?

Surprise! Medicare isn't worried. If the service meets the coverage requirements, it doesn't matter to Uncle Sam where the care is provided—the doctor's office, your home, a mountain top—any location in the nation is fine. (Under very specific circumstances, care in Canada and Mexico also are covered—see your *Medicare Handbook* for the rules on care in a foreign country.)

✦ ✦ ✦

What Doctors Does Part B Cover?

Not only must the type of service provided be acceptable to Medicare, but the type of doctor providing the service must also be okay. Doctors of medicine (M.D.) and doctors of osteopathy (D.O.) are acceptable; others may not be.

Dentists, optometrists, podiatrists, and chiropractors are sometimes acceptable; we'll talk about these below. Christian Science practitioners and naturopaths may provide services to you, but they don't pass for Medicare coverage.

❖ GEM: A Doctor Must Only Perform Authorized Service

Even if the doctor is acceptable and the service is acceptable, there must be a match. Medicare will only pay if the doctor is performing a service he or she is legally authorized to offer. If you let your chiropractor operate on your knee, your friends will question your sanity and Medicare will question the bill.

✦ ✦ ✦

Chiropractors' Services. Don't get "bent out of shape" when you read this. Medicare covers only *one* service provided by a licensed chiropractor: "manual manipulation of the spine to correct a proven subluxation" (misalignment or abnormal spacing of vertebrae). How can you prove you have this condition? An X-ray is required, but Medicare *won't* pay for that. Medicare will only pay if the X-ray is by a "real" doctor (doctor of medicine or osteopathy).

Podiatrists' Services. Treatment for injuries and diseases of your foot by a licensed podiatrist should be covered (*e.g.*, hammer toes, bunions, in-grown toenails). But here's a "rule of toe": Medicare will *not* pay for any care it classifies as routine. If your podiatrist bills you for basic hygienic services—trimming your toenails, corns—you will foot the bill.

❖ GEM: Get Coverage for Podiatric Service Related to Another Medical Condition

If you have a medical condition that affects your legs or feet (such as diabetes or circulatory disorders), the podiatric costs are considered necessary and *should* be covered. However, treatment for putting your foot in your mouth on a routine basis is not eligible!

Dentists' Services. Medicare offers you very little when it comes to dental coverage. Even if this strikes a raw nerve, Medicare will still *not* pay for: cleanings, fillings, removal or replacement of teeth, root canals, or any surgical procedures related to your teeth or gums.

Medicare should pay for:

- Dental services provided in cases where your medical problem is more extensive than the teeth or the structures supporting them (*e.g.,* you require surgery on your gums to remove a tumor).
- Hospital care if the severity of a dental procedure requires hospitalization. Your stay should be covered under Part A benefits even though the dental services are *not* eligible for reimbursement.

In summary, Medicare dental coverage is pretty toothless, and you will be too if you wait for Uncle Sam to pick up your dental bills.

Optometrists' Services. You and Medicare probably won't see eye to eye on coverage for eye care. Routine services such as eye exams, fittings for eyeglasses or contact lenses, and the eyewear itself are *not* covered. Medicare will only pay for:

- Prosthetic lenses that are needed to *replace* the natural lens of your eye.
- Eyeglasses required after cataract surgery.
- An optometrist to provide a service that is already covered by Medicare. The optometrist must also be licensed by the state to perform the service.

What Other Health Care Providers Are Covered?

Medicare should also lend a hand for certain services provided by other Medicare-approved practitioners, such as certified registered nurses, physician assistants, nurse practitioners, and clinical psychologists. Of course, there are specific requirements. The service generally must be:

- A Medicare-covered service.
- Supervised by a physician.
- Provided in a hospital, intermediate care facility, or SNF. (Nurse practitioner services are only covered when provided in an SNF.)
- An integral part of your prescribed plan for care.

Golden Rule: Generally, Medicare should contribute to the cost when the service would have been covered if a physician had provided the care.

Treatment and diagnostic services by Medicare-certified psychologists may be covered. You can receive psychological services as an outpatient at a hospital, rural health clinic, community mental health center, or HMO. However, Medicare does "shrink" from its responsibility when it comes to reimbursement. Only 50 percent (not the usual 80%) of approved charges are covered; you pay the rest. But talk can still be cheap (at least cheaper) because your Medicare-certified psychologist *must* accept assignment.

Services by Medicare-certified clinical social workers may also be covered, but the reimbursement is even less. Services provided to diagnose and treat psychiatric problems are covered when a doctor would have been covered for doing the same job. Medicare will pay a social worker up to 75 percent of the fee a qualified psychologist would have received, or the actual service charge (whichever is less). In all cases, accepting assignment is a must.

What Supplies and Drugs Are Covered?

Supplies, drugs, vaccinations, and biologicals (such as blood) may be covered by Medicare Part B. Table 4.17 shows when you can and can't cash in. As the table shows, Medicare will pay for an inoculation against a specific, immediate harm. It's nice to know that Uncle Sam will give you a shot in the arm when there is a clear-cut injury or health risk.

TABLE 4.17

Supplies, Drugs, Biologicals, and Vaccinations Covered/Not Covered by Medicare Part B

	Covered	Not Covered
Supplies	Any special materials a doctor must buy and use to diagnose and treat you (*e.g.,* surgical dressings, casts, oxygen, special creams). These items must appear on the physician's bill.	Common first aid supplies (Band-Aids, antiseptics, tape); supplies *you* buy and give to a doctor to administer.
Drugs and Biologicals	The drug must be: (1) an approved medication for your condition, (2) supplied and administered by the doctor or his nurse, (3) an extra expense for the doctor.	Prescription or nonprescription drugs you buy. Drugs that can be self-administered (*e.g.* insulin, pills), unless it's an emergency situation.
	Hemophilia clotting factors and related items for hemophilia patients.	Experimental drugs. Even if the drug has been approved for other uses, the medication must be on the books with the FDA as an approved treatment for *your* condition.

	Covered	Not Covered
	Antigens prepared and administered by a doctor to treat allergies.	
	Immunosuppressive drugs for recipients of Medicare-covered organ transplants for one year (beginning with the date of discharge).	
Vaccinations and Inoculations	Tetanus, rabies, and other shots when responding to a specific injury or immediate risk.	Shots given to prevent illness or disease if there is no specific risk to you. (This is the reason why flu shots are not paid for.)
	Pneumococcal shots: Medicare will pay the entire approved charge for the vaccine and administration. No deductibles or co-insurance payment is needed.	
	Hepatitis B vaccine, if there is a reasonable likelihood that you might contract the disease.	

Source: The Medicare Handbook, page 24.

EXAMPLE 53

You step on a rusty nail and get a tetanus shot or you are bitten by a mad dog and receive anti-rabies treatment. Since these treatments are a response to a particular injury or risk, Medicare should cover.

But what if you know you will end up in an elevator filled with sneezing, coughing passengers at the height of flu season? Shouldn't a flu shot count as an immediate risk? Tough luck! Medicare does not consider it a threat worth paying for, no matter how susceptible you are to the virus.

MEDICARE PART B: OUTPATIENT HOSPITAL SERVICES

Medicare Part B will help pay for outpatient care, at a Medicare-approved hospital, when ordered by your doctor. Charges for the use of the facility, nurses, and other aides, as well as any supplies necessary for treatment, should all be included. Tables 4.18 and 4.19 list the major outpatient hospital services covered and not covered by Medicare.

TABLE 4.18

Major Outpatient Hospital Services Covered by Medicare Part B

- Services in an emergency room or outpatient clinic, including ambulatory surgical procedures
- Laboratory tests billed by the hospital
- Mental health care in a partial hospitalization psychiatric program, if a physician certifies that inpatient treatment would be required without it
- X-rays and other radiology services billed by the hospital
- Medical supplies, such as splints and casts
- Drugs and biologicals that cannot be self-administered
- Blood transfusions furnished to you as an outpatient

Source: The Medicare Handbook, page 21.

TABLE 4.19

Sample of Outpatient Hospital Services
Not Covered by Medicare Part B

- Routine physical examinations and tests directly related to such examinations (except some pap smears)
- Eye or ear examinations to prescribe or fit eyeglasses or hearing aids
- Immunizations (except pneumococcal and Hepatitis B vaccinations, or immunizations required because of an injury or immediate risk of infection)
- Most routine foot care

Source: The Medicare Handbook, page 21.

❖ GEM: Bring Your Most Recent Explanation of Benefits

The outpatient facility will want to know if you have already met your $100 annual deductible before services are provided. They'll want this information because if you haven't met it yet, and the fee for treatment is less than $100, chances are you will be asked to pay the entire bill. So avoid delays and problems by bringing along your most recent Explanation of Medicare Benefits (EOMB) notice, which shows your deductible balance.

EXAMPLE 54

You have already paid $25 toward your Medicare deductible. This means you must pay for $75 in approved services before Medicare will even begin sharing your bills. If the charge for your outpatient care is going to be $100, you must pay $75 out of your own pocket ($75 + $25 = $100) to meet your deductible. Now that leaves $25 of service fees that you and Uncle Sam must divide: Medicare's share will be $20 (80% of $25) and you must pay your $5 co-insurance (20% of $25 = $5).

This brings your total costs for the outpatient service to $80. By bringing along your EOMB (which shows how much you have left on your deductible), you will reduce your out-of-pocket expenses by $20 ($100 – $80) because the hospital can't make you pay the full amount.

If you don't have the EOMB and the hospital requests payment in full to cover the deductible you really don't owe, the hospital should eventually refund the amount you overpaid. But who needs the added nuisance of keeping track of the I.O.U.? Wouldn't you rather have that money sitting in your bank account instead of the hospital's?

MEDICARE PART B: OTHER COVERED SERVICES AND SUPPLIES

This category of Medicare Part B coverage is a real potpourri; there are quite an assortment of services and supplies eligible for reimbursement. Read on and you are bound to uncover a gem or two.

Comprehensive Outpatient Rehabilitation Facility Services (CORF)

Medicare will help pay for services provided at a CORF when your doctor has certified that you need this type of care. You will still need to pay the $100 annual deductible and 20 percent of all Medicare-approved charges. Covered services include doctors; physical, speech, occupational, and respiratory therapies; and counseling. Mental health care provided by doctors, physicians' assistants, or psychologists at a CORF are also covered, but Medicare will only pay 50 percent of the approved charges (not the usual 80%).

Ambulatory Surgical Center (ASC) Services

These centers can be independent facilities or affiliated with a hospital. Their sole purpose is to perform outpatient surgical procedures. Before going under the knife, you will want to make sure: (1) the facility is participating in the Medicare program; and (2) the surgery you are having is on Medicare's list of approved outpatient procedures. If the answer to both of these questions is yes, Medicare's answer to your bill should be "yes," too.

Table 4.20 lists ASC services that should be covered by Medicare Part B.

TABLE 4.20

Ambulatory Surgical Center Services

Covered

- Physicians, nurses, and other technical personnel services
- Use of the facilities (*e.g.,* operating and recovery room)
- Drugs, surgical dressings, splints, or other supplies necessary for the surgical procedure and aftercare

Not Covered

- Diagnostic tests; with the exception of simple urinalysis and blood work (which are usually included in the base price of your surgery), Medicare will not pay for any testing done at an ASC.
- Items such as ace bandages, support hose, and surgical leggings are not classified as surgical dressings. They are considered secondary coverings and Medicare does not pay for this layer of care.

Note: The services must be provided at a Medicare-participating center in order to be eligible for coverage.

Rural Health Clinic Services

These clinics are located in areas defined by the Census Bureau as rural and by the Secretary of Health and Human Services as being medically underserved. If you receive care from a rural health clinic, Medicare should help pay for:

- Physician's services
- Nurse practitioners, physician assistants, clinical psychologists, and clinical social workers
- Services and supplies "incident to" the care provided by your doctor or any of the professionals listed above
- Visiting nurses when care by a home-health-care agency is not available

❖ GEM: Get Coverage for Rural Services

Essentially, any services Medicare would cover in a doctor's office or hospital should be covered when furnished at a rural health clinic. Clinics submit claims directly to Medicare. You pay any unmet annual deductible and the 20 percent co-insurance on Medicare's approved charges.

✦ ✦ ✦

Independent Clinical Laboratory Services

First, the good news: Medicare will pay the entire approved fee for diagnostic tests. Now, the better news: the lab must accept assignment and can't bill you; the same goes for your doctor if he's the one furnishing the test. Unfortunately, good news is always tempered by bad news when it comes to Medicare. The bad news is that the laboratory you use must be Medicare approved. Note that some laboratories are Medicare approved only for certain kinds of tests.

❖ GEM: Check Out an Independent Lab for Medicare Coverage

You or your doctor must find out if the lab is covered for the test(s) your doctor is ordering. If you make the mistake of assuming that a Medicare-approved lab will cover *all* your lab tests, you could end up being stuck with more than a needle.

✦ ✦ ✦

Warning: Government studies show that doctors who own their own labs tend to recommend more lab services than necessary. Before going for lab services, ask the doctor who advised you to go whether he or she has a financial interest in the lab.

Portable Diagnostic X-Ray Services

When your doctor orders X-rays "to go," they should be covered when provided by a Medicare-approved supplier.

Other Diagnostic Tests and X-Rays

When your doctor orders medically necessary diagnostic tests to evaluate your condition, Medicare should help pay.

Radiation Therapy

Medicare should cover these costs when treatment is performed under your doctor's supervision.

Kidney Dialysis and Transplants

Medicare has extensive rules and regulations concerning coverage. Refer to the *Medicare Coverage of Kidney Dialysis and Kidney Transplant Services Guide,* available from Social Security.

Ambulance Transportation

What are Medicare's "rules of the road" for ambulance reimbursement? The path to coverage is bumpy; here's a road map to follow:

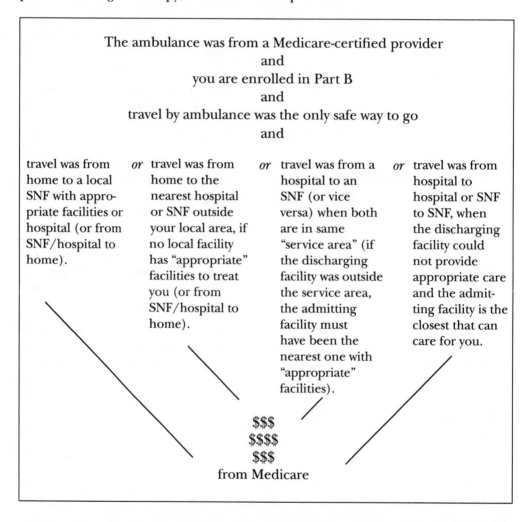

The ambulance was from a Medicare-certified provider
and
you are enrolled in Part B
and
travel by ambulance was the only safe way to go
and

travel was from home to a local SNF with appropriate facilities or hospital (or from SNF/hospital to home). *or* travel was from home to the nearest hospital or SNF outside your local area, if no local facility has "appropriate" facilities to treat you (or from SNF/hospital to home). *or* travel was from a hospital to an SNF (or vice versa) when both are in same "service area" (if the discharging facility was outside the service area, the admitting facility must have been the nearest one with "appropriate" facilities). *or* travel was from hospital to hospital or SNF to SNF, when the discharging facility could not provide appropriate care and the admitting facility is the closest that can care for you.

$$$
$$$$
$$$
from Medicare

You will probably have to pay for a trip to the doctor's office by ambulance. The *only* exception to this rule is if you can show that the service provided by the doctor was medically necessary and unavailable at the hospital or SNF where you were receiving inpatient care.

If the ambulance service was not a Medicare-certified provider, you are out of luck. There are no exceptions to this rule for coverage. If the company you used doesn't fit the bill, *you* will pay the bill.

❖ GEM: Find a Certified Ambulance Company Before You Need It

Now is the time to do your research—*before* you have an emergency. Check the yellow pages under the heading Ambulance Service—Emergency and Medical; find two or three companies serving your area with ads that include the words "Medicare Approved." Call and confirm that they are, and that they service the medical facilities in your area. Write the phone numbers down and post with your other emergency information so that you'll have it when needed.

◆   ◆   ◆

Durable Medical Equipment (DME)

Medicare should help pay for durable (nondisposable) medical equipment like walkers and wheelchairs, but you'd better first read Medicare's fine print because there's a lot of it! Before Medicare will contribute to the costs, according to the Center for Medicare Advocacy, you must show that the equipment:

- Is prescribed by your doctor because it is a "necessary and reasonable" part of your home treatment program
- Can be used over and over
- Is no fun or comfort for healthy people
- Is appropriate for home use
- Is from a Medicare-certified provider

The DME must have a medical purpose. Medicare will not pay for any equipment designed particularly to make a healthy person's life more pleasant, no matter how helpful it might be to you or your caregiver. This means that items such as room heaters, humidifiers, air conditioners, elevators, and seat boosters generally are no-go.

❖ GEM: Bend the "No Fun Allowed" Rule

You may be able to get Medicare to show some flexibility and grant coverage for DME that is not primarily medical. But your doctor had better be able to clearly show that, in your case, the equipment is therapeutic and not purely for comfort.

EXAMPLE 55

A water mattress can be used by anyone to enhance a night's sleep, but if your doctor prescribes one to help alleviate your severe case of bedsores, Medicare should consider its therapeutic value. The same goes for heat lamps, if (and only if) your need for heat therapy can clearly be proved as a necessary part of your home-treatment plan.

On the other hand, Medicare is completely cool to the idea of air conditioning as humidity and breathing therapy. No matter how helpful a lower room temperature would be for your overall health status, Medicare won't pay because an air conditioner's main use is nonmedical.

✦ ✦ ✦

For the DME to be covered, those good old standards of "necessary and reasonable" must be satisfied, too. Medicare bureaucrats will ask questions like:

- Is the item really necessary for treatment or therapy to improve your functioning?
- Will the equipment make a significant difference in your health status?
- Are the therapeutic benefits worth the price, or is this the least expensive way to meet your needs? (Why buy a Cadillac when a Chevy will get you there?) Uncle Sam will do a cost-benefit analysis.

EXAMPLE 56

If you install a whirlpool to help your arthritis, enjoy it but don't count on Medicare to help. The expense will probably be called unreasonable because a warm bath would work, too.

❖ GEM: Chair Lifts—Raise Expectations but Buyer Beware!

Before renting or purchasing a chair lift, know the rules or you could lose your pants on the deal! In spite of what the ads say, Medicare won't automatically pay.

The fact that one of these chairs would make your life more convenient isn't enough incentive for Medicare to foot the bill. The same standards for DME coverage apply—the seat lift must be prescribed by your doctor as a reasonable and necessary part of your treatment. Its use must either improve or stabilize your condition so that you can avoid confinement to a bed or chair.

Also, in Uncle Sam's eyes not all chairs are created equal. Don't catapult yourself into debt by purchasing the wrong type of seat. Medicare will pay for a chair that enables you to safely stand or sit without help. Medicare will *never* pay for a chair lift that uses a spring release mechanism because the catapult-like motion can be dangerous. In any event, Medicare pays only for the lift mechanism, not the chair itself.

✦ ✦ ✦

Once you and Medicare agree that the DME meets all the requirements for coverage, the next question is: "To buy or not to buy." The folks at Medicare, not you, decide whether you rent or purchase the DME.

Medicare has divided all DME into six categories, which helps Medicare determine whether to pay for rental or purchase. The categories are described in Table 4.21. The amount of time you will need the DME should be a key factor in Medicare's decision. When the doctor predicts that your needs will be short term, Uncle Sam is more likely to opt for rental.

In addition, Medicare has set a reimbursement price ceiling on fees for each category. When items are approved for rental, Uncle Sam will want to know the DME's purchase price. He then checks his books to see if that exceeds his price ceiling for that category. The cheaper of the two prices (the supplier's or Medi-

TABLE 4.21

Medicare Payment Options for DME

Category of DME	Form of Payment
Inexpensive or routinely purchased rental equipment—items less than $150 (noncustomized power-driven wheelchairs are now included here)	Lump-sum purchase or monthly
Items requiring frequent servicing (any item that needs frequent care to assure safe operation, such as aspirators)	Monthly rental
Customized items (DME that must be adapted to meet your specific health needs)	Lump-sum purchase
Prosthetic and orthotic devices (items needed to substitute for a body part or internal body organ)	Lump-sum purchase
Capped rental items ("capped" means Medicare has put a limit on the length of time and amount of money to be paid: 15 months at 10 percent of the base price)	Monthly rental (after 15 months, only maintenance and servicing fees reimbursable)
Oxygen and oxygen equipment	Monthly rental (rate of reimbursement based on local rates)

care's) will become the base price; Medicare will then pay 10 percent of this base price directly to the supplier each month for rental costs.

If Medicare opts to pay a lump-sum payment for purchase, Medicare will calculate what it believes should be the "average reasonable charge" for the item in your neighborhood. It's too bad if the actual price of the item is more; you will not get a higher level of reimbursement.

❖ GEM: Don't Buy Until Uncle Sam Says Yes

If you have jumped the gun and purchased an item, and then Uncle Sam decides it should be rented, too bad for you. Medicare will only contribute the approved monthly rental fee, and only for as long as the DME is needed or until Medicare's approved purchase price is reached (whichever comes first). You will have to pay any additional money owed. Another downside to buying is that if you then die, Medicare will stop payments, no matter how much you still owe on the purchase. (Try to stick around just to break even!)

Before shelling out your money, call your Part B Medicare Carrier (Appendix 17) to find out how Uncle Sam wants to pay.

◆ ◆ ◆

If Medicare decides that the DME should be purchased and you disagree, you can still opt to rent the item and Medicare will contribute to the fees, but only up to the equivalent of its "reasonable purchase price." Find out what that amount is before making a final decision, because if you later change your mind and decide to buy, you will be penalized for not listening. Uncle Sam will not credit the entire amount of the money he's been shelling out for rental to help purchase the item. You end up paying more.

❖ GEM: Watch Out for DME "House Rules"

Medicare has "residency requirements" you must meet. If you're not home enough, Uncle Sam will decide it's not worth his money to rent supplies for you, and you will lose coverage.

EXAMPLE 57

You have rented an aspirator (with Medicare's blessing). After three weeks of home use, complications arise and you enter a nursing home for a week. In this situation, because you were at your residence for part of the month, Medicare will contribute to the full month's DME rental. But if you are out of the home for an entire month, Medicare will take a "use it or lose it" stand and won't pay a penny.

◆ ◆ ◆

Because DME falls under Part B, *you* are still responsible for paying a 20 percent share of the costs (co-insurance) and any unmet deductible. When this involves expensive equipment, your share could run into hundreds—even thousands—of dollars.

❖ GEM: Negotiate If You Can't Afford to Buy

What if Medicare says buy, but you can't afford to? When a lump-sum payment is required and you can't come up with your share of the lump, you can negotiate. Write to your Medicare carrier and explain why the money required would cause you "undue financial burden" (fancy Medicare language for saying you'll go broke!). If no monthly installment plan can be worked out with the supplier, then the carrier must let you rent the equipment for up to three months while you figure out how to come up with the purchase money. The rental fees paid will then be subtracted from the purchase price.

What if you still can't afford to pay your share? Medicare will tell you to prove it! You must show that:

- no other financial arrangements (*e.g.,* charging or monthly installment plans) could be negotiated
- no cheaper sources were available
- no Medicare assignment was acceptable to the supplier(s)

If Medicare agrees, you will not be required to purchase the DME and your share will be based on a monthly rental plan instead.

❖ GEM: Find an Accepting Supplier

Some suppliers accept assignment, others don't. Cut your costs by finding a supplier that does.

❖ GEM: A Better Bet—Buy It Used

When you buy any *new* DME, you are required to pay your 20 percent co-insurance. But if you get the carrier's okay to purchase an item *used,* Medicare should let you off the hook, and you just pay any unmet deductible.

❖ GEM: Don't Forget Part A

The cost of doctor-prescribed DME may be paid entirely by Medicare under Part A. Check with your doctor about getting the necessary DME under Part A. Why? Under Part A, you pay no co-insurance. For example, let's say you need a wheelchair. During your stay in an SNF, it is included. But what should you do when it's time to go home? If the SNF is also a DME supplier, arrange to get the chair before you leave and you won't have to pay any extra!

✦ ✦ ✦

Nondurable items (items that cannot be used over and over) related to DME may sometimes be covered, too. Here are two gems to help you collect for items needed for the operation, maintenance, and repair of DME.

❖ GEM: Get Repaid for
Supplies and Accessories for DME

Nondurable items that are essential for the operation of your DME should be reimbursed by Medicare when obtained from a Medicare-approved supplier. You might be able to get coverage for oxygen or therapeutic drugs that are put into the equipment as part of your treatment (*e.g.,* drugs used for chemotherapy and kidney dialysis). Your costs to replace essential nondurable parts, like mouthpieces or hoses, can also be shared with Medicare if you purchase or own the DME.

❖ GEM: Collect for Repairs,
Maintenance, and Related Costs

Nondurable items that are necessary to the upkeep and use of the DME may also be covered. Table 4.22 shows how.

TABLE 4.22

Repairs, Maintenance, and Related Costs for DME

Repairs

- Covered   Loaner costs—While your DME is in the shop, Medicare should pay for a substitute.

- Not Covered   Excessive costs—When it would be cheaper to rent or buy another one, Medicare won't pay the repair bill.

  Abuse—If DME needs repair because you have purposely damaged or neglected to maintain it, you pay.

Maintenance

- Covered   Complex tasks—When the instruction manual tells you a skilled technician is needed for the job, take their word for it because Medicare will pay.

- Not Covered   Routine tasks—Whatever owner maintenance tasks are listed in the instruction manual, Medicare figures you can manage. If you want someone else to do the work, that's fine too, but you pay the bill.

Replacement

- Covered   When DME wears out, is damaged beyond repair, lost, or no longer useful because of a change in your condition, a doctor can authorize replacement, at Medicare's cost.

- Not Covered   If Medicare suspects you've abused or purposely lost the DME, sorry Charlie.

Delivery and Service Charges

- Covered   Delivery charges on leased and purchased items should be covered if it's the common practice to have a separate charge for this service.

- Not Covered   When Medicare thinks the supplier has already calculated the cost of delivering and servicing a DME in its price, you pay. For example, separate delivery charges for oxygen are usually denied unless the supplier has to travel outside his usual service area to deliver the oxygen to you and there is no other supplier available.

❖ GEM: Maintenance of Rental Items Used Beyond 15 Months

If you continue to require the DME beyond the 15-month rental time limit (see Table 4.21), Medicare will help pay for any service and maintenance not covered by a warranty once every six months. But you must have the work done during the first month of eligibility.

EXAMPLE 58

You start renting the DME on April 1, 1991. To be reimbursed for service and maintenance after 15 months, you must have the work done by September 1992 (six months after the 15-month rental cap, and every six months thereafter). If you procrastinate, you lose.

◆ ◆ ◆

Prosthetic Devices

The bionic man would have been pleased to know that Medicare Part B covers the costs of a wide range of body repair and replacement parts. (Depending on the circumstances, coverage may also be provided under Part A.) Certain sup-

TABLE 4.23

Covered Prosthetic Devices

- Artificial limbs.
- Body braces—*e.g.*, arm, back, leg, neck.
- Internal body organs (*e.g.*, corrective eye lenses needed after cataract surgery). Note: even if your own lens was removed *before* your entitlement to Part B benefits, a prosthetic lens received afterwards is covered. Also, prosthetic eyeglasses and contact lenses can be covered when your doctor states that they are medically necessary. But keep your choice of frames simple; Medicare sees no reason to pay the high price of "designer label" lenses.
- Breast prosthesis and surgical bras after mastectomies.
- Cardiac pacemakers. Medicare does have a heart and will cover the installation costs of an approved pacemaker. Uncle Sam will also pay for the followup visits to monitor you, but limits are set on how often. In most cases, "reasonable monitoring" is once a week for the first month; then every two months until 80 percent of the pacemaker's life expectancy is reached (your doctor and Medicare decide this); and then monthly. Unless you can show "good cause" for more frequent monitoring (like your heart is skipping beats), Medicare will be skipping payments.
- Colostomy, ileostomy bags.

TABLE 4.24

Uncovered Prosthetic Devices

"See no evil, hear no evil, speak no evil—walk the path of truth," but Medicare still won't pay for these:

Vision	Prescription lenses. Although these costs might be out of sight, glasses and sunglasses used to correct routine vision problems (*e.g.,* nearsighted and farsightedness) are not covered.
	Cataract sunglasses. Medicare figures you can squint.
	Optician's services. These are on your bill even if the visit was to fit or service prosthetic glasses (opticians are *never* covered by Medicare anyway).
Hearing	Hearing aids. What did you mumble? You think hearing is essential and should be covered? So far, Medicare has turned a deaf ear to requests for reimbursement.
Speech	Dentures. Bite your tongue, because no matter what you say, Medicare won't pay (unless the dentures are an essential part of a medically necessary mouth reconstruction).
Walking	Orthopedic shoes. You will foot the bill. The sole exception is when shoes are an integral part of leg braces and their cost is included in the fee for the brace. (Medicare is currently paying for orthopedic shoes needed by diabetics with foot disease in a few states with demonstration projects.)

plies, repairs, and replacements that enable you to use the prosthetic device effectively, and are integral to the operation of the prosthetic device, can be included too (*e.g.,* batteries used in an artificial larynx). Tables 4.23 and 4.24 list some of the more commonly required "parts" that Medicare will and will not lend a helping hand to you with payment. Example 59 illustrates how this works.

EXAMPLE 59

As a result of permanent urinary incontinence, Mr. Walters needs a urinary collection and retention system. Medicare should pay for the Foley catheter (a nondurable component) as a prosthetic device because it is an essential supply to enable the urinary collection system to take over the bladder's job. On the other hand, the rubber sheets, diapers, and antiseptic wipes Mr. Walters needs are helpful but *not* covered as prosthetic supplies because they aren't integral to the urinary collection system's operation.

Are prosthetic devices considered DME? As Table 4.23 showed, Uncle Sam sometimes says yes. But sometimes Medicare classifies prosthetic devices separately under Part B. Why does this matter? Because Uncle Sam might deny your perfectly legitimate claim simply because it was filed under the "wrong" code. To avoid frustration, check to make sure your doctor uses the correct Medicare vocabulary for coverage.

Navigating around the Medicare Monopoly board is like walking through a mine field. The tips we've provided should signal the mines and enable you to turn the Medicare mine field into a gold mine.

·5·

The Appeal of Medicare Appeals

It's a safe bet that if you are reading this chapter, it's not for pure pleasure. You have had the "joy" of playing Medicare Monopoly and you know the sad truth: Uncle Sam doesn't play fair.

In the last chapter we discussed the rules of the game and offered gems to help you win the Medicare coverage you deserve. But even if you've done everything right and played according to Uncle Sam's rules, why are you constantly getting unfair denial notices? Because the system is grossly inexact and unjust.

The following tale should help explain why Medicare is such a mess, and why appeals should be tremendously appealing to you.

THE BIRTH OF A "PROBLEM CHILD"—
THE TRUTH (ALMOST) ABOUT WHY MEDICARE IS A MISFIT

In 1965, when the legislation for Medicare was being drafted, there were lots of nervous relatives "laboring" in the delivery room along with Congress—lobbyists from senior-rights organizations, insurance companies, and, of course, the medical profession. Each group was anxious to make sure baby Medicare would come out most closely resembling "their side of the family." The commotion was tremendous; everyone had been so busy grabbing for body parts—an arm here and a leg there—that the poor child came out grossly misshapen, resembling no one but costing an arm and a leg. Today no one wants to take responsibility for causing Medicare's disabilities.

When first conceived, the federal Medicare laws borne by Congress were very generally drawn, and actually fairly liberal in concept. But once Medicare's adoption papers were signed by President Johnson, Congress declared the birth a great success, hired a "nanny" to raise the child, and went back to work on other important issues.

The "Nanny" chosen for Medicare was the Health Care Financing Administration (HCFA), a subdivision of the Social Security Administration. Congress gave HCFA a limited budget and said "you worry about the details of how to feed and clothe this kid." In other words, it became HCFA's job to translate those noble but general concepts of care that Congress had mandated into specific and cost-efficient rules and policies. Since child rearing is so difficult, HCFA decided mother's helpers were needed. So she wrote a job description and hired private insurance companies to lend a hand, serving as her Medicare baby "carriers" and handling the messy job of claims processing (the bureaucratic equivalent of laundering millions of messy diapers).

Because HCFA also has other children to look after, she delegates. There's no time to watch every step. As a result, her underlings have a lot of freedom on the job. For example, "Nanny" might provide the spending money and shopping list of needed health-care products and services. But her handwriting isn't always legible, so it's left up to her mother's helpers to interpret the list (Medicare's rules and policies). Being so busy, perhaps "Nanny" (HCFA) won't even notice when a few items are "forgotten" or a less expensive brand of care is substituted for the "higher priced spread."

The moral of this long tale of surrogate parenting is that the baby gets thrown out with the bath water. Who gets hurt? *You do,* because Uncle Sam's left hands (he has two—Part A intermediaries and Part B carriers) are illegally denying you benefits provided by Uncle Sam's right hand (the actual Medicare rules and regulations). Unless *you* slap Uncle's hand by appealing incorrect claims, you won't get paid money you are entitled to by law.

THE "HOW-WAS-I-SUPPOSED-TO-KNOW" DEFENSE, OR IGNORANCE CAN BE BLISS

When your Medicare claim for coverage is denied, you probably think you have only two options: pay the bill and figure you're out of luck, or appeal. But there's actually a third option: the "how-was-I-supposed-to-know-that-Medicare-wouldn't-pay?" defense.

Before you get into the appeals process, you should always consider whether this defense applies to you. If it does, you don't have to pay the medical bills—you're done!

How come you never heard about this defense before? Because the Government and—more important—health-care providers don't want you to know about it. But this is a Golden Opportunity that should *not* be kept secret.

"How was I supposed to know Medicare wouldn't pay?" Do you believe that this excuse, under certain circumstances, is actually a perfectly legal basis for refusing to pay bills? *It is!* You can't be forced to pay for services that "you could not reasonably have been expected to know" would not be covered by Medicare.

EXAMPLE 1

You were admitted to a nursing home and treated there. No one ever told you that the treatment is considered "unskilled" and so won't be covered by Medicare. You read *The Medicare Handbook,* but nothing there explained in English that the particular care you were receiving would not be covered. How about trying the "I-didn't-know" defense? In this case, it works!

This defense has been kept well hidden by the Government. But it can offer a wonderful opportunity to avoid paying big money for medical costs.

Not surprisingly, to use the "I-didn't-know" defense, your case must meet certain requirements. You should not have to pay if you did not know, and could not reasonably have known, that the care you received was not covered by Medicare. In addition, the service you received must:

- Not have been reasonable and necessary according to Medicare's standards
- Have been classified as unskilled or custodial care
- Have been covered under home health care, but you must not have been eligible for coverage because you did not meet *all* the home health requirements (*e.g.,* you were not housebound or receiving skilled care on an intermittent basis)

Does the "I-didn't-know" defense apply to *all* service providers? No. You are not quite that lucky. The "I-didn't-know" defense can be used only when the provider was a:

- Medicare participating provider
- Nonparticipating provider who had agreed to take assignment on the claim
- Nonparticipating provider who (i) should have known the service wasn't reimbursable; (ii) failed to notify you in writing; and (iii) did not get your written permission to provide the service

We now outline how an "I-didn't-know" defense works for Part A and Part B claims.

Part A Claims

Let's say you received care from a hospital, and then Medicare denied the claim for coverage because it was not "medically necessary and appropriate." So the hospital billed you. You had no idea that the care wouldn't be covered, and you had no practical way to find out; the other requirements described above are also met. What should you do?

The bill should *not* be your problem. In fact, you should not even have been sent a bill. Return the bill, *without payment,* but *with* an explanation of why you're not paying (see sample letter). Make copies or write a dated note for your files outlining your action.

Here's a sample letter that you can use:

Date

Dear Sirs:

> I am returning the enclosed bill unpaid. As explained in *The Medicare Handbook* under the Limitation of Liability Provision, I am not responsible for paying the costs of services that I "could not reasonably be expected to know were not covered by Medicare." I was never informed by the hospital, or my doctor, that this service was ineligible for coverage. I thought the care I received was medically necessary and appropriate for my case.

> Sincerely,

> Your name
> Address
> Medicare Claim Control #
> Health Insurance Card #

Chances are you will continue to receive bills, even after sending the letter. (The hospital hopes to wear you down!) Return them unpaid, with a note citing the date of your first letter of explanation. If the harassment continues, contact a lawyer who is experienced with Medicare for advice. *Don't pay anything.*

The key phrase for this very special defense is "reasonably be expected to know." What is reasonable? Your definition and Medicare's might differ. To succeed with this defense, you must not have been informed, in writing, that your care would not be covered (by, for example, your doctor, hospital, or insurance intermediary). If *The Medicare Handbook* stated in black and white that a service wasn't covered, you won't be able to use the "I-didn't-know" defense. But if you were never advised that the service would not be covered, you cannot be expected to be a Medicare expert—you may have yourself a real Golden Opportunity.

Part B Claims

Medicare participating service providers. Let's say you received care from a doctor, and then Medicare notified the doctor (or other provider) that reimbursement was denied. Again, you had no reason to know that the services would not be paid by Medicare, and the denied claim met the other standards described on page 213. When the provider sends you the bill, what should you do?

DO NOT PAY. Chances are the provider is first going to try to pass the buck, hoping you will assume responsibility. But the bill is not your problem. Contact the provider. Since you both had expected the service to be covered, suggest that the provider submit a "waiver of liability appeal" to the carrier. Providers are permitted to try to get paid by Medicare, but they are not allowed to bill you for their work [HCFA Pub. 13-3 §3789].

Document your case. Show that you had every reason to believe the service was covered. For example, if before agreeing to the procedure you asked your doctor if Medicare would pay, and he said that previous surgeries for the same problem had been reimbursed, you should be protected. You relied on the doctor's word; he relied on Medicare's past track record.

Even though you aren't liable to pay the bill, a provider's billing department will make you *think* you must pay by continuing to send bills or nasty letters. If this happens, you might want to discuss the problem with a lawyer and have him send the provider a letter outlining the "I-didn't-know" defense. Situations like these are not pleasant because you are now pitted against your service provider. But this is your money we're talking about. Can you afford to pay hundreds of dollars that you are legally not responsible for, just to remain a "good patient"? Hopefully, your doctor will understand that this is not a *personal* complaint. Your doctor should not be angry with you for protecting your legal rights. If the situation becomes too uncomfortable, you might end up hunting for a new physician. That should be the highest price you pay.

Nonparticipating service providers. Let's say you received care from a doctor who did *not* accept assignment. Medicare denied your claim for coverage because it was not a "reasonable" or "necessary" service. The doctor billed you for the entire cost and expects payment in full from you. What should you do?

Do not grab your checkbook yet. You might still be protected under the "I-didn't-know" defense (see page 213). The most critical requirement is that the doctor should have known Medicare wouldn't pay.

How do you prove that? Good question. You can't exactly ask him, but you can ask the insurance carrier. Or you can do a little undercover work. Call another doctor's office or two and say you have been told that you need a particular procedure (the one already provided), and you want to know if the service is covered by Medicare. If they all answer "No, Medicare will not reimburse," then you have a good way to show that your doctor should have known better.

You will need to write the doctor a note that explains your reasons for either (1) not paying the bill or (2) requesting a refund. (If you've already paid, the law requires that the provider refund your money!) If the dollar amount in dispute is large, you might feel more comfortable having a lawyer handle the "dirty work" for you.

Here's a sample letter (of course, you will want to modify it to suit your circumstances):

Date

Dear Dr. _____:

    I am writing concerning my bill for _____ (name of service) on _____ (date). As you know, Medicare has denied the claim as "not reasonable and necessary." According to Medicare law, when a service is not eligible for reimbursement, you are obliged to notify me in writing and to obtain my written agreement to pay for the uncovered procedure *before* it is performed. You did not fulfill these requirements. I relied on your experience, and had no reason to believe this procedure was not necessary.

    Under these circumstances, Medicare does not require a patient to pay the bill, even when the doctor is a non-participating provider. I regret the inconvenience and hope this information will be helpful to you in the future.

Sincerely,

Your name

cc: Insurance carrier

Make two copies: one for your files, one to send to the insurance carrier.

When you receive additional bills, DO NOT CAVE IN AND PAY! Simply photocopy another copy of your letter of explanation, attach it to the bill, and return both to the doctor.

The "I-didn't-know" defense won't cover you for every denial, but in many instances it can save you a lot of money. And it makes sense, too. After all, if you had no reasonable way to learn that the service wasn't covered, why should you be stuck for the bill? This defense provides a Golden Opportunity for fairness that should not be missed.

If this defense is not available, it's time to consider an appeal.

THE APPEAL OF APPEALS

Congratulations! All of your Medicare claims have been filed. You pat yourself on the back because you think you are actually getting the hang of this game of Medicare Monopoly. You are feeling pretty good—that is, until the Medicare mail starts arriving. The first note informs you that your hospital admission was not considered medically necessary so you must pay the entire bill. Upon opening the second envelope, you find another "notice of noncoverage" because the doctor's care you received was "not reasonable." Or perhaps you do get a reimbursement check, but the amount is only a fraction of what you shelled out.

What's going on? The rainbow pointing to the pot of Medicare gold is fading. You are frustrated, you feel defeated. You fantasize about burning all those Medicare papers, but instead you throw the entire mess into a box and hope the problems will magically disappear. Anyway, who are you to argue with Uncle Sam? He knows the rules and you don't. Why bother fighting city hall? Right?

Wrong! Wrong! Wrong!

Throw away any assumptions that the authorities in the Medicare system have a method to their madness and really do know what they are doing. If you haven't figured it out by now, here are the facts: You are dealing with a *very* imperfect system staffed by imperfect people who are relying on imperfectly programmed computers for answers. No, most of these folks aren't out to "get you" on purpose. But they will "get you" by accident, oversight, and ignorance of the Medicare laws. As a result, the burden is on you to protect yourself. You are not defenseless. You do have a weapon for battle; it is the appeals process.

We hear you asking: "I can't really win, can I?" Yes, you can! If you think the odds are against you, take a look at these statistics and you will change your mind: In 1990, the reversal rate for Part A claims was 52.1 percent—not bad. But the odds were even more appealing for Part B: almost 7 million requests for reviews were filed and two-thirds (65.8%) of these appeals were successful!* Put in human terms, over 4,600,000 frustrated Americans, no different from you, fought the system and struck gold with Medicare appeals. These people recovered hundreds—even thousands—of dollars per claim. The dollars represent money that was unfairly and wrongly denied—the culprits should "go directly to jail" without "passing Go." But they won't, so if you don't appeal, you can't win— and you may lose hundreds or thousands of dollars that rightfully belong to you.

*1991 HCFA Statistics, Health Care Financing Administration, Bureau of Data Management and Strategy (September 1991), page 41.

Isn't filing an appeal difficult? No. Filing a basic appeal is actually pretty easy. There's no risk. It's free. You don't need a lawyer (unless your case is complex). Remember, Uncle Sam's game strategy is counting on the fact that you are too tired, sick, or lazy to keep playing! He wants you to think you can't win. Don't fall into his trap. Appeal!

This chapter explains the various appeals procedures and gives you some gems on how to be most effective. We don't expect you to become an expert, but we do want you to become familiar and comfortable with the general rules of this part of the game. We devote a lot of attention to this subject because appeals have become the most important phase of the Medicare Monopoly game. Having the appeals "card" in your hand is like owning the "Boardwalk" of Medicare Monopoly. It's the best card in the deck and everyone is entitled to it. Don't forfeit your turn to reach the Medicare treasure through ignorance.

Introduction to the Medicare Appeals Process

Just like Medicare's insurance coverage, the appeals structure is based on the Part A, Part B division of labor. While the later stages of the appeals process are largely the same for Parts A and B, there are significant differences in the initial step onto the Appeals Ladder. You need to know the game strategies for both Parts A and B in order to cash in on the golden opportunities of Medicare coverage. We have organized our discussion to address appeals under first Part A, then Part B.

Keep in mind that Part A Hospital Insurance is really a large umbrella that also covers care provided in other settings, not just hospitals. To keep the game challenging, Uncle Sam has varied the Part A appeals rules based on where the treatment is provided. But fear not, we have highlighted these variations in the Part A appeals game for you, too.

Obviously, because everyone's medical situation is unique, our job is to help you recognize the red flags that signal you to take a closer look at a denied claim. Certain categories of supplies and services have unusually high rates of unfair denials; you'll want to know these trouble spots.

When appropriate, we have also included references to the rules and regulations that provide the legal rationale for your appeal (the specific citations from the Government's documents appear in brackets). Although we certainly don't expect you to be a lawyer (heaven forbid!), we think it is important that you have these legal facts at your fingertips. This way, if you are challenged, you can point right to the source. The information can also be a handy starting point for simple Medicare research.

Remember, there are many good reasons to appeal a claim and only a few valid excuses not to! Don't procrastinate—file those appeals! You can't win if you don't play the game.

Try Informal Resolution Before Starting the Formal Appeals Process

When you are denied coverage, your first step should be to try to handle the problem *informally*. Put on your Sherlock Holmes hat—your goal is to uncover information needed to successfully resubmit your claim. If you can win coverage without going through the formal appeals process, you'll save time and paper.

Start with a call or letter to Medicare. We don't have to tell you the obvious: when you must speak on the phone with anyone who has anything to do with Medicare, expect to wait! Unfortunately, we can offer no magical advice for avoiding this unpleasantry (knitting?). Social Security recommends calling at off-peak hours. Is there really such a time?

We *can* remind you that it's important to prepare *before* you even pick up the phone. Pick a convenient time and quiet location. Gather your "tools"—pens, paper (no small scraps, please), eyeglasses, Medicare card, and claim(s) in question. Write down *all* the questions you have. Don't rely on your memory—it's too easy to get flustered. The excitement of finally hearing a real human voice can turn the most competent of us into a stammering fool! Table 5.1 provides a Checklist for Action.

TABLE 5.1

Tools of the Trade—A Checklist for Informal Action

Basic Tools	Yes	No
Telephone in a quiet location	_____	_____
Paper (no tiny scraps, please) and pens (that work)	_____	_____
Telephone numbers of key players in the Medicare Monopoly game (SSA, Medicare Intermediary, Carrier, PRO)	_____	_____
Claim form(s) or correspondence to be discussed	_____	_____
All your questions written down	_____	_____
Medicare card/Health Insurance Claim Number	_____	_____
Eyeglasses (don't laugh; if you wear glasses for reading, you'll need them at hand)	_____	_____
Time, patience, a book to read, or paperwork to do in case you are put on hold	_____	_____

Try to keep your cool. No matter what bad news the service representative gives you, blowing off steam won't help. You're the one who needs advice, and the person on the other end has the power of the hold button!

Example 2 shows a sample phone conversation; of course, you will have to modify the details to suit the unique circumstances of your case. But the point we want to make is that Medicare is just interested in facts. You need to provide specific information and ask specific questions.

EXAMPLE 2

Here's a sample phone conversation: "Hello. I am calling to obtain more information about a claim. The Claim Control Number is _____. The Medicare Claim Number is _____." (This information can be found on the denial notices or Explanation of Medicare Benefits you have received.)

The voice on the other end will probably ask what exactly you want to know. You will then need to identify the specific service and problem. For example,

"The claim for my post-surgical visit to Dr. Walsh was denied. Why?"

Have a pencil and pad ready to write down the reason given. If no adequate explanation can be found, request that the claim be refiled.

- Take notes on what was said during your conversation.
- Ask the representative for his or her name and write it down, along with the date and time of your call.
- Clip this information to your claim form so that you will have all the facts handy when you need to follow up.

For example, perhaps the explanation you receive is that the claim was coded as a routine office visit and routine visits are ineligible for coverage. Now you know where the likely problem spot is—the doctor's office goofed. You will need to call whoever is in charge of the physician's Medicare billing, tell the person what you learned, and request that the claim be corrected and resubmitted. Hopefully, your troubles now will be over, but just in case the claim gets booted out again, you will have a written record of the facts.

If your telephone call doesn't resolve the matter, try a letter. Whenever you correspond with Medicare, be as *specific* as possible. For example, if your *Medicare Handbook* states that ambulance service is covered when your health is in jeopardy, refer to the page number in the handbook and include a letter from your doctor confirming the severity of your condition. If your claim for appeal is based on a conversation you had with someone at Medicare, then include the person's name and the date you spoke.

Your letter can be very basic if the claim denial was due to a simple coding or computer processing error. It will need to be more detailed if the denial is based on interpretations of the Medicare rules. But don't let that scare you—stick to the facts and be brief.

To document the "rightness" of your side of the story, you might need to include additional information, such as:

- Medical records
- Letters of support from experts—doctors, therapists, or other service providers
- Copies of prescriptions or other supply orders

A sample letter is printed here. Of course, you will want to tailor the wording to meet the specifics of your case, but it can serve as a helpful frame of reference.

Date

Dear Sir or Madam:

    This is a request to review a Medicare Claim Control Number _____. My Health Insurance Claim Number is _____.

    I believe there was a processing mistake because this service should be covered by Medicare. (Then refer to *The Medicare Handbook* or any other documentation to support your claim.) If you disagree with my opinion on this claim, please provide me with a clear explanation for the basis of your decision.

Sincerely,

Name
Address
Medicare #

____I am enclosing additional information.

If your phone call and/or letter doesn't get you the right result, it's time to take more serious action. It's time to start up the Appeals Ladder.

PART A APPEALS PROCESS: OVERVIEW

There are two doors that must be opened before you get into the formal Part A appeals process. First, you must actually receive the service you need. Second, you must be given a written notice that the service will not be covered by Medicare.

❖ GEM: Get the Care You Need

Hospitals, nursing homes, and home-health-care agencies don't want to get stuck with big bills that Medicare won't pay. Rather than take a financial risk, they may simply deny you service. And when there's no service provided, there's nothing to appeal.

How can you get around this serious problem? Tell the provider that you'll agree in writing to pay for the service if Medicare refuses coverage; that should be enough to get the service you need. (Waiver forms, saying you'll pick up the tab, should be attached to bills from skilled nursing facilities.) Then demand that the provider bill Medicare—that's your right. If the claim is then denied, you're ready to move into the appeal process.

❖ GEM: Don't Pay Anything Without a Written Denial!

If the provider just told you orally that your service won't be covered by Medicare but didn't put the denial in writing, you don't have to pay a penny! A *no* is not official—and you have no obligation to pay—until you see the news in black and white. (If the provider tries to collect from you without giving you a written denial, report the provider to the Medicare Fraud Hotline: 800-368-5779.)

❖ ❖ ❖

If your claim for Part A services is wrongfully denied by Medicare, you get not one, not two, not three, but four more chances to get the problem straightened out. These four steps up the Appeals Ladder—Reconsideration, Administrative Hearing, Appeals Council Review, and Federal District Court—are each described, and we give you lots of "gems" to help you reach a successful conclusion.

The first step up the Appeals Ladder, called a RECONSIDERATION, is the most confusing. The rules for hospital claims differ from the rules for SNF and home-health-care claims, so for the first appeal step, we'll talk about hospital claims separately from SNF and home-health-care claims. The next three steps are the same for all Part A claims, so we talk about these together. Ready to get started? Let's Go!

Your Medicare claim has been denied. Who uttered the big bad words "we won't pay"? There are three possibilities:

1. The service provider (*e.g.,* hospital, nursing home, home-health-care agency)

2. The hospital's Peer Review Organization (PRO) (doctors and other health-care professionals hired by the government to handle the initial appeals for Medicare hospital claims)

3. The Medicare Part A intermediary (insurance company designated to handle initial appeals for skilled nursing facility, home-health, and hospice-care claims)

What you do next depends on who denied your claim.

If the Service Provider Says No

Let's say the hospital denied your claim. The denial is called a "Notice of Noncoverage." You can't appeal to Medicare yet. Why not? Because *Medicare* hasn't yet denied your claim.

The first appeal is called a Request for Reconsideration. Medicare can't "reconsider" before it has "considered." The provider—a hospital, doctor, etc.—is not Medicare. So before you start climbing the Appeals Ladder, you must first ask the provider to file a claim with the Medicare PRO or intermediary. The PRO or intermediary will then make an "official Medicare decision," and if it denies your claim you *then* can appeal. Unfortunately, this added step can sometimes cause costly delays. For example, if you are out money and are looking for a sizable reimbursement, delays can be a real problem.

NOTE

There are two basic speeds of travel for a review request—fast and slow. An "expedited" review is Medicare's version of the fast track. You are allowed to choose this option when you must have an answer quickly. The PRO must give you an answer within three working days of your request.

To ask the PRO for an immediate review you, too, must act immediately. You are given three days from the date you receive written notification (*e.g.,* if you are informed on Monday, you need to contact the PRO by Thursday). The telephone number and address are on the Notice of Noncoverage.

A "routine" review is the appeal speed you must use when time is not of the essence. You are given up to 60 days from the date on your "no"-tice to file a routine appeal. The PRO must give you an answer within 30 days.

❖ GEM: Avoid Delays by Asking
for Consideration and Reconsideration Together

To save time, you can request Reconsideration at the same time your claim is first officially submitted to Medicare. Medicare can consider and reconsider your claim at the same time. Odd but true!

✦ ✦ ✦

Hospitals and other providers can't just assume your claim will be denied by Medicare and charge you directly, skipping the claims process. *Make* the provider file the claim with the Medicare PRO (you have a legal right to insist), and then make your Request for Reconsideration. And ask for an expedited review, because time may be critical.

If you are receiving care from a hospital, and then you are told the service won't be covered, you can't be kicked out immediately. But the Notice of Noncoverage will tell you that if you don't leave by a particular day, *you* will be responsible for the costs. Again appeal immediately to the PRO and ask for an expedited review.

If the PRO Says No

The PRO is Medicare's official voice, so if the Notice of Noncoverage comes from that source, you can file a Request for Reconsideration—*without* first asking the provider to submit a claim. You can only hope the PRO will change its mind.

The address and telephone number of the PRO in your state can be found in Appendix 18. Call the PRO promptly for a reconsideration.

If the Medicare Intermediary Says No

If the denial of your claim comes on an Explanation of Medicare Benefits (EOMB), rather than a Notice of Noncoverage, you know that your claim was denied by a Medicare intermediary (the insurance company chosen by Medicare to handle Part A claims). A denial on an EOMB is an "official" no, and you can file a Request for Reconsideration directly to the intermediary.

Generally, only the provider or PRO will deny claims for care at a hospital. An intermediary generally handles Part A claims for skilled nursing, home health, or hospice care.

PART A APPEALS: STEP 1—RECONSIDERATION
OF INPATIENT HOSPITAL CARE CLAIMS

If your claim for inpatient hospital care was denied and you can answer yes to *either* of these two questions, you'll want to consider starting up the Appeals Ladder with a Request for Reconsideration.

- Did your condition require a level of care and services that could *only* be provided in a hospital setting?
- Did you require the skilled services available at a skilled nursing facility (SNF) but no bed was available, so hospitalization was required?

All the basic information about starting a Part A hospital appeals process is located in an official-looking document called "An Important Message from Medicare." You will receive this Masterpiece of Medicarese when you enter a hospital.

In the following paragraphs, we will provide our translation of "An Important Message from Medicare." We will review each section of the document so you will know what all that Medicarese means in practical terms. Our goal is to demystify the process and show you there truly are options for action. You can then make informed decisions about which appeals strategies are best suited for you when playing the "hospital inpatient appeals" round of Medicare Monopoly. You might not feel up to handling all the details yourself, but at least you will be an informed backseat player. You can roll the dice and let someone else carry out the moves for you.

SECTION I: "YOUR RIGHTS WHILE YOU ARE A MEDICARE HOSPITAL PATIENT"

This section outlines three basic rights all Medicare hospital patients must receive by law.

Your Right to Care

You are entitled to receive all care that is medically necessary for your condition. Note the statement: "*your discharge date must be determined solely by your medical needs,* not by DRG's or Medicare payments." By law, the *only* reason you can be discharged from a facility is because your medical condition no longer requires that level of care. A hospital can't make you leave just because Medicare will no longer pay for your stay.

Most of the focus of Medicare appeals is on denials of claims for coverage. But you may also appeal a wrongful attempt to discharge you. To understand why improper ejections happen, just take a quick look at how Medicare reimburses hospitals.

The government has grouped all the illnesses in the medical books into categories, called Diagnostic Related Groups (DRGs). Each DRG is assigned a price tag—Uncle Sam's estimate of the average cost to treat patients with this type of condition. Medicare pays the hospital based solely on the DRG price tag, without regard for how long your individual stay is. A hospital makes the same amount from Medicare whether you stay two days or two weeks, so the sooner you're out, the better for the hospital (even if not for you).

Although the law says you can only be discharged when it's "medically appropriate," the hospital may try to discharge you when it's "financially appropriate." Of course, hospitals won't tell you this; instead, they'll tell you you're well enough to go. If you and your doctor disagree with the hospital's decision, start up the Appeals Ladder with a Request for Reconsideration to the PRO (see page 224).

Your Right to Know

You are entitled to be "fully informed about decisions affecting your Medicare coverage and payment for your hospital stay and for any post-hospital services." This means you have the right to know what is in your medical files. When you must fight a hospital's decision, the law recognizes that you need access to the information that was used as the basis for denying your claim.

❖ GEM: Get Your Medical Records

Don't let anyone tell you that a patient can't see his or her medical records. The Medicare law is on your side. Point out Right #2 in the "Important Message from Medicare." If that isn't convincing, pull out the big guns: refer directly to the law—Title 20 of the Code of Federal Regulations (C.F.R.) Section 404.1710; and the Federal Freedom of Information Act.*

◆   ◆   ◆

Your Right to Fight

If the hospital gives you a written Notice of Noncoverage that states Medicare is no longer going to pay for your treatment, you have the right to stay and fight. Request a review by the PRO. The address and telephone number of the nearest PRO will be printed right on the Notice.

Keep in mind that your reasons for appealing must be based on *medical* facts. If you just don't feel well, that's not a "bad" enough excuse. Your physician must document that a hospital is the ONLY place that can provide the level of care you require and a discharge at this time would jeopardize your health.

---

*The C.F.R. and the United States Code (U.S.C.) are documents that contain the fine print of our federal laws and regulations. The sections mentioned here deal specifically with Medicare. The rationales for Medicare coverage decisions are supposed to be drawn from these sources and the Health Care Financing Administration (HCFA) manuals.

The need for your doctor's active support leads us to the next major section in "An Important Message from Medicare":

SECTION II: "TALK TO YOUR DOCTOR ABOUT YOUR STAY IN THE HOSPITAL"

This is probably the best advice Medicare will ever give you. Medicare law states that your *doctor* (not the hospital or PRO) is the ultimate medical expert on matters concerning your medical condition. This means, by law, that his word carries great weight when decisions are being made about your treatment.

Because of this authority, your doctor is your *best ally*. If you do need to request Reconsideration with a PRO, the magic words for Medicare coverage are "medical necessity." A detailed letter of support from your doctor that explains why your case meets Medicare's coverage requirements is your best key to success.

SECTION III: "IF YOU THINK YOU ARE BEING ASKED TO LEAVE THE HOSPITAL TOO SOON"

In this section, Medicare talks about the importance of a written Notice of Noncoverage to trigger your right to start an appeal. The Notice is the very first Medicare Monopoly game piece you need for the appeals process. This document contains the hospital's explanation for why Medicare coverage is ending. If you received the bad news only by word of mouth, it isn't legal and doesn't count. The PRO won't look at your case without this document.

❖ GEM: No Pay Without "No"-tice

Until you get a written Notice of Noncoverage, you don't have to pay for any days the hospital claims are not covered.

◆ ◆ ◆

Once you have the Notice in your hands, look for the date of notification. Make sure it corresponds with the day you actually received the written Notice. There are very tight deadlines for requesting an expedited review—the three-day countdown begins from the date printed on your notification.

If you disagree with the decision, *you must act quickly* and request an *immediate review*. If you do nothing and don't leave by the date given, the hospital can start billing you for *all* the costs of your continued stay!

SECTION IV: "HOW TO REQUEST A REVIEW
OF THE NOTICE OF NONCOVERAGE"

This section explains what you must do to start an appeal when you get a Notice of Noncoverage. As you will see, there are three different "exit" scenarios, each with different "actors" and deadlines for action (depending on whether your doctor or the PRO has agreed with the hospital's decision). Most important, the time when *your* financial responsibility begins during the fight will also vary. Knowing Medicare's deadlines is critical; in some situations, you will not even have a full day to respond.

After reading "How to Request a Review" in *The Medicare Handbook*, chances are you will be tempted just to pack your suitcase and go. *Don't.* The basic appeals process is really not overwhelming; Medicare just makes it sound that way. This is no accident. The Government's game strategy is to discourage people. But, if you are right, requesting a Reconsideration is your *only* option for correcting Medicare hospital mistakes.

❖ GEM: Submit Bills to Medicare During Appeals

If you disagree with a Notice of Noncoverage and are requesting a review, make sure the hospital continues to submit all bills to Medicare during the dispute. This is essential so that you can continue to exercise your "right to a review" for those bills too. Remember, only claims that have been submitted to Medicare are eligible for the appeals process.

❖   ❖   ❖

Scenario 1: Your physician agrees with the hospital's decision. You receive a Notice of Noncoverage that states your doctor and hospital *both* think hospital care is no longer medically necessary. In this situation, the PRO's approval is *not* required before the Notice can be issued. This scenario is less than ideal because it requires the fastest action on your part—you must request a review by the PRO immediately to avoid getting stuck with hospital payments. You only have until noon of the first *work* day after you receive the Notice to request a review.

EXAMPLE 3

You are notified by the hospital on Monday that you'll have to leave. Your doctor agrees that hospital care is no longer needed. Better hurry to appeal—you must contact the PRO for a Reconsideration by 11:59 A.M. Tuesday.

❖ GEM: Act Fast, but Not Too Fast

Although you don't have much time to appeal, wait until the last minute. In Example 3, you must ask for a reconsideration by 11:59 on Tuesday. *Don't* appeal on Monday. Since you can't be charged until noon of the day *after* the PRO makes its decision, waiting a day to appeal will give you an extra free day in the hospital!

◆ ◆ ◆

The reason why Medicare is so stingy with giving you time to act is simple: the assumption is that the hospital and physician are right and you can go home. Uncle Sam figures, in all likelihood, the PRO is going to agree with the decision. Since an appeal costs the government and hospital money, Medicare doesn't want to give you any more time than is absolutely necessary.

Those are the facts but, if you feel strongly about the medical rightness of your view, don't let Uncle Sam's tactics scare you off: *Call your doctor immediately.* If he is unavailable, tell the secretary it is essential you speak with him as soon as possible about your Notice of Noncoverage. When you do talk with him, politely ask for an explanation (remember he still can be your ally). Perhaps there was an error, or upon hearing your view, he might even change his mind (in which case have him notify the hospital and you can skip the appeal). You need to be open minded, but you also need facts. And if the notice came as a complete surprise, there's been a serious communication gap between you and your doctor and there is good cause to complain!

❖ GEM: Talk to Your Doctor Before Problems Arise

The situation of fighting the hospital *and* your doctor shouldn't happen. Good communication with your physician can avoid any unpleasant surprises and can help ensure the doctor will be on *your* side.

Unless you are comatose, you should *always* be informed about your health status. But don't wait for a doctor to initiate a heart-to-heart talk. If your physician peeks his head in the door, asks how you are, and leaves before you have time to answer, your needs are not being met. You must take the lead. Try this: "Doctor, I see you look rushed, and I want a few minutes with you to discuss my case. What time would be convenient for you? I'll be here all day." (Just because you are ill doesn't mean you need to lose your sense of humor.)

When you set a time to talk, don't waste it. Prepare a list of your questions. Ask about discharge plans—when does he think you will be ready? If you disagree, *now* is the time to talk it over. Once your doctor knows your personal circumstances, he might be willing to adjust the schedule to suit your needs rather than the hospital's. *You will never know unless you communicate with your doctor.*

❖ GEM: Get Hospital Records

You are legally entitled to have your hospital records. Get them—the information may be critical to your appeal.

Once you have more facts from the doctor and/or hospital records, pick up the phone and call the PRO (phone number is on the notice) to tell them you want an expedited Reconsideration.

❖ GEM: Reach Out and Touch Medicare

The notice states that you can "phone or write" to request Reconsideration. But how fast is the U.S. mail in your neighborhood? Unless the PRO is right next door to your hospital, you'd better not rely on Medicare's untimely suggestion to pick up a pen; use the phone, or you will surely lose by default!

❖ ❖ ❖

Explain why you disagree with the decision. The PRO must ask; it's the law. Try not to get emotional—stick to the facts of your condition, since that's all that counts. The PRO must respond to your request by phone and in writing. You cannot be held responsible for hospital care received before you get the PRO's decision, even if you lose. But once you get the PRO's decision, it's a whole new game. If the PRO agrees with the Notice of Noncoverage, you *can* be billed for all your hospital costs beginning at noon of the day *after* you get the PRO's decision.

EXAMPLE 4

The PRO rejected your appeal on Monday. If you stay in the hospital past Tuesday at 12:00 noon, the financial burden gets shifted to you.

❖ GEM: Appeal Later

Even if you decide to quit and go home by the hospital's discharge date, skipping this emergency Request for Reconsideration, you still have 60 days to file for any billing problems that call for a routine (nonexpedited) appeal. Do it!

❖ ❖ ❖

Scenario 2: The PRO agrees with the hospital's decision. Before the Notice of Noncoverage was issued, the PRO may also have reviewed your case. If the PRO agrees with the hospital that Medicare can stop paying because further care is not a medical necessity, what should you do?

Again, call the PRO immediately (phone number is on the Notice of Noncoverage) and ask for an expedited Reconsideration. Although you have three days to ask for an expedited appeal, DON'T DELAY.

❖ GEM: Ask for an Immediate Review Immediately

The PRO is allowed to take up to three working days to respond to your request for expedited Reconsideration. Whether or not the PRO has finished its review, the hospital can start billing *you* on the third day from the date on your Notice of Noncoverage. (Medicare allows this because Uncle Sam operates on the assumption that the PRO's first look was right and you are wrong.) If you wait two days before calling, and the PRO takes its three days to reply, *you* may get stuck paying for at least one day of care. (If you win the appeal, you are entitled to be reimbursed. If you lose, the bill is yours.) By moving quickly, you can avoid costly bills.

❖ GEM: Appeal Later

Just as in Scenario 1, if you don't ask for an expedited review, you are still entitled to request a routine appeal up to 60 days after notification. Do it!

❖ ❖ ❖

Scenario 3: Your doctor disagrees with the hospital's decision. We have saved the best of the worst for last. In this scenario, the hospital (not the PRO) has notified you in writing that it's time to go, but your doctor disagrees because he thinks a discharge at this time would be medically unsound. At least someone's on your side.

When you first get the hospital's Notice telling you to leave, contact the hospital's patient representative, or whoever handles Medicare-related issues, and say you want the *hospital* to request an *immediate PRO review.* Remember, by law you are entitled to an "official Medicare determination"—*you* can't appeal directly to the PRO until you first get its official "no, you must go."

The hospital must then notify you *in writing* that it has requested a review. The PRO has three working days to respond. Use the time while you are waiting for this reply to plot your battle plan. Speak to your doctor; he should be your best ally. Ask his advice about options available. Chances are, he has been through all this before.

❖ GEM: An Appeal Gets You Extra Free Time

While you are waiting for the PRO decision, you have no legal responsibility for the hospital costs—you can't be forced to leave or pay. Don't let the hospital intimidate you! Even if you lose the appeal, you'll have received an extra day or two of coverage!

◆　◆　◆

If the PRO agrees with you, you WIN! But if the PRO agrees with the hospital, you'll need to decide what to do next. Should you appeal further? Quit? Here are three options to consider:

Option 1: Leave the hospital. Perhaps filing the appeal provided the extra day or two you needed to recuperate. So, if the PRO says "go," you might decide that going home would be okay. On leaving the hospital, if you could use some extra assistance, remember, Medicare can also cover home health care services (see page 162 to find out if you meet eligibility requirements). Hospital social workers and discharge planners should be able to assist you and your doctor in forming the necessary home-health-care plan that meets Medicare's reimbursement requirements (if you have not already been contacted by the planner, now's the time to call).

❖ GEM: Continue the Appeal from Home

If you have any bills which are being charged to you, you may choose to leave the hospital and continue the appeal from home. If you are well enough to be discharged, you may as well leave.

◆　◆　◆

Option 2: Stay and pay. Remember, no one is going to force you out of the hospital. The issue is, who will be *paying* for your continued care—Medicare or you? If you're in good shape financially, perhaps it would be worth it to stay and pay for an extra day or two.

Option 3: You are right—stay and fight. You can ask the PRO to take a second look (request a Reconsideration). But since it has already said no once, Medicare operates on the assumption that you are wrong. The hospital is permitted to start billing you on the third day after you received the notice. So, if the PRO takes its full three-day time limit to review your case, you might get stuck paying for one or two days of hospital care. (If you do win, the money will be reimbursed.)

❖ GEM: Appeal If You Plan to Stay

If you believe that you should stay in the hospital longer, ask the PRO for a second look. The worst that will happen is that you'll again be denied. But even if you are given a second no, you may pick up another couple of *free* hospital care days. Remember, you can't be held liable for the days while the PRO reconsiders. So appeal—even if you lose, you win!

❖ GEM: Show Medical Necessity

Medical necessity is the key to coverage. When you appeal, your doctor must document why hospital care is essential and respond very specifically to the PRO's reasons for denying your claim.

SECTION V: POST-HOSPITAL CARE

This last section of "An Important Message" attempts to answer the question: "Is there life after hospitalization" as far as Medicare is concerned?

If you still need medical care, but no longer require hospitalization, your doctor can discharge you to either a skilled nursing facility or your home with care services. Hospital discharge planners or social workers can help with this process. In either situation, some supplies and services you need might be eligible for insurance coverage under Medicare or supplemental insurance policies. But the reimbursement rules are strict, so you better make sure you know what is covered, or you will get stuck paying. Ask for help—you'll need it!

SECTION VI: ACKNOWLEDGMENT OF RECEIPT

Medicare wants your signature. When you sign on the line, you are simply agreeing that someone handed you "An Important Message from Medicare." Uncle Sam isn't interested in whether you understand his message or not; he just wants to know whether the hospital has met its legal obligation. It's okay to sign— you aren't giving any rights away, so don't worry.

If your first step up the Appeals Ladder for a hospital claim is not successful, don't panic. There are three more "bites at the appeal." We'll tell you about your remaining appeal options for hospital claims starting at page 239.

PART A APPEALS: STEP 1—RECONSIDERATION OF SNF AND HOME-HEALTH-CARE CLAIMS

The first appeal step—Request for Reconsideration—is much simpler for SNF and home-health-care claims. The reason is simple: unlike hospital appeals, there is no PRO involved with these claims.

In this section, we tell you how you can start up the Appeals Ladder if you have been wrongfully denied coverage for SNF or home health care, and when you should consider doing so. The *Golden Rule* is: if you want to win, you have to play the game. This means you have to file papers; we will tell you when and how.

How Do You Begin an SNF or Home-Health-Care Appeal?

You must first get an official no from Medicare. If the SNF or home-health-care agency tells you that a service will not be paid for by Medicare, that is *not* an official denial. You are legally entitled to a decision by Medicare. (Section 3439.1 of the Medicare Intermediary Manual.)

Tell the SNF or home-health-care agency to submit a "no-payment" claim to the Medicare intermediary. This request forces the provider to file your claim so that you can get an official decision from Medicare. The intermediary's response is called an "official initial determination." If the intermediary then says "the SNF or HHA is right; the service isn't eligible for coverage," the news may not be good, but at least you have an official Medicare denial. Now you can ask Medicare for a Reconsideration of the decision.

❖ GEM: Don't Pay Until Medicare Decides

The SNF or HHA probably will keep sending you bills. Hang on to your checkbook—you don't have to pay until the official Medicare decision arrives.

❖ ❖ ❖

Once you receive the official no from Medicare on SNF or home-health-care claims, it's not too difficult to start the appeals process. Uncle Sam has prepared a form called Request for Reconsideration of Part A Health Insurance Benefits (Form HCFA-2649). This is the same form, mentioned earlier, that can be used for services or a hospital. This multipurpose form also can be used for all Part

A–covered services received at a skilled nursing facility (SNF), home-health agency (HHA), or health maintenance organization (HMO).

Actually, you are not even required to use the form. A letter from you is fine too, as long as it contains all the basic information. A letter should include your Medicare card number, the date(s) of service, a simple explanation about why you are asking for a review, and any documentation to support your request. Staple your letter to a *copy* of the EOMB (*never* part with your original forms). Since HCFA 2649 is pretty simple, if you have one handy use it. You then won't have to worry about accidentally omitting some needed fact and having your claim rejected again.

You can find a copy of Form HCFA-2649 in Appendix 13, along with an easy-to-read explanation of how to fill it out.

When Should You Appeal SNF Claim Denials?

If your claim for SNF care was denied and you can answer yes to these four questions from *The Medicare Handbook* (page 15), you'll want to consider an appeal.

- Were you hospitalized first for at least 3 days and entered the SNF within 30 days of your hospital discharge?
- Was the SNF Medicare certified?
- Did your doctor certify that you needed SNF care?
- Did you need and receive SNF level care (*e.g.,* skilled nursing or rehabilitation services that could only be provided by trained professionals such as physical therapists or registered nurses) on a *daily* basis (at least 5 days per week)?

When Should You Appeal Home Health Service Denials?

If your claim for home health services was denied and you can answer yes to these four questions from *The Medicare Handbook* (page 16), you should appeal.

- Are you housebound? (Although you don't need to be bedridden, Medicare is very literal about this. Leaving home must require a considerable and taxing effort. You meet the standard if you cannot get out without assistance from others or you need a wheelchair, crutches, etc. Trips out for medical treatment are okay as are occasional "walks" outside.)
- Did your doctor prescribe the care because it was medically necessary, and was a home-health-care plan developed?
- Do you need intermittent or part-time skilled care? (Skilled services are those tasks that can only be performed by, or under the supervision of, a nurse or therapist; housekeepers do *not* meet the standard.) See page 149 for an explanation of this type of care.
- Is the home health agency (HHA) a Medicare-certified provider?

What Are the Red Flags for Identifying Unfair Denials?

When it comes to SNF and home health care, there's good news and bad news. First, the good news: if you are eligible, Medicare will cover a wide range of skilled services in a nursing home or your own home. The bad news is that the Medicare insurance intermediaries who process your claims are often overly strict in interpreting the rules. As a result, many valid claims are unfairly denied. (Remember, Medicare law *requires* that your *overall condition* must be considered [42 C.F.R. §409.33(a)(1)].

There are a number of red flags that should alert you to an unfair denial. Be particularly suspicious if your claim for SNF or home health care is denied for any one of these reasons:

▶ ▶ ▶ **RED FLAG 1.** *"Your condition is 'stable' or 'not improving.'"*

Restorative potential cannot be used as the deciding factor for coverage. If SNF or home-health-care services will help maintain your present functions or slow deterioration, you should be entitled to coverage. [42 C.F.R. §409.32(c)]

Action: Resubmit claim (fill out a Request for Reconsideration form) along with a note stating that, under Medicare law, "no improvement" denials are illegal. Also include an explanation of why the service is needed to maintain health.

▶ ▶ ▶ **RED FLAG 2.** *"The amount of time allowed for reimbursable home health care has been exhausted."*

As Table 5.2 shows, there are limits on Medicare reimbursement for SNF coverage. But you can receive up to 35 hours per week of home-health-care services for as long as necessary (if you meet the eligibility criteria outlined on page 162). Home health agencies will often try to impose arbitrary ceilings on the number of weeks of care you can receive at home. These limits are unfair and *not legally authorized.* Don't accept this reason for a denial.

Action: Insist that the home health agency continue to provide care. Have your doctor write a letter explaining why you need the services and why it would be unsafe for the agency to stop. If the agency ignores you, call your State Department of Health, or agree to sign a form saying you'll pay privately if Medicare denies the claim and then demand they bill Medicare.

▶ ▶ ▶ **RED FLAG 3.** *"Service provided was not medically reasonable or necessary."*

This is one of the most popular excuses for denying a claim. Your physician is the expert. If he believes the service was essential for your care, then don't let the insurance intermediary "play doctor" and deny your claim as unnecessary.

Action: Have the SNF or home health agency resubmit the claim along with a letter from your doctor explaining why the care is essential.

▶ ▶ ▶ **RED FLAG 4.** *"Services received could have been performed by family members."*

There is *no* Medicare law that requires your family to perform health-care services. It is illegal to penalize you for having relatives.

Action: Have the SNF or home health agency resubmit the claim along with a letter from your doctor stating that it is inappropriate for family to provide the services you need.

▶ ▶ ▶ **RED FLAG 5.** *"Services provided were available elsewhere."*

The intermediary is telling you that you didn't need SNF or home-health-care services because you could have received the same services, for example, as an outpatient at a hospital. Even if this is true, you have the *right* to choose where to receive a service.

Action: Resubmit the claim along with a letter from your doctor, SNF, or home-health-care provider stating that you are entitled to receive the services at a location of your choice.

▶ ▶ ▶ **RED FLAG 6.** *"The care you received does not meet Medicare's definition of a 'skilled service.'"*

Medicare looks very closely at the type of care you receive and will only reimburse for services that *must* be provided or supervised by a nurse or other health-care professional. If you *only* need custodial, nonskilled care, you are out of luck.

But as we explained in Chapter 4, Medicare wrongfully denies many perfectly legitimate claims for SNF and home-health-care coverage based on a misreading of the definition of skilled care or a misunderstanding of the care you received. We have described many common situations in which you should be covered for SNF (pages 147–173) and home health care, and we suggest you go back to those sections now.

A particularly high number of wrongful denials for SNF and home-health-care services occur because intermediaries fail to recognize that Medicare will pay for skilled care to oversee unskilled services and observe and assess a patient's condition. Take a look at the following examples:

EXAMPLE 5

The plan of care developed by your physician to promote recovery and ensure your safety consists solely of a health professional overseeing several unskilled personal care services (*e.g.,* bathing and feeding). You are entitled to coverage, as long as the doctor can show that the complexity of your case requires observation and management by a skilled professional [42 C.F.R. §409.33) (a) (1)].

EXAMPLE 6

You have just arrived at home after lung surgery. Your condition is not completely stable. You need to be monitored by someone trained to recognize postoperative treatment complications, so that necessary modifications in care can be made promptly. Your doctor is justified in requesting skilled professional observation [42 C.F.R. §409.33(a)(2)].

EXAMPLE 7

You are a newly diagnosed diabetic, and you need training in insulin injection as well as other health-care techniques. Or your leg was amputated, and you must learn how to walk and care for your prosthesis. Only a trained professional can adequately perform these educational tasks. Teaching of essential self-maintenance skills should be covered, and a denial of claims for these services is wrong [42 C.F.R. §409.33(a)(3)].

Action: Resubmit claim, add any helpful documentation, and note that service is covered as "skilled care."

▶ ▶ ▶ **RED FLAG 7.** *"You were not 'housebound.'"*

Perhaps this is a new form of faith healing. If Medicare tells you that you don't really need to be home, you then will be able to throw away your crutches and walk out the door! Does Uncle Sam actually think people would become prisoners at home just to collect a few dollars?

Action: Resubmit the claim along with a letter from your doctor or home-health-care provider that verifies your homebound status. (See page 165 for definition of housebound.)

▶ ▶ ▶ **RED FLAG 8.** *"Services do not meet Medicare's definition of 'intermittent or part-time care.'"*

Intermediaries became so overly zealous in their use of this excuse that the HCFA was sued. A coalition that included angry congressmen, the AARP, and the National Association of Home Health Care Agencies took the complaint to court *and won!* The judgment required that all past claims denied using the "not-part-time" excuse be reopened.

Action: If you have been unfairly denied coverage for this reason, dig out your papers. Resubmit your claim, explaining that your care meets the Medicare requirements. (See page 164 for definition of intermittent or part-time care.)

We have now told you how to take the first step up the Part A Appeals Ladder for hospital care appeals and for SNF and home-health-care appeals. Unfortunately, you may not get satisfaction after only one step. To reach approval of your claim and get the coverage that's legally yours, you'll probably have to continue up the ladder.

The steps for hospital, SNF, and home-health-care appeals are the same from this point forward, so we discuss them together. Tables 5.2 and 5.3 summarize the steps up the Appeals Ladder for Part A claims. The steps are also similar to the corresponding steps described in Chapter 3 for Social Security disability appeals, and the gems there are generally applicable here, too.

STEP 2—THE ADMINISTRATIVE HEARING

The second appeal step (after Reconsideration) is an Administrative Hearing by an Administrative Law Judge (ALJ) from Social Security. Starting at this second level, "money talks." The ALJ will only listen to your complaint if your claim meets a *$100 minimum* ($200 for hospital claims). Arriving at this figure is not as simple as you might think; any unmet deductible and co-insurance will reduce your claim, perhaps below the minimum.

EXAMPLE 8

Your bill for service is $100. But $50 still remained on your annual deductible. So your claim is really only $50, which is too little for an Administrative Hearing. Sorry.

❖ GEM: Accumulate Claims to Meet the Minimum

Several Part A denials can be lumped together to reach the minimum. For example, you can add the fees for a series of home health visits to qualify for an Administrative Appeal.

❖ ❖ ❖

Once you have done Medicare math and determined that you meet the dollar minimum, you have 60 days from the date on the denial notice to ask for an Administrative Hearing. To start the process, you need to get a Part A Request for Hearing form (Form HA 5011) from the Social Security office. (See Appendix 11 for a copy of this form.)

TABLE 5.2

Step by Step up the Medicare Appeals Process

Part A Appeals: Hospital Care

Appeals Step Rules of the Game	Step 1 Request a Reconsideration	Step 2 Request a Hearing	Step 3 Request an Appeals Council Review	Step 4 Request a Federal Court Review
What is my time limit for filing an appeal?	Routine (nonemergency) appeal—60 days from date you received Notice of Medicare Claim Determination Expedited appeal—3 days; use when speed is essential: a. Your preauthorization for hospitalization is denied b. While hospitalized, your hospital inpatient coverage is terminated	60 days* from date you received results of Step 1 Reconsideration Determination	60 days* from date you received results of Step 2 Hearing Decision	60 days* from date you received results of Step 3 Appeals Council Decision
Is there a minimum dollar amount?	No. Claim can be any amount	$100 minimum when Intermediary denies $200 when Hospital PRO denies	Dollar minimums same as Step 2	$1,000 minimum when Intermediary denies; $2,000 when Hospital PRO denies
Where do I file my appeal?	Hospital Peer Review Organization (PRO) or local Social Security office	Hospital PRO or local Social Security office	Social Security Appeals Council, Arlington, Virginia (address on form)	U.S. Federal District Court
What do I need? 1. A lawyer? 2. Special forms?	1. No. You or your appointed representative can handle 2. Optional; (a) Written explanations from you or service provider accepted but using Form HCFA 2649 recommended; (b) Appointment of Representative Form SSA-1696-U4 if needed	1. Yes, when issues are complex; no, when case is simple or you can get expert advice if needed 2. Optional: (a) written explanations accepted but using Form HA-5011 recommended; (b) Appointment of Representative Form SSA-1696-U4 if needed	1. Yes. To prepare, review and submit written documentation for case 2. Yes; (a) Form HA-520; (b) Appointment of Representative Form SSA-1696-U4, if needed	1. Definitely yes! 2. Yes; (a) Lawyer must file a legal brief; (b) Appointment of Representative Form SSA-1696-U4 if needed
Who reviews my case?	Hospital's PRO or Part A Intermediary	Administrative Law Judge from SSA Office of Hearings & Appeals	Social Security Administration Appeals Council	U.S. Federal District Court Judge
How soon will I hear the results?	30 days routine appeal, 3 days expedited appeal	No time deadline	No time deadline	No time deadline

*Or 65 days from date on your notice.

TABLE 5.3

Step by Step up the Medicare Appeals Process

Part A Appeals: Skilled Nursing Facility and Home Health Care

Appeals Step Rules of the Game	Step 1 Request a Reconsideration	Step 2 Request a Hearing	Step 3 Request an Appeals Council Review	Step 4 Request a Federal Court Review
What is my time limit for filing an appeal?	60 days* from date you received Notice of Medicare Claim Determination	60 days* from date you received results of Step 1 Reconsideration Determination	60 days* from date you received results of Step 2 Hearing Decision	60 days* from date you received results of Step 3 Appeals Council Decision
Is there a minimum dollar amount?	No. Claim can be any amount	$100 minimum	$100 minimum	$1,000 minimum
Where do I file my appeal?	Insurance Intermediary or local Social Security office	Same as Step 1. Case is then forwarded to SSA Office of Hearings and Appeals	Social Security Appeals Council, Arlington, Virginia (address on form)	U.S. Federal District Court
What do I need? 1. A lawyer? 2. Special forms?	1. No. You or your appointed representative can handle 2. Optional; (a) Written explanations from you or service provider accepted but use of Form HCFA 2649 recommended; (b) Appointment of Representative Form SSA-1696-U4, if needed	1. Yes, when issues are complex; research often needed to cite legal basis for coverage 2. Optional: (a) Written explanations accepted but use of Form HA 5011 recommended; (b) Appointment of Representative Form SSA-1696-U4, if needed	1. Yes; to prepare, review and submit written documentation for case 2. Yes; (a) Form HA 520; (b) Appointment of Representative Form SSA-1696-U4, if needed	1. Definitely yes! 2. Yes; (a) Lawyer must file a legal brief; (b) Appointment of Representative Form SSA-1696-U4, if needed
Who reviews my case?	Insurance Intermediary	Administrative Law Judge from SSA Office of Hearings and Appeals	Social Security Administration Appeals Council	U.S. Federal District Court Judge

*Or 65 days from date on your notice.

What Should You Do with the Form?

The Request for Hearing form is pretty simple to complete. You check off what Part A service the claim is for (*e.g.,* hospital, SNF, home health care); whether you are submitting new evidence; and whether you want to attend the hearing. There is also space for you to explain why you disagree with the initial decision. Of course, you need to have a "good" reason for requesting a hearing. For example, you might write: "The service in question was medically necessary. Attached is a letter of documentation from my doctor." Editorial comments such as "I think you are wrong; Medicare doesn't know what it is doing" might be true, but won't win you a reversal!

✦ GEM: Use Medical Records for Support

We have already told you that you have a legal right to request your medical files so you can see all documents the insurance carrier used as the basis for making its decision. (Requests can be made using the federal Freedom of Information Act; 42 U.S.C. §1305, 20 C.F.R. §404.1710.) Check your medical records and use them to support your appeal.

✦　✦　✦

Once you have completed the form, bring or mail it to the local Social Security office. (As always, make sure you keep a copy of everything you submit.) You will then be contacted by the ALJ about setting up a time and place to study the evidence and take testimony. The ALJ is not a local Social Security office employee; he or she is assigned a region to tour.

An Administrative Hearing can be held in various places, such as the local Social Security office, a hotel room, or even your own home, if necessary. You might want to request that a location be selected as convenient to you as possible.

If necessary, Medicare will also conduct hearings over the phone. This can save time, but you need to decide if the telephone is the most effective way to present your case. For example, if you are hard of hearing, a telephone hearing would not be the best choice!

While it is not always necessary to attend a hearing, your chances of success are better when you meet the judge face to face. For example, if your claim for physical therapy was denied as unnecessary, you and your doctor might want to demonstrate the range of your mobility to substantiate the need for treatment. Or an ALJ might benefit by coming to your home to see why receiving services there is more suitable for you than going to an outpatient care facility.

What Happens at a Hearing?

The rules are really very loose. First, the ALJ will look at all the facts that were previously considered. He or she then can look at new evidence. If the additional information is submitted by the service provider, the judge must notify you ahead of time so that you have time to respond to the new facts presented. If possible, before the hearing date, make an appointment with the ALJ to review your case file. You can copy any documents free of charge [20 C.F.R. §404.946(b)].

At the hearing you can introduce any information that relates to your claim; you will not be limited by the usual evidence rules that apply in court [20 C.F.R. §404.950(c)]. Documentation doesn't need to be presented in a fancy lawyer's brief. You may bring statements from any folks with useful information. For example, if you are contesting a "not-housebound" denial, a letter from a "nosey" neighbor supporting the fact that you are confined to home would be perfectly appropriate. Or you might want the neighbor to appear as a witness for you, describing how he or she only sees you out two times a month when the home health aide lifts you onto the wheelchair and takes you out for some air. Your witnesses *don't* have to have official titles to be legitimate [20 C.F.R. §404.950(e)].

Unwilling witnesses can even be subpoenaed, and the Government will pay for all the costs to do it [20 C.F.R. §404.950(d)]. You will need to put your request to subpoena witnesses to the judge in writing, in advance of the hearing, explaining why this person's presence is essential to your case. Although an ALJ may give you a hard time, the right to subpoena witnesses is yours. But think twice before trying to force unwilling witnesses to the hearing; they probably won't be too happy, and may not help your case.

The judge can ask questions of any witness. He is allowed to bring in an outside medical expert who will look at the facts of your case and offer his opinion. You or your representative can also question this expert. If this advisor's views differ from your own doctor's, you might remind the judge that Medicare law requires your own physician's views to be given stronger consideration because he has cared for you and knows your case better than anyone else.

Who Attends the Hearing?

No, it's not like a Perry Mason trial—you won't find yourself in a courtroom packed with curious bystanders. Medicare hearings are "intimate affairs," closed to the public. You will find the ALJ, an assistant to help with a tape recorder and paperwork, and perhaps the court's medical advisor.

Do You Need Professional Help?

No. If you decide to ask for help, you can choose anyone to be your advocate— a person doesn't need a Harvard law degree (or any degree for that matter!) to be a patient's representative. However, whoever you choose must be officially appointed by you. This can be done at the time you submit your request for a hearing. Simply attach a note signed by you or use the Appointment of Representative form (Form SSA-1696-U4). (See Appendix 15 for a copy of the form.) Additional forms can be obtained from your local Social Security office.

Of course, you want to choose someone you trust, but the person also should be assertive because it will be the advocate's job to prepare your case for the hearing. This includes obtaining and submitting all appropriate documentation, making sure he or she knows or learns the rules, checking filing deadlines, and meeting any other requirements for the hearing. By law, your representative must be given access to your appeal file when it is requested, so he or she shouldn't take no for an answer [20 C.F.R. §404.1710]!

You should also know that advocates are entitled to be paid for their work. Although it might be a labor of love, don't assume your representative is doing this job for free. Make sure you both understand and agree to terms in writing. Medicare puts a ceiling on how much an advocate can be paid—25 percent of the past due benefits awarded to you. It is illegal to be charged more [20 C.F.R. §404.1720].

If you have hired a lawyer and win your case, Uncle Sam will reimburse fees at the rate of $100 an hour. The lawyer must file certain forms to get paid. Again, don't assume anything. Talk over fees and who will pay beforehand, so you don't get stuck with a bill. Always get a lawyer *experienced with Medicare* (not your friend's fresh-out-of-law-school nephew); a specialist should be familiar with the system and what needs to be done.

While you can handle the hearing yourself, we generally don't advise it. Unless the claim is too small to warrant getting anyone else involved, get an experienced advocate to help.

Do You Have to Attend the Hearing?

No. If you have chosen someone to serve as your representative, you don't have to be there. Also, if your case "speaks for itself"—the evidence you have submitted is extremely strong and the use of witnesses won't add anything—you can request that the judge rule *without* having an oral hearing. Opting for this can protect you from surprises. Remember, the judge is allowed to ask your witnesses *any* questions he desires (does witness Aunt Sophie talk too much?), and he can also bring in his medical expert (someone who is not "on your side"). You eliminate these unknowns when you skip the oral hearing.

On the other hand, the hearing gives you a chance to make your case forcefully. Your presence and testimony, and the testimony of others, may be very useful to convince the ALJ to approve your claim.

❖ GEM: Pursue an Administrative Hearing

If even the thought of going before a judge makes your knees quake, take courage by thinking of this statistic: Your chance of winning after only the first appeal Reconsideration is one in two—50 percent.* When people persevere and go on up to the second step, an Administrative Hearing, the chance of striking gold is even higher. Those odds are too good to pass up, so don't!

STEP 3—THE SOCIAL SECURITY APPEALS COUNCIL REVIEW

If your Administrative Hearing did not resolve your complaint satisfactorily, your next step up the Appeals Ladder is a request for an Appeals Council Review. Keep in mind that, at this point, you are getting down to really serious business. You definitely will want assistance. You need either a professional with expertise in Medicare or a lawyer to prepare your case.

What Happens at a Review?

The review (held at the Appeals Council's office in Arlington, Virginia) is a "paper hearing"; no oral testimony is allowed. Your case will stand or fall based solely on what written facts are presented. Clear documentation and citation of the specific Medicare law(s) that support your case (or that have been violated) are essential. The Appeals Council is allowed to choose which cases to review; not every appeal request is accepted. The council also may decide to send your case back to step two, for a new review by an ALJ.

What Are the Basic Requirements?

To pursue an Appeals Council Review, you will need:

1. Medicare expertise—guidance from someone knowledgeable in Medicare law, preferably a lawyer.
2. An accurately completed Form HA-520—Request for Review of Hearing Decision/Order (see Appendix 12 for a copy of form), or a letter to the ALJ requesting a review.
3. To submit any additional written evidence to support your claim. These materials can be attached to your form or mailed within 15 days of filing. (Given the high risk of papers getting separated and lost, it's wiser to send

---

1991 HCFA Statistics, Health Care Financing Administration, Bureau of Data Management and Strategy (September 1991), page 41.

your entire case at the same time. If you can't, make sure any items being mailed separately are clearly marked with your name, Social Security number and claim number; attach a note stating that Form HA-520 has already been mailed and this material is to be added to your appeal documents.)

4. To make copies of all materials you have submitted, so that you will have an accurate record.
5. To use registered mail.
6. To meet filing deadlines. After receiving your ALJ hearing decision, you have 60 days to request an Appeals Council Review.

STEP 4—THE REQUEST FOR JUDICIAL REVIEW

This is the "Supreme Court" of the Medicare appeals process. It is your last step up the Appeals Ladder—your final chance to make sure justice is done.

What Happens at a Judicial Review?

You are taking your case to Federal District Court, and you *must* be represented by a lawyer. Your attorney will prepare a detailed brief and argue your case. Obviously, you only proceed to this stage when the legal merits of your claim are very strong. If you win your case, Medicare will reimburse your legal fees (but at Uncle Sam's approved rates, which are probably lower than your own lawyer's, so discuss fees with your attorney beforehand).

What Are the Basic Requirements?

To pursue a Request for Judicial Review, you will need:

1. A minimum claim of $1,000 or more.
2. Medicare expertise: a lawyer experienced with the Medicare appeals process.
3. To meet filing deadlines. You have 60 days after the Appeals Council Decision to request a Judicial Review.

PART B APPEALS: OVERVIEW

When you believe a claim is unfairly denied or paid at less than you were due for any service that falls under the Part B umbrella (see page 177 for detailed list of services), you should first try to identify the source of the error and to work out the problem informally. Because a claim passes through many hands, there are lots of opportunities for human error. Unfortunately, the mistake that took only a second to make may take weeks or months to correct.

Was the claim form completed properly? That's a possible source of the problem. Ask the service provider who submitted the claim to check for any error. Or request a copy so you can double check. Is all the information there? Is it legible?

If the claim form was accurately completed, and the service should be covered, resubmit the claim. Just write a cover note: "Please review. This is a covered service."

If the problem can't be resolved informally, you must climb the Part B Appeals Ladder to reach the pot of gold. Table 5.4 summarizes the steps up the Part B Appeals Ladder. The steps are very similar to those for Part A. To correct Medicare's mistakes, you must start at the bottom rung of the ladder (a Request for Reconsideration) and if necessary work your way up to the fifth step (a Judicial Review). As you might guess, each step up gets increasingly complex. But fear not, the first level is *very do-able.* You *do* need patience—you do *not* need a law degree.

The tips provided in this section will focus on the bottom steps of the ladder—what you can do yourself. If you are not satisfied with the outcome of a review and want to move up to the higher steps, it's a wise idea to seek advice from "appealing" individuals—folks with some Medicare expertise. (Check with your community's nearest senior citizen center, contact AARP, call the county bar association, or get recommendations from friends for lawyers who handle these kinds of claims.)

Remember, it's part of Uncle Sam's Medicare Monopoly strategy to intimidate you. He doesn't want you to think it's an easy climb up the Appeals Ladder. Although it's not effortless, we are not talking Mount Kilimanjaro, either. It's worth a try. Remember the *Golden Rule:* you can't win if you don't play the game!

When Should You Appeal?

There are many reasons why Medicare claims can be denied. Some are valid excuses and some are not. Unfortunately, when an unfairly denied claim arrives on your doorstep, it does not present itself in a color-coded envelope with neon lights that flash "UNFAIR." An incorrect decision comes disguised looking like any other Medicare correspondence—official—and as a result, too many of us believe the information inside must be the official last word on the matter. Don't let appearances fool you. There is plenty of room for official error!

Since Medicare's mistakes will never be as glaringly apparent as neon lights, we must look for more subtle signs of bureaucratic bungling. So, what should you keep your eyes open for?

Locate and carefully read Medicare's reason for limiting or denying reimbursement of your claim on the Explanation of Medicare Benefits (discussed on page 224). Certain official-sounding explanations can conceal an unfair denial. Compare the reason your claim has been denied with the following list of common red flags (the closest we can get to neon lights). When you spot excuses similar to these on your denial notice, sit up and take a closer look. You may have been wrongly denied.

TABLE 5.4

Step by Step up the Medicare Appeals Process

Part B Appeals

Appeals Step Rules of the Game	Step 1 Request a Carrier Review	Step 2 Request a Carrier Hearing	Step 3 Request an ALJ Hearing	Step 4 Request an Appeals Council Review	Step 5 Request Federal Court Review
What is my time limit for filing an appeal?	6 months after Explanation of Medicare Benefits received; EOMB will state exact date including deadline information	6 months from date of Step 1 Carrier Review Decision[†]	60 days from date of Step 2 Carrier Hearing Decision	60 days from date of Step 3 ALJ Hearing Decision	60 days from date of Step 4 Appeals Council Decision
Is there a minimum dollar amount?	No. Claim can be any amount	$100* (But you can combine several small claims to reach)	$500 minimum*	$500 minimum*	$1,000 minimum*
Where do I file my appeal?	Part B Insurance (address is on EOMB) or local Social Security office	Same as Step 1	Local Social Security Office	Social Security Appeals Council, Arlington, Virginia (address on Form)	U.S. Federal District Court
What do I need? 1. A lawyer? 2. Special forms?	1. No. You or your appointed representative can handle 2. Optional; (a) Written explanation from you or service provider accepted but using Form HCFA-1964 recommended; (b) Appointment of Representative Form SSA-1696-U4, if needed	1. Yes, when issues are complex; no, when case is simple or you can get expert advice if needed 2. Optional: (a) Written explanations acceptable but using Form HCFA-1965 recommended; (b) Appointment of Representative Form SSA-1696-U4, if needed	1. Same as Step 2 2. Same as Step 2	1. Yes; to prepare, review and submit written documentation for case 2. Yes; (a) Form HA 520; (b) Appointment of Representative Form SSA-1696-U4, if needed	1. Definitely yes! 2. Yes; (a) Lawyer must file a legal brief; (b) Appointment of Representative Form SSA-1696-U4, if needed
Who reviews my case?	Part B carrier	Part B Carrier Hearing Officer	Administrative Law Judge from Social Security Office of Hearings and Appeals	Social Security Administration Appeals Council	U.S. Federal District Court Judge

* When appeal is on a question of entitlement of Part B benefits, minimum is waived.
† Longer if there's "good cause" for late filing—see Appendix 13 (HCFA 2649).

▶ ▶ ▶ **RED FLAG 1.** *"Approved amount limited by item 5c on back."*

Put simply, the amount Medicare reimbursed is less than the provider's bill. This fact shouldn't come as a surprise. Remember, Medicare has reimbursement fee schedules and will only pay up to the amount that Uncle Sam has decided is a "reasonable" charge for that service—the "approved amount." Since providers and Medicare usually have different views of what's reasonable, you can expect a price gap. But if the gap is more than 20 percent (*e.g.*, your bill was $175 and Medicare's approved charge was only $50, so the gap is greater than 20%), a "red flag" should go up. There is an error, either on Medicare's or your doctor's part. Here are three possible causes:

- *Inaccurate coding of treatment.* Medicare might be reimbursing you for the wrong service—one that is less complex and less expensive. If the claim form wasn't specific in its description, Uncle Sam will choose the least expensive code for that category of care and then base its 80 percent payment on that rate. You lose money.

  Action: Don't assume the approved amount is correct. Call your physician to double-check whether this is the going rate of reimbursement for the level of care you received. If not, ask that the record of your visit be pulled to see if someone goofed in the coding description and checked off the wrong diagnosis or treatment. If your doctor's paperwork is correct, then the fault probably lies with Medicare—the claims processor applied the wrong code. It's time to appeal.

- *Inaccurate, outdated data.* Although it might sometimes seem so, Uncle Sam isn't totally arbitrary when establishing his rates for the "approved amount." These figures are based on complicated formulas that supposedly consider data such as inflation and the going rates for services in the region where you live. Since this information is rarely up to date, the result can be a level of reimbursement that is unreasonably low. Because reversing the decision would be like admitting that the basic rules of Medicare's game were wrong, appeals based on unrealistic fee schedules are not big winners. But your complaint is valid. You are entitled to fight.

  Action: Your doctor will need to submit proof that Medicare's "approved amount" is entirely out of line with today's real health care costs.

- *Physician overcharge.* By law, doctors cannot charge more than 20 percent above the amounts set in Medicare's fee schedules. If they do, you don't have to stand for it.

  Action: First call your doctor and remind him about this legal limit. If he doesn't cut the bill, call your Medicare Part B carrier (Appendix 17) and insist on a reduced fee. Beware: Don't assume the carrier knows the rules; some have not been enforcing this limit. Stand firm—you are right!

▶ ▶ ▶ **RED FLAG 2.** *"Service is not 'reasonable and necessary' for this condition," or "Procedure is not covered for 'diagnosis given.'"*

In Uncle Sam's eyes, the "punishment didn't fit the crime." The treatment provided didn't make medical sense and Medicare won't pay. This may signal that the information on your claim form was not sufficiently detailed or an inaccurate diagnostic code was mistakenly applied by your doctor; an appeal should correct the problem.

Action: Confirm the accuracy of the information on the original claim (call the provider if you don't have your copy). If it's incorrect, resubmit with the necessary changes. If it's correctly completed, resubmit with documentation showing why this service was essential (*e.g.,* letter from physician, copies of medical records, prescriptions).

▶ ▶ ▶ **RED FLAG 3.** *"Too many services or doctors"; "Medicare does not pay for this service because it is part of another covered service done on the same day."*

Medicare is barely willing to pay for medically necessary treatment once, so if claims are submitted by more than one provider for similar sounding care, chances are the Government will use that (often unfairly) to deny a claim. Medicare will assume that if something looks duplicative or excessive, it is.

EXAMPLE 9

You are in the hospital for a hip replacement. Both the surgeon and your doctor examine you. Medicare denies one of the claims as duplicative. That's a wrongful denial *if* you can show that both visits were necessary.

Action: Show that the complexity of your condition required more than one doctor (*e.g.,* specialists, consultants). A letter from your doctor outlining why the services are separate and essential, and copies of relevant medical records, will be helpful in refuting the denial. Attach these materials to the Request for Reconsideration.

▶ ▶ ▶ **RED FLAG 4.** *"Therapy (or other service) is no longer considered necessary."*

Frequently, Medicare will initially pay for services like speech or physical therapy and then, just when life begins to get easier, your claims for these services are suddenly denied. What happened? It's likely that Medicare has downgraded your condition from "acute" to "routine." This means Medicare has decided the service no longer offers therapeutic value. Since the benefits of treatment to you are now defined as maintenance, you will pay. Often, Medicare's downgrading is unfair.

Action: Your doctor, therapist, or health-care agency will need to explain why the service is necessary to promote recovery or prevent further deterioration. Copies of pertinent medical files should be included with your appeal.

▶ ▶ ▶ **RED FLAG 5.** *"Number of visits to your doctor was excessive for the nature of your illness."*

Medicare has decided what frequency of treatment is reasonable for a particular medical condition and, if you deviate from this norm, your claim will be denied or reimbursement limited to the "correct" amount. Again, this often leads to unfair results.

Action: When you request a review, include a letter from your doctor that explains why the visits were needed. Perhaps you developed complications that required additional follow-up care. Medicare needs to know. As long as the visits are reasonable and necessary, Medicare must pay!

▶ ▶ ▶ **RED FLAG 6.** *"Treatment provided is considered experimental."*

For every health problem in the book, Uncle Sam has a list of treatments that are considered appropriate and acceptable medical practice for that particular condition. If a newer procedure used by your doctor is not yet included on that list, your claim will be denied. This holds true even when the treatment is approved for use with another illness! For example, claims for drugs that have been approved to treat one form of cancer have been denied when a doctor prescribes the same drug for treating another form of the disease. Why? Because it is not yet on the FDA's list *for this purpose.* Does this sound fair to you?

Action: Your physician will need to show why Medicare is in the dark ages. He or she must document that this treatment has been recognized by credible medical professionals as reasonable and effective *for your condition.* Submit this proof along with your Request for Reconsideration.

▶ ▶ ▶ **RED FLAG 7.** *"Durable Medical Equipment (DME) was not necessary or appropriate."*

Because Medicare has at least six criteria that must be met before Uncle Sam will pay a penny for DME, there is plenty of room for wrongful denials. If your DME claim met all of the following standards but was still denied, get out your "appeal armor" and prepare to fight!

- Your doctor prescribed the equipment as medically necessary.
- The equipment was appropriate for home use.
- Its *primary* purpose was medical.
- A healthy person would not benefit from its use (in other words, the DME is no fun!).

- You could use it repeatedly (it was durable).
- The supplier was a Medicare-certified provider.

Action: To appeal your claim, you need to know the specific reason for denial. Which of the above standards was considered missing? If the EOMB does not clearly explain this, call the carrier and find out. When you request a review, submit the necessary documentation to show why Medicare's reason for denial was unfair (*e.g.,* letter of explanation from your doctor or supplier).

▶ ▶ ▶ **RED FLAG 8.** *"Ambulance service was used but not necessary"; or "You did not go to the nearest appropriate facility."*

Medicare is very fussy about spending money on transportation. You and the ambulance company must meet specific criteria. If you don't, you won't get the green light for coverage. To avoid heartache (or heart attack), it pays to know the rules of the road before an emergency trip is ever needed (see page 200 for details).

Medicare may deny your claim because travel by ambulance was not "necessary." Perhaps you could have taken a car, bus, or taxi instead. In a real emergency, this Medicare denial should be easily overcome.

Medicare may also deny your claim because you did not go to the nearest appropriate facility. The criteria for "appropriateness" is the facility's ability to treat *your* condition. For example, if you are a 68-year-old male having a coronary, but the nearest facility is a hospital for women, you have good cause to be driven ½ mile farther to the general hospital.

Even if you didn't go to the nearest appropriate facility, your claim still should not be denied entirely. If you have "gone the distance" with Medicare (and then some) by choosing a hospital that exceeds the travel limits, you are still entitled to receive *partial* reimbursement for the ambulance service. Let's say you use an ambulance to travel from a distant hospital to your home. Medicare should calculate what the transportation would have cost had you used the nearest "appropriate" facility, and reimburse for that amount.

Action: Unfair denials are sometimes simply due to lack of documentation. You might need a letter from your doctor that explains why an ambulance was medically necessary and a taxi or bus wouldn't do, or why the closest hospital wasn't appropriate for you. Call the ambulance service and ask if proof of Medicare certification was mailed with the claim. If not, when you request a review, make sure you include copies of the necessary proof.

Did any of the preceding "red flags" sound familiar? If your claim was unfairly denied for one of those reasons (or any other, for that matter) and your first actions did not resolve the problem, then it's time to move onward and upward in the appeals process. Get out your hiking boots!

STEP 1—THE REQUEST FOR REVIEW

The first step up the Part B Appeals Ladder is the Request for Review. Once again, in order to play the Medicare Monopoly appeals bonus round, you need the right card—you must have an Official Medicare Determination to enter the game. In this case, the card is the Explanation of Medicare Benefits (EOMB) notice you receive from the Medicare Part B insurance carrier. When your Part B provider tells you that a supply or service is ineligible for coverage, that is *not* an official Medicare decision. Only after Uncle Sam's *carrier* has reviewed your claim, and you have received an EOMB denial notice, can you request a Medicare Review.

How Can You Decode the EOMB?

The EOMB is supposed to provide you with an explanation of Medicare's coverage or denial of coverage. Unfortunately, EOMBs are written in Medicarese "secret code," making it very confusing to read (are you surprised?). In many cases, it's difficult even to know if your claim has been unfairly denied or underpaid.

You need to be a bit of a detective to decode the secret message in the EOMB. To make your job easier, pull the bills that correspond to the services included in your EOMB. Look for a sentence at the beginning of the EOMB that reads something like: "Assignment was (or was not) taken on your claim for $_____ (dollar amount) from _____ (name of service provider). See item ____ on back." This shows whether your doctor agreed to take assignment. If so—good news—he must accept as payment in full the amount Medicare has approved as a reasonable charge for the service.

Next, look on the EOMB for the words *billed* and *approved*.

Billed $_____	The dollar figure that appears under this heading is the *actual* fee your doctor charges for the service.
Approved $_____	This amount is the fee Medicare has determined is a reasonable cost for that service.

Medicare calculates reimbursement based on the lesser of the billed or approved charge. (Can you guess which will be less?)

If the amount the doctor billed is greater than the approved charge, look for the sentence "Approved amount limited by item 5c on back." When you turn the EOMB over and read 5c, you will be reminded that reimbursement is based on 80 percent of *Medicare's* approved amount for that service and *not* your doctor's higher fee.

Medicare pays	80 percent of approved amount
You pay	20 percent of approved amount

EXAMPLE 10

Your doctor billed you $120 for a service, but Medicare approved only $100. Medicare's share will be $80 (80% of $100). If your doctor accepted assignment, your share will be $20 (20% of $100). If assignment was *not* taken, you will have to fill the gap between 80 percent of Medicare's approved charge and the provider's full fee (you pay $40). Remember, the doctor cannot bill any more than 20 percent above the amounts set in the fee schedule.

Examine the figures on the EOMB to determine whether Medicare is paying the correct amount.

The EOMB should also tell you whether Medicare is not providing any benefits and, if that is the case, why not. Again, the explanation may be tough to understand. Contact your doctor or other provider for an interpretation.

How Do You Request a Review?

A Request for Review asks the Medicare carrier to take a second look. Just like Part A, at this first step Medicare is not fussy; you do *not* need to file any special forms to request a review. A signed letter saying "please review" will do just fine. However, there is a government form that was created for the process. It's called Request for Review of Part B Medicare Claim—Form HCFA-1964. (See Appendix 14 for a copy of this form.)

The form is brief and, by using the form, you can be assured that all the necessary information will be included. At the very least, keep one handy to use as a guide when preparing your appeal letter. You don't want to risk having your claim rejected because of incomplete documentation. (Many claims are denied just for that reason.)

The price is right for this appeal. The cost of a postage stamp and a few minutes of time is all you need to invest for a first-stage review.

❖ GEM: Just Do It!

This first-level appeal has a lot of appeal. The odds are stacked in your favor—60 percent of folks (just like you) who file a Request for Review *win!* The average reimbursement is $122 in additional benefits!

✦   ✦   ✦

Table 5.5 is our Checklist for Action. It outlines all the basic steps you need to take for Requesting a Review.

TABLE 5.5

Request for Review of Part B Medicare Claim

Checklist for Action

1. Complete Form HCFA 1964 *or* write a letter including all necessary information.

2. Obtain additional written documentation to support my claim (if necessary).

3. Photocopy the EOMB and any other enclosures for my records.

4. Move quickly to meet the six-month filing deadline or provide a "good cause" explanation for the delay (see page 256 for more information).

5. Staple Form HCFA 1964 (or the letter) and any other documents to the EOMB.

6. Put the correct postage on the envelope (if your argument is weighty, you might need extra stamps).

7. Use the carrier's correct address (it can be found at the top of your EOMB), and include a return address on the envelope.

8. Create an appeals file for the claim (use date of service and name of provider as file heading), and insert all pertinent materials.

9. Mail the form or letter.

❖ GEM: Get the Facts and Nothing but the Facts

As we've said before, you can build your best appeal only if you have the facts to support your claim, and many of those facts lie in your medical records. You (or your representative) are legally entitled to copies of your health records that served as the basis for the carrier's decision. You can be sure that the carrier isn't going to tell you this information voluntarily—or jump at the chance to help you. You will need to ask, and if necessary cite the law—refer them to the source, the Government's own books of rules and regulations [Federal Freedom of Information Act, 42 U.S.C. §1305 and 20 C.F.R. §404.1710]. Your records will be very useful when preparing an appeal. After all—you can't hit the bull's eye if you don't know where your target is.

✦   ✦   ✦

You can expect a Step 1 Review to take at least 45 days. If you haven't heard anything within that time, call the carrier for a status report. If you are not satisfied with the outcome of the Review, and your claim is at least $100 (several smaller claims can be bunched together to reach the minimum—see Gem on page 239), you can move up to the next step in the appeals process.

STEP 2—THE CARRIER HEARING

After receiving the bad news, you have six months to initiate the next step: requesting a Carrier Hearing of your case. At this level, you would be wise to get help from a lawyer or someone with expertise in the Medicare appeals process, particularly if your case is complex. You will need to make decisions such as whether you or others should appear before the hearing officer and what additional evidence must be obtained and submitted. An experienced professional can help you build your best case and make the right decisions.

❖ GEM: Just Do It, Again!

Even though the hearing officer is hired by the carrier, the odds of winning are still heavily in your favor. You have a 60 percent chance of receiving additional benefits. And awards average $825.

✦ ✦ ✦

For a Carrier Hearing, your claim must be at least $100. You must file a Request for Hearing—Part B Medicare Claim Form HCFA 1965. You should attach any additional information to support your case, such as letters from doctors or therapists. The hearing officer will review all evidence submitted (old and new) and then issue a decision.

STEP 3—THE ADMINISTRATIVE HEARING

If more than $500 is at stake, you are entitled to climb up the next step of the Appeals Ladder: bringing your case to an ALJ appointed by the Social Security Office of Hearings and Appeals. You have 60 days from the date you receive the Step 2 Hearing Decision to file. The format is exactly the same as described for the Part A Administrative Hearing (see page 239).

Although by this time you are probably feeling discouraged, hang in there, because Administrative Law Judges are more likely to base their decisions on the actual Medicare laws, rather than the insurance carrier's own profit-motivated interpretations of Medicare's rules and regulations. In other words, with an ALJ, chances are even better that your case will be viewed with eyes that are not also focused on the corporate bottom line.

STEP 4—THE APPEALS COUNCIL REVIEW

This step is also the same as for Part A (see page 245). Your case will be handled strictly through the mail—it is sent to the Social Security Administration Appeals

Council in Virginia. Because you do not plead your case in person, it is essential that the facts be available in black and white. This is why the trained eye of a Medicare lawyer is invaluable. The Council might choose to review your case or send it back down to an ALJ for another look. Again, $500 is the minimum price of admission, and you only have *60* days from the date you receive your Administrative Hearing (Step 3) decision to file your claim.

STEP 5—THE REQUEST FOR JUDICIAL REVIEW

You have reached the top of the Appeals Ladder when you take your case to the U.S. District Court. Again, this step is similar to Part A (see page 246). There are three basic requirements. You must:

- Have at least $1,000 at stake.
- File within 60 days of your Appeals Council Review (Step 4) denial.
- Hire a lawyer.

At this level, if you win your appeal, in addition to the benefits due you, Uncle Sam will pay your lawyer's fees. That's the good news. The bad news is that the Government's rate for reimbursement is usually lower than what most lawyers charge. Make sure you discuss and agree upon any additional fees with your attorney, so that all those hard-earned winnings aren't eaten up by legal bills!

❖ GEM: It Ain't Over 'till It's Over

If you haven't met with any success on appeal there's one final action you can take: request that your appeal file be kept open, just in case new information comes to light or the rules of the game change. An appeal can be reactivated. So don't throw away all those papers you've accumulated—you just might need them again. Isn't that something to look forward to?

AN UNAPPEALING CONCLUSION

It is a national embarrassment that the imperfections of Medicare are so gross that seniors, at a time when they are most vulnerable, must find the physical and financial resources to fight for benefits they legally deserve. We cannot say it any clearer: *You must view the appeals process as an essential strategy in playing the Medicare Monopoly Game.* You will never win unless you are ready to call Medicare's bluff and challenge the hand Uncle Sam has dealt you. If you forfeit your turn at the appeals table, the cards will remain stacked in Medicare's favor.

Remember, when the Medicare program was created, the needs of America's seniors (the legitimate beneficiaries) were not the sole consideration. The shape of this country's health-care delivery system was excessively influenced by those who most benefit from our ills—the medical, hospital, and insurance industries. The fact that our Government officials have continued to build upon this flimsy house of cards should be considered a form of elder abuse. In light of this sad truth, the appeals process becomes not an interesting footnote but the main theme of any Medicare story. It is up to you to supply the happy ending.

DEATH: THE FINAL APPEAL

We've talked about the appeals process, which is available to help you avoid paying your hefty medical bills. Perhaps the thought has crossed your mind (in exasperation with the system) that at least death would bring an escape from all the debts and forms.

Don't count on it. The folks at Medicare have given new meaning to the phrase "buried in paperwork," because your Medicare mess can follow you to the grave. Unless you know your rights, chances are your family will be haunted, not by your ghost but by your bills, and nasty collection agencies demanding payment.

Here's what you need to know to assure that the legacy you leave behind will only be your good deeds, not expenses for your family.

❖ GEM: The Family Has No Legal Duty to Pay

At your death, your children, nieces, nephews, cousins, etc. do *not* automatically become responsible for paying all your medical debts. Your estate, and in some states a surviving spouse, may be legally liable, but other individual family members are not.

When there is a large estate, there's no problem. All debts will be paid. But when the estate is not large enough to cover the medical bills, your family cannot be forced to pay unless they have signed an agreement to assume financial responsibility for your unpaid bills.

Not surprisingly, unpaid doctors, hospitals, and service providers aren't likely to tell you about this family "Bill of Rights"; they'd prefer to follow a "Rights of Bill." Chances are, your family will be made to feel as if it *is* their legal duty to pay. The pressure will be intense to "tidy things up as quickly as possible." As a result, bills often get paid with money out of the deceased family's pockets. If the relatives are rich, no problem; but it's another story when families must put their own financial futures at risk to pay bills owing to undue pressure.

◆　◆　◆

The issue of whether your heirs feel a *moral* obligation to pay is entirely separate, and clearly it is sensible for you to consider with your family how accounts will be settled. But the law puts no obligation on the family.

HELP!

All these facts and strategies may sound overwhelming. Don't despair; as we've said, the Government has done its best to make the system confusing. There's help available, and you should use it to your advantage. After all, your goal is to solve your problem in the most energy-efficient way possible. This means reducing unnecessary trips and phone calls.

The obvious trick is to make sure you ask the right person the right question in the first place. Calling Social Security, being put on hold for 20 minutes, and then learning that you called the wrong place is no sane person's idea of fun. Neither is hanging up and two minutes later discovering a question that's just right for Social Security in your next pile of papers.

These situations can only be avoided if you are organized (sorry, there's no other way!). So, your strategy for problem solving must include plotting your war on paper:

Divide and Conquer

Try to separate your troubles by type. Call your doctor to find out the status of your claims; doctors can be slow to file. You need to know where things stand— get the dates for when your bills were submitted to Medicare and copies of any claims that you don't already have. Now you can divide your health insurance papers into two or three groups: Medicare Part A, Medicare Part B, and Supplemental Insurance (if applicable). Then subdivide each group based on a claim's current status in the system:

- Claims not yet filed
- Claims filed (sort by date, oldest first)
- Claims completed correctly (*e.g.*, proper reimbursement received)
- Problem claims (*e.g.*, coverage unfairly denied or reimbursement too low)

Going through this paper-sorting process will serve several purposes. You will gain a sense of control (maybe there *is* hope), feel a small measure of satisfaction at having devised a workable system, and have an easier way to recognize the trouble spots. Your organizational efforts will prove invaluable when you seek help because the facts will all be in a file at your fingertips. To help with your organizational efforts, use our Health Insurance Claims Activity Log in Appendix 16.

Pack Up Your Troubles

Now look at the problem's level of difficulty and the source of the trouble. Try to think like a bureaucrat, and ask yourself: "How can I solve this problem, expending the least amount of time and effort. Can I do it or can I pass the buck to someone else?" When considering where to turn for help, think "small and local" first, then work your way up the bureaucratic scale.

Here is a list of possible resources for help:

- Family and friends
- Social workers or discharge planners at any health-care facilities used
- Local offices on aging or your community senior citizen center (if not listed in the telephone directory, call city hall)
- Local chapter of AARP
- Lawyers with expertise in Medicare (to get names: ask friends, call Legal Aid Society or the County Bar Association)
- Peer Review Organizations (see Appendix 18 for state by state listing)
- Part B Medicare Insurance Carrier (see Appendix 17 for toll-free numbers)
- Medigap or Supplemental Insurance service representative (check policy for address and telephone number for inquiries)
- Social Security (800-772-1213)

Another source of help worth considering is a Medicare claims assistance service. For a fee, these businesses will take over managing your Medicare mess. Prices and level of efficiency vary, so check a company out before signing on. (Get references.) A good service can be worth every penny. Your increased rate of return on claims filed should more than offset the cost of fees, and an added no-cost bonus is that you'll sleep much better because you're no longer battling the Medicare bureaucrats yourself.

Finally, we have provided a list of Health Care Financing Administration Regional Offices (Appendix 19). Personnel in these offices should be able to answer your questions.

·6·

Retirement Plans:
An Alphabet Soup That Spells Big Benefits

Social Security alone doesn't provide enough "security" for most older Americans. Many retirees depend on pension benefits, IRAs, and other retirement plans to gild their golden years. In this chapter, we tell you how you can mine your resources to add some glitter to your retirement.

First, we briefly explain the different types of retirement programs and how they work, just so we all understand each other. Then we get into the good stuff. We tell you how you can take money out of your retirement plan without giving too much of it to Uncle Sam. And we let you in on some Golden Opportunities for your retirement funds, like how to get an interest-free and tax-free loan from a pension plan or IRA; how to get to your pension funds before age 59½ *without a penalty;* and how to delay withdrawals from retirement funds until age 72. And there's lots more—just read on. Any one of our gems can save you thousands of dollars.

TYPES OF RETIREMENT PLANS

There is a wide variety of retirement plans, many with acronyms that sound more like brands of motor oil—IRAs, SEP, ESOP, HR10, pension, profit-sharing, 401(k), stock bonus, target benefit, and Keogh plans. How do you know which "brand" to choose? It's confusing, so we describe each one briefly.

IRA (Individual Retirement Account). Retirement plan designed to let individuals sock away money for the future. Anyone with earnings can set up an IRA; earnings do not include interest or dividends. You can put in as much as $2,000 each year ($2,250 for a couple with one spouse working, and $4,000 for a couple when both work). All money in an IRA grows tax-free until withdrawn from the account. Also, contributions may be deductible depending on income and other pension coverage.

Pension. Standard type of plan that requires the employer either to make annual contributions to a fund for your retirement (a defined-contribution plan), or to guarantee a particular benefit for you at retirement (a defined-benefit plan).

Profit-sharing. Just as it sounds, this retirement plan allows employers to share profits with employees. The employer decides on a total amount to contribute for employee retirement, based on the amount of profits, available cash, and employee relations. Once a total amount is decided, that amount is allocated to pension accounts for employees based on their compensation.

401(k). This is really a profit-sharing plan that lets employees set aside part of their wages, up to either 25 percent of pay or $8,728 (in 1992; the amount goes up each year), whichever is less. Because you don't receive the deferred wages, you don't pay income tax, and the amount set aside grows tax-free until withdrawn. The employer may also contribute.

Stock bonus. Another type of profit-sharing plan where at least part of the company's contribution is made as stock of the company. This plan may have tax benefits for employees, particularly if stock appreciates, because no tax is due on the appreciation until the stock is sold. See page 287.

Simplified Employee Pension (SEP). Yet another type of profit-sharing plan, this is primarily designed for small employers (fewer than 26 employees), although larger ones may use it. The employer contributes to IRA accounts for each employee. You pay no tax on the contribution, and your money grows tax-free until withdrawn. Employees have complete control and ownership of the account.

Employee Stock Ownership Plan (ESOP). Similar to stock bonus plans. Employer contributes company stock to retirement plans for employees, instead of cash. Employees get voting rights in stock held in the plan. May have tax benefits for employees, particularly if stock appreciates, because no tax is due on the appreciation, even when withdrawn, until the stock is sold.

Target benefit plan. A pension plan sometimes used by small employers (usually under 25 employees) to allow larger contributions to owners of the business and smaller amounts to other employees.

Keogh or HR-10. Retirement plans for self-employed individuals and partners who have not incorporated their business. You contribute a part of your wages or profits into a retirement fund. The contribution is tax deductible, and the money grows tax-free until withdrawn. The terms Keogh or HR-10 are no longer used in the pension laws, since the rules for retirement plans for individuals and companies aren't much different anymore. Now the terms that apply to company plans—pension, profit-sharing, 401(k), etc.—apply to individuals, too.

With the exception of IRAs, all of the retirement plans can be divided into two basic categories: defined-benefit and defined-contribution plans. We'll hold our detailed discussion of IRAs for later, since they're different.

In order to know where to begin digging for retirement gems, you first need to know whether you have a defined benefit or contribution plan. Check with the individual in charge of employee benefits where you work.

What Is a Defined-Benefit Plan?

A defined-benefit plan is based on a clearly defined "bottom line." Your employer promises to pay a certain fixed benefit to you upon retirement. The company then is supposed to set aside money each year so that there will be enough to pay you when the time comes. You are entitled to the promised benefit even when the company has failed to manage its finances well.

The amount of your benefit at retirement is based on a formula that considers your years with the company. The company has a choice of different formulas; Example 1 shows how this might work.

EXAMPLE 1

Your company has a defined-benefit plan, which sets your pension like this: you get 2 percent of your average highest pay, multiplied by years of service. You started work at age 25, and now 30 years later at 55 you're ready to retire. Your pay averaged $45,000 each year for the last three years, which was the most you had received.

Figure your retirement benefit like this: 2 percent per year multiplied by 30 years is 60 percent. Take 60 percent of $45,000, and your annual pension will be $27,000 per year (or $2,250/month). This is your guaranteed pension, regardless of how well or poorly the pension fund investments have done.

What Is a Defined-Contribution Plan?

A defined-contribution plan is based on employer contributions. The company does not guarantee you a particular benefit. Instead, the company agrees to make a certain contribution each year into a retirement account for you; usually the contribution is a percentage of your pay. Monies in your retirement account are invested. Your retirement account is like a bank or stock brokerage account: you benefit by gains in the account, but you lose if it goes down. Your benefit monies are *not* locked in until you retire—you get whatever is in your account at the time. This type of plan often is riskier.

EXAMPLE 2

You made $45,000/year for the last 10 years, and each year your employer contributed 15 percent of your pay to the plan. Assuming the funds in the plan earned 7 percent interest each year, the funds available to you at retirement would be $93,260.

But you can't count on any particular interest rate. Your pension investments might earn 10 percent, or they might lose money! Whatever is there when you retire, that's what you get. Timing is everything!

HOW MUCH WILL YOU GET?

How much will you get from a retirement plan? If you have an IRA, or if the contributions to some other retirement plan were all made by you, the answer is easy—whatever is there is what you get. But understanding the amount of your benefits available from a company pension plan when the company contributes is much tougher.

Years of Service

Whether you are in a defined-contribution or defined-benefit plan, the amount of your pension benefits will be based on the number of years with the company. The longer you work, the larger the pension.

As you near retirement, find out from the plan administrator (usually in the company benefits or personnel office) how many years they show you as working for the company. Make sure the records are right. Usually you get a full year of credit with 1,000 hours or more of work. And time off with pay, such as vacations, sickness, disability, or military duty, counts as work.

Your first year of work with an employer usually won't count; some exclude up to two years. And if you leave your employer for a year or more and then return, you may have to go through another waiting period of one to two years to rejoin the plan, and you might even lose the credits you had already earned for your years of work.

❖ GEM: Get Credit Where Credit Is Due

The rules for crediting service prior to a break are a little confusing, and plan administrators sometimes make mistakes. Don't let them! Your pre-break service must be counted after you've been back at work a year if either:

- You were vested (as of the time of the break) in the pension plan and the break was less than 5 years.
- You had no vested interest in the plan (at the time of the break), and the break was less than 5 years.
- You had no vested interest in the plan (at the time of the break), and the break was less than the number of years of pre-break service.

(If you were off work before 1976, the rules of the pension plan apply. If the plan says that you lose credit for earlier work, then, unfortunately, you're probably stuck.)

EXAMPLE 3

You started a new job at 48, and you worked for three years before suffering a serious injury. You were off work for two years before you were able to return. You then worked for 10 years, and now you're ready to retire.

When you check with the plan administrator, he says you've got 10 years of work credits. Of course you didn't expect to get credited for the two years you were out. But what about the three years before your injury—those should be counted, shouldn't they?

The answer is yes! Whether or not you were vested at the time of the break, your pre-break service should be counted since the break was less than 5 years. If the first year of work doesn't count for the pension, you should have 12 years of participation in the plan for purposes of calculating your benefits. If the company refuses to give you proper credit, get yourself a lawyer experienced in pension law.

✦ ✦ ✦

Some businesses used to set age limits for participating in a plan. If you continued working past 65, for example, your pension would not increase. After 1987, pension plans can no longer set maximum age limits. As long as you work, you benefit.

There are two other rules you should know about when trying to understand your retirement plan: vesting and integration.

Vesting: Only a Time In-Vestment Gets You Full Benefits

To get your full retirement benefits, under either a defined-benefit or defined-contribution plan, you must stay with your company for a fixed number of years—at that time, you're "fully vested." If you leave earlier, you will only get a portion of your retirement benefit.

There is no single rule establishing the time it takes to "vest." The law gives employers some leeway, and you'll have to check with your plan administrator to find your plan's rules. Tables 6.1 and 6.2 show typical vesting schedules:

TABLE 6.1

Typical Six-Year Vesting Schedule

Years of Service	Percentage Vested
1	0
2	20
3	40
4	60
5	80
6	100

TABLE 6.2

Typical Seven-Year Vesting Schedule

Years of Service	Percentage Vested
1	0
2	0
3	20
4	40
5	60
6	80
7	100

Let's say you are in a defined-contribution plan, and you leave the company after four years. Although your retirement account has $20,000, you won't get the whole amount. Using the six-year vesting schedule in Table 6.2, you'd get 60 percent, or $12,000; under the seven-year vesting schedule in Table 6.3, you'd get 40 percent or $8,000.

A defined-benefit plan works the same way. Let's say the benefit is 2 percent for each year of service multiplied by your average highest salary. After four years during which you earned $40,000 each year, your benefit at retirement would be $3,200 per year (8% of $40,000). But since you weren't "fully vested," your benefit is reduced; using the vesting schedule in Table 6.2, you'd only get $1,920 per year (60% of $3,200).

Vesting is an important protection. Your employer can't fire you a year before retirement age and bar you from any pension. Once you've put in the time, and your pension is vested, you have a legal right to it at retirement.

❖ GEM: Don't Let Them Exclude You Because of Your Age

If you take a job later in life, can your new employer keep you from joining the pension plan because you're "too old"? The answer is *no,* although some companies have tried. As of January 1, 1988, the rule is that you *cannot* be excluded because of age.

Vesting rules may limit the amount you actually receive, but at least if you've put in your time you can't be completely blocked from participating in the pension plan.

◆ ◆ ◆

Integration

Integration is a nasty rule allowing the employer to *cut* your retirement benefit by figuring in Social Security benefits. Integration can be used against you under either defined-contribution or defined-benefit plans. Examples 4 and 5 show how this sinister rule works.

EXAMPLE 4

You are in a defined-contribution plan. Your employer is to make contributions of 15 percent of your pay each year to your retirement account. If you made $20,000 last year, the contribution should be $3,000, right?

What you didn't know is that the plan is integrated with Social Security. Your employer's contributions will be linked to the Social Security wage base (currently $55,500). He is allowed to reduce his contribution on your behalf by about 5 percent. So instead of getting $3,000 (15% of $20,000), your retirement account only gets $2,000 (5% less).

EXAMPLE 5

You are in a defined-benefit plan, with the same facts as Example 1. Except this time the plan is integrated with Social Security.

Your pension will be about $18,000/year (or $1,500/month). Compare that to the $27,000 you would receive if the plan were not integrated (Example 1)—a 33 percent cut—and you can see the vile effect integration can have on your future income.

The impact of integration is even more severe for lower paid employees. An employee whose pay is under $25,000 can expect a reduction in retirement benefits of as much as *50 percent* due to integration!

As a result of a change in federal law, the portion of your pension attributable to years worked after 1988 can't be slashed to less than half. But you are unprotected for earlier years. You could possibly be left with no pension benefit at all!

Table 6.3 describes the basic rules for common types of retirement plans.

BEST WAYS TO TAKE YOUR IRA OR PENSION MONEY

As a result of many years of hard work, you've put together a retirement fund. How long should you let it sit? When should you start withdrawing money? What's the best way to do this? The answers to these questions may be worth many thousands of dollars to you and your family.

❖ GEM: Let Your Money Grow Tax-Deferred

As a general rule, the longer you can leave your money in an IRA or other retirement fund, the better off you'll be. Money in these plans grow *tax-deferred!* That means your nest egg grows quickly, while all the interest earned in these funds is allowed to accumulate until the time it's withdrawn.

EXAMPLE 6

Let's say you have $100,000. Put in a bank account, CD, or any other investment—but not in a retirement plan—you would have $172,000 after 10 years (assuming 8% interest rate and you are in a 28% tax bracket). The same money in an IRA would grow to $216,000—$44,000 more!

And the longer money is in a retirement fund, deferring taxes, the better. After 15 years, your money would be $226,000 if not in a retirement fund, but $317,000 if it was in a retirement fund.

◆ ◆ ◆

TABLE 6.3

Basic Rules for Most Common Retirement Programs

	Defined Contribution						Defined Benefit	Other
	SEP	Profit-sharing	Pension	401(k)	Keogh Profit-sharing	Keogh Pension	Pension Plan	IRA
Typical eligible participant	Worked for 3 of last 5 years and earned $374 in 1992	Age 21 and 1 year of service over 1,000 hours	Same as profit-sharing	Same as profit-sharing	Same as profit-sharing	Same as profit-sharing	Same as profit-sharing	Have earned income
Maximum deductible contribution	Lesser of 15% of pay or $30,000	Lesser of 25% of pay or $30,000 subject to employer limit of 15% of eligible wages	Lesser of 25% of pay or $30,000	Lesser of 25% of pay or $8,728 in 1992 adjusted for inflation, employer may add subject to limits	Lesser of $30,000 or 13.043% of earned income less ½ the self-employment tax	Lesser of $30,000 or 20% of earned income less ½ the self-employment tax	Amount necessary to fund for a benefit of $112,221 per year at age 65 (in 1992) adjusted for inflation	$2,000 or $2,250 if you have non-working spouse with a maximum of $2,000 per IRA. Deductible if not covered by a plan or if adjusted gross income is under $25,000 if single or $40,000 if married
Non-deductible contribution allowed?	No	No[1]	No[1]	No[1]	No[1]	No[1]	No[1]	Yes
Borrowing allowed?	No	Yes[2]	Yes[2]	Yes[2]	Yes,[2] except owner	Yes,[2] except owner	Yes[2]	No, except as a rollover
Vesting	Immediate	3 years 100% or 5 years 100% or 6 years graded or 7 years graded	Same as profit-sharing	Immediate except employer portion same as profit-sharing	Same as profit-sharing	Same as profit-sharing	Same as profit-sharing	Immediate

[1] The plan may allow for a nondeductible contribution, but such a provision is very unlikely.

[2] Borrowing is allowed if the plan contains a loan provision.

At some point, though, you will want to (or be required to by tax rules) withdraw funds from an IRA, pension, or profit-sharing plan. How and when you do this depends in part on your personal situation and in part on legal requirements.

IRAs

The rules covering IRAs are much simpler than the rules for company pension and profit-sharing plans; they provide a great deal of flexibility. Once you reach age 59½, you can take money from your IRA at *anytime* and in *any amounts* (though there are minimum withdrawal rules at age 70½—see page 279). You can withdraw the funds before age 59½, but you will pay a penalty for the early withdrawal. For each distribution you take from an IRA, whether before or after 59½, you pay income tax at your regular rate.

Pension and Profit-sharing Plans

The rules for getting your funds from a company pension or profit-sharing plan are not as simple. You can only collect your money in a company pension or profit-sharing fund when you reach the retirement age under the plan, leave the job, suffer a disability, or die. You can also take money from a profit-sharing plan (but not a pension) if you need the money due to a "hardship." A hardship withdrawal is allowed, at any age, if you have a pressing, immediate financial need that can't be satisfied from other sources—for example, payment of medical expenses (for you, your spouse, and dependents), purchase of a home (for you only), and payment of tuition for college or other post–high school education (for you, spouse, children or dependents) may all qualify. Of course, you will need to provide hard proof of your hardship.

You have much less flexibility in withdrawing funds from a pension or profit-sharing plan than from an IRA. With an IRA, you can take as much or as little as you want at any time after you reach 59½ (but before age 70½); for instance, you could take $4,000 one month; $300 the next; and then a year later take $10,000.

Most company pension or profit-sharing plans give a choice when you retire: you may either take all of your benefits all at once (called a lump sum), or you may take fixed monthly installments (called an annuity). And if you choose monthly installments, you may get them for either a fixed number of years, your lifetime (called a single-life annuity), or both you and your spouse's lifetimes (called a joint and survivor annuity). Once you have made the decision, you are locked in.

Will a lump sum or an annuity give you and your family the most money? Which type of annuity will yield the most benefits? Examples 7 to 10 illustrate the different options. For each example, we consider a 61-year-old man married to a 57-year-old woman.

EXAMPLE 7: LUMP SUM

You take $180,000 in one lump sum. If you invest that $180,000 at 8 percent and take interest and principal over 15 years, you and your spouse receive $1,720/month. The total payout over 15 years actually is $309,000.

EXAMPLE 8: MONTHLY PAYMENTS FOR A FIXED PERIOD

Instead of taking a lump sum, you choose monthly payments of $1,637 for 15 years; then payments will stop and there will be nothing left. (This is what a current commercial annuity pays.) Over the course of 15 years, you'll receive total payments of $294,660. If you die before 15 years are up, your heirs will get the rest of the payments; if you live beyond 15 years, the payments will still stop. You need a lump sum today of $171,297 (taking the present value) to yield those payments (interest and principal) over 15 years (assuming an 8% interest rate).

EXAMPLE 9: MONTHLY PAYMENTS FOR YOUR LIFE

You take your pension as monthly payments for the rest of your life. A current commercial annuity for a 61-year-old man pays $1,469/month (based on a life expectancy of 17½ more years). If you actually live 15 more years, you will receive $264,420 in total payments. If you live 19 more years (age 80), you will receive a total payout of $334,932. You need a lump sum today of $171,913 to yield those same payments over 19 years.

EXAMPLE 10: MONTHLY PAYMENTS
FOR YOUR AND YOUR SPOUSE'S LIVES

If you opt for a joint and 50 percent survivor annuity, you will receive $1,334/month for your life, and then after you die your wife will receive $667/month (half your benefit) until her death. If you live for 15 more years, and your wife lives for five years after your death, payments will total $280,140.

If you live 19 years, and your spouse lives 24 years, then you and your wife will receive a total payout of $344,172. You need a lump sum today of $163,344 to yield those same payments. Keep in mind that your monthly payments will be *less* if made over both your lives. That's because the pension plan will try to keep the total it would pay out about the same, whether paying just to you or for your spouse's life too. Simply extending the number of years of the payout will not increase the value of your pension.

Table 6.4 compares the results in Examples 7 to 10, as well as a few additional options.

TABLE 6.4

Retirement Payment Options*

Type of Payout	Amount of Payment	Value of Lump Sum Today
Lump sum	$180,000	$180,000
Lump sum of $180,000 invested at 8% and paid out over 15 years	$ 1,720/mo.	$180,000
Monthly payments over 15 years, fixed payout	$ 1,637/mo.	$171,297
Annuity for your life and you live 15 years	$ 1,469/mo.	$153,717
Annuity for your life and you live 19 years	$ 1,469/mo.	$171,913
Annuity for your life and you live 25 years	$ 1,469/mo.	$190,330
Annuity for your life but guaranteed payments for 15 years and you live exactly 15 years	$ 1,368/mo.	$143,148
Joint and 50% survivor annuity for lives of you and spouse; you live 15 more years and spouse lives 20 more years	$ 1,334/mo., then $667/mo.	$147,219
Joint and 50% survivor annuity for lives of you and spouse; you live 19 more years and spouse lives 24 more years	$ 1,334/mo., then $667/mo.	$163,344
Joint and 100% survivor annuity (which means your spouse gets the same benefit you were receiving) for lives of you and spouse; and second spouse to die lives another 20 years	$ 1,221/mo.	$145,976
Joint and 100% survivor annuity for lives of you and spouse, and second spouse to die lives another 24 years	$ 1,221/mo	$156,127

*Assumes 61-year-old male and 57-year-old female; male is retiring with $180,000 pension; and 8 percent discount factor.

As you can see from Table 6.4, you need a crystal ball to predict which is the best way to take your pension. So much depends on how long you will live. If you've got a foolproof way to predict life expectancy, write to us *immediately*—we'll make you rich!

While we can't tell you exactly which option is best for you, the following guidelines should help you to make the most of your pension or profit-sharing decision:

Consider taking a lump sum if:

- You are good at investing, or you want to give it a try (manage the funds yourself).

oundness of the insurance company that will be

ioney in the foreseeable future.
ig as the projections.
ites are likely to go up over the rest of your life.
ayments will be fixed and won't keep pace with

oth your and your spouse's lives are too little to
er monthly benefits over just one of your lives.)
it (less than $50,000). (If your total pension is
s your employer to *require* you to take it in one

; for your life if:

isks of investing. (The pension will be invested
be fixed.)
shot at living longer than the average person
guarantees, think *honestly* about your current
and longevity in your family.)
use, and it's your pension.

; for your and your spouse's joint lives if:

e pension, and you expect to outlive him. *Don't*
over his lifetime alone (unless you use our gem
on pages 275–276). You can't risk being left with nothing when he dies. You often have a legal right to demand he take payments to cover both your lives.
- Your spouse is the one with the pension, and neither of you is very good at holding on to your money. (Otherwise, a lump sum may be gone while you're still alive.)

Consider taking monthly payments for a fixed number of years if:

- You are in very bad health at the time you retire.

❖ GEM: A Spouse Gets Legal Protection

Many retirement plans automatically give special rights to spouses of covered workers. As the spouse of a worker, you may have a right to insist that your spouse take an annuity from his company for both your lives (a joint and 50% survivor annuity), so that you won't be left with nothing in case your spouse dies. If your husband or wife dies, you will be guaranteed for life at least half the amount you were receiving together.

To be entitled to these special spousal rights, you must have been married for at least a year before your spouse either started taking his pension or died ("close friends" is not close enough). As a result, your wedding date can be key to eligibility.

EXAMPLE 11

You dated for a number of years, but didn't get married until June 1, 1991. On February 1, 1992, your husband started taking his pension. On May 15 of the same year, he died. You would have no right to any part of his pension, because you weren't married for a full year before he started taking his pension or died. Had you two tied the knot just a few weeks earlier, you wouldn't have such a knotty problem now because you'd be protected under his pension plan.

❖ GEM: Take a Single Life Annuity When Spouse Is Older and Sick

As Example 12 shows, in some situations you may not need an annuity to protect a spouse.

EXAMPLE 12

You (the worker) are 60 and in good health; your spouse is 65 and in poor health. Should you choose a joint life or single life annuity?

If you choose a joint and 50 percent survivor annuity, you'd get $1,700/month for life, and on your death your spouse would get $850/month. An annuity for your life alone would be $2,000/month. Since you are likely to outlive your spouse, the higher annuity for your life alone makes a lot more sense.

✦ GEM: A Joint Life Annuity Is Better When Your Spouse Is Likely to Outlive You

Compare Example 13 for a situation where a joint life annuity is better than one for your life alone.

EXAMPLE 13

Let's reverse the facts of Example 12: you (the worker) are 65 and in poor health, and your spouse is fit as a fiddle and only 60. Now you'd be better off taking the joint and 50 percent survivor annuity which pays you $1,700/month for your life, and then pays your spouse $850/month on your death. Since your spouse is likely to outlive you, you don't want to leave her without sufficient income.

✦ GEM: Take a Single Life Annuity and Life Insurance

While a joint annuity offers your spouse added protection, it may cost you a lot of money. If you take an annuity for the lives of both you and your spouse, the monthly payments will be less than if you took the annuity for your life alone. And if your spouse dies first, you'll continue to get the *lesser* amount for the rest of your life—and then the payments will end when you die.

Here's a better idea for many couples. Take an annuity for your life only. Now use the extra monthly payments—the amount over what you'd get on a joint life annuity—and buy life insurance on your life, with your spouse as the beneficiary. If you die before your spouse, she gets the life insurance money, which should be enough to provide her at least as much monthly income as she would have received under a joint life annuity. So far, you and your spouse are no worse or better off than if you had opted for a joint life annuity.

But if your spouse dies first, you can now stop paying for your life insurance coverage and keep the entire monthly payments—which are higher than what you would be getting under a joint life annuity. Or you could keep the insurance policy and name your children or other heirs as the beneficiary. Either way, you're better off! Be careful that the insurance is not too costly because of your age or health.

EXAMPLE 14

You and your wife are both 55. At retirement, you can either take an annuity of $2,000 a month for your life only, or you can opt for an annuity that pays $1,700/month for your lifetime and $850/month to your wife after you die. You like the idea of providing for your wife after you're gone, but $300 a month ($2,000 minus $1,700) for the rest of your life is a stiff price to pay.

Take the $2,000/month annuity from the company for your life, and use the $300/month difference to buy whole or universal life insurance on your life. If you died at age 70, your wife would receive about $175,000 from the policy. Invested at 7 percent, she could draw monthly income of more than $1,000/month—*more* than she would have gotten under the company pension—*plus* she's got an extra $175,000 in the bank!

What if your wife dies before you? If you had opted for the joint annuity, you'd be stuck with $1,700/month. But if you had taken the $2,000/month single life annuity, using $300/month to buy life insurance, you could either: keep the insurance, which would pay your heirs at least $175,000 when you die; or cash in the insurance for $80,000 (cash value at age 70), and keep the entire $2,000/month pension for your personal use.

❖ GEM: Take a Lump Sum to Protect Retirement Funds from a Nursing Home

As you will see in Chapter 11, discussing catastrophic illness, almost all of your income must be used to pay the bills if you must enter a nursing home. The retirement funds you take as monthly payments for life will be spent on your long-term-care costs. But if you take your pension as a lump sum, the funds can be protected using the gems presented in Chapter 11.

EXAMPLE 15

You are retiring from your job with a nice pension fund. Your choice is to take a $180,000 lump sum or monthly payments of $1,467 for life.

If you opt for monthly checks and wind up in a nursing home ten years later, almost the entire amount of your monthly income will have to be turned over to the nursing home.

More important, if you take monthly pension payments and live in an income cap state (see Table 11.3), watch out! You could be locking yourself out of every nursing home in the state by permanently making yourself ineligible for Medicaid. See page 466.

Here's a better idea. Take a lump sum payment at retirement and put it into a Medicaid trust. The funds then will be protected from your long-term-care bills. For more information on Medicaid trusts, see page 490.

◆ ◆ ◆

You're not done figuring the best way to take your retirement funds until you consider the terrible *T* word—taxes. Depending on the state you live in, you may have to give up more than 40 percent of your retirement dollars to income taxes, and *more* to other penalty taxes. But if you take advantage of our gems, you can avoid costly, hidden tax traps into which many retirees fall. There are two types of taxes to worry about: income and excise taxes. We begin with income taxes, and tell how you can minimize or avoid them completely!

INCOME TAXES

The income tax rules are almost the same for IRAs, pension, and profit-sharing plans. The general rule is that all monies you receive are taxed as regular income.

If you had deducted from your income tax all contributions to your IRA when you made them, then all withdrawals are taxed. So on a $100,000 withdrawal, Uncle Sam gets $28,000 (28%).

When you receive payments from a pension or profit-sharing plan—either in a lump sum or on a monthly basis—you'll also pay income tax on the entire amount. There are some exceptions to this rule, which we'll discuss shortly.

Since income tax rates go up based on income received, wouldn't you be better off always taking lower monthly payments (to keep you in a lower tax bracket) rather than one larger lump sum payment? Most people think so. Unfortunately, that's too simple an approach and can cost you a lot of money. In many cases, you pay a *higher* tax on lower monthly retirement benefits than on a larger lump sum. This is due to two reasons: the hidden tax on pension payments, and the availability of some special tax-cutters for lump-sum distributions.

❖ GEM: Watch Out for
the Hidden Tax on Pension Payments

If you are receiving Social Security, as most older Americans are, your "effective" tax on monthly pension payments may be higher than you think, because the pension makes Social Security benefits taxable.

Example 16 demonstrates the hidden tax on monthly retirement benefits. While this example shows taxes jumping from 2 to 20 percent, the rate can go even higher. You can't ignore the hidden tax when deciding whether to opt for monthly payments or a lump sum.

EXAMPLE 16

Let's say you are single and collecting $12,000 of Social Security. You earn $8,000 from a part-time job, and you receive $17,000 of tax-exempt interest from your investments. In this case, $3,000 of your Social Security benefits would be taxable, and your total federal income tax would be $630. This means you'd be paying tax on less than 2 percent of your total income.

Now you elect to take pension payments of $10,000/year. With the pension, $6,000 of your Social Security benefits become taxable, and your total federal income tax would skyrocket to $2,580. In other words, you'd be paying tax on the pension at a rate of almost 20 percent—*ten times* the tax rate on your income before you took the pension.

◆ ◆ ◆

While the tax on monthly payments is likely to be *higher* than you suspected, the tax on a lump sum may be lower—with our special tax-cutting gems. *Golden Rule:* Take your lumps and save on taxes.

When you get a lump sum, reduce or eliminate income tax with these little-known money-saving techniques:

- Rollover to IRA
- Five-year averaging
- Ten-year averaging
- Special capital gains treatment
- Distributions for tax-deductible expenses
- Stock distributions
- Distributions to cover underpaid withholding taxes
- Distributions of nondeductible contributions
- Move to Florida or Texas

The five-year and ten-year averaging and special capital gains treatment options are available for lump-sum distributions from a pension or profit-sharing plan; they are *not* available for withdrawals for IRAs. To use these three options, you must fill out IRS Form 4972. (We have provided completed sample calculations in Appendix 20.) Now let's discuss each of these valuable tax-cutters.

Tax-Cutter 1: Rollover to IRA

For most people who don't need to use their company retirement money right away, rolling it into an IRA (or other retirement plan) is the best strategy. This option allows you to build your wealth quickly and easily. And you can use it at any age. Here's how it works:

You take the company retirement funds in one lump sum and deposit them into a "rollover IRA" at your bank, broker, or other financial institution. The rollover IRA can be an existing one, but it's usually best to open a new IRA since there are some restrictions on mingling. Also, as we will explain later (pages 292, 302–303), there are some advantages to having more than one IRA. If deposited into a rollover IRA within 60 days of the payment, you pay *no tax* at that time. You don't have to deposit the whole amount of the distribution, but you'll pay tax on any portion that is not rolled over.

Beginning in 1993, the retirement funds will have to be transferred directly from the company plan to the IRA custodian in order to avoid a new 20 percent federal tax withholding. If the transfer is not direct (you take the company retirement funds yourself and deposit them into a rollover IRA within 60 days), the Government will take 20 percent of the entire amount off the top. To roll your retirement funds over tax free, you would then have to replace the 20 percent withholding amount from your own bank account. You don't lose the 20 percent forever—if you are making quarterly estimated tax payments, you could reduce your next payments by the 20 percent withheld, or at worst you would "recover" the withheld money when you file your federal income tax return the following April 15. For an example of how this works, see pages 301–302.

As long as the money sits in the rollover IRA, it accumulates income—interest and/or dividends—and you don't pay any tax on the income. Here's how this powerful tool can work for you.

EXAMPLE 17

You retire at age 61 and receive a lump-sum pension of $180,000 and roll the entire amount into an IRA. You pay no tax at that time.

The money earns 8 percent interest in various investments. You don't pay tax as the money grows, because it's in an IRA. By age 70½ (nine years after rolling the money over), your pension will have *doubled*—you now have $360,000. That's the beauty of a rollover.

At age 70½, the tax rules require you to start taking money out of the IRA. As you take money out, that's when you pay tax—at your regular income tax rates

(5- or 10-year averaging won't be available). But if you take out only the smallest amount possible, your IRA actually will continue to *grow!*

EXAMPLE 18

You and your spouse are 70½. You have $360,000 in your IRA and you must begin taking distributions.

If the fund earns 8 percent and you take the smallest amount required ($22,000 in the first year), the balance in your IRA will be $420,000 in 5 years; $434,000 in 10 years; and $407,000 in 15 years! For more on taking money from IRAs, see pages 289–293, 297–298, 300–303.

If you get a lump-sum payment before you reach age 59½ (unless it's due to the death of another), you are almost always best off rolling it into an IRA. Otherwise, you're sure to get socked with a stiff income and excise tax.

The IRA rollover has another benefit: once the money is in the IRA, you can get to it very easily. You may take out as little or as much as you like or need at *any time* (except there are minimum withdrawal rules at age 70½—see pages 296–299).

What are the down sides? A rollover can only be used if you leave your employer, your employer terminates the entire company's pension plan, you become disabled, or you die, and (in 1992) the distribution into the IRA is at least half of your total in the retirement plan. (Beginning in 1993, partial distributions of *any* amount from a company plan or IRA, other than under a plan to take out substantially equal periodic payments over a long period [see pages 289–292], are eligible for rollover.) Also, you cannot use 5- or 10-year averaging when taking money from the IRA.

❖ GEM: If a New Job Is in Your Future, Roll Over into a Temporary IRA or Keogh

As we have explained, if you are leaving a company, the money in your 401(k), Keogh, or other pension or profit-sharing plan may be distributed to you in a lump sum. You then have the choice of paying income tax on the entire amount or rolling the funds into an IRA and deferring any tax. But when you finally withdraw money from your rollover IRA, you will pay income tax at your current rates; five- and ten-year averaging (discussed below) can't be used to cut the tax.

Here's a way out of that problem. When you roll your lump sum into an IRA, set up a new one just for these funds; don't roll into an existing IRA. And don't make additional contributions to your new IRA in the future.

If you keep the rollover IRA totally separate from other funds, and you later go back to work, you may roll that money back into another company 401(k), Keogh, or other pension or profit-sharing plan (if the new plan permits). If you go into business for yourself, you can set up a Keogh and roll the IRA into that plan. Once you've been in the new retirement plan for five years, you regain the opportunity to use five- or ten-year averaging. As we discuss below, this can save you thousands of dollars in taxes.

✦ ✦ ✦

You may cut the tax on lump-sum distributions from pension, profit-sharing, stock bonus, Keogh, and ESOP plans (but not IRAs or SEPs) using five- or ten-year averaging, and 20 percent capital gain treatment if:

- You were 50 years or older on January 1, 1986 (56 or older on January 1, 1992).
- You participated in the retirement plan for at least five years (unless you die before).
- The lump sum is being paid because you died, reached age 59½ (or older), are disabled, or left the job (for any reason).

You can roll a lump-sum payment into an IRA at *any* age. But you can't use ten-year averaging unless you were at least 50 on January 1, 1986, and you can't use five-year averaging until you reach age 59½. If you are the beneficiary of a lump sum earned by someone else, you can still use these tax-savers if the employee who earned the money satisfied the requirements listed above. For example, the employee, not you, must have been 50 on January 1, 1986.

NOTE

Averaging and capital gains tax-cutters are *not* available for withdrawals from IRAs.

Tax-Cutter 2: Five-Year Averaging

As you can see from the example that follows, if you had to pay tax at regular rates on the entire amount of a lump-sum pension, few would ever take that option—the price would be too high.

EXAMPLE 19

You are single, your only income is the pension, and you receive a $200,000 one-time distribution. If you paid tax at regular rates on the entire amount, your tax would be more than $55,000!

Compare the tax on monthly distributions for life of $1,250. Your tax would be much less: only about $1,400/year. After 14 years, you would have received more than $200,000, while your total tax paid would amount only to $19,600. That's quite a difference!

Fortunately, you may not have to pay tax at regular rates on the full lump-sum distribution. If you are at least 59½ when you take the pension money, you can cut the tax on a lump-sum distribution by using five-year averaging. Here's how five-year averaging works:

Let's say you are entitled to a $100,000 lump sum. Divide your lump sum by 5—in this example that would be $20,000. You then calculate the tax on $20,000 using tax rates for a single person (even if you are married). Multiply by 5, and that's what you must pay when April 15 arrives. In other words, you still pay tax on $100,000, but at the lower rates for $20,000 rather than for $100,000. The calculation is done on IRS Form 4972. Sound complicated? To make things easier, we've prepared Table 6.5, which tells you the tax on lump-sum distributions using five-year averaging.

TABLE 6.5

Five-Year Averaging*

Distribution	Tax You Must Pay on Distribution
$0–$20,000	7.5% of distribution
$20,000–$70,000	$1,500 plus 18% of excess over $20,000
$70,000–$107,250	$10,500 plus 15% of excess over $70,000
$107,250–$259,500	$16,088 plus 28% of excess over $107,250
over $259,500	$58,718 plus 31% of excess over $259,500

* Numbers in Table 6.5 are based on 1992 tax rates; amounts will differ slightly in future years.

As you can see from Table 6.5, on a lump sum payment of $100,000, you would pay tax of $15,000 using five-year averaging ($10,500 + 15% of 30,000). Without five-year averaging, you'd pay $24,825 tax on the same amount (assuming you are single with no other income). The tax savings is most dramatic for lump sums of less than $250,000. You pay tax only one time—after that, the money is yours, just like any other monies you have.

If you were at least 50 years old on January 1, 1986 (56 or older on January 1, 1992), you have two more options to cut your tax on a lump-sum payment: ten-year averaging and 20 percent capital gain.

Tax-Cutter 3: Ten-Year Averaging

Ten-year averaging works just like five-year averaging, except that you can spread the amount (for tax purposes) over ten years, and you use 1986 tax rates. Table 6.6 shows the tax on lump-sum payments using ten-year averaging.

TABLE 6.6

Ten-Year Averaging

Distribution	Tax You Must Pay on Distribution
0–$ 20,000	5.5% of the distribution
20,000– 21,583	$ 1,100 plus 13.2% of excess over $20,000
21,583– 30,583	1,309 plus 14.4% of excess over 21,583
30,583– 49,417	2,605 plus 16.8% of excess over 30,583
49,417– 67,417	5,769 plus 18.0% of excess over 49,417
67,417– 70,000	9,009 plus 19.2% of excess over 67,417
70,000– 91,700	9,505 plus 16.0% of excess over 70,000
91,700– 114,400	12,977 plus 18.0% of excess over 91,700
114,400– 137,100	17,063 plus 20.0% of excess over 114,400
137,100– 171,600	21,603 plus 23.0% of excess over 137,100
171,600– 228,800	29,538 plus 26.0% of excess over 171,600
228,800– 286,000	44,410 plus 30.0% of excess over 228,800
286,000– 343,200	61,570 plus 34.0% of excess over 286,000
343,200– 423,000	81,018 plus 38.0% of excess over 343,200
423,000– 571,900	111,342 plus 42.0% of excess over 423,000
571,900– 857,900	173,880 plus 48.0% of excess over 571,900
857,900– -------	311,160 plus 50.0% of excess over 857,900

❖ GEM: Take Ten-Year Averaging for Smaller Amounts

With lump-sum payments of less than $390,000, you'll almost always be better off choosing ten-year averaging rather than five-year averaging. For larger distributions, five-year averaging is usually better. For example, a $100,000 payment will cost you $15,000 in taxes under five-year averaging and only $14,471 with ten-year averaging—a savings of more than $500!

❖ GEM: Use Ten-Year Averaging for Distributions Before Age 59½

You can use ten-year averaging (but not five-year averaging) if you take a lump-sum pension before reaching age 59½ *if* the payment is made due to death, disability, or termination of employment (for any reason, including retirement, firing, or layoff). But don't rush to take a pension before reaching 59½—you'll still be forced to pay a 10 percent excise tax unless the payment is made due to death or disability (see pages 289–290).

❖ GEM: Save State Taxes Too!

As an added bonus, a few states such as Ohio won't charge any state income tax if you use five- or ten-year averaging. Those same states probably *will* charge income tax if you don't average.

❖ GEM: Take Your Lumps All at Once

You can use five- or ten-year averaging only once in a lifetime. So don't get caught in a costly trap if you're covered by more than one pension plan. Take all lump-sum payments in one year, then you can apply five- or ten-year averaging to the combined amounts.

If you can't take all lump sum payments in one year, think carefully before using averaging. Decide whether you'll be better off using it now or waiting for a larger distribution.

There's an exception to this rule allowing only one-time use of averaging: if you took a lump-sum pension and used income averaging (five- or ten-year) before 1987, you may still use this tax-cutter one more time.

❖ GEM: It May Not Be Too Late, Even If You Took the Lump Sum Years Ago

Five- and ten-year averaging may sound good to you, but what if you took your lump-sum distribution a couple of years ago—before reading this book—and didn't take advantage of these gems. Is it too late?

No! You usually have until three years after the federal tax return was filed or two years after you paid the tax, whichever is longer, to go back and use averaging. For example, if you retired in 1989, and filed your tax return on April 15, 1990, you have until April 15, 1993, to amend the return and use the averaging strategy. Uncle Sam will have to give you some money back!

◆ ◆ ◆

Tax-Cutter 4: Capital Gains

If you were covered by a pension plan before 1974, you can have part of your lump-sum payment taxed at a maximum 20 percent rate. This 20 percent capital gains tax may be better than five- or ten-year averaging for some people.

Here's how to calculate how much of your pension payment is eligible for the 20 percent capital gains rate. Figure the total number of months you've been in the plan, and divide that number into the number of months you were in the plan before 1974. Multiply that fraction by the total pension payment, and that tells you how much is eligible for the 20 percent capital gains tax. How about an example to help you through this confusing calculation?

EXAMPLE 20

You've been in the pension plan for 216 months (18 years), and 36 months (three years) of this time were pre-1974. The lump-sum payment is $286,000. Divide 36 into 216; that gives ⅙. Multiply ⅙ by $286,000, and the result is $47,700. So $47,700 is eligible for 20 percent capital gains tax.

If you used 20 percent capital gains for $47,700 and ten-year averaging for the rest, your tax would be $56,800. If you used ten-year averaging for the whole payout, your tax would be $61,570—almost $5,000 more!

The pension administrator will figure the capital gains if you'd like. Form 1099R, which you get in January of the year following the year of distribution (*e.g.,* if you get the money June 1991, you'll get the form January 1992), will also list how much of the lump sum is eligible for the 20 percent capital gains tax.

When you opt for the 20 percent capital gains tax for a portion of your lump sum, you may still choose to use five- or ten-year averaging for the rest.

❖ GEM: Take 20 Percent
Capital Gains If You've Got Capital Losses

Five- or ten-year averaging on the entire distribution usually is better than the 20 percent capital gains tax unless the portion of the distribution earned after

1974 is more than $114,000 or so. But if you've got capital losses, such as losses on the sale of stock or real estate, then the 20 percent capital gains tax may be a big benefit at any level!

EXAMPLE 21

Your lump-sum pension is $180,000, and $30,000 of that is eligible for the 20 percent capital gains tax. You also have other taxable income of $35,000, and you sold stock this year at a loss of $20,000.

Are you better off taking the 20 percent capital gains tax, or should you use five- or ten-year averaging for the full amount? With a sizable capital loss like this, you're almost always better off with the 20 percent capital gains tax. Let's run the numbers:

Strategy	Tax You Must Pay
20% capital gains tax on $10,000 ($30,000–$20,000), 10-year averaging for the rest	$26,570
20% capital gains tax on $30,000 (no capital loss), 10-year averaging for the rest	$30,570
10-year averaging on whole amount	$31,722
5-year averaging on whole amount	$36,458

✦ ✦ ✦

Tax-Cutter 5: Distributions for Tax-Deductible Expenses

Can you take money out of your pension, IRA, or other retirement fund without paying even the regular income tax? The answer is yes with this valuable tax-cutter!

Take taxable distributions and use them for tax-deductible costs. That way, you end up getting your pension money tax-free!

EXAMPLE 22

You would like to add a family room and a new roof to your home. So you take a loan on your home for construction costs, and you must pay it back at $600/month.

Now withdraw $600/month from your IRA or other retirement plan to make the payments. The income tax on the distributions will be offset by the loan repayment, most of which is deductible interest. What's the result? You get to use your pension funds with almost no tax!

This technique works regardless of the use of the money. Instead of adding a family room, you might want to take a trip, pay off medical bills, or give gifts to your kids. Whatever the reason, you can fund it through a deductible loan against your home and then pay it off with a virtually tax-free retirement fund distribution.

Tax-Cutter 6: Stock Distributions

Many companies, particularly large ones, contribute shares of their stock to employee retirement plans, or use company retirement funds to invest in their company stock. If you participate in this type of plan, you will probably get the choice to take your distribution in company stock or cash. In many cases, "taking stock" of your situation can save you a lot of money.

EXAMPLE 23

You are ready to retire, and your company plan has $100,000. You are going to take a lump sum and use five-year averaging for the tax. But you may take $80,000 of company stock and $20,000 of cash, or all $100,000 in cash—is there any difference?

If you take the $100,000 in cash, you'll pay a tax of $15,000 (using five-year averaging). That's not too bad, but you can do better!

The company figures that the value of the stock, at the time it was added to your retirement fund over the years, totals $50,000 (the stock has appreciated since). If you take the stock as part of your lump-sum distribution, you will be taxed only on $70,000 ($50,000 of stock and $20,000 of cash). That's because you will be taxed on the cost of the stock to the company, not on the current appreciated value. The tax you'll pay is $10,500—an immediate savings of $4,500 over taking the entire lump sum in cash.

You then hold the company stock for five more years, and the stock continues to go up in value. You pay no tax on the appreciation until you sell. If you sell the stock for $100,000, you'll pay long-term capital gains tax on $50,000 ($100,000 minus the original values of $50,000), as you normally would do. But you've deferred the tax for a good many years.

Tax-Cutter 7: Distribution of Nondeductible Contributions

If a portion of your IRA (or pension) contributions were nondeductible when you made them, then some of your withdrawals will be income tax–free. Here is an example of how it works:

EXAMPLE 24

You have $100,000 in IRAs; of that, $15,000—or 15 percent of the total—was not deductible when you contributed to the IRA.

You now withdraw $5,000. You must pay income tax, but *not* on the whole amount. Since 15 percent of your IRA was from nondeductible contributions, 15 percent of your withdrawal is not taxable. So $750 (15% of $5,000) of your withdrawal escapes income tax; only $4,250 will be taxed.

If you are making IRA contributions, tell the bank or IRA manager whether or not the contribution is deductible; let them keep track of the totals for you. If you make a nondeductible contribution, file an IRS Form 8606 with your regular income tax return. That form shows the total market value of the IRA and the amount of nondeductible contributions. From this information, you should be able to figure the portion of your IRA distribution that is tax-free.

Tax-Cutter 8: Move!

Folks living up North often consider the greatest benefit of retiring to the South to be a warmer climate. Here's another hot tip: if you move to Florida or Texas before taking money from your retirement fund, you won't pay any *state* income tax, since those states don't have one.

PENALTY OR EXCISE TAXES

In addition to the regular income tax on retirement fund—pensions, IRAs, 401(k)s, Keoghs, etc.—payments or withdrawals, you may get hit with three types of penalty or excise taxes if you're not careful:

1. A 10 percent penalty tax on distributions (monthly or lump sum) taken before age 59½.
2. A 15 percent excise tax on a distribution over $150,000 that is not a lump sum (you can take $150,000 with no 15 percent penalty); $750,000 if taken as a lump sum and five- or ten-year averaging is used.
3. A 50 percent penalty tax for failing to take required distributions starting at age 70½.

Again, we tell you what these income drainers are—and how to minimize or avoid them.

10 Percent Penalty Tax

The 10 percent penalty taxes can really hurt. In most cases, you shouldn't take a retirement-fund distribution until after you're 59½. If you retire or leave your employer before age 59½ and get a lump sum, you'll usually be smart to immediately roll it into an IRA or other retirement plan so there won't be any penalty.

EXAMPLE 25

You are 50 years old and have $100,000 in pension funds. You're buying a house and take $50,000. Since you are under 59½, you pay the 10 percent excise tax—$5,000—*plus* income tax on that $50,000.

There are a number of situations where early distributions before age 59½ avoid the 10 percent penalty tax. These include:

- Payments to a beneficiary after the death of an employee, regardless of the employee's and beneficiary's ages
- Payments to a disabled employee regardless of his age
- Substantially equal payments made at least annually over your life expectancy (or you and a beneficiary's joint life expectancies), no matter how old you are when they start
- Payments if you are at least 55 and have left your employer (this exception applies to all retirement funds except IRAs)
- Payment of an amount equal to your deductible medical expenses, over the 7½ percent adjustable gross income floor (see page 292)
- Payments after a divorce pursuant to court order

The following gems can help you use these rules to avoid the 10 percent excise tax.

❖ GEM: Before 59½, Take Substantially Equal Payments to Get Your Money Without a Penalty!

After age 59½, you can take as much or as little from your pension, IRA, or other retirement funds, and you'll only pay regular income tax—at most. But if you are younger than 59½, you're looking at a stiff 10 percent penalty tax. Would you like a way around this nasty problem? Then take "substantially equal periodic payments."

Generally, you can avoid the 10 percent penalty tax on early distributions from any retirement plan by taking substantially equal periodic payments, at least annually, over your life (or the lives of you and a designated beneficiary). While there are several ways to calculate the payments, the easiest is just to take the total amount in the fund (on the first day of the year) and divide by your life expectancy as found in Table 6.7.

TABLE 6.7

Life Expectancy (Without Regard to Sex)

Age	Life Expectancy	Age	Life Expectancy
50	33.1	75	12.5
51	32.2	76	11.9
52	31.3	77	11.2
53	30.4	78	10.6
54	29.5	79	10.0
55	28.6	80	9.5
56	27.7	81	8.9
57	26.8	82	8.4
58	25.9	83	7.9
59	25.0	84	7.4
60	24.2	85	6.9
61	23.3	86	6.5
62	22.5	87	6.1
63	21.6	88	5.7
64	20.8	89	5.3
65	20.0	90	5.0
66	19.2	91	4.7
67	18.4	92	4.4
68	17.6	93	4.1
69	16.8	94	3.9
70	16.0	95	3.7
71	15.3	96	3.4
72	14.6	97	3.2
73	13.9	98	3.0
74	13.2	99	2.8
		100	2.7

Source: Treasury Regulation Section 1.72–9.

EXAMPLE 26

You are 50 years old and have $150,000 in your IRA (rolled over from your company's pension plan). You'd like to buy a house, and you could use some help with the monthly payments.

At your age, your life expectancy is 33.1 years. (See Table 6.7.) Take $150,000 and divide by 33.1; the result is $4,532. That's the amount you can take from your IRA in the first year (or $377/month) without paying any penalty tax. If the IRA has $160,000 at the beginning of the next year (having gone up due to accumulated interest and dividends), you divide that amount by 32.2 (life expectancy at age 51), to get a $4,969 or $414/month payment. You would do a calculation like this each year.

Although you pay no 10 percent penalty tax, you normally would still pay regular income tax on equal periodic distributions. But in this example, you don't even pay income tax because the distributions are used to pay deductible mortgage payments. The deduction offsets the income tax, so you get your pension money tax-free—at age 50!

Equal periodic distributions are based on your life expectancy, but that doesn't necessarily mean you must continue them for life. You must take these distributions for at least five years and you cannot alter or stop the payout until you reach 59½. At that point you may change the payment schedule, stop payments altogether, or take a lump sum.

EXAMPLE 27

You are 50 years old and have $150,000 in your IRA. Your child is starting college, and you could use some help paying the costs.

Using equal periodic payments from your IRA, you can take $4,532 the first year, adjusted each year after that. Although you'll pay income tax on that amount (say $1,300/year), you'll escape any penalty tax and you'll have enough left to help pay the school tuition.

Once your child is done with school and you have reached age 59½, you don't need to continue taking the pension payments. You can halt the payments and let your money grow in the IRA.

To cash in on this periodic payment gem, you usually must have your funds in IRAs, Keoghs (if you are the owner and can control the payment), or SEPs. Company pension rules generally won't let you start taking funds early.

❖ GEM: Maximize Flexibility by Splitting Retirement Funds

By splitting your retirement funds among IRAs, Keoghs, or SEPs, you can increase your options to take money before age 59½, *without* paying any excise taxes. Example 28 shows how.

EXAMPLE 28

You are 55 and would like to add about $250/month to your income. How about tapping your retirement funds?

You've got $150,000 in an IRA, and your life expectancy is 28.6 years. Using equal periodic payments to avoid any penalty would mean you'd have to take $5,245 the first year (more after that), which is more than you need.

How about rolling your funds into two IRAs, one with $90,000 and the other with $60,000? Now you can take equal annual payments from the $90,000 IRA, giving you $3,146 in the first year—about $260/month. And you can leave the other IRA to grow tax-free.

❖ GEM: Use Distributions to Pay Deductible Medical Expenses

We've already described how you can avoid income tax on retirement-fund distributions used to pay tax-deductible expenses (page 286). If the expenses are medical expenses over 7½ percent of your adjusted gross income, you can *also* avoid the 10 percent penalty tax.

EXAMPLE 29

You are 55 and require expensive medical care that is not covered by insurance. Your bills total $50,000.

The first 7.5 percent ($3,750) you pay from your regular savings account. The rest you take from your IRA, even though you haven't reached 59½. No problem! You will avoid any penalty tax because you used the IRA funds for deductible medical expenses.

❖ GEM: A Divorce Might Not Be a Taxing Experience

You are 50 and would like to get to your pension funds without paying the 10 percent tax. Think about getting a "friendly" divorce. Example 30 explains how.

EXAMPLE 30

You are ready to retire, and you and your wife want to buy a boat and travel the world. You are only 53, though, and would pay a $20,000 (10%) penalty tax on your $200,000 pension fund if you took the money now.

You and your wife decide to divorce; since you are a nice guy you give your wife the $200,000 pension as the settlement. Since the funds come to her through a divorce, she pays no penalty tax (though she still pays income tax). Your ex-wife buys a boat and sets sail for Australia. Maybe, if you're nice, she'll invite you to join her as her "first mate"!

◆ ◆ ◆

15 Percent Excise Tax

The 15 percent excise tax doesn't affect too many people since it only applies to very large distributions ($150,000 if not taken as a lump sum; $750,000 if taken as a lump sum). And there are simple ways to avoid the tax.

Rolling the money into an IRA or another retirement plan avoids the 15 percent excise tax. Taking less than these amounts in one year, and the rest in another year, also avoids the tax. You avoid the tax on a distribution of more than $150,000 (but less than $750,000) if taken as a lump sum and five- or ten-year averaging is used. Payments made as a result of the employee's death also won't get socked with a penalty tax, no matter how large. But large amounts accumulated in a retirement plan and not distributed will be clipped at a 15 percent excise tax rate at the time of your death, unless all is left to a surviving spouse.

EXAMPLE 31

You are 50 years old and withdraw $200,000 from your pension fund to buy a house. What's the tax hit?

- Income tax = $60,000 (30% × $200,000)—this is figured by looking at standard tax tables.
- 15 percent excise tax = $7,500 (15% × [$200,000 – $150,000])—you pay the 15 percent excise tax on the amount over $150,000 (see page 288).

- 10 percent penalty tax = $15,000 (10% × $150,000) (the 10% penalty tax does not apply to the $50,000 which is subject to the 15% excise tax)—the 10 percent tax is a penalty for "early withdrawals" (see page 288).

The total tax would be $82,500, or almost half of your entire retirement pot. Wow!

The 10 percent penalty and 15 percent excise taxes can devastate your retirement funds. If you are leaving a job before age 59½ and have accumulated a sizable pot of money, here are some gems on how to bury your stash, so you won't lose cash!

❖ GEM: If You Don't Need the Money Right Away, Roll It into an IRA and Take Out Smaller Amounts

If you won't need to use a big chunk of your retirement funds right away, you're usually best off rolling the funds into an IRA.

EXAMPLE 32

You leave your job at 58, and your retirement plan has $600,000. If you took it all out immediately, you could use five- or ten-year averaging. You'd also avoid the 15 percent excise tax because you used averaging with a lump-sum payout of less than $750,000. But because you're under 59½, you'd still pay a 10 percent penalty tax. Total income and penalty taxes would be about $225,000.

Here's a better idea. Take the lump sum and roll it into an IRA. Since you don't need the money right away, it continues to grow tax-deferred. And after you reach age 59½, the law says you can take up to $150,000/ year without paying any penalty or excise tax at all (see page 289). By age 65, you could withdraw all your funds, and you'd pay a total income tax of only about $180,000—a $45,000 savings!

❖ GEM: If You Do Need a Large Amount Right Away, Don't Fall into the IRA Trap

Many people make a big mistake when they leave a job. They roll their lump sum into an IRA without anticipating big expenses ahead. This is often a very costly error.

EXAMPLE 33

Let's start with the same facts as in Example 32. You leave your job at 58 and roll your funds into an IRA. Why? You are smart—you want to avoid the 10 percent (early withdrawal) penalty tax.

At age 60, you need the money for a major purchase, maybe a boat and condo in Hawaii. So you withdraw the entire amount. Of course, you always pay income tax, though no five- or ten-year averaging is available now. You have managed to avoid the 10 percent penalty tax because you are now 60. Congratulations are in order, right? Wrong!

Now you've bought yourself a 15 percent excise tax. Since you can't use five- or ten-year averaging, you must pay a 15 percent excise tax on any withdrawal over $150,000. So you've got a total income and excise tax of about $250,000—*more* than if you had taken the money immediately (and paid the income tax and 10% penalty tax) when you retired!

Before deciding how to handle your retirement funds, think about your needs in the next few years. If you won't need a large sum (over $150,000) right away, roll into an IRA. But if you can see the need to take out big amounts right away, pay the 10 percent penalty tax rather than the 15 percent excise tax.

❖ GEM: Freeze a Retirement Fund Until the Upper Excise Tax Limit Catches Up

If you have retirement funds of more than $150,000 in pension and profit-sharing plans, you have still another option to cut your distribution costs.

EXAMPLE 34

You own a business, and you have $300,000 in a profit-sharing plan and $650,000 in a pension plan. Since you are only 58, you don't do anything yet.

At age 60, you start taking $75,000/year—the total of the interest and dividends from *both* retirement funds—but you take the whole amount from the profit-sharing plan. In about seven years, the profit-sharing plan will be used up, while the pension plan has grown to $950,000.

By that time, the $750,000 excise tax threshold for lump-sum distributions should have gone up to more than $950,000 (owing to indexing). You then could take a lump-sum distribution from the pension plan and elect five- or ten-year averaging to cut the income tax. You'd pay *no* excise tax at all.

◆   ◆   ◆

50 Percent Penalty Tax

Once you reach age 70½, Uncle Sam requires that you begin taking some of your retirement money out and pay tax on it. This applies to money in IRAs as well as Keoghs and company pension plans. The rule is firm, even if you are still working. In order to force you to do so, the Government imposes a whopping 50 percent excise tax on the difference between what you withdrew and what you were supposed to withdraw.

EXAMPLE 35

You are 70½ and widowed, with a retirement fund of $360,000. The law requires you to take $22,500 (¹⁄₁₆). If you only distribute $10,000, you will owe a 50 percent tax on $12,500 ($22,500 − $10,000)—or $6,250. And that's in *addition* to income tax. Ouch!

You can take your benefits all at once or in monthly installments. If you choose equal installments, you can't arbitrarily pick some small amount. The least you will be required to take is an amount calculated on your life expectancy or the joint life expectancies of you and a beneficiary. For example, if your life expectancy is 10 years and your IRA has $100,000, you must take at least $10,000 a year (based on ¹⁄₁₀ of your life expectancy).

The 50 percent penalty tax is extremely harsh because it requires payments to start at 70½ and sets a floor (minimum) on amounts you must withdraw. Many older Americans would be better off delaying distributions past 70½ or taking lesser amounts. For example, your income may be too high right now because you are still working. If you could delay or reduce your benefit payments until your income is lower, you'd pay less tax, and more of your hard-earned retirement funds would end up in *your* pocket rather than Uncle Sam's. Also, since your money grows tax-free in the retirement fund (IRA, pension, etc.), you would have more to distribute if you could delay or reduce distributions.

Is there any way to delay distributions and beat the 50 percent penalty tax, or at least to cut its harsh impact? The answer is yes. Our gems will help you put off some of your retirement payments, allowing more of your money to grow tax-free—*without* getting hit with the 50 percent penalty tax.

❖ GEM: Delay Withdrawals
Until April 1 of the Next Year

Most people think they've got to take their first withdrawal of retirement funds at age 70½, but that's not true. You may actually have until almost age 72!

You are legally entitled to wait until April 1 of the year *after* you reach age 70½ to start taking your retirement money. This may mean you can delay until you are almost 72 to start withdrawing your retirement funds, with no penalty.

Let's say you'll be 70½ on January 5, 1993. You don't have to take your first withdrawal until April 1994—at that time, you'll be almost 72 years old!

❖ GEM: Refigure Life Expectancy Each Year

The longer your life expectancy, the longer you'll be able to extend your retirement payments, and the less you'll have to pay now while the tax hit would be greater. Life expectancy is a strange thing—the older you get, the longer you're expected to live. Take a look at Table 6.7: at age 71, Uncle Sam's actuarial chart says you're expected to live until 86; at 80, you're expected to live until 89½.

By recalculating your life expectancy each year, you can save yourself money!

EXAMPLE 36

You have $100,000 in an IRA, and you have just reached age 70½. Right now, you're in the 28 percent tax bracket. Your life expectancy is 15.3 years.

A lifetime annuity would pay you $6,535 in year 1, $7,026 in year 2, and increasing somewhat each year as the fund earns interest. After five years, you would have received $39,547, on which you'd pay tax of $11,073.

You guess that five years from now you'll quit work, and your tax bracket will only be 15 percent at that time. The trick is to push as much of your retirement money off until after you actually retire.

Using Table 6.7, you recalculate your life expectancy each year. By doing that, you can reduce the amount of retirement dollars you must take each year. After year 1, your life expectancy would be 14.6 years, so you could recalculate the payouts from the lifetime annuity.

If you recalculated life expectancy each year for five years, your total retirement receipts would be $37,718 and the tax would only have been $10,561. In other words, by recalculating your life expectancy each year, you deferred $1,829 and saved tax of $512—you get the double bonus of knowing you gained money and a longer life!

After your tax rate drops (at retirement), you can stop using this gem and either take a lump sum or stick with the same monthly payments. No five- or ten-year averaging would be allowed (for an IRA), though.

❖ GEM: Pick a Young Beneficiary

Let's say you are 70 with a 16-year life expectancy and $100,000 in your IRA. You would have to take at least $6,250 (1/16 of $100,000) in the first year, based on your life expectancy.

You can reduce your distribution by recalculating your life expectancy each year. But since you are still working and earning a salary, you would like to reduce your distribution—and the tax—even more.

One way to do this would be to add a younger person as beneficiary and take pension distributions over *both* your life expectancies. Let's say you make your 50-year-old daughter a beneficiary. Now you can take your distributions over 26.2 years, which is the maximum period allowed by law (the only exception is that a longer period is allowed when the beneficiary is a young spouse—hmmm . . .). You'd only take $3,816 the first year (a little more in the following years as the IRA increases) from your IRA, cutting your taxes and leaving the rest to grow tax-free.

What happens when you stop working and need more income from the IRA? No problem! You can always take more. You can take *any* amount over the minimum at *any* time (as long as you don't run into the 15% excise tax for distributions over $150,000).

❖ GEM: If You Have More Than One IRA, Allocate Minimum Distribution to Fit Your Needs

Let's say that the minimum IRA distribution you must take this year is $9,000, based on your life expectancy. You've got two IRAs, each with equal amounts. Do you have to withdraw $4,500 from each? You really don't want to take anything from one IRA because you're getting a higher interest rate on your long-term CDs in that one.

Don't worry—you can take the whole $9,000 from one IRA and nothing from the other, if you want. As long as you withdraw the right *total*, you won't get hit with a 50 percent penalty tax.

MONIES LEFT AT DEATH

It's true. The two things you can't escape forever are death and taxes. Death won't help you avoid the income or 15 percent excise taxes on your retirement fund; the monies will go to your beneficiaries and they will pay income tax and any applicable 15 percent excise tax. In addition, your funds don't escape estate or inheritance tax, either. But there's a gem that can save your heirs some money.

❖ GEM: Pass Out Funds Before You Pass On

In situations where you know death is imminent, you may be wise to take a lump-sum distribution and give the money to your heirs. This strategy may save you money two ways.

First, your income-tax rate may be much lower than your heirs' rates. If you take a distribution, you'll be charged income tax at your rate, perhaps saving money for your beneficiaries. And second, if you then give the funds to your heirs, you may avoid your state's estate or inheritance taxes.

GET YOUR RETIREMENT FUNDS WITHOUT PAYING INCOME, PENALTY OR EXCISE TAXES

Any time you take a distribution from your retirement plan, there's a cost. As we've explained, you will always pay income tax. If you're not yet 59½, you'll usually get stuck with a 10 percent penalty tax on top of that. If you take out too much, you may get socked with a 15 percent penalty tax. Sure would be nice if there was some way to get the money *without* paying tax, right?

There is! Here's a way to take your money at no cost.

❖ GEM: Borrow from a Company Plan— It's in Your Self-interest!

Many company pension and profit-sharing plans allow employees to borrow against their pension monies. Borrowing gets you the money *without having to pay any tax,* whether you are 50 or 80.

The money is almost completely cost-free. Sure, there will be interest charged by the plan. (The rate may be several points less than what a bank would charge.)

But here's the best news of all: since you borrowed from yourself, you'll be paying yourself back. You're paying interest to yourself, so you get the money cost-free!

EXAMPLE 37

You need $50,000 to make home improvements. You could take a bank loan, but you'd end up paying $13,700 in interest (at 10%) over five years while repaying the loan.

If you took the $50,000 from your pension plan, you'd pay $15,000 income tax and, if you are younger than 59½, $5000 in excise tax, too.

If you *borrow* the funds from your pension plan, you'll repay with interest over the same five years—but the interest would all go into your retirement fund. In other words, you'll borrow the funds *at no cost!*

The law places no limits on the purpose for the loan. You can use the money for anything—a new house, debt payments, college tuition. But tax rules do limit the amount you can borrow to a maximum of $50,000, or one-half of your vested (guaranteed) pension benefit, whichever is less (although if the plan permits, you may borrow up to $10,000 even if that's more than half the vested benefit). Loans generally must be repaid within five years, unless the loan is being used to buy a home (in which case the repayment term may be as long as 30 years).

Pension-plan loans are easier to get, interest rates are cheaper, and interest generally is deductible (or not deductible) just as on any commercial loan. If you are a highly paid owner or officer of the company, or if your loan is from a 401(k) plan and is secured with your contributions, then interest will not be deductible under any circumstances.

If your pension plan allows loans, don't walk into a bank, run to your company—you're almost always better off borrowing from yourself!

❖ GEM: Take a Short-term Loan from Your IRA

As we just explained, borrowing from a company retirement plan can be a great way to get your money tax-free. Unfortunately, IRAs, SEPs, and self-employed plans generally don't permit borrowing—at least not in the traditional sense. But don't give up.

If you need a short-term loan, here's a great tip that lets you use money from your IRA, SEP, or self-employed plan without paying any tax or interest. How? Take a nontraditional loan by "rolling over" (moving) retirement funds from one fund to another.

If you are rolling funds from a plan other than an IRA into an IRA, you must roll at least 50 percent of your funds (this limit will be eliminated beginning in 1993). If you are moving funds from one IRA into another IRA, you may move any amount. If you are rolling funds into anything other than an IRA, you must move *all* monies in the fund. But in any case, the rollover must be complete—the monies put into a retirement fund—within 60 days.

The 60-day period is key. During that time, you can "borrow" your retirement money interest-free and tax-free. Just like in *Cinderella,* you can use your money to live like a prince or princess for 60 days. But when the clock strikes 60 (days), you'd better have the money back into an IRA or other retirement fund, or else your mean step-Uncle (Sam) will come after you for taxes.

EXAMPLE 38

You need to pay off an $8,000 loan. You've got the money in a CD, but the CD doesn't come due for another month; if you take the money now, you'll lose a lot of interest.

So you roll over an $8,000 IRA. You take the money from the IRA and pay off your bill. Then when the CD comes due, you can take the $8,000 and put it back into an IRA. And just like that, you've accessed your retirement money interest-free and tax-free!

Remember that traditional borrowing from a pension plan is limited to $50,000 or half the fund (see page 300). Short-term nontraditional loans are not limited; you could use some or all of your funds, no matter how much.

The Government has made it a little harder to use this gem beginning in 1993 if your retirement funds are in a company plan: Uncle Sam will withhold 20 percent off the top. This new wrinkle may cost you unless you first make a direct transfer to an IRA.

EXAMPLE 39

Take the same situation as in Example 38, except the money is in a company plan. Beginning in 1993, if you take a $10,000 distribution, the Government withholds $2,000 (20 percent), and you get $8,000 to pay off your loan. When the CD comes due, you take $10,000 and put it into an IRA.

What happens to the $2,000 withheld by the Government? You don't lose that money—it's just temporarily withheld to cover potential income taxes. Since you are rolling over to the IRA rather than taking your retirement funds permanently, there won't be any income tax to pay on the rollover, and you'll get the withheld funds back when you file your next federal income tax return. If you pay quarterly estimates, you can reduce your next payment(s) by $2,000 (the amount withheld). But in either case, you temporarily lose the use of your funds.

To avoid the 20 percent withholding entirely, roll the funds from a company plan directly to an IRA, then take a loan from the IRA.

We mentioned that you can roll money from an IRA into an IRA to cash in on the short-term borrowing gem. Can you roll funds from an IRA into the *same* IRA? The IRS says yes. You should be able to take money from your IRA, use it for 60 days, then replace it in the *same* IRA.

❖ GEM: Extend the 60-Day Loan

A 60-day loan is nice, but can you get more? You sure can! Example 40 shows how you can extend the 60-day loan. We have used the new 20 percent withholding rules that go into effect in 1993.

EXAMPLE 40

You have just bought a new home, and the deal closes this week. You need $50,000 to put down, which you expected to get from the sale of your existing house. Unfortunately, the market is soft and you still haven't sold. Where can you get the $50,000 to complete your purchase? One option would be to take out a bridge loan from a bank. *If* you could get one, the loan would cost you about $385/month (assuming 8.5% interest).

You've got $150,000 in a pension plan. If you took $50,000 and rolled over the rest, the cost would be about $15,000 in taxes (assuming 30% tax rate) and another $5,000 excise tax if you are under 59½. That's a stiff price to pay.

You could take the 60-day free loan for the entire $150,000, then roll it into an IRA. But that only gets you 60 days, and you may need the money for a longer period. In addition, you will have to send $30,000 (20%) to the IRS in withholding.

Here's how you can do better—extend the 60-day loan and cut the withholding. Take the $150,000 and roll it directly into three IRAs rather than one, putting $50,000 into each. Then take $50,000 from IRA number 1 and use it for the down payment. That gives you 60 days. If you haven't sold your home within 60 days, then you take the money from IRA number 2 and repay IRA number 1. Again, withdrawals from an IRA do not trigger withholding. That gets you another 60 days to repay IRA number 2. If you still haven't sold your home, you can take the money from IRA number 3 and repay IRA number 2. That will extend your interest-free, tax-free loan another 60 days.

Using this technique, you'll be able to get an interest-free, tax-free loan from your retirement funds for 180 days, not just 60 days! If your funds are in a company plan, be sure to roll them directly into one or more IRAs first, to avoid any withholding. Then take the loans from the IRAs.

You can roll over money from an IRA only once in 12 months. But you can move money from a pension or profit-sharing fund into an IRA, and then from an IRA into another IRA, within the same 12 months without violating this rule.

We've discussed how you can take maximum advantage of your retirement plan; now let's look at the flip side—what to do when your company takes advantage of you!

BENEFIT CUT-OFF

If you take your retirement money as a lump sum, or you have an IRA, the money is yours. Period. You needn't worry about pension surprises.

But if you opt to take company retirement funds as an annuity for a fixed period or for your lifetime, is the money guaranteed for that period? Not necessarily. If you go back to work or if your company terminates the plan, you may find your benefits cut off!

Returning to Work—Requires Re-Working Your Benefits

Let's say you retire, start taking a monthly pension from your company, and then go back to work for a different employer or for yourself. In that case, you can keep both your wages and pension. No problem.

But if you go back to work for your former employer—where you earned the pension—and put in more than 40 hours a month, your monthly pension checks may be suspended. Although you can restart the monthly payments once you re-retire, the payments for the months you worked are gone. By returning to work, you will need to recalculate your benefits. It could cost you thousands of dollars.

❖ GEM: You Can't Go Home Again— Don't Return to Former Employer

The solution to this problem is simple. If you want to go back to work, go elsewhere. Money you earn at another company will be *added* to your pension; money you earn from your old employer will just *replace* your pension.

✦　✦　✦

Plan Termination

What if your company goes out of business or gets bought out, or your pension plan goes bankrupt? Are you out of luck?

No, at least not completely. If your company is bought by another company that continues a pension plan, your prior years of credit and benefits must be preserved. Although changes can be made for future work, you can't be cheated out of retirement benefits already earned.

Even if the company or plan ends, don't lose hope. Most pensions are at least partly insured by Uncle Sam, through the Pension Benefit Guaranty Corporation. Your pension should be protected if:

- You are in a defined-benefit plan. In a defined-contribution plan, you will get only what is already in your account, and nothing more (see page 263).
- You have worked enough so that your pension has vested (see page 265).
- Your employer is a professional service organization with at least 25 employees or employer of any size, and the pension is not provided by the Government, a religious organization, or a union.

The amount of your pension may be cut. The government insurance covers all vested benefits for nonkey (nonmanagement) employees, but the interest rates Uncle Sam uses to calculate benefits may be less. Only retirement benefits are usually protected; other benefits, such as disability and death benefits, typically are not covered by the federal insurance.

If you have any problems getting your pension after the company or plan shuts down, contact the Pension Benefit Guaranty Corporation at: Coverage and Inquiries, 2020 K Street, N.W., Washington, D.C. 20006; (202) 778-8800.

APPLYING FOR A COMPANY PENSION

After you get your gold watch, don't sit back and wait for your pension checks to start rolling in. Benefits don't start automatically—you've got to apply. Contact the company's retirement-plan administrator for information about your company's application process.

You should also review your rights under the pension plan, so that you can make sure you get all you're entitled to. Look at the:

- *Pension plan document,* which is the legal description of the plan
- *Summary plan description,* which is a simplified explanation of your pension plan
- *Personal benefit statement,* which tells you the status of your pension benefits

These documents are available from the plan administrator. You have a right to see this information. If the plan administrator gives you a hard time, contact the U.S. Department of Labor, Division of Technical Assistance and Inquiries, Room N-5658, Pension and Welfare Benefits Administration, U.S. Department of Labor, 200 Constitution Ave., N.W., Washington, D.C. 20210; (202) 523-8784.

After you apply for benefits, you wait for a response. But you don't have to wait forever. The plan must respond within a "reasonable time," usually no more than 90 days.

It is hoped the company plan will approve your benefits. But if your application is rejected, or the amount of benefits approved is not as much as you thought, the plan must give you an easy-to-understand explanation. It must also tell you how you can appeal this decision.

Don't delay your appeal. File within 60 days, or you will lose your appeal rights. At this point, you might want to enlist the help of a lawyer to make the best possible argument for why the plan is wrong. If you are again denied, then you can take your complaint to federal court.

Don't count on getting your benefits the minute you walk out the company door. Even if promptly approved, you can often expect delays of a year or more. To avoid problems, discuss your retirement plans with the employer as soon as visions of condos and golf carts start appearing on a regular basis.

SURVIVING OR DIVORCED SPOUSE

So far, we've been talking about how a worker can maximize return on retirement funds. What rights does a surviving spouse have after the worker dies? What rights does a divorced spouse have to a worker's retirement funds? The answers to both these questions may mean a lot of money to you.

Surviving Spouse

We have already explained your right in defined-contribution and defined-benefit pension plans to insist that, when your spouse takes his pension, he take a monthly annuity to be paid over both your lives (see page 274). If your spouse elected a joint and 50 percent survivor annuity, you'll get 50 percent of his monthly pension when he dies.

What if your spouse dies before he started taking his pension? In that case, you'll usually have some or all of the following options:

- If the funds are in a defined-benefit or defined-contribution pension plan, you can start taking monthly retirement benefits (one-half the amount your late spouse would have received) whenever he could have begun.
- If the funds are in a defined contribution (pension or profit-sharing) company plan, IRA, SEP, Keogh, or other retirement plan, and you are the beneficiary, you almost always will have the option to take the money in a lump sum and either pay tax now or roll it into your IRA.
- If the money is in a profit-sharing plan, you generally will *not* be able to elect to take your funds in the form of a monthly annuity.
- In any plan, if your retirement funds are $3,500 or less, the plan administrator may *force* you to take a lump sum regardless of the option you wish to choose.

❖ GEM: Roll Over Late Spouse's Retirement Funds

If you take your late spouse's retirement funds as a lump sum, you'll pay tax immediately. But if you roll the funds into your own IRA, they will continue to grow tax-deferred. You can take the monies as needed (after 59½), sheltering the rest.

Only a surviving spouse can cash in on this gem. No other beneficiary can roll over someone else's retirement funds.

❖ GEM: Leave Late Spouse's Funds in His or Her Name

In most cases, you'll benefit by taking advantage of our last gem, rolling your late spouse's retirement funds into your own IRA. But if you are older than your late spouse, rolling his retirement funds into your IRA will just mean that you'll have to start taking the funds out earlier (when you reach 70½). In this situation, you're usually better off leaving the funds in your late spouse's retirement fund to continue to grow tax-deferred.

✦   ✦   ✦

Divorced Spouse

You cooked, cleaned house, and raised the kids for years. Although you never expected a pension for the work, you had planned on "retirement benefits" like relaxation and travel with your spouse. Your husband had the same idea, but unfortunately he picked another woman to spend his retirement with. If you get divorced, do you have a right to your spouse's pension?

In a divorce, you can claim a portion of your spouse's pension, which often is the most valuable property you and your spouse have. But the pension must be covered by a court order, a Qualified Domestic Relations Order (QDRO).

Before you can begin discussing your spouse's pension, you should get as much information about it as you can. Contact the plan administrator and ask for general information about the plan and specific information about your spouse's status. Try to get the information informally; an attached statement from your spouse (if he'll cooperate), authorizing you to get this information, will be helpful. If you have trouble getting the information informally, you can ask the divorce judge to order that the information be released.

Also, tell the plan administrator that you are getting divorced and demand that no funds be disbursed to your spouse until the divorce goes through. That way, you won't later be surprised to find the pension money gone.

You can choose to collect payments under the plan, or you could have your spouse buy you out right now. In other words, if the pension is worth $100,000 today, your soon-to-be ex-spouse might pay you $50,000 from other assets, and then he gets to keep the entire pension when he retires.

❖ GEM: Take Your Share in Assets Other Than a Pension

Most divorce judges try to split the couple's total assets 50–50. If there are other assets besides the pension available to give you your 50 percent share, you may be better off taking them and leaving your ex-spouse the pension.

Remember, money in most retirement plans will be taxed when withdrawn (reducing how much you actually put into your pocket). If you can get a full share from nonpension assets, you will come out ahead.

If you decide to take a portion of your spouse's pension, you will need to obtain a QDRO from the divorce judge. A QDRO must satisfy the requirements of the federal Employee Retirement Income Security Act (ERISA).

Protecting your pension rights in a divorce can be complicated. Make sure you use a lawyer who understands the pension rules. Your QDRO should deal with all sorts of contingencies, such as what happens if your ex-spouse quits his job early, becomes disabled, or dies. The QDRO will protect your rights to your spouse's pension. Without it, you may wind up with nothing.

❖ GEM: Protect Your Right to Early Retirement Incentives

Many businesses offer special financial incentives to entice workers to retire early. You should make sure your QDRO gives you the right to a portion of those incentives, even if you are already receiving pension benefits at the time your former spouse retires.

❖ GEM: Pass On Benefits to Your Family in Case You Die

If you die before your ex-spouse, you don't want your right to his pension to die with you. Put into the QDRO that your heirs will get your benefits when you die.

After the divorce is final, send the QDRO to the plan administrator. Once he gets the order, he must comply with it.

CONTRIBUTIONS TO RETIREMENT PLANS

In the first part of this chapter, we talked about taking money out of retirement plans. Now let's take a look at contributions to retirement plans.

If you are age 50 or older and approaching retirement, does it make sense at your age to contribute to a pension plan or IRA? Or if you are already retired but still working part time, is there any reason to add to your retirement savings plan?

Many people believe that saving for retirement is only for younger people; and many people are dead wrong. In most cases, the older you get, the *more* reason exists for adding to retirement plans. If you are still working full time, you are probably making more than ever before, and surely your income is higher now than it will be after retirement. Putting money into retirement plans lets you defer taxes until your income is lower—and at that time the tax you'll pay will be lower, too! Even when you are *already retired,* and just working part time, you have a lot to gain by adding to a retirement savings plan (if you don't need the cash to live on).

401(k) Company Plan

Here's how the 401(k) works. You tell your employer to pay a part of your salary to the retirement plan rather than to you. Since you don't actually get the money, you don't pay any income tax on it until you withdraw it later. The most you can contribute generally is 25 percent of your pay, up to a maximum of $8,728 a year (in 1992). Your employer may contribute from its funds, too. While the money is in the plan, it will be invested—and you pay no tax on the income that is generated (until later, when you take it out).

❖ GEM: Put Money into a 401(k)

If your company offers a 401(k) option, take advantage of this Golden Opportunity.

EXAMPLE 41

Let's say you earn $10,000/year and are in the 20 percent tax bracket. You will pay $2,000 in income tax, leaving you $8,000. If you put $500 into regular savings, you'll have $7,500 spendable income.

If you put that $500 into a 401(k) plan, your taxable income will go down to $9,500, so the tax will be $1,900. In other words, you immediately save $100 on taxes by putting the same $500 into a 401(k) rather than a regular savings account. *Plus,* the interest you get on the money in the 401(k) grows tax-deferred, while the interest on regular savings is taxed every year.

❖ ❖ ❖

IRAs

You may have the choice between putting money into a 401(k) or an IRA. As Table 6.8 shows, you're usually better off with the 401(k).

TABLE 6.8

Comparison of IRAs and 401(k)s

	IRA	401(k)
Can you withdraw early (without penalty)?	Not before age 59½	Not before age 55 and have 6 years in plan
What are contribution limits?	$2,000 or amount of earned income if less	25% or $8,728
Is there income tax on withdrawals?	Taxed at ordinary income tax rates	Special 5-year (and 10-year) averaging allowed
Can you take loans from the fund?	No	Yes
Do you pay plan expenses?	Yes	No

But you may not be covered by a 401(k) at your business, particularly if you have already retired and are just working part time; many 401(k) plans exclude part-timers. Don't worry—contributions to IRAs often provide the shelter you need. And in some cases, you may want to contribute to an IRA even if you are covered by a 401(k) plan.

The rules governing IRAs are fairly simple (for government rules). You may contribute to an IRA the lesser of:

- 100 percent of your earned income (like wages, but not interest, dividends, or Social Security)
- $2,000 ($4,000 for a couple when both work)

If you work and your spouse doesn't (or your spouse makes less than $250), you and your spouse may, in one year, contribute up to $2,250 to IRAs for you and your spouse. The amount may be split between two IRAs (one for you and one for your spouse) in any way you choose, as long as neither gets more than $2,000. In other words, even if your spouse isn't working, you could put $2,000 into her IRA and $250 into yours.

Why contribute to an IRA? Two important reasons: Your contribution may be deductible, and the money grows tax-deferred. A few years ago, IRAs were a hot investment tool because all contributions were tax-deductible. The deductions made IRAs *very* attractive. For example, if you contributed $2,000 to an IRA,

Uncle Sam would give you back about $500 (assuming 25% tax bracket). But when that benefit went up in smoke, many investors turned away from the IRA.

You may not know that your IRA contribution is *still fully deductible today* if either:

- You and your spouse both are not covered by a company pension plan (it's easy to find out if you are covered by a company plan—just look at your W-2 form; if the box for "pension plan" is checked, you're covered).
- Even if you are covered under a company plan, your federal adjusted gross income is under $25,000 ($40,000 if married) before taking an IRA deduction.

If your income is a little over the limits, falling between $25,000 and $35,000 ($40,000 to $50,000 for couples), your IRA contribution may be partly deductible.

EXAMPLE 42

You are married and recently retired. You receive pension payments of $10,000/year and Social Security benefits of $12,000 per year. You also receive annual tax-exempt interest of $17,000. To supplement your income, and to keep busy, you took a part-time job that pays $8,000/year.

Your federal adjusted gross income, which is your income before itemized deductions and personal exemptions are subtracted, is $22,500 ($10,000 pension + $8,000 wages + $4,500 of Social Security benefits). The tax you'd pay on that amount is $1,785.

But if you put $2,000 into an IRA, you could deduct the whole amount—even if covered under a company plan—because your income is less than $40,000. The deduction would mean that your tax would be $1,335, for a savings of $450—think you could find some way to use that?

How is the tax break figured? The deduction itself is worth $300 to you. Plus by reducing the amount of your taxable income, the amount of your Social Security benefits subject to tax also is reduced, and that's worth another $150 to you.

EXAMPLE 43

Let's take the same facts, except you have an additional $21,000 of taxable income—maybe because you sold appreciated stock or because you are working full time. Now your adjusted gross income is $45,000 ($8,000 wages + $10,000 pension + $6,000 Social Security + $21,000 added).

Remember, with income between $40,000 and $50,000, you can take a partial deduction. Since $45,000 is halfway between $40,000 and $50,000, you can take half of the full deduction—$1,000 of your IRA contribution is deductible. (If your income is one-quarter of the way between $40,000 and $50,000, you could take 25% of the full deduction.)

❖ GEM: Use Tax-free Investments to Maximize IRA Deductions

In some situations, cutting your taxable investments can *increase* your IRA deduction. In other words, Uncle Sam may make the yield on tax-free investments more attractive.

EXAMPLE 44

Let's say your taxable income is $50,000, $10,000 of which is interest from CDs. None of your IRA contribution is deductible.

But if you shift your investment from CDs to tax-free bonds, your adjusted gross income is only $40,000, and your $2,000 IRA contribution is now fully deductible. And that means the government returns about $700 to you (assuming 28% federal tax rate and 7% state tax rate)!

Don't forget that you may get less interest income from tax-free investments than you were getting before, but you pay no regular income tax on the income, either. In most cases, the reduction in taxes should at least cover the lost earnings—and the IRA deduction is gravy.

❖ GEM: Make Tax-deductible IRA Contributions

If you can set up or add to an IRA, and get a tax deduction for the amount you put in, do it! Take a look at how valuable this is.

EXAMPLE 45

You are 60 years old and working. You take $1,500 each year and invest in CDs, stocks, bonds, or other regular investments—not an IRA. At age 70, you'll have $19,500.

Now let's say you instead open an IRA and make a $2,000 tax-deductible contribution each year for 10 years. A $2,000 contribution to an IRA is the same as a $1,500 regular investment; since the $2,000 is deductible, each contribution cost you only $1,500. The IRA monies are invested in CDs, stocks, or bonds and they grow tax-deferred. When you are ready to stop making contributions and to start using your retirement pot of gold, you've got $29,300. In other words, the IRA added $9,800 to your retirement fund! Not bad, right?

❖ GEM: After 59½, Use an IRA as Your Savings Account

The one drawback to an IRA is that you can't freely make withdrawals before you hit age 59½. But after you reach that age, that drawback disappears; if you need your money, you can get it—without penalty. You can remove money as often as you want. Putting extra dollars into an IRA is far better than just adding to a regular savings account.

❖ GEM: Make IRA Contributions Even Without a Deduction

Being able to deduct your IRA contributions is great. But even if you can't get a deduction (maybe you're covered by a company plan and your income is too high), IRA contributions may still be—to quote Wilfred Brimley—"the right thing to do!"

EXAMPLE 46

You are 60 years old and working. You contribute $2,000 each year to an IRA, but the contributions are not deductible. They will still grow tax-free, and at the end of 10 years, you'll have $29,300.

Now compare what you'd have if you put $2,000 each year into the same investments, but without the benefit of an IRA. Since taxes would have to be taken out on the investment earnings, you'd have only $26,000.

Or let's look at it another way. If you took the same $2,000 each year and bought tax-free bonds, you'd still only have about $26,000 at the end of 10 years. Why? Because even though you don't pay tax, the rate of return is less on tax-free bonds than on taxable investments. With an IRA, you can make taxable investments tax-deferred!

❖ GEM: Only Make Nondeductible IRA Contributions When the Money Can Sit

Although you'll be saving some money by making nondeductible IRA contributions, you'll lose more than you gain if you promptly make withdrawals. In that case, you are better off with a regular savings account. This example shows why.

EXAMPLE 47

Your IRA stands at $18,000, with $2,000 from nondeductible contributions and the rest from deductible contributions.

If you put in $2,000 more on a nondeductible basis, and then turn around and take $1,500 out, you'll pay tax on $1,200 of the withdrawal. That's because 20 percent of the total in the IRA is from nondeductible contributions ($4,000 of $20,000), so 80 percent of the withdrawal is taxable. (See page 311 for discussion on withdrawals from IRAs that are made up of both deductible and nondeductible contributions.)

You would have been better off not making the contribution at all. By making a contribution and promptly withdrawing most of it, you leave little in the IRA to grow tax-free, and you pay a tax that wouldn't otherwise have had to be paid yet.

✦　✦　✦

Self-employed Plans

Let's say you are working as a real estate agent, consultant, or independent contractor, or are otherwise self-employed. Maybe the work is part time, maybe full time. You may shelter income from taxes by setting up an IRA, but that will be limited to $2,000 a year, and the contribution may not be deductible. There may be other options that are even better.

You can set up your own profit-sharing or pension plan, similar to plans set up by a company. These self-employment retirement plans (often called Keoghs or HR-10 plans) are *great* because contributions are tax-deductible, your money grows tax-free until you take the funds out, and you can cut the tax on withdrawals using five- and ten-year averaging (see Tables 6.3, 6.5, and 6.6). As long as you are the only person in the plan, the rules are simple.

Any type of self-employment income may be sheltered. Consulting fees, sales commissions, management fees, or director's fees paid to you may all go into a self-employed plan. (Rental income and royalties don't count as self-employed earnings.)

Self-employment retirement plans, like plans sponsored by corporations, can be defined-contribution or defined-benefit plans. As we explained on page 263, a defined-benefit plan guarantees a particular benefit at retirement, while a defined-contribution plan requires certain contributions each year. In most cases, you should opt for a defined-contribution plan. A defined-benefit plan is much more complicated and will require you to hire an actuary and/or an experienced pension lawyer to help you figure the annual contributions. A defined-benefit plan should be used only if your income is over $20,000 and you want to sock away most of it in a retirement account; while it may allow you to shelter more of your income from tax, the complicated rules make it unattractive and more expensive to set up and administer.

Once you've decided on a defined-contribution plan, you're still not done. You may choose either a pension or a profit-sharing plan, or some combination (which is probably best). With a self-employed pension plan, you can set aside a fixed percentage of your net income (total income less expenses including one-half of the self-employment tax) each year, up to 20 percent. (The maximum contribution is $30,000.) Once you set the percentage, you must contribute that amount each year or get socked with a prohibitive excise tax on the shortfall.

With a self-employed profit-sharing plan, you can set aside a percentage of your net income each year, up to 13 percent. But unlike the pension plan, each year you can change the percentage you set aside, to fit your needs. For example, if your net income is $10,000, you can make a maximum contribution of $2,000 to a pension plan, but only $1,300 to a profit-sharing plan. But the percentage contribution to the pension plan is fixed; the percentage contribution to a profit-sharing plan can be changed. The most you can contribute in a year under either plan is $30,000.

❖ GEM: Contribute Self-employment Income to Both a Pension and Profit-sharing Plan

Let's say you want to shelter 20 percent of your self-employment income. Are you better off putting it all into a pension plan, or using both a pension and profit-sharing plan? The answer is: mix and match—use both! Put the first 13 percent into a profit-sharing plan, and the last 7 percent into a pension.

Here's why: Although you still cannot contribute a total of more than 20 percent of self-employment income—or $30,000, whichever is less—this mixing gives you added flexibility. You can vary contributions to a profit-sharing plan, depending on your circumstances each year. But with a pension plan, you must make a fixed annual contribution.

EXAMPLE 48

You are in business for yourself, and last year you earned $100,000 (before deductions for any retirement plan contribution and self-employment tax). Since you had a good year, you would like to maximize your retirement contribution without locking yourself into a 20 percent contribution in future years.

So you create two Keoghs, contributing about $7,000 (7%) into a pension plan and about $13,000 (13%) into a profit-sharing plan. (Actual contributions will be slightly less after considering self-employment tax.)

In future years, you will be locked into only minimal contributions to the pension plan of 7 percent; you don't have to contribute anything to the profit-sharing plan. This allows you to make a maximum contribution now and allows you flexibility in the future.

What's the benefit of contributing to a pension or profit-sharing plan rather than a normal investment? Take a look at Example 49.

EXAMPLE 49

You put $1,000 in a Keogh (pension or profit-sharing), with investments yielding 8 percent. In nine years, your savings will have grown to $2,000. If you then withdraw the funds and pay tax at 30 percent, you'll still be left with $1,400—and don't forget, you may be eligible to cut your tax by a lot, using our gems.

Compare a regular investment *not* in a Keogh. The interest or dividends will be taxed each year. Assuming the same interest and tax rates, you'd have only $1,140 after nine years. In other words, using a retirement plan put at least an extra $260 into your pocket.

✦ ✦ ✦

Do You Use IRAs with Self-employment Plans?

How do IRAs fit in with these self-employment plans? If your self-employment income is less than $2,000, you can use an IRA to shelter the whole amount. In that case, you might as well just use an IRA because they are much simpler than pension or profit-sharing plans.

If your income is more than $25,000 ($40,000 for a couple), you're probably best off using just self-employed retirement plans. That's because the plans allow you to contribute more than $2,000, all of which is deductible. If you are in a plan, you probably wouldn't use an IRA too because, at these income amounts, your contribution would not be deductible.

But if your income is between $2,000 and $25,000, you might benefit by having a retirement plan *and* an IRA.

EXAMPLE 50

You are single and 65 years old. You get $12,000/year in Social Security benefits and $1,500/year in interest and dividends from investments. You also do odd jobs in the neighborhood and earn about $7,000 net income each year.

You could contribute $2,000 to an IRA, and the whole amount is tax deductible. That's not bad, but you can do even better!

You may contribute about $1,300 to a self-employed retirement plan, which is just under 20 percent of your self-employment income (slightly under 20% because you must deduct self-employment tax). That contribution is also tax-deductible, and the income is tax-deferred, just like in an IRA.

Using *both* an IRA and a self-employed plan, you can shelter $3,300 of the $7,000 self-employment income (47%). That's much more than the amount you can protect using either an IRA or self-employment plan alone. If you made these contributions each year for five years, at the end of that time you'd have $19,310 socked away (at 8% yield). If you took those same amounts and put them into taxable CDs or stocks *without* sheltering them, you'd have only $15,595 after taxes. The IRA and self-employment plan together added $3,715 to your retirement kitty in just five years!

❖ GEM: Parlay a Profit-sharing Plan and Deductible IRA

As we've discussed, an IRA is fully deductible only if your income is less than $25,000 ($40,000 as a couple) or you are not covered under a company plan. But even if your income is higher than these amounts, you may be able to make tax-deductible contributions to both an IRA and a self-employed profit-sharing plan. Profit-sharing plans have special rules that allow you to contribute and still make a deductible IRA contribution.

EXAMPLE 51

You want to make retirement contributions for 1992. Between January 1, 1993, and April 15, 1993, you can make a contribution (up to

13%) to a profit-sharing plan, and you can *also* make a *deductible* IRA contribution for 1992.

You can't play this game every year. But under the IRS Golden Rules, you can take advantage of this gem every three years.

✦   ✦   ✦

Setting Up a Self-employed Plan and Making Contributions

Setting up a self-employed defined-contribution profit-sharing or pension plan is pretty easy. Just go to your banker or broker and say what you want to do. Banks and brokerage houses have standard plans, and they are happy to help you set up a plan, often for little or no fee. (The IRS may charge a small fee to register your plan.) You will have to fill out a legal form, called an Adoption Agreement. Use this form to describe the plan, including eligibility and vesting requirements. There are no annual forms to file as long as your plan covers only you (and your spouse) and the value of the assets in your plans (not including IRAs) is no more than $100,000. If the law changes, the bank or broker should help you satisfy any new requirements.

You can wait to contribute to any self-employed retirement plan until April 15 of the next year, just as you can with an IRA. But that's where the similarity ends. You can only contribute to a self-employed retirement plan after the end of the year if it was set up by December 31. For example, if you want to make a contribution for 1992, you can make it in 1993 *as long as the plan was set up by December 31, 1992.* To be set up, the plan must be signed and funded with some money (as little as $5 or $10 should be enough).

If you get an extension to file your tax return later than April 15, you can make your contribution up to the *extended* due date for your tax return. (September 15 is the latest for contributions to a self-employed pension plan; you can wait even longer for contributions to a profit-sharing plan.) With an IRA, you *must* make a contribution by April 15.

❖ GEM: Take Extra Time to Fund Pension or Profit-sharing Plans

You don't have to decide whether or how much to contribute to a retirement plan until at least April 15 (March 15 for a corporation with December 31 year-end) of the following year. And if you take an extension to file your return, you can wait much longer. Take advantage of the extra time to review your income and cash needs—the added flexibility should let you make the best decision to fit your needs.

✦   ✦   ✦

Simplified Employee Pension Plans

Here's one more strategy you can use to shelter self-employment income from income tax. It's called a Simplified Employee Pension (SEP). This is similar to a profit-sharing plan in that you can contribute up to 13 percent of your net income. So if your income is less than $15,000, you may as well just put $2,000 into an IRA—because 13 percent of $15,000 is less than $2,000. Like a profit-sharing plan, contributions to an SEP are flexible—you can contribute as much or as little as you like each year. And like a profit-sharing plan, you can make contributions after year end, up to the extended due date of your tax return.

Why have a SEP rather than a profit-sharing plan? For one, a SEP is a little easier to set up and maintain. It requires no special legal documents to set up; you need only sign a one-page IRS form (Form 5305). The SEP costs nothing to establish and you don't have to bother with later IRS filings. (With a profit-sharing plan you do have to fill out a legal form to set it up, and annual IRS forms must be filed if other employees are covered or your assets in the plan total more than $100,000. Also, a bank or broker helping you might charge a fee for a profit-sharing plan.)

Most important, a SEP does *not* have to be set up before year-end. If you are reading this book in March 1993, and you haven't set up any retirement plan, you can still get yourself a deduction for 1992 by using a SEP.

Don't close the book quite yet and rush off to get a SEP. A SEP has an important disadvantage when compared to a profit-sharing plan: distributions are not eligible for five- or ten-year averaging. Generally, SEP distributions are taxed at regular tax rates, just like distributions from an IRA. Table 6.9 compares IRAs, Keoghs (pension and profit-sharing plans), and SEPs.

TABLE 6.9

Comparison of Options for Self-employed Person

	IRA	SEP	Keogh
Is the plan easy to set up?	Easy	Easy	Easy if a prototype at a bank or institution is used; complex if many employees
What are costs to maintain?	Low	Low	A little more expensive than SEP
Must you report to IRS?	No	No	Yes, if assets over $100,000 or more than one employee
Is there flexibility in dealing with multiple employees?	N.A.	Some	Most

(Continued)

TABLE 6.9 (Continued)

Comparison of Options for Self-employed Person

	IRA	SEP	Keogh
Can you extend date of required contribution past April 15 of following year?	No	Yes	Yes
Can you contribute very large amounts?	No	Yes	Yes
Can you choose to make contribution vest over a period of years?	No	No	Yes

As you can see, your private retirement funds can offer tremendous benefits. There are lots of hidden gems available to get the most for and from your money. We've uncovered them—now it's up to you to use them!

• 7 •

COBRA: *Insurance Protection That Takes a Licking and Keeps on Ticking*

Y ou *must* have health insurance if you are going to enjoy security in your golden years. If you are 65 or older, at least you'll get Medicare; if you are totally broke, Medicaid is available at any age.

What if you are under 65 and *not* destitute? Most Americans get insurance through their own or their spouse's employment. But if you stop working before 65, you are likely to have a terrible time obtaining insurance coverage.

Why? As your age creeps up, so do the odds for serious ailments. When you apply for insurance at age 50, 55, 60, or whatever, you may get a "thanks, but no thanks" letter from an insurance company afraid to take a chance on your health. Or if you are lucky enough to get accepted, the premiums may be back-breaking. At the least, it may take you a long time to find an acceptable insurance policy— leaving you at risk in the meantime.

If you go without insurance, even for a short time, you are risking your entire life savings. A stroke, heart attack, or any other catastrophic illness can wipe you out in no time. But here's a Golden Opportunity, compliments of Uncle Sam, that can help you avoid losing everything to catastrophic medical bills. It's called COBRA.

Under COBRA (which stands for Consolidated Omnibus Budget Reconciliation Act of 1985), when you leave your job for almost any reason, including retirement, layoff, or a job change, your former employer must allow you to continue your medical coverage under the company's group plan while you look for a new insurance policy. You don't get the coverage for free—you'll have to pay—but at least you won't have to requalify. You are guaranteed coverage for a reasonable period, and at relatively low group rates.

Whether you are rich or poor, COBRA is crucial. It will help you bridge the gap between policies when you leave a job. COBRA is a Golden Opportunity that you can't afford to miss.

ELIGIBILITY

You, your spouse, and/or your dependent child(ren) may be able to cash in on COBRA. To qualify, you must have been working for, and getting your insurance from, a business that:

- sponsors a group health plan;
- had 20 or more employees on a typical day during the prior year

Even if you were not an employee in the usual sense, you (and your spouse and dependents) may still qualify for COBRA. Independent contractors, corporate directors, partners, and other self-employed individuals who were covered by a group health plan should be eligible for COBRA.

EXAMPLE 1

You have finally decided to give up your law practice and retire. (We envy that decision!) Even though you were a partner, and not really an employee, you can use COBRA to continue health-care benefits for you and your spouse as long as you were covered by a group health plan while working.

Your former employer does not have to be a private business—local and state governments are all included. The federal government has its own special rules for continuing benefits under the Federal Employees Health Benefits Plan.

If your former employer is small, you may be out of luck. But even a small business may owe you COBRA rights.

❖ GEM: Count All Employees for Cobra

To qualify for COBRA, your employer must have had at least 20 employees in the past year. Here are a few tips to help build up the numbers:

- Part-time employees count. If you worked for a retail store that had only 5 full-time employees, but there were at least 15 part-time workers who were eligible for health benefits, you can get COBRA.
- You can get COBRA as long as the business had 20 employees for half the working days of the year. So don't let the boss hoodwink you by pointing out that, when you left, there were only 15 employees. Look at the entire year.

- Aggregate all your company's offices. There must only have been 20 employees *total.*
- If your company participates in a group plan with other businesses, depending on the business arrangement, you may qualify for COBRA if *any* of the affiliated businesses have 20 or more employees.

❖ GEM: Sign Up for Your Business's Health Insurance Plan *Before* You Retire

To qualify for COBRA after you retire, you must have been participating in your company's health plan while you were working. Compare Examples 2 and 3 to see how you can avoid the two-worker trap and gain important protection.

EXAMPLE 2

You and your husband are getting ready to retire. You have been on your husband's insurance plan because it's a little cheaper, so of course you're not on your own company's, too. When you and your husband retire, you get an unpleasant surprise. Your husband's office is small, so it doesn't offer COBRA. And you can't get COBRA from your company because you weren't participating in the plan when you were working.

EXAMPLE 3

Same facts as Example 2, except that you read our book and planned ahead. Right before retiring, you joined your company's health insurance plan. Now when you quit, you and your husband both qualify for COBRA coverage under *your* company's plan!

❖ GEM: For Two-Worker Couples, Plan Ahead for Retirement

For most two-worker couples, it doesn't make sense to carry two insurance plans. So you'd usually compare costs, pick the best plan, and drop the other. But this can be another two-worker trap for the unwary—in some cases, when retirement is coming, you may be better off picking the more expensive plan of the younger spouse.

EXAMPLE 4

You and your wife are both working. You both are covered by your insurance plan, since the premiums run $200/month for your plan and $300/month under your wife's plan. You are 60 and your wife is only 53; you are planning to retire much earlier than she will. Consider switching to your wife's plan *now*.

Here's what happens if you wait: At age 62, when you retire, you can either go onto COBRA under your company's insurance plan at $400/month (COBRA costs are more than for working participants), or switch to your wife's policy for $300/month. But if you or your wife has become ill, you may no longer have the option to join your wife's plan. Instead, you may be stuck paying a lot more for COBRA!

If you switch to your wife's plan now, while you're both healthy, you'll pay a little more until your retirement. But you'll lock in your right to continue your coverage under her plan after you retire—at a lower price than you'd have to pay for COBRA.

✦　✦　✦

Events Triggering COBRA Protection

COBRA protection is triggered when any of the following events would cause you to lose your health benefits:

- You leave your job.
- You reduce your hours.
- You were retired and covered by a retiree health plan when the employer went into bankruptcy.

These are called qualifying events—events which qualify you for COBRA—and you are called a qualified beneficiary. Whether you leave your job because you retire, quit, strike, are fired, or are laid off makes no difference. You qualify for COBRA when you leave for any reason except gross misconduct. (Don't worry too much about gross misconduct; terminations for this reason are *very rare*. You must have broken the law or violated an important company rule to even get close to gross misconduct.)

Bankruptcy will sometimes—but not always—trigger COBRA coverage. If you were covered by retiree health benefits when the company goes into bankruptcy, and the company terminates retiree benefits *but continues health benefits for active employees,* then you are entitled to COBRA benefits for life. But if the company terminates health benefits for *everyone,* active and retired employees, you get no COBRA benefits.

Your spouse or dependent child may also cash in on COBRA (as a qualified beneficiary) when any of these qualifying events happens:

- You leave your job (other than for gross misconduct) or reduce your hours and so would lose regular health coverage.
- You die.
- You divorce or legally separate.
- You become eligible for Medicare (and so lose your group health coverage).
- Your dependent child no longer qualifies for dependent coverage under the group health plan.
- Your company files for bankruptcy and you were covered by retiree health benefits.

❖ GEM: Your Children Are Covered Between Graduation and Their First Job

Your group health plan at work probably covers health care for your children while in college or graduate school, as long as they are still dependents. (Don't worry, there will come a time when they'll stop being dependents!) Many policies will stop the coverage at a specific age, such as 23.

When your child graduates or hits the age limit, normal health coverage will end. But your child may not yet be covered by some other health insurance plan. For example, his or her first job may not have started, or the employer may not offer health insurance.

COBRA can be crucial. You can continue COBRA coverage for your child for three more years. In the meantime, your child should be looking for alternate coverage. But until he or she finds a good plan, COBRA can bridge the gap.

✦ ✦ ✦

Qualified beneficiaries are determined as of the date of the qualifying event— the date the worker retires, dies, or so on. The timing of these qualifying events can be extremely important to make sure you and your family receive the COBRA benefits you're entitled to.

❖ GEM: Marry Before Retirement, Not After

If you marry after leaving your job, your spouse might be covered under *your* COBRA plan, but she would not be a qualified beneficiary with her own COBRA coverage—and the difference could mean a lot of money. Compare Examples 5 and 6.

EXAMPLE 5

You have met a wonderful woman and decide that life's too short not to fully enjoy. So you quit your job and the next month you get married. At the time you retired, you were not married. You qualify for COBRA coverage, but your new wife doesn't qualify for herself. Remember, the law looks to see who is covered on the date of the qualifying event—your retirement—and since you were single at the time, only you are a qualified beneficiary.

Fortunately, you can cover your spouse under *your* COBRA policy. The law says that as long as the plan allows active workers to cover spouses, then retirees can also cover spouses. So what's the big deal that your wife isn't herself a qualified beneficiary? Two months later, you die a happy man, but your wife loses COBRA coverage because she was covered under *your* plan and was not a qualified beneficiary herself.

EXAMPLE 6

Same facts as Example 5, except you marry *before* leaving your job rather than after. At the time you retire, your spouse is a qualified beneficiary herself. If you die, she'll get to *keep* her COBRA coverage (and even *extend* it for a longer period—see page 332).

❖ GEM: Consider Coverage Under Your Spouse's Plan

If both you and your spouse are working, you probably can choose between your own or your spouse's insurance coverage. Even though your plan is less expensive, you may be better off paying more under your spouse's plan. Take a look at Example 7.

EXAMPLE 7

Your company offers a nice health insurance program, and the premium is $100/month less than your spouse's. Of course, you'd stay with your own plan, right?

Maybe not! Your marriage is a little shaky and may not last much longer. And since your company is pretty small—fewer than 10 employees—you won't have the chance to get COBRA. If you and your husband are divorced, you can get COBRA benefits under his company plan *only* if you were covered by his plan before the divorce. So if the marriage is coming apart, consider tying into his insurance plan now.

✦   ✦   ✦

Choosing COBRA After Qualifying Events

Each qualified beneficiary must choose whether or not to take COBRA coverage at the time of the qualifying event; otherwise, the opportunity to use COBRA will be forever lost. Sometimes the decision is easy, such as when the qualifying event is a divorce and COBRA is necessary to avoid the immediate loss of health insurance benefits.

EXAMPLE 8

You are covered by your husband's health insurance plan when you get divorced. After the divorce, you are no longer a covered spouse under his plan, so you would lose your benefits—*unless* you take COBRA coverage. With COBRA, you can continue coverage under the same plan while you find your own policy.

In Example 8, the decision to take COBRA coverage is easy. But in some cases, the decision can be much less clear.

❖ GEM: Take COBRA to Protect Yourself in Case of Divorce

You may be smart to opt for COBRA coverage under your spouse's company policy at his retirement, even if you have cheaper coverage under your own company plan. Why? So you don't get caught short in case your marriage doesn't last until "death do you part."

EXAMPLE 9

Your husband is retiring from his job. He takes COBRA coverage for himself, but you take a pass because you're covered under your own employer's health insurance plan. A few months later you quit your job.

Your company was very small and doesn't offer COBRA, so your husband adds you to his COBRA plan. Since you didn't elect to get your own COBRA coverage when your husband retired, you lost your chance to be a qualified beneficiary with your own COBRA coverage, but you get the same benefits under his plan. So far, no problem.

Then one day your husband runs off with the cashier at the local bowling alley. After the divorce, your husband won't be your only loss: you lose your health insurance coverage too because you are no longer covered as a spouse under your husband's plan. If you had opted to take your own COBRA coverage as a qualified beneficiary when your husband left his job, the divorce would not affect your coverage.

❖ GEM: Sometimes It Pays to Double Your Coverage

Many older Americans are wasting money with two or more duplicative health insurance policies. Yet when it comes to COBRA, you may be smart to double your coverage temporarily.

Look again at Example 9. Had you known you would be leaving your own job (which didn't offer COBRA), you should have taken COBRA coverage when your husband retired. Though you would have doubled your coverage for a period of time, at least you would have bought yourself "divorce insurance."

Warning: This GEM has recently become tarnished. At least two federal appeals courts have ruled that people covered under their own group health plan are ineligible to elect COBRA unless they can show COBRA is necessary to avoid gaps in their health-care coverage. Before buying "divorce insurance," check with a lawyer to find out the current rule in your state.

❖ GEM: With Your Own COBRA, You Can Add a New Spouse

By electing COBRA after your spouse leaves a job, you protect not only yourself, but maybe others, too!

EXAMPLE 10

When your husband retires, both he *and you* take COBRA coverage. That way, if he dies or divorces you, you can continue your coverage.

Let's say the worst happens, and shortly after retirement your husband dies or you are divorced. Later you meet another man and decide to get remarried. Even though your new spouse never had any involvement with your former husband, no less his employer, you can bring him onto your COBRA policy. Welcome to the family!

❖ GEM: Watch Out for Paid Health Coverage—A "Snake in the Grass"

If you have the choice between electing COBRA benefits or taking free, company-paid health benefits, which should you do? Again, the answer might surprise you, as Example 11 shows.

EXAMPLE 11

When you retire, your company provides fully-paid lifetime health coverage for you; your wife also is given paid health benefits, but for only six months. Because your wife is given paid health benefits, she fails to elect COBRA benefits. Unfortunately, when her free benefits run out after six months, she may not be able to opt for COBRA at that time—the insurance company may argue that she's too late.

While it's not clear whether the law would prohibit her from electing COBRA benefits *after* the free coverage runs out, she could have avoided any problems by electing COBRA immediately upon your retirement. She still would have received the six months of free, company-paid benefits, and when those ran out she'd still receive COBRA protection (for 12 more months).

Don't let short-term paid benefits lull you into a false sense of security so that you miss out on the opportunity to take COBRA. Elect COBRA coverage even if your employer will provide paid health benefits for a short-term period.

COVERAGE

If you qualify for COBRA coverage, here's what you get:

1. The *identical* health-care benefits available to others who are still working.
2. Coverage for at least 18 months, and often as much as 36 months (extended with the help of our gems).
3. A guarantee that the premium will run no more than 102 percent of the regular cost for participation in the health plan.

4. No requirement of insurability.

5. The opportunity to convert to individual coverage after the COBRA coverage ends, again without having to show insurability.

Identical Benefits

You cannot be treated unfairly just because you retired. You must be given the chance to get the *same benefits* as active employees.

You are subject to the same deductibles and co-payments as working employees—no more and no less. If your former employer changes (or eliminates) the health plan for *all* employees, then you are stuck with those same results. But he can't reduce benefits or increase deductibles just for retirees generally or you particularly. And if he eliminates your group health plan but offers other plans for active employees, you must be given the chance to choose coverage in one of those other plans.

While you are legally entitled to choose to continue the same coverage you had before retiring, you don't have to. In some cases you might want to cut your benefits in order to cut your costs.

What if you are covered by an HMO that serves only your city, and you move away? Generally, you are out of luck. But here's a gem that might save the day.

❖ GEM: If Active Employees in Your New City Get Coverage, You Can Too

Let's say you move from Michigan to Florida following retirement because you're tired of fighting snow in the winter. Your Michigan HMO can't cover you in your new location.

But you're in luck. Your former employer has a factory in your new area, and active employees working there are covered by a different health-care program. You must be given the chance to opt for the same coverage. Remember—you can't be treated any worse than an active employee in the same location.

◆ ◆ ◆

When you elect to take COBRA benefits, you get "credit" for any deductibles and co-payments you have already satisfied while an active employee; you also get stuck with limits on any benefits you've already used up as an active employee.

EXAMPLE 12

Your group health plan applies separate $100 annual deductibles to you and your wife. You retire midway through the year; at the time, you had paid $80 toward your deductible, and your wife had gone over her $100. When you begin COBRA coverage, you only have $20 more of your deductible to meet, and your wife has nothing more to pay. Your employer or the health plan can't make you and your wife each start with new $100 deductibles.

EXAMPLE 13

Your health plan pays for up to 150 hospital days. You had used 20 days at the time you retired. Under COBRA, you get coverage for only 130 more hospital days.

❖ GEM: Delay Expenses After a Divorce

The rules get trickier for divorce. Wise timing of medical expenses may allow you to add some money to the joint pot to be split.

EXAMPLE 14

Your health-care plan pays a maximum of $20,000 of medical expenses per year, for either a family or an individual. You and your husband had $15,000 of expenses when he announced he wants a divorce. You have surgery coming up which is likely to cost another $5,000. If you undergo the surgery before the divorce is final, that will use up the rest of the $20,000 coverage for you and your spouse. After the divorce, neither you nor your ex-husband will have any more benefits for the year.

But let's say you delay the surgery until after the divorce. At the time the divorce goes through, you and your husband have used a total of $15,000 of your benefits. After the divorce, you will *each* get $5,000 coverage. If you then pay $5,000 for the surgery, you'll have used up your benefits, but your ex-husband will still have $5,000 coverage left. In other words, by wise timing of medical expenses, you may *double* the total benefits for you and your husband following the divorce.

So far in this example we've showed how you can get an extra $5,000 benefit for your ex-husband. Why should you be so generous? In order to get a benefit for yourself, negotiate with him before the divorce. Tell him that if he wants you to delay your surgery, he'll have to pay $2,500 more of your medical expenses that you incur during the year (or give you an extra $2,500 of the marital property as part of the settlement). That way, he still benefits by $2,500, and you benefit, too!

✦ ✦ ✦

Period of Coverage

The bad news is that, in most cases, COBRA won't last forever. But you'll be covered for at least 18 months, and maybe more!

You get COBRA:

- For 18 months if triggered by you or your spouse leaving the job or reducing hours
- For 36 months if triggered by your or your spouse's death, divorce, eligibility for Medicare, or loss of qualification as a dependent child
- For 29 months if you or your spouse was disabled at the time COBRA coverage began
- For life if you or your spouse were covered under a retiree health plan and the company went into bankruptcy

These time periods run from the date of the qualifying event—the day you first become eligible for COBRA—even if you don't lose regular coverage immediately. For example, if your employer pays health benefits for six months after you retire, you can cash in on COBRA for 12 more months, not 18 months.

❖ GEM: Extend Your COBRA Coverage

In some situations, you can get *more* COBRA coverage than the 18 month maximum for retirement, as Example 15 shows:

EXAMPLE 15

You retired on December 31, 1990, and you and your wife opted for COBRA coverage. The most you can get is 18 months, which will take you to June 30, 1992. But if you die, or hit age 65 and so become eligible for Medicare, before the COBRA period expires, your wife will get an *extra 18 months*—until December 31, 1993 (a total of 36 months).

❖ GEM: A Divorce Can Add Coverage

As we've said throughout this book, divorce might be a home wrecker but it is also sometimes a financial lifesaver. The benefits of breaking the knot also apply to COBRA.

EXAMPLE 16

Same facts as Example 15. You retire on December 31, 1990, and you and your wife take 18 months COBRA coverage. Your wife becomes ill and needs very expensive medical care. It's now May 1992, and your COBRA coverage is about to expire. While you could convert to an individual plan (pages 338), the cost is just prohibitive. By divorcing (a qualifying event), your wife gets COBRA coverage for another 18 months. The added time can save you thousands of dollars!

✦ ✦ ✦

If you were disabled at the time you or your spouse left the job or reduced hours, and so lost regular health benefits, you can continue COBRA for 29 months—11 months longer than the period generally allowed following retirement. (The plan may increase the premium for the last 11 months, as discussed on page 337). The same rules for disability under Social Security (see Chapter 3) apply to COBRA. To get your extra 11 months of COBRA disability coverage, you must be certified by Social Security as disabled as of the date of the qualifying event. This can be a very tough hurdle to overcome.

❖ GEM: Apply for Disability ASAP!

Don't waste any time applying for Social Security disability. You only have 18 months from the date of the qualifying event (retirement, divorce, etc.) to get a favorable ruling from the Government—and the way the Government works, that's not much time.

Start preparing for the disability process even *before* the qualifying event. For example, if you are getting set to quit in two months, get everything you'll need for the application (see page 340) so you'll be able to apply as soon as you leave. You may even apply *before* the qualifying event, to give yourself extra time.

❖ GEM: Make Sure the Decision Says You Were Disabled as of the Qualifying Event

To extend your COBRA benefits, you must be certified as disabled *on or before the date of the qualifying event.* Make sure you ask Social Security to certify your disability as of that date.

EXAMPLE 17

You retire January 1, 1992, and immediately apply for Social Security disability. You also elect COBRA coverage. In May 1993, before 18 months have lapsed, Social Security certifies that you are now disabled. Unfortunately, that decision won't get you the extra 11 months of COBRA protection. For you to cash in on the added benefits, Social Security must state that you were disabled as of January 1, 1992, or earlier.

◆ ◆ ◆

The only time you can continue COBRA for more than 36 months is when the company goes into bankruptcy. If you were covered by a company retirement health plan when the company went into bankruptcy, and the company terminated health benefits for retirees but not active employees, then you can use COBRA for the rest of your life. And when you die, your spouse can continue COBRA for another 36 months.

There are also situations where COBRA can *stop* before you reach the maximum period. You may lose coverage when:

- Your former employer drops group health coverage for everyone, including active employees.
- You fail to pay your COBRA policy premium.
- After starting COBRA coverage you become covered by (not just eligible for) some other group health plan.
- You become eligible for Medicare.
- Social Security decides you are no longer disabled, *if* you were in the final 11 months of the 29-month disability coverage period.

❖ GEM: Avoid the "Preexisting Conditions" Trap

If you become covered by another group plan, you can't stay with COBRA, even if your COBRA coverage is better. But there's an exception that can save your life savings: preexisting conditions.

You can and should stay in COBRA, even though you are eligible for coverage under another plan, if that plan will not cover "preexisting conditions." This rule is very important. If you fail to understand it, you could lose COBRA coverage when you come under another plan, and yet the new plan would not insure you for the very problems for which you *need* insurance.

EXAMPLE 18

You have been covered by COBRA since your husband died a year ago. You have been suffering from heart problems that require frequent medical care. Thankfully, the COBRA policy has been covering the costs. You are now getting remarried and will be eligible for coverage under your new husband's health policy. But the new policy says something about not covering preexisting conditions. Do you need to worry about that? You bet!

One of the main reasons for COBRA is to provide continuing protection for older Americans who can't get substitute insurance. Many policies exclude coverage, for at least some period of time, for preexisting health problems. If you lost your COBRA coverage by coming under your husband's policy, you could wind up with no coverage for your expensive heart condition. The law protects you by letting you continue COBRA coverage when you become covered by another policy that has a preexisting condition exclusion.

❖ GEM: Find a New Policy Early!

As long as we're talking about preexisting conditions, here's a very valuable gem: As soon as you begin COBRA coverage, start looking for another policy. Don't wait!

Unfortunately, many people lose lots of money by delaying. They think, since they've got 18 months or more on COBRA, why worry about other insurance until COBRA is about to run out? That's a *major mistake*. Here's why:

When you find another health insurance policy (either individual or group) at a reasonable premium, you can bet dollars to doughnuts that the policy will *not* cover preexisting health problems for at least six months, and maybe longer. If you wait until COBRA is about to expire, you could go "bare" until the limitation for preexisting conditions expires. And if you get sick during that period, kiss your savings goodbye.

But if you pick up a new policy with a preexisting conditions limitation at the *start* of your COBRA coverage, you will never be uncovered. You will have COBRA until the limitation period under the new policy runs out!

EXAMPLE 19

You retired from your job almost 1½ years ago, and you've been using COBRA health coverage ever since. Now that the coverage is about to expire, you figure it's time to find another policy. After much research, you find a good policy, at a reasonable cost; the only problem is that it won't cover preexisting conditions for six months. That's nothing to worry about, right?

Three months later your leg starts giving you problems, landing you in the hospital. Your diabetes is acting up, causing poor circulation. The medical costs will be sky-high. At least you're covered by insurance—or so you think. But your insurance company refuses to pay. The diabetes is a preexisting condition, and you are still within the six-month period for which you can't get coverage. Kiss your savings goodbye!

If only you had obtained the insurance earlier, this financial disaster could have been avoided. All you would have had to do was obtain the same policy at least six months before your COBRA coverage was set to expire. The six months noncoverage period for preexisting conditions would have run while you were still covered by COBRA. You never would have been without coverage.

Of course, if you keep COBRA coverage after purchasing another policy, you'll be paying for both. Only you can decide whether the extra costs are worth it. But in our view, the risk of going "bare" until the period for preexisting conditions has expired is too great to bear.

NOTE

Starting a new job after taking COBRA does not, in itself, end your COBRA coverage. Only if you obtain health insurance from the new employer, *and* the health insurance does *not* exclude coverage for preexisting conditions, will you lose COBRA.

✤ GEM: Medicare Ends COBRA for You, but Not Your Spouse

When you become eligible for Medicare, your COBRA coverage will end. And that's okay, since Medicare is probably sufficient. But here's a gem you won't want to miss: your spouse may continue COBRA if he or she is under 65 (and not eligible for Medicare). In fact, as we explained on page 332, your Medicare eligibility may even *extend* your spouse's COBRA coverage.

✦ ✦ ✦

Premiums

Remember, "There ain't no such thing as a free lunch." Well, that holds true for COBRA. You can, and usually will, be charged for COBRA coverage. But while you'll have to pay, the cost will almost always be much lower than what you'd pay without COBRA. And most important, you're guaranteed the coverage that you might not be able to buy for any price based on your health.

You can be charged premiums up to 102 percent of the cost that active employees pay in the plan. This doesn't mean you will only pay 102 percent of the premiums you paid before retirement; if your employer was picking up part of the cost, that portion can also be charged to you under COBRA.

EXAMPLE 20

You and your co-workers each have been paying health insurance premiums of $200/month. Your employer has been paying another $200 a month for each active employee. Now that you've retired, you can buy COBRA coverage for $408/month: the total cost of $400, plus 2 percent ($8) to cover administrative costs.

You don't have to pay the entire annual premium at once. The law gives you the option to pay in monthly installments. You may also pay in other intervals (quarterly, etc.) if the plan allows.

There is one exception to the 102 percent ceiling on premiums. If you are disabled and take COBRA for more than 18 months, you may be charged up to 150 percent of the cost for active employees for the final 11 months (months 19 through 29). The first 18 months are still limited to 102 percent.

❖ GEM: Never Go Naked

Even if you are 64½ years old and close to getting Medicare, you can't go even a few months without health insurance. That's like betting your life savings on the Cleveland Indians winning the pennant—the odds are much too long. COBRA charges can be expensive, but you've got to find a way to pay.

EXAMPLE 21

You are retiring from your job and looking forward to a wonderful retirement. You're almost 65—just a few months more. You just had a complete checkup, and everything looked fine. You've decided to pass on COBRA. It sounds too expensive; at $300 a month, you could use the money for other things. And at 65, you'll get Medicare. What can go wrong in just a few months?

Plenty! Just before your 65th birthday you get a terrible stomach pain. After a series of tests, the doctor finds a malignant tumor. When you try to get insurance coverage, you find that no policy will insure you for the cancer treatments—they all exclude preexisting conditions. By passing on COBRA, you made a very costly mistake.

COBRA will almost always be more expensive than the group rates you were paying while actively employed (because you pay your employer's contribution plus a 2 percent administrative fee). But in today's world, you *can't* afford to go uninsured. Two words—preexisting condition—can cost you your life's savings.

✦ ✦ ✦

Insurability

The most valuable gem in the COBRA treasure chest is that you can continue your health coverage without proof of insurability. No matter what your health condition is, COBRA must be made available for a minimum of 18 months at 102 percent of the actual group rate.

Even if you are about to begin costly medical care—or are in the midst of expensive care—the same COBRA rules apply. You can maintain your coverage for the full period allowed by law.

Conversion to Individual Policy

When your COBRA coverage runs out, you can convert to an individual policy if that option is generally available under the employer's health plan or required by state law. The coverage is likely to be much less favorable and much more expensive than your group coverage had been. It will probably limit coverage for preexisting conditions, and you can expect deductibles and co-payments to be higher. Although most states provide some limit on premiums, you may still find your premium costs for an individual policy are double or triple.

But at least you'll be insured. And if you've got health problems, this conversion option can be priceless.

EXAMPLE 22

You've been paying $300 a month for COBRA coverage, but that will run out soon. Since you've got some serious health problems, you can't find another insurance policy—every company tells you you're uninsurable.

Thankfully, you can convert your COBRA coverage to an individual plan. Although the cost will be a whopping $600 a month, at least you'll be protected. And once you hit 65, you can switch to Medicare.

❖ GEM: Don't Wait for the Plan to Tell You to Convert

The law requires a representative of the insurance plan to tell you about your right to convert sometime during the last six months of your COBRA coverage. That means the plan may wait until the last day. By that time, you may already have bought replacement insurance for a higher premium than even the conversion policy would cost, or one that provides much less coverage than a conversion policy.

Or you may have done nothing, and now that COBRA is about to end, you find that you don't have time to look for a better policy than the one available through the company. You can't afford to go without coverage, and since it is likely to take a while to find another individual policy, you may have no choice but to accept a less favorable conversion policy.

Don't fall into this trap. Start looking for another policy long before it's time to convert.

❖ GEM: Get a Separate Policy for a Healthy Spouse

If you are unhealthy, your COBRA conversion policy is likely to be expensive. Don't add a healthy spouse to your insurance policy. Even though you may always have been on the same health insurance policies before, now is the time to split up (we mean health insurance here!). When you convert your policy under COBRA, your spouse should go out and get a separate, less expensive policy for herself. The savings will be substantial.

❖　❖　❖

Not every company must offer conversion coverage, but if your employer offers individual coverage to workers who leave, then it must give you the chance to get an individual policy when your COBRA coverage ends. At this writing, more than 30 states *require* employers to offer individual policies, including California, Illinois, Maryland, Minnesota, Missouri, New York, Ohio, Texas, Virginia, Washington, and Wisconsin.

❖ GEM: Get Replacement Coverage Early!

Here's another reason why you should start searching immediately for replacement coverage, even if your company offers a conversion option: your health may deteriorate. If you become ill during the time you're on COBRA, you may not be able to get alternative insurance when COBRA runs out because you are now a poor risk. Conversion coverage might be your only option, and if it isn't available, you might be left uncovered.

EXAMPLE 23

You retire and take COBRA coverage. Although you've got 18 months, you read our book and immediately start searching for other insurance. Within 9 months you find another policy. Even though it's a little more expensive than the rate you're paying for COBRA, it's a lot less than conversion insurance will be. So you make the switch and start paying more.

Was that dumb? No! Two months later your doctor finds cancer. If you had waited until COBRA ran out, you would not have been able to get any other insurance, except conversion insurance (if available). And conversion insurance would have been *lots more expensive!*

Shopping around early can't hurt. If your company offers a good conversion plan and you don't find anything better, you can stay with COBRA and then convert. But if you do find something better, grab it—even if COBRA hasn't expired. Otherwise, the better policy might no longer be available by the time COBRA ends.

HOW TO GET COBRA

You must let the company benefits plan administrator know, in writing, if you want COBRA coverage. The plan administrator is usually someone in the company's benefits or personnel office. By law, you are entitled to get a brochure from the employer describing your health benefits, and the name and location of the plan administrator should be identified there.

You generally have 60 days from the qualifying event—that is, the date you retired, became divorced—to notify the plan administrator of your decision to take COBRA. If you don't get a notice describing your rights under COBRA until after the qualifying event, then the 60 days runs from the date of the notice.

Generally, the employer has 30 days from the qualifying event to alert the plan administrator that you are eligible for COBRA. The only exceptions are that *you* must alert the plan administrator (within 60 days of the qualifying event) if the qualifying event is a divorce, legal separation, or termination of coverage for a dependent child.

The plan administrator then has 14 days to notify you of your right to COBRA coverage. As Table 7.1 shows, this string of events may mean that you don't actually have to decide to take COBRA until long after you retire.

TABLE 7.1

Time Limits for Making COBRA Decision

1. Qualifying event (retirement, etc.)	
2. Employer has 30 days to notify plan administrator of a qualifying event*	30 days
3. Plan administrator has 14 days to notify you of your COBRA rights	14 days
4. You have 60 days to decide whether to take COBRA coverage	60 days

*If you must notify the plan administrator (because the qualifying event is a divorce, separation, or termination of coverage for a dependent child), you get 60 days.

Here's an example of how these time periods affect the timing for your COBRA decision.

EXAMPLE 24

You retire on June 1, 1991, and your health coverage ends at that time. The employer notifies the plan administrator of your retirement on June 20, and the plan administrator notifies you of your COBRA rights on June 30. You've got until August 29—60 days from June 30—to decide whether to take COBRA coverage.

In other words, rather than having just 60 days, if everyone takes the maximum time allowed (see Table 7.1) you may end up with a much longer time—as much as 104 days (134 days in the event of separation or divorce)—to decide on COBRA coverage. This delay is important for two reasons: you get a period of free health insurance coverage, and your money can work for you, not the insurance company.

❖ GEM: Pick Up Free Coverage

We've already said—twice—to start searching for another policy as soon as you start COBRA. In fact, you should start looking *before* you go on COBRA. If you are relatively healthy, and you are able to find another policy quickly, you may pick up a couple of months of coverage *free!*

EXAMPLE 25

Let's take the same facts as in Example 24. You retire on June 1 and you have until August 29 to decide on COBRA coverage. If you become ill during that time, you can elect COBRA on August 29 and your coverage will date back to June 1.

But let's say you are healthy and you find another policy that costs you about the same as the COBRA plan. You can wait to start the new policy until August 30. If you become ill before then, you can take COBRA; you'll have to pay for the months of June, July, and August (which can be hefty), but at least you'll be covered. If you make it to August 29, you can start the new policy. And you'll never have to pay for June–August. You've had the protection of COBRA for three months after your retirement—*without having to pay for it!*

When you elect to take COBRA benefits, you've then got 45 days to pay the first premium. But the first payment *must* cover the period starting with the qualifying event; you can't apply the premium to future coverage only. So if you want to take advantage of *free* health coverage, have your new policy all lined up but arrange to begin coverage after the COBRA election period runs out.

❖ GEM: Get Another Free 45 Days

Waiting the full 45-day period to pay for your COBRA policy may buy you more "free" coverage.

EXAMPLE 26

Let's continue the same facts as in Example 25. You retire on June 1 and elect COBRA coverage on August 29. You've now got until October 13—another 45 days from the election of benefits—to pay.

If you become ill before October 13, you can send in your check (which, again, will be hefty), and the medical costs will be covered by your COBRA plan. If you make it to October 13 without getting sick, you can start a new insurance policy—and you'll never have to pay for June, July, August, September, and half of October. You've had the protection of COBRA for more than four months—*for free!*

✦ GEM: Keep Your Money Working for You

By delaying your COBRA election, you can keep your money in the bank working for *you* rather than for the insurance company. This gem works even if you decide to take COBRA benefits.

If you wait until the last possible day to elect coverage, and then wait to pay until 45 days later, you can save *at least* 3½ months of interest on your premium payments, and maybe more.

EXAMPLE 27

Let's start with the same facts as in Examples 24 to 26. You retire on June 1, but you don't pay anything then. You elect COBRA on August 29, but you still don't pay anything. You wait until the last possible day, October 13 (45 days after the election), to pay for the coverage which dates all the way back to June 1.

How much have you saved? If your premium is $400 a month, you will have saved $20 (assuming 6% interest)—just by delaying your payment as long as possible. While that's not a fortune, it's just about enough to cover the cost of this book!

✦ GEM: Look a Gift Horse in the Mouth

If you qualify for COBRA, your employer may try to fool you into accepting less than you're entitled to by enticing you with free health care. Don't accept a few crumbs when you should get the whole loaf.

EXAMPLE 28

When you retire from your job, your boss gives you three months of paid health coverage. Even though you aren't losing your benefits immediately, don't wait to elect COBRA coverage. After three months have passed, you may have lost your chance to claim COBRA benefits and you will be stuck finding a new policy. Elect COBRA immediately at retirement, then get three months free (from the company) and 15 months of COBRA.

EXAMPLE 29

Your former employer offers you accident insurance in lieu of COBRA health insurance. He says he'll pay for 12 months if you give up your COBRA rights. Take a page from the anti-drug campaign and "just say no." Accident insurance will *not* cover you for illnesses—and that's the very coverage older Americans need most.

❖ GEM: Don't Let Your Employer Force You into a Bad Decision

Let's say your former employer owes you some money, and threatens to hold it back unless you give up your COBRA coverage. In that case, go straight to your friendly lawyer. That kind of intimidation is illegal!

WHAT IF THE EMPLOYER OR HEALTH PLAN DOESN'T FOLLOW RULES?

Contact the benefits plan administrator of the health plan and complain. If you don't get satisfaction, you usually will then follow the appeal process provided by the plan (the procedure should be described in your benefits book).

Sometimes the insurer drags out the appeals. If that happens, wait no more than four months; after that time, you can file a lawsuit in court (usually state or federal court).

Before starting the appeals process, which can get fairly complicated, get yourself a good lawyer experienced in employment law. In many cases, the employer or plan will have to pay your legal fees if you win. To decide on attorney fees, the court will look at how unfair the employer or plan insurer was, what the basis is for your claim, whether others will benefit from your case, and whether your opponent can afford to pay fees.

When you leave a job, you don't have to leave your health insurance coverage, too. COBRA provides invaluable protection which may not be available anywhere else.

·8·

Tax Treats for Older Americans

All taxpayers are not created equal. Uncle Sam has given some special tax breaks to older Americans. But here's the *Golden Rule:* if you want the benefit of these breaks, you've got to act. The tax bonuses won't come automatically.

We are not going to discuss every tax break available to all Americans, no matter their ages; otherwise, we'd need a separate volume just on taxes. What follows are the most important federal income tax–saving gems for seniors. To avoid tax hassles and put money into your pocket, read on!

FILING

Do you even have to file a federal tax return? The answer may be no! At any age, an individual who earns below a certain amount in a year isn't required to file a tax return. But once you or your spouse hit age 65, you get a golden tax break: Uncle Sam raises the maximum income you may receive before you must file a tax return. Table 8.1 shows the tax-filing benefit you get; Table 8.2 describes the different ways to file returns.

❖ GEM: Sometimes It Pays to File Anyway

Of course, no one likes to file an income tax return. Yet you may sometimes come out ahead by filing a return even if you don't *have* to. If income tax has been withheld from your pay, the *only* way to get a refund is by filing a return. And if you can get the Earned Income Credit (page 389), filing a return may get you a check from Uncle Sam.

◆　◆　◆

Filing requirements are based on income. What is included in income? Almost everything. If you are working, count your total salary or wages. If you are a land-

346

TABLE 8.1

Income Tax Filing Requirements

Filing Status	If You Are Under 65, You Must File a Return If Your Income Is	If You Are 65 or Older, You Don't Have to File a Return Unless Your Income Is	Age 65 Benefit
Single	$ 5,900	$ 6,800	$900
Married, file joint return, your spouse is under 65	10,600	11,300	700
Married, file a joint return, your spouse is 65 or over	11,300	12,000	700
Married filing separately	2,300	2,300	0
Married but not living together at end of year or when spouse died	2,300	2,300	0
Head of household	7,550	8,450	900
Surviving spouse	8,300	900	700

Note: Somewhat different rules apply if you are claimed as a dependent on another person's tax return.

TABLE 8.2

Filing Status

Single
 You are unmarried (widow, widower, divorced) or legally separated on December 31, the last day of the year.

Married Filing Jointly
 You and your spouse file a single joint tax return, which combines your incomes and deductions. You can file a joint return even if one spouse has no income or deductions.

Married Filing Separately
 You and your spouse file separate tax returns, each reporting your own income, exemptions, and deductions.

(Continued)

TABLE 8.2 (Continued)

Filing Status

Surviving Spouse (also called Qualifying Widow or Widower)

For the two years following the year in which your spouse died (*e.g.,* if your spouse died in 1990, you could file as surviving spouse for 1990, 1991 and 1992), you may file your tax return as a surviving spouse if you:

- Were entitled to file a joint return with your spouse for the year he or she died (doesn't matter whether you actually filed jointly)

- Have not remarried

- Have a dependent child, stepchild, adopted child, or foster child living with you

- Pay more than half the cost of the upkeep of your home

Head of Household

You are unmarried,[1] and you pay more than half the cost of keeping up a home which was the main residence for more than half the year for you and one or more of the following relatives:[2]

- Your child, grandchild, stepchild, or adopted child who is: (1) single (does not have to be dependent (see page 354) on you); or (2) married (in most cases must be your dependent).

- These relatives, if dependent on you: mother, father, stepmother, stepfather, mother-in-law, father-in-law, sister, brother, brother-in-law, sister-in-law, stepbrother, stepsister, grandparent, son-in-law, daughter-in-law, or (if related by blood) uncle, aunt, nephew, or niece.

[1]You will be considered unmarried for purposes of filing as head of household if you were actually unmarried on the last day of the year, *or* all of the following:
- You file a separate return.
- You paid more than half the cost of keeping up your home for the year.
- Your spouse did not live in your home during the last 6 months of the year.
- Your home was, for more than half the year, the main home for your dependent child, stepchild, or adopted child.

[2]You may qualify as a head of household if you are unmarried and caring for a dependent parent, even if the parent is *not* living with you. As long as you paid more than half the cost of keeping up your parent's main home, you should qualify. These costs include property taxes, utilities, mortgage interest or rent, insurance, and repairs. If your parent is in an assisted living or nursing facility, you can qualify as head of household by paying more than half of these costs.

lord, count total rent (without any deduction for expenses). If you are self-employed, include gross profit (gross receipts minus cost of goods sold). Even some Social Security benefits may be taxable (see page 27).

❖ GEM: Timing a Separation from Spouse May Avoid Tax Hassle

Your marital status (married, separated, or divorced) can affect the filing requirements. If you are thinking about separating from your spouse, watch the timing.

EXAMPLE 1

You and your wife are both 65. Your income during the year is $7,000; your wife's income is $3,500. Because the $10,500 total is below the $12,000 filing minimum, you wouldn't be required to do the IRS tax paperwork (see Table 8.1).

But in November, you decided you couldn't remain together anymore, and so you moved out. Now the tax picture changes. You will have to file a return for the year because, as "married but not living together," your income must fall below $2,300 to avoid the filing (see Table 8.1).

Remember, your tax filing status for the year is determined on the last day of the year. If you had waited to separate until after December 31, you would have avoided this hassle because your joint income for the year would be less than $12,000.

❖ GEM: Sign for Spouse If Necessary

If you and your spouse file a joint return, you generally must both sign. But what if your spouse is incapacitated and can't sign? No problem—you can sign your spouse's name and note "by husband" or "by wife." You should also attach a letter to the IRS explaining why your spouse couldn't sign.

On an individual return, another person can sign only when legally authorized by a guardianship or durable power of attorney. You can use IRS Form 2848, Power of Attorney and Declaration of Representative.

STANDARD DEDUCTION

You can reduce your taxable income by either taking a standard deduction or itemizing your deductions. The standard deduction allows many taxpayers to avoid the time-consuming process of listing all tax-deductible items. You benefit by taking the standard deduction when it is more than the total of your itemized deductions (discussed on pages 350–351).

TABLE 8.3

Standard Deduction

Check the items below that apply to you. Then go to the chart.

- You are   65 or older _____   Blind[1] _____
- Your spouse is   65 or older _____   Blind _____

Total number of items you checked: _____

If Your Filing Status Is	And the Number in the Box Above Is	Your Standard Deduction Is[2]	If You Were Under 65 (and Not Blind), Your Standard Deduction Would Only Be
Single	1 2	$4,500 5,400	$3,600
Married filing joint return or surviving spouse	1 2 3 4	6,700 7,400 8,100 8,800	6,000
Married filing separate return[3]	1 2 3 4	3,700 4,400 5,100 5,800	3,000
Head of household	1 2	6,150 7,050	5,250

[1]The test for blindness is the same as that used for Social Security benefits: You must show that you cannot see better than 20/200 in the better eye, even with glasses or contact lenses, or your field of vision is not more than 20 degrees.

[2]Different rules apply if you can be claimed as a dependent by another taxpayer, such as a child (see pages 353–361).

[3]You cannot take a standard deduction if you are married and filing a separate return, and your spouse itemizes deductions.

Older Americans get a Golden Benefit—Uncle Sam gives a *higher* standard deduction, and that can mean a major savings, as Table 8.3 demonstrates.

Examples 2 and 3 show how to figure your standard deduction.

EXAMPLE 2

You are a widow and age 65. Your standard deduction is $4,500 (see Table 8.3). If you were under 65, your deduction would only be $3,600. In other words, Uncle Sam gives you a $900 "gift" on your 65th birthday.

EXAMPLE 3

You are married and file a joint tax return. You and your wife are both 66, and your wife is legally blind. Your standard deduction is $8,100 (Table 8.3), an increase of $2,100 over the "standard" standard deduction.

❖ GEM: Happy Birthday for New Year's Babies!

Let's say you are 65 on January 1, 1993. That made you 64 at the end of 1992, so you won't get the benefit of the increased standard deduction for 1992, right? Wrong!

The IRS has some screwy rules, and here is one. You are considered 65 on the day *before* your birthday. So if you were 65 on January 1, 1993, you can ring in the New Year and get the age 65 tax benefits for 1992!

FILING STATUS

Your filing status—single, married filing jointly, etc.—can have a big impact on the amount of tax you pay. In many cases, older Americans may choose to file in different ways. Which is best for you? Here are some filing status tips to save you money.

Married Filing Jointly or Separately

As a married couple, you and your spouse may either file jointly or separately. Which is better? In almost all cases, filing separately will cost you. For example, if your taxable income is $20,000 and your spouse has no taxable income, the tax if you file jointly is $3,000; filing separately the tax is $3,273—in other words, separate filing costs you *$273!*

In addition, if you file separately you cannot take some added benefits that could lower your tax even more, such as the special credit for older Americans (see pages 387–389).

❖ GEM: File Separately If You or Your Spouse Has High Medical Costs

You may more than make up for the higher separate rate if you or your spouse has very high medical costs. Medical expenses are only deductible to the extent they exceed 7.5 percent of adjusted gross income (see page 394). By filing separately, your individual incomes are lower, and so it's easier to hit that 7.5 percent. The likelihood that you can cash in on medical deductions is increased.

❖ GEM: Divorce Can Be Less Taxing Than You Think

When money is tight, you may have to look at all of your options. Since two single people sometimes pay less tax than a married couple, divorce may, sadly, be an option.

EXAMPLE 4

Your income is $20,000/year and your husband's is the same. On a joint return, you pay tax of $6,546. If instead you were two single people, you would each pay tax of $3,000—the total would be $6,000. In other words, a divorce would let the two of you keep $546 extra each year.

❖ ❖ ❖

Filing Status for the Year a Spouse Dies

If your spouse died during the year, you again may have options with respect to how to file your tax return for the year: as married filing jointly, single, or head of household. In most cases, you'll come out ahead making your tax return as married filing jointly.

Why? The tax rates for filing jointly usually are lower than for singles or heads of household. Also, the standard deduction you can take generally is higher, and you are still allowed to take an exemption for your late spouse.

**Surviving Spouse, Single or Head of Household
for Years After a Spouse Dies**

For the next two years after a spouse's death, you may continue to get the same low tax rates by filing as a surviving spouse. Example 5 shows how you benefit.

EXAMPLE 5

You are 65, and your adjusted gross income for 1992 was $50,000. Your wife died in 1991, and you continued to take care of a dependent child at home. As a surviving spouse, your taxable income would be $38,700 ($50,000 − $2,300 exemption for you − $2,300 exemption for child − $6,700 standard deduction).

Now let's compare your taxable income if you filed as head of household or single. As head of household, your taxable income would be

$39,250 ($50,000 – $4,600 exemptions for you and your child – $6,150 standard deduction), which is $550 higher than the income as a surviving spouse because the standard deduction is lower. Filing as single, your income would be even higher—$40,900—because the standard deduction is even lower.

The tax you pay as a surviving spouse is $6,182; the tax as a head of household is $7,252.50—a difference of over $1,000! And the tax as single is $8,663.50—a difference of more than $2,400!

Single or Head of Household

Between single or head of household, file as head of household if you can. As head of a household, your tax rate is lower than the rates for single (or married filing separately), and you may also qualify for the earned income credit. In addition, you get a higher standard deduction. Example 5 demonstrated how you get "ahead of the game" by filing as head of household instead of as single.

DEPENDENT EXEMPTION

As we live longer, it is becoming more and more common to see 50- and 60-year-old adults caring for their parents and grandparents. We also see the reverse: grandparents caring for young grandchildren. The burden of caring for a parent, grandparent, or grandchild can be very difficult. To help, Uncle Sam offers a golden tax break, called a dependency exemption. (Two other tax benefits may also be available: you may file as head of household, which we just discussed, and you may deduct some of your costs for care, discussed on page 356.)

You can take a $2,300 tax exemption (for 1992) for each person you can claim as a dependent—and that can put hundreds of dollars back in your pocketbook, compliments of Uncle Sam. To get the dependency exemption, you must pass five tests:

- Citizenship test
- Joint return test
- Household or relation test
- Gross income test
- Support test

The first two tests are the simplest. Your parent, grandparent, grandchild, or other dependent must be an American citizen or a resident of the U.S., Canada, or Mexico, and must not file a joint tax return with anyone else. The other three tests are described below.

Household or Relation Test

Under the household test, you may claim *anyone* as a dependent if he or she lived with you year-round. Temporary absences are no problem—a short stay in a hospital or nursing home will not alter your dependency claim.

What if your dependent dies mid-year—can you still get a full $2,300 exemption even though he (or she) did not live with you for the entire year? The answer is yes. As long as he lived with you right up until his death, you can take the full exemption.

Most close relatives don't even have to live with you. You can get a dependency exemption if you provide care outside your home for any of the following relatives: grandparents, stepparents, brothers, sisters, children, fathers-in-law, mothers-in-law, brothers-in-law, or sisters-in-law. Also, your uncles, aunts, nieces and nephews—*if* they are related to you by blood (not marriage)—qualify without having to live with you.

Gross Income Test

You can claim a dependency exemption only for someone who had gross income of less than $2,300 for the year. Though that's not much, it's often more than enough to get you a dependency exemption for a parent or grandparent. Here's why: gross income does *not* include tax-exempt income, such as Social Security and SSI payments.

EXAMPLE 6

Your father is 85 years old and still manages to live on his own. He receives $800/month in Social Security and a small pension of $100/month. You can claim him as a dependent (if the other tests are met) because his gross income is less than $2,300. None of the Social Security is taxable since his total income is less than $25,000/year, and so the Social Security doesn't count in his gross income.

❖ GEM: Tax-free Investments Can Get You an Exemption

Wise use of tax-free investments might make a lot of sense, as Examples 7 and 8 show.

EXAMPLE 7

Your mother is living on $500 a month Social Security and interest dividends from her $30,000 mutual fund. The mutual fund is invested at 8 percent, and gives her $2,400 of interest income.

You are not able to claim her as a dependent. Although her Social Security income of $6,000 a year doesn't count, she receives more than $2,300 of taxable interest and dividend income (even though she won't pay any tax on the income).

EXAMPLE 8

This is the same as Example 7, except your mother leaves only $20,000 in the mutual fund and invests $10,000 in tax-free municipal bonds yielding 6 percent interest.

Now your mother gets only $2,200 income ($1,600 from the mutual fund and $600 from the bonds)—that's $200 less than she was getting before. But you can take a $2,300 exemption because her gross income is only $1,600—the income from the tax-free bonds doesn't count. The exemption will *more* than make up for your mother's lost income.

❖ GEM: Giving Away Money Can Be Rewarding

As Examples 7 and 8 demonstrate, tax-free investments, if used wisely, can gain you a valuable tax break. Another way to reach the same result is for your parent to give away income-producing assets.

EXAMPLE 9

Your mother gets $5,000/year Social Security, plus her $50,000 savings generates $3,500 interest income. She fails the income test because $3,500 of interest income is too high.

But if she gave you the $50,000, then the interest income would also be yours, and she would meet the gross income test. You could give her the income back as cash gifts, and your mother would still qualify (because gifts don't count in gross income). For some people, this yields a valuable benefit.

Giving away funds is surely not for everybody. First and foremost, an individual puts himself or herself at risk by giving away savings. And depending on your tax bracket, the added tax the recipient pays on the income may wipe out the benefits of the dependency exemption.

◆   ◆   ◆

Support Test

You satisfy the support test by providing more than half of a person's total support during the year. Support includes amounts spent to benefit an individual, such as food, lodging, utilities, telephone, clothing, laundry, medical and dental care (including insurance premiums), adult day care, recreation and entertainment, transportation (including purchase of a car), nursing home charges, and other necessities.

First total all the support received by your dependent, then figure your share of the total. If your share is more than 50 percent, you meet the support test. Your dependent's own funds are counted toward part of his total support *only* if they are actually spent for his support.

EXAMPLE 10

Your mother received $6,400 in Social Security benefits and $2,000 in interest from her savings. She used those funds to pay $7,700 for rent, $300 for recreation, and $400 for life insurance premiums.

Though she received income of $8,400, she only contributed $8,000 to her support. Life insurance premiums are not considered support since they don't contribute to her maintenance, enhance her life-style, or benefit her in any other way. If you contributed more than $8,000 for her support, you would have passed the support test.

When we looked at the gross income test, we explained that tax-exempt income did not count. All income, including tax-exempt income, counts when figuring support. Even savings and proceeds from loans that are not income are counted if used for support.

EXAMPLE 11

Your mother has taxable income of $600, nontaxable Social Security benefits of $1,800, and tax-exempt interest of $200. She used all these, plus $500 from her savings, for her support. You provided $3,000 for your mother's support.

You *cannot* claim her as a dependent, since you paid only $3,000 of her total $6,100 support.

When determining support, compare the amount of your contributions to *total* support for the year.

EXAMPLE 12

You paid $2,000 for your mother's support during the last three months of the year. During the first nine months, she used $1,800 of her own funds for her support. You pass the support test, even though you did not pay anything for nine months of the year. The important thing is you paid more than half the total *amount*.

Support is more than just money. In-kind contributions, such as food or shelter, also count as support.

EXAMPLE 13

Your mother has been living with you and your husband rent-free. To figure the value of the lodging, estimate the amount you would have expected to receive from a stranger renting the same room—say that's $1,000. Calculate her share of your total household food costs—say that's $1,000 (one-third of $3,000). So your contribution to her support is $2,000. If your mother herself contributed less than $2,000 to her own support, you pass the support test.

❖ GEM: Contributions to Maintain a Dependent's Home Carry a Double Benefit

If the dependent lives in his own home, the fair rental value—that is, the amount he could get by renting to a stranger—is considered support he contributes to himself. And that can make it tough for you to meet the support test. But if you help maintain the home (by paying for maintenance, repairs, taxes, etc.), your contribution has a double benefit.

EXAMPLE 14

Your father lives in his own home, which could rent for $3,600/year. Uncle Sam counts that as your father's contribution. You provide $3,000 for his support. Since that is less than 50 percent, looks like you don't pass the support test, right? WRONG!

Your father used $800 of your support money to pay his real estate taxes. That *reduces* your father's contribution to his own support by $800, so his total contribution to his own support was only $2,800. Your contribution carries a double benefit: it adds to your support and it reduces his contribution at the same time. You now pay more than half his support, so you pass the test!

✦ ✦ ✦

If you are helping pay for your parent's costs in a nursing home or home for the aged, you may get the dependency deduction. Private payments to these institutions often don't cover all the costs of care; the institutions often receive subsidies from religious or charitable organizations to make up the difference. Find out what the real cost of care is, then compare that figure to the amount you paid to determine whether you pass the support test.

EXAMPLE 15

Your parent is living in a home for the aged. You pay $2,500/year, but the actual cost of care is $4,300/year—$1,800 is subsidized by the home. You pass the support test because your contribution of $2,500 is more than half the total cost of $4,300.

✦ GEM: Amortize Lump-Sum Payments to Nursing Homes

Some institutions require a lump-sum advance payment. By amortizing this payment over your parent's life expectancy, you may be able to claim an amount toward your parent's support *each year.*

EXAMPLE 16

Your parent entered a nursing home, and you made a one-time $45,000 payment. The home subsidizes his care $2,000/year. If you counted the $45,000 as support all in one year, you would qualify for an exemption once, but never again.

Your father has a 15-year life expectancy, according to standard tables. If you divide the $45,000 by 15 years, that means you actually contributed $3,000 a year for each year of his expected life. Using this calculation, your $3,000 exceeds the 50 percent support contribution requirement because the home pays only $2,000; you would qualify for an exemption every year for 15 years!

✦ ✦ ✦

Many payments are *not* counted in support. When you calculate, do not add in payments for:

- Federal, state, and local income taxes
- Social Security taxes
- Life insurance premiums
- Funeral expenses
- Medical insurance *benefits,* including Medicare and Medicaid (though medical insurance *premiums are* counted as support)

EXAMPLE 17

You contributed $8,500 for your parent's support. He also received $3,000 in Medicare and private medical insurance benefits and $6,000 in Social Security retirement benefits, which he paid for his support. You meet the support test, because your father's $3,000 medical benefits don't count toward his support.

❖ GEM: A Little Savings Can Mean a Lot to You

Your dependent does not have to spend all of his or her income on support. By adding to his or her savings, your dependent can fatten both of your accounts.

EXAMPLE 18

Your mother receives $5,000/year in Social Security benefits, which she uses for her entertainment, travel, clothing, and other support. She lives with you, and the value of the room and board you provide is $400/month, or $4,800/year. Too bad—you don't pass the support test.

Let's say your mother took $150 of her Social Security benefits and put it into a savings account rather than spending it on her support; you made up that amount for her by contributing an extra $150 to her support. Now you pass the test—she's contributing $4,850 to her own support, and you're contributing $4,950.

❖ GEM: Share and Share Alike

Sometimes several people contribute to another's support, but no one provides more than half. Does that mean no one gets the dependency exemption?

The answer is no. You may agree among yourselves who should get the exemption; anyone contributing more than 10 percent may take the exemption if the others agree (and the other tests are met). You might even agree to shift the exemption to a different person each year.

EXAMPLE 19

Your mother pays $3,000 toward her own support. You and your two sisters each pay $1,200 toward your mother's support. No one pays more than half, but together the three children contribute enough to pass the support test.

You can get together with your sisters and agree who should get the exemption. Only one can get it; the other two must file a Form 2120 with the IRS, agreeing not to claim the exemption for that year.

INCOME

The federal tax rules require citizens to pay taxes on their income. And most income is taxable—that's the starting point. Wages, interest, dividends, rents, trust payments, and much more is taxable. But some types of income commonly received by older taxpayers are *not* taxable. Don't report these on your tax return:

- Monies received from a state fund for victims of crime
- Benefits to reduce costs of winter energy use
- Food you receive under a nutrition program for the elderly
- Worker's Compensation
- Damages paid (through a lawsuit or settlement) to compensate you for an injury or illness
- Benefits under an accident or health insurance policy
- Disability benefits paid for injuries under a no-fault car insurance policy
- Disability benefits attributable to your payments into a disability insurance plan
- Gifts from others
- Inheritances
- Life insurance lump-sum death benefits
- Veterans benefits
- Employment awards (like a gold watch) up to $400
- Payments from these volunteer programs: Retired Senior Volunteer Program (RSVP), Foster Grandparent Program, Senior Companion Program, Service Corps of Retired Executives (SCORE), Active Corps of Executives (ACE)

Also, as we've already discussed, some or all of your Social Security benefits may not be taxable; see pages 27–30.

Tax-exempt investments are often confusing. In general, interest that you receive on state, county, or municipal obligations (like bonds) is *tax-exempt*—this is not counted in your income for most tax purposes. Interest from U.S. Savings Bonds and obligations of any agency of the United States is *taxable*. Dividends from stocks and money market funds are also usually taxable.

Rents tend to be confusing, too. If you rent out one unit of a two-family, for example, the *gross* income is not taxable; you are taxed only on the *net*. That means you can subtract from income amounts spent for repairs, maintenance, advertising, utilities, insurance, real estate taxes, interest, and necessary transportation costs. You may also reduce taxable rents by depreciation.

AGE 55 TAX LOOPHOLE

Does it seem like only the rich can take advantage of generous tax loopholes to avoid paying income tax? We're going to let you in on two Golden Opportunities that are specially designed for older Americans, whether rich or poor.

If you are like most people, your home is your most valuable asset. Over the years, you've probably made a nice "profit" on your residence(s). You may have bought your first home 30 years ago for $5,000, and today your house is worth at least 10 or 20 times greater—and you probably have never paid any tax on the increased value.

The federal income tax laws usually require citizens to pay taxes on profits (called capital gains) when they sell any item for more than they paid. For example, if you buy a share of stock for $10 and it goes up to $100, you owe a hefty tax on the $90 "profit" when you sell. Now's the time to plan so you *never* have to pay tax on the profit in your home.

There are two loopholes that can save you and your family a bundle: the Age 55 Loophole and the Death Tax Loophole. First we talk about the Age 55 Loophole; in the next section we explain the benefits of the Death Tax Loophole.

EXAMPLE 20

Your kids have grown and left the nest, and you don't need such a large place anymore. You sell your home and move into an apartment.

Fortunately, you made a nice profit on the sale. You bought the home in 1950 for $10,000; you sold it for $150,000. Real estate commissions and closing costs were $15,000, so your total gain was $125,000 ($150,000 − $15,000 − $10,000).

Normally, you would pay tax on that profit. Under present capital gains tax rules, you would owe $35,000. But with the Age 55 Tax Loophole, you can avoid *any* tax—you save the entire $35,000.

The Age 55 Tax Loophole allows you to escape paying tax on up to $125,000 of the profit from the sale of your house. To qualify, you generally must pass four tests:

1. You must be 55 years or older when you sell (age test).
2. You must have owned and lived in the house for at least three of the five years before the sale (ownership and use test).
3. The home must be your principal residence (residence test).
4. Neither you (nor your spouse) may have taken advantage of the Age 55 Tax Loophole before (one-time test).

These tests are very important. We discuss each below.

Age Test

You must have reached your 55th birthday on or before the date your home transfers to someone else. If you own the home jointly with your spouse, only one of you needs to meet all the tests.

❖ GEM: Keep Your Birthday Happy, Transfer Title After Age 55

If you are approaching age 55 and selling your home, make sure you structure the sale so that title doesn't transfer before your birthday. Other dates, such as the date you are to move out of the house or the date the buyers are to move in, mean nothing—the title transfer date means everything.

EXAMPLE 21

You have sold your house, and the date for title transfer is August 21, three days *before* your 55th birthday. Even though you won't be moving out of the home until September 1, and the new owners won't be moving in until September 3, you lose the benefit of the Age 55 Tax Loophole. If you had only postponed the title transfer a few days, Uncle Sam would have given you a nice birthday present.

If you're cutting things close to your 55th birthday, make sure your sales contract sets the proper date for title transfer and the buyer, real estate agent, and escrow agent handling the transaction understand the importance of the closing date so they don't close early.

✦ ✦ ✦

Ownership and Use Test

You must own and use the house for three of the last five years before the sale. But the three years don't have to be continuous. As long as you can show that you were in the home for 1,095 days (365 days a year multiplied by three years) during the five-year period, you're okay.

And don't worry about short, temporary absences—those are still counted as part of your three years of use.

EXAMPLE 22

For many years you owned homes in Miami and Cleveland. Your primary residence was in Cleveland; you rented out the Florida house most of the year. On January 1, 1989, you sold your Cleveland home (didn't use the Age 55 Loophole) and moved into your Florida house, making it your primary residence. Three years later, in January 1992, you sold the Florida house and moved into an apartment. Can you use the Age 55 Loophole to avoid taxes on the profits for the Florida home?

Since you owned the Florida place for at least five years, and it was your main residence for three years, you get the Age 55 Tax Loophole exclusion.

But what if you spent two months each year back in Cleveland? That's fine—short absences still count as time you lived at home. Besides showing very good sense in choice of vacation location (remember, we're from Cleveland), you also still get the Age 55 Tax Loophole.

You can meet the ownership and use requirements at different times during the five-year period before the sale and still get the Age 55 Tax Loophole, as Example 23 shows.

EXAMPLE 23

In 1982, you lived in a rented apartment. The building later changed to condominiums and you bought your apartment in December 1985. In April 1987, after a serious illness, you moved in with your daughter, where you've been ever since. In February 1989, you sold your condo. Do you qualify for the Age 55 Tax Loophole?

Let's look back five years from February 1989, when you sold the residence—that takes you to February 1984. During that period you lived in the apartment from February 1984 through April 1987—more than three years. So far so good.

But you didn't own the apartment during all of that particular three-year period—from February 1984 until December 1985, you rented. No problem, though, because you owned the residence from December 1985 through February 1989—more than three years.

The fact that the three years you lived there and the three years you owned the residence are not exactly the same makes no difference. As long as you lived in the residence for three of the five years before the sale *and* owned the residence for three of the five years before the sale, you can qualify for the Age 55 Tax Loophole.

❖ GEM: Get the Age 55 Tax Loophole at 53!

You decide to move into an apartment at age 53. You'll miss out on the Age 55 Tax Loophole, right? Not necessarily. If we just got done telling you that you must be 55 to get the tax break, how can you get a benefit at 53? The answer involves good planning.

You can move out of your home at age 53—and not sell it until you reach age 55. As long as you lived in the house for three of the five years before the sale, you can qualify for the Age 55 Tax Loophole under the ownership and use test.

EXAMPLE 24

You are 53 and decide to get an apartment. Your home has appreciated $100,000 since you first moved in; to sell now without the Age 55 Tax Loophole would cost you more than $25,000.

Instead of selling, you rent out the home for two years. At your 55th birthday, you sell it. Although you haven't lived in the house for almost two years, you were there for the prior three years. And since you are now 55—*bingo*—you get the Age 55 Tax Loophole and pay *no* tax.

❖ GEM: Extra Two Years for Disabled Homeowners

Let's say you've been ill and have spent a prolonged period in a hospital or nursing home. In a short time you won't be able to say that you've lived in the house for three of the last five years. Do you have to rush and sell your home so you don't lose out on the Age 55 Tax Loophole? The answer is no—a special rule protects disabled homeowners.

EXAMPLE 25

You suffered a series of strokes beginning in March 1990, and since that time you've spent most of your time in hospitals and nursing homes. You don't really want to sell your home yet because you are still recovering and hope to return home. But it's now February 1992, and you've been out of your home for almost two years—in another month you will no longer meet the Age 55 Loophole residence requirement.

Don't panic. Persons who are in a care facility licensed by a state or political subdivision, like a hospital or nursing home, get extra time. You can qualify for the Age 55 Tax Loophole as long as you owned and lived in your home for as long as *one* year during the five-year period before a sale.

In other words, if you are disabled you get an extra two years to decide whether to sell your home. If you sell your home within four years (rather than just two years) of entering an institution, you still pass the ownership and use test.

♦ • ♦

To take the Age 55 Tax Loophole, you generally must own and live in the *same house* for three of the five years before the sale. The only exception is if your prior home was destroyed or condemned; in that case, you can add the time you owned and lived in your prior home to the time you owned and lived in the present home.

❖ GEM: Hindsight Is 20/20— Take Your Age 55 Tax Loophole Late

The requirement that you must have owned and lived in the same house for three of five years can cost you lots of money, *unless* you know the Golden Rules.

EXAMPLE 26

Last year you sold your home. Although you had a $100,000 profit, you didn't pay tax because you bought a new home of greater value (see page 381). You didn't take your Age 55 Tax Loophole since you figured you'd be living in your new home for many years.

But you've become ill and you can't keep up your new home any longer; you are forced to sell immediately. Unfortunately, you don't qualify for the Age 55 Tax Loophole because you haven't lived in the new house for three years. When you sell, you'll have to pay $28,000 tax on the $100,000 profit.

But wait. You can still go back and take the Age 55 Tax Loophole for the sale of your prior house last year. When you sell the new house, the only tax you'll pay is on any *additional* profit you've made since you've lived in the new home, which will probably be negligible.

As Example 26 shows, you can change your mind even if you had decided not to take the Age 55 Tax Loophole. You may make a choice to take your Age 55 Tax Loophole at any time before the latest of:

- Three years from the due date of the tax return covering the year of sale
- Three years from the actual filing date of the tax return for the year of sale
- Two years from the date any tax was paid

As long as you are within these time periods, you can claim the Age 55 Tax Loophole—even though you may have bought another home in the meantime. In other words, the rules may allow you more than four years to change your mind and claim the Age 55 Tax Loophole.

EXAMPLE 27

You sell your home in February 1992; the return for that year is due by April 15, 1993. Even if you don't take the Age 55 Tax Loophole on your 1992 tax return, you can change your mind until April 15, 1996—more than four years after the sale!

♦   ♦   ♦

Residence Test

You can use the Age 55 Tax Loophole to avoid paying tax only on your main residence. That can include a house, condo, co-op apartment, mobile home, or even a boat (if you live there). But you can only have one main home. If you spend eight months in Cleveland and four months in Miami, your main residence is Cleveland because that's where you spend most of your time.

❖ GEM: Turn a Vacation Home into Primary Residence

Nothing prevents you from turning your vacation home into your primary residence. For some, that may be a valuable strategy.

EXAMPLE 28

Your main home is in Cleveland. You've lived there for 20 years, and the value has gone up $80,000. About 10 years ago you bought a condo in Florida, and you spend about four months there each year; the value of that home has gone up $125,000.

Now you're ready to give up home ownership and take up apartment life. Plus you need the equity locked in your homes. So you sell. The total profit is $205,000 ($80,000 plus $125,000). You'll pay no tax for the Ohio residence (using the Age 55 Tax Loophole), but you'll pay $35,000 tax on the Florida home.

You could do better. Before selling, you make the Miami home your main residence by spending most of the year there. Maybe you even rent out the Cleveland home for a year. Now when you sell, you pay only $22,000 tax—a saving of $13,000. The tax is paid only on the Cleveland residence, and the Age 55 Tax Loophole avoids any tax on the Miami home.

❖ GEM: Don't Sell Off Land

Generally, when you sell your residence, the land on which it sits goes with it. Even if you own 100 acres, you can avoid tax on the entire property if it is sold as a whole with your home. But if you sell off part of the land separately, watch out!

EXAMPLE 29

Your home sits on 50 acres in a rapidly developing community. You purchased the whole property 20 years ago for $10,000; today it's worth $170,000 (for a gain of $160,000). To earn some cash, you sell off 25 acres of vacant land for $85,000 (and you keep the rest). You can't take any Age 55 Tax Loophole for the sale of the land alone, so you'll pay $20,400 tax on the profit (half of $160,000, or $80,000).

A year later you sell your home with the remaining 25 acres for another $85,000. This time you take the Age 55 Tax Loophole for the remaining $80,000 of profit. You save about $20,000.

While that's not bad, you could have done better. By selling the entire property together for $170,000, you could have avoided tax on profits of $125,000, rather than just on $80,000. In other words, you would have pocketed an *additional* $15,000.

♦   ♦   ♦

If you use your home partly for business, you won't be able to entirely escape tax on the profit when you sell. For example, if you use part of home as an office, or rent a floor of a two-family, or live on a working farm, you'll only be able to use the Age 55 Tax Loophole for the residence portion of the property.

But the IRS looks at the use of the property during the year you sell it. And that leads to a Golden Opportunity.

❖ GEM: Turn Business into Pleasure

You can change your property from business to residential use and avoid paying taxes!

EXAMPLE 30

You've been renting the upstairs of your home to boarders, which earns you $300/month. Your home has appreciated by $90,000, and when you sell, you claim the Age 55 Tax Loophole. Since one-third of your home has been used for business, you still must pay $8,400 (tax on one-third of the profit).

But let's say that, instead, you go out of the rental business for a year before you sell. You lost the $3,600 of rentals, but when you sell and take the Age 55 Tax Loophole, you pay *no* tax—the $8,400 tax savings more than offsets your lost rentals.

♦   ♦   ♦

One-Time Test

You can use the Age 55 Tax Loophole to avoid tax on the sale of a home only *once* in your life. But as with every rule, there's an exception.

❖ GEM: Second Chance on Home Sales on or Before July 26, 1978!

If you or your spouse chose to avoid tax on home sale profits from a sale after July 26, 1978, you've used up your Age 55 Tax Loophole. But a sale on or before

July 26, 1978, doesn't count against you. If you were lucky enough to use the Age 55 Tax Loophole before that date, you still can take it again!

◆ ◆ ◆

Married couples and divorced individuals face dangerous traps surrounding the one-time test. Here are the gems you'll need to avoid these traps and cash in on the Age 55 Tax Loophole:

Marriage trap. If either spouse used the Age 55 Tax Loophole before the marriage, *neither* can use it again during the marriage.

EXAMPLE 31

You and Sam are set to marry; both of you own your own homes. The plan is for Sam to sell his and move in with you. When he sells, he uses the Age 55 Tax Loophole to avoid tax; you're not involved at all because you're not yet married.

After a few years, you and Sam decide to sell your home and move to an apartment. You bought your home for $25,000, and now it's worth $150,000; of course, you want to avoid paying tax, too. Unfortunately, you've blown your chance. Since Sam already used his Age 55 Tax Loophole—even though before the marriage—you can't use the Loophole to sell your house (still in your name alone) now.

❖ GEM: Sell Both Homes Before Marriage

Don't get caught in the trap described in Example 31. Sell *both* homes before marriage.

EXAMPLE 32

Same facts as Example 31. But before you and Sam exchange wedding vows, you *both* sell your homes. Since each of you is unmarried, you can *both* avoid tax on up to $125,000 of profit. Now you can buy a new love nest with your money!

Example 32 shows how you can both use your Age 55 Tax Loopholes to avoid tax. But what if you want to live in one of the homes? Is there any way to use your Age 55 Tax Loopholes without giving up both homes?

The answer is yes, as Example 33 shows.

EXAMPLE 33

Same facts as Example 32, except that six months before the wedding, you sell your home to Sam (for full market value). Both of you use your Age 55 Tax Loopholes, avoiding taxes. And you can still live in your former home (now Sam's) after the wedding.

If you later go to sell the home, you won't have the Age 55 Tax Loophole available anymore. But you'll only pay tax on any profit earned *from the time you sold to Sam.*

Go back to Example 31. You bought your home originally for $25,000 and sold it to Sam for $150,000 (market value). Under the Age 55 Tax Loophole, you paid no tax. Now the home is worth $175,000. By keeping the sale "in house," you'll pay tax *only* on the $25,000 profit—*not* the whole $150,000 gain. (Note: Although this gem is perfectly legal, sell to your spouse-to-be as far as possible ahead of the wedding date in order to minimize any risk of an IRS audit.)

❖ GEM: With Two Homes, Avoid the Higher Tax

If you didn't mine the gold with our last gem, and both you and your spouse brought a home into the marriage, you'll only get to use the Age 55 Tax Loophole for one. Use it wisely and avoid the higher tax. Though this may seem obvious, lots of folks blow this Golden Opportunity.

EXAMPLE 34

You and Sam have just married. You both own homes, but you only need one. Yours has increased $125,000 since you bought it; Sam's has gone up $50,000. Which should you sell?

Since you've only got one chance to use the Age 55 Tax Loophole, sell your home. You'll save $35,000 taxes on yours and only $14,000 on Sam's—that $21,000 difference is a nice wedding gift from Uncle Sam!

❖　❖　❖

What if you or your spouse had sold a home and used the Age 55 Tax Loophole before the marriage, and now you want to sell your current residence. Have you lost the Age 55 Tax Loophole? The answer is yes—but you may be able to get it back!

❖ GEM: You Can Go Home Again— Revoke a Prior Use of the Loophole

You can revoke your use of the Age 55 Tax Loophole at any time before the latest of either:

- Three years from the due date plus extensions of the tax return covering the year of sale
- Two years from the date any tax was paid on the sale

Revoking your use of the Loophole sometimes can pay big dividends, as Example 35 shows.

EXAMPLE 35

Let's take the same facts as in Example 31. You blew your Age 55 Tax Loophole because Sam used his when he sold his house before the marriage. By avoiding tax on his profit of $50,000, he saved $14,000; but now you're going to pay tax of $35,000 on your $125,000 profit.

Wait! Tell Sam to revoke his use of the Age 55 Tax Loophole. Although he'll have to pay the $14,000 tax, you will now be able to avoid the $35,000 tax on your home sale. In other words, if he revokes his Loophole and you use yours, together you'll make an extra $21,000! Use the profits from this gem to finance an extra diamond or two for your wedding ring! (Note that you may also have to pay a few thousand dollars in interest and penalties, but you'll still be way ahead.)

❖ ❖ ❖

Divorce trap. So far, we've been talking about the problems that can arise when one spouse uses the Age 55 Tax Loophole before the marriage. Now let's look at the divorce trap: if either spouse uses the Age 55 Tax Loophole during the marriage, *both* lose the opportunity ever to use it again.

EXAMPLE 36

Your husband, Fred, owned a house at the time of your marriage. Shortly after the wedding, he sold it and took the Age 55 Tax Loophole. Since the house was in Fred's name, not yours, you didn't have to do anything except agree (one spouse must agree in order for the other to take the Age 55 Tax Loophole).

Eight years later you divorced Fred. You bought yourself a small condo, where you've lived for a number of years. The place has gone up in value, and you're ready to sell. Can you use the Age 55 Tax Loophole to avoid tax, since you've never used it before? The answer is no—you're out of luck. When Fred sold his house *while you were married,* you used up your Age 55 Tax Loophole.

In fact, the trap can be even worse than as shown in Example 36. A new spouse may also lose the Age 55 Tax Loophole.

EXAMPLE 37

Let's take the same facts as in Example 36. After you divorced Fred, you married Bob and moved into his home. Ten years later, you both want to sell Bob's home and move into an apartment. Can Bob avoid paying tax on the profits?

The answer is no because you were married to your first husband, Fred, at the time Fred sold his house and took the Age 55 Tax Loophole. You lost your Age 55 Tax Loophole, and now neither you *nor your present husband, Bob,* can use the loophole. Poor Bob—he probably never suspected a thing!

❖ GEM: Sell Home Before Marriage

The lost Golden Opportunities in Examples 36 and 37 could have been avoided. If only you had told Fred to sell his house before the wedding, today you would still be free to take your own Age 55 Tax Loophole for the condo.

❖ GEM: Untie the Knot at the Right Time

If you and your spouse are getting divorced, timing the sale of the house just right can mean a lot of money to you.

EXAMPLE 38

You and Cal are getting divorced. The house has gone up $250,000 since you first bought it. You both meet the test for the Age 55 Tax Loophole. Since neither of you want to keep the house, you sell it. Together, you avoid tax on $125,000 of the $250,000 profit. But you pay $35,000 tax on the remaining $125,000 gain.

If only you had waited to sell, you each could have pocketed another $17,500, compliments of Uncle Sam. By selling the house *after* the divorce was completed, rather than before, you could each have avoided tax on $125,000 profit—the entire $250,000 gain would have been tax-free!

❖ GEM: Divorce May Put Money into Your Pocket

We always hate to offer divorce as a money-saving option. But remember the old expression: "the devil made me do it." Here, the Government makes us do it. Example 39 shows how divorce sometimes can be the only way to protect your financial security.

EXAMPLE 39

Tom sold his home in 1984 and used his Age 55 Tax Loophole. In 1987, you and Tom married, and Tom moved into your house. Now you would like to sell and move into an apartment. You've got a $125,000 gain, and tax would run $35,000.

Unfortunately, as long as you and Tom are married you can't take advantage of your Age 55 Tax Loophole. That's because Tom's already used his Loophole. But there is a solution: you and Tom could divorce. After the divorce is complete, you can sell your home and use your Age 55 Tax Loophole! Since Tom sold his house *before* the marriage, his use of the Age 55 Loophole doesn't stop you from using yours now that you are single again.

Once you take advantage of the Loophole, you and Tom could remarry. For a $35,000 savings, the hassle of a divorce and remarriage might be worth it! Or you could live together in sin—the choice is yours. After all, you're old enough to make your own decisions.

USING THE AGE 55 TAX LOOPHOLE

We've just described the four tests for the Age 55 Tax Loophole and given you some gems along the way. Now let's talk some more about using these tests to your advantage.

Married Couples

If you are married, file a joint tax return, and you and your spouse both own the property (joint tenants, joint with survivorship, tenants by entirety, or community property), then the Age 55 Loophole will be available as long as *either one* of you passes the tests. But if the house is in one spouse's name alone, then *that spouse* must pass the Age 55 Loophole tests.

❖ GEM: Shift Ownership to Qualify

Sometimes changing the names on the deed can put money in your pocket, as Example 40 shows.

EXAMPLE 40

You and your spouse have been married for 10 years. You are 50 and your spouse is 56. The house is and has been in your name, and you've never had any reason to change it.

You and your husband are thinking about selling the house and taking an apartment in sunny Arizona. Since the house is in your name alone, you must pass the tests for the Age 55 Loophole. Since you don't, the profit will be taxed, costing you thousands of dollars.

But what if you put your husband's name on the deed? Your husband is 56, but he hasn't owned the home for three of the last five years, so he doesn't pass the ownership and use test; you still don't qualify for the Loophole.

But in three years, your husband *will* pass the test. You still won't be 55, but that doesn't matter. By putting your husband's name on the deed and then waiting to sell, you'll buy a lot of extra sunshine.

◆　◆　◆

As Example 40 demonstrates, planning ahead can save you money. If you think you may be selling before you are eligible to take advantage of the Age 55 Loophole, check to see if you can save money by adding your spouse to the deed.

If you are married and file a separate income tax return, you can use the Age 55 Loophole, but only for $62,500 of profit, half of the full $125,000. And if your spouse doesn't use the Loophole at the same time, your spouse will lose his or her right to use the Age 55 Loophole in the future, even for the remaining $62,500.

Your spouse must agree to the Age 55 Loophole before you can claim it—even if the house is in your name alone, even if you don't live together, and/or even if you file separate tax returns. This is because your decision to use the Loophole prevents *either of you* from ever using the Loophole in the future.

EXAMPLE 41

You and your husband sell your jointly owned home. Your husband is 62 and meets all the Age 55 Loophole tests, but you are only 50 and don't yet qualify.

If you file a joint return, together you can avoid tax on $125,000 of profit because only one of you must meet the tests. If you file separate returns, your husband can avoid tax on profits of $62,500, and you get no benefit at all.

Unmarried Co-owners

Unmarried co-owners (parent-child; siblings; friends; etc.) may *each* take advantage of the Age 55 Loophole, so long as each meets the tests.

EXAMPLE 42

You and your son are both on your deed and live in the house. You are 85 and your son is 60. You both meet all the Age 55 Loophole tests.

The house has gone up in value since you originally bought it—from $25,000 to $275,000 today. When you sell it, you can avoid tax on $125,000 and your son can avoid tax on $125,000—a total of $250,000! If you qualify but your son didn't, you could still protect $125,000. Your son would not have to consent, and your decision to use the Loophole would not have any affect on your son's ability to use the Loophole on another home in the future.

The availability of the Age 55 Loophole to nonmarried joint owners opens up a number of planning options, as Example 43 shows.

EXAMPLE 43

You have lived in your home for 35 years, and it has increased in value by $375,000. You would like to avoid paying taxes when you sell, but you can only protect $125,000 of the profit—the remaining $250,000 of profit would be taxed. Instead of getting $375,000, you'd only keep $305,000—Uncle Sam would take $70,000.

To protect more, you add your two daughters to your deed. Three years later, you sell the property. Now, assuming you all meet the Age 55 Loophole tests, you can avoid paying *any* tax—each of you can protect $125,000 of the profit!

If you own a property jointly with someone else, you don't have to use the Age 55 Loophole even if the co-owner does. Sometimes, there's good reason to hold out.

EXAMPLE 44

You own a home with your brother. The original price was $30,000; today you are selling the house for $150,000. Your brother is going to use the Age 55 Loophole, but you aren't ready to do that. Here's what happens:

Your half of the profit is $60,000, and your brother's half is $60,000. He uses the Age 55 Loophole, moves into an apartment, and pays no tax. You don't want to use your Loophole because the profit is only $60,000. The Loophole avoids tax on up to $125,000 of profits, but it can only be used once. Why not defer paying tax on the profit by buying another home for more than $75,000 (your half of the sale price of the present home)?

Let's say you buy another house for $100,000. Five years later you sell it for $150,000. Your profit on the sale of the second home is $110,000: $60,000 from the first home and another $50,000 on the second home. Now you can use the Age 55 Loophole to avoid tax on the entire amount. By waiting to use the Loophole, you put an extra $14,000 in your pocket! (See pages 380–381 for an explanation of deferred profits.)

Widow or Widower

When a spouse dies, the survivor often decides to sell the home. To help grieving widows and widowers face the financial strains following a death, Uncle Sam offers a break to surviving spouses who don't meet all of the Age 55 Loophole tests.

The Government allows you to use the Age 55 Loophole even if you haven't owned and lived in the home for three of the last five years, as long as your late spouse met those requirements on the date of the sale. Example 45 shows how important this break can be.

EXAMPLE 45

You and Bill were married January 1, 1987. After the wedding, you moved into the home Bill had owned since 1980. Bill died on January 1, 1989. You inherited the house and lived in it until May 1989. But it was too big for one person, and you really needed the money, so you sold it on June 10, 1989. The profit on the sale was $125,000.

You didn't live in and own the home for three of the last five years, so you don't pass the ownership and use test. Does that mean the sale will cost you $35,000 tax on the profit? *No.* Since Bill had lived in and owned the home for three of the five years before the sale, you can take advantage of the Age 55 Loophole.

To take advantage of the special break for surviving spouses, you must still be at least 55 when you sell, you must not have remarried, and both you and your late spouse must not have used the Age 55 Loophole before.

CALCULATING PROFITS FOR THE AGE 55 LOOPHOLE

When you use the Age 55 Loophole, you need to figure the profit on your home. Since you can only avoid tax on profits up to $125,000, you don't want to *over*estimate your profit, or you may pay tax unnecessarily.

In the simplest terms, you figure your gain or profit by taking the sale price and subtracting the original purchase price (called the basis). But if that's all you do, you'll pay too much tax. Let's see if we can help you save some money.

Basis

Figuring the starting basis usually is easy—that's the price you paid for the house when you bought or built it.

If you received the house as a gift or inheritance, you didn't pay anything for it. But don't worry, your basis isn't zero. When you get a gift, your basis generally is the same as the basis of the person who gave it to you. For example, let's say your mother gave you the house, and her original purchase price was $5,000—that's her basis. Your starting basis then also would be $5,000—the same as her basis when she gave it to you.

If you inherited the property, your starting basis is probably much higher—the market value at the time you received it. That's because of the death tax break, discussed on page 382. For example, if your mother's basis was $10,000, and the house was worth $50,000 when she died and left it to you, your starting basis is $50,000, not $10,000. As you'll see in a moment, the higher the starting basis, the better for you.

Adjustments to Basis

Before calculating your profit on the sale of your home, you may be able to add to the basis, which will reduce your profit (and your tax) when you sell. First, add purchase costs you paid when buying the home. These include expenses for:

- Loan charges which you paid (such as points), if not deducted at the time you took the loan
- Legal services
- Appraisal
- Inspection
- Escrow services
- Title recording
- Title insurance
- Surveys
- Transfer taxes
- Real estate taxes owed by the seller that you agreed to pay

Next, add the costs you paid over the years for improvements to the property. Improvements are things that add to the value of the property, lengthen its life, or change its use; they generally must last more than a year. Common improvements include:

- Adding a bathroom, bedroom, or den
- Finishing the basement or attic
- Putting up a fence
- Putting in new plumbing or wiring
- Installing a new roof
- Paving your driveway
- Building cabinets
- Adding aluminum siding
- Planting trees or shrubs
- Installing central air conditioning or a new furnace
- Enclosing your porch
- Waterproofing the basement
- Adding storm windows

WARNING

You *cannot* add costs of repairs and maintenance to the basis. Repairs and maintenance simply maintain the condition of the property rather than add to its value, and generally last no more than a year. These include costs for painting inside or outside, fixing leaks, plastering, and replacing broken windows.

Reductions to Sale Price

Once you've figured the starting basis and adjustments to the basis, you should turn to the sale price and see whether there's any way to cut the amount for purposes of figuring your profit. You can reduce the sale price by the amounts of most selling expenses, including:

- Commissions
- Advertising
- Legal fees
- Loan charges you paid (such as points)
- Escrow fees

You can also reduce the sale price by the amounts of fixing-up expenses (decorating and repairs) you paid to help sell the home, *if* these costs were both:

- for work done during the 90-day period before you signed the sale contract
- paid before or within 30 days after the sale

Figuring the Gain

Ready to try your hand at figuring your profit? Take a look at Example 46.

EXAMPLE 46

You originally bought your home 30 years ago for $10,000. When you bought the home, you paid loan charges, appraisal and escrow fees, and title insurance, for a total of $500. Over the years, you finished the basement ($2,000), replaced the furnace and added air conditioning ($3,000), installed a new roof ($3,500), redid the kitchen ($8,000), added living room blinds ($1,000), and built a landscaped patio ($3,000). You also painted the house inside and out many times.

You have just sold the house for $200,000, but you won't actually receive that much. You've first got to subtract the real estate commission ($14,000), the fee to have your lawyer review the closing documents ($500), and the cost to paint the house and garage just a month before the house sold ($2,500).

If you didn't know your rights, you might have assumed your profit on the house was $190,000 ($200,000 minus your $10,000 purchase price). After avoiding profits on $125,000, you'd still pay $18,000 tax on $65,000 of "profit."

But now you know better. Your basis is not just the $10,000 purchase price. Add:

	$10,000	Purchase Price
+	500	Purchase Expenses
+	20,500	Improvements
	$31,000	Adjusted Basis

Your sale price isn't the $200,000. Subtract:

	$200,000	Sale Price
−	14,000	Commission
−	3,000	Sale Related Costs
	$183,000	Adjusted Sale Price

Your profit is $152,000 ($183,000 − $31,000). After excluding $125,000, your taxable profit is $27,000, and the tax you will pay is about $7,500. By taking full advantage of the adjustments to basis and reductions to the sale price, you saved more than $10,000 of taxes!

**WARNING: DON'T FORGET
DEFERRED TAXES FROM PRIOR HOMES**

So far, we've been discussing the sale of the only home you ever owned. But most older Americans have owned more than one home, and they have deferred paying taxes on earlier profits. When you calculate your profit for the Age 55 Loophole, you can't forget earlier gains. These reduce your basis.

EXAMPLE 47

You bought your first home for $20,000, added $20,000 of improvements, and sold it years later for $100,000. You made a $60,000 profit, but you didn't pay any tax because you bought your current home for more—$150,000. Now you are selling it for $200,000.

Your profit is figured like this: First, take the cost of your new home ($150,000) and reduce it by the untaxed profit on your first home ($60,000); the result ($90,000) is the adjusted basis in your new home. Subtract the adjusted basis ($90,000) from the sale price ($200,000) to get the total profit ($110,000).

Since the profit in this example is less than $125,000, you can avoid paying any tax by using the Age 55 Loophole.

❖ GEM: Avoid Taxes When Buying Down

Most of our examples have involved the use of the Age 55 Loophole where no new home is purchased. This is not unusual—for many people, the time to use the Age 55 Loophole is when trading home ownership for a rental.

Some folks "buy down" as they wind down. They sell their residences for smaller, more manageable houses or condominium units. You can use the Age 55 Loophole when you "buy down," too.

EXAMPLE 48

You originally paid $10,000 for your family home; now you sell for $200,000. You buy a condominium for $50,000, which is all on one floor and will have much lower maintenance costs. Will you have to pay any tax?

You can reduce the sale proceeds ($200,000) by the basis of the old house ($10,000), which gives you a profit of $190,000. You can avoid tax on $125,000 with the Age 55 Loophole, leaving a $65,000 profit ($190,000 – $125,000). Do you have to pay tax on $65,000? The answer is no.

You used $50,000 of that profit for a new residence, so you would pay tax on only $15,000 of the profit. Tax on the $50,000 you used to buy the new home is deferred, not eliminated. If you later sell the home, you'll pay tax on the $50,000 profit (plus any additional gain in the coming years). But in the meantime, you escape additional taxes. And if you die before selling the home, your heirs will *never* have to pay *any* more tax, thanks to the magic of the Death Tax Loophole, discussed on page 382.

HOW DO YOU APPLY FOR THE AGE 55 TAX LOOPHOLE?

You must notify the IRS by attaching IRS Form 2119, Sale of Your Home, to your federal income tax return for the year in which you sell. That form asks for:

1. Your name, age, Social Security number, and marital status on the date of the sale. If the house was jointly owned, give this information for both.
2. The dates you bought and sold the home.
3. The adjusted basis and reduced sales price of the property.
4. The dates of any extended absences from the home during the five years before the sale.
5. Whether you or a joint owner ever used the Age 55 Loophole before, and if so, when.

If you decide to use the Age 55 Loophole *after* you have already filed your tax return for the year of the sale, you can do so by filing an amended tax return on IRS Form 1040X; you'll also have to send in a Form 2119 with the amended tax return.

DEATH TAX LOOPHOLE

The Government offers a little-known, and even lesser-understood, tax benefit that we call the Death Tax Loophole. This tax break can save a lot of money for the spouse, children, and other survivors when a loved one dies.

As we've said, taxes must generally be paid on profits made when an appreciated asset (one which has gone up in value) is sold. This applies to houses and other real estate, stocks, bonds, antiques, coins, and other assets that increase in value over time. These taxes are often called capital gains taxes—paid as part of your income taxes.

EXAMPLE 49

Your mother bought General Motors stock years ago for $3,000, and today it's worth $53,000. When she sells, she'll have a $50,000 profit. Unfortunately, she won't get to keep all $50,000—Uncle Sam will take $14,000 in taxes.

Gifts of appreciated assets do not avoid capital gains taxes on the profits when the recipient of the gift sells the items. The basis (generally, the original cost of the asset, plus any improvements—see page 377) is the same for the recipient of the gift as it was for the original owner.

EXAMPLE 50

Same facts as in Example 49, except your mother gives the shares of GM to you. You get your mother's $3,000 basis in the stock. If you sell the shares for $53,000, your profit is still $50,000 ($53,000 − $3,000), and your tax is still $14,000.

But a gift made at death, either under a will, a trust, a beneficiary payment, joint ownership or laws of intestacy (for a person who dies with no will or trust), generally "steps up" the basis of appreciated assets. The basis becomes the market value at the time of the owner's death. This Death Tax Loophole can provide a *tremendous* tax benefit to beneficiaries.

EXAMPLE 51

Same facts as in Example 49, except your mother leaves the stock to you in her will. Your new basis is $53,000—the market value of the shares at the time of her death. After you receive the stock, you immediately sell it for $53,000. You have no profit ($53,000 sale price minus the new $53,000 basis is $0). So you pay no tax.

In other words, in Example 50 you end up paying through the nose for your mother's gift to you. But by waiting until her death to pass on the stock to you, she saves you $14,000 in taxes.

As you can see from Examples 49, 50, and 51, the Death Tax Loophole can provide a big tax savings. Unfortunately, many people lose out because they don't understand the Golden Rules.

❖ GEM: Don't Make Gifts Without Considering the Death Tax Loophole

Many older Americans give away assets during their lifetimes, for a variety of reasons. Some do it so their kids can enjoy the benefit of their wealth before the kids themselves are too old; some do it to avoid probate of their assets; some do it to reduce estate taxes at death; some do it to qualify for Medicaid or SSI. There are often very good reasons to make lifetime gifts.

But gifts should *never* be made without first considering the tax consequences. And one of the biggest consequences can be loss of the Death Tax Loophole.

384 • *Golden Opportunities*

EXAMPLE 52

You are unmarried, and your only valuable asset is your home. You bought it 40 years ago for $10,000, and today it's worth $300,000. You've heard about the perils of probate, and you don't want your children to have to suffer with the probate system when you die. So you put the house in their names today.

When you die, the house does avoid probate. You've saved your family maybe $5,000 of probate costs, and maybe another $10,000 of state estate or inheritance taxes.

But you cost them a lot more! When the children sell your home after you die for $300,000, they'll have a $290,000 profit ($300,000 minus your $10,000 basis); on that they'll pay more than $81,000 taxes! If you had left the house to them under your will or in a living trust, they would have paid *no* taxes on the profit, thanks to the Death Tax Loophole.

◆ ◆ ◆

The Death Tax Loophole allows heirs to avoid paying tax on profits made when appreciated assets are sold. Used wisely, it can open up a number of useful planning options.

❖ GEM: Shift Assets to Ill Spouse

When you own appreciated assets jointly with a spouse, you'll get the assets when the spouse dies. Typically, the Death Tax Loophole applies to the deceased spouse's half of the asset.

EXAMPLE 53

You and your husband own a home. You bought it 10 years ago for $70,000 and today it's worth $150,000. You've already used the Age 55 Loophole for a prior property.

Your husband dies, leaving you with the home. The basis for your husband's half of the home is stepped up at his death, from $35,000 (half the original basis) to $75,000 (half the market value at his death). The basis for your half of the home remains at $35,000. The combined basis for the home is $110,000 ($75,000 + $35,000).

When you sell the home for $150,000, the profit to you is $40,000 ($150,000 less the combined basis of $110,000). Since you've already used the Age 55 Exclusion, you'll have to pay $11,000 tax on the profit.

If you have a good idea which spouse may die first, you may benefit by putting the house entirely in that spouse's name. Compare Example 54 to Example 53.

EXAMPLE 54

Let's take the same situation as Example 53, except that your husband becomes very ill. Before he dies, you put the deed in his name alone. You figure that you'll want to sell the house after he dies, and you want an added tax break.

When he dies, he leaves the house in his will to you. Since the home was entirely in his name, the entire house gets a step-up in basis, from $70,000 to $150,000, under the Death Tax Loophole. When you sell for $150,000, you pay *no* tax. Your savings: $11,000!

Comparing Examples 53 and 54, you can see the tremendous tax benefits gained by putting assets into the name of the spouse who is likely to die first. While you may not like to think about death, it's better to prepare beforehand rather than hoping beyond hope that it will never happen. On the death of your spouse, you may need the extra cash a little more than Uncle Sam.

This same gem works with other assets besides a house, too.

EXAMPLE 55

You and your wife jointly own stocks worth $100,000. You've been lucky—the stocks cost only $10,000 when you bought them originally.

Your wife has heart trouble and probably won't outlive you. When she dies, her half of the stock will be stepped up in basis under the Death Tax Loophole. If you then sell, you'll pay taxes of about $12,600. Here's how we calculate the amount:

Stepped-up basis for your wife's half of the stock $50,000
(market value
of her half)

Basis for your half   5,000
                                                          (half of the
                                               original purchase price)

$100,000 Selling price
− 55,000 Combined basis
$ 45,000 Net total

Tax at 28% on $45,000 = $12,600

Want to save $12,600? Transfer the stock to your wife. When she dies, she'll leave all of the shares to you under her will—with a stepped-up basis under the Death Tax Loophole. When you sell, you'll have *no* profit and *no* tax.

❖ GEM: Shift Assets to Parent

The same idea can work to benefit children. A child can shift appreciated assets to a parent; when the parent dies, he or she leaves the assets back to the child under the will. The Death Tax Loophole allows the child to avoid paying tax on any profits when the assets are sold.

EXAMPLE 56

You bought some land 20 years ago for $20,000, and today it's worth $150,000. When you retire, you'll need to sell and live on the proceeds. But you won't get to keep the entire $150,000. You'll pay a stiff tax on the $130,000 profit—more than $36,000. That's money you could really use.

Why not ask your father for help? He's 85 years old, and although it's not something you like to think about, he's not going to live forever.

Transfer the real estate to him. When he passes away, he'll leave it back to you. Only now it comes with a basis that has been stepped up to the market value of the property, thanks to the Death Tax Loophole. When you sell, you'll pay *no* tax on the profit! (Your father's estate will pay an estate or inheritance tax on the property in most states. But the estate or inheritance tax runs about 2 percent to no more than 10 percent of the value; the capital gains tax on the profit will probably be 28 percent. So despite the estate or inheritance tax, you'll come out ahead by using this gem.)

WARNING: DON'T WAIT TOO LONG!

The IRS doesn't want to make it too easy for you to avoid taxes. Are you surprised? So the Government has adopted a rule that says if you transfer or give appreciated assets to someone who dies *within one year* of the gift, the Death Tax Loophole won't apply. There's no penalty; you just get the asset back without the benefit of any step up in the basis. But if you're a little creative, you can avoid even this one-year hurdle.

❖ GEM: Get a Third Person Involved

The one-year limit only applies when you give assets to someone who dies within one year and leaves the assets back to you (or your spouse). But if the deceased leaves the assets to someone else—maybe your child—the one-year limit doesn't apply.

EXAMPLE 57

Let's go back to Example 55. Your wife is very ill, so you take your name off the $100,000 of stocks, putting them all in your wife's name. Since she may not survive a year, she makes a will leaving them all to your son, not you. Even if she dies within a year, your son will get the shares of stock with a stepped-up basis, and *no* tax will be paid when he sells. And if he decides to give you a $100,000 gift later, that would be nice, too.

If your wife lives for more than a year, then she can again change her will leaving everything to you. Once the year has passed, you are assured of the benefit of the Death Tax Loophole.

CREDIT FOR THE ELDERLY OR DISABLED

Could you use $1,125? Of course you could! If you are at least 65 or disabled, you can cut your taxes by as much as $1,125 (based upon rules in effect for 1991 returns) by taking advantage of a little-known tax break called the Credit for Elderly or Disabled (CED).

This CED won't help everyone. If your adjusted gross income is more than $17,500 ($25,000 for married couples), or if your Social Security benefits are more than $5,000 ($7,500 for couples), you can skip this section—you won't qualify. But if your income and Social Security benefits are less than these amounts, read on. You may be able to cash in on a secret tax break.

The CED is a tax credit, not a tax deduction, and that means more money to you. If you qualify for a CED credit of $500, that means $500 is taken off your tax bill, leaving $500 more for *you!* (A deduction of $500 means $500 is subtracted from your taxable income, and your tax is then figured on that reduced amount. This might only put $75 into your pocket.)

To get the CED, you must be either 65 or older, or you must:

- Be retired with a permanent and total disability
- Receive taxable disability benefits

The definition of disability here is similar to the definition we've discussed before for Social Security disability (pages 85–86): you must be unable to do any substantial work, owing to a physical or mental condition that is expected to last at least a year or to result in death. A doctor will have to sign IRS Schedule R, Part II, confirming your disability (or Schedule 3, Part 2, if you file IRS Form 1040A for your regular taxes). The doctor has two choices: he can say either that your disability is expected to last at least a year, or he can go further and say your disability will last for your entire life. If the doctor says that there is no reasonable probability that your condition will ever improve, then he won't have to sign Schedule R again in future years. A copy of Schedule R is in Appendix 21. (If the Veterans Administration has decided you are disabled, you can file IRS Form 6004, Certification of Permanent Total Disability, instead of getting a doctor to sign Schedule R.)

Generally, if you are married when applying for the CED, you must file a joint federal income tax return, even if only one of you qualifies for the CED. If you and your spouse didn't live together at all during the year, you may file a separate return.

Figuring the Credit

The IRS never does anything simply, and figuring the CED is no exception. But in general, here's what you do:

Start with the base amount, which the law has set at $5,000 for a single person, $7,500 for a married couple. Then subtract:

- Social Security benefits that are not taxed

- Nontaxable veterans pension
- Any other pension or annuity that is excluded from income

If your adjusted gross income is more than certain income limits set by the Government ($7,500 if you are single or $10,000 if you are married filing a joint return), then you will also have to subtract one-half of the amount over the limit. (Adjusted gross income is shown on line 32 of IRS Form 1040.)

After you have reduced the base amount as we've described, multiply what's left by 15 percent, and that is your CED. Let's look at a simple example.

EXAMPLE 58

You are married, so your base amount is $7,500. Both of you are over 65. Your nontaxable Social Security benefits are $2,000 a year, and your adjusted gross income is less than $10,000. Guess what? Uncle Sam owes you $825! ($7,500 − $2,000 = $5,500; 15% of $5,500 is $825.)

If this sounds too complicated for you, don't give up. The IRS will figure your CED for you if you file Schedule R with just your name and age filled out, and signed by your doctor if you are disabled.

Unfortunately, the IRS has been known to make a mistake or two. Try to fill out all of Schedule R yourself; it's really no more difficult than we've just described. To make it even easier, we have provided easy-to-follow, step-by-step instructions in Appendix 21.

EARNED INCOME CREDIT

The IRS may have a check for you of up to $1,192—and all you have to do is ask! Yes, you read this right, the IRS may pay *you*. You never heard of such a thing? Unfortunately, you're not alone. This year millions of Americans will lose out on over $1 billion of benefits, just because they don't understand the Earned Income Credit.

Don't let this happen to you. Here are the gems that will help you add to your retirement treasure chest.

The Earned Income Credit (EIC) is a federal tax credit available to citizens who worked during the year. You don't have to work full time—part-time is enough. The credit can be used to reduce your tax bill or, if you don't pay tax, to pay you cash.

Eligibility

Based on rules in effect for 1991 returns, to get the EIC benefit your adjusted gross income can't exceed $21,250. But don't let that amount fool you—Social Security and tax-exempt interest income don't count, so your actual income can be lots more.

You must also have had a child or grandchild living with you for more than half the year (all year for a foster child). Your child generally must be:

- Your son, daughter, stepchild, legally adopted child, foster child or grandchild
- And: under 19, a full-time student under 24, or permanently and totally disabled

There are a few other requirements you must satisfy to get the EIC, but these usually pose no problems:

1. Your main home must be in the United States.
2. Your tax return must cover a full 12 months.
3. If you are married, you must file a joint return, unless you file as head of household.
4. You must have some earned income from work.
5. Your earned income and your adjusted gross income must each be less than $21,250.

Let's take a closer look at the last two requirements.

Earned income includes wages, salaries, tips, net earnings from self-employment, union strike benefits, and anything else of value (money, goods, or services) you get from an employer for your services, even if it is not taxable. Earned income does *not* include: veterans benefits, interest, dividends, pensions, annuities, Social Security benefits, Worker's Compensation, or unemployment compensation.

Adjusted gross income is your total income (earned and unearned) minus certain adjustments, including an IRA deduction for you and your spouse and any alimony you paid; it is found on line 16 of Form 1040A or on line 31 of Form 1040.

Your adjusted gross income must be less than $21,250. But that isn't hard for many older Americans, since Social Security benefits and tax-free investment income generally don't count.

If you satisfy these requirements, congratulations! You should be able to get a check from Uncle Sam—up to $1,192 with one child, and up to $1,235 with two or more children who pass the tests described above.

Figuring Your Check from Uncle Sam

Use the worksheet we've provided in Table 8.4 and the Earned Income Credit Table in Appendix 22 to figure your EIC.

TABLE 8.4

EIC Worksheet

1. Enter the amount of your earned income from line 7 of Form 1040 or 1040A (wages, salaries, tips, etc.), plus any other compensation from your employer.

    $_____

2. If you are self-employed, enter the amount of earned income (or loss) shown on Schedule SE, Section A, line 3 (line 3 if you use the Long Schedule SE).

    $_____

3. Add the amounts from lines 1 and 2 (or subtract any loss), and that gives you your total earned income. Enter that amount here.

    $_____

4. Enter the amount of your adjusted gross income from line 31, Form 1040 (line 16, Form 1040A).

    $_____

5. If the amount entered on line 4 is *less* than $11,250, use the amount entered on line 3 to find your credit in the Earned Income Credit table (Appendix 22), and enter that amount here—that is your Earned Income Credit.

    $_____

6. If the amount entered on line 4 is $11,250 or more:

    a. Use the amount entered on line 3 to find the credit in the table (Appendix 22) and enter the number here.

    $_____

    b. Use the amount entered on line 4 to find the credit for that amount in the table (Appendix 22) and enter the number here.

    $_____

    c. Enter the smaller of the amounts entered on lines 6a and 6b—that would be your Earned Income Credit.

    $_____

Let's take a look at a couple of examples to see how the EIC can help you.

EXAMPLE 59

You and your wife have a dependent, handicapped child living with you. You earn $11,935/year. Your wife is self-employed and has a loss of $400 from her business. You also received $100 of interest income. Using the Worksheet (Table 8.4):

1. Line 7 of Form 1040 or 1040A would show: $11,935
2. Your wife's loss from her business goes here: (400)
3. Earned income (adding lines 1 and 2): $11,535
4. Adjusted gross income (wages plus interest): $11,635
5. This would not be applicable, since the amount entered on line 4 above is more than $11,250.
6 a. The credit in the Earned Income Credit table for $11,535 is: $1,160
   b. The credit in the table for $11,635 is: $1,148
   c. Since $1,148 is smaller than $1,160, your Earned Income Credit is: $1,148

EXAMPLE 60

You and your daughter are living in your home. She works full time, earning more than $50,000/year. You get Social Security retirement income of $600/month, tax-free municipal bond interest of $800/month, and you earn another $500/month. Your total income is $22,800/year.

1. Line 7 of Form 1040 would show your wages (your daughter's don't count) of: $6,000
2. Not applicable.
3. Repeat the amount in line 1: $6,000
4. Your adjusted gross income, from line 32 of Form 1040, would include only your wages—your Social Security benefits and tax-free interest wouldn't count: $6,000
5. Since the amount on line 4 above is less than $11,250, you can use the amount ($6,000) to find your credit in the EIC table (Appendix 22): $1,006

> Even though your total income is over the $21,250 limit, you still get a
> check from Uncle Sam for $1,006.

As you can see from Example 60, don't let the $21,250 income limit discourage you from taking a close look at the EIC—you may qualify even if you have lots more income.

❖ GEM: Shift from Taxable to Nontaxable Income

Sometimes you can get the EIC benefit by changing taxable investments into nontaxable investments.

EXAMPLE 61

> Same facts as Example 60, except you receive $800/month *taxable* interest. Now plug into the worksheet and see what happens:
>
> 1. Line 7 of Form 1040 would show wages of: $ 6,000
> 2. Not applicable.
> 3. Repeat the amount in line 1 above: $ 6,000
> 4. Your adjusted gross income would include both
>   your wages *and* your taxable interest: $15,600
> 5. Not applicable.
> 6. a. Credit for the amount on line 3 above: $ 1,006
>   b. Credit for the amount on line 4 above: $ 670
>   c. Earned Income Credit $ 670
>
> In other words, with taxable interest you received over $300 *less* from Uncle Sam than with the same tax-exempt interest. Switching from taxable investments to nontaxable investments can add dollars to your pocket. (Of course, you've got to consider how much less interest you'll receive from a nontaxable investment; typically, tax-exempt investments pay less than taxable ones. Compare the loss of interest with the gain in the EIC benefit to decide whether shifting investments makes sense for you.)

❖ ❖ ❖

Collecting

To cash in on the EIC, you *must* file a tax return. This is where many citizens make a critical mistake. Even if you don't owe any tax, you have to file a return to get this benefit. No pain—no gain!

To claim the EIC benefit, just use your regular tax return—no special form is necessary. Put the amount of your EIC on line 56 of Form 1040 or line 28c of Form 1040A.

EXAMPLE 62

You are retired, but you still work part time. Your earnings come to only $7,100/year—not a lot, but it sure helps. Since your other income is not very much (a little Social Security), you don't owe any tax. But you file an income tax return anyhow. Why? Because the IRS will then send you a check for $1,192.

❖ GEM: Get Extra Credit for Health Insurance Payments

If you paid for health insurance for a child who passed the tests described above, then you can get an extra credit of up to $428. As long as your adjusted gross income is less than $11,250, you should get "full credit." If over that amount, the credit will be reduced.

MEDICAL DEDUCTIONS

Do taxes make you sick? One prescription for the tax-payment blues is to deduct all eligible medical expenses.

The costs for medical and dental care today, even with Medicare and other health insurance, can put a terrible strain on your budget. But you can reduce the pain by taking advantage of the medical expense deductions—for yourself, your spouse, your parent, and any others when you are contributing to their health care.

Of course, medical-expense deductions are available to everyone, but they are particularly important to older Americans. While the wonders of modern science have added many years to our lives, the costs for longevity can be staggering. Getting sick is enough to tarnish your golden years—don't add to your troubles by paying a penny more than you must.

The IRS tries to make it tough to qualify for a medical-costs deduction on your federal income tax return. The biggest hurdle is that you can only deduct unreimbursed medical costs that exceed 7.5 percent of your adjusted gross income.

(On Form 1040, adjusted gross income is found on line 32 and reflects total taxable income minus a few adjustments for alimony, IRA, and Keogh deductions.) For example, if your adjusted gross income is $25,000, only your unreimbursed medical costs over $1,875 would be deductible.

But don't be discouraged. If you consider *all* your medical expenses from A to Z—for you, your spouse, *and* your dependents—you may get yourself a "healthy" write-off.

Deductible Expenses

Take a look at Tables 8.5 and 8.6, which list deductible and nondeductible expenses. We discuss some of the more important deductible expenses, and give some tips about how to beat the 7.5 percent hurdle.

TABLE 8.5

Deductible Medical Expenses from A to Z

Have you received any of the following supplies and services? If so, pull out your bills and start adding!

1. Acupuncture

2. Alcoholic treatment, including contributions to Alcoholics Anonymous and transportation to meetings and treatment at a center for alcoholics

3. Ambulance

4. Artificial limb

5. Braille books and magazines, to the extent the cost exceeds the price for regular books and magazines

6. Car: costs for special equipment installed for a handicapped person

7. Chiropractors

8. Crutches and canes

9. Dental costs, including X-rays, fillings, dentures, extractions

10. Doctor's fees, including for chiropodists, ophthalmologists, osteopaths, podiatrists, psychiatrists, surgeons, anesthesiologists, gynecologists, and neurologists

11. Elastic stockings

12. Eyeglasses, prescription sunglasses, and contact lenses, including fees for exams and insurance

13. Facelifts, tummy tucks, and other cosmetic surgery (but only if necessary for medical reasons, not just personal appearance)

(Continued)

TABLE 8.5 (Continued)

Deductible Medical Expenses from A to Z

14. Guide dog, including costs to care for the dog

15. Gym equipment, a whirlpool, a swimming pool, and other home improvements, if installed for medical reasons on the advice of a physician, and only to the extent the cost exceeds the value added to your home*

16. Hair transplant by a doctor

17. Health club, but only on doctor's advice for particular medical condition

18. Hearing aids, and the batteries to operate them

19. HMO fees

20. Hospital services

21. Insulin

22. Insurance premiums for health-care policies, such as Blue Cross and Blue Shield*

23. Jamaican vacation, but only on doctor's advice for particular medical condition*

24. Kitchen cabinet lowering, ramp installation, door widening, and other home alterations to accommodate a physical limitation*

25. Lab fees

26. Laetrile, if purchased and used where legal

27. Legal fees paid to get authority to treat mental illness or obtain other medical care

28. Lifetime nursing or medical care paid in a lump sum or monthly for self, spouse, or dependent in a retirement facility

29. Lodging and meals at hospital or similar institution if there for medical care

30. Lodging and meals not in an institution, up to $50 per person per night, if for and essential to medical care (for example, you may claim this deduction if living in a hotel to be near your parent in a hospital)

31. Medicare Part A premiums paid voluntarily, and Medicare Part B*

32. Medicines and drugs that require a prescription

33. Nursing-home charges, including meals and lodging, for yourself, your spouse, or your dependents*

34. Nursing services, even if provided by a family member at home*

35. Operations

36. Orthopedic shoes

37. Oxygen

38. Psychoanalysis

39. Psychologist

40. Quiet games, magazines, TV rentals, or flowers for patient in hospital if doctor confirms these are medically therapeutic

41. Removal of hair when by a doctor or licensed technician

42. Telephone and equipment for deaf

43. Television equipment to provide subtitles

44. Therapy

45. Transplants

46. Travel costs to get medical care, drugs, or medicines*

47. Unusual medical services, including treatment by Christian Science practitioners and Indian medicine men

48. Vaccines and vitamins prescribed by an M.D.

49. Wheelchairs

50. Wigs and hairpieces if a doctor says they're important to normal health

51. X-ray fees

52. Zesty exercise or weight-loss programs, or costs for special diet (such as salt-free diet), if undertaken for specific medical reasons on the advice of doctor

*See discussion in text for further information.

TABLE 8.6

Nondeductible Health-Related Expenses

1. Legal fees for guardianship or estate management

2. Travel for general health improvement, not for specific medical reason

3. Smoking program for general health improvement

4. Weight-loss program for general health improvement

5. Medications that don't require prescription

6. Funeral expenses

7. Housekeeping services

✦ Golden Opportunities

TABLE 8.6 (Continued)

Nondeductible Health-Related Expenses

8. Health club dues, YMCA dues, or country club dues which are not related to any specific medical condition

9. Life insurance premiums

10. Toothpaste and toiletries

Some of the deductible expenses listed in Table 8.5 require more explanation:

Home Improvements and Equipment

Home improvements and special equipment installed in your home are deductible *if* the main purpose is for medical care. Under this rule, deductions have been allowed for such common home improvements as elevators for people with heart disease, air conditioning for persons suffering from allergies, and swimming pools for people with polio.

Less exotic deductible expenses include:

- Constructing doorway entrance ramps
- Widening doorways
- Installing support bars in bathrooms
- Lowering kitchen cabinets
- Changing locations of electrical outlets
- Adding fire alarms or smoke detectors

You may deduct only the cost of equipment and improvements above any increase to the value of your property. For example, let's say you install an elevator owing to a serious arthritic problem. The cost is $2,000. When it is installed, an appraisal shows that the value of the house has gone up $1,200 as a result. You can deduct the difference—$800.

❖ GEM: Deduct All Expenses as Renter

If you are renting and make changes in the apartment for medical reasons, you can deduct the *entire* amount of your costs, regardless of how much the property goes up in value. That's because you don't get any financial benefit from the equipment or improvements.

◆ ◆ ◆

You also can deduct the cost of operating and maintaining equipment and improvements—even if none of the installation costs were deductible. For example, if you pay $1,000 to install a whirlpool for medical reasons, but your home goes up in value by $1,000 as a result, you can't deduct the initial costs. But you could still deduct costs to run and maintain the whirlpool.

❖ GEM: Get Backup Support Lined Up

Uncle Sam may look suspiciously on a claimed deduction for a sauna, swimming pool, or luxury improvement. Plan ahead to protect yourself. Get your doctor to write a recommendation to make the home improvement for medical reasons. And get an independent appraisal of your home after the improvement is made to confirm the amount of any increased value, if any.

◆ ◆ ◆

Medical Insurance

Medical insurance premiums, such as for Blue Cross, are deductible. Premiums for Medicare Part B can be deducted; even premiums for Part A, *if* voluntarily paid, are deductible. But you cannot deduct the portion of Social Security tax that covers you for Part A.

Premiums are also deductible when you pay for policies covering prescription drugs and replacement of contact lenses.

When you buy a multipurpose health or accident policy, you must be careful *only* to deduct that part of the premium paid for medical care expenses—you *cannot* deduct any amount for coverage for loss of earnings, limbs, or sight.

❖ GEM: Get Your Employer
to Pick Up the Tab for Insurance—Cost Free!

Businesses often approach medical benefits in one of two ways: (1) the employer pays for the cost of insurance; or (2) the employer offers an insurance plan for which the workers pay.

If your medical costs aren't high enough to qualify you for a deduction, you may still get yourself a break by getting your employer to pick up the tab. Example 63 shows how.

EXAMPLE 63

You pay $2,500 for health insurance offered through your company. That's a big hit on your budget. And even with all of our tips about deductible expenses, your expenses are under 7.5 percent of your income.

Ask your employer to pay for the insurance; tell him you'll be happy to have your salary reduced by the same $2,500. That way, this plan won't cost your company a penny extra. But *you* benefit, thanks to Uncle Sam. Since your income is $2,500 less, you save $700 (in the 28% tax bracket). The insurance premiums paid by the company are *not* included in your income (or taxed).

◆ ◆ ◆

Travel Expenses

As you get on in years, it may seem that you spend half your time going to or coming from doctor appointments. If you use your car to go to the doctor, lab, hospital, or other medical facility, you can deduct your costs for gas, oil, parking, fees, and tolls. Or you may deduct nine cents per mile (plus parking and tolls). You can take this same deduction when you take a parent for medical care.

If you use a bus, taxi, or train, those costs are also deductible.

❖ GEM: Let Uncle Sam Bring Sunshine to Your Life

Wouldn't it be nice to deduct the expenses for your trip to Florida this winter? You may be able to do just that! If there is a *real* medical reason for your trip, the travel costs should be deductible.

EXAMPLE 64

You have a medical condition that makes it very difficult to breathe during the cold winters up north. So your doctor advises you to spend a few months in sunny Florida—for medical reasons, of course. You can deduct the travel costs. The costs for food and lodging are not deductible, but you can't have everything.

◆ ◆ ◆

Even travel expenses for a permanent move may be deductible, if the move is being made to alleviate a particular illness.

Plan ahead—talk to your doctor about your medical condition and have him recommend your travel in writing. That should keep the IRS at bay.

Nursing Services and Nursing Homes

You can deduct amounts paid for nursing services, even if not performed by a nurse. If you are paying someone to help with giving medications, changing dressings, bathing, and grooming, the costs are deductible.

Payments made to a family member (other than a spouse) who is providing nursing services are also deductible. For example, if your daughter moves into your home to care for you after surgery, you can deduct any reasonable payments you give her (including Social Security tax payments, or FICA). You also can deduct costs for her meals and any added utility costs and rent you pay because of her presence. But if she spends time doing housework, you must figure what portion of her time is involved with nursing or caregiving, and deduct only that portion of her expenses. Housekeeping services and routine nonmedical care are not deductible.

❖ GEM: Take Along a Helping Hand

You have terrible arthritis, which is at its worst during the winter. Your doctor says a trip to Florida would reduce your arthritis problem, but you can't travel alone. So you invite your daughter, who cares for you on the trip. You can deduct your travel expenses *and* the expenses of your daughter. Even the costs for a spouse can qualify.

✦   ✦   ✦

Nursing home costs can be very high. If you (or your dependent) is in a nursing home for medical care (rather than just because he can't care for himself), all costs are deductible. Medical care doesn't have to be the only reason for being in the nursing home, just an important reason. For example, if your parent is in a nursing home, at least in part because he's not able to take his medications on his own, the costs all should be deductible. Most people in nursing homes require at least some medical care and attention. Have a doctor state, in writing, the medical reason(s) for the nursing home stay.

Expenses for Spouse and Dependents

When toting up your medical expenses, include amounts you paid for your spouse and dependents, including your parents. Including these costs may put you over the 7.5 percent limit.

You can include medical expenses you paid for a spouse, as long as you were married either at the time your spouse received the care or at the time you paid.

❖ GEM: Juggle Medical Costs When Getting Married

If you are getting married, make sure you maximize your chances to take a medical deduction.

EXAMPLE 65

You are going to marry Sally next month, January 15. She just had some surgery, which cost $3,000 above the insurance coverage. Based on her income, though, she won't be able to deduct any of that amount.

But if you tell her to hold off payment until after the wedding, you may do better. Depending on your and Sally's medical expenses next year, when you file a joint return, the entire $3,000 may qualify for a deduction. That would put $840 into your pocket—a nice wedding present from Uncle Sam!

❖   ❖   ❖

You also can include in your medical expenses costs paid for a dependent, such as a parent. The dependency tests are discussed on page 353. You can count the medical costs even if the individual fails to qualify as your dependent because his income exceeds $2,300, as long as the other dependency tests are met.

EXAMPLE 66

Your mother earned $2,400. You can't claim her as a dependent because she earned more than $2,300, although she passes the other dependency tests. You paid $800 of her medical expenses. If you count the $800 when figuring your medical deduction, your pocketbook will get a healthy boost.

You actually get two shots at taking a deduction for medical expenses you paid for someone else. As long as the person passed the dependency tests (other than income) *either* in the year you paid the costs *or* in the year the costs were incurred, you can take the deduction.

EXAMPLE 67

Your father had a stroke in 1991, and he moved in with you for four months while he recovered. In 1992, you paid $3,000 for therapy provided to him during 1991.

For the year 1992, even counting the $3,000 you paid for his medical costs, you didn't pay for half his support, so he's not a dependent. Does that mean you lose out on the $3,000 medical deduction? No!

In 1991, when the therapy was provided, you did provide more than half your father's support. Since he was a dependent when the services were provided, you can take the medical deduction for the year you pay (1992).

Many children today find themselves paying for nursing care for their parents, either at home or in a nursing home. As we stated in Table 8.5, typical nursing home care qualifies for a medical deduction. You can include the entire fee; you don't have to deduct for food or lodging.

If you are paying for nurses to come in to your parent's home, or if you are paying others to perform nursing services, these costs are also deductible as medical expenses. Nursing services include bathing and dressing your parent.

❖ GEM: Combine Medicaid and Tax Planning

If your parent gives assets to you, which is often done to qualify for Medicaid (see Chapter 11), to avoid probate, to reduce income or estate taxes, or for other reasons, the assets are yours. If you then use some or all of those funds to care for your parent, you are using *your* money—and you may be able to deduct the costs.

EXAMPLE 68

Your mother has bad arthritis and doesn't get around very easily anymore. She's still living in her apartment, but she recognizes that she may need to enter a nursing home at some time in the future. So she turns her cash assets over to you.

She has made it clear to you she wants to stay at home as long as possible. To do that, she now needs nurses to come in several hours a day to help. You use the funds from your mother to pay. Uncle Sam will help cover the costs. You can take a medical deduction for the expenses (assuming the total costs pass 7.5% of your income).

◆ ◆ ◆

Beat the 7.5 Percent Limit

The most difficult, most aggravating thing about medical-expense deductions is the requirement that your medical expenses exceed 7.5 percent of your adjusted gross income. Here are several gems to help you beat this unfair limitation.

❖ GEM: Bunch Expenses

Moving medical expenses from one year to the next may enable you to satisfy the 7.5 percent income limit.

EXAMPLE 69

Your adjusted gross income in 1991 is $20,000; 7.5 percent is $1,500. Your income in 1992 is the same. Your unreimbursed medical expenses each year are $1,200. Unfortunately, that's not quite enough to qualify for a deduction in either year, since it's not 7.5 percent of your income.

But let's change the facts a little. You postpone $800 of nonemergency medical expenses from 1991 to 1992. Although you still get no tax deduction in 1991, you are now able to deduct $500 ($2,000 − $1,500) on your 1992 tax return.

Bunching expenses, as shown in Example 69, can put some much-needed cash into your pocket. But how can you do this?

Planning medical treatment usually isn't easy; you can't control when you will get sick! But some medical treatment can be planned. Can you wait a few months for cataract surgery? Does it pay to replace your dentures or glasses this year or next? Would it make sense to postpone your trip to Florida (for medical reasons) from December to January? As you can see, the timing for some medical expenses can be adjusted.

And the timing for *payment* of medical expenses can be made to fit your needs, too. You can deduct medical expenses in the year you *pay* them, not in the year you receive the care. So postponing payments may make sense.

EXAMPLE 70

You had some extensive dental work done in September, and you just received the bill in October. Should you pay it?

You go through your unreimbursed medical expenses, and you find that, even including the dental costs, you won't reach the 7.5 percent limit this year. Make arrangements with the dentist to pay in January of the following year. Although you often can't tell in advance whether you'll have enough medical expenses to reach the 7.5 percent limit next year, you've got nothing to lose by delaying payment. And you might end up with a tax break to help you cover the costs!

WARNING

If you pay by credit card, the payment is counted in the year you put the cost on the charge, *not* the year you pay the card balance.

❖ GEM: Reduce Adjusted Gross Income

Since you can deduct medical costs that exceed 7.5 percent of your adjusted gross (taxable) income, you might benefit by taking steps to cut your taxable income.

EXAMPLE 71

It's February, and you are facing substantial medical costs that will not be reimbursed. You are widening the hallways and door entrances in your home, lowering cabinets and light switches, and making other improvements to accommodate your wife who is confined to a wheelchair. Your total unreimbursed medical costs this year will be in the $4,000 range.

Your taxable income is about $50,000 annually, which means that you can only deduct medical expenses over $3,750 (7.5% of $50,000). In other words, only about $250 of your huge expenses will be deductible.

But if you shift some taxable investments into tax-exempt or tax-deferred investments, the benefits could be great. Let's say you change investments so $10,000 of your income is nontaxable and $40,000 is taxable; that reduces your 7.5 percent limit to $3,000. Instead of only $250 qualifying for a deduction, now $1,000 is deductible. Depending on the difference in interest rates (tax-free investments are likely to pay a lower return), you could wind up pocketing more cash at the end of the year through this gem.

❖ GEM: File Separate Returns

If you are married and one of you has much higher medical expenses than the other, you are likely to be better off paying expenses out of separate funds and filing separate returns rather than a joint return. On your separate returns, each of you can deduct the medical expenses actually paid. And the 7.5 percent limit applies only to that spouse's income.

EXAMPLE 72

Your adjusted gross income is $25,000 and your husband's is the same. You had only $500 of medical costs. But your husband was extremely ill, and his Medicare and Blue Cross didn't cover $4,000 of his costs.

On a joint return, only expenses over $3,750 (7.5% of $50,000) would be deductible. So only $750 ($4,500 − $3,750) would qualify. But on a separate return, your husband's 7.5 percent limit would be $1,875, and he could take a deduction for $2,125.

The total tax the two of you would pay is $385 *less* by filing separate returns instead of joint returns.

❖ GEM: Start a Part-time Business to Cover Insurance Costs

If you are self-employed, the law allows you to deduct 25 percent of your insurance costs as a *business* expense, rather than as a medical expense. You don't have to worry at all about the 7.5 percent limit.

The amount of your deduction is limited to the net earnings from your business (in other words, you can't deduct more than you make). Example 73 shows how important this benefit can be.

EXAMPLE 73

You are spending $2,500 a year on health insurance costs, which aren't deductible. And you've been looking for something to do with your time. So you start doing odd jobs for people in the neighborhood, earning $200 to $300/month. Now, as a self-employed individual you can deduct $625 (25% of the $2,500 premiums), without worrying about the 7.5% income limit. (The remaining portion of your $2,500 premiums may still be taken as medical deductions, subject to the 7.5% limit.)

MORE INFORMATION

For more information about these Golden Opportunities to cut your taxes, take a look at these *free* IRS publications:

- Publication 17—Your Federal Income Tax
- Publication 501—Exemptions, Standard Deduction, and Filing Information
- Publication 502—Medical and Dental Expenses
- Publication 503—Tax Information on Selling Your Home
- Publication 524—Credit for the Elderly or the Disabled
- Publication 525—Taxable and Non-Taxable Income
- Publication 530—Tax Information for Homeowners
- Publication 544—Sales and Other Dispositions of Assets
- Publication 551—Basis of Assets
- Publication 554—Tax Information for Older Americans
- Publication 596—Earned Income Credit
- Publication 907—Tax Information for Handicapped and Disabled Individuals
- Publication 929—Tax Rules for Children and Dependents

While these are some of the most useful, there are many more. Publication 920—Guide to Free Tax Services—lists all of the IRS publications. You can get any of these publications by calling the IRS toll-free 800-829-3676, or by stopping at the nearest IRS office.

The IRS also offers an automated information service, called Tele-Tax, which can answer many questions. A list of the 140 Tele-Tax subjects is included in Publication 17 and is available at your IRS office. To use this service, just pick out the tape you want to hear and punch into your telephone the Tele-Tax number. With a touch-tone telephone, Tele-Tax is available seven days a week, 24 hours a day; otherwise, it's available during regular office hours.

For those of you with VCRs, there even is a videotape available with line-by-line instructions on how to complete your return. You can get this at some libraries and videotape outlets.

Lastly, the IRS also has trained "real people" to answer your specific questions. Table 8.7 lists toll-free numbers you can call for help.

Although death and taxes are inevitable, paying taxes shouldn't be the death of you. Using our tax-saving gems will provide a welcome Rx from the pain of excessive IRS-itis.

TABLE 8.7

Numbers to Call for Tax Help

Alabama
800-829-1040

Alaska
Anchorage, 561-7484
Elsewhere, 800-829-1040

Arizona
Phoenix, 257-1233
Elsewhere, 800-829-1040

Arkansas
800-829-1040

California
Oakland, 839-1040
San Francisco, 839-1040
Elsewhere, 800-829-1040

Colorado
Denver, 825-7041
Elsewhere, 800-829-1040

Connecticut
800-829-1040

Delaware
800-829-1040

District of Columbia
800-829-1040

Florida
Jacksonville, 354-1760
Elsewhere, 800-829-1040

Georgia
Atlanta, 522-0050
Elsewhere, 800-829-1040

Hawaii
Oahu, 541-1040
Elsewhere, 800-829-1040

Idaho
800-829-1040

Illinois
Chicago, 435-1040
In area code 708, 312-435-
1040
Elsewhere, 800-829-1040

Indiana
Indianapolis, 226-5477
Elsewhere, 800-829-1040

Iowa
Des Moines, 283-0523
Elsewhere, 800-829-1040

Kansas
800-829-1040

Kentucky
800-829-1040

Louisiana
800-829-1040

Maine
800-829-1040

Maryland
Baltimore, 962-2590
Elsewhere, 800-829-1040

Massachusetts
Boston, 523-1040
Elsewhere, 800-829-1040

Michigan
Detroit, 237-0800
Elsewhere, 800-829-1040

Minnesota
Minneapolis, 644-7515
St. Paul, 644-7515
Elsewhere, 800-829-1040

Mississippi
800-829-1040

Missouri
St. Louis, 342-1040
Elsewhere, 800-829-1040

Montana
800-829-1040

Nebraska
Omaha, 422-1500
Elsewhere, 800-829-1040

Nevada
800-829-1040

New Hampshire
800-829-1040

New Jersey
800-829-1040

New Mexico
800-829-1040

New York
Bronx, 732-0100
Brooklyn, 596-3770
Buffalo, 685-5432
Manhattan, 732-0100
Nassau, 222-1131

(Continued)

TABLE 8.7 (Continued)

Numbers to Call for Tax Help

New York
Queens, 596-3770
Staten Island, 596-3770
Suffolk, 724-5000
Elsewhere, 800-829-1040

North Carolina
800-829-1040

North Dakota
800-829-1040

Ohio
Cincinnati, 621-6281
Cleveland, 522-3000
Elsewhere, 800-829-1040

Oklahoma
800-829-1040

Oregon
Portland, 221-3960
Elsewhere, 800-829-1040

Pennsylvania
Philadelphia, 574-9900
Pittsburgh, 281-0112
Elsewhere, 800-829-1040

Puerto Rico
San Juan Metro Area,
766-5040
Isla, 766-5549

Rhode Island
800-829-1040

South Carolina
800-829-1040

South Dakota
800-829-1040

Tennessee
Nashville, 259-4601
Elsewhere, 800-829-1040

Texas
Dallas, 742-2440
Houston, 541-0440
Elsewhere, 800-829-1040

Utah
800-829-1040

Vermont
800-829-1040

Virginia
Richmond, 649-2361
Elsewhere, 800-829-1040

Washington
Seattle, 442-1040
Elsewhere, 800-829-1040

West Virginia
800-829-1040

Wisconsin
Milwaukee, 271-3780
Elsewhere, 800-829-1040

Wyoming
800-829-1040

Phone Help for Hearing-Impaired People with TDD Equipment

All areas in U.S., including
   Alaska, Hawaii, Virgin
   Islands, and Puerto Rico,
   800-829-4059

Hours of Operation:
8:00 A.M. to 6:30 P.M. EST
   (Jan. 1–April 4)
9:00 A.M. to 7:30 P.M. EDT
   (April 5–April 15)
9:00 A.M. to 5:30 P.M. EDT
   (April 16–Oct. 24)
8:00 A.M. to 4:30 P.M. EST
   (Oct. 25–Dec. 31)

✦9✦

Home Sweet Home:
Treasures Right Under Your Roof

On paper, your net worth is pretty decent. Yet you never seem to have enough money to do all those things you want, or need, to do. How can this be?

The answer is simple. Many older Americans are short on cash but have built up a lot of equity in their home. Sound familiar? Over 16 million older Americans own their homes free and clear. Of those, at least 5 million, and probably more, qualify as house rich and cash poor.

How can you get the equity from your home? Most people think that the only way to cash in on their home equity is either to sell or borrow against the home, but neither option is very appealing. Owning a home means comfort and security; selling is often terribly traumatic. When you've lived in a home for 10, 20, even 30 years or more, you're comfortable with the house and you know the neighborhood. Memories abound in every room. Moving can be both emotionally and financially costly!

Standard borrowing usually is no better an option. The pressure of large monthly payments imposes serious strains on older Americans. And you may not be able to get a conventional mortgage or home equity loan, even if you wanted to. To qualify for those loans, you must meet certain income requirements—and that may be impossible on a fixed income from Social Security, pension, interest, and dividends.

Even when you do qualify, your problems aren't over; in fact, they may just be starting. With a standard loan, you must make monthly payments. If you become ill, are laid off, or for some other reason can't meet your obligations, the lender can foreclose and force a sale of the home—your worst nightmare come true.

Wouldn't it be nice if you could keep your home and increase your monthly income at the same time? Sure it would! What would you do if you could add

$200, $300, even $500 or more to your monthly income? Take a trip to Hawaii? Buy a new car? Or maybe just maintain your current life-style in spite of rising taxes, insurance, utilities, and home maintenance costs?

Believe it or not, there may be a way that you can accomplish these objectives without having to rob a bank! When Dorothy (in *The Wizard of Oz*) tapped her heels together and chanted "There's no place like home," she was absolutely right. Your home is full of gold, and we're going to help you get to it *without* having to move or pay a monthly mortgage. How? By using the following gems: reverse mortgages, sale and leaseback, home sharing, co-signor, and special-purpose loans.

REVERSE MORTGAGES

When we say the word *mortgage,* what's the first thought that comes into your mind? Monthly payments, of course. With a usual mortgage or home equity loan, you borrow a lump sum, using your house as security. As you repay the loan each month, your debt to the bank shrinks, slowly but surely, and your share of ownership increases until the home is yours free and clear.

A reverse mortgage works just the opposite: it pays *you* money each month. Your debt to the bank grows, rather than shrinks. The monthly payments to you can be a wonderful supplement to your income. And you generally don't have to worry about paying the loan back until you die. At that time, the home typically will be sold and the proceeds used to pay off the debt.

Reverse mortgages have been around for years, yet very few older Americans have taken advantage of them. These loans have not been widely available since banks, savings and loans, and mortgage companies have been hesitant to offer them. But all that is changing, thanks to Uncle Sam.

The Federal Housing Administration (FHA) is now guaranteeing reverse mortgages for homeowners 62 years of age or older. Any one of the 10,000 lenders that regularly do business with the FHA is allowed to make reverse mortgages guaranteed by the FHA, which means important protection for both you and the lender. Most important, if the amount of your debt grows to be more than the value of your home, you don't have to worry—no one can ever try to collect more than the value of the home. If the lender can't collect the entire debt from the proceeds of a sale of the house, the Government makes up the difference.

The FHA guarantees three primary types of reverse mortgages: tenure, term, and line of credit. Each is a little different. We tell you about each of these, and then we discuss the types of reverse mortgages that are not FHA insured.

Tenure Reverse Mortgage

A tenure reverse mortgage makes monthly payments to you for life or, if you choose, until you leave the home, such as if and when you must enter a nursing home. The amount you receive is paid based on a complicated formula that considers your age, the interest rate, and the value of your home. You can see how the tenure reverse mortgage works in Example 1.

EXAMPLE 1

You are 65, and your income from Social Security doesn't give you enough to meet your needs. Your home is worth about $80,000, but that doesn't help you take a vacation to visit your grandchildren. So you get a tenure reverse mortgage paying you $185/month for life. If the interest is 10 percent per year, compounded monthly, here is what you will owe after each year:

Year	You Received	You Owe*	Interest
1	$ 2,222	$ 4,129	$ 292
2	4,444	6,937	850
3	6,666	10,054	1,702
4	8,888	13,515	2,882
5	11,110	17,357	4,425
10	22,220	43,934	19,154
20	44,440	164,358	112,680

*These figures assume $1,600 closing costs and a small amount of mortgage insurance included in mortgage.

As you can see, if you live five years, you'll only owe $17,357. If your house is worth $100,000 at your death, it may be sold and your heirs will get in the neighborhood of $82,643 (after the $17,357 is paid to the lender). If you live 20 years, you'll owe the lender more than $160,000.

But what if the house is worth only $150,000 after 20 years? Can the lender grab your bank accounts and other assets? No! Any shortfall is made up by good old Uncle Sam.

Term Reverse Mortgage

With a term reverse mortgage, you get monthly payments for a fixed number of years, not for life. When that time expires, the paychecks stop coming in. *But you don't have to pay the loan balance and you don't have to move out.* The loan just sits (accruing interest) until you die or move out—only then can the house be sold to pay the loan.

Since payments are for a fixed period rather than for your entire life, the payments you receive are higher than you'd get under a tenure reverse mortgage.

EXAMPLE 2

Let's assume the same facts as in Example 1, except you get a term reverse mortgage paying you for 10 years. Instead of $185/month, you get paychecks of $278/month. At the end of 10 years, you'll owe $63,720.

Should you die at that time, your house would then be sold and the debt paid from the proceeds. If the house sells for $130,000, your heirs would get about $66,280 and the lender would get the rest.

But let's say you live another 10 years. That's okay—in fact, it's great! You can live in the house without paying anything to the lender. When you die, the loan balance would be more than $180,000, as interest accumulated on the $63,720 balance. If the house value hasn't gone up enough to cover the balance, the Government will pick up the tab.

Line of Credit Reverse Mortgage

A line of credit reverse mortgage looks a little like a typical home equity line of credit that you can get from almost any bank. With both types of loans, the lender sets a maximum amount you can borrow, based primarily on the value of your home. Rather than getting steady monthly payments, you borrow as you need to.

So far, the line of credit reverse mortgage and the standard home equity line of credit sound the same. But here's the important difference: with a standard home equity credit line, you must make regular monthly payments to repay the loan. This means your monthly income has to be high enough to make the payments. And if you fail to make the payments, the lender can foreclose and force a sale of your home. Finally, you may be required to requalify for a standard home equity loan each year; if you don't requalify, the lender could demand repayment of the entire loan balance immediately.

An FHA-insured line of credit reverse mortgage cuts the risks. You do *not* have to make any monthly payments. The loan balance sits (accruing interest for the lender) until you sell or move out; only then will the lender be repaid. *You cannot be forced out of your home!* Also, you don't have to requalify every year. Once you qualify, you can draw on the credit line until you reach the maximum.

Here's one more nice benefit: your credit limit may increase each year by a percentage agreed to by you and the lender. For example, if your credit line is $30,000 and you don't use it for a year, the line may increase to $33,000 for the following year.

A line of credit reverse mortgage is not designed to provide a monthly income supplement—a tenure or term reverse mortgage is better for that. But if you just want to have money available in case your spouse becomes ill and needs nursing care, or in case your furnace blows and you must suddenly replace it, or if you decide to splurge on a big, one-time vacation, then a line of credit reverse mortgage might be just right.

EXAMPLE 3

You are doing just fine on your regular monthly income. But every year or two something seems to go wrong. Last year the roof on your home sprung a leak and the repair job cost more than $2,000. This year, your dear old car died, and you have to come up with $15,000 to replace it. Unfortunately, your income isn't enough to qualify for a standard bank loan to cover these costs, so you take out a line of credit reverse mortgage. The credit limit is $20,000, which is more than enough to cover your needs.

Let's say this year you borrow $15,000 for the car. Next year, when the sewer line to your home breaks, you need another $3,000. And two years later, for your grandchild's wedding present (and first house purchase), you take another $2,000.

Here's how your loan account would stand after four years: You borrowed a total of $20,000, and your loan balance would be about $35,000 (assuming 10% interest). If you lived another five years and didn't borrow any more funds, you would owe about $62,000. The loan does not have to be repaid until you die or move out.

Reverse Mortgage Questionnaire

We have described three types of reverse mortgages insured by the FHA. The specific terms of each loan must be worked out between you and the lender. To get the most for your money, you should ask a number of questions before signing on the dotted line. Here's our questionnaire to help you:

1. *How much cash will I receive?* It depends on a number of factors that you and the lender evaluate. You must consider the monthly supplement you

desire. Lenders will look at your age, home value (determined by a licensed independent appraiser), amount of any remaining mortgage, interest rate applied to your repayment, terms and limits on adjustable rate interest (if applicable), and length of time you'll be receiving payments. You know how life insurance becomes less attractive as you get older owing to rising premium costs? Well, reverse mortgages become *more* attractive. The older you are, the more you can get each month with a tenure reverse mortgage.

2. *What closing costs must I pay?* As with other loans, points and fees will be charged. Make sure you understand how much. FHA-insured mortgages carry mortgage insurance requirements that will add to your costs. At this writing, you must pay up-front premiums of 2 percent of the value of your home, up to certain limits which can be no higher than $124,875, and ½ percent per year. Most of the initial costs can be made part of your loan balance.

3. *What rate of interest will be charged?* The higher the interest rate you must pay, the less your monthly income checks are likely to be. And remember that even though you don't have to make monthly payments to the lender, your house will be used to repay the loan eventually—and the higher the interest rate, the more you'll owe. With adjustable-rate loans, your monthly income checks will *not* vary—only the amount added to your loan balance will change as the interest charge increases or decreases.

4. *Can you repay the loan early?* You may want the flexibility to pay off all or some of the loan balance before you die or move. For example, if interest rates drop, or if you come into extra money, early repayment of the reverse mortgage may make sense. The FHA program gives you the right to prepay the loan at any time with no penalties.

Eligibility

To qualify for an FHA-insured reverse mortgage, you must:

- Be at least 62 years or older (if joint owners, each must be 62)
- Own your own home (condominiums included)
- Reside in your home
- Have maintained your home in good condition
- Go through mortgage counseling with a counselor approved by the U.S. Department of Housing and Urban Development

Qualifying for a reverse mortgage is much easier than for a regular mortgage because there are *no income or credit requirements!*

Benefits

We have already mentioned a number of glittering opportunities provided by all of these reverse mortgages insured by the FHA, but let us summarize the advantages that make reverse mortgages a gem of a deal:

- They supplement your income.
- You make no monthly payments.
- You can live in your home as long as you like.
- There's no chance of foreclosure for nonpayment.
- No payments are due until you die or permanently leave the house.
- There is no obligation on your part or your heirs to pay any debt greater than the value of the house.

In addition, the reverse mortgage checks you receive are *not* taxable and should *not* affect your Social Security or Medicare benefits. These payments also should not affect SSI or Medicaid (in most states), as long as you spend the money as you get it. If you save the money, though, it may become an asset that can harm your SSI or Medicaid eligibility.

The most important benefit of an FHA-insured reverse mortgage is that you are guaranteed the right to remain in the home until you sell or permanently move out. What happens if you become ill and must enter a hospital and/or a nursing home, and you're out of the home for five months? Will the lender nail you with a foreclosure lawsuit? No! Under the FHA program, you must be out of the house for at least a full year before the lender can claim you've permanently left. Note that if you take a reverse mortgage that is *not* insured by the FHA (see below), the lender may apply different rules to decide when you've left the home. Check them out before agreeing to the mortgage.

Reverse Mortgages Not Insured by FHA

Reverse mortgages not insured by FHA do not have to comply with the same requirements, and do not have to give you the same protections. Some plans are offered by banks and savings and loans; others are sponsored by state or local government agencies.

Although noninsured programs may be just fine, in many cases they are not. Ask these questions.

1. *Can the lender force you to move out and sell your home to pay the loan back before you die or voluntarily leave?* The reverse mortgage agreement may require you to repay the loan after a set number of years. For example, you may get a term reverse mortgage, which gives you monthly paychecks for 10 years,

and then at the end of that time you must repay the loan. In that case, you'll have to sell and move out if you don't have other available cash to pay the balance. (Of course, if you intend to move in a few years, then a requirement that you must repay the loan after a fixed term should not be a problem.)

2. *Can you be forced to pay off the loan if you transfer your interest to your spouse?* Transferring your interest in the house to your spouse, which might make sense in your planning (see Chapter 11 discussing Medicaid), will not make the balance of the loan immediately due under the FHA program. But reverse mortgages that are not insured by the FHA may allow the lender to call the loan when transfers between spouses are made. Ask before you sign. (Note: If you sell or give your home to your kids for any reason, all reverse mortgages will be due and must be paid—whether or not insured by FHA.)

3. *Is repayment limited to the value of the home?* The FHA program assures that you or your heirs will not have to pay any more than the value of the home. Check to make sure you get the same protection from other programs before signing on.

4. *Can you repay the loan early?* Unlike FHA loans, which allow early repayment, other programs may not give you the same flexibility.

5. *What if the lender goes under?* In these days of bank and S&L closings, what would happen if the lender goes out of business in the middle of a reverse mortgage plan? Under FHA insurance, you're protected; without that insurance, you could find yourself with a legal mess. Talk to the lender about what obligations you have before taking on an uninsured reverse mortgage.

Where to Get a Reverse Mortgage

Reverse mortgages are a new, though growing, field. For names of lenders in your area offering FHA-insured or uninsured reverse mortgages, send a self-addressed stamped envelope and $1 to the National Center for Home Equity Conversion, 1210 East College, Suite 300, Marshall, MN 56258. The NCHEC will send you a monthly updated list of lenders offering reverse mortgages. You can then contact the lender directly to initiate the application process.

We have provided a list of lenders that have offered FHA-insured reverse mortgages in Table 9.1. Please keep in mind that these are not the only lenders authorized to make FHA-guaranteed reverse mortgages; most other lending institutions (banks and mortgage companies) can make reverse mortgages. Table 9.2 lists lenders currently making uninsured reverse mortgages. These two tables are constantly changing and growing. For up-to-date information, write to the NCHEC.

TABLE 9.1

FHA-Insured Reverse Mortgage Lenders

State	Lender
Alabama	United Savings; 205-237-6668
Arizona	Directors Mortgage; 800-442-4966; extension 2201 Sun American; 602-832-4343
California	ARCS Mortgage; 800-237-2727 Bank of Lodi; 209-367-2075 Beachfront Funding; 714-492-5000 CFE Mortgage; 818-577-0233 Directors Mortgage; 800-442-4966; extension 2201 Farwest Mortgage; 714-579-1177 Interstate Mortgage; 818-810-2665 Mical Mortgage; 619-452-8200 Northpoint Mortgage; 209-225-6762 Western Residential; 916-485-1900
Colorado	Wendover Funding; 303-843-0480 Directors Mortgage; 800-442-4966; extension 2201
Connecticut	Prudential Mortgagee; 800-473-6467
Delaware	International Mortgage; 301-484-6016 Boulevard Mortgage; 215-331-6900
DC	International Mortgage; 301-484-6016
Florida	Sterling Savings; 407-968-1000 Brasota Mortgage; 813-746-6119 Chateau Mortgage; 813-545-3523 Homestead Federal; 305-556-1100 IDL Mortgage; 813-482-8686 TST Harms; 904-398-4476
Georgia	Capital One Mortgage; 404-934-9790 Homestead Mortgage; 404-324-2274 Unity Mortgage; 404-493-1041
Hawaii	ARCS Mortgage; 808-263-6602 First Hawaiian; 916-581-5626
Idaho	Directors Mortgage; 800-442-4966; extension 2201 Investors West; 800-281-3338

(Continued)

TABLE 9.1 (Continued)

FHA-Insured Reverse Mortgage Lenders

State	Lender
Illinois	Senior Income; 312-214-2540 WestAmerica; 708-916-9299
Indiana	Merchants Mortgage; 317-237-5100
Iowa	Commercial Federal; 402-554-9200
Kansas	James B. Nutter; 816-531-2345
Kentucky	Tri-County Mortgage; 606-523-1076
Massachusetts	Prudential Mortgagee; 800-473-6467
Maine	ME State Housing; 207-623-2981
Maryland	International Mortgage; 301-484-6016 Home Equity Conversions; 410-269-4322
Michigan	Unity Mortgage; 404-493-1041
Minnesota	Executron Mortgage; 612-854-7676 Richfield Bank; 612-861-8339
Missouri	James B. Nutter; 816-531-2345
Montana	Intermountain Mortgage; 406-652-3000
Nebraska	Commercial Federal; 402-554-9200
Nevada	Directors Mortgage; 800-442-4966; extension 2201
New Hampshire	Chittenden Bank; 802-660-2123
New Jersey	Interchange State Bank; 201-845-5600 ARCS Mortgage; 201-795-0100 Pioneer Mortgage; 800-222-0057 Prudential Mortgagee; 800-473-6467 Boulevard Mortgage; 215-331-6900
New Mexico	Charter Bank; 505-291-3758 Sunwest Bank; 505-765-2211
New York	ARCS Mortgage; 800-237-2727 Onondaga Savings; 315-424-4011 Rockwell Equities; 516-334-7900 Prudential Mortgagee; 800-473-6467
Ohio	Mid-America Mortgage; 216-861-4040

State	Lender
Oregon	ARCS Mortgage; 800-640-4773 Directors Mortgage; 800-442-4966; extension 2201
Pennsylvania	Boulevard Mortgage; 215-331-6900 Hart Mortgage; 215-628-3131 Landmark Savings; 412-553-7727 Pioneer Mortgage; 609-546-1700 Prudential Mortgagee; 800-473-6467
Rhode Island	RI Housing & Mortgage; 401-751-5566
South Carolina	First Citizens Mortgage; 803-733-2747
Tennessee	Mortgage South; 615-624-3878 Randolph Mortgage; 615-622-8303
Utah	AIM Mortgage; 801-485-9355 Directors Mortgage; 800-442-4966; extension 2201
Vermont	Chittenden Bank; 802-660-2123 Prudential Mortgagee; 800-473-6467
Virginia	International Mortgage; 301-484-6016 VA Housing; 804-782-1986 Ameribanc Savings; 703-658-5500 Crestar Mortgage; 804-498-8702 Mortgage Capital; 703-941-0711 Tidewater First; 800-282-4326
Washington	ARCS Mortgage; 206-462-7055, 744-2727 Directors Mortgage; 800-442-4966; extension 2201
West Virginia	International Mortgage; 301-777-1400
Wyoming	Key Bank; 307-635-7724

Source: Reprinted with permission from *Retirement Income on the House* (NCHEC Press, November 1991), as updated by the *Reverse Mortgage Locator* (NCHEC Press, Edition 2—February 1992).

TABLE 9.2

Lenders Currently Making Uninsured Reverse Mortgages

State	Area	Lender
Arizona	Northern Arizona	Reverse Mortgage Program 602-997-6105
	Southern Arizona	Reverse Mortgage Program 602-623-0344; extension 376
California	Alameda and Contra Costa Counties	ECHO Housing—RAM 415-930-0989
	San Francisco	Independent Living 415-863-0581
	San Mateo County	Human Investment 415-348-6660
	Santa Clara County	Project Match 408-287-7121
	Sonoma County	Sonoma Council on Aging 707-525-0143
	Southern California	Life Services 818-547-0585
Connecticut	Middlesex and New London	Farmers & Mechanics 203-346-9677
Massachusetts	Massachusetts	H.O.M.E. Program 617-451-0680
Minnesota	Minneapolis–St. Paul metro area	Senior Housing 612-645-0261
New Jersey	Bergen, Passaic, and Morris Counties	Boiling Springs Savings 201-939-5000
New York	Nassau County	CHEC Program 516-485-5600
	Suffolk County	Dept. on Aging 516-853-3626
	Westchester County	Residential Housing Opportunities 914-428-0953

Source: Reprinted with permission from *Retirement Income on the House* (NCHEC Press, November 1991), as updated by *The Reverse Mortgage Locator* (NCHEC Press, Edition 2—February 1992).

If you would like more information about reverse mortgages, you can write to the AARP for a free copy of the guide: "Home Made Money," AARP Home Equity Conversion Service, 1909 K Street, N.W., Washington, D.C. 20049. An excellent full-length book discussing reverse mortgages, which we highly recommend, is *Retirement Income on the House* (NCHEC Press, November 1991); for information about how to get this book, call toll-free (800) 247-6553.

SALE AND LEASEBACK

A sale and leaseback is another gem that allows you to cash in on your home equity, making your life more comfortable, while allowing you to live in the house. This technique is especially useful if you've got a child or children who have a little spare cash.

The major drawback to a reverse mortgage is the cost. As we explained, the lender benefits by charging interest on the monies you receive. And although the lender won't get paid right away, there's a chance the bank will later end up with the entire house equity, leaving your kids with nothing at your death.

A sale and leaseback avoids this problem. No bank need be involved, so there are no fees. Only you and the buyer (probably your child) are involved. And even if your child finances the purchase with a bank, your child—not the lender—will get the house. You supplement your income, and your child gets the house when you die.

Overview

A sale and leaseback is just like it sounds: you sell your home and then lease it back. Sale and leasebacks are legally binding arrangements usually made with a child, though they can be done with a nonfamily member, too.

The best way to explain how a sale-and-leaseback arrangement works is with an example.

EXAMPLE 4

Your costs are rising much faster than your income. Though you've got a nice "buried treasure" in your house, you can't get at it. So you arrange a sale and leaseback with your son.

You sell the house to him for $100,000, which is the market value. Since your child bought it, there are no real estate commissions or advertising fees. Your son goes to the bank to finance the purchase, just as he would with any sale. He puts down 20 percent and finances the balance over 30 years at 9½ percent, paying points and closing costs to the lender. You get the $100,000 in cash, tax-free (using your Age 55 Tax Loophole—see page 361).

You take your $100,000 and invest it at 9 percent; you receive $9,000/year or $750/month. At the same time, your child rents the house back to you, under a long-term lease, for a fair market rental of $600/month. The lease is for a period far longer than your life expectancy.

So how do you benefit? You have $150/month more spending money ($750 − $600). *Plus* you save the costs for property taxes, homeowner's insurance, and upkeep, which could easily save you another $200 or more each month. And depending on how you invest the sale proceeds, your income might be even higher, and some or all of your assets could be much more liquid (and so available to you) than when they were buried in your home. At the same time, the lease assures that you can remain in the home until you die.

What's your son get out of the deal? This is a business arrangement, and he can and should do well, too. His income ($600) is less than his payments to the bank ($700/month, at 9.5% interest) by $100/month. And he's also paying $200/month property taxes, insurance, and maintenance—so his apparent loss is $300/month, or $3,600/year.

But that's not what he really loses, because Uncle Sam offers tax benefits. Your son can deduct his $300/month loss, and he can depreciate the value of the house (but not the land it sits on)—let's say that's $80,000—allowing him to take a further loss on his tax return of $2,900/year, or $242/month. In the 28 percent income tax bracket, your son's deductions for the house would result in a cash benefit of $150/month—so he's really only losing about $150/month out of his pocket (after taxes).

So far, this isn't a very good deal for your son. But remember, he owns the house and will benefit by any appreciation. If you die 10 years later, and the house appreciated just 5 percent each year over that time, he could sell it for $163,000—$63,000 more than the purchase price. That gives him a profit of $40,000 ($63,000 − $23,000 out-of-pocket losses, including the points and closing costs he initially paid). If his original investment was $20,000, his return would be 100 percent in ten years, or 10 percent per year. And the investment couldn't be much safer, now could it?

Example 4 shows how a sale and leaseback can be a Golden Opportunity for both you and a child. You supplement your income; you get to stay in the house for as long as you live; your child gets the house when you die; and your child receives a safe and, it is hoped, lucrative investment.

In Example 4, your child went to a bank for the financing, so he needed a down payment and was required to pay fees and interest, too. All of those costs can be avoided if *you* take back the financing, as shown in Example 5.

EXAMPLE 5

As in Example 4, you sell the house to your child for $100,000. Rather than have him get a bank loan, you act as the bank. He pays you just $5,000 for a down payment, and you finance the $95,000 balance at 9 percent over 20 years (you don't charge closing costs or points). Your child's mortgage payments to you are $855/month. You pay him back $600/month rent. In other words, you get an extra $255/month cash, which is more than you receive (Example 4) if he finances through a bank. The interest payments, which would have gone to the lender, now go to supplement your income. And you still save an additional $200/month in property taxes, homeowner's insurance, and upkeep.

What if you live longer than the 20-year financing? Where would you get the money to pay the $600/month rent? If you purchased a single-premium deferred annuity with the $5,000 down payment when your child first gave it to you, the annuity would start paying you more than $750/month for five more years (following the end of the 20-year financing).

What does your child get, other than a big debt? Again, this is an investment for him. He can deduct his out-of-pocket loss of $455/month ($855 − $600 = $255, plus $200 taxes, insurance, and upkeep). And he can deduct $242/month depreciation. The deductions (in the 28% tax bracket) would result in a cash benefit of $195/month—so he's really only losing $260/month.

If the house appreciates just 5 percent/year and he sells (when you die) in 10 years, he'll receive $163,000. That gives him a profit of $8,400 ($63,000 − $54,600 out-of-pocket losses in 10 years). His return on his $5,000 investment would be 68 percent in 10 years, or 6.8 percent per year. Not too bad, right? (And if the house appreciated 7 percent/year, his return would be 700 percent, or 70 percent per year!)

Congress has made investments in rental property less attractive over the last few years. But as you can see from Examples 4 and 5, the benefits to a purchaser can still be worthwhile. Just looking around at the market bears this out. There are still many absentee landlords reaping the advantages offered by rental property. And the biggest concern for landlords—problems with a bad tenant—are avoided in the sale and leaseback arena where an older resident who has lived in and maintained the house for years plans to continue. The investment a buyer makes in your home is about as safe as purchasing U.S. Treasury Bonds.

If your child has the funds to contribute $455 a month to your support, as in Example 5, why go through the hassle of a sale and leaseback? Why not just have him give you the money? You can leave him the house when you die, and everybody's happy.

While we strongly believe in simplicity, and in some circumstances gifts from your child may be all that you need, there are good reasons to make a sale and leaseback arrangement. Maybe most important is that Uncle Sam helps by giving tax breaks to your child. Consider Example 5: you get $455 a month, but your child only pays $260—Uncle Sam pays the other $195.

Also, your child gets the assurance that you won't later change your mind and leave the house to someone else (although that assurance might be provided by you giving your child the house, perhaps keeping a "life estate"—a lifetime right to live there). And a sale and leaseback can be done with a third party, while gifts typically would only be made by a family member.

Are There Tax Benefits?

As you can see from Examples 4 and 5, a sale-and-leaseback arrangement can provide a variety of tax benefits. If the sale and rent is at a fair market rate, the buyer should be able to deduct interest, expenses, and depreciation.

At the time of the sale, you should be able to avoid paying tax on the profit up to $125,000, using the Age 55 Tax Loophole. And since the sale price is at the fair market value, the buyer (your child) gets a stepped-up basis (see page 377), which allows him to reduce or eliminate any capital gains tax on the profit, at least up to the date of the sale.

On the downside, you will also be receiving more income, which may increase your income tax. If you receive a lump sum that you invest, as in Example 4, the interest is counted as income; if you finance the sale, as in Example 5, part of each payment you receive is counted as income again.

You probably can't escape income tax by financing the deal and not charging any interest. The IRS will most likely charge you tax on the income you should have received in a regular deal with a nonfamily member.

Will Your Other Benefits Be Affected?

A sale-and-leaseback arrangement might have an impact on Social Security, SSI, and Medicaid benefits. For example, interest that you receive by taking back financing for the buyer (Example 5) would be income—which could make part of your Social Security benefits taxable and could harm your eligibility for SSI and Medicaid. But only the *interest* portion matters, *not* the entire monthly payment you get.

NOTE

You might be able to avoid receiving income for tax purposes if you give the home to your child, instead of selling it, and then your child makes cash gifts to you each month in return. Gifts are not income. The reason we are telling you this as a "note," rather than a Gem, is because it is a diamond in the rough and probably won't work. The IRS is likely to say this is really a sale, so the cash gifts are really income. Talk to an accountant or tax lawyer before trying this.

Also, the down payment and any mortgage note you receive might be counted as an asset for Medicaid and SSI eligibility. We say *might* because it may be possible to prepare the sale-and-leaseback documents to avoid these problems. As we mention in the next section, an experienced lawyer can help protect your Social Security, Medicaid, and SSI benefits.

How Do You Get a Sale and Leaseback?

If you decide to use a sale-and-leaseback arrangement to supplement your income, you'll need the help of a lawyer to put the deal together. Make sure the documents protect you against a variety of possible problems. The arrangement should:

1. Allow you the legal right to live in the house for life. If the buyer changes his mind and decides to throw you out, you need to be protected.
2. Protect you in case the buyer dies or sells the property while you're still there. The new owner can be bound to follow your deal *if* the documents are properly made and recorded.
3. Include a due-on-sale clause, which gives you the right to cancel if ownership changes.
4. Provide remedies for you in case the buyer fails to make his mortgage payments to you or another lender.
5. Protect you from unexpected rent increases. You may want to provide for *no* rent increases, but that might cause you and the buyer to lose tax benefits. Instead, you might be better off providing for fixed rent increases, matched by increasing mortgage payments by the buyer.

428 ◆ *Golden Opportunities*

6. Clearly spell out the buyer's responsibility for taxes, insurance, repairs, and maintenance.

7. Give you the right to have someone move in with you, perhaps to provide you with nursing care or to share expenses.

8. Specify what occurs if you choose to move, or if you must enter a nursing home.

You will probably not be surprised to learn that a lawyer will charge you for preparing these papers. If you have an experienced lawyer who has done this before, a simple arrangement will probably run about $500. Take it from us—that's money well spent. You can purchase a good set of model sale-and-leaseback forms from the National Center for Home Equity Conversion by sending $39 to the NCHEC at 1210 East College, Suite 300, Marshall, MN 56258.

Sale and Leaseback vs. Reverse Mortgages

Sale-and-leaseback arrangements may be better or worse than a reverse mortgage, depending on your circumstances. Let's compare the pros and cons of each.

1. A sale and leaseback is much more complicated and requires the help of a lawyer; a reverse mortgage can be done between you and a lender.

2. A sale and leaseback requires you to find a willing buyer; a reverse mortgage requires you to find a willing lender. Today, lenders are much easier to find.

3. A sale and leaseback can be less costly, particularly if you provide the financing. Reverse mortgages can carry stiff interest charges that you *don't* pay with a sale and leaseback.

4. With a sale and leaseback, you must protect your right to live in the home in writing; with a reverse mortgage you must also protect via documents your right to live in the home. Without these protections, you could wind up sleeping on a park bench.

5. You don't have to worry about real estate taxes, insurance, and maintenance after a sale and leaseback; you're not off the hook for these obligations with a reverse mortgage.

6. If your house has appreciated more than $125,000 in value since you bought it, you could wind up paying tax on part of the profit if you use a sale and leaseback; with a reverse mortgage, you and your heirs will pay no tax on profit, but there may be no house for them, either.

7. Your child gets the house if he buys under a sale and leaseback; your heirs could completely lose out under a reverse mortgage.

8. Your Social Security, SSI, and Medicaid will not be affected by a reverse mortgage; a sale and leaseback might cost you a portion of those benefits.

HOME SHARING

Another gem to supplement your income is to rent out a room in your home. This technique provides not only cash but also companionship, which some see as a plus and some as a minus.

The financial piece of the arrangement is fairly simple: you look in the rental ads in your local newspaper, figure a fair rental, and find a tenant. If you get $150 a month, that's an extra $1,800 a year you didn't have before; $300 a month would add $3,600 a year to your budget.

The money you receive is income for tax purposes, and the extra income may also impact your Social Security, SSI, and Medicaid benefits. But you may also get some tax breaks, since you are now a landlord.

The most important issue in home sharing is personal, not financial: you have someone living with you. You may find that attractive, particularly if the empty house has started to seem a little lonely lately. If you fall or become ill, having someone who can call the doctor or ambulance is useful, too. On the other hand, you may enjoy your privacy. The added money may not be worth the loss of peace and quiet around the house. And if you get a "bad apple," watch out.

Home sharing makes you a landlord, with the responsibilities and risks that go with it. If a leak develops in your renter's room, you can't put off repairing it. If your renter stops paying and won't move out, you may have to evict him.

No matter how nice and trustworthy the person appears, you should have a written lease between you and your renter that spells out your rights and your renter's rights. For example, it should specify whether your renter must use a particular entry to the home, where he can park his car, which room or rooms he may use, whether he has access to the kitchen, when he must pay his rent and what happens if he's late, and whether he can have guests or pets. You must also make sure you comply with any state or local laws governing rentals.

Home sharing can be a wonderful way to supplement income, especially with the right tenant. But make sure you understand all the risks before cashing in on this gem.

HAVE YOUR CHILD CO-SIGN A LOAN

Consider this situation. Your income generally is enough for you to live on, but once in a while you need additional money to repair the roof, replace the furnace, or go on a nice trip. Your kids would like to help, but they just don't have the savings to give you. You don't need a regular income supplement provided by a reverse mortgage or a sale and leaseback. Instead, a standard bank loan might be enough. The problem is that you can't qualify based on your income.

Having your child co-sign a loan might be all you need. Even though you don't qualify on your own, your child's signature could help you get the loan. And if you are able to pay back the loan out of your income, the loan won't cost your child a penny. For many older Americans, this is the easiest and least expensive way to cash in on the equity in their homes.

This gem probably won't help if you need regular monthly income supplements, because you could never repay the debt. Normal loans or mortgages aren't designed to handle growing balances—that's the purpose for reverse mortgages. But for a one-time or occasional cash supplement, take a look at getting a child (or someone else) to co-sign a standard loan for you.

If your child wants some protection in case you can't pay it off, you could give him a mortgage on your home. While it's unlikely you'd ever default or he'd ever foreclose, the protection is there.

If the lender won't approve the loan to you, even with your child's co-signature, you might give the home to your child and have him take out a standard mortgage or home equity loan in his own name. In most cases, that step shouldn't be necessary; if your child can qualify for a loan, then his signature on your loan should be enough.

SPECIAL-PURPOSE PROGRAMS

Many states and communities offer special programs designed to allow older homeowners to cash in on their home equity for specific purposes, including home repairs or improvements (but not decoration), weatherization, and property tax relief.

While there are no standard benefits, most programs have in common:

- Loans at low or no interest and no fees or points.
- No repayment until you die or permanently move out.
- Income, asset, age, and/or home value limits.

EXAMPLE 6

You need a new roof, and the cost will be $10,000. Your state offers a program that will loan you the $10,000 at 3 percent interest—that's a deal you can't pass up.

You gladly take the money and make the home repairs. You make no payments during your lifetime. When you die five years later, the house is sold and used to pay the loan balance, which at that time will be $11,600.

If you use a special-purpose loan to repair or improve your property, the value of your property may increase, and the added value may more than make up for the cost.

EXAMPLE 7

These days the stairs in your home seem like mountains and you can't keep climbing. If you added a bathroom on the first floor, you wouldn't have to move. The cost is $10,000, which is beyond your budget. Your state offers special-purpose loans with no interest and no repayment required until you die or move. You are a little concerned about taking on $10,000 of debt, but you go ahead.

The added bathroom immediately increases your home value by $5,000. You live another 15 years, and your home appreciates an average of 5 percent each year. During this time *you* have appreciated the convenience and your independence. By the time the house is sold, the bathroom has actually added *more* than $10,000 to the sale proceeds. The increase in value covers the entire amount of the loan, and then some. The amount you will be able to leave your spouse or children has gone *up*, not *down*, as a result of the borrowing.

Most of the loan programs that cover property taxes work the same way; you borrow the amount to cover your property taxes each year, but you don't pay the money back until you sell the home or move. These Golden Opportunities allow some older Americans to use their resources for other purposes; for many, special-purpose property tax loans make the difference between moving and staying.

EXAMPLE 8

Your property taxes run $2,000/year. That breaks down to more than $160/month. When you add that to your other expenses, you might have no choice but to give up your home of 30 years.

Fortunately, your state offers a special program that will loan you the money for the taxes. The charge is 6 percent per year, but you don't pay until you die. After five years, you would owe $11,000 ($1,000 of which is interest); after 10 years, the balance due would be $25,156 (including interest of more than $5,100).

But don't forget the wonderful magic of appreciation. If your home was worth $80,000 when you first took the property tax loan, and it increases in value by just 3 percent each year, it would be worth $12,000 more in 5 years and $27,000 more in 10 years—in other words, the increased value is more than enough to cover the loan.

So instead of thinking about a special-purpose loan as a burden, think of it as an investment. If the difference between staying in your home and moving is the property tax, you can use a special-purpose loan to pay the tax, and the appreciation you gain should more than cover the eventual cost.

At this time, special-purpose loans to pay property taxes are available in all or parts of California, Colorado, Connecticut, Florida, Georgia, Illinois, Iowa, Massachusetts, Maine, New Hampshire, Oregon, Tennessee, Texas, Utah, Virginia, Washington, and Wisconsin. To find out whether your state offers special-purpose loans to pay property taxes, and if it does, on what terms, call the local agency to which you pay property taxes. Someone there should be able to point you in the right direction. (While you're on the phone, ask about any other benefits that might be available.)

For other special-purpose loans, there's no easy place to look for information. You should start with your city housing department or aging office. If that doesn't work, try your area agency on aging or your state department on aging. Even your local consumer affairs office might be able to help.

Your home contains a "treasure chest" of riches; the trick is getting to them. By using a reverse mortgage, sale-and-leasehold arrangement, home sharing arrangement, child co-signature, or special-purpose loan, you can literally avoid having the roof cave in on you. These home advantages will enable you to cash in on the equity in your home to supplement your income and pay your bills.

·10·

Supplemental Security Income:
A Little Extra to Make Ends Meet

Are you having trouble making ends meet on Social Security or other retirement benefits? Relief could be available from a surprising source: your Uncle Sam may have a monthly check for you under the Supplemental Security Income (SSI) program!

SSI is not for everyone. The program is primarily for folks with fairly low income. But despite income limitations, a lot of people are missing out on this wonderful program. As many as *half* of all eligible persons are *not* receiving money that is rightfully theirs—usually because they don't even realize there's money set aside for them. Don't you pass up this Golden Opportunity.

OVERVIEW

Since most people don't have the foggiest notion about the SSI program, let's start with the basics. SSI is a federal program that pays monthly checks to people who meet a few requirements. It was designed to provide an income safety net, to catch older Americans falling through holes in the Social Security program. Although the program is run by Social Security, it has nothing to do with standard Social Security benefits.

Benefits are *not* dependent on your past work record. And the amount of payment is *not* based on prior earnings. Benefits *are* based primarily on your income and assets—you can't have too much of either. But as we explain, the limitations are not as difficult as they seem.

If you qualify, you may receive basic federal benefits of as much as $422 per month for one person (widowed, divorced, never married), $633 for a couple. Many states supplement these amounts. In New York, for example, the state supplement adds $86 for an individual and $102.50 for a couple.

Table 10.1 lists SSI benefits including state supplements. Your SSI benefit is the amount of the federal benefits plus any state supplements; benefits are reduced by income you receive. Factors such as age, blindness, or disability influence the level of benefits you receive from the state supplements; the basic federal benefits remain the same regardless of the reason for qualification.

TABLE 10.1

Maximum SSI Payment Amounts (to Individual/Couple)[1]

State	Aged	Blind	Disabled
California	$645/$1,190	$719/$1,395	$645/$1,190
Hawaii	426.90/641.80	426.90/641.80	426.90/641.80
Iowa	422/633	444/677	422/633
Maine	432/648	432/648	432/648
Massachusetts	550.82/834.72	571.74/1,143.48	536.39/813.06
Michigan	436/654	436/654	436/654
Montana[2]	422/633	422/633	422/633
Nevada	458.40/707.46	531.30/1,007.60	422/633
New Jersey	453.25/658.36	453.25/658.36	453.25/658.36
New York	508/735.50	508/735.50	508/735.50
Pennsylvania	454.40/681.70	454.40/681.70	454.40/681.70
Rhode Island	488.79/757.53	488.79/757.53	488.79/757.53
Utah	427.30/643.60	427.30/643.60	427.30/643.60
Vermont	486.99/751.24	486.99/751.24	486.99/751.24
Washington	450/655	450/655	450/655
Washington D.C.	437/663	437/663	437/663
Wisconsin	514.72/778.86	514.72/778.86	514.72/778.86

[1]The states listed in Table 10.1 provide SSI supplements administered through the federal SSI program. The following states administer their own SSI supplements: Alabama, Alaska, Arizona, Colorado, Connecticut, Florida, Idaho, Illinois, Indiana, Kentucky, Louisiana, Maryland, Minnesota, Missouri, Nebraska, New Hampshire, New Mexico, North Carolina, North Dakota, Ohio, Oklahoma, Oregon, South Carolina, South Dakota, Virginia, and Wyoming. Contact your local welfare or human services office to find out the amounts.
[2]Supplements available only to persons in protective care arrangements.

Qualifying for SSI may also open up a variety of other Golden Opportunities too, such as Medicaid, food stamps, rehabilitation, hot meal programs, and home care.

To obtain SSI benefits, you must first pass three tests:

- Status test
- Income test
- Assets test

STATUS TEST

To satisfy the status test, you must be either 65 or older, blind, or disabled.

Age 65 or older—that's easy to understand. The test for blindness is similar to that described in Chapter 3 regarding Social Security disability: your vision must be 20/200 or worse in the better eye, or your visual field must be 20 degrees or less, even with glasses or contacts.

❖ GEM: If You Are Blind, Don't Overlook SSI Even If You Can't Get Social Security Disability Benefits

To qualify for Social Security disability benefits due to blindness, you must show that you can't work (see pages 89–90). For SSI, you can still be working and earning money; as long as you are blind, you pass the status test for SSI.

◆ ◆ ◆

The definition of disability for SSI is the same as for Social Security: you must have a physical or mental impairment that prevents you from working and earning at least $500 a month, and which is expected to last (or has lasted) for at least one year or to result in death (see pages 85–86). If you qualify for SSI because you are disabled, you do *not* have to wait five months before starting to collect, as you do for Social Security disability.

INCOME TEST

The income test is easy: if your income is less than the maximum benefits payable, you qualify for SSI and get the difference. We've already told you that the maximum federal benefits are $422 a month for singles and $633 a month for couples, and many states supplement these amounts. If your income is less than these amounts, you can get SSI.

Don't be scared off because these numbers seem so low. Even with *much higher income,* you may still pocket SSI money. First, many types of income don't count for SSI purposes. Second, we give you some gems to help you cut your income (pages 438–441).

Income That Does *Not* Count

There's plenty of income that does *not* count as income for purposes of figuring SSI. Knowing these can help ensure your SSI eligibility. Table 10.2 lists types of income which do not count.

Knowing what is not income can provide you with some Golden Opportunities.

EXAMPLE 1

You receive $200/month Social Security and $300/month in German War reparations. A state assistance program pays your home heating costs, which average $60/month. Your son pays $80/month for a gardener to take care of your lawn. And your daughter who lives 1,000 miles away in California buys you airline tickets to visit her twice a year.

In reality, your monthly income is about $700/month. But if you know your rights under SSI, only $200/month (Social Security) "counts" for SSI.

◆ ◆ ◆

Income That Counts

There are three types of income that will be counted for SSI: earned income, unearned income, and deemed income.

Earned Income. Earned income is cash or "in-kind" payments you receive in exchange for work performed. As an employee, include your gross income before taxes and expenses. If self-employed, figure your net income after deducting work expenses. In-kind payments include the value of food, clothing, and shelter provided as part of your compensation.

EXAMPLE 2

You work part time for a family-style restaurant. Your wages and tips run about $200/month. In addition, you get dinners free; the value of those meals is around $50/month. Costs include purchase and cleaning of uniforms and transportation. Your earned income for SSI purposes is $250/month; you must include the meals, but the work-related costs do not reduce income.

TABLE 10.2

Income Not Counted for SSI

- Infrequent or irregular earned income of up to $10/month and unearned income of up to $20/month. Income is infrequent if you receive it no more than once in three months, or if you really can't count on receiving it. For example, you could ignore a $20 gift (unearned) or a $10 payment for a one-time job.
- Weatherization assistance (for such things as insulation, storm doors and windows).
- Income tax or property tax refunds.
- Grants, scholarships, and fellowships paid for education tuition and fees.
- Food you raised for yourself or your family to eat.
- Disaster relief.
- Home energy assistance if based on need and certified by the state.
- Medical care and services if given to you for free or if paid for by another, including an insurance company.
- Room and board during a medical confinement.
- Reimbursement of medical payments previously made by you. For example, if you have paid for prescription drugs and get the money back from your health insurance, the money is not income.
- Payment of your medical insurance premium by anyone for you.
- Food stamps.
- Payments for work in the foster grandparents program, the Retired Senior Volunteer Program, or the Senior Companion Program.
- Housing assistance from a federal housing program.
- Payment for sales of property (real or personal). The amount you receive will be an asset (subject to the assets test), but not income.
- Insurance or court-ordered damages to reimburse for loss of health, property or income.
- Assistance by the state, county or city, or a nonprofit organization, based on need.
- Payments by a credit life or credit disability policy (i.e., insurance on charge accounts or other credit accounts).
- Loan proceeds (amounts you borrow). For example, payments you get under a reverse mortgage are not income.
- Repayments of principal on a loan you made. Interest you receive *is* income.
- Payments of your bills (telephone, medical, etc.) by someone else for things other than food, clothing or shelter.
- Domestic airline or other transportation tickets received as gifts and used.
- If disabled or blind, the amount of income necessary for fulfillment of a government-approved plan to achieve self-support.
- Restitution payments made by the U.S. government to Japanese-Americans and Aleuts who were interned or relocated during WWII.
- Agent Orange settlement payments.
- Reparations payments received by Holocaust survivors on or after November 1, 1984, from Germany or Austria.
- Interest which accumulates on excluded burial funds.

Unearned Income. Unearned income includes income that is not payment for work. Examples of unearned income are Social Security retirement, disability, and life insurance benefits; pensions; VA benefits based on your own military service; Worker's Compensation; unemployment; alimony; rents; interest; dividends; annuities; gifts; inheritances; proceeds of life insurance (unless used to pay expenses for last illness or funeral); and prize winnings.

Regular contributions of food, clothing, and shelter also "count." For example, if your son pays for your food each month, you are receiving unearned income. But rather than use the market value of the contribution, the government *assumes* the value of food, clothing, or shelter to be $160.66 a month ($231 for a couple).

❖ GEM: Prove You Don't Get Expensive or Regular Gifts

If you actually receive contributions of less than $160.66 a month, don't let the Government assume you get that much. By showing that the market value of what you receive is, say, only $50 a month, you can cut your countable unearned income. How can you prove the value? Have the person who provides the contributions save bills and receipts for the items he or she buys for you.

And if you only get very irregular gifts, you probably won't have to count any income. For example, if your daughter only takes you out for dinner once in a while (it wouldn't hurt if she called more often!), the value of those meals should not count.

❖ GEM: The More You Get, the Less the Government Counts

As we just said, the Government will assume you are getting income of $160.66 a month ($231 a month for a couple) if you regularly receive food *or* shelter. But if you regularly get food *and* shelter, the Government, in its great wisdom, only assumes that value to be $140.66 ($211 for a couple)—$20 *less!* What's the *Golden Rule?* Getting more from family can mean more for you from Uncle Sam too!

EXAMPLE 3

You can't get around like you used to, so you've moved in with your son and his wife. They don't charge you any rent, but you pay for your own food. In that situation, the Government will assume that you are receiving unearned income of $160.66 for the shelter.

But if you stopped paying for your food and let your son pay, your income (for SSI) would *drop* by $20. Not only will that help you qualify for SSI by reducing your income but, as we discuss soon, cutting your income by $20 will raise your SSI benefits by $20. You might then gift the extra $20 to your son, if you choose to.

❖ GEM: Have Your Child Give You a Life Estate

Let's say you move in with a child. As we've told you, the Government will assume that you have income of $160.66 a month because you are receiving shelter. But if you have an ownership interest in the residence, then you have a legal right to live there, and your child is not making any contribution to you.

How can you use this to your benefit? If your child owns a house, have him give you a life estate—a legal right to live in the home for as long as you live (you'll need a real estate lawyer to help). When you die, your child still owns the residence. In the meantime, you avoid having the Government assume you have $160.66 a month income, which helps you get SSI.

❖ GEM: Take Food and Shelter as a Loan

The Government's practice of assuming unearned income when you receive food and/or shelter can be a catch-22—since you have "income," you don't receive any (or as much) SSI; because you don't get SSI, the next month you can't afford to pay for shelter or food, so you need to have your kids (or others) provide these, and again you won't qualify for SSI; and on it goes. Example 4 shows how to break the cycle and cash in on SSI.

EXAMPLE 4

Your Social Security is $300/month, hardly enough to live on. So you move in with your son, and you pay no food or rent costs. Adding the assumed value for these contributions ($140.66/month), the Government will say you have too much income for SSI (your $440.66/month income exceeds the $422 limit).

But let's say your son "loaned" you the value of the food and rent, with you agreeing to pay it back. Then your income would only be $300/month, and you'd be entitled to $122/month SSI. You could then use some or all of the $122 to pay your son on the "loan."

To use this technique, make a formal, written loan agreement. An oral arrangement by itself probably won't get by the Government bureaucrats.

WARNING

If you are institutionalized in a public facility, such as a city or county rest home, halfway house, mental hospital, or prison, the Government says you are receiving more than enough, and you will not get any SSI. If you are in a medical facility (hospital or nursing home) and Medicaid is paying for more than half your care, the most you can get from SSI is $30 a month—with two exceptions. You may still get full SSI benefits if:

- You need the money to pay expenses related to your permanent living arrangement (like rent, utilities, property taxes, and maintenance).
- A doctor certifies that your institutionalization won't last more than three months.

Income Reductions. So far, we've been discussing earned and unearned income. Uncle Sam gives you a break by letting you reduce these amounts.

❖ GEM: Take Your $85 Reduction!

You can reduce your monthly income by $20 when calculating your SSI eligibility. This $20 reduction applies first to unearned income, if any. If you don't have any unearned income, then you can reduce your earned income by $20. Don't ask why—that's the law!

In addition, you can reduce the amount of your earned income by $65 a month, plus one-half of the remainder of your monthly earned income.

❖ GEM: Reduce Earned Income by Work Expenses Related to an Impairment

If you suffer from an impairment, you may "deduct" from your earned income the cost for items and services you need to enable you to work. These are the same items as can be used to qualify for Social Security disability (page 87), and include wheelchair, cane, crutches, inhalator, pacemaker, prosthetic devices, modifications to car or van, bandages and other expendable medical supplies, and drugs to control your impairment. One-time costs may be taken all in one month or spread (¹⁄₁₂ per month) over a year.

In addition, if you are working and blind, you may deduct federal, state, and Social Security taxes on the earnings; routine transportation costs to and from work; and union dues.

WARNING

When you *first* apply for SSI, you must satisfy the income test *without* the benefit of these impairment-related deductions. So you may have to cut your income—perhaps by waiting to work—until after you first qualify for SSI.

Table 10.3 shows how these reductions help you qualify for SSI—and increase your monthly check!

TABLE 10.3

Calculation for SSI

1. Subtract $20 from your monthly unearned income. The amount of your reduced unearned income is $_____.

2. If you work and have earnings, subtract another $65 (deduct $85 if you have no unearned income). The amount of your reduced earned income is $_____.

3. Take the reduced earnings in line 2 and subtract any impairment-related work expenses. The amount is $_____.

4. Take the reduced earnings in line 3 and cut it in half. The amount is $_____.

5. Add the amount in line 4 to the amount in line 1: $_____.

6. If the total dollars in line 5 is less than the maximum SSI payment for your state, you're due a check for the difference.

Examples 5, 6, and 7 illustrate how to figure your income and SSI check.

EXAMPLE 5

You are unmarried, get $200 per month Social Security or pension, and earn $400 monthly wages. You are not disabled. You would:

1. Deduct $20 from $200 (your unearned income) = *$180.*
2. Deduct $65 from $400 (your earned income) = *$335.*
3. There are no impairment-related work expenses, so reduced earnings remain *$335.*
4. Take half the amount in line 3 ($335) = *$167.50.*
5. Add $167.50 to $180 = *$347.50.*
6. Since $347.50 is less than $422 (which is the maximum SSI for one person without any state supplement), you are entitled to a monthly SSI check for the difference: *$74.50.*

EXAMPLE 6

Neither you nor your spouse is working and you both are over 65. You are living on your combined Social Security payments of $350/month. After deducting $20, the amount is $330. Since that is $303 less than the $633 maximum for a couple, you'd be entitled to an additional $303 each month.

EXAMPLE 7

You are working and earning $365/month. You also receive $200/month Social Security, making your total income $565/month—well over the SSI limits. Clearly, you don't qualify for SSI, right? WRONG. If you know the rules, you can put additional cash in your pocket.

You subtract $20 of unearned income and $65 of earned income, which brings the total down to $480. That's still over the limit, but you're not through.

You pay $50/month for medications to control your severe arthritis, which allows you to work. That amount can be deducted, bringing earned income down to $250. And you can deduct half of the remaining earned income ($125). Now the total income that is counted for SSI is only $305 ($180 unearned and $125 earned)—not only do you qualify, but you will get a monthly check for $117!

WARNING

You must apply for other benefits you are entitled to—you can't cash in on SSI just by refusing other options. For example, if you qualify for Social Security retirement benefits at age 62, you must apply before taking SSI. You can't delay Social Security until age 65 (to build it up) and take full SSI in the meantime.

Deemed Income. We've mentioned earned and unearned income; there's a third type of income called deemed income (when using Table 10.3, this will be part of your *unearned* income).

If you and your spouse are both 65, blind or disabled (you both pass the status test), both your incomes are counted and you use the higher SSI limit that applies to couples. But what if only one of you is eligible for SSI? The ineligible spouse's income will be "deemed" to (counted against) the eligible spouse.

Table 10.4 illustrates the impact of an ineligible spouse's income, and Example 8 shows how to use the table.

TABLE 10.4

Deeming Income

1. The ineligible spouse's income is $_____.

2. If the ineligible spouse's income (the amount in line 1) is equal to or less than $211, then ignore that income and just figure the eligible spouse's benefits as if he were unmarried, using Table 10.3. If the ineligible spouse's income is more than $211, then continue.

3. Add the couple's unearned income and subtract $20; the result is $_____.

4. Add the couple's earned income and subtract $65 ($85 if no unearned income); the result is $_____.

5. Take one-half of the number in line 4; the amount is $_____.

6. Add lines 3 and 5 together; the amount is $_____.

7. If the total amount in line 6 is less than the maximum SSI payment for a couple in your state, you're due a check for the difference.

EXAMPLE 8

You are 65 and receive $200 Social Security benefits. Your wife is younger and so is not yet eligible for SSI; she works and earns $600/month. Here's how to figure your benefits:

1. Your ineligible spouse's income is $600/month.
2. Since $600 is well over $211, you must continue through the table.
3. Your total unearned income ($200) less $20 is *$180*.
4. Your total earned income ($600) less $65 is *$535*.
5. One-half of $535 is *$267.50*.
6. Add $267.50 to $180 = $447.50.
7. Since $447.50 is less than $633 (the maximum a couple may receive in your state), you are entitled to a check for the difference, *$185.50*.

Example 8 demonstrates the evil impact of deeming income against you. Using the same facts, if your wife's earnings were not counted, you would be entitled to $242—an increase of more than $55 a month.

❖ GEM: Separation or Divorce Can Pay Off with SSI

As you can see, a spouse's income can cost you money—money which may be critical to your survival. While you probably won't like the idea, a separation or divorce could get you out of the "deeming trap."

Your ineligible spouse's income is only deemed against you if you are living together as husband and wife. If you are divorced, or even just living apart for a month, your spouse's income won't reduce your SSI benefits. Take a look at Example 9.

EXAMPLE 9

You are 65 and have no income of your own. Your husband is 64, and so is not eligible for SSI. He receives an $800 monthly pension.

Using Table 10.4, you would not be entitled to *any* SSI benefits. But if you and your husband separated, you'd get $422/month and he'd still receive his $800/month. Then when he reaches 65, you could get back together. For $422/month, this plan might prove to be a lifesaver.

Separation or divorce might even make sense if you and your spouse both pass the status test. Take a look at Example 10.

EXAMPLE 10

You and your husband are both 65, so you both pass the status test. He receives a $600/month pension; you get $100/month in interest. Your combined income is more than the $633/month allowed for a couple. So even though you have trouble making ends meet on $700/month, SSI is *not* available.

But now you divorce. Maybe you even continue to live together. Your husband still can't get SSI, but you *can!* Expect a $342 ($422 – $80) check *every month.*

ASSETS TEST

Here's the biggest SSI hurdle for most people. The government tries to make it very tough to cash in on SSI by saying that a single person can have no more than $2,000 of assets and a couple can have no more than $3,000. Assets are defined broadly as "cash or other liquid assets or any real or personal property that an individual (or spouse) owns and could convert to cash." As you can see, that definition includes a lot.

Your and your spouse's assets both are included—even if only one of you qualifies or intends to apply for SSI. Whether the assets are in your name, your spouse's name, or joint names with you and your spouse makes no difference— $3,000 is the limit for a couple.

Long-term CDs are counted against you, even if you'd get socked with a penalty if you had to cash them in. IRAs are counted against you, even if you would be penalized for removing the cash. The SSI rules are pretty harsh.

But don't give up; not all assets are counted for the SSI calculation and the numbers aren't quite as tough as they appear. By using our gems, you may still be able to make SSI a Golden Opportunity for added income.

In addition to the base $2,000 ($3,000 for a couple), you may *also* keep the assets listed in Table 10.5. Wise use of the protected assets listed in Table 10.5 can help you get SSI benefits while receiving more than $2,000 (single) or $3,000 (couple) of money and property. Let's see how.

TABLE 10.5

Protected Assets

- *Your residence.* The family home, whether in your or your spouse's name, is not counted under the SSI assets test, *regardless of its value!* Adjoining land is also exempt.

- *Household goods and personal effects.* Household goods and personal effects, including furniture, clothing, and jewelry, are protected up to an additional $2,000; if your goods and personal effects exceed $2,000, only the excess is counted in your assets for SSI eligibility. In addition, you can keep a wedding and an engagement ring of *any* value, and all personal items needed for medical reasons (such as wheelchairs, dialysis machines, hospital beds, and prosthetic devices), also regardless of value.

- *One car.* You (and your spouse) may keep one car with a current market value up to $4,500 (anything over that amount is counted in your assets).

- *Life insurance.* Cash surrender value of life insurance is not counted if the total face value of all life insurance on any one person is $1,500 or less. Term and burial insurance are not counted in your assets since they generally have no cash value.

- *Burial and funeral costs.* You may keep burial spaces for you and your immediate family. This protection not only covers the grave sites but also headstones, markers, caskets, vaults, crypts, urns, and other repositories. You may also set aside up to $1,500 for funeral expenses for you and $1,500 for your spouse, but the funds must be kept separate from other resources. (Note that this $1,500 limit will be reduced by the face value of life insurance or an irrevocable burial contract.)

- *Jointly owned real estate.* Real property which you own with someone else is not counted against you if the property is a co-owner's principal residence, a sale would force the co-owner to move, and that co-owner has no other readily available house to move into. Jointly held real estate is also protected if you cannot sell your share without permission of the other owners.

- *Real estate that can't be sold.* You may keep, and not count, real estate that you aren't able to sell despite your reasonable efforts.

- *Property essential to self-support.* You can protect up to $6,000 equity in property (personal and real estate) if necessary for your support. To be considered necessary for support, the property should either produce income, goods, or services necessary for your daily activities (such as land to grow food for your own use). Income-producing property should produce net annual income of at least 6 percent of the amount of the protected equity (*i.e.*, $360/year if the equity of the property is $6,000).

- *Retroactive SSI or Social Security payments.* Back payments of SSI or Social Security benefits are not counted as assets for SSI purposes for six months after you receive them. After six months, monies left unspent *will* count against you.

Home Sweet Home

The most important protection is for the family home. By far, the residence is typically the major asset that most people own. You may own a home worth $50,000, $100,000, or more, and still qualify for SSI if your other assets are below the $2,000 ($3,000 for couple) limit.

You do not have to own the entire property. Any ownership interest in your residence—a life estate (legal right to live in the house for life) or a partial interest (for example, if you own the home with a child)—is protected.

The residence remains protected as long as you live there. Even if you are not currently living in the home—you may be in a hospital or nursing home—the home maintains its protection as long as either:

- You intend to return.
- Your spouse or dependent relative lives there.

❖ GEM: Promise to Come Home—in Writing

If you leave home, keep it protected by stating *in writing* your intent to return. Don't leave any room for question.

If you enter a nursing home, try to get your doctor to state, in writing, that there is at least some chance you'll be able to return home. That, coupled with your stated intent to return, should allow you to keep the house and qualify for SSI.

✦   ✦   ✦

If you sell your home, the cash from the sale is *not* protected—that is, unless you use the funds to purchase another residence. You have three months from the time you receive the sale proceeds to buy another place.

Household Goods and Personal Effects

You can have $2,000 of household goods and personal effects *in addition* to the base $2,000 you can keep.

Don't get too uptight if you think the value of your personal items may go over $2,000. Rarely have we seen the Government deny someone SSI based on the value of household and personal items. Usually the Government doesn't look too closely at these.

Car

If you or a member of your household uses the car for any of the following reasons, it will be protected *regardless of value:*

- Employment
- Treatment of a specific medical problem
- Transportation of a handicapped person
- Essential daily activities

In most cases, you should be able to protect the entire value of the car. If you live too far to walk to shopping, then it's necessary for essential daily activities. If you need it to get to your doctor for treatment of a chronic illness, then, again, it's fully protected—even if it's a Mercedes Benz!

❖ GEM: Get a Job

If there's no other way to protect the entire value of your car, you may want to get a part-time job. The car is protected if you or any member of your household uses it to get to work. There is no required number of hours—for example, if you work one day a week for three hours, that should be enough.

◆ ◆ ◆

Insurance

If the face value of all your life insurance policies (that's the amount that will be paid out on your death) is less than $1,500, you can forget about them—they won't count for SSI. Your spouse can also have life insurance with $1,500 face value without worrying.

But if the face values of your policies exceed $1,500, then you'll have to check to see if there is any cash-surrender value—any amount you could receive by cashing them in today. Cash value is then considered an asset and can be counted against you for SSI.

Burial and Funeral Costs

You can buy burial spaces (any amount) not only for yourself and your spouse but also for your adult children, brothers, sisters, parents—and their spouses. None of these will be counted as part of your assets.

Up to $1,500 can be set aside for funeral expenses, but only if the money is really set aside—you can't designate a CD for funeral expenses, then use the money for other purposes unless you immediately designate a substitute account worth the same amount.

If you set aside a $1,500 investment today, and it earns interest and grows to $2,500, the entire amount remains protected—but only if you don't withdraw the interest. If you take the interest and use it for other purposes, your SSI benefits will be reduced by the amount withdrawn.

Finally, we note that $1,500 isn't enough for a decent burial in most places today. Some states have expanded protection for funeral costs, allowing you to protect the entire cost of an irrevocable prepaid funeral contract; check with your local Social Security office for further information.

Jointly Owned Real Estate

As we showed in Table 10.5, property that you own with someone else will not be counted against you in many cases. You can protect property by adding a co-owner, as Example 11 shows.

EXAMPLE 11

You and your sister have been living in your home for years. After you enter an assisted living facility, the Government decides that you have no intent to return, so no SSI will be paid.

But if you add your sister to the deed, then the home will not be counted against you; you can keep the home and *still* get SSI. As long as your sister doesn't own another residence, the house is protected.

WARNING

While owning real estate jointly with someone else may be a benefit, owning liquid assets jointly may cost you. In most cases, bank accounts, CDs, stocks, and bonds that are in both your and another person's name (such as a child's) will be considered *entirely yours*. You always have the right to prove that it isn't all yours—that a portion really belongs to your child, for example—but if the account is in your Social Security number, and it was your money initially, and you claim the interest or dividends on your tax returns, the asset will be considered yours and yours alone. And that may make you ineligible for SSI.

Real Estate You Can't Sell

If you own real estate that is not protected, you will have to sell it and use (or dispose of) the proceeds before qualifying for SSI. But if you just can't sell the property for a fair price after making reasonable efforts, then the property won't count against you—and you can get SSI.

What will the Government consider a "reasonable effort" to sell? You must list the property with an agent or try to sell it yourself. If you try on your own, you must:

- Advertise in at least one of the local media
- Put up a "For Sale" sign, if allowed by your community
- Conduct open houses
- Show the property to interested prospects

Feel free to reject offers below two-thirds of the current market value. But if you get an offer that's more than two-thirds of the value, the Government may say that your rejection is *not* reasonable unless you can show why the price offered isn't fair.

You don't have to keep advertising forever. After nine months of reasonable efforts, you can keep the property *and* your SSI benefits too!

Property Essential to Your Support

This protection usually doesn't offer much help. Example 12 illustrates how it is supposed to work:

EXAMPLE 12

Your mother has a small business in her house making handwoven rugs. The looms and other equipment used in the business have a value of $7,000, and her equity is $5,500 since she owes $1,500 on the looms. Your mother's income from selling the rugs (net of expenses) is $400 per year. Since her equity in the looms and other equipment ($5,500) is under the $6,000 limit for property essential to her support, and since her net income ($400) is greater than 6 percent of her equity, your mother's looms and other equipment will not be counted against her for SSI.

A rental property or vacation home usually will be counted against you—that is, unless you use our gems!

❖ GEM: Borrow and Rent Your Second Home!

Let's say you live in Ohio and have a vacation home in Florida. Can you protect the second home? The answer may be *yes*.

Your first problem is that the equity is $50,000, a far cry from the $6,000 maximum. That can be solved by borrowing to reduce the equity. Take a $45,000 loan, and your equity in the property will be below $6,000. Now you need to show that the property generates income for your support. All you need is a few hundred dollars a year. Rent it for a couple of weeks, maybe to a child, and the property has "magically" become protected.

But what do you do with the $45,000 which you borrowed? That answer comes on pages 452–457.

❖ GEM: Grow Crops on Vacant Land and Reap Benefits!

Let's say you have a vacant lot worth $5,000. Can you protect it? Not as it is. But why not plant a vegetable garden? Even if it's in the middle of the city, who cares? Not Uncle Sam! As long as you sample the fruits of your labor, the property should be protected!

❖ GEM: Protect Your Property Rights—Go to Court

If you have property that is "essential to your support," such as income-producing property, but your equity is more than $6,000 or your income is less than 6 percent, you may still qualify for SSI. Two courts in recent years have ruled that the $6,000 and 6 percent limits are invalid. A lawsuit may be the way to get SSI payments. If you can't afford a lawyer, talk to Legal Aid.

✦   ✦   ✦

Retroactive SSI and Social Security Payments

Back payments of SSI or Social Security benefits won't count as assets for six months. After you get a payment for "past-due" benefits, you've got six months to spend it or find some other way to protect it.

❖ GEM: Convert Back Benefit Payments into Other Protected Assets

Let's say you get $3,000 in past-due Social Security benefits. Any part of that left after six months will count against you for SSI. And if you just put it in the bank or use it to buy other countable assets, say goodbye to SSI after six months.

But if you buy *protected* resources, like household goods (TV, stereo, etc.), car, or prepaid funeral contracts, the assets will remain protected even after six months!

CASHING IN ON SSI

If your income or assets are too high to get SSI benefits, does that mean you're out of luck? No! By using our gems, you may be able to cash in on hundreds of dollars each and every month!

❖ GEM: Use a Little Alchemy to Change Countable Assets into "Gold"

You can take money from bank accounts, stocks, bonds, CDs, and so on—all of which would count against you for SSI—and put it into your home. No, we *don't* mean that you should take cash out of the bank and hide it under the bed. But because a home generally is protected, adding to your equity can qualify you for SSI.

EXAMPLE 13

You own your home, which today is worth $85,000. You also have $10,000 in CDs, but not much else. An extra $200 or $300/month from SSI would sure help.

Take the $10,000 and pay off your mortgage, put on a new roof, build on a family room, add aluminum siding, or make other necessary improvements to your home. By these simple steps, you can qualify for SSI. The $10,000 CDs no longer exist, so they don't count against you. And the house, even with $10,000 of improvements, is protected. (Added bonus: when you do sell, your home will be in much better shape!)

Putting countable assets into the home can have a double benefit because it reduces both assets and income. This helps you kill two of the SSI requirement birds with one stone.

EXAMPLE 14

Same facts as in Example 13. Your income from Social Security is $350/month, and you get $50/month interest from your $10,000 CD.

Since your assets exceed $2,000, you get no SSI. And even if you passed the assets test, you would only qualify for SSI of $42/month. But by putting the $10,000 into the house, you pass the assets test *and* reduce your income. Now you can get SSI payments of $92/month.

If you don't own a home, you could buy one. Using cash from CDs, stocks, bonds, or other "countable" assets for a home can be a way to protect most or all of your assets and get SSI. But in many cases the costs of purchasing a home may outweigh the SSI benefits.

Once your cash is "in" your home, what are you going to do if you need money? Although you'll be adding SSI benefits to your income, you may need more for some emergency.

In that case, you may take a loan on the house. The loan might be in the form of a standard mortgage, a home equity line, or a reverse mortgage (see Chapter 9). Remember, loan proceeds are *not* counted as income!

❖ GEM: Buy Part of Your Child's Home

Many older Americans live with a child, brother, sister, or other relative. Example 15 shows how you can benefit from this situation.

EXAMPLE 15

You have been living with your son and his wife for years. You've got $75,000 (CDs and money market funds), so you clearly don't qualify for SSI.

You take the $75,000 and "buy" a portion of your child's home, paying him the money. Suddenly, you do qualify for SSI (and you've purchased a legal lifetime guarantee that you may live in the house as well). Even if you must later enter an assisted living or nursing facility, your SSI should continue; remember, jointly held real estate doesn't count against you, even if you are not living there. And again, if you ever need more cash, you could take a loan on the property.

❖ GEM: Buy a Home for Your Child

If you've got too much cash to qualify for SSI, you can get yourself an SSI check by using that money to buy a home for a family member! Example 16 shows how.

EXAMPLE 16

You've got $50,000, so you don't qualify for SSI. Your child has been renting and would like to buy a home. You can get your child a home, and get yourself an SSI check at the same time, by buying a home for her.

Take the $50,000 and buy a home for your daughter, putting both your names on the deed. The house will not be counted against you, so you've "protected" your $50,000. And you've bought yourself a monthly SSI check at the same time!

❖ GEM: Buy Other Protected Assets

Let's say you've got $15,000—which is well over the $2,000 SSI threshold. You could put those funds into other protected assets, so they will not count against you for SSI qualification.

Need a new refrigerator? Is the stove on its last leg? Time to buy a new coat for the winter? You'd be amazed (or maybe you wouldn't) how easy it is to spend money on personal and household goods you really could use. You can "shelter" at least $2,000 in household goods and personal effects—and often more, because the Government doesn't look too hard here.

How about a new car? If you need the car to get to medical appointments or work, or for transportation of someone who is handicapped, the vehicle is protected no matter how much it costs. You can protect $10,000 to $15,000 easily, just by buying a new set of wheels.

And we're sure this won't come as a shock, but you will die someday. Funerals cost money. You could set aside $3,000, and possibly more in some states, for you and your spouse. Shifting money into protected assets can pay off by qualifying you for SSI.

❖ GEM: Give Assets Away

The easiest way, and in many cases the best way, to protect your savings and qualify for SSI is to give your savings away! Here is a time when less makes more.

EXAMPLE 17

You have $80,000 which you've been able to save over the years. That savings provides you with income (interest and dividends) of

$430/month. While you get by, you could sure use another $422/ month. Unfortunately, you don't pass the SSI tests because both your assets and income are too high.

But let's say you give the $80,000 to your son. That's right, just give it away. Now you have no income or assets. How are you better off? Thanks to Uncle Sam, you get SSI! You qualify for SSI payments of $422/ month—that almost completely replaces your lost income. So far you're about even.

But that's not all. Now your son makes you a "loan" which pays you the monthly income you were receiving before—$430/month. It won't cost your child anything because he's just paying you the income from the $80,000 you gave him. And since loan proceeds do not count against your income, you can get SSI *plus* the "loan" income. The result: your income *doubles*, from $430 to more than $800 each month.

What happens to the "loan" when you die? No problem—at that time your son can forgive the debt. And if that's not enough, here's another benefit: your child already has the $80,000 when you die. There will be no estate tax to pay or probate to suffer through!

This gem provides a Golden Opportunity to enhance your income because you can give money or property away with no fuss, muss, or problems. This was not always the case. Until recently, making a gift or transfer would cause you to be disqualified for SSI for up to two years. But now there is *no* disqualification period for SSI. You can give your money away and *immediately* qualify for SSI!

NOTE

The rules for getting Medicaid benefits generally are very similar to those for SSI. But here's an important difference: transfers or gifts will still, in most cases, cause you to be disqualified for Medicaid for as much as 30 months.

Are you afraid of giving your money and property away to your kids? What if they take the money and run? The next day you get a call from the Bahamas and it's your kids telling you they're having a great time with your money!

There are surely risks with giving your savings away to your children—no question. If you expect to continue to receive the interest from your investments, as in Example 17, you are dependent on the honesty of your children. But you can minimize the risks by making your children commit, in writing, to make payments to you.

EXAMPLE 18

You've got $100,000, which is invested in CDs, money markets, and mutual funds. You are living on the $500/month interest and dividends you receive. If you gave the $100,000 away to your daughter, you would qualify for $422/month SSI payments. And as we explained in Example 17, your daughter could loan you $500/month to supplement your SSI. But you would be dependent on the goodwill of your daughter to do so.

You can minimize this risk by loaning your daughter the $100,000, rather than giving it to her. She is required by the written loan agreement to pay you $500/month. As long as that is a return on *principal*, and you are not getting any interest from her on your loan, then the $500/month payments will not prevent you from receiving SSI. You will get $422 *plus* $500 each month! And you've minimized your risk by making your daughter a formal loan that she is legally obligated to pay back, rather than a gift.

DON'T WORRY ABOUT GIFT TAXES

A lot of people ask: "If I give away more than $10,000, won't there be a gift tax?" The answer for most people is no! As long as your total wealth is under $600,000, you will never pay any gift tax no matter how much you give away.

The reason is this. Uncle Sam allows you a $600,000 "unified credit" during your lifetime. Gifts over $10,000 reduce your credit (gifts of less than $10,000 don't). But until you give away more than $600,000, using up your entire credit, you won't pay any gift tax. And the person who receives a gift of any amount never pays any gift tax.

❖ GEM: Create an Irrevocable Trust

Another way to minimize the risks involved in giving money to children is to set up an irrevocable trust. In Chapter 11 we tell you about the benefits of a Medicaid Trust to qualify for Medicaid benefits; the same type of trust can be used to obtain SSI payments.

EXAMPLE 19

You have $10,000 in the bank, which is too much to qualify for SSI payments. You don't like the idea of giving it to your daughter, because her financial condition is a little shaky and you don't want her creditors getting those funds. So you set up an irrevocable trust with your daughter as trustee. Immediately after putting your $10,000 into the trust, you qualify for SSI.

How much will SSI pay? Your Social Security checks are $200/month. In addition, your $10,000 was generating interest of $600/year or $50/month. When you set up the trust, you have a choice: you can require the trust to pay you the interest, or you can have the interest paid to your daughter.

If the interest goes to you, your SSI paychecks will be $192/month (see Table 10.2); if the interest is paid to your daughter, SSI will make up the $50 loss and pay you $242/month. And if your daughter decides to gift you back some or all of the income—all the better! (For gifts of this amount, you don't have to worry about documentation.)

❖ GEM: Check Medicaid!

Creating a Medicaid Trust is not the only Medicaid gem that can be a gold mine for SSI benefits. Because the Medicaid rules are so much like the SSI rules, the gems are almost interchangeable. For more ways to cash in on SSI benefits, take a look at Chapter 11. In fact, by opening up the treasure chest of one program, you should be able to find the gold in the other as well.

APPLICATION

The application form and process for SSI is similar to that for Social Security retirement and disability. Apply at your local Social Security office. Bring with you the documents listed in Appendix 6, including your Social Security card or number; birth certificate or other proof of age; and your spouse's Social Security card and birth certificate (if applicable).

Since SSI is dependent on income and assets, you will also have to bring proof of those amounts, such as:

- Tax bill, assessment, or appraisal for your home and other real estate
- Mortgage or lease
- Deeds
- Payroll slips or other evidence of income
- Bank books and statements
- Life insurance policies
- Car registration
- Burial fund records
- Rent receipts

If you are applying for SSI as disabled or blind, provide the same information necessary for Social Security disability (pages 106–108). Include names, addresses and phone numbers of doctors, hospitals, and clinics that treated you; medications; medical records; and names and addresses of employers.

❖ GEM: Don't Delay or You Lose Pay!

Call Social Security—1-800-772-1213—for an SSI application *today* (or as soon as you qualify). Even though it may take you several weeks to get the information together to support your application, get the application now. Why rush?

The Government will only pay you SSI benefits from the date of your application (or the date you became eligible, whichever is later). But the Government will treat your telephone call asking for SSI information and an application form *as your application.*

EXAMPLE 20

You are eligible for SSI benefits, so you call the local office on March 1 to get an application. By the time you gather the supporting material and file your application, it's April 1. You should get SSI benefits back to March 1—an extra four weeks of benefits—just because you made the call without waiting!

To have your call to the Government trigger your eligibility, you must do two things:

1. Give your name. A blind call won't do you any good.
2. File your application within 60 days of the call.

❖ GEM: Get One Month Emergency Cash

Once you file your application, be prepared to wait. It may take months for your application to be granted or denied, especially when it is based on disability. Once approved, the Government will pay you back to the date you applied, so the delay won't cost you anything.

But what if you really need the money in the meantime? You may get a one-time check up to $422 ($633 for a couple) *plus* any state supplement if:

- it is likely, based upon information in your application, that your application will be approved; and
- you *need* the money for food, clothing, shelter, or medical care.

Make sure the Government bureaucrats understand that you want and need your one-month emergency payment. When your application is approved, the first check will be reduced by the amount of any emergency payment. And if your application is *not* approved, the Government may come after you for a repayment.

❖ GEM: Get Three Months of Disability Payments

The longest delays come with applications based on disability or blindness. You can collect SSI for six months, *before* your application is approved, if:

- You clearly satisfy the income and assets tests.
- You have submitted enough information about your disability to show that your application is likely to be approved.

Certain impairments, listed in Table 10.6, will almost surely get you six months of advance payments. Don't worry about having to return the funds if the Government decides you don't qualify for SSI. Once paid, this money is yours!

TABLE 10.6

Impairments Allowing Advance SSI Payments

- Amputation of two limbs
- Amputation of a leg at the hip
- Total deafness or blindness
- Confinement to a bed
- Immobility without a wheelchair, walker, or crutches owing to a long-standing condition
- Limited movement of hand, arm, or leg owing to a stroke
- Difficulty walking, speaking, or coordination owing to cerebral palsy, muscular dystrophy, or muscular atrophy
- Amputation of a foot due to diabetes
- Down's syndrome
- Severe mental deficiency
- AIDS

❖ GEM: Stop the Presses and Press Your Claim

Once your application for SSI is approved, there will still be a short delay—usually about 10 days—before you get the check. According to the law, you can get up to $200 immediately if you face a financial emergency, *or* the Government will suffer bad publicity. That's right—Uncle Sam is camera shy.

So how can you get the Government bureaucracy to move faster? First, explain you have a financial emergency and need the money now. If that doesn't work, call the local media (of course, only do this if your claim is strong). Some bad publicity for the Government can mean good news for you!

APPEALS

Many valid applications are wrongfully denied. Just as we said in talking about Social Security disability, you *can* fight city hall and win, but you've got to be persistent.

The steps up the Appeals Ladder for SSI are very similar to the appeals for Social Security disability. You again have four steps to climb: Reconsideration, Administrative Hearing, Appeals Council, and Federal Court. Don't give up—perseverance can pay big dividends. Look to Chapter 3 for our gems on how to handle the appeals process.

WARNING: COOPERATE WITH GOVERNMENT REVIEWS

After you've been approved, you're not completely out of the woods. The Government will periodically recheck to make sure you still qualify and to confirm the amount you should receive. You can expect to hear from the Government every 12 to 18 months.

You may be asked to provide the same type of information required in your original application—income, assets, living arrangements, and (if disabled) medical condition. You may even have to undergo a medical exam to establish your continued disability.

In most cases, the Government review is all done by telephone or mail. Occasionally, you'll have to go down to the local Social Security office. But no matter what's involved, *cooperate.* Don't be worried—these reviews usually are just routine, standard procedure.

Generally, all appeals must be filed within 60 days from the date you received the unpleasant news. If you're a day or two late, don't worry—there's usually a five-day grace period.

❖ GEM: Move Quickly If You're Appealing a Cut-off of Benefits

If your benefits have been reduced or eliminated and you want to appeal, don't delay! By appealing within 10 days, you can keep your benefits during Reconsideration.

Don't let Government personnel convince you that it's not worth continuing your benefits during the appeal process. Sometimes they try to scare you, saying you'll just have to repay all the benefits if you lose. Take a look at page 115; even if you lose your appeal, you may be able to avoid repaying these benefits!

OVERPAYMENTS

The Government might surprise you someday by claiming it has paid you too much in SSI benefits, and telling you that you now owe Uncle Sam a pot of dough. In fact, this is a much more common problem with SSI than with Social Security retirement, survivors, or disability payments.

In Chapter 1, pages 47–49, we explained how to respond to a Government attempt to collect overpaid Social Security benefits; the same rules and gems apply to SSI. If you show the Government you were not at fault, and that forcing you to repay would be against "equity and good conscience," or would violate the purpose of the SSI program, you should get off the hook.

EXAMPLE 21

After being notified that you were eligible for SSI benefits, you signed a lease for an apartment that cost $15/month more than you were paying before. A year later, the Government tells you there's a mistake and you should not have received SSI benefits.

Even if the Government is right about your eligibility, you should not have to repay the benefits. You changed position to your financial detriment, taking on a higher monthly obligation in reliance on the benefits. Don't let them tell you otherwise.

EXAMPLE 22

The Government tells you that you owe $3,000 in SSI overpayments. Your income, including SSI, is less than $422/month plus the state SSI supplement. In this case, you should not be forced to repay the overpayment. As long as your income is low enough to qualify for SSI, you have a very good argument that forcing you to make repayment would defeat the purpose of the program.

Most people know nothing about SSI. And that's sad, because a lot of folks are missing out on money that is there for the asking. The Golden Opportunities we've presented in this chapter can add enough income to make a real difference in your everyday life-style.

·11·

Invaluable Aid from Medicaid

Health-care costs have skyrocketed and are now out of reach for most middle-class Americans. As we explained in Chapter 4, Medicare offers invaluable financial aid for health care, but it's not enough. As a safety net, Medicare is full of holes.

Despite the benefits of Medicare coverage, your entire life savings—everything you've worked so hard for—can be wiped out by bills from a catastrophic illness. Medical costs resulting from Alzheimer's, senility, strokes, falls, arthritis, and many other illnesses and injuries are often a one-way ticket to the poorhouse.

But this financial and personal disaster is avoidable—if you take steps to protect yourself and your family. That's what this chapter is all about. We'll let you in on some Golden Opportunities available under the Medicaid program that help you protect your life savings.

WHAT IS MEDICAID?

Medicaid is a public program designed to cover medical costs, including the biggest of these: nursing-home care. But Medicaid covers much more. In fact, in most states almost all medical needs are covered. Table 11.1 lists the types of services for which Medicaid will pay.

ELIGIBILITY

Here's the rub: to qualify for Medicaid, you've got to have no money. Many people who have worked hard and put away a little for the "golden years" wind up spending everything on medical costs—particularly nursing-home charges—before Medicaid comes into play.

TABLE 11.1

Medicaid Covered Services

All States Cover

- Skilled care in a nursing home
- Intermediate or custodial care in a nursing home (the typical care most people in nursing homes need)
- In-hospital services, including costs for a semiprivate room and doctors
- Outpatient hospital services
- Lab tests and X-rays, in or out of a hospital
- Doctors' care and treatment

Most States Also Cover

- Prescription drugs
- Transportation to and from medical appointments
- Eye exams and glasses
- Dental care
- Podiatric care
- Physical therapy
- Speech therapy
- Prosthetic devices and dentures
- Diagnostic tests, screening, preventive care, and rehabilitation

Some States Also Cover

- Private nurses in a hospital, nursing home, or at home
- Emergency hospital services
- Personal care services at home, including cooking and cleaning help
- Adult day-care services
- Home-delivered meals
- Respite care (to relieve the caregivers at home)
- Hospice care for the terminally ill

In most states, if you qualify for Supplemental Security Income (SSI) (see Chapter 10) you also can get Medicaid; the same basic income and asset limits apply. A few states (listed in Table 11.2) use even tougher standards. If you live in one of the more restrictive states, contact your local Medicaid office to find out the income and asset requirements.

TABLE 11.2

States Using Tougher Eligibility Standards Than Under SSI

• Connecticut	• New Hampshire
• Hawaii	• North Carolina
• Illinois	• North Dakota
• Indiana	• Ohio
• Minnesota	• Oklahoma
• Missouri	• Utah
• Nebraska	• Virginia

We won't repeat the SSI income and asset limits described in Chapter 10. After all, why repeat bad news?

If your income and assets are too high, does that mean you can't get Medicaid? The answer in most states is no. You are allowed to "spend down"—that's a nice way of saying you can spend virtually your entire income and assets on medical or nursing-home costs until you're down to the Medicaid limits, and then the benefits will start.

All states allow you to spend down assets (money and property). But a few states impose strict limits on *income* and will *not* allow a Medicaid applicant to spend down; these states are listed in Table 11.3. This rule can create unbearable hardships; if you are one penny over the income limit, you can't get Medicaid. Sadly, that leaves some people with too much income for Medicaid but not enough to pay the nursing home.

TABLE 11.3

States Imposing Strict Income Limits of $1,266/Month or Less

• Alabama	• Louisiana
• Alaska	• Mississippi
• Arizona	• Nevada
• Arkansas	• New Jersey
• Colorado	• New Mexico
• Delaware	• Oklahoma
• Florida	• Oregon
• Idaho	• South Dakota
• Iowa	• Texas
• Kansas	• Wyoming

EXAMPLE 1

Your mother has spent all of her savings on medical costs. She gets $700/month in Social Security and $600/month in pension benefits. Unfortunately, the state says that no one with income over $1,266/month can get Medicaid.

Nursing homes in her area are running $3,000/month. She can't afford to pay the cost herself, and you don't have the funds to make up the difference. What happens? Must she be thrown into the street? One thing is clear—she won't get Medicaid.

The severe income limits set by the states listed in Table 11.3 create terrible problems for older Americans. At the end of this chapter (pages 493–494), we offer three gems that may help.

We have previously written a book, *Avoiding the Medicaid Trap: How to Beat the Catastrophic Costs of Nursing-Home Care* (Holt, 1990), which provides a thorough discussion of the income and asset limits in each state. (A series of important tables list state-by-state variations.) Space limitations prevent us from providing that same detail here. In most states, once you use up your income and assets on medical bills, Medicaid will step in. Your goal is to get Medicaid *before* you've lost everything.

HOW MUCH CAN YOU KEEP?

We don't want to be accused of overstating the case. The Government in its great generosity throws a few crumbs to older Americans and their families, allowing them to keep a small amount of income and assets. But the meat and potatoes must go to pay the medical and nursing-home bills.

Let's focus on the Medicaid rules as they involve nursing homes because those are the biggest costs you will face.

Today you generally can't find a decent nursing home for under $35,000 per year in most parts of the country—and if you're lucky enough to live in New York, Los Angeles, Chicago, or just about any other large city, expect to pay more like $50,000 per year and up!

A report published in the respected *New England Journal of Medicine* showed that the chance of needing nursing home care is 50-50—a flip of a coin—for people 65 and up. And the risk is even greater as you get to 70 or 75 years old.

The average nursing-home stay is about 2½ years, but many elderly citizens need care for much longer. For example, a patient with Alzheimer's disease lives eight years, on average, after the symptoms first appear, and much of that time often is spent in a nursing home. What's it all mean? High costs + high risk + long stays = trouble.

As you've already noted in our discussion of Medicare, don't count on that program to pay for nursing-home charges. Medicare pays for less than 2 percent of all nursing-home bills. And standard Medicare supplement insurance policies pay almost *no* nursing home costs. Medicaid is it!

The Medicaid rules differ for unmarried (widow, widower, divorced, never married) and married people. Here's a sketch of each:

Unmarried

In most states, all of your income will go to pay the nursing-home (or other medical) bills. Medicaid only steps in if your income isn't enough. You can keep a token amount of income, including:

- An allowance of $30 to $70 per month (depending on the state) to cover personal needs like haircuts, clothing, toiletries, and magazines
- Funds to pay health insurance premiums, including Medicare, and other medical expenses not covered by Medicaid, such as over-the-counter drugs
- Money to maintain your home

EXAMPLE 2

Your mother's income is $400/month from Social Security. Her income (less a small amount for her personal allowance) will go to pay her nursing-home bill. Medicaid will cover the rest.

EXAMPLE 3

Your mother's income is $2,000/month. In most states, she'll still qualify for Medicaid. But her income will cover most of the nursing-home costs, and Medicaid will only cover the difference. She'll still be left with almost nothing.

Not only your income must go to pay the bills; almost all assets (cash and property) must be turned over to the nursing home before Medicaid will pay a penny. If a senior isn't poor going into a nursing home, it won't take long to get there.

Again, the Medicaid law allows unmarried older Americans to keep a small amount of their assets—generally about $2,000, depending on the state.

You also can keep a few specific items, called protected or exempt assets. For unmarried people, these are pretty limited. Although these vary a little from state to state, Table 11.4 lists the most common.

TABLE 11.4

Typical Unmarried Exempt Assets

- The house. Until recently, the house was given only limited protection; in most states it would remain protected as long as you intended to return *and* as long as there was a reasonable chance (stated by a doctor) that you would return. Otherwise, the house would have to be sold after a reasonable time, usually six months, and the money spent on the nursing home. However, a regional office of the Health Care Financing Administration (HCFA) has now ruled that the home may remain protected as long as you intend to return, even if that intent is not realistic and you are likely to live out your days in a nursing home. The impact that this HCFA ruling will have is not yet clear.
- Household goods and other personal items of a reasonable value.
- One car (some states limit the value to about $4,500).
- Up to $6,000 in property (personal and real estate) if the property either produces income or goods and services for personal use (such as land used to grow your own food).
- Life insurance policies if the total death benefits don't exceed $1,500 (amounts vary by state).
- Burial plots for you and spouse.
- Funeral costs (sometimes limited in amount).

As you can see, these exempt or protected assets are just about the same as the protected assets for SSI (Table 10.5, page 446). For more information on each of these, turn to pages 447–452. (You should be aware of the specific rules for your state. *Avoiding the Medicaid Trap* [Henry Holt & Co., 1990] has very important state-by-state tables.)

Married

If your spouse goes into a nursing home, you don't have to worry about your income going to pay your spouse's bills. Almost all states use the "name-on-the-check" rule: only income in the name of your spouse will go to the nursing home; income in your name remains yours. (Only three states—Indiana, Nebraska, and West Virginia—require the spouse remaining at home to use any of his or her income for the nursing-home bill.)

But what if the spouse at home doesn't have enough income in her own name to make ends meet? In many cases, the husband enters the nursing home and the wife remains at home, but her Social Security and pension income (if any) is much lower since she may not have worked or earned as much as her husband.

Thankfully, the law often allows the spouse at home to get some of the nursing-home spouse's income. If you are at home, you should be allowed to get enough of your spouse's income to bring your monthly income up to at least $1149, and possibly as much as $1,718. Check with your state Medicaid office for the exact amount.

You will also get to keep more of your cash and property than an unmarried person would. First, you get to keep more in the way of exempt assets, as you can see from Table 11.5.

TABLE 11.5

Typical Married Exempt Assets

- The house, for as long as one spouse lives there
- Household goods and other personal items without regard to value
- One car without regard to value
- Up to $6,000 in property (personal and real estate) if the property either produces income or goods and services for personal use
- Life insurance policies if the total death benefits don't exceed $1,500 (amounts vary by state)
- Burial plots for you and spouse
- Funeral costs (sometimes limited in amount)

The biggest difference in exempt assets for unmarried and married people is the house: the family residence is exempt as long as one spouse is living there. Now don't get greedy—only one house is protected. A part-time home in Florida, for example, is not protected.

❖ GEM: If You Own Two Homes, Make the More Expensive One Your Legal Residence

Let's say you live in Ohio six months and in Florida six months. You've always considered Ohio your residence. Maybe it's time to rethink that, as Example 4 shows.

EXAMPLE 4

Your home in Ohio is worth $75,000, and the condo in Florida has a value of about $150,000. Since you can only protect one residence, wouldn't it make sense to make that Florida? It sure would!

How do you make Florida your residence? Start by registering to vote, getting a driver's license, and opening bank accounts there. When you make out your next income tax return, put Florida as your residence. That way, if your spouse enters a nursing home, the more expensive home will be protected.

In addition to the exempt assets, you also can keep half of your combined (husband and wife) assets up to a maximum of $68,700; the least you are permitted is $13,740. Here's how this works:

1. Take the total of your assets on the day your spouse enters a nursing home. Count assets in your name, your spouse's name, or assets in both your names. Don't count exempt assets.
2. Now cut the total in half. If the result is less than $13,740, then $13,740 can be sheltered. If the amount is more than $68,700, then $68,700 can be protected. And if the amount falls in between, that's what you can keep.

A growing number of states, including New York, Illinois, Georgia, Kansas, Vermont, Wisconsin, North Dakota, Washington, and California, will allow you to keep $68,700 without going through this rigmarole of figuring your total worth and cutting it in half.

EXAMPLE 5

Your parents have total (nonexempt) assets of $80,000 on the day your father enters a nursing home. In most states, they will not qualify for Medicaid until $40,000 (one-half) of their savings has been spent.

Although the law is a little more humane for married couples than it is for unmarrieds, it is still very harsh. If you've been challenged by making ends meet on the income from your CDs and stocks, try living on *half*. When one spouse enters a nursing home, the costs of the spouse remaining at home often are hardly reduced. Whether it's one or two living under one roof, certain expenses won't change: the rent or mortgage payments, real estate taxes, and utilities stay about the same. Car-related costs often go up (owing to driving to and from the nursing home). As Example 6 demonstrates, even married couples often end up with nothing.

EXAMPLE 6

At the time your husband entered a nursing home, your combined assets were $60,000. The money was invested in CDs and money funds, and you were getting about $4,000/year in interest and dividends.

After "spending down" half of your assets to $30,000, which didn't take long, Medicaid started paying your husband's nursing home costs. But you couldn't make ends meet anymore. Suddenly you were getting only about $2,000/year from your investments, and that just wasn't enough. Pretty soon, your $30,000 was used up too. Now what can you do? Not much!

The Medicaid rules will devastate most older Americans who don't take steps to protect themselves. The gems we provide in this chapter can save you thousands of dollars!

Gifts and Transfers

Before we get to the "good stuff"—the gems—there's one more rule you should know. You (and your spouse, if applicable) can't give all your money away and immediately qualify for Medicaid. Sorry!

Most gifts (by either you or your spouse) will make you ineligible for Medicaid for some period of time, up to *30 months* (2½ years). Note that we said *up to* 30 months. Many people are under the mistaken view that any transfer or gift triggers a full 30-month ineligibility period, and that's not so.

Here's how to figure out how long you'll have to wait for Medicaid after making a gift: Divide the amount of the gift by the average monthly nursing-home cost in your state (call Medicaid to get the amount). That will tell you the number of months you can't get Medicaid. The ineligibility period starts to run from the day of the gift, not from the entry into a nursing home.

EXAMPLE 7

Your father gave you $25,000 on December 31. Your state says that the average monthly cost for nursing homes is $2,500 (not very realistic, but many states actually use this figure). He would not be eligible to get Medicaid for 10 months ($25,000 divided by $2,500/month). On

November 1 of the following year he'd be eligible for benefits (assuming he had no other money).

EXAMPLE 8

Your father gives you $100,000. No matter how you cut it, he'll be ineligible for Medicaid for the full 30 months.

Although most transfers or gifts trigger a Medicaid waiting period, some do not. A few types of gifts, listed in Table 11.6, will *not* affect your eligibility for Medicaid.

TABLE 11.6

Transfers That Do Not Trigger a Medicaid Waiting Period

- Transfers of a home to any of the following:
  1. A spouse
  2. A child who is under 21, blind, or permanently and totally disabled
  3. A sibling who already has some ownership interest in the house and who was residing in the home for at least one year immediately before the Medicaid applicant was admitted to a nursing home
  4. Any child who was residing in the house for at least two years immediately before the parent's admission to a nursing home and who provided care for the parent that allowed him or her to stay at home rather than in an institution
- Transfers of any other assets to:
  1. A spouse
  2. A child who is under 21, blind, or permanently and totally disabled
- Transfers of any *exempt* assets (listed in Tables 11.3 or 11.4), other than the house, to anyone.
- Sales or exchanges where market value is received in return.
- Transfers made solely for a purpose other than to qualify for Medicaid. (The Medicaid applicant has a very tough burden to prove this to the state Medicaid bureaucrats.)
- Transfers of any type, to any person, if denying Medicaid assistance would cause an undue hardship. (Again, this is very difficult to prove, and you will need the help of an experienced Medicaid lawyer.)

That's the law in a nutshell. As you can see, it's very harsh. As a result, millions of older Americans have lost everything they owned when struck by a catastrophic illness.

AVOIDING THE MEDICAID TRAP

You can "avoid the Medicaid trap." You don't have to stand idly by as nursing-home costs eat away at all of your life savings. Following are more than 20 gems that can save you many thousands of dollars.

Gems Providing Immediate Benefits

Let's start with some gems that have an immediate payoff. If you, a spouse, or parent is about to enter or is currently in a nursing home, these first gems can be very useful.

❖ GEM: Shelter Money in Your House

For most people, the home is their largest asset, and it can be protected as long as a spouse is living there. For a married couple, this rule makes the family home a treasure chest for savings. Even for unmarried people who intend to return home, putting money into the residence can protect those funds. Compare Examples 9 and 10 to see how this works.

EXAMPLE 9

You are married and your husband must enter a nursing home. On the date he enters, together you have $100,000 plus a house. You must first spend $50,000 (one-half the liquid assets) before he can get Medicaid to cover his nursing home bills; you will only be permitted to keep the remaining $50,000 plus the residence—if you do nothing to protect yourself.

To lose $50,000 would hurt and would leave you in a precarious financial position. Is there any way to protect more of your savings? The answer is yes.

You could take some or all of the $100,000 and put it "into" the house. What do we mean? You could pay off a mortgage; make home improvements, such as putting on a new roof, redoing the kitchen, adding aluminum siding, or adapting the home for easier handicapped living; or sell your existing home and buy a more expensive residence.

All of these suggestions have one thing in common: you are taking money which would have to be spent on nursing-home costs and "sheltering" it in the home. You're not losing anything, because you're adding value to your home, but you will qualify for Medicaid, as Example 10 shows.

EXAMPLE 10

Same facts as Example 9, except you take the $100,000 and put it into the house. The next day you go to Medicaid and apply for benefits. Since you've got no cash, your husband qualifies *immediately;* your entire $100,000 is fully protected, because the house is "exempt." No gift or transfer to a third person was made, so there's no waiting or ineligibility period. By this one simple technique, you've protected $50,000 that otherwise would have been spent.

Of course, money in a home isn't as liquid as money in stocks or bank accounts. But you could still get at it if needed. For example, combining this Medicaid technique with a reverse mortgage (see page 412) might be a perfect way to shelter assets while giving yourself a reasonable income.

In fact, you really only have to put part of your funds into the home, and you may still protect everything! Timing is the key, as Example 11 shows.

EXAMPLE 11

Let's again take the same facts as in Examples 9 and 10. But instead of putting funds into the home *before* your husband enters a nursing home, you wait until after.

On the day he goes in, you have $100,000 plus the home—your husband won't qualify for Medicaid until you've spent $50,000. The next day, you take $30,000 and pay off the remaining mortgage, and you pay $20,000 for various home improvements.

Now he qualifies for Medicaid—no more waiting. You've spent down to $50,000, but without really losing a penny. And because you timed the expenses right, you still get to keep the remaining $50,000.

❖ GEM: Use Other Exemptions

There are other exempt assets besides the house (Tables 11.4 and 11.5) that you can use to protect part of your savings.

EXAMPLE 12

At the time your father enters a nursing home, he and your mother have $30,000 and a home. Your mother would have to spend $15,000 before Medicaid would cover his bills.

Instead of pouring the $15,000 down the nursing-home drain, your mother purchases exempt assets. She spends $7,000 to prepay for funerals for her and your father. The stove, refrigerator, washer, and dryer are 20 years old, so she spends $2,500 to replace them. She needs a new car, so she spends $5,000 (plus her trade-in) for that. Finally, neither your mother nor father have bought new clothes in years, so $500 goes for a few items.

Now they've spent down and your father immediately qualifies for Medicaid. Rather than going to the nursing home, their $15,000 has been used to make your mother's and father's lives a little more comfortable.

Even for an unmarried person, purchasing exempt assets can be a useful way to avoid losing everything to a nursing home.

EXAMPLE 13

Your mother, a widow, has just entered a nursing home. She has $10,000 in the bank—well over the $2,000 Medicaid limit. If she does nothing, her $10,000 will be spent on the nursing home in no time flat.

Her first step is to prepay for her funeral—that is $4,000. She doesn't drive, so getting a car doesn't seem to make much sense for her. But you would like to visit her and have no easy way to get to the nursing home— so she might want to spend $4,500 to get a car that you could use. And what do you know? Your mother now qualifies for Medicaid!

❖ GEM: Buy an Annuity

We've already explained how harsh the Medicaid laws can be on one spouse when the other must enter a nursing home. Spending down half the assets, to no more than $68,700, often leaves the at-home spouse without enough to live on. Here's another gem to protect the home front.

EXAMPLE 14

On the day your spouse goes into a nursing home, you've got $100,000. He won't qualify for Medicaid until you've spent down to $50,000.

You take $50,000 and purchase an annuity that pays you, say, $600 per month for life. The income is yours because it comes in your name, and so it won't be used to pay your spouse's nursing-home costs. With an annuity, you'll be getting *more* income than you ever were before, and your husband immediately qualifies for Medicaid because you've spent $50,000. Since no transfer to any third person occurred, there should be no Medicaid ineligibility period.

To take advantage of this gem, the annuity generally must meet two requirements: it must be irrevocable and nonassignable. This gem has not yet been accepted in many states, so find out how your state Medicaid office views annuities.

❖ GEM: Take and Pay a Mortgage

Example 15 shows how taking a mortgage can pay off.

EXAMPLE 15

Your husband will be going into a nursing home shortly. Together you have $50,000 and a house you own free and clear. If you do nothing, you'll have to spend down $25,000 before Medicaid will cover his costs.

The week before he enters a nursing home, you take a $50,000 mortgage on the home. If you can take the loan from your kids, you can avoid paying any points or fees. You now have a $50,000 mortgage on your house and another $50,000 cash.

When your husband enters a nursing home, Medicaid takes a "snapshot" of your assets. On that day, you and he have combined assets of $100,000 (not $50,000) plus the house. Medicaid won't subtract your debts (*e.g.,* mortgage) from your cash assets.

Now you've got to spend $50,000 before he qualifies for Medicaid. You take $50,000 from your cash and pay off the mortgage. Voilà—your husband qualifies for Medicaid, and you get to keep the entire $50,000 which you originally had!

Timing is critical when using this gem. You must take the loan *before* one spouse enters a nursing home.

This gem may be very useful for married couples who didn't plan for catastrophic care coverage well in advance, but it will be of little use for unmarried individuals.

A WORD OF WARNING

While this gem has been used very effectively in some states, there is no guarantee that this will work in all states. Talk to a lawyer before trying to cash in on this gem.

✦ GEM: Don't Give Up Income-generating Assets

When describing the amount of income you may keep, we explained that the law guarantees the spouse at home a minimum amount of income—at least $1,149 a month, and in some states as much as $1,718 a month. If the spouse at home doesn't have enough income to reach the minimum, the difference generally is made up from the income of the spouse in the nursing home. For example, if you receive $300 a month in your name, and your spouse's income is $1,500 a month, you should be entitled to an additional $849 a month, which generally comes from your husband's income.

But there's another—and often much better—way to gain the minimum income: keep enough assets to generate enough income for the spouse at home.

EXAMPLE 16

Your income from Social Security is $399/month; your husband, who has just entered a nursing home, gets $900/month. In addition, the two of you have assets of $150,000. You could spend down your assets to $68,700; at that point, your husband would qualify for Medicaid. Your husband would give you $750/month from his income to bring your monthly income up to $1,149.

But here's a better idea. Your husband *refuses* to give you anything from his income (which he has a legal right to do). Since you still need an additional $750 of income each month to bring you up to the minimum of $1,149, you can keep sufficient assets to generate that income. At 6 percent interest, you would need *all* of your $150,000. In other words, your husband would qualify for Medicaid immediately—without spending down assets. You can keep the entire $150,000!

Example 16 depended on your spouse's refusal to give you any of his income. If your spouse in the nursing home has become incompetent, then he (or she) cannot authorize his income to be given to you. In that case, you should be allowed to retain enough of your savings to bring your income up to the minimum level.

❖ GEM: Pay Children for Their Services

Has your child been helping you with a variety of chores—driving to the store, doing banking, preparing meals, handling medical insurance claims, providing nursing care? Have you been living with one of your kids? If so, here's a gem you can use whether you are married or unmarried. Transfer assets to your kids—without any Medicaid waiting period—by paying them for services and/or rent!

This gem is more likely to work prospectively rather than retrospectively. What we mean is, if you agree to pay your kids—from now on—$2,000 a month for rent and the help they provide, and you put the agreement in writing, Medicaid shouldn't have much to complain about.

But what happens when a child has been working for the parent for the last two years for free and now the parent is about to go into a nursing home. Can a payment of $50,000 be made for the past services? Can you turn over money for past rent? The answer is less certain because the Medicaid bureaucrats could argue that any money a parent gives now is a gift. And that would mean no Medicaid.

Surprisingly, though, payment for past services and rent is often allowed. You and your child may say that the understanding was always that the child would be paid, but he or she was never in any hurry to collect. You gave your child the money now because your increasing costs make it apparent that the funds won't be there in the future.

When figuring how much can be paid for services or rent, don't guess. Get independent estimates from third parties. Call a bookkeeping company, nursing service, or insurance claim service, and get a written estimate as to what they would charge for the same things your child has been doing. Check the local real estate listings or call a real estate agent to get a realistic rental price for the room you've been using.

❖ GEM: Withdraw Money from Joint Accounts

Many elderly citizens have put children on their accounts, with the accounts in their names "and/or" their children. If the money was the parent's originally, and if the parent's Social Security number is on the account, then the *entire* account usually will be considered the parent's by Medicaid.

But a withdrawal of the cash by the child can be a wonderful gem, since a number of states, including Florida, Georgia, Maryland, and Washington, D.C., will allow a parent to get Medicaid benefits *immediately* after funds are withdrawn from a joint account.

EXAMPLE 17

Your mother, a widow, has $100,000 in a bank account. Several years ago, she added your name to the account so that you could help her pay bills from the account if necessary. You and your mother both have unrestricted access to the cash; only one signature is required to withdraw funds. The account is in the names of your parent "and/or" you.

Just having your name on the account probably won't help protect the assets from nursing-home costs. Although in a few states your mother and you might be considered each to own one-half, most states would say that your mother owns the entire $100,000 account. In that case, she would not qualify for Medicaid until all but about $2,000 had been spent.

But before your mother applies for Medicaid, you withdraw the entire $100,000 and put it into your name alone. Now when your mother applies for Medicaid, she qualifies. Your withdrawal will not be considered a transfer, so she will not have to wait thirty months!

Your state Medicaid office may say that a withdrawal from a joint account by a child (who is not the Medicaid applicant) is not a transfer or gift by the parent. Since only transfers or gifts by a Medicaid applicant are penalized with a 30-month waiting period, withdrawals can qualify a parent for Medicaid *immediately,* with no waiting period!

This gem works only with "or" accounts, in which the child can withdraw all the funds with only his or her signature. If the account has the names listed as parent "and" child, and both must sign to withdraw funds, then the rules are different: the parent and child each own only one-half of the funds; if a parent signs, giving the child all the funds, then the parent has made a gift or transfer of one-half.

EXAMPLE 18

You and your mother are named on her stocks, worth $100,000. Both of your signatures are required to sell them. The day before your mother enters a nursing home and applies for Medicaid, you sell the stocks. You sign for yourself and use your mother's durable power of attorney to sign for her.

Since your mother did not sign her own name, can you claim that she made no transfer and so should qualify immediately for Medicaid? The answer is no. By signing for your mother using the durable power of attorney, you were acting for her, not for yourself—she would be ineligible for Medicaid for 30 months.

Let's say your mother has kept all of her assets in her name alone. If she added your name to the account and then, the very next day, you withdrew the funds, could she immediately qualify for Medicaid? Consider Example 19.

EXAMPLE 19

Your mother knows she will be entering a nursing home on Friday. On the Monday before, she goes to the bank and adds your name to her accounts, totaling $100,000. On Tuesday you withdraw the entire amount. And on Wednesday she applies for Medicaid.

In a few states, like Georgia, your mother would be considered eligible for Medicaid. Although this approach has not been tested in most states, we believe that Medicaid offices generally will say that a transfer occurred when your mother added your name to the account. The longer the joint account has been set up, the more likely your withdrawal of funds will avoid any Medicaid ineligibility period.

Placing assets into joint ownership may be a very valuable gem, because a co-owner (usually a child) may withdraw the assets later without any Medicaid penalty. Keep in mind, though, that giving a child free access to accounts carries risks. Also, this is not available in every state; check with the local Medicaid office before using it. If a state allows this planning technique, it can be, literally, a lifesaver.

❖ GEM: Get a Divorce

Sad as it is, for some couples, the best step they can take to protect their savings is a divorce.

We recently saw a couple with the following situation: George and Mary had been happily married for 50 years. George has a degenerative muscle disease. Mary has been caring for him for years at home, but it is becoming clear that pretty soon a nursing home will be needed.

They have about $200,000 in cash, stocks, CDs, and T-bills. Mary doesn't want to give the money to the children or set up a Medicaid trust, because she'd lose control of the assets; but even if she did give away the funds, they'd have to pay the nursing home for 30 months. In the area where they live, a good nursing home runs $45,000 per year. In 2½ years, they'd spend more than $110,000.

Their best plan is to get divorced. They can file for an uncontested divorce, providing that Mary gets all the savings. When George goes into a nursing home, he will *immediately* qualify for Medicaid—assets divided under a divorce decree do not cause any Medicaid waiting period.

Divorce is a very unpleasant option; it was very hard for us to call the strategy a gem. But when it comes to protecting your life savings, a divorce may be necessary to avoid financial devastation.

❖ GEM: Don't Get Married: When You Say Yes, Medicaid Says No!

More and more, older persons are getting married or remarried later in life. Usually, that's just wonderful. But if your new spouse becomes ill, watch out!

EXAMPLE 20

You have just remarried, and you are very happy. To protect your savings for your children from a prior marriage, you and your husband signed a premarital contract. Your will leaves everything to the kids. You feel peaceful knowing that they'll be protected in case anything happens to you. No problem, right? Wrong! The honeymoon was too much for your husband; he suffered a stroke and must go into a nursing home.

You have $150,000 in savings and your husband has nothing—you were marrying him for love and companionship, not money. He won't be eligible for Medicaid until your savings are spent down to $68,700. But all the savings were yours. The marriage is only two weeks old, and you both signed a premarital agreement. Too bad, none of those facts matter. The moment you say "I do," all of your assets are at risk if your spouse becomes ill. A premarital agreement will *not* protect your assets from nursing-home costs.

So before getting married, think long and hard about the risk to your life savings. Marriage may be hazardous to your financial health.

Gems with Long-term Benefits

So far, we've provided 10 gems with immediate benefits. Now let's mine some gems with longer-term benefits.

GIVE ASSETS AWAY AND TAKE YOUR CHANCES

❖ GEM: Give Your Money Away

Giving your money away can be a valuable gem, even though gifts and transfers will carry risks and will trigger a period of Medicaid ineligibility. Example 21 shows why.

EXAMPLE 21

Your father has $150,000, and his income (Social Security, interest, and dividends) is $20,000/year. If he goes into a nursing home and fails to use our gems, he'll spend all but about $2,000 before Medicaid will pay a penny.

If he gives away the assets, he won't be eligible to receive Medicaid benefits for 2½ years from the date of the gift. But after that 2½ years has passed, Medicaid will cover his costs.

Even if he has done no advance planning, and is about to enter a nursing home, giving away assets may be very wise. Let's say he gives away the $150,000 on the day he enters a nursing home. The home costs $40,000/year—$20,000 more than his income.

The first year you'll use the interest and dividends, as well as his Social Security, to pay the nursing home. You'll have to supplement the income with $20,000 of principal from his transferred assets. The second year you do the same thing: use his income and about $25,000 of principal (probably slightly more than the year before owing to increased prices and reduced income) to pay the nursing-home costs. And for half of the third year, the same thing happens. At the end of 2½ years, the $150,000 pot has been cut to about $90,000.

But here's the gem: after the 2½ years have passed, the remaining $90,000 is protected, and Medicaid will start to pay your father's costs. Remember, without the transfer, your father's assets would continue to dwindle to nothing!

Giving away assets isn't perfect. If you wait until the last minute, you'll end up paying the nursing home for 2½ years. But at least the drain will end after that time, and the rest of your life savings will remain protected.

DON'T WORRY ABOUT GIFT TAX

We are often asked: "If I give away more than $10,000, won't I have to pay tax?" The answer is *no,* unless your total estate is worth $600,000 or more.

Federal law gives each person something called a unified transfer-tax exemption. That allows anyone to make $600,000 in gifts during his or her lifetime without any tax. The person receiving the money never pays any tax on the gift. Of course, the person receiving the gift will pay income tax in the future on any income (interest and dividends) generated by the funds.

❖ GEM: Don't Get Trapped by Giving Away Appreciated Assets

While you usually don't have to worry about gift tax, you may have to think about capital gains tax if you give away appreciated assets, like your home. Capital gains taxes are charged (at normal income tax rates) on profits made when anything that has increased in value is sold. Stocks, real estate, paintings, and any other appreciated assets are included. Giving these assets away, to children or others, will mean that the recipients will pay these taxes when they sell. You may be better off *not* making a gift. Compare Examples 22, 23, and 24.

EXAMPLE 22

Your parents bought their house 30 years ago for $20,000; today it's worth $220,000. Your father has died, and your mother is worried about nursing-home costs. So she gives you the home as a present. Remember, there's no gift tax.

After she dies, you sell the house for $220,000. At that time—watch out! You'll owe Uncle Sam capital gains tax on the $200,000 profit ($220,000 – $20,000). The tax will cost you about $56,000.

EXAMPLE 23

Same facts as Example 22, except your mother keeps the house until she dies; you receive it under her will. When you sell the home, you pay *no* capital gains tax.

Here's why: When your mother leaves the house to you at death, the Death Tax Loophole eliminates the capital gain (see page 382 for a discussion of how this works). This tax break applies to *any* type of appreciated assets passing to heirs at death (there's no limit on amount).

EXAMPLE 24

Same facts again, except your mother sells the house and gives you the proceeds. When she sells the house, she can avoid paying tax on $125,000 of the profit; she'll only pay tax on $75,000 of the $200,000 profit (see page 361 for a discussion of the Age 55 Tax Loophole). So she'll pay about $21,000—a lot less than the $56,000 tax in Example 22.

Before giving away appreciated assets, think about the capital gains tax on the profits. If you want to minimize or eliminate the tax on a home but still give the property away so that you won't lose it to nursing-home costs, you should sell first and give away the cash (Example 24) or put it into a trust (see page 490). For appreciated assets other than your home, putting them into a trust may be your best option.

❖ GEM: Make Overlapping Gifts

As we've said, a gift or transfer of money or property generally triggers a Medicaid ineligibility period of up to 30 months. We also explained how to calculate the exact length of the ineligibility period (page 471). Consider Example 7, which shows that a gift of $25,000 would trigger a Medicaid ineligibility period of 10 months, and Example 8, which demonstrates that a gift of $100,000 would trigger a 30-month waiting period.

Here's a way you might make a gift of more than $100,000 and still become eligible for Medicaid after a waiting period of only 10 months:

EXAMPLE 25

You've got savings of $90,000. If you simply give all of it away in January 1993 to your child, you won't qualify for Medicaid until July 1995, after 30 months had passed. Instead, you give your money away like this (assuming your state says average nursing-home care is $2,500 a month):

January	$32,500	creates 13-month ineligibility
April	25,000	creates 10-month ineligibility
July	17,500	creates 7-month ineligibility
October	10,000	creates 4-month ineligibility
December	5,000	creates 2-month ineligibility

The total given away is the same $90,000. But by using this technique, you should be eligible for Medicaid benefits starting February 1, 1994—after only 3 months of ineligibility.

Why should this work? Because the law says that the ineligibility period starts from the date of each gift; the law says nothing about adding the ineligibility periods for overlapping gifts. Note that, so far, this gem has been tried and approved in very few states.

❖ GEM: Get Money Back After Medicaid Qualification

Let's say you and your spouse decide to take advantage of the gems we just discussed, and you give your money away. After the ineligibility period (up to 30 months) has run, Medicaid will cover the nursing-home bills for you or your spouse. Once one of you qualifies for Medicaid, the other can get the money back—without losing Medicaid benefits!

EXAMPLE 26

Your husband has become ill and is likely to require nursing-home care. Your combined assets are $150,000, which you give to your daughter.

Thirty months later, your husband qualifies for Medicaid, and the rest of the funds (about $90,000 at that time) are protected. But now they belong to your daughter, not you. If she is sued, gets divorced, or dies, the assets may not be available if you ever need them.

As soon as your husband qualifies for Medicaid, you can get the assets back. Your daughter can give you the remaining $90,000 without causing your husband to lose his Medicaid benefits. You regain control of your funds!

This gem is wonderful because it allows you to regain control of your assets. Of course, it depends on the willingness of your child to give them back—we hope that won't be a problem.

❖ GEM: Shuffle Assets
Between Spouses and Change the Will

Shifting assets from one spouse to another, in and of itself, won't protect a couple's life savings when one must enter a nursing home. And whether stocks, bonds, or CDs are in your name, your spouse's name, or joint names won't make any difference. If your spouse enters a nursing home, all you'll be allowed to keep is half of the total amount (up to $68,700).

But transferring assets from a spouse who enters a nursing home to the spouse still at home can be very useful, as Examples 27 and 28 demonstrate.

EXAMPLE 27: THE WRONG WAY

At the time your father enters a nursing home, he and your mother have jointly held assets of $170,000. Your father and mother will be able to protect a total of $68,700 under the Medicaid rules for married individuals.

Two years after your father enters the nursing home, they have $110,000 left; the rest has been spent on the nursing home and on your mother's living expenses. Then your mother dies. Since the assets were held jointly, your father now owns them all. And since your father is no longer married, the Medicaid rules for *unmarried* individuals take over. Now your father is allowed to keep only about $2,000; that's the total of your parents' life savings that would be protected. Kiss the rest goodbye.

EXAMPLE 28: THE RIGHT WAY

At the time your father enters a nursing home, he and your mother have total assets of $170,000; your father doesn't qualify for Medicaid. As soon as he enters, he transfers everything into your mother's name. That transfer won't help him qualify for Medicaid immediately, but it will help later as you'll soon see. Your mother also changes her will, taking him out.

Two years after he enters the nursing home, your mother has $110,000 left in her name; the rest went toward payment of their bills. Then she dies. Under her will, all $110,000 would pass to the children (or other named beneficiaries); your father would then qualify for Medicaid, which would pick up the remaining nursing-home costs.

Most married couples own most of their assets jointly with rights of survivorship. They also usually have reciprocal wills: each person's will leaves everything to the other spouse. This can be the *worst* way to hold assets—particularly the house—when one spouse must enter a nursing home.

As soon as it becomes clear that one spouse will have to be institutionalized, put everything into the name of the healthy spouse. That transfer won't make the ill spouse eligible for Medicaid, but it also won't create any period of Medicaid ineligibility. (Assets are counted against the Medicaid eligibility limits regardless of whether they're in the husband's or wife's name, so transfers between them don't help for qualification. But transfers between spouses also do not trigger any ineligibility period.)

The spouse at home also must change her will, deleting her spouse. She will leave everything to other heirs such as her children. She should also change the beneficiary on the life insurance and IRAs, so that assets will not end up with her spouse.

If the spouse at home dies first, which sometimes happens, the assets will pass under the will to the heirs, rather than to the spouse in the nursing home. He will immediately qualify for Medicaid, because he's got nothing; passing assets at death under a will should not be considered a gift or transfer which makes anyone ineligible for Medicaid. Everything would go to the heirs (typically the children) and would be fully protected.

There's one hitch: if the spouse in the nursing home is incompetent at the time the spouse at home dies, he or she may be forced by the probate court to elect against the will and take a significant portion of the assets (usually one-third to one-half). The spouse in the nursing home would choose not to take anything if competent to make a choice, but if not competent, then the probate court may step in. How can you get around this risk? Instead of making a will, the spouse at home can leave assets to heirs in a revocable living trust. A living trust avoids probate—and should be able to get assets to the heirs without risk that a probate judge could cause problems.

Giving money away, especially to children, can be an excellent planning tool. Your money is safe from nursing-home costs and you can get it back later if you need it (and if the kids will return it). But giving money away carries significant risks. You give your money to your son, and the next day he may call from Hawaii, telling you that your money is doing just fine!

Even if your children are trustworthy, giving away money carries potential pitfalls. Your child may be in an auto accident and may be sued, and "your" money could be taken. Children these days have this nasty habit of becoming divorced, or your child may die before you, and now his or her spouse may get some or all of your funds. If you like the idea of being dependent on your child, you'll love the thought of becoming dependent on your son-in-law or daughter-in-law!

GIVE MONEY AWAY, BUT KEEP SOME CONTROL

The next four gems, involving a life estate, a durable power of attorney, a Medicaid trust, and a testamentary trust, can minimize the risks inherent in giving your money and property away while providing long-term benefits.

❖ GEM: Keep a Life Estate

You are afraid to give your house to your child because of the risks. Your child (or his spouse if he dies) could throw you out or sell the house without your permission. What can you do? You may want to create a life estate (with the help of a lawyer), which gives you a legal right to live in the house for as long as you live. You transfer a "remainder interest" in the house, which means that your children will own the home automatically when you die. Until then, your life estate protects your right to live there.

By giving away a "remainder interest," you are getting rid of most of the value of the house. If you enter a nursing home, only the value of the life estate (which Medicaid will calculate based upon your life expectancy and the home value) would be counted against you.

EXAMPLE 29

You are widowed and your only significant asset is the house, worth $100,000. You give away the remainder interest to your son, but keep a life estate. According to the American Experience Tables of Mortality (available at your local library), the life estate is worth $20,000, and the remainder is worth $80,000.

If you later go into a nursing home, you can transfer the life estate to your son. That transfer would make you ineligible for Medicaid for only about 10 months (see page 471). If you had given away the entire $100,000 home when entering a nursing home, you'd be unable to get Medicaid for 2½ years.

Note that a few states say that a life estate has no value, because nobody would pay good money to buy it. But most states use life expectancy tables to put a value on a life estate. Check with your local Medicaid office.

❖ GEM: Make a Durable Power of Attorney

We've already told you that giving money and property away can be a valuable gem. But it's not risk-free, and many older Americans prefer holding onto their assets—and remaining in control—for as long as possible.

You may decide to keep your funds in your names until either you or your spouse need to go into a nursing home. Even giving away assets at that late date usually can protect a good portion of your savings.

Unfortunately, you may never get the chance. The reason many people enter nursing homes is that they've become so physically or mentally impaired that they can no longer care for themselves. The law in *every* state bars someone who is incompetent from making gifts or transfers. If you can't understand what you are doing, assets can't be given away.

EXAMPLE 30

Your mother suffered a stroke and has become incompetent. You'd like to help her protect some of her assets, including CDs, stocks, bonds, and real estate, all of which are in her name. Sadly, there's nothing she or you can do. It's too late; the assets are stuck in her name and can't be transferred. Within a short time, her life savings will be gone.

Perhaps the best gem we can offer in this book is: make a durable power of attorney. This document can *guarantee* that you and your loved ones will not have to pay a nursing home for more than 30 months.

A durable power of attorney lets you authorize someone else to handle your financial affairs. You can give your spouse, child, or anyone else the power to do anything you can do, including endorse checks, take money out of your bank accounts, transfer stocks, or sell real estate. You aren't giving up your rights to do these things; you're just giving someone else power to handle financial matters for you.

If you give someone a durable power of attorney, you won't fall into the "Medicaid trap" described in Example 30. Someone will be able to give your assets away, even if you can't, when you enter a nursing home. And at least after 30 months, you'll get Medicaid.

EXAMPLE 31

Same facts as in Example 30. Your mother has become incompetent and is entering a nursing home. She has assets of $150,000 in her name, but she can't give them away.

Fortunately, she gave you a durable power of attorney several years earlier, when she was well. The durable power of attorney specifically authorizes you to give her money away. With this document, you can legally transfer the assets for her. In 30 months, she will qualify for Medicaid; the remainder of her nest egg, perhaps $90,000, will be saved.

A durable power of attorney allows you to retain control of your assets—and your life—for as long as possible. Once it's clear you must go into a nursing home, the assets can be transferred. If you can give them away yourself, fine, but if you can't, the durable power of attorney gives you a guarantee that someone else will be able to get rid of them for you. And until you clearly need nursing-home care, you can keep your life savings for yourself.

NOTE

A *durable* power of attorney is not the same as a power of attorney. The difference is critical: a power of attorney becomes ineffective and stops working the moment you become incompetent—the time you need it the most, it can't be used. A *durable* power of attorney remains valid even after you become incompetent.

❖ GEM: Trust a Medicaid Trust to Protect Savings

You can put some or all of your money and property into a Medicaid trust, and anything in the trust will be protected from the reach of the state or the nursing home. Medicaid will cover the nursing-home bills, and the assets in the trust will pass to your heirs at your death.

A Medicaid trust is the only type of trust that you can use to protect your life savings from the nursing home while you're alive. The most common type of trust, a revocable living trust, provides *no protection at all* during your life (although it can be useful when passing assets at death—see page 487).

You create a Medicaid trust by signing a legal paper. Once created, you can put assets (cash, CDs, stocks, bonds, house, car, and just about anything else) into the trust by changing the name on the asset to the name of the trustee. For example, if your child is going to be the trustee, you go to the bank and change the name on the accounts to your child as trustee.

A Medicaid trust may be set up in a variety of different ways, but three rules must always be met:

1. The trust must be irrevocable. Once set up, you can *never* change your mind.
2. Neither you nor your spouse can be the trustee. The trustee, the person who will manage the trust, may be a child, another relative, a friend, or a bank. Anyone but you or your spouse.
3. You can't have any access to the money and property you put into the trust (although you can get the income generated by your investments). It is illegal for the trustee to give you $20,000 from the principal, even if you ask very nicely.

As you can see, these are severe restrictions. No one would ever want one of these trusts, right? Wrong! While they are not for everybody, they have proved to be very valuable for many people. Example 32 shows one common way a Medicaid trust can be designed.

EXAMPLE 32

You are a widow and your entire nest egg consists of CD, stocks, and bonds worth $150,000. These investments generate annual income of $10,000; when added to your Social Security benefits of $10,000 per year, your total annual income is $20,000.

You put the entire $150,000 into a Medicaid trust. As part of the trust, you require that you be paid the entire income (interest and dividends) generated from the trust during your lifetime, and on your death the children receive the $150,000. (Nothing prevents you from getting the income.)

Then you suffer a stroke and are confined to a nursing home that charges $40,000 per year. Your $20,000 income will pay a portion of the charges, but who pays the rest? The answer is Medicaid! Your $150,000 savings cannot be spent down.

Without a Medicaid trust, the $20,000 annual nursing-home costs not covered by your income would have to come from your savings, and your nest egg would completely disappear. Most people are willing to pay their fair share, but the Government doesn't give you that option.

A Medicaid trust can be a precious gem. Let's say you must go into a nursing home for rehabilitation—after nine months, you are able to return home. Nine months in a nursing home could run $30,000 or more. Without a Medicaid trust, much of your nest egg could be spent in that time; when you come out, what are you returning to? A life of poverty.

A Medicaid trust can avoid this financial disaster. After returning home following a nursing-home stay your entire savings would still be intact. If you were living on the income, all of your income would remain available after you come back home.

And with a Medicaid trust, your savings will go to your heirs when you die. There's nothing "unAmerican" about wanting the money you worked so hard for during your life to pass to your kids.

But why not just disperse the savings directly to your children? With a trust, you don't have to worry about the pitfalls of giving money to kids. Though your child may be the trustee, in control of your assets, he doesn't own them—the trust owns your savings. This means your child can't take the money and use it for a vacation in Hawaii. If your child is sued, creditors can't get the funds; if your child is divorced or dies, your in-laws don't get the money. The assets belong to the trust and stay there—protected—until you die.

Putting assets into a Medicaid trust triggers a waiting period of up to 30 months, but by then your savings will be fully protected and Medicaid will pay the nursing-home bills.

❖ GEM: Set Up a Testamentary Trust

The biggest drawback to a Medicaid trust is the fact that you and your spouse can't get access to the principal. One possible way around that problem is a testamentary trust.

A testamentary trust will be set up as part of a will, so no money or property goes into the trust until you die. As long as you are alive, everything you own remains yours. When you die the assets go into the trust. The money and property in the trust will be protected in case the surviving spouse later must enter a nursing home.

EXAMPLE 33

Your wife has Parkinson's disease. You have been caring for her at home for the last 20 years, and you expect to continue for the rest of your life. But if you were to die first, she probably would have to go into a nursing home.

You and your wife put everything you own into *your* name, and you create a testamentary trust. Nothing goes into the trust until your death; as long as you remain alive, the assets are yours. When you die, everything goes into the testamentary trust. Let's say you name your child as trustee. The trust can give your child substantial discretion over the income and principal—he can take out these funds from the trust for your wife.

> If your wife needs money to pay for care at home, your son as trustee can make it available to her. If she must enter a nursing home, then the trustee has discretion to provide nothing to her. The trust protects your joint life savings in case your wife must enter a nursing home and can *immediately* qualify her for Medicaid, because assets passing on death do not trigger a 30-month waiting period. None of the principal *or income* goes to the nursing home, except maybe to pay for things Medicaid won't cover, like a private room. The assets remain in the trust until your wife dies—unaffected by the nursing-home bills—and will then go to the heirs.

A testamentary trust actually provides greater control, flexibility, and protection than a Medicaid trust. The trust can protect both principal and income from the nursing home. In other words, assets in the trust may actually increase over time. The drawback is that this trust only works after one of you dies. If you or your spouse goes into a nursing home while the other is still alive, *nothing* is protected by the trust.

And you've got to correctly guess which one—you or your spouse—will die first. For that reason, a testamentary trust normally should not be considered until one of you has become ill or has been diagnosed with a terminal illness.

◆　◆　◆

Gems to Avoid Harsh Income Limits

Earlier we explained that a few states (Table 11.3) impose severe, unbending income limits, which can lead to disastrous financial consequences. The following three gems may help you and your loved ones to avoid the income limits trap.

❖ GEM: Transfer Income-producing Assets

A nursing-home resident may be able to bring income down by getting rid of assets.

EXAMPLE 34

> Your father is in a nursing home. He gets $1,000/month from Social Security and $300/month from $50,000 of funds (stocks, CDs, etc.) in his name. Your mother also gets some income, but hers doesn't affect his Medicaid qualification.
>
> Although they have spent down enough of their assets to qualify for Medicaid, your father's income is slightly over the $1,266/month limit imposed by the state. As long as his income is too high, he can't get Medicaid.

Your parents simply have to shift the $50,000 to your mother, so the interest and dividend checks come in her name. Now Dad is below the income limit, and he immediately qualifies!

Single people obviously can't shift income-producing assets to a spouse, but they can give away assets to others to cut their income.

EXAMPLE 35

Your father receives $1,000/month from Social Security and $300 a month from his savings—just over the income limit for his state. If he gives away the savings, at least enough to bring his income below the state cap, then he can qualify for Medicaid (although the transfer of assets will create an ineligibility period).

❖ GEM: Ask a Judge to Reduce Income

The last gem, transferring income-producing assets, works fine for interest and dividends. But how can you get rid of other income, like pensions?

In a few instances, judges have "removed" pension income from Medicaid applicants, directing the income to either a spouse, a guardian, or into a trust. This technique is extremely complicated and requires the assistance of an experienced lawyer, but it may, quite literally, prove to be a lifesaver.

❖ GEM: Move!

As a last resort, move your residence to another state. We are not being flip. In many instances in which a person had too much income for Medicaid eligibility, but too little to pay the nursing home, there has been no other real choice.

❖ ❖ ❖

Medicaid was not originally designed for the middle class. But times change, and now Medicaid provides some of the most important benefits available for older Americans with moderate income and assets. We hope you and your loved ones will never suffer a catastrophic illness. But it's always best to be prepared.

·12·

Civil Service:
It's Time for Uncle Sam to Give Something Back

Most people who go into government work do so because they want to serve the public and help make life better for others, not because they want to get rich. Government jobs typically pay less than comparable work in the private sector, but there is generally one big bonus to working for Uncle Sam. The payoff comes when you leave the job! Most government retirement systems combine generous benefits with the chance to retire as early as 55.

The largest of the government retirement programs is the Civil Service Retirement System (CSRS) for federal employees. Here, we discuss the CSRS and explain how to maximize benefits under this program. Local and state government retirement programs generally are very similar; for details on how those plans operate, contact the personnel or retirement benefits advisor where you work.

OVERVIEW

The CSRS retirement plan takes the place of Social Security for government workers. The benefits, though, are generally *much better!* For example, while the average Social Security check for retirees from private-sector jobs is about $600 a month, the average CSRS check is *double* that amount.

Unfortunately, Congress has again done its best to undercut the financial security of our public servants, replacing CSRS with the Federal Employees' Retirement System (FERS) for federal employees hired after December 31, 1983. As often occurs when Congress creates a new program, it is more complicated and less generous than what previously existed. Thankfully, most older federal workers who have retired or are considering retirement in the next 10 to 15 years will still be covered by CSRS, so we will focus our discussion on that program.

CSRS, like Social Security, is not welfare; Uncle Sam is not giving you something for nothing. You've been paying toward CSRS over the years through payroll deductions, and now it's time to collect.

RETIREMENT BENEFITS

CSRS retirement benefits, like Social Security benefits, are based on your age, years of service, and the amount of salary you earned while working. If you have worked at least 30 years for the Government, you can start taking retirement benefits at age 55. With at least 20 years of service, you can retire at 60. And with as little as five years of work, you can retire at 62. Five years (of civilian service) is the minimum you must put in to get a CSRS retirement pension.

Amount of Benefits

Your Government pension will be a percentage of your highest average salary over three consecutive years. For example, if you earned $27,000 in 1985, $30,000 in 1986, and $33,000 in 1987, your average for those years is $30,000. Table 12.1 shows the amount of benefits you may receive, based on a percentage of your highest average salary.

NOTE

Here's some good news. When you calculate your benefits, remember that government retirement pensions increase each year with the cost of living, just like Social Security. This is a big plus over private pensions, which don't go up with time.

A few examples show how to use Table 12.1 to figure your retirement benefit.

EXAMPLE 1

Your highest average wages over three years was $30,000, and you have worked for the Government for 35 years. You could retire as early as age 55 with annual benefits of $19,875 (66.25% of $30,000).

TABLE 12.1

CSRS Retirement Benefits

Years of Service	% of Highest Salary
41 years 11 months or more	80.00
41	78.25
40	76.25
39	74.25
38	72.25
37	70.25
36	68.25
35	66.25
34	64.25
33	62.25
32	60.25
31	58.25
30	56.25
29	54.25
28	52.25
27	50.25
26	48.25
25	46.25
24	44.25
23	42.25
22	40.25
21	38.25
20	36.25
19	34.25
18	32.25
17	30.25
16	28.25
15	26.25
14	24.25
13	22.25
12	20.25
11	18.25
10	16.25
9	14.50
8	12.75
7	11.00
6	9.25
5	7.50

EXAMPLE 2

Your highest average wages over three years again was $30,000, and you have 15 years of Government service. If you are at least 62, you may start taking retirement checks of $7,875/year (26.25% of $30,000).

EXAMPLE 3

Your highest average salary for three years is $45,000 and you worked for the Government for 20 years. At age 60, you could retire with annual benefits of $16,313 (36.25% of $45,000).

❖ GEM: Extra Work Doesn't Always Pay Off

Because of the way CSRS benefits are figured, it often doesn't pay to work longer than you have to.

EXAMPLE 4

Your three highest salary years were 10 years ago, when you averaged $45,000/year. Since that time, you switched positions, your salary dropped, and now you're making only $40,000/year. You've worked 20 years and just hit age 60. Should you retire?

Right now, you'd be entitled to retirement pay of $16,313/year (36.25% of $45,000; see Table 12.1). If you work an extra year, you'll add less than $1,000/year to your pension—$20/week (38.25% of $45,000 is $17,213/year, which is $900 more than $16,313). In this situation, the answer seems clear, doesn't it?

❖ GEM: When Your Salary Is Increasing, It Pays to Stay

If your salary is going up each year, raising your highest three-year average, there is more incentive for you to keep working.

EXAMPLE 5

Let's take the same facts as in Example 4. You could retire at age 60 with retirement pay of $16,313/year. But instead you work another year for $51,000, and that increases your highest three-year average salary to $48,000. Your annual retirement pension would go up to $18,360—an increase of more than $2,000/year!

❖ GEM: If You Leave Government Service, Leave Your Pension Too

Once you've worked for Uncle Sam for five years, you're entitled to a Government pension. If you leave the Government but haven't reached retirement age, you can either wait until reaching retirement age (62 with five years of service) to start taking monthly retirement benefits, or take a lump sum when you leave.

Most people who leave the Government before retirement age take their money with them—and most are making a big mistake!

EXAMPLE 6

You worked for 10 years for the Government, earning an average of $25,000/year for the 10 years. You left at age 57, which is too early to take your government pension.

You could take your contributions to the retirement system in a lump sum, which would be about $17,500 (the 7% portion of your total salary contributed over the years). If you invested these funds, by age 62 your money will have grown to about $26,000. If you started to draw the interest, you'd take a little more than $2,000/year.

If you did *not* take any lump sum, at age 62 you'd be entitled to a pension of $4,550/year (16.25% of $28,000, which was your highest average earnings for three years); see Table 12.1. If you live more than 10 years, past age 72, you'll be better off with the annual pension. Why? Because if you took the extra $2,550/year you'd get from the Government pension ($4,550 − $2,000) and put these funds in the bank, you'd have more than $26,000 in about 10 years. Although nobody has a crystal ball, life expectancy statistics say you'd be much better off leaving your benefits with the Government, rather than taking them with you.

❖ GEM: Buy Back Lost Time

Let's say you took your contributions as a lump sum when you left the Government, but several years later you rejoined federal service. Too bad—you lost all credit for past service time as soon as you took your retirement pay. Is it gone forever? No!

You can recover your lost credit by repaying all your prior contributions (the amount of the lump sum) with interest. In almost every case, you'll be better off financially if you take advantage of this gem.

And here's the best news of all. You don't have to repay the contributions when you rejoin the Government—you can wait until you retire. Even at retirement, you don't have to make the repayment in one lump sum. If the prior contributions were for service before October 1, 1990, you can pay monthly installments from your retirement checks! Your checks will be reduced using a calculation based on your life expectancy. Contact the benefits advisor where you work to make arrangements.

✦   ✦   ✦

Years of Service

As you can see from Table 12.1, the amount of your retirement pension will depend, in part, on the number of years you served the Government. You generally get credit for one year of service for each 12-month period you put in for the Government. The time doesn't have to be for any one particular agency or branch—when calculating the benefit you can add together all your years of service. Even military service may be included *if* you have also put in five years of civilian Government service.

EXAMPLE 7

You have worked five years for NASA, and you are now ready to retire. Your average salary for the three best years was $35,000. And you previously served four years in the military.

You would be entitled to a Government pension based on nine years of service—$5,075/year (14.5% of $35,000); see Table 12.1. But if you had worked just one year less for NASA, you'd get *no* pension (because you didn't have five civilian years)!

❖ GEM: Forgetting Sick Days Can Make You Sick!

When you calculate your years of service, you can get "extra credit" for unused sick time. Every eight hours of unused sick time gets you one additional day of credit toward your CSRS pension. But unused sick time cannot be applied toward the five years needed for vesting in CSRS.

EXAMPLE 3

You worked for the Department of Labor for 35 years. Your highest three years' salary was $35,000. At retirement, you get a pension of $23,188/year (66.25% of $35,000); see Table 12.1.

But don't forget those unused sick days. Let's say you've got enough to add another one year. Your pension now would be $23,888/year—an increase of $700/year. That sure is a healthy bonus!

✦　✦　✦

"Early" Retirement for Laid-off Employees

Earlier we told you that you could retire and start collecting pension benefits at age 55 with 30 years of service; age 60 with 20 years of service; and age 62 with five years of service. But there are a number of exceptions allowing "early" retirement at even younger ages.

The most important exception covers employees who were laid off for a reason other than misconduct or delinquency. In these days of budget cuts and reductions in force, layoffs are not unusual. If you fall within this exception and have 25 years of service, you may start taking your monthly benefits, no matter what your age. You also qualify if you've got 20 years of service once you have reached age 50. Employees caught in office reorganizations or closings will find this exception very helpful. If you retire before age 55, the benefits will be slightly reduced—generally by 2 percent for each year before age 55.

Other exceptions allowing "early" retirement involve specific types of employees, such as FBI or DEA officers, air traffic controllers, and employees of the Bureau of Indian Affairs. If you have been laid off, check with your Government employer to determine the minimum retirement age allowed for your agency or department.

SPOUSE RETIREMENT BENEFITS

Remember in Chapter 6 we talked about joint and 50 percent survivor annuities (monthly pension payments for life)? We explained how you could reduce your monthly pension during your lifetime, and then when you died your spouse would be entitled to continue receiving half of your monthly pension amount.

Government pensions work much the same way. You could opt to take your entire monthly pension for your life alone (with your spouse's consent), but when you die your spouse gets nothing. Or you could choose to take a *smaller* annuity for your life and then your spouse would continue to receive an annuity after you die.

You may remember that we weren't too crazy about joint-life annuities for *private* pensions. We offered a gem that explained how you might be better off taking an annuity for your life alone and purchasing life insurance with the money you save.

❖ GEM: Take a Joint-Life Government Pension

Our view on Government pensions is different. Most married older Americans *should* opt for joint-life government annuities. You generally get a *much better deal.* Typically, the reduction in your annuity is much less, and the amount your spouse gets is much more, than under private pension joint and survivor arrangements.

Under a joint-life Government annuity, your spouse will get 55 percent of your regular pension (before any deductions), starting at your death. The pension during your lifetime will be reduced by 2.5 percent of the first $3,600 of retirement benefits and 10 percent of any amount over that. Here's how it works:

EXAMPLE 9

You retire at age 65 with 30 years of Government service, and your highest average three-year salary is $40,000. If you took a pension for your lifetime only, you'd get $22,500/year, but your spouse would get *nothing* after you die.

Instead, you choose a joint-life annuity. Your pension is reduced by $1,980/year (2.5% of the first $3,600 is $90; 10% of the next $18,900 is $1,890), and you wind up with annual benefits of $20,610, rather than $22,500. But when you die, your spouse continues to benefit. She will still receive $12,375/year (55% of $22,500).

◆ ◆ ◆

Joint annuities are a great bonus under the CSRS program. You should *always* opt for a joint annuity unless your spouse is very ill or much older than you, and so is not likely to outlive you.

A joint annuity may be available even if you get married *after* taking retirement. You would reduce your pension at that time, and your spouse would then be entitled to benefits at your death.

❖ GEM: Watch Out for Remarriage

After you die, your spouse's annuity will generally continue until he or she dies. But if your spouse remarries before becoming 55 years old, he or she had better really be in love, because the pension will be cut off!

SURVIVOR BENEFITS

If you worked for the Government for at least 18 months and died before retiring, your spouse is entitled to monthly survivor payments for the rest of her life (or until she remarried, if remarried before age 55). The amount of the payments is based on 55 percent of your regular pension (see Table 12.1) or, if it will result in a higher amount, 55 percent of the *lesser* of:

- 40 percent of your highest three-year average pay
- Your pension had you worked until age 60

EXAMPLE 10

You die at age 58, after 30 years of service with the Government. You were still working at the time of your death. Your three highest years of earnings averaged $45,000. In this case, your spouse would get $13,922/year, which is 55 percent of $25,313. ($25,313 is 56.25% of $45,000, based on Table 12.1.)

EXAMPLE 11

You die at age 56 after 13 years of Government service. Your three highest years of earnings averaged $45,000. In this case, your spouse would get $7,487/year, which is 55 percent of $13,613; $13,613 is 30.25 percent of $45,000. Why did we use 30.25 percent? Had you worked until age 60, you would have had 17 years of service, so according to Table 12.1 you'd get 30.25 percent of $45,000.

EXAMPLE 12

You die at age 49 after 13 years of Government service. Your three highest years of earnings averaged $45,000. In this case your spouse would get $9,900/year, which is 55 percent of $18,000; $18,000 is 40 percent of $45,000.

Had you worked until age 60, your pension would have been $19,913, 44.25 percent (under Table 12.1) of $45,000. Since $19,913 is more than $18,000, the law says take 55 percent of the lesser of the two amounts.

Your surviving spouse gets survivor benefits at your death *regardless* of her or his age. This is different from—and much better than—Social Security survivor benefits, which don't pay a surviving spouse until age 60.

DISABILITY BENEFITS

Let's say you aren't yet at retirement age, but you just can't keep working due to a physical or mental impairment. Under CSRS, you should be entitled to a very nice disability pension.

We've already explained how tough it is to get a disability pension under Social Security. The rules are usually *much* easier under CSRS—another benefit for our civil servants. To qualify for disability benefits, you must:

- Have become disabled while working in a government job
- Have five years or more civilian government service
- Be unable to do useful service in your current job or in another vacant job in the same agency at the same grade or pay level

Under Social Security, you generally won't be considered disabled if you can do *any* job in which you could earn at least $500 a month, whether or not there are job openings, anywhere in the country. Under CSRS, you may be considered disabled even if you could do other work and earn up to 80 percent of your last salary. As long as you can't continue in your present job or in another vacant position at the *same* agency, in the *same* geographic area, in the *same* pay or grade level, you should be considered disabled.

To apply for disability benefits you should contact your agency personnel office. They should help you file the correct forms and evidence. You will have to provide evidence of your disability. A doctor who examined you will have to document, in writing, your medical condition, including the history of the problem and the possibility that you will recover. The physician's statement must be fully supported by your medical records.

If you qualify for disability benefits and are 60 or older, your benefits will be permanent—they won't be taken away, even if your condition improves. If you are younger, you may have to undergo periodic physical exams to see if you've recovered.

Your disability pension will be the amount of your regular pension (Table 12.1) or, if it will result in a higher amount, the lesser of:

- 40 percent of your highest three-year average pay
- Your pension had you worked until age 60

If you are under age 60 when you begin disability, there is no reduction in benefits.

Here is a *Golden Rule* to help you figure your disability pension: If you are over 60, or if you have more than 21 years 11 months of Government service at the time of your disability, your disability pension will be the same as your regular pension (Table 12.1).

❖ GEM: A Workable Solution: Collect Disability While on the Job!

While the CSRS disability benefits aren't bad, you can make some money on the side without reducing your benefits at all. And the amount you can earn by working can be substantial—up to 80 percent of your last salary!

EXAMPLE 13

Your aching back has gotten increasingly worse from all the lifting involved with your job; at age 58 it has finally become so painful that you have to retire. Your highest three-year average pay is $40,000, and you've got 25 years on the job, so you collect $18,500/year as your disability pension (46.25% of $40,000).

Even though you can't continue doing your same job, you can still work, so you find an easier job with a private company paying $28,000/ year. You can keep the entire amount—and now, without breaking your back, your total income (earnings and disability benefits) is $46,500— *more* than you were making at your old position!

But don't get greedy. If you earn more than 80 percent of your last salary, the Government will say that you've recovered from your disability and cut you off.

❖ GEM: Don't Work for Uncle Sam Again

As Example 13 shows, you can supplement your disability pension by working. But if you take a Government job, your income will be reduced by the amount of your benefits.

EXAMPLE 14

Same facts as in Example 13, except your new job is with the Government. Your $46,500 income will be cut by $18,500 (the amount of your disability), reducing the total income you get to the amount of your salary. While that's still more than just the disability benefits, you could do a lot better choosing another boss.

APPLICATION

When you are ready to retire, or if you think you are entitled to CSRS survivor or disability benefits, follow the *Golden Rule:* you must apply—benefits don't come automatically.

For Government retirement benefits, you apply with your department or agency; your supervisor should be able to get you the right form or forms (Standard Form 2801 for retirement). If you are applying for retirement benefits after you left your job, you may apply to the U.S. Office of Personnel Management (in Washington, D.C., [202] 606-0400).

While there are no outside time limits for retirement applications, you may only apply for disability benefits within one year after you leave the Government (unless you are considered incompetent). This is very important: *don't delay a disability application!*

Retirement benefits should start the month after you leave the government; disability benefits should start the day after you leave.

APPEALS

If you don't like the decision made on your application, ask the Office of Personnel Management to review its decision. After you get a final decision, if you're still not satisfied you can appeal to the Merit Systems Protections Board, Office of the Clerk, MSPB, 1120 Vermont Ave., N.W., Washington, D.C. 20419. Write a letter describing why the decision is wrong, and state that you have sent a copy of your letter to the opposing party. If you are still not satisfied, your next appeal is to the U.S. Court of Appeals for the Federal Circuit (in Washington, D.C.). You generally have no more than 30 days to file an appeal, so don't waste time.

Get yourself a good lawyer, one who knows something about CSRS. Once you get into the appeals process, you need experienced help. If you win, Uncle Sam may have to pay your legal fees.

❖ GEM: Get Free Help from OPM

If you are still working, you can get information on retirement and disability from the personnel office of your department or agency. If you are separated from service, you can call the Office of Personnel Management in Washington, D.C., at (202) 606-0400, for recorded messages or (202) 606-0500 for a person who can answer your specific questions. If you want more general information, ask for their series of booklets called *Retirement Facts*. And for detailed information, take a look at the *Federal Personnel Manual,* available at your agency personnel office.

· 13 ·

Railroad Retirement:
Benefits to Keep Your Retirement on Track

You've been working on the railroad, all the livelong day.
You've been working on the railroad, just to reach retirement day.
Can't you hear Hawaii calling, no more rising up so early in the morn.
Don't you fear your budget stalling, 'fore your pension's born.

Those older Americans who have worked for a railroad at some time during their lives may be in line for a "free ride" (well, not exactly free—you paid a lot of money into the system over the years). The Golden Rules for getting railroad benefits are similar to those for Social Security, but if you qualify, the benefits generally are *higher!* So if you've "been working on the railroad," make sure you get your due.

RETIREMENT BENEFITS

Railroad retirement benefits, like Social Security retirement benefits, are based on the time you worked and the amounts you earned. You must have at least 10 years of railroad service to collect any benefits. Now don't get too depressed if you have less—your years won't be wasted. Railroad time less than 10 years is transferred to the Social Security system.

❖ GEM: If You Are Close to
10 Years of Service, Stay on Track

While it's true that you won't completely lose your railroad credits if you retire without 10 years of service, railroad benefits typically are higher than Social Security benefits. So if you're close to the 10-year minimum, work those extra months to reach the magic plateau—it'll be worth it.

Your years of service need not be consecutive. Add up your total railroad time to figure your service years.

❖ GEM: Don't Forget Military Time

You only have seven years of railroad service—not quite enough for the 10-year minimum. Are you out of luck? Maybe not!

If you served in the military during a war or national emergency, and you worked for a railroad just prior to entering the military, all of your military time could count toward your railroad service.

❖ ❖ ❖

Basic Pension

If you meet the 10-year railroad service minimum, you can retire at age 65 with a full regular pension, or earlier with a reduced basic pension. Table 13.1 shows this.

TABLE 13.1

Basic Pension

Retirement Age	Years of Service	Amount of Pension
65	10 years or more	Full
62	10–29 years	Reduced pension*
62	30 years or more	Full
60	30 years or more	Reduced pension*

* Reductions are the same as under Social Security: you lose $\frac{1}{180}$ of full retirement benefits for each month before age 65 (age 62 if 30 years of service).

Note: You must leave railroad work to collect any retirement benefits. You can't continue to work for a railroad and collect benefits at the same time.

❖ GEM: If You're Close to the "Brass Ring" of 30 Years, Grab It!

While there's not a lot of incentive to work more than 30 years, you get a big break by reaching that final stop, as Example 1 shows.

EXAMPLE 1

You are 62 years old with 29 years of rail service. Your full age 65 pension would be $800/month, but you can retire now and still get a $640 monthly annuity. Not bad, but if you work just one more year, and reach the 30-year mark, you can then get the full $800 monthly pension even though you'll only be 63. Your one more year of work adds $160/month or almost $1,920 every year!

✦ ✦ ✦

What Is a Supplemental Pension?

You may be entitled to more than a basic pension. If you have at least 25 years of railroad service, you can collect a supplemental pension too. Table 13.2 shows the years of service required to cash in.

TABLE 13.2

Supplemental Pension

Age	Years of Service
60	30 or more years
65	25–29 years

In addition to the years of service requirement, there are two other requirements for a supplemental pension: (1) you must have a "current connection" with the railroad industry; and (2) you must have put in some rail service before October 1981. If you meet the requirements, you'll get from $23 to $43 added to every monthly paycheck for the rest of your life. The amount depends upon the number of your years of rail service; the base is $23 and you add $4 for each year of service over 25 years to a maximum of $43.

A "current connection," for purposes of getting a supplemental pension, means that you worked for a railroad for at least 12 of the 30 months before the pension starts. In other words, within the last 2½ years you must have worked for a railroad for at least one year.

❖ GEM: Get the Added Pension
Even If You're Late Coming Aboard

Let's say you don't have a year of work for a railroad during the last 2½ years. Maybe you retired from rail work several years ago and haven't worked since. Or maybe you got a different job. In some cases, you may still qualify for the supplemental pension. Here's how.

If you worked for a railroad for 12 months during any 30-month period, and you haven't worked since, you can still get the supplement. And even if you did work since the end of the 30-month period, you can get the supplement if the work was for:

- Yourself in any unincorporated business
- The U.S. Department of Transportation, National Transportation Safety Board, Interstate Commerce Commission, National Mediation Board, or Railroad Retirement Board
- *Any* employer, if you had at least 25 years of rail service and you were involuntarily terminated without fault

EXAMPLE 2

You stopped working for the railroad in 1986. Since then, you've been self-employed, doing odd jobs around the neighborhood. Although you haven't worked for the railroad during the last 2½ years, you did work on the tracks up until 1986.

You satisfy the current connection requirement because your work since 1986 has been for yourself. As long as you did rail work 12 out of the last 30 months before you left the railroad in 1986, you should be eligible for a supplemental pension.

✦ ✦ ✦

Can Your Spouse Benefit Too?

You may be able to collect a railroad pension, even if you never worked for a railroad. As long as your spouse (of at least a year) has worked for a railroad, you may collect a pension based on his or her work record. Again, this is similar to the Social Security retirement spouse benefit program. Table 11.3 is a timetable for pension eligibility as a railroad spouse.

Your spouse pension will end if:

- You go to work for a railroad.
- You die.
- Your spouse dies (though you may now get a widow benefit).
- Your spouse's pension stops for any reason (such as if your spouse goes back to a railroad job).

TABLE 13.3

Spouse's Railroad Pension

Rail Worker's Spouse Starts Collecting at Age	Rail Worker's Age	Rail Worker's Years of Service	Spouse's Pension*
60	60	30	Full or reduced
60	62	30	Full
60	62	10–29	Reduced
65	62	10–29	Full

*Full pension will be paid if the worker reached 60 and had 30 years of service before July 1, 1984, or if the worker was 62 and had 30 years of service when his pension started. Otherwise, the spouse's pension will be reduced by $\frac{1}{144}$ for each month she is under 65.

What Happens to a Divorced Spouse?

If you were married to a rail worker for at least 10 years, your ex-spouse has retired, and you have reached age 62, you may be entitled to some money—even if you've been "derailed" for many years! As long as you are not remarried when you apply, you should qualify for a divorced spouse pension. (Look at our gems on pages 23–24, discussing how to maximize divorced spouse benefits under the Social Security system; the same gems can put money in your pocket here, too.)

The pension will be the same as it would under the Social Security system, though that's *less* than you'd get if you were still married. Why? Because a railroad spouse who is not divorced gets *higher* benefits than Social Security would pay!

How Are Retirement Benefits Calculated?

Just as under Social Security, calculation of benefits under the railroad retirement system is complicated. You can get an estimate by contacting your nearest U.S. Railroad Retirement Board (Table 13.5).

The basic railroad retirement pension is figured in two stages, or tiers. The first stage figures basic retirement benefits in pretty much the same way as Social Security retirement benefits and is based on *all* of your earnings—railroad and non-railroad. The amount figured under this stage of the railroad retirement calculation will be about the same as you'd get if you were under Social Security.

The second stage is based *only* on your railroad service—and it is this component which generally boosts your basic rail benefits higher than if you had been covered under Social Security. Together these two stages give you your basic rail benefits. And then don't forget the supplemental pension too!

The average monthly benefit for a 65-year-old with 20 years of service was about $780 in 1991. For a 60-year-old with 35 years of service, the average payout was more than $1,400 a month. For both a 62-year-old with 40 years of service and his spouse, the average benefit was more than $2,400 a month in 1991.

Can You Get Both Social Security and Railroad Retirement Benefits?

If you've got time in under both the Social Security and railroad retirement systems, surprise! Your retirement ticket won't get punched twice—you generally won't get double benefits. For example, if you retire from your rail job now and take up nonrailroad employment, you won't get any added benefits, and you'll probably get less than you would have received if you had stayed with the railroad.

If you switch from a railroad job to a job covered by Social Security, you'll probably receive only railroad retirement benefits at retirement. Earnings at your new job will increase your railroad benefits only as much as the same earnings would have added to Social Security retirement benefits. The same earnings in a railroad job would have put *more* retirement benefits in your pocket.

❖ GEM: Stick with the Railroad for Better Benefits

If you've got less than 30 years of rail service, you'll increase your retirement benefits more by continuing to work for the railroad than by switching jobs. The reason: your rail job will boost railroad retirement benefits *more* than the same earnings would add to Social Security retirement benefits.

◆ ◆ ◆

The prohibition against collecting double benefits (rail pension for rail earnings and Social Security retirement for Social Security–covered job earnings) wasn't always there. The law used to permit rail workers to switch jobs and collect both rail pensions *and* Social Security—and they'd usually come out way ahead.

The old law is not completely gone. If you had qualified for both railroad and Social Security retirement benefits before 1975 (which would make you at least 80 today), then you may still be able to double up on your benefits.

Can You Work After Retirement?

When we discussed Social Security retirement benefits, we explained that work after retirement may reduce or eliminate your benefits. The same rules apply here. If you are 65 to 69, your benefits will be reduced by $1 for every $3 over $10,200 that you earn; if you are under 65, your benefits will be reduced by $1 of every $2 of earnings over $7,440 (1992 figures)—just like under the Social Security rules (see page 34). After age 70, Uncle Sam figures if you can you can work, you can keep the money!

Since the Social Security and railroad retirement rules covering postretirement work are the same, the gems we described to enhance Social Security retirement benefits and avoid the Working Whammy (pages 34–36) can provide Golden Opportunities here too. Here are a few more gems specifically cut for railroad workers.

❖ GEM: Don't Retire and Go Back to the Railroad

If you decide to work after retiring, don't take another railroad job. If you find rail work, your benefits will stop, no matter how much you make. If you go with a nonrail job, your benefits may continue, though reduced.

EXAMPLE 3

You are 65 and retire. Your benefits are $800/month. But then you get itchy to do something, and you'd like to supplement your income, so you get a part-time job paying $6,000/year. If the job is *not* with the railroad, you keep the paychecks and *all* of your benefits. But if you chose rail work, you get *no* benefits—not a penny!

❖ GEM: Watch Out for Your Last Nonrail Job

Let's say that before you retired you had a nonrailroad job. If you reboard with the same employer after retiring, your railroad retirement benefits will probably be significantly reduced, even though the job is not with a railroad. And the reduced benefits start with the very first $1 you earn—there's no annual exempt amount ($10,200 in 1992). To make matters worse, the reduction applies even after age 70.

The moral of this story is clear: if you decide to go back to work after retiring, don't rejoin your last employer. Try a new nonrail employer—you'll be dollars ahead!

SURVIVOR BENEFITS

When you die, your survivors (spouse, parent, child) may be able to get survivor benefits based on your work for the railroad. Table 13.4 shows who's eligible for this benefit.

TABLE 13.4

Survivors Eligible for Railroad Survivor Benefits

Relation to Railroad Worker	Age of Survivor	Other Conditions
Widow or widower	60 or older	Unmarried when apply[1]
Widow or widower	50–59	Permanently and totally disabled; unmarried when apply[2]
Widow or widower	Any	Caring for child who is under 18 or disabled since before age 22
Parent	60 or older	Dependent on worker for at least half support
Unmarried child	Under 18	
Unmarried child	18 or older	Permanent and total disability since before age 22

[1]If widow or widower remarried after age 60, may receive reduced benefits.
[2]If widow or widower remarried after age 50, may receive reduced benefits.
Note: Definitions of terms here, like *widow* or *widower* and *dependent*, generally are the same as the definitions we used in Chapter 2 to discuss Social Security survivor benefits.

For survivors to receive railroad survivor benefits, the deceased worker must:

- have worked at least 10 years with the railroad; and
- have had a current connection with the railroad at the time of his death.

The current connection requirement is discussed on page 516.

The current connection requirement can be a terrible trap. As we said earlier, a current connection generally requires at least 12 months of rail work in the 30 months before starting a pension; for a family to receive survivor benefits, the deceased must have worked 12 of the 30 months before his death. If the current connection requirement is not met, survivors can lose all rail benefits. Take a look at Example 4 to see what can happen.

EXAMPLE 4

Your husband left the railroad four years ago to take a job in the private sector. He recently died, and you want to know your right to a railroad pension.

Since he hadn't done rail work for at least 12 of the 30 months before his death, there's no current connection; that means you get no railroad survivor benefits. This doesn't mean you won't get any survivor benefits, but your railroad benefits will be gone. You should still qualify for survivor payments under the Social Security system (your husband's railroad credits will be transferred to Social Security), but the amount probably will be much less—*you may lose 30 percent or more of your benefits!*

❖ GEM: Avoid the Current Connection Trap!

What can you do to avoid the "current connection trap"? First, make sure your spouse maintains a current connection with the rail industry, if possible (e.g., part-time work). If that can't be done, arrange to make up the future benefits. For example, if your spouse is insurable, buy life insurance on his life in an amount that will generate enough income to pay the difference between Social Security and railroad survivor benefits. Or at least put some money aside to protect you in case he dies.

✦ ✦ ✦

There actually are three types of railroad survivor benefits available: monthly benefits, a lump-sum residual payment, and a lump-sum death benefit. You should be very interested in the monthly and the lump-sum death benefits; forget the residual lump-sum option.

Monthly Benefits

The best and most common railroad survivor benefit is the monthly benefit, paid like a pension. The average railroad survivor award for a widow or widower in 1991 was about $675 a month. That's a benefit you don't want to miss.

The amount is calculated the same way railroad retirement benefits are computed for a living employee. There again are two stages in the calculation. And again, benefits under the railroad survivor program will be higher than Social Security payments would have been.

Your monthly railroad survivor payments will be reduced by the amount of any Social Security benefits to which you are entitled. You'll get the higher benefit, but you'll only get one benefit—you can't double up on the payments. Your monthly survivor payments will also be reduced if you work, just as with retirement benefits ($1 for $3 of earnings over $10,200 if 65 years old; $1 for every $2 of earnings over $7,440 if under 65 years old).

Since the rules covering railroad and Social Security survivor benefits are very similar, the same gems can prove quite beneficial. Backtrack and take a look at Chapter 2!

❖ GEM: Watch Out for Remarriage

Let's say your husband died several years ago, and you're finding life a little lonely. You've met a nice man and he's proposed to you. Should you remarry? Well, we wouldn't possibly try to answer this personal question for you. But we can tell you that if you've been getting railroad survivor payments, tying the knot again may be very costly. When you take the vows, your pension will be reduced, and possibly eliminated. Financially speaking, you'd be better off not remarrying.

❖   ❖   ❖

Residual Lump Sum

This is a one-time payment that, in effect, is a refund of the worker's railroad retirement taxes—the amounts he paid in to the system over the years. This option is available if your spouse (or parent or child) dies and you don't yet qualify for monthly survivor benefits (see Table 13.4). The average residual payment is about $5,000. That's not bad, so why at the start of this section did we say to pass by this money? Here's your answer.

❖ GEM: Don't Stop the Train for the Residual Lump Sum

If you take this option, you give up all rights to future monthly payments—which is likely to cost you thousands of dollars over your lifetime. And maybe even more significant, you also lose your right to Medicare based on the deceased worker's railroad service.

EXAMPLE 5

Your husband died and you are only 55. You could use some extra money, and someone at your husband's railroad company told you that you could pick up spare cash by taking a lump sum residual payment. After doing some checking, you were told that the amount you'd receive is $6,000. If you wait until age 60, you could opt for a monthly pension of $400 based on your husband's record. Which option gives you more dollar mileage?

This one's easy. Wait for the monthly payments and skip the one-time residual benefit. You'll be much further ahead that way. Try to find another way to make ends meet right now.

❖   ❖   ❖

Lump-Sum Death Benefit

Survivors can cash in on one more benefit, a one-time death payment, if:

- The worker had 10 years with a railroad.
- The current service connection requirement is satisfied (see page 516).
- No one is immediately eligible for monthly survivor benefits (see Table 13.4).

For example, if your husband died and you are not yet 60, you can't get immediate monthly payments, but you still qualify for a one-time check. And that payment does *not* affect your right to collect monthly survivor benefits later—this check is *extra*.

The amount of the death benefit will be at least $255 (just like under Social Security). But if your late spouse had put in at least 10 years with a railroad before 1975, the payment will be much higher, usually about $800.

❖ GEM: Get a Lump-Sum Check If You're Working

Let's say you qualify for monthly survivor payments, but you are still working and your job earnings reduce or eliminate the monthly benefits. In that case, you can and should take a lump-sum death benefit check. Don't lose out—this benefit is easy to overlook!

DISABILITY

Many people "retire" from jobs because their health just doesn't permit them to continue. In that situation, a disability pension might be available.

We talked a lot about Social Security disability benefits, and we don't want to rehash all that we said. Most of the rules and tips we gave there apply to railroad disability (including the five-month waiting period). But there are some differences you should understand.

There are actually *two* types of railroad disability benefits. First is *general disability*, which is a lot like Social Security disability. To get a general disability pension, you must prove—like Social Security—that you are unable to do any substantial work with any employer. See Chapter 3.

The second type of railroad disability is different—and much easier to show. To qualify for *occupational disability*, you must:

- Be age 60 if you have 10 to 20 years of rail service; you can be any age if you have at least 20 years of service

- Have a "current connection" with the railroad; see page 516
- Be unable to continue your regular railroad job

❖ GEM: Occupational Disability—the Best Way to Go!

Occupational disability benefits are a gold mine. If you have at least 10 years of rail service (20 years of service if under 60 years old), you can retire and get full disability benefits—and all you have to show is that a physical or mental problem prevents you from doing your regular railroad job.

The disability doesn't even have to be work related. If you injured your back playing golf or fixing your roof at home, and can no longer do your rail job, you can collect disability. Occupational disability is *much easier* to qualify for than Social Security disability, as Example 6 illustrates:

EXAMPLE 6

Years of working on the tracks has taken a toll on your knees, and you can no longer continue the same line of work. You are 60 with 15 years of service.

Under Social Security, you'd have to show you couldn't do any other job, for the railroad or any other employer—a tough standard. But luckily you're under the railroad system and have more than 10 years service. Now you only have to show that you can't keep working the tracks like you've been doing. You can retire with full benefits, even if you are physically able to switch gears and work at a desk job.

❖ ❖ ❖

If you qualify for disability benefits—of either type—your benefits will be figured like those for railroad retirement. Your disability pension will be higher than the amount you'd get under the Social Security system.

All right—let's say you qualify for a railroad disability pension, but you can still work at another job. Will the earnings affect your pension? The answer in many cases is yes. You will lose your disability pension for any month in which you earn more than $400 (after subtracting work-related expenses). Now don't get too upset yet: if your earnings for the year are less than $5,000, you'll get all your lost disability pension payments back.

If your earnings for the year are over $5,000, you will lose one month pension for every $400 over $4,800 you go. Here's how it works:

EXAMPLE 7

You qualified for and are receiving a railroad disability pension. But to make a little extra spending money, you find a job at a local department store on the weekends. Since you only make about $200 month, you keep it all—and your pension too!

EXAMPLE 8

You find employment paying $500/month, and you lose your disability pension *every month* (because your income is over $400). At the end of the year, you've earned $6,000 (12 × $500). Since $6,000 exceeds $4,800 by $1,200, you should only have lost three months of pension payments ($1,200 ÷ $400 = 3 months). You will be entitled to have nine months of disability pension checks returned.

❖ GEM: Keep Track of Earnings or You Will Lose $

As you can see, working can be hazardous to your pocketbook. In fact, many people don't understand just how much can be lost.

EXAMPLE 9

You earned $9,600 last year to supplement your railroad disability pension—or so you thought. But since $9,600 exceeds $4,800 by $4,800, you lose your entire pension ($4,800 ÷ $400 = 12 months).

Now, if you had only been getting a $300 monthly pension, totaling $3,600/year, you're still ahead by working. You lost $3,600, but you earned $9,600, leaving you $6,000 richer.

But what if your railroad disability pension was $850/month, or $10,000/year? You earned $9,600, but gave up $10,000 in benefits. In other words, a full year's work left you with $400 *less* than if you hadn't worked at all!

GETTING YOUR DUE

If, after reading this far, you think you should be getting railroad retirement, survivor, or disability benefits, now's the time to apply. Applications are available from any of the local offices of the Railroad Retirement Board. Table 13.5 lists the cities with local offices. To find the address and phone number, look in the Government Offices section of the white pages. The Railroad Retirement Board will be listed under U.S. Government. Most offices are open from 9:00 A.M. to 3:30 P.M., Monday through Friday.

Personnel in the local office can tell you what information you'll need to provide. Generally, you'll need the same items as we listed for Social Security benefits, including proof of:

- The employee's age (for example, a certified copy of a birth certificate or church record)
- Any military service, which may increase the benefits (for example, a Certificate of Discharge)
- Marriage, if spouse is seeking benefits (for example, a certified copy of marriage certificate or church record)
- Divorce, if ex-spouse is seeking benefits (for example, a copy of final divorce decree)
- Disability (by supporting medical information)
- Death of worker, if trying to get survivor benefits
- Support by worker for parent, if parent is trying to get survivor benefits
- Child's disability, if child is seeking survivor benefits

❖ GEM: Don't Wait to Hop on the Benefits Gravy Train!

Waiting too long to apply can cost you money. For example, you can only collect a railroad retirement pension for, at most, the six months prior to the date of application. That means if you delay more than six months after eligibility, you'll lose benefits, and in many cases, no retroactivity is allowed. A disability pension can only go back a year from the application date. Lump-sum death benefits must be claimed within two years, or they go up in smoke.

APPEALS

Within 30 days after a decision is made on your application (by the same local office with which you filed your application), you must receive written notice of whether your request is approved or denied, along with reasons for the Railroad Board's decision. If you don't agree, ask (in writing) for a reconsideration (write

TABLE 13.5

U.S. Railroad Retirement Board Offices

Alabama
Birmingham
Mobile

Arizona
Phoenix
Tucson

Arkansas
Little Rock

California
Fresno
Oakland
Sacramento
San Bernardino
West Covina

Colorado
Denver

Connecticut
New Haven

District of Columbia

Florida
Fort Lauderdale
Jacksonville
Tampa

Georgia
Atlanta
Savannah

Idaho
Boise
Pocatello

Illinois
Chicago

Missouri
Kansas City
St. Louis
Springfield

Montana
Billings

Nebraska
Omaha

New Jersey
Newark

New Mexico
Albuquerque
Gallup

New York
Albany
Buffalo
Hicksville
New York
Syracuse

North Carolina
Charlotte
Raleigh

North Dakota
Fargo

Ohio
Cincinnati
Cleveland
Columbus
Toledo
Youngstown

Oklahoma
Oklahoma City
Tulsa
Decatur

Granite City
Joliet
Rock Island

Indiana
Fort Wayne
Indianapolis

Iowa
Des Moines

Kansas
Topeka
Wichita

Kentucky
Louisville

Louisiana
New Orleans
Shreveport

Maine
Portland

Maryland
Baltimore

Massachusetts
Boston
Springfield

Michigan
Detroit
Escanaba
Grand Rapids

Minnesota
Duluth
St. Paul

Mississippi
Jackson

Oregon
Klamath Falls
Portland

Pennsylvania
Altoona
Harrisburg
Philadelphia
Pittsburgh
Scranton

Tennessee
Knoxville
Memphis
Nashville

Texas
Amarillo
El Paso
Fort Worth
Houston
San Antonio

Utah
Salt Lake City

Virginia
Norfolk
Richmond
Roanoke

Washington
Bellevue
Spokane

West Virginia
Huntington

Wisconsin
Eau Claire
Milwaukee

to address on notice)—you have 60 days to do this. Feel free to provide additional evidence that responds to the reasons for the denial.

If you're still not satisfied with the reconsideration decision, you can appeal to the Railroad Board's Bureau of Hearings and Appeals—you again have 60 days. At this stage (if not before), we would strongly urge you to get a lawyer to help you. There will be a hearing, and your lawyer can help organize the strongest evidence to support your claim.

If you again lose, there are two more steps up the Appeals Ladder: to the Railroad Board itself, and then to a federal appeals court. Don't wait until these appeals to get legal help. Generally, your last chance to add new evidence is at the Bureau of Hearings and Appeals. You should have an experienced attorney no later than this stage.

As you can see, taking advantage of the gems offered in the Railroad Retirement program can be your ticket to a financially sound future.

·14·

Veterans' Benefits:
Uncle Sam's Reward for Military Service

As a veteran, you have contributed to the welfare of your country through military service. Now it's time for Uncle Sam to return the favor.

Our Government makes available an assortment of benefits to veterans and their families. The most important of these include pensions for older veterans, disability payments, and free or low-cost medical services. Although almost 4 million Americans are receiving these benefits, many more are missing out on the Golden Opportunities available to them.

If you (or your spouse or parents) are entitled to veterans' benefits, make sure you get them. Here are our gems for coverage.

DISABILITY AND SURVIVOR PAYMENTS

You may be entitled to a monthly check from Uncle Sam if:

- You are disabled.
- You served in the armed forces.
- You were not discharged dishonorably.

Many older Americans with military, naval, or air service mistakenly think they don't qualify. Even if you served only in peacetime, your disability had nothing at all to do with the service, or you have significant income, you may be able to collect!

Any service can make you eligible, including service as:

- Field clerk
- Army, Navy, Air Force, and Marine nurse

- Cadet and Midshipman
- Member of the Coast Guard
- Lighthouse Service personnel
- Member of National Guard
- AWAC
- Member of Women's Army Auxiliary Corps
- Civilian employees of Pacific Naval air bases who participated in the defense of Wake Island in WWII
- Participant in American Merchant Marine in Oceangoing Service from December 7, 1941, to August 15, 1945

Monthly veterans' payments can be divided into four types: pensions for veterans with disabilities unrelated to their military service, pensions for survivors of veterans, compensation for veterans with service-related disabilities, and compensation for survivors of veterans who died from service-connected disabilities. Let's take each separately.

Pensions for Veterans with Disabilities Unrelated to Their Service

You can get monthly pension payments from the VA, regardless of your age, if you pass these three tests:

- You are permanently and totally disabled.
- You served at least briefly during wartime.
- Your income is below current pension levels listed in Table 14.1.

Service during wartime generally means that you must have served at least 90 consecutive days of active duty, at least one day of which was during:

- Mexican border period—May 9, 1916, through April 5, 1917, in Mexico, on its borders, or in adjacent waters.
- World War I—April 6, 1917, through November 11, 1918 (the regular period). The regular period is extended to April 1, 1920, for those veterans who served in Russia. The regular period is also extended through July 1, 1921, for those veterans who served after November 11, 1918, and before July 2, 1921, provided they had at least one day of service during the regular period.
- World War II—December 7, 1941, through December 31, 1946.
- Korean conflict—June 27, 1950, through January 31, 1955.
- Vietnam era—August 5, 1964, through May 7, 1975.

TABLE 14.1

Basic Veteran Pensions

Veteran Status	Annual Pension
Veteran without dependent spouse or child	$ 7,397
Veteran with one dependent (spouse or child)	9,689
Veteran in need of regular aid and attendance[1] without dependents	11,832
Veteran in need of regular aid and attendance with one dependent	14,124
Veteran permanently housebound[2] without dependents	9,041
Veteran permanently housebound with one dependent	11,333
Two veterans married to one another	9,689
For veterans of World War I and the Mexican Border Period, add an extra	1,673
For each additional dependent child, add an extra	1,258

[1]A veteran generally is considered to need regular aid and attendance if he or she can't dress or undress without help, can't cook meals without someone to help, can't go the toilet without help, or would pose a danger to himself or herself.
[2]A veteran generally is considered housebound if confined to the home due to a disability that is likely to last throughout the veteran's life.

❖ GEM: Any Military Service Triggers Benefits

You are eligible for pension benefits even if you never fired a shot at the enemy. Being in a war zone is not required. You just need 90 days of military service, which is at least partially during one of the above periods of wartime.

❖ GEM: Check Your Military Record and Fix Mistakes

As we've said before, the Government makes mistakes and the military is no different. Request your military record and check it for accuracy; for example, make sure your dates of service are correctly stated. You can get a copy by contacting the local VA office. A mistake may cost you a lot in veterans' benefits.

If you find a mistake, fix it as soon as possible. Use Form DD-149 to make the correction.

❖ GEM: Upgrade Your Discharge

A dishonorable discharge will prevent you from collecting veterans' pension payments. If you did not receive an honorable or general discharge, or a discharge under honorable conditions, and you disagree with the decision, you may now apply for an upgrade. Contact your local office of the Veterans Administration (VA), now Department of Veterans Affairs, for Form DD-293.

If your request for an upgrade is denied, you may "make a federal case" out of it by filing a lawsuit. It's not just a matter of honor; it's dollars too!

❖ ❖ ❖

You must also be disabled to qualify for a monthly pension. This is new. Up until November 1, 1990, veterans who were at least 65 years old could qualify for a pension without any disability. The test for disability is similar to the test under the Social Security program, described in Chapter 3. You must be unable to engage in "substantial gainful employment."

Not every disabled veteran is eligible for a monthly pension. You and your spouse's total income (including Social Security, pension, interest, dividends, and rents) must be below the maximum amount of the veterans' pension payments, listed in Table 14.1.

The Government may also consider your net worth—the value of your assets other than your home and personal effects—and may deny you a pension if your net worth is high. Don't worry too much about this requirement. Uncle Sam focuses primarily on your income, not your assets. If your income is low, you should get this pension. And even if the Government gives you a hard time about the amount of your "wealth," you could give your assets to your children or place them into an irrevocable trust (as we explained in Chapter 11 on Medicaid) and immediately qualify for the pension, as long as the gift is not to someone living with you. Unlike the Medicaid rules, there should be no waiting or ineligibility period for veterans' pension benefits after a transfer.

❖ GEM: If You Qualify Now or in the Future, Get Your Pension

Even if you served 40 or 50 years ago, and even if your income had been too high to qualify while you were working, you can still get your pension now if you qualify (i.e., you are disabled, served during wartime, and have low enough income). When you retire and your income drops, a veterans' pension may be just the income supplement you need!

❖ ❖ ❖

Pensions for Surviving Spouse and Children

If your late husband or wife served 90 days, at least part of which was during wartime, *you* should be entitled to a veterans' pension if all of the following:

- You were married at least one year before your spouse's death.
- You are not remarried at the time you apply for benefits.
- Your income is below the surviving spouse pension amounts listed in Table 14.2.

Neither you nor your late spouse need be disabled. Your age, and your late spouse's age at the time he or she died, are both irrelevant; you can collect this pension *at any age!* Table 14.2 shows the payments you can get if you qualify.

TABLE 14.2

Basic Surviving Spouse Pension

Spouse Status	Annual Pension
Surviving spouse without dependent children	$4,957
Surviving spouse with one dependent child	6,494
Surviving spouse in need of regular aid and attendance[1] without dependent child	7,929
Surviving spouse in need of regular aid and attendance with one dependent child	9,462
Surviving spouse permanently housebound[2] without dependent child	6,061
Surviving spouse permanently housebound with one dependent child	7,594
For each additional dependent child, add an extra	1,258

[1]A surviving spouse generally is considered to need regular aid and attendance if he or she can't dress or undress without help, can't cook meals without someone to help, can't go to the toilet without help, or would pose a danger to himself or herself.
[2]A surviving spouse generally is considered housebound if confined to the home due to a disability which is likely to last throughout her (or his) life.

As a surviving spouse, your pension will be reduced by the amount of your other income, including Social Security based on your late spouse's work record. Medicaid and SSI benefits (discussed in Chapters 11 and 10) will not reduce your pension.

❖ GEM: Watch Out for Remarriage

A veterans' pension provides a nice income supplement for a surviving spouse. But if you remarry, you will lose out. You can't ever again qualify for a survivor pension from your late spouse.

❖   ❖   ❖

Children of a deceased veteran who served 90 days, at least part during wartime, also are entitled to a small government pension ($1,258 a year) if the child is either:

• Under age 18 (23 if in school)
• Any age if the child became permanently incapable of self-support before reaching age 18

Compensation for Veterans with Service-related Disabilities

Here the rules are different. If you've got a service-related disability, you may be entitled to a monthly check regardless of your age, regardless of your income, and regardless of whether you served in war or peacetime.

Service connection is often pretty easy to show. If your injury or disease first happened or was aggravated while in military service (during wartime or peacetime), you should have a good argument that it's service connected. The main exception is that a disability brought on by your own misconduct may not qualify as service related.

Your disability must limit your ability to do "substantial gainful work" (see Chapter 3, page 86) in civil (nonmilitary) occupations. The Government will evaluate your condition based on your medical records and, usually, an examination by one of its own doctors. The amount of your compensation will depend on how seriously disabled the Government thinks you are. Table 14.3 lists the monthly payments based on the extent of your disability.

While the test for disability under the veterans' program is similar to that under Social Security, you might have an easier time getting veterans' benefits. Why? Because the veterans' program considers "partial" disabilities.

The Government uses a long set of tables that assigns a percentage disability to different injuries or illnesses. For example, the loss of one hand and one foot qualifies for a 100 percent disability. The loss of one hand alone will render you 60 to 70 percent disabled, according to the Government's charts. The amputation of a thumb makes you 20 to 40 percent disabled, depending on the extent of the loss; loss of your little finger makes you only 10 to 20 percent disabled.

TABLE 14.3

Disability Compensation

Extent of Disability	Monthly Payment*
10%	$ 83
20	157
30	240
40	342
50	487
60	614
70	776
80	897
90	1,010
100	1,680

*These amounts may be increased for a spouse who is in need of aid and attendance, and for dependents *if* veteran is at least 30 percent disabled. These amounts also may be increased, up to $4,899, for certain severe disabilities or combination of disabilities.

How about a few more? Rheumatoid arthritis which flares up once or twice a year makes you 20 percent disabled, more if it is worse. A hip replacement will make you at least 30 percent disabled, and possibly as much as 100 percent depending on how much pain and weakness follows. A moderately severe ulcer, with pain once a month, would get you a 40 percent rating, but an ulcer that completely incapacitates you would make you 100 percent disabled.

These are just examples. Get the help of an experienced advocate or attorney; talk to your doctor about your disability, and make sure he or she provides the information necessary to get you the highest disability rating for which you qualify.

Disabilities—and ratings—can change! Even though you may not have been disabled at the time of your injury or the onset of an illness, the impairment may have gotten worse over the years. Changes in your disability can qualify you for changes in the level of benefits.

EXAMPLE 1

You suffered a knee injury during your military service while lifting crates in a warehouse. That was 50 years ago. When you left the service, you got a job—the injury never slowed you down.

But over the years, the pain has gotten worse. Your knee stiffens up more and more often, making it hard to walk. Your doctor says it's likely that the condition first arose from the knee injury years ago.

You may be entitled to a veterans' disability pension of as much as $614 a month (60% rating). That's money you could use, right? Don't give it up!

Compensation for Survivors of Veterans Who Died from Service-connected Disabilities

If your husband, wife, mother, father, or child died from a service-connected disability or while in active service, you may be entitled to monthly compensation from Uncle Sam, called dependency and indemnity compensation (DIC). In fact, you may even be able to collect a monthly Government check if your disabled spouse or parent died from something *unrelated* to a service-connected disability. Table 14.4 describes when you are likely to be eligible for DIC.

TABLE 14.4

Eligibility for Disability Survivors' Payments

You generally can collect monthly compensation following the death of a disabled veteran if any of the following apply:

- Your late spouse died from a service-connected disability or while in active service.
- Your late parent, a veteran, died from a service-connected disability or while in active service, and you are either under 18, under 23 and in school, or permanently incapable of self-support and have been since before reaching 18.
- The cause of the death of your late spouse or parent was unrelated to a service-connected disability, and he or she had been totally disabled for at least 10 years before the death (five years if he or she was disabled from the date of discharge).
- Your child died from a service-connected disability or while in active service and your income is less than $8,414 ($11,313 for two parents together).

Payments to a surviving spouse, who has never remarried, will depend on the veteran's pay grade. Table 14.5 shows the amounts available as of 1992.

MEDICAL BENEFITS

Veterans and their families may also be eligible for free or low-cost hospital, nursing-home, outpatient, and at-home medical care. Hospital or nursing-home care will usually be provided at VA facilities, though the Government may sometimes pay for care at a non-VA institution. These benefits are limited because

TABLE 14.5

Death Payments to Surviving Spouse Based on Veteran's Salary[1]

Pay Grade	Monthly Payment
E–1	$ 616
E–2	635
E–3	652
E–4	693
E–5	711
E–6	727
E–7	762
E–8	805
E–9[2]	841
W–1	780
W–2	811
W–3	835
W–4	884
O–1	780
O–2	805
O–3	862
O–4	912
O–5	1,005
O–6	1,134
O–7	1,225
O–8	1,343
O–9	1,440
O–10	1,580

[1]Additional payments are available if surviving spouse has young children, is housebound, or requires regular aid and attendance by another person. Also, if the veteran died before 1957, other payment rates are used.
[2]Certain individuals in this group get special (added) amounts.

there are many more veterans needing help than there are resources available. But if you know your rights, you will have a better chance to cash in on this Golden Opportunity.

Hospitalization

If you can get into a VA hospital, all of your costs should be covered. These include medical exams, wheelchairs, prescription drugs, and even reasonable travel expenses to the hospital. The trick is to get in.

Because demand for VA hospital care far exceeds supply, the Government must rank veterans. In an emergency, you should gain entrance. For veterans not needing emergency care, the Government has created two categories: veterans in the Mandatory category *must* be given care at the closest possible hospital; veterans in the Discretionary category may be given care if space is available. Table 14.6 describes the two categories.

TABLE 14.6

Medical Care Categories

Category	Who Is Included:
Mandatory	Veterans with service-related disabilities
	Veterans who were discharged for disabilities incurred or aggravated in the line of duty
	Former POWs
	Veterans of WWI
	Veterans getting a pension (see pages 525–527) or disability payments (see pages 529–531)
	Veterans with nonservice-connected disabilities and income of less than $18,843 ($22,612 if married, plus $1,258 for each additional dependent)
Discretionary*	Veterans with nonservice-connected disabilities and income above $18,843 ($22,612 if married, plus $1,258 for each additional dependent)

*A Discretionary category veteran must pay for the cost of care or the Medicare deductible ($652 today), whichever is less, for the first 90 days of care. For each additional 90 days, the veteran will be charged half the Medicare deductible. The *most* a veteran may be charged in a year is four times the Medicare deductible. (For a discussion of the Medicare deductible, see page 129.)

Nursing-Home Care

VA nursing-home benefits are even more limited than hospital coverage. Admission to a VA nursing home is based on the same priorities as in Table 14.6, except that even those in the Mandatory category will only be admitted on an "as available" basis. You will only be admitted to a private nursing home at VA expense if any of the following apply:

- You were in a VA hospital and are being discharged into a nursing home.
- Your need for a nursing home stems from a service-connected disability.
- You were receiving VA medical center–based home health services.

Even if you qualify, don't expect much. VA nursing-home benefits generally won't last for more than six months, unless your care is for a service-related disability.

Outpatient Medical Treatment and Home Health Services

Uncle Sam will provide you with outpatient services at VA facilities if you qualify. These services include medical exams, drugs and medicine, rehabilitation, counseling, and mental health services. In some cases, even dental care will be provided.

Home health services needed for your treatment may also be included, and may even cover home improvements (such as changes to the bathroom which facilitate accessibility). Costs for structural changes are generally limited to $2,500.

TABLE 14.7

Requirements for Outpatient and Home Health Service

The VA *must* furnish service to a veteran who:

- Needs treatment for any service-connected disability
- Needs treatment for a nonservice-connected disability, if the veteran is 50 percent or more disabled from a service-connected disability
- Needs treatment for a nonservice-connected disability if both:
  1. The treatment is necessary to prepare for hospital admission, to complete hospital treatment, or to avoid hospitalization.
  2. The veteran is 30 to 40 percent disabled from a service-connected disability, or has income less than the maximum monthly pension for veterans who need aid and attendance (now $11,832 for singles, $14,124 for a person with one dependent).

The VA *may* furnish service to a veteran who needs treatment
for a nonservice-connected disability and:

- Is a former prisoner of war
- Is a veteran of WWI
- Is receiving a pension for housebound veterans or for those who need aid and attendance
- Is participating in a VA-approved rehabilitation program
- The treatment is necessary to prepare for hospital admission, to complete hospital treatment, or to avoid hospitalization; and the veteran either is less than 30 percent disabled from a service-connected disability, was exposed to a toxic substance or radiation, is in the Mandatory category (Table 14.6) with income over the maximum pension for veterans in need of regular aid and attendance, is in the Discretionary category, or is eligible for hospital care and is not otherwise included above

Table 14.7 lists the eligibility requirements for outpatient and home health treatment. If outpatient services can't be made available to everyone listed in Table 14.7, they will be provided on a priority basis, generally in the order listed in the table.

You may also be eligible for other nonmedical benefits at home (called domiciliary care), including food and clothing, if you are disabled but do not require hospitalization or nursing-home care. The coverage is much broader than under the Medicare program (*i.e.,* Medicare will never cover food and clothing). To be eligible, your income must be less than the maximum veteran pension (currently $7,397 for single veterans or $9,689 for person with one dependent).

Health-related Travel

You may be able to have Uncle Sam cover your costs for travel in connection with Government-paid health care. The first $3 for each one-way trip will be your responsibility, but anything over that amount will be covered by the Government. If you travel by ambulance, wheelchair van, or other transportation specially designed for disabled individuals, you won't even have to pay the $3. How do you qualify? Table 14.8 lists the eligibility requirements for health-related travel coverage.

TABLE 14.8

Requirements for Health-related Travel Benefits

You are eligible for travel coverage if you are:

- At least 30 percent disabled by a service-connected disability

- Less than 30 percent disabled and traveling for treatment of a service-connected condition

- Receiving a veteran's pension

- Receiving an income that is less than or equal to the maximum veteran's pension rate ($7,397 for single veterans, $9,689 for person with one dependent)

- Required because of your medical condition to use transportation specially designed for disabled persons and either you are unable to pay the cost, the VA has pre-authorized its use (contact your registered VA office, listed in Table 14.10), or you need emergency care

Prosthetic Appliances

Uncle Sam may provide prosthetic appliances (false leg, etc.). To qualify, you must meet the requirements for outpatient care set forth in Table 14.7, and the appliance must be required for one of the reasons listed in Table 14.9.

TABLE 14.9

Requirements for Prosthetic Appliances

The prosthetic appliance must be necessary for a veteran:

- With a service-connected disability
- With a disability for which the veteran was discharged
- As part of an approved rehabilitation program
- As part of outpatient care to complete treatment
- With any medical condition, if the veteran is at least 50 percent disabled by a service-connected condition
- Who is receiving a veteran's pension based on need for aid and attendance of permanently housebound
- Of WWI
- Who is a former prisoner of war

Benefits for the Blind

You may receive an assortment of benefits if you are blind. These include compensation for home improvements to make living easier, low-vision aids, electronic and mechanical aids, guide dogs, talking books, tapes, and braille literature.

To qualify you must have less than 20/200 vision in your better eye, or a visual field of 20 degrees or less after correction. You must also meet the requirements for disability compensation for a service-related disability, or you must be eligible for hospitalization or outpatient treatment.

Medical Benefits for Family Members

A veteran's family members may also be entitled to medical coverage, compliments of Uncle Sam. The Government will help pay for medical services and supplies from your regular doctor, pharmacy, and so on, if you fit into one of these categories:

- Your spouse or parent is a veteran with a permanent, total, service-connected disability.
- Your late spouse or late parent died from a service-connected disability.
- Your late spouse or late parent had a permanent, total, service-connected disability at the time of his death, though he died from something else.
- Your late spouse or late parent died in the line of duty.

To qualify based on your late spouse's service, you must be unmarried at the time you apply for benefits.

MISCELLANEOUS BENEFITS

Uncle Sam offers lots more to older veterans than just pensions and medical benefits. Here are a few of the better, but little known, Golden Opportunities. To apply, contact your regional office (Table 14.10).

Home Remodeling

If you are disabled and want to remodel your home to make it more liveable and accommodate your disability, Uncle Sam may pay for all or part! For example, there may be money available to add a bedroom or bathroom on the first floor, install railings, lower cabinets, and much more.

Uncle Sam may pay for half the costs, up to $38,000, if you have a permanent and total service-connected disability due to:

- Loss of use of both feet or legs, so that you need braces, crutches, canes, or a wheelchair
- Loss of use of one leg or foot, plus blindness
- Loss of use of one hand or arm which, coupled with other problems, causes the need for braces, canes, crutches, or a wheelchair

The VA also has another more limited home-remodeling grant program. To qualify, you must be blind in both eyes or have suffered the loss of use of both hands as the result of a permanent and total (100%) service-connected disability. If you are eligible, you may receive up to $6,500 for home remodeling.

New Car

The Government may pay up to $5,500 toward purchase of a car *if* you have a service-connected loss of use of one or both hands or feet, or (believe it or not) severe loss of vision in both eyes.

Clothing

If you wear out or tear clothing faster than usual, due to use of prosthetic devices, wheelchairs, or medications and creams that damage clothing, Uncle Sam may pick up part of the costs for new duds, up to $452.

Life Insurance

The government offers life insurance, under a variety of different plans, to veterans. Even if you haven't been enrolled because you don't think you are covered, it might be worth a few minutes of your time to check with the VA.

For example, veterans who are totally disabled before reaching age 65 might be entitled to a premium waiver—so even if you haven't been paying, you may still be insured. In fact, disabled veterans may even be entitled to disability payments under a rider to their life insurance.

Check your insurance now, before any more time passes. In some cases, lapsed policies may be reinstated, but there's usually a time limit. The longer you wait, the less likely you'll be able to reinstate lapsed insurance.

Funeral and Burial Benefits

Death can be an expensive proposition. Uncle Sam may help defray the costs for veterans' families. Here's what's available:

- Up to $300 for burial expenses. Far from the entire cost, but at least it's something. If your spouse or parent died within the last two years, you may still make a claim with the VA.
- $150 for the plot, unless the veteran is buried in a national cemetery.
- Transportation to, and burial in, a national cemetery. This benefit is available for the veteran, and his spouse, widow or widower (who is unmarried at the time of his or her death), and children.
- Headstone or grave marker.
- American flag to drape the casket.

APPLICATION FOR BENEFITS AND APPEALS

Serving your country should be rewarding, but you won't get *any* benefits unless you apply. Application forms generally are available at all VA offices, hospitals, medical centers, and nursing homes. Hopefully, your application will be approved, and that will be that. But what if the system fails?

If your application is turned down and you don't agree with the VA's decision, you can file a Notice of Disagreement (Form 21–4138) with the VA office that denied your claim. You typically have one year from the denial. If you are still not successful, you can appeal to the Board of Veterans Appeals by filing a Substantive Appeal (using Form 1–9) with the regional VA office. You generally must also file this appeal within one year from the initial rejection of your application.

You may choose to have your appeal decided by the Board of Veterans Appeals in Washington, D.C., or by a panel of the board at a regional office, or by a single hearing officer at the regional office. Convenience usually dictates appealing at the regional VA office.

Your next stop is the U.S. Court of Veterans Appeals, located in Washington, D.C. Once you get here, chances of your winning are slim. If you are still unhappy with the results, you may appeal to the U.S. Court of Appeals for the Federal Circuit, also in Washington.

When you get involved in appeals at any level, you'd be smart to: (1) get as much information as you can, and (2) have an experienced advocate or lawyer. Attorney fees are limited by law, so you don't have to worry about all your benefits going to the lawyer. Generally fees are contingent on your winning; if you don't collect, neither does the lawyer.

For more information, and for help with specific problems, contact the National Veterans Legal Service Project (NVLSP), a nonprofit organization providing valuable services to veterans. The address is 2001 S Street, N.W., Suite 610, Washington, D.C. 20009-1125; (202) 265-8305. The NVLSP maintains a list of veterans' advocacy groups and attorneys throughout the country who are experienced in serving the needs of veterans.

All major veterans' organizations will provide help. Contact the Veterans of Foreign Wars (202) 543-2239; American Legion (202) 861-2700; Disabled American Veterans (202) 208-1360; Jewish War Veterans (202) 265-6280; Viet Nam Veterans of America (202) 628-2700; AmVets (301) 459-9600; and your local state or county veterans' service office.

Table 14.10 lists VA regional offices. For more information, or to apply for benefits, contact the office nearest you. In addition, the VA offers a booklet entitled "Federal Benefits for Veterans and Dependents." That booklet contains a wealth of information about available benefits.

TABLE 14.10

VA Regional Offices

Alabama

Montgomery 36104 (474 S. Court Street; local 205-262-7781; statewide 800-392-8054. Direct dial from Birmingham 205-322-2492, Huntsville 205-539-7742, Mobile 205-432-8645)

Alaska

Anchorage 99501 (235 E. 8th Avenue; local 907-279-6116, statewide 800-478-2500); Benefits Office: Juneau 99802 (P.O. Box 20069, Federal Building, Room 103, 907-586-7472)

Arizona

Phoenix 85012 (3225 N. Central Avenue; local 602-263-5411, statewide 800-827-2031)

Arkansas

North Little Rock 72115 (Building 65, Ft. Roots, P.O. Box 1280; local 501-370-3800, statewide 800-827-2033)

California

Los Angeles 90024 (Federal Building, 11000 Wilshire Boulevard, counties of Inyo, Kern, Los Angeles, Orange, San Bernardino, San Luis Obispo, Santa Barbara and Ventura. Direct dial from central Los Angeles 479-4011; other areas of these counties 800-827-2013) Benefits Office: East Los Angeles 90022 (5400 E. Olympic Boulevard, Commerce, 213-722-4927)

San Diego 92108 (2022 Camino Del Rio North, counties of Imperial, Riverside and San Diego. Direct dial from: Riverside 686-1132, San Diego 297-8220; other areas of these counties 800-532-3811)

San Francisco 94105 (211 Main Street; recorded benefits 415-974-0138, 24-hour availability; local 415-495-8900, other Northern California areas 800-827-0641)

Counties of Alpine, Lassen, Modoc, and Mono served by Reno, Nev.; RO, 800-648-5406

Colorado

Denver 80225 (44 Union Boulevard, P.O. Box 25126; local 303-980-1300, statewide 800-332-6742. Direct dial from: Colorado Springs 475-9911, Pueblo 545-1764)

Connecticut

Hartford 06103 (450 Main Street; local 203-278-3230, statewide 800-842-4315)

Delaware

Wilmington 19805 (1601 Kirkwood Highway; local 302-998-0191, statewide 800-292-7855)

District of Columbia
  Washington, D.C. 20421 (941 N. Capitol Street, N.E., 202-872-1151)

Florida
  St. Petersburg 33701 (144 1st Avenue S.; local 612-898-2121; statewide 800-827-2204); Benefits Offices: Jacksonville 32206 (1833 Boulevard, Room 3105, 800-827-2204) Miami 33130 (Federal Building, Room 120, 51 S.W. 1st Avenue, 800-827-2204) Pensacola 32503-7492 (312 Kenmore Road, Room IG 250, 800-827-2204)

Georgia
  Atlanta 30365 (730 Peachtree Street, N.E.; local 404-881-1776, statewide 800-282-0232. Direct dial from: Albany 439-2331, Augusta 738-5403, Columbus 324-6646, Macon 745-6517, Savannah 232-3365)

Hawaii
  Honolulu 96813 (PJKK Federal Building, 300 Ala Moana Boulevard, Mailing: P.O. Box 50188, Honolulu 96850; Kauai, Lanai, Maui, Molokai 800-232-2535. Direct dial from: Oahu, 541-1000, Hawaii 961-3661)

Idaho
  Boise 83724 (Federal Building & U.S. Courthouse, 550 W. Fort Street, Box 044; local 208-334-1010, statewide 800-632-2003)

Illinois
  Chicago 60680 (536 S. Clark Street, P.O. Box 8136; local 312-663-5510, statewide 800-827-0466)

Indiana
  Indianapolis 46204 (575 N. Pennsylvania Street; local 317-226-5566, statewide 800-827-0634)

Iowa
  Des Moines 50309 (2600 Walnut Street; local 515-284-0219, statewide 800-362-2222)

Kansas
  Wichita 67218 (5500 E. Kellogg; local 316-264-9123, statewide 800-827-0445)

Kentucky
  Louisville 40202 (600 Martin Luther King, Jr. Place; local 502-584-2231, statewide 800-827-2050)

Louisiana
  New Orleans 70113 (701 Loyola Avenue; local 504-561-0121, statewide 800-462-9510. Direct dial from: Baton Rouge 504-343-5539, Shreveport 318-424-8442); Benefits Office: Shreveport 71130 (510 E. Stoner Avenue, 318-424-8442)   *(Continued)*

TABLE 14.10 (Continued)

VA Regional Offices

Maine

Togus 04330 (Route 17 East; local 207-623-8000, statewide 800-452-1935. Direct dial from Portland 207-775-6391)

Maryland

Baltimore 21201 (31 Hopkins Plaza, Federal Building; local 301-685-5454, other areas 800-492-9503); counties of Montgomery & Prince Georges served by Washington, D.C., RO 202-872-1151

Massachusetts

Boston 02203 (JFK Federal Building, Government Center; local 617-227-4600, other areas 800-392-6015. Direct dial from: Brockton 588-0764, Fitchburg/Leominster 342-8927, Lawrence 687-3332, Lowell 454-5463, Springfield 785-5343, Worcester 791-3595)

Towns of Fall River & New Bedford, counties of Barnstable, Dukes, Nantucket, Bristol, part of Plymouth served by Providence, R.I., RO 800-556-3893

Michigan

Detroit 48226 (Patrick V. McNamara Federal Building, 477 Michigan Ave.; local 313-964-5110, statewide 800-827-1996)

Minnesota

St. Paul 55111 (Federal Building, Fort Snelling; local 612-726-1454. Direct dial from: Duluth 722-4467, Rochester 288-5888, St. Cloud 253-9300). Counties of Becker, Beltrami, Clay, Clearwater, Kittson, Lake of the Woods, Mahnomen, Marshall, Norman, Otter Trail, Pennington, Polk, Red Lake, Roseau, Wilkin served by Fargo, N.D., RO 800-437-4668

Mississippi

Jackson 39269 (100 W. Capitol Street; local 601-965-4873, statewide 800-827-2028)

Missouri

St. Louis 63103 (Federal Building, 1520 Market Street; local 314-342-1171, statewide 800-392-3761); Benefits Office: Kansas City 64106 (Federal Office Building, 601 E. 12th St., 816-426-5763, 800-392-3761)

Montana

Fort Harrison 59636 (local: Fort Harrison/Helena 406-447-7975, statewide 800-332-6125. Direct dial from Great Falls 761-3215)

Nebraska

Lincoln 68516 (5631 S. 48th Street; local 402-437-5001, statewide 800-827-6544)

Nevada

Reno 89520 (1201 Terminal Way; local 702-329-9244, statewide 800-992-5740. Direct dial from Las Vegas 702-386-2921)

New Hampshire

Manchester 03101 (Norris Cotton Federal Building, 275 Chestnut Street; local 603-666-7785, statewide 800-562-5260)

New Jersey

Newark 07102 (20 Washington Place; local 201-645-2150, statewide 800-242-5867. Direct dial from: Clifton/Paterson/Passaic 472-9632, Long Branch/Asbury Park 870-2550, New Brunswick/Sayreville 828-5600)

New Mexico

Albuquerque 87102 (Dennis Chavez Federal Building, 500 Gold Avenue, S.W.; local 505-766-3361, statewide 800-432-6853)

New York

Buffalo 14202 (Federal Building, 111 W. Huron Street; local 716-846-5191, western New York areas 800-827-0619); Benefits Offices: Rochester 14614 (Federal Office Building & Courthouse, 100 State Street, 800-827-0619); Syracuse 13202 (344 W. Genesee St., 800-827-0619)

New York City 10001 (252 Seventh Avenue at 24th Street; local 212-620-6901; counties of Albany, Bronx, Clinton, Columbia, Delaware, Dutchess, Essex, Franklin, Fulton, Greene, Hamilton, Kings, Montgomery, Nassau, New York, Orange, Otsego, Putnam, Queens, Rensselaer, Richmond, Rockland, Saratoga, Schenectady, Scholharie, Suffolk, Sullivan, Ulster, Warren, Washington, Westchester 800-827-8954); Benefits Office: Albany 12207 (Leo W. O'Brian Federal Building, Clinton Avenue & N. Pearl Street, 800-827-8954)

North Carolina

Winston-Salem 27155 (Federal Building, 251 N. Main Street; local 919-748-1800, statewide 800-642-0841. Direct dial from Asheville 253-6861, Charlotte 375-9351, Durham 683-1367, Fayetteville 323-1261, Greensboro 274-1994, High Point 887-1202, Raleigh 821-1166)

North Dakota

Fargo 58102 (655 First Avenue North; 2101 North Elm Street—mail only, local 701-293-3656, statewide 800-342-4790)

Ohio

Cleveland 44199 (Anthony J. Celebrezze Federal Building, 1240 E. 9th Street; local 216-621-5050, statewide 800-827-8272); Benefits Offices: Cincinnati 45202 (Society Bank Center, Suite 210, 36 East 7th Street, 800-827-8272); Columbus 43215 (Federal Building, Room 309, 200 N. High Street, 800-827-8272)

(Continued)

TABLE 14.10 (Continued)

VA Regional Offices

Oklahoma

Muskogee 74401 (Federal Building, 125 S. Main Street; local 918-687-2500, statewide 800-827-2206); Benefits Office: Oklahoma City 73102 (200 N.W. 5th St., 800-827-2206)

Oregon

Portland 97204 (Federal Building, 1220 S.W. 3rd Avenue; local 503-326-2431, statewide 800-452-7276)

Pennsylvania

Philadelphia 19101 (RO & Insurance Center, P.O. Box 8079, 5000 Wissahickon Avenue; local 215-438-5225; counties of Adams, Berks, Bradford, Bucks, Cameron, Clinton, Columbia, Cumberland, Dauphin, Delaware, Franklin, Juniata, Lackawanna, Lancaster, Lebanon, Lehigh, Luzerne, Lycoming, Mifflin, Monroe, Montgomery, Montour, Northampton, Northumberland, Perry, Philadelphia, Pike, Potter, Schuylkill, Snyder, Sullivan, Susquehanna, Tioga, Union, Wayne, Wyoming, York 800-869-8387; recorded benefits information 215-951-5368, 24-hour availability); Benefits Office: Wilkes-Barre 18701 (19–27 N. Main Street, 800-869-8387) Pittsburgh 15222 (1000 Liberty Avenue; local 412-281-4233, other western Pennsylvania areas 800-242-0233)

Philippines

Manila 96528 (1311 Roxas Boulevard, APO San Francisco—air mail; local 810-521-7116; ext. 2577 or 2220; from U.S. 011632 521-7116, ext. 2577 or 2220)

Puerto Rico

San Juan 00936 (U.S. Courthouse & Federal Building, Carlos E. Chardon Street, Hato Rey, GPO Box 48567; local 809-766-5141, island-wide 800-462-4135. Direct dial from U.S. Virgin Islands 800-474-2976)

Rhode Island

Providence 02903 (380 Westminster Mall; local 401-273-4910, statewide 800-322-0230)

South Carolina

Columbia 29201 (1801 Assembly Street; local 803-765-5861, statewide 800-922-1000. Direct dial from Charleston 723-5581, Greenville 232-2457)

South Dakota

Sioux Falls 57117 (P.O. Box 5046, 2501 W. 22nd Street; local 605-336-3496, statewide 800-952-3550)

Tennessee

Nashville 37203 (110 9th Avenue South; local 615-736-5251, statewide 800-342-8330. Direct dial from: Chattanooga 267-6587, Knoxville 546-5700. Memphis 527-4583)

Texas

Houston 77054 (2515 Murworth Drive; local 713-664-4664, counties of Angelina, Aransas, Atacosa, Austin, Bandera, Bee, Bexar, Blanco, Brazoria, Brewster, Maverick, Medina, Menard, Montgomery, Nacogdoches, Newton, Nueces, Orange, Pecos, Polk, Real, Refugio, Sabine, San Augustine, San Jacinto, San Patrico, Schleicher, Shelby, Starr, Sutton, Terrell, Trinity, Tyler, Uvalde, Val Verde, Victoria, Walker, Waller, Washington, Webb, Wharton, Willacy, Wilson, Zapata, Zavala: 800-827-2021); Benefits Office: San Antonio 78229-2041 (3601 Bluemel Road, 512-225-5511, 800-827-2021)

Waco 76799 (1400 N. Valley Mills Drive, 817-772-3060; direct dial from Austin 477-5831, Dallas 824-5440, El Paso 545-2500, Ft. Worth 336-1641; Bowie County served by Little Rock, AR, RO, 800-643-5688. Other counties 800-792-3271); Benefits Offices: Dallas 75242 (U.S. Courthouse & Federal Office Building, 1100 Commerce Street, 214-824-5440); Fort Worth 76102 (819 Taylor Street, 817-336-1641); Lubbock 79401 (Federal Building, 1205 Texas Avenue, 800-792-3271)

Utah

Salt Lake City 84147 (P.O. Box 11500, Federal Building, 125 S. State Street; local 801-524-5960, statewide 800-662-9163. Direct dial from: Ogden 399-4433, Provo/Orem 375-2902)

Vermont

White River Junction 05001 (N. Hartland Road; local 802-296-5177, statewide 800-622-4134)

Virginia

Roanoke 24011 (210 Franklin Road, S.W.; local 703-982-6440; northern Virginia counties of Arlington and Fairfax, cities of Alexandria, Fairfax, Falls Church served by Washington, D.C., RO 202-872-1151. Other areas 800-827-2018)

Washington

Seattle 98174 (Federal Building, 915 2nd Avenue; local 206-624-7200, statewide 800-827-0638)

West Virginia

Huntington 25701 (640 Fourth Avenue; local 304-529-5720, statewide 800-827-2052; counties of Brooke, Hancock, Marshall, Ohio served by Pittsburgh Pa., RO)

Wisconsin

Milwaukee 53295 (5000 W. National Avenue, Building 6; local 414-383-8680, statewide 800-827-0464)

Wyoming

Cheyenne 82001 (2360 E. Pershing Boulevard; local 307-778-7396, statewide 800-442-2761)

✦ APPENDIX 1 ✦

Calculating Retirement Benefits

Make sure Uncle Sam is giving the right amount in your retirement checks. Table 1.3 (page 8) gives an estimate of what your benefits should be. But that's just an estimate. To be more exact, use Tables A, B, and C (pages 550–552).

Here's how to use Table A. Columns A, B, and D are already filled in for you; all you have to do is fill in Columns C and E.

1. In Column C, list your annual earnings for each year from 1951 to the present; if you plan to continue working, fill in estimated earnings for each future year. But in no instance should the earnings listed in Column C exceed the amount in Column B. For example, even if you earned $35,000 in 1980, list only $25,900 (from Column B) in Column C. For any year with no earnings, put a zero ($0) in Column C.

2. Multiply the amount in Column C by the appropriate number in Column D, and write the result in Column E. You see that Column D is broken down by year; select the number under the year in which you reached 62. For example, if you reached 62 in 1991, multiply the amounts in Column C by the numbers in the last subcolumn of D.

3. Look at Table B and find the number of years that count for your Social Security benefits.
   Write the number of years counted for your birth date here:_____.

4. Once you have found the appropriate number of years from Table B, go back to Column E of Table A and cross off the years with the lowest earnings until you have only the number of years corresponding to that from Table B. For example, if you were born in 1925, you would leave the highest 31 years of earnings listed in Column E, crossing out the rest.

5. Add all the earnings still showing in Column E. The total is _____.

6. Divide the total in line 5 by the number of years in line 3. The amount is _____.

7. Divide the number in line 6 by 12; the result is _____. That gives you your Average Indexed Monthly Earnings (AIME).

8. Take the AIME in line 7 and look at Table C to find the monthly retirement benefit you would receive if you retired at age 65.

Here's an example of how to figure your age 65 retirement benefit.

EXAMPLE

You were born in 1925 and reached 62 in 1987. You've been working steadily since you were a kid, earning the maximum for Social Security benefits. Your Average Earnings Worksheet (Table A) looks like this:

Worksheet for Average Earnings

(A) Year	(B) Maximum Annual Earnings	(C) Your Annual Income	(D) You Reach 62 in: 1987	(E) Indexed Earnings
1951	$ 3600	$ 3600	6.0	$21,600
1952	3600	3600	5.7	20,520
1953	3600	3600	5.4	19,440
1954	3600	3600	5.3	19,080
1955	4200	4200	5.1	21,420
1956	4200	4200	4.8	20,160
1957	4200	4200	4.6	19,320
1958	4200	4200	4.6	19,320
1959	4800	4800	4.4	21,120
1960	4800	4800	4.2	20,160
1961	4800	4800	4.1	19,680
1962	4800	4800	3.9	18,720
1963	4800	4800	3.8	18,240
1964	4800	4800	3.7	17,760
1965	4800	4800	3.6	17,280
1966	6600	6600	3.4	22,440
1967	6600	6600	3.2	21,120
1968	7800	7800	3.0	23,400
1969	7800	7800	2.9	22,620
1970	7800	7800	2.7	21,060
1971	7800	7800	2.6	20,280
1972	9000	9000	2.4	21,600
1973	10,800	10,800	2.2	23,760
1974	13,200	13,200	2.1	27,720
1975	14,100	14,100	1.9	26,790
1976	15,300	15,300	1.8	27,540

(A) Year	(B) Maximum Annual Earnings	(C) Your Annual Income	(D) You Reach 62 in: 1987	(E) Indexed Earnings
1977	$16,500	$16,500	1.7	$28,050
1978	17,700	17,700	1.6	28,320
1979	22,900	22,900	1.5	34,350
1980	25,900	25,900	1.3	33,670
1981	29,700	29,700	1.2	35,640
1982	32,400	32,400	1.2	38,880
1983	35,700	35,700	1.1	39,270
1984	37,800	37,800	1.0	37,800
1985	39,600	39,600	1.0	39,600
1986	42,000	42,000	1.0	42,000
1987	43,800	0	1.0	0
1988	45,000	0	1.0	0
1989	48,000	0	1.0	0
1990	51,300	0	1.0	0
1991	53,400	0	1.0	0
1992	55,000	0	1.0	0

Your AIME is $2,200. Adding the highest 31 years (from Table B) of Indexed Earnings from Column E (dropping 1954 and 1962 through 1965) totals $818,650. Dividing that by 31 gives $26,408, and dividing that by 12 gives $2,200. Table C shows that your age 65 monthly retirement benefit would be about $827.

By figuring your own monthly benefits using Tables A, B, and C, you'll be able to double-check the Government's figures. If you find that your calculation is a few dollars different from the Government's, don't get upset—remember, this book is only providing a way to get an estimate. But if your number is more than $20 higher, better call the Social Security office (800-772-1213)—you may be due for an increase!

TABLE A

Worksheet for Average Earnings

(A) Year	(B) Maximum Annual Earnings	(C) Your Annual Income	(D) You Reach 62 in: 1984	1985	1986	1987	1988	1989	1990	1991	1992	(E) Indexed Earnings
1951	$ 3600		5.2	5.4	5.8	6.0	6.2	6.6	6.9	7.2	7.5	
1952	3600		4.9	5.1	5.4	5.7	5.8	6.2	6.5	6.8	7.1	
1953	3600		4.6	4.9	5.1	5.4	5.5	5.8	6.2	6.4	6.7	
1954	3600		4.6	4.8	5.1	5.3	5.5	5.8	6.1	6.4	6.7	
1955	4200		4.4	4.6	4.9	5.1	5.2	5.6	5.9	6.1	6.4	
1956	4200		4.1	4.3	4.6	4.8	4.9	5.2	5.5	5.7	6.0	
1957	4200		4.0	4.2	4.4	4.6	4.8	5.1	5.3	5.5	5.8	
1958	4200		4.0	4.1	4.4	4.6	4.7	5.0	5.3	5.5	5.7	
1959	4800		3.8	4.0	4.2	4.4	4.5	4.8	5.0	5.2	5.5	
1960	4800		3.6	3.8	4.0	4.2	4.3	4.6	4.8	5.0	5.2	
1961	4800		3.6	3.7	3.9	4.1	4.2	4.5	4.7	4.9	5.1	
1962	4800		3.4	3.6	3.8	3.9	4.0	4.3	4.5	4.7	4.9	
1963	4800		3.3	3.5	3.7	3.8	3.9	4.2	4.4	4.6	4.8	
1964	4800		3.2	3.3	3.5	3.7	3.8	4.0	4.2	4.4	4.6	
1965	4800		3.1	3.3	3.5	3.6	3.7	3.9	4.2	4.3	4.5	
1966	6600		2.9	3.1	3.3	3.4	3.5	3.7	3.9	4.1	4.3	
1967	6600		2.8	2.9	3.1	3.2	3.3	3.5	3.7	3.9	4.0	
1968	7800		2.6	2.7	2.9	3.0	3.1	3.3	3.5	3.6	3.8	
1969	7800		2.5	2.6	2.7	2.9	2.9	3.1	3.3	3.4	3.6	
1970	7800		2.3	2.5	2.6	2.7	2.8	2.9	3.1	3.2	3.4	
1971	7800		2.2	2.3	2.5	2.6	2.7	2.8	3.0	3.1	3.2	
1972	9000		2.0	2.1	2.3	2.4	2.4	2.6	2.7	2.8	2.9	
1973	10,800		1.9	2.0	2.1	2.2	2.3	2.4	2.6	2.7	2.8	
1974	13,200		1.8	1.9	2.0	2.1	2.2	2.3	2.4	2.5	2.6	
1975	14,100		1.7	1.8	1.9	1.9	2.0	2.1	2.2	2.3	2.4	
1976	15,300		1.6	1.7	1.7	1.8	1.9	2.0	2.1	2.2	2.3	
1977	16,500		1.5	1.6	1.6	1.7	1.8	1.9	2.0	2.1	2.2	
1978	17,700		1.4	1.4	1.5	1.6	1.6	1.7	1.8	1.9	2.0	
1979	22,900		1.3	1.3	1.4	1.5	1.5	1.6	1.7	1.8	1.8	
1980	25,900		1.2	1.2	1.3	1.3	1.4	1.5	1.5	1.6	1.7	
1981	29,700		1.1	1.1	1.2	1.2	1.3	1.4	1.4	1.5	1.5	
1982	32,400		1.0	1.0	1.1	1.2	1.2	1.3	1.3	1.4	1.4	
1983	35,700		1.0	1.0	1.1	1.1	1.1	1.2	1.3	1.3	1.4	
1984	37,800		1.0	1.0	1.0	1.0	1.1	1.1	1.2	1.2	1.3	
1985	39,600		1.0	1.0	1.0	1.0	1.0	1.1	1.1	1.2	1.2	
1986	42,000		1.0	1.0	1.0	1.0	1.0	1.1	1.1	1.2	1.2	
1987	43,800		1.0	1.0	1.0	1.0	1.0	1.0	1.0	1.1	1.1	
1988	45,000		1.0	1.0	1.0	1.0	1.0	1.0	1.0	1.0	1.1	
1989	48,000		1.0	1.0	1.0	1.0	1.0	1.0	1.0	1.0	1.0	
1990	51,300		1.0	1.0	1.0	1.0	1.0	1.0	1.0	1.0	1.0	
1991	53,400		1.0	1.0	1.0	1.0	1.0	1.0	1.0	1.0	1.0	
1992	55,500		1.0	1.0	1.0	1.0	1.0	1.0	1.0	1.0	1.0	

Note: This Table can be used if most of your earnings were after 1951. But if most of your earnings were before 1951, call Social Security and ask about a special formula to use to calculate your retirement benefits—don't use this Table if most of your earnings are from before 1951.

TABLE B

Years Counted for Retirement Benefits

Year You Were Born	Years Counted	
	Male	Female
1908	17	14
1909	18	15
1910	19	16
1911	19	17
1912	19	18
1913	19	19
1914	20	20
1915	21	21
1916	22	22
1917	23	23
1918	24	24
1919	25	25
1920	26	26
1921	27	27
1922	28	28
1923	29	29
1924	30	30
1925	31	31
1926	32	32
1927	33	33
1928	34	34
1929 or later	35	35

TABLE C

Monthly Age 65 Full Retirement Benefit

Year in Which You Reach 62

AIME	1984	1985	1986	1987	1988	1989	1990	1991	1992
$ 300	$ 250	$ 258	$ 268	$ 270	$ 270	$ 270	$ 270	$ 270	$ 270
400	282	290	300	307	313	324	334	342	352
500	314	322	332	339	345	356	366	374	384
600	346	354	364	371	377	388	398	406	416
700	378	386	396	403	409	420	430	438	448
800	410	418	428	435	441	452	462	470	480
900	442	450	460	467	473	484	494	502	512
1000	474	482	492	499	505	516	526	534	544
1100	506	514	524	531	537	548	558	566	576
1200	538	546	556	563	569	580	590	598	608
1300	570	578	588	595	601	612	622	630	640
1400	602	610	620	627	633	644	654	662	672
1500	634	642	652	659	665	676	686	694	704
1600	666	674	684	691	697	708	718	726	736
1700	683	704	716	723	729	740	750	758	768
1800	698	719	746	755	761	772	782	790	800
1900	713	734	761	782	793	804	814	822	832
2000	728	749	776	797	811	836	846	854	864
2100	743	764	791	812	826	859	878	886	896
2200	758	779	806	827	841	874	901	918	928
2300	773	794	821	842	856	889	916	938	960
2400	788	809	836	857	871	904	931	953	981
2500	803	824	851	872	886	919	946	968	996
2600	818	839	866	887	901	934	961	983	1011
2700	833	854	881	902	916	949	976	998	1026
2800	848	869	891	917	931	964	991	1013	1041
2900	863	884	911	932	946	979	1006	1028	1056
3000	878	899	926	947	961	994	1021	1043	1071
3500	953	974	1001	1022	1036	1069	1096	1118	1146
4000	1028	1049	1076	1097	1111	1144	1171	1193	1221
4500	1103	1124	1151	1172	1186	1219	1246	1268	1296

The amounts computed using Table C will go up with cost of living increases.

*For survivor benefits, use the year in which the deceased reached age 62; for disability benefits, use the year you became eligible for disability benefits.

✦ APPENDIX 2 ✦

Special Minimum Benefit

The Special Minimum Benefits Rule can add to your regular retirement benefits. Table A shows how to figure the Special Minimum Benefit.

TABLE A

Calculating Special Minimum Benefit

1. Add up your income for each year from 1937 through 1950 and divide the total by $900. This provides the number of points you get for purposes of this calculation (14 points is the most anyone is allowed for work through 1950).

2. For work after 1950, you get one point for each year in which you earned at least the following amounts (up to a maximum of 30 points):

Year	Earnings	Year	Earnings
1951–1954	$ 900	1979	$4725
1955–1958	1050	1980	5100
1959–1965	1200	1981	5550
1966–1967	1650	1982	6075
1968–1971	1950	1983	6675
1972	2250	1984	7050
1973	2700	1985	7425
1974	3300	1986	7875
1975	3525	1987	8175
1976	3825	1988	8400
1977	4125	1989	8925
1978	4425	1990	9525
		1991	9900

3. Take your total points from 1 and 2 above and check the amount of your Special Minimum Benefits listed on the next page.

Points	Special Benefits Payable in 1992
11	$23.80
12	47.50
13	71.60
14	95.50
15	119.40
16	143.30
17	167.20
18	191.20
19	215.10
20	238.90
21	263.10
22	286.80
23	310.90
24	334.80
25	358.60
26	382.80
27	406.70
28	430.40
29	454.30
30 or more	478.20

(Amounts will increase slightly each year.)

Here's how the table works. Let's take the same facts as in the example in Appendix 1. From 1945 through 1950, you earned $4,500. Plugging into item 1 above, you get five points ($4,500 divided by $900 equals 5) for work through 1950.

From 1951 through 1975, you earned at least the amounts listed in item 2 above. So you get one point for each of the 25 years after 1950 that you worked.

Your total points from items 1 and 2 are 30. Using Table A, you find that with 30 points, your Special Minimum Benefits should be $478 a month. Your Social Security retirement checks should be *no less* than this.

✦ APPENDIX 3 ✦

Calculating Spouse Retirement Benefit

You should understand how much you're entitled to if you're eligible for benefits on both your own work record and your spouse's record. Table A explains how to calculate your benefit so you can make sure you're receiving the right amount.

TABLE A

Calculate Your Benefit

1. Your spouse's full age 65 retirement benefit is $_____.

2. One-half of line 1 is $_____.

3. Your full age 65 retirement benefit is $_____.

4. Subtracting line 3 from line 2 equals $_____.

5. When you take spouse benefits, you are _____ months under 65.

6. Multiplying line 5 by .694% equals _____%.

7. Subtracting line 6 from 100% equals _____%.

8. Multiplying line 7 by line 4 equals $_____.

9. The amount of your own benefit which you would be entitled to receive is $_____.

10. Adding lines 8 and 9 equals $_____.

Let's look at an example to illustrate how to figure your spouse benefit.

EXAMPLE

You and your spouse are both 62; your spouse has just retired, and now it's your turn. Your spouse's age 65 retirement benefit is $800/month and yours is $300/month. He'll take his retirement benefit of $640/month (80% of $800). How much do you receive?

1. Your husband's age 65 retirement benefit is $\underline{\$800}$.
2. One-half is $\underline{\$400}$.
3. Your age 65 retirement benefit is $\underline{\$300}$.
4. Subtracting line 3 from line 2 equals $\underline{\$100}$.
5. When your husband retires, you are $\underline{36}$ months under age 65.
6. Multiplying 36 by .694% equals $\underline{25\%}$.
7. Subtracting 25% from 100% equals $\underline{75\%}$.
8. Multiplying 75% by $100 equals $\underline{\$75}$.
9. The amount of your own benefit which you would be entitled to receive is $\underline{\$240}$ (80% of $300).
10. Adding $75 and $240 equals $\underline{\$315}$.

You would be entitled to receive a spouse retirement benefit of $315/month.

✦ APPENDIX 4 ✦

Calculating the Maximum Family Benefit

For a worker reaching age 62 or dying in 1992, the Maximum Family Benefit ("MFB") is calculated by adding:

150% of the first $495 of full age 65 retirement benefits

+

272% of the next $219 of full age 65 retirement benefits

+

134% of the next $217 of full age 65 retirement benefits

+

175% of the rest.

These numbers will be increased slightly each year.

For disabled workers, the MFB is calculated somewhat differently. It is the lesser of

- 85 percent of the worker's Average Indexed Monthly Earnings
- 150 percent of his full age 65 retirement benefit

But the MFB for a disabled worker's family can never be less than 100 percent of his full retirement benefit.

✦ APPENDIX 5 ✦

Calculating Survivor Benefits

Your Social Security survivor benefits are based on your late spouse's (or your late parent's or child's) work record. Use Tables A and B to check the Government's calculation of his full age 65 retirement benefit.

Here's how to use Table A. Columns A, B, and D are already filled in for you; all you have to do is fill in Columns C and E.

1. In Column C, list the deceased's annual earnings for each year from 1951 to the present. But in no instance should the earnings listed in Column C exceed the amount in Column B. For example, even if the deceased earned $35,000 in 1980, list only $25,900 (from Column B) in Column C. For any year with no earnings, put a zero ($0) in Column C.

2. Multiply the amount in Column C by the appropriate number in Column D, and write the result in Column E. You see that Column D is broken down by year; select the number under the year in which the deceased reached 62. For example, if your late spouse reached 62 in 1992, multiply the amounts in Column C by the numbers in the last subcolumn of D.

3. Use Table B below to find the number of years that will count for your Social Security survivor benefits.

4. Once you have found the appropriate number of years from Table B, go back to Column E of Table A and cross off the years with the lowest earnings until you have only the number of years corresponding to that from Table B.

5. Add all the earnings still showing in Column E. The total is _____.

6. Divide the total in line 5 by the number of years in line 3. The amount is _____.

7. Divide the number in line 6 by 12; the result is _____. That gives you the deceased's Average Indexed Monthly Earnings (AIME).

8. Take the AIME in line 7 and look back at Table C of Appendix 1 to find the deceased's full age 65 retirement benefit. (Use the year in which the deceased reached age 62.)

TABLE A

Worksheet for Average Earnings

(A) Year	(B) Maximum Annual Earnings	(C) Deceased's Annual Income	(D) Deceased Reached 62 in:									(E) Indexed Earnings
			1984	1985	1986	1987	1988	1989	1990	1991	1992	
1951	$ 3600		5.2	5.4	5.8	6.0	6.2	6.6	6.9	7.2	7.5	
1952	3600		4.9	5.1	5.4	5.7	5.8	6.2	6.5	6.8	7.1	
1953	3600		4.6	4.9	5.1	5.4	5.5	5.8	6.2	6.4	6.7	
1954	3600		4.6	4.8	5.1	5.3	5.5	5.8	6.1	6.4	6.7	
1955	4200		4.4	4.6	4.9	5.1	5.2	5.6	5.9	6.1	6.4	
1956	4200		4.1	4.3	4.6	4.8	4.9	5.2	5.5	5.7	6.0	
1957	4200		4.0	4.2	4.4	4.6	4.8	5.1	5.3	5.5	5.8	
1958	4200		4.0	4.1	4.4	4.6	4.7	5.0	5.3	5.5	5.7	
1959	4800		3.8	4.0	4.2	4.4	4.5	4.8	5.0	5.2	5.5	
1960	4800		3.6	3.8	4.0	4.2	4.3	4.6	4.8	5.0	5.2	
1961	4800		3.6	3.7	3.9	4.1	4.2	4.5	4.7	4.9	5.1	
1962	4800		3.4	3.6	3.8	3.9	4.0	4.3	4.5	4.7	4.9	
1963	4800		3.3	3.5	3.7	3.8	3.9	4.2	4.4	4.6	4.8	
1964	4800		3.2	3.3	3.5	3.7	3.8	4.0	4.2	4.4	4.6	
1965	4800		3.1	3.3	3.5	3.6	3.7	3.9	4.2	4.3	4.5	
1966	6600		2.9	3.1	3.3	3.4	3.5	3.7	3.9	4.1	4.3	
1967	6600		2.8	2.9	3.1	3.2	3.3	3.5	3.7	3.9	4.0	
1968	7800		2.6	2.7	2.9	3.0	3.1	3.3	3.5	3.6	3.8	
1969	7800		2.5	2.6	2.7	2.9	2.9	3.1	3.3	3.4	3.6	
1970	7800		2.3	2.5	2.6	2.7	2.8	2.9	3.1	3.2	3.4	
1971	7800		2.2	2.3	2.5	2.6	2.7	2.8	3.0	3.1	3.2	
1972	9000		2.0	2.1	2.3	2.4	2.4	2.6	2.7	2.8	2.9	
1973	10,800		1.9	2.0	2.1	2.2	2.3	2.4	2.6	2.7	2.8	
1974	13,200		1.8	1.9	2.0	2.1	2.2	2.3	2.4	2.5	2.6	
1975	14,100		1.7	1.8	1.9	1.9	2.0	2.1	2.2	2.3	2.4	
1976	15,300		1.6	1.7	1.7	1.8	1.9	2.0	2.1	2.2	2.3	
1977	16,500		1.5	1.6	1.6	1.7	1.8	1.9	2.0	2.1	2.2	
1978	17,700		1.4	1.4	1.5	1.6	1.6	1.7	1.8	1.9	2.0	
1979	22,900		1.3	1.3	1.4	1.5	1.5	1.6	1.7	1.8	1.8	
1980	25,900		1.2	1.2	1.3	1.3	1.4	1.5	1.5	1.6	1.7	
1981	29,700		1.1	1.1	1.2	1.2	1.3	1.4	1.4	1.5	1.5	
1982	32,400		1.0	1.0	1.1	1.2	1.2	1.3	1.3	1.4	1.4	
1983	35,700		1.0	1.0	1.1	1.1	1.1	1.2	1.3	1.3	1.4	
1984	37,800		1.0	1.0	1.0	1.0	1.1	1.1	1.2	1.2	1.3	
1985	39,600		1.0	1.0	1.0	1.0	1.0	1.1	1.1	1.2	1.2	
1986	42,000		1.0	1.0	1.0	1.0	1.0	1.1	1.1	1.2	1.2	
1987	43,800		1.0	1.0	1.0	1.0	1.0	1.0	1.0	1.1	1.1	
1988	45,000		1.0	1.0	1.0	1.0	1.0	1.0	1.0	1.0	1.1	
1989	48,000		1.0	1.0	1.0	1.0	1.0	1.0	1.0	1.0	1.0	
1990	51,300		1.0	1.0	1.0	1.0	1.0	1.0	1.0	1.0	1.0	
1991	53,400		1.0	1.0	1.0	1.0	1.0	1.0	1.0	1.0	1.0	
1992	55,500		1.0	1.0	1.0	1.0	1.0	1.0	1.0	1.0	1.0	

Note: This table can be used if most of the deceased's earnings were after 1951. But if most of the deceased's earnings were before 1951, call Social Security and ask about a special formula to use to calculate your survivor benefits.

TABLE B

Years of Earnings Counted for Survivor Benefits

1. Go back to Table 2.2, Line 7, and get the number of credits needed to *qualify* for survivor benefits. The number is _____.

2. Subtract 5 from the number in line 1 above. The result is _____.

3. If the result in line 2 is less than 2, write 2 here; if the result in line 2 is more than 2, write the result in line 2 here: _____.

This gives the number of years to be counted in figuring the deceased's AIME.

By figuring the deceased's full age 65 retirement benefit, or at least a close estimate, you'll be able to double-check the Government's computers. If you find that your calculation is a few dollars different from Social Security's, don't get upset—remember, this book is only providing a way to get an estimate. But if your number is more than $20 higher, better call the Social Security office (800-772-1213)—you may be due for more money.

✦ APPENDIX 6 ✦

Checklist of Important Documents and Information for Application

_____ Proof of your age*

_____ Proof of spouse's age

_____ Certified copy of your marriage certificate (if applying for spouse retirement or life insurance)

_____ Copy of your latest income tax withholding statement (Form W-2), or federal income tax returns if self-employed

_____ Tax return of deceased child if you are applying as dependent parent

_____ Your checkbook or savings passbook if you want to have your benefits deposited directly into your account

_____ Certified copy of birth certificate of each child for whom a benefit is sought

_____ Certified copy of adoption order (if a child is adopted)

_____ Death certificate of worker who dies

_____ Receipt for funeral bill if someone other than a spouse claims lump-sum life insurance payment

_____ Divorce papers (where applicable)

_____ Military discharge papers

_____ Your Social Security number (or card)

_____ Your spouse's Social Security number (or card)

_____ Social Security numbers (or cards) for anyone else for whom a claim is being filed

_____ An estimate of your expected earnings for this current year

_____ Dates of any railroad employment of you or your spouse

_____ Names and addresses of school, and dates of schooling, for any child who is between the ages 18 and 22 and eligible for benefits

*For proof of age, you must have a *certified copy* of your birth certificate *or* baptismal certificate (that was recorded before age 5) if it exists. Social Security won't take regular photocopies. If *neither exists,* then locate at least two documents that show your name and age. Usually records established early in life are best. Some records you might use are:

- delayed birth certificate
- child's birth certificate (showing your age)
- family bible with birth dates
- immigration or naturalization record
- hospital record
- labor union or employer record
- insurance policy
- school record
- state or federal census record
- passport

✦ APPENDIX 7 ✦

The Grids

Tables A, B, and C which follow are excerpted from the Government Grids used to determine disability. Terms included in the three tables are defined as follows:

- *Limited education*—generally means you have completed up to 7th through 11th grade of formal education. Some ability in reasoning, arithmetic, and language skills, but not enough to handle semiskilled or skilled jobs.

- *Marginal education*—generally means less than 7th grade of formal education.

- *Unskilled work*—generally needs little or no judgment to do simple duties that can be learned on the job within 30 days. Includes, for example, placing materials in or removing materials from automatic machines. Unskilled work gives you no skills that could be transferred to another job.

- *Semiskilled work*—requires some skills for activities that are less complex than skilled work but more than unskilled work. May require: alertness and close attention to watching machine processes, inspections and testing; guarding equipment, property, or persons against damage or injury.

- *Skilled work*—requires independent judgment. For example, skilled work may require laying out items; estimating quality; determining suitability and quantities of materials; making precise measurements; reading blueprints; making computations or mechanical adjustments; or dealing with people, facts, figures, or abstract ideas. The skills take at least 30 days, and often more, to learn.

- *Transferable skills*—skills learned on one job that can be used to meet the requirements of other jobs. In looking to whether skills are transferable, the Government will consider whether a similar degree of skill is required in the new job; similar tools and machines are used; and similar raw materials, products, processes or services are involved.

TABLE A

Disability Determination Where Capacity Limited to Sedentary Work

Age	Education	Previous Work Experience	Disabled or Not Disabled
55 or over	Limited or less	Unskilled or none	Disabled
55 or over	Limited or less	Skilled or semiskilled—skills not transferable	Disabled
55 or over	Limited or less	Skilled or semiskilled—skills transferable	Not disabled
55 or over	High school graduate or more—does not provide for direct entry into skilled work	Unskilled or none	Disabled
55 or over	High school graduate or more—provides for direct entry into skilled work	Unskilled or none	Not disabled
55 or over	High school graduate or more—does not provide for direct entry into skilled work	Skilled or semiskilled—skills not transferable	Disabled
55 or over	High school graduate or more—does not provide for direct entry into skilled work	Skilled or semiskilled—skills transferable	Not disabled
55 or over	High school graduate or more—provides for direct entry into skilled work	Skilled or semiskilled—skills not transferable	Not disabled
50–54	Limited or less	Unskilled or none	Disabled
50–54	Limited or less	Skilled or semiskilled—skills not transferable	Disabled
50–54	Limited or less	Skilled or semiskilled—skills transferable	Not disabled
50–54	High school graduate or more—does not provide for direct entry into skilled work	Unskilled or none	Disabled
50–54	High school graduate or more—provides for direct entry into skilled work	Unskilled or none	Not disabled
50–54	High school graduate or more—does not provide for direct entry into skilled work	Skilled or semiskilled—skills not transferable	Disabled

Age	Education	Previous Work Experience	Disabled or Not Disabled
50–54	High school graduate or more —does not provide for direct entry into skilled work	Skilled or semiskilled— skills transferable	Not disabled
50–54	High school graduate or more —provides for direct entry into skilled work	Skilled or semiskilled— skills not transferable	Not disabled

TABLE B

Disability Determination Where Capacity Limited to Light Work

Age	Education	Previous Work Experience	Decision
55 or over	Limited or less	Unskilled or none	Disabled
55 or over	Limited or less	Skilled or semiskilled— skills not transferable	Disabled
55 or over	Limited or less	Skilled or semiskilled— skills transferable	Not disabled
55 or over	High school graduate or more —does not provide for direct entry into skilled work	Unskilled or none	Disabled
55 or over	High school graduate or more —provides for direct entry into skilled work	Unskilled or none	Not disabled
55 or over	High school graduate or more —does not provide for direct entry into skilled work	Skilled or semiskilled— skills not transferable	Disabled
55 or over	High school graduate or more —does not provide for direct entry into skilled work	Skilled or semiskilled— skills transferable	Not disabled
55 or over	High school graduate or more —provides for direct entry into skilled work	Skilled or semiskilled— skills not transferable	Not disabled
50–54	Illiterate or unable to speak in English	Unskilled or none	Disabled
50–54	Limited or less—at least literate and able to communicate in English	Unskilled or none	Not disabled

(*Continued*)

Disability Determination Where Capacity Limited to Light Work (Continued)

Age	Education	Previous Work Experience	Decision
50–54	Limited or less	Skilled or semiskilled— skills not transferable	Not disabled
50–54	Limited or less	Skilled or semiskilled— skills transferable	Not disabled
50–54	High school graduate or more	Unskilled or none	Not disabled
50–54	High school graduate or more	Skilled or semiskilled— skills not transferable	Not disabled
50–54	High school graduate or more	Skilled or semiskilled— skills transferable	Not disabled

TABLE C

Disability Determination Where Capacity Limited to Medium Work

Age	Education	Previous Work Experience	Decision
60 or older	Marginal or none	Unskilled or none	Disabled
60 or older	Limited or less	None	Disabled
60 or older	Limited	Unskilled	Not disabled
60 or older	Limited or less	Skilled or semiskilled— skills not transferable	Not disabled
60 or older	Limited or less	Skilled or semiskilled— skills transferable	Not disabled
60 or older	High school graduate or more	Unskilled or none	Not disabled
60 or older	High school graduate or more —does not provide for direct entry into skilled work	Skilled or semiskilled— skills not transferable	Not disabled
60 or older	High school graduate or more —does not provide for direct entry into skilled work	Skilled or semiskilled— skills transferable	Not disabled
60 or older	High school graduate or more —provides for direct entry into skilled work	Skilled or semiskilled— skills not transferable	Not disabled
55–59	Limited or less	None	Disabled
55–59	Limited or less	Unskilled	Not disabled
55–59	Limited or less	Skilled or semiskilled— skills not transferable	Not disabled

Age	Education	Previous Work Experience	Decision
55–59	Limited or less	Skilled or semiskilled—skills transferable	Not disabled
55–59	High school graduate or more	Unskilled or none	Not disabled
55–59	High school graduate or more—does not provide for direct entry into skilled work	Skilled or semiskilled—skills not transferable	Not disabled
55–59	High school graduate or more—does not provide for direct entry into skilled work	Skilled or semiskilled—skills transferable	Not disabled
55–59	High school graduate or more—provides for direct entry into skilled work	Skilled or semiskilled—skills not transferable	Not disabled
50–54	Limited or less	Unskilled or none	Not disabled
50–54	Limited or less	Skilled or semiskilled—skills not transferable	Not disabled
50–54	Limited or less	Skilled or semiskilled—skills transferable	Not disabled
50–54	High school graduate or more	Unskilled or none	Not disabled
50–54	High school graduate or more—does not provide for direct entry into skilled work	Skilled or semiskilled—skills not transferable	Not disabled
50–54	High school graduate or more—does not provide for direct entry into skilled work	Skilled or semiskilled—skills transferable	Not disabled
50–54	High school graduate or more—provides for direct entry into skilled work	Skilled or semiskilled—skills not transferable	Not disabled

✦ APPENDIX 8 ✦

Calculating Disability Benefits

Calculating Social Security disability benefits is similar—but not identical—to figuring Social Security retirement benefits. Use the following Tables A and B to calculate your benefits.

TABLE A

Worksheet for Average Earnings

(A) Year	(B) Maximum Annual Earnings	(C) Your Annual Income	(D) You Become Eligible for Disability Benefits in:									(E) Indexed Earnings
			1984	1985	1986	1987	1988	1989	1990	1991	1992	
1951	$ 3600		5.2	5.4	5.8	6.0	6.2	6.6	6.9	7.2	7.5	
1952	3600		4.9	5.1	5.4	5.7	5.8	6.2	6.5	6.8	7.1	
1953	3600		4.6	4.9	5.1	5.4	5.5	5.8	6.2	6.4	6.7	
1954	3600		4.6	4.8	5.1	5.3	5.5	5.8	6.1	6.4	6.7	
1955	4200		4.4	4.6	4.9	5.1	5.2	5.6	5.9	6.1	6.4	
1956	4200		4.1	4.3	4.6	4.8	4.9	5.2	5.5	5.7	6.0	
1957	4200		4.0	4.2	4.4	4.6	4.8	5.1	5.3	5.5	5.8	
1958	4200		4.0	4.1	4.4	4.6	4.7	5.0	5.3	5.5	5.7	
1959	4800		3.8	4.0	4.2	4.4	4.5	4.8	5.0	5.2	5.5	
1960	4800		3.6	3.8	4.0	4.2	4.3	4.6	4.8	5.0	5.2	
1961	4800		3.6	3.7	3.9	4.1	4.2	4.5	4.7	4.9	5.1	
1962	4800		3.4	3.6	3.8	3.9	4.0	4.3	4.5	4.7	4.9	
1963	4800		3.3	3.5	3.7	3.8	3.9	4.2	4.4	4.6	4.8	
1964	4800		3.2	3.3	3.5	3.7	3.8	4.0	4.2	4.4	4.6	
1965	4800		3.1	3.3	3.5	3.6	3.7	3.9	4.2	4.3	4.5	
1966	6600		2.9	3.1	3.3	3.4	3.5	3.7	3.9	4.1	4.3	
1967	6600		2.8	2.9	3.1	3.2	3.3	3.5	3.7	3.9	4.0	
1968	7800		2.6	2.7	2.9	3.0	3.1	3.3	3.5	3.6	3.8	
1969	7800		2.5	2.6	2.7	2.9	2.9	3.1	3.3	3.4	3.6	
1970	7800		2.3	2.5	2.6	2.7	2.8	2.9	3.1	3.2	3.4	

(A) Year	(B) Maximum Annual Earnings	(C) Your Annual Income	(D) You Become Eligible for Disability Benefits in:									(E) Indexed Earnings
			1984	1985	1986	1987	1988	1989	1990	1991	1992	
1971	7800		2.2	2.3	2.5	2.6	2.7	2.8	3.0	3.1	3.2	
1972	9000		2.0	2.1	2.3	2.4	2.4	2.6	2.7	2.8	2.9	
1973	10,800		1.9	2.0	2.1	2.2	2.3	2.4	2.6	2.7	2.8	
1974	13,200		1.8	1.9	2.0	2.1	2.2	2.3	2.4	2.5	2.6	
1975	14,100		1.7	1.8	1.9	1.9	2.0	2.1	2.2	2.3	2.4	
1976	15,300		1.6	1.7	1.7	1.8	1.9	2.0	2.1	2.2	2.3	
1977	16,500		1.5	1.6	1.6	1.7	1.8	1.9	2.0	2.1	2.2	
1978	17,700		1.4	1.4	1.5	1.6	1.6	1.7	1.8	1.9	2.0	
1979	22,900		1.3	1.3	1.4	1.5	1.5	1.6	1.7	1.8	1.8	
1980	25,900		1.2	1.2	1.3	1.3	1.4	1.5	1.5	1.6	1.7	
1981	29,700		1.1	1.1	1.2	1.2	1.3	1.4	1.4	1.5	1.5	
1982	32,400		1.0	1.0	1.1	1.2	1.2	1.3	1.3	1.4	1.4	
1983	35,700		1.0	1.0	1.1	1.1	1.1	1.2	1.3	1.3	1.4	
1984	37,800		1.0	1.0	1.0	1.0	1.1	1.1	1.2	1.2	1.3	
1985	39,600		1.0	1.0	1.0	1.0	1.0	1.1	1.1	1.2	1.2	
1986	42,000		1.0	1.0	1.0	1.0	1.0	1.1	1.1	1.2	1.2	
1987	43,800		1.0	1.0	1.0	1.0	1.0	1.0	1.0	1.1	1.1	
1988	45,000		1.0	1.0	1.0	1.0	1.0	1.0	1.0	1.0	1.1	
1989	48,000		1.0	1.0	1.0	1.0	1.0	1.0	1.0	1.0	1.0	
1990	51,300		1.0	1.0	1.0	1.0	1.0	1.0	1.0	1.0	1.0	
1991	53,400		1.0	1.0	1.0	1.0	1.0	1.0	1.0	1.0	1.0	
1992	55,500		1.0	1.0	1.0	1.0	1.0	1.0	1.0	1.0	1.0	

Note: This table can be used if most of your earnings were after 1951. But if most of your earnings were before 1951, call Social Security and ask about a special formula to use to calculate your disability benefits.

Here's how to use Table A. Columns A, B, and D are already filled in for you; all you have to do is fill in Columns C and E.

1. In Column C, list your annual earnings for each year from 1951 to the present. In no instance should the earnings listed in Column C exceed the amount in Column B. For example, even if you earned $35,000 in 1980, list only $25,900 (from Column B) in Column C. For any year with no earnings, put a zero ($0) in Column C.
2. Multiply the amount in Column C by the appropriate number in Column D and write the result in Column E. You see that Column D is broken down by year; select the number under the year in which you became eligible for disability benefits. For example, if you became eligible in 1992, multiply the amounts in Column C by the numbers in the last subcolumn of D.

3. Look at Table B and find the number of years which will count for your Social Security disability benefits. The number is _____.

4. Once you have found the appropriate number of years from Table B, go back to Column E of Table A and cross off the years with the lowest earnings until you have only the number of years from Table B.

5. Add all the earnings still showing in Column E. The total is _____.

6. Divide the total in line 5 by the number of years in line 3. The amount is _____.

7. Divide the number in line 6 by 12; the result is _____. That gives you your Average Indexed Monthly Earnings (AIME).

8. Take the AIME in line 7 and look at Table C in Appendix 1 to find the amount of your monthly disability benefit. (Use the year you became eligible for disability benefits.)

If you find that your calculation is a few dollars different from the Government's, don't get upset—remember, this book is only providing a way to get an estimate. But if your number is more than $20 higher, better call the Social Security office (800-772-1213)—you may be due for more money.

TABLE B

Years Counted for Disability Benefits

1. Go back to Table 3.1 and find the number of credits you need to qualify for disability benefits. The number is _____.

2. Calculate the reduction number:

If You Become Disabled at Age	The Reduction Number Is
Under age 27	0
Age 27–31	1
Age 32–36	2
Age 37–41	3
Age 42–46	4
Age 47 or older	5

3. The number of credits in line 1 minus the reduction number in line 2 is _____, the number of years counted. (The number may be slightly different if you were disabled before age 37 with young kids at home.)

✦ APPENDIX 9 ✦

Social Security Disability Questionnaire

PERSONAL HISTORY

Name:_____ Social Security No. _____

Maiden and prior married names: _____ When? _____

Address:_____

Number & Street   City   State   Zip

Phone: (___)_____ - _____ Date of birth: _____

Height: _____ Weight: _____ Right or left handed: _____

Present marital status: _____ Spouse's name: _____

Spouse's Social Security No. _____

Previously Married to: From When to When:

_____   _____

_____   _____

_____   _____

Children's name(s) &

birthdates: _____

_____

Other dependents: _____

Military (branch & dates): _____

EDUCATIONAL HISTORY

Highest grade completed: _____ Where: _____

GED: ____ yes ____ no   Vocational: ____ yes ____ no   (If yes, describe:)

_____

_____

Other education or training (please describe):

_____

_____

Can you read? _____ yes _____ not well _____ no

If so, check if you can read:

_____ newspapers _____ magazines _____ comic books _____ novels

_____ technical journals _____ other (describe)

Can you write? _____ yes _____ not well _____ no

If so, check if you can write:

_____ letters _____ grocery lists _____ checks

Can you do math? _____ yes _____ not well _____ no

If so, check if you can:

_____ make change _____ manage own finances

SOCIAL SECURITY HISTORY

Local Social Security office: _____

Applied for disability benefits before? _____

When? _____

Nature of disability: _____

Received disability benefits before? _____ When? _____

Nature of disability: _____

EMPLOYMENT HISTORY

Dates of last employment—from _____ to _____

Occupation: _____

Last employer: _____ Address: _____

Salary before leaving: $ _____ per _____

Reasons for leaving: _____

_____

Job demands (such as lifting, bending, pushing, pulling, carrying, hours, special tools or equipment, etc.): _____

_____

Supervisory responsibility? _____ yes _____ no (if yes, describe)

_____

Any medical leaves of absence? _____

   If so, when and why? _____

For each other employer for the past 15 years, starting with the most recent and working backwards, state:

Employer: _____ Address: _____

Dates of employment: _____ Salary: $_____ per _____

Reasons for leaving: _____

_____

Occupation: _____

Job demands: _____

_____

Supervisory responsibility? _____ yes _____ no (if yes, describe)

_____

Any medical leaves of absence? _____

    If so, when and why? _____

Employer: _____ Address: _____

Dates of employment: _____ Salary: $_____ per _____

Reasons for leaving: _____

_____

Occupation: _____

Job demands: _____

_____

Supervisory responsibility? _____ yes _____ no (if yes, describe)

_____

Any medical leaves of absence? _____

    If so, when and why? _____

Employer: _____ Address: _____

Dates of employment: _____ Salary: $_____ per _____

Reasons for leaving: _____

_____

Occupation: _____

Job demands: _____

_____

Supervisory responsibility? _____ yes _____ no (if yes, describe)

_____

Any medical leaves of absence? _____

    If so, when and why? _____

MEDICAL DISABILITY HISTORY

Description of disability:_____
_____
_____

PHYSICIANS (for the past five years)

Name:_____ Phone no.: _____
Address:_____
      Street   City   State   Zip
Date first seen:_____ Date last seen: _____
Type of treatment(s):_____
_____

Name:_____ Phone no.: _____
Address:_____
      Street   City   State   Zip
Date first seen:_____ Date last seen: _____
Type of treatment(s):_____
_____

Name:_____Phone no.:_____
Address:_____
      Street   City   State   Zip
Date first seen:_____Date last seen:_____
Type of treatment(s):_____
_____

Name:_____ Phone no.: _____
Address:_____
      Street   City   State   Zip
Date first seen:_____ Date last seen: _____
Type of treatment(s):_____
_____

Name:_____ Phone no.: _____
Address:_____
      Street   City   State   Zip
Date first seen:_____ Date last seen: _____
Type of treatment(s):_____
_____

Name:_____ Phone no.: _____
Address:_____
      Street   City   State   Zip

Date first seen: _____ Date last seen: _____

Type of treatment(s): _____

_____

Name: _____ Phone no.: _____

Address: _____
        Street   City   State   Zip

Date first seen: _____ Date last seen: _____

Type of treatment(s): _____

_____

HOSPITALS/CLINICS (for the past five years)

Name: _____ Dates: _____ to _____

Address: _____
        Street   City   State   Zip

_____ Inpatient _____ Outpatient _____ Emergency room

Reason for visit: _____

Doctor in charge (if known): _____

Name: _____ Dates: _____ to _____

Address: _____
        Street   City   State   Zip

_____ Inpatient _____ Outpatient _____ Emergency room

Reason for visit: _____

Doctor in charge (if known): _____

Name: _____ Dates: _____ to _____

Address: _____
        Street   City   State   Zip

_____ Inpatient _____ Outpatient _____ Emergency room

Reason for visit: _____

Doctor in charge (if known): _____

Name: _____ Dates: _____ to _____

Address: _____
        Street   City   State   Zip

_____ Inpatient _____ Outpatient _____ Emergency room

Reason for visit: _____

Doctor in charge (if known): _____

Name: _____ Dates: _____ to _____

Address: _____
        Street   City   State   Zip

_____ Inpatient _____ Outpatient _____ Emergency room

Reason for visit: _____

Doctor in charge (if known): _____

CURRENT MEDICATIONS

Drug:_____ Dosage:_____ Times per day:_____

Reason:_____ When first prescribed: _____

Who prescribed:_____

Side effects:_____
       (dizzy, nervous, tired, nauseous, can't sleep, etc.)

Drug:_____ Dosage:_____ Times per day:_____

Reason:_____ When first prescribed: _____

Who prescribed:_____

Side effects:_____
       (dizzy, nervous, tired, nauseous, can't sleep, etc.)

Drug:_____ Dosage:_____ Times per day:_____

Reason:_____ When first prescribed: _____

Who prescribed:_____

Side effects:_____
       (dizzy, nervous, tired, nauseous, can't sleep, etc.)

Drug:_____ Dosage:_____ Times per day:_____

Reason:_____ When first prescribed: _____

Who prescribed:_____

Side effects:_____
       (dizzy, nervous, tired, nauseous, can't sleep, etc.)

Drug:_____ Dosage:_____ Times per day:_____

Reason:_____ When first prescribed: _____

Who prescribed:_____

Side effects:_____
       (dizzy, nervous, tired, nauseous, can't sleep, etc.)

Drug:_____ Dosage:_____ Times per day:_____

Reason:_____ When first prescribed: _____

Who prescribed:_____

Side effects:_____
       (dizzy, nervous, tired, nauseous, can't sleep, etc.)

OTHER MEDICAL TREATMENT

1. Do you presently use a cane, brace, wheelchair, home traction, oxygen machine, or any other device on a regular basis? If so, explain.

_____

_____

    Doctor who prescribed device(s):_____

2. Have you ever seen a mental health professional? If so, please provide name, address, date(s) seen and reason.

_____

_____

_____

Would counseling of this type help you now?_____

Why?_____

3. Have you ever been through vocational rehabilitation?_____

    If so, specify counselor, address, date(s) seen and results:

_____

_____

_____

DAILY ACTIVITIES

Are you presently able to:

Get dressed	_____ yes	_____ no	_____ only with help
Tub bathe	_____ yes	_____ no	_____ only with help
Shower	_____ yes	_____ no	_____ only with help
Make beds	_____ yes	_____ no	_____ only with help
Cook	_____ yes	_____ no	_____ only with help
Wash dishes	_____ yes	_____ no	_____ only with help
Vacuum	_____ yes	_____ no	_____ only with help
Do laundry	_____ yes	_____ no	_____ only with help
Shop for food	_____ yes	_____ no	_____ only with help
Put out trash	_____ yes	_____ no	_____ only with help
Mow lawn	_____ yes	_____ no	_____ only with help
Garden	_____ yes	_____ no	_____ only with help
Walk	_____ yes	_____ no	For how long at one time? _____
Stand	_____ yes	_____ no	For how long at one time? _____
Sit	_____ yes	_____ no	For how long at one time? _____
Climb stairs	_____ yes	_____ no	For how long at one time? _____
Drive a car	_____ yes	_____ no	For how long at one time? _____
Sleep	_____ yes	_____ no	For how long at one time? _____
Lift	_____ yes	_____ no	Weight: _____

TYPICAL DAY

Describe your activities during a typical day:

When you wake up to 11:00 a.m.: _____

_____

_____

11:00 a.m.–3:00 p.m.: _____

_____

_____

3:00 p.m.–7:00 p.m.: _____

_____

_____

7:00 p.m.–bedtime:_____

_____

_____

Do you have any help (nurses, homemakers, family, etc.) to assist you? If yes, describe:

_____

Hobbies or sports before your disability began:_____

How has your disability affected your hobbies or sports?_____

For what reasons do you leave the house (shop, visit, religious activities, appointments, etc.)?_____

_____

Do people come to visit you? If so, who (relatives, friends, etc.) and how often?

_____

_____

_____

INCOME

	AMOUNT MONTHLY	SPOUSE MONTHLY
Social Security	_____	_____
Unemployment	_____	_____
Worker's Compensation	_____	_____
Private pension	_____	_____
State or local pension	_____	_____
Federal Civil Service Retirement	_____	_____
Railroad Retirement	_____	_____
Black Lung	_____	_____
VA Pension	_____	_____
Insurance annuity	_____	_____
Welfare	_____	_____
Other (specify)	_____	_____
_____	_____	_____
_____	_____	_____
_____	_____	_____

✦ APPENDIX 10 ✦

Form for Request for Reconsideration

DEPARTMENT OF HEALTH AND HUMAN SERVICES
SOCIAL SECURITY ADMINISTRATION

TOE 710

REQUEST FOR RECONSIDERATION

(Do not wirte in this space)

The information on this form is authorized by regulation (20 CFR 404.907 – 404.921 and 416.1407 – 416.1421). While your responses to these questions is voluntary, the Social Security Administration cannot reconsider the decision on this claim unless the information is furnished.

NAME OF CLAIMANT

NAME OF WAGE EARNER OR SELF-EMPLOYED PERSON *(If different from claimant.)*

SOCIAL SECURITY CLAIM NUMBER

SUPPLEMENTAL SECURITY INCOME (SSI) CLAIM NUMBER

SPOUSE'S NAME *(Complete ONLY in SSI cases)*

SPOUSE'S SOCIAL SECURITY NUMBER *(Complete ONLY in SSI cases)*

CLAIM FOR *(Specify type, e.g., retirement, disability, hospital insurance, SSI, etc.)*

I do not agree with the determination made on the above claim and request reconsideration. My reasons are:

SUPPLEMENTAL SECURITY INCOME RECONSIDERATION ONLY *(See reverse of claimant's copy)*

"I want to appeal your decision about my claim for supplemental security income, SSI. I've read the back of this form about the three ways to appeal. I've checked the box below."

☐ Case Review   ☐ Informal Conference   ☐ Formal Conference

EITHER THE CLAIMANT OR REPRESENTATIVE SHOULD SIGN – ENTER ADDRESSES FOR BOTH

SIGNATURE OR NAME OF CLAIMANT'S REPRESENTATIVE

☐ NON-ATTORNEY
☐ ATTORNEY

CLAIMANT SIGNATURE

STREET ADDRESS

STREET ADDRESS

CITY | STATE | ZIP CODE | CITY | STATE | ZIP CODE

TELEPHONE NUMBER *(Include area code)* (— — —) | DATE

TELEPHONE NUMBER *(Include area code)* (— — —) | DATE

TO BE COMPLETED BY SOCIAL SECURITY ADMINISTRATION

See reverse of claim folder copy for list of initial determinations

1. HAS INITIAL DETERMINATION BEEN MADE?   ☐ YES ☐ NO

2. CLAIMANT INSISTS ON FILING   ☐ YES ☐ NO

3. IS THIS REQUEST FILED TIMELY? *(If "NO", attach claimant's explanation for delay and attach only pertinent letter, material, or information in social security office.)*   ☐ YES ☐ NO

RETIREMENT AND SURVIVORS RECONSIDERATIONS ONLY (CHECK ONE) REFER TO (GN 03102.125)

SOCIAL SECURITY OFFICE ADDRESS

☐ NO FURTHER DEVELOPMENT REQUIRED   (GN 03102.125)

☐ REQUIRED DEVELOPMENT ATTACHED

☐ REQUIRED DEVELOPMENT PENDING, WILL FORWARD OR ADVISE STATUS WITHIN 30 DAYS

ROUTING INSTRUCTIONS (CHECK ONE)

☐ DISABILITY DETERMINATION SERVICES *(ROUTE WITH DISABILITY FOLDER)*
☐ INTPSC, BALTIMORE

☐ ODO, BALTIMORE
☐ DISTRICT OFFICE RECONSIDERATION

☐ PROGRAM SERVICE CENTER
☐ OCRO BALTIMORE

NOTE: TAKE OR MAIL COMPLETED COPIES TO YOUR SOCIAL SECURITY OFFICE

FORM **SSA-561-U2** (9-85)

✦ APPENDIX 11 ✦

Form for Request for Hearing by Administrative Law Judge

DEPARTMENT OF HEALTH AND HUMAN SERVICES
SOCIAL SECURITY ADMINISTRATION
OFFICE OF HEARINGS AND APPEALS

Form Approved
OMB No. 0960-0269

REQUEST FOR HEARING BY ADMINISTRATIVE LAW JUDGE
[Take or mail original and all copies to your local Social Security Office]

**PRIVACY ACT NOTICE
ON REVERSE SIDE OF FORM.**

1. CLAIMANT	2. WAGE EARNER, IF DIFFERENT	3. SOC. SEC. CLAIM NUMBER	SPOUSE's CLAIM NUMBER

5. I REQUEST A HEARING BEFORE AN ADMINISTRATIVE LAW JUDGE. I disagree with the determination made on my claim because:

_____

_____

_____

_____

You have a right to be represented at the hearing. If you are not represented but would like to be, your Social Security Office will give you a list of legal referral and service organizations. (If you are represented, complete form SSA-1696.)

An Administrative Law Judge of the Office of Hearings and Appeals will be appointed to conduct the hearing or other proceedings in your case. You will receive notice of the time and place of a hearing at least 20 days before the day set for a hearing.

6. Check one of these blocks.	7. Check one of the blocks:
☐ I have no additional evidence to submit.	☐ I wish to appear at a hearing.
☐ I have additional evidence to submit. (Please submit it to the Social Security Office within 10 days.)	☐ I do not wish to appear and I request that a decision be made based on the evidence in my case (Complete Waiver Form HA-4608)

[You should complete No. 8 and your representative (if any) should complete No. 9. If you are represented and your representative is not available to complete this form, you should also print his or her name, address, etc. in No. 9.]

8.	9.
(CLAIMANT'S SIGNATURE)	(REPRESENTATIVE'S SIGNATURE/NAME)
ADDRESS	(ADDRESS) ☐ ATTORNEY; ☐ NON ATTORNEY
CITY STATE ZIP CODE	CITY STATE ZIP CODE
DATE AREA CODE AND TELEPHONE NUMBER	DATE AREA CODE AND TELEPHONE NUMBER

TO BE COMPLETED BY SOCIAL SECURITY ADMINISTRATION—ACKNOWLEDGMENT OF REQUEST FOR HEARING

10.
Request for Hearing RECEIVED for the Social Security Administration on _____ by: _____

(TITLE)	ADDRESS	Servicing FO Code	PC Code

11.	Request not timely filed-Attach (1) claimant's explanation for delay, (2) any
☐ Request timely filed	☐ pertinent letter, material, or information in the Social/Security Office.

12. Claimant not represented –	13. Interpreter needed –
☐ list of legal referral and service organizations provided	☐ enter language (including sign language): _____

14.
Check one: ☐ Initial Entitlement Case
☐ Disability Cessation Case
☐ Other Postentitlement Case

15.
Check claim type(s):
☐ RSI only .... (RSI)
☐ Disability—worker or child only .... (DIWC)
☐ Disability—Widow(er) only .... (DIWW)
☐ SSI Aged only .... (SSIA)
☐ SSI Blind only .... (SSIB)
☐ Disability only .... (SSID)
☐ SSI Aged/Title II .... (SSAC)
☐ SSI Blind/Title II .... (SSBC)
☐ SSI Disability/Title II .... (SSDC)
☐ HI Entitlement .... (HIE)
☐ Other—Specify: (_____)

16.
HO COPY SENT TO: _____ HO on _____.
☐ CF Attached: ☐ Title II; ☐ Title XVI; or
☐ Title II CF held in FO to establish CAPS ORBIT; or
☐ CF requested: ☐ Title II; ☐ Title XVI
(Copy of teletype or phone report attached).

17.
CF COPY SENT TO: _____ HO on _____.
☐ CF attached: ☐ Title II; ☐ Title XVI
☐ Other attached _____

FORM **HA-501-U5** (5-88)
Issue old stock

✦ APPENDIX 12 ✦

Form for Request for
Review of Hearing Decision/Order

DEPARTMENT OF HEALTH AND HUMAN SERVICES
SOCIAL SECURITY ADMINISTRATION/OFFICE OF HEARINGS AND APPEALS

Form Approved
OMB No. 0960-0277

REQUEST FOR REVIEW OF HEARING DECISION/ORDER
(Take or mail original and all copies to your local Social Security office)

See Privacy Act
Notice on Reverse

CLAIMANT

(Check ONE) Initial Entitlement ☐ Termination or other Postentitlement Action ☐

WAGE EARNER (Leave blank if same as above)

Type Claim (Check ONE)

Retirement or Survivors . . . . Only ☐ (RSI)
Disability, Worker or Child . . . . Only ☐ (DIWC)
Disability, Widow or Widower . . . . Only ☐ (DIWW)
Health Insurance, Part A . . . . Only ☐ (HIA)

SOCIAL SECURITY NUMBER

SPOUSE'S NAME AND SOCIAL SECURITY NUMBER
(Complete ONLY in Supplemental Security Income Case)

SSI, Aged . . . . . . Only ☐ (SSIA) With Title II Claim ☐ (SSAC)
SSI, Blind . . . . . . Only ☐ (SSIB) With Title II Claim ☐ (SSBC)
SSI, Disability . . . Only ☐ (SSID) With Title II Claim ☐ (SSDC)

NAME   SSN

Other (Specify)

I disagree with the action taken on the above claim and request review of such action by the Appeals Council of the Office of Hearings and Appeals. My reasons for disagreement are:

ADDITIONAL EVIDENCE

Any additional evidence which you wish to submit must be either attached to this form or forwarded within 15 days to the Appeals Council at the address shown below. It is important that you write your Social Security number on any letter or material you send us. Where the evidence is not submitted within 15 days of this date, or within any extension of time granted by the Appeals Council, the Council will proceed to take its action based on the evidence of record.

Knowing that anyone making a false statement or representation of a material fact for use in determining the right to payment under the Social Security Act commits a crime punishable under Federal law, I certify that the above statements are true.

Signed by: (Either the claimant or representatives should sign—Enter addresses for both)

SIGNATURE OR NAME OF CLAIMANT'S REPRESENTATIVE
☐ ATTORNEY
☐ NON-ATTORNEY

CLAIMANT SIGNATURE

STREET ADDRESS

STREET ADDRESS

CITY, STATE, AND ZIP CODE

CITY, STATE, AND ZIP CODE

AREA CODE AND TELEPHONE NUMBER   DATE

AREA CODE AND TELEPHONE NUMBER

Claimant should not fill in below this line

TO BE COMPLETED BY SOCIAL SECURITY ADMINISTRATION

Is this request filed timely? ☐ Yes ☐ No

If "NO" is checked: (1) attach claimant's explanation for delay; (2) attach any pertinent letter, material or information in Social Security Office.

ACKNOWLEDGEMENT OF RECEIPT OF REQUEST FOR REVIEW OF HEARING DECISION/ORDER

This request for Review of Hearing Decision/Order was filed on _____ at _____
The APPEALS COUNCIL will notify you of its action on your request.

For the Social Security Administration:

SIGNATURE BY:

TITLE

STREET ADDRESS

CITY

APPEALS COUNCIL
OFFICE OF HEARINGS AND APPEALS, SSA
P.O. BOX 3200
ARLINGTON, VA 22203

STATE   ZIP CODE

SERVICING SOCIAL SECURITY OFFICE CODE

Form HA-520-U5 (11-90)
Prior editions may be used until supply is exhausted

✦ APPENDIX 13 ✦

Tips for Using HCFA 2649

You can get Form HCFA 2649 from any Social Security office. Keep a stack handy. (We have also reproduced one for you on page 587; photocopy it if necessary.) The questions asked are not complex, but a few sections that might need further clarification are outlined below:

- Box 2—*Health insurance claim number.* Copy this number from the upper right corner of the Notice of Medicare Claim Determination. If you can't read it, use your Health Insurance (Medicare) card number.
- Box 3—*Representative's name.* If someone else is helping you, here's the place to identify their relationship to you. You will also need to complete and attach the Appointment of Representative Form (see page 586 for explanation).
- Box 5—*Which Part A provider is this claim for.* You need to identify the service provider (*e.g.*, hospital, SNF, Home Health Agency).
- Box 6—*Name and address of provider and provider number.* Look for this information in the "services provided by" section of your Notice of Medicare Claim Determination.
- Box 7—*Name and address of intermediary and intermediary number.* Fill in the name of the insurance company that sent you the denial notice (if the intermediary number is not included, don't worry, just skip it).
- Box 8—*Date of admission or start of services.* When did you arrive? If you can't recall, have the SNF check its records.
- Box 9—*Date(s) of the notice(s) you received.* You will find this date in the upper right corner of the Notice of Medicare Claim Determination.
- Box 10—*I do not agree with the determination on my claim.* At last, you have arrived at the heart of the matter. Now is the time to plead your case. It's a good idea to speak with your doctor or service provider about the possible cause for denial. If you believe the reason was due to a basic computer

coding error or misreading of facts, simply write: "The service *does* meet the standards for coverage under the Medicare Act."

- Box 11—*Additional evidence.* If you do (or do not) have additional documentation to support your claim, note that here.
- Box 12—*Filing deadline.* If your claim was denied because you missed the 60-day appeal deadline, this is the place to explain why. Medicare will make exceptions to the rules if you have a "good cause" excuse.

> Here are three examples of good causes that Uncle Sam has determined are valid:

1. I was over 75 when I received the service [Health Insurance Manual 13, Section 3781.8(c)(2)]. At last, you can use old age as a valid excuse!
2. I never received the denial notice; it arrived after the deadline; or reasons beyond my control were to blame (then explain, *e.g.,* your house burned down) [Health Insurance Manual 13, Section 3781.8(c)(3)].
3. My illness was so severe (state the medical condition), I was unable to manage my personal affairs [Health Insurance Manual 13, Section 3781.8(c)(1)].

> If you are late and need to show "good cause," check "No," write your explanation on a separate piece of paper, or use Box 10 and write "See above."

- Box 13—*Signature.* If you are handling the appeal, check off the beneficiary box and sign your name. Only one signature is needed. If someone is acting as your representative, have him or her check the representative box, sign and in parentheses write the nature of the relationship to you (husband, child, friend). As a safety precaution, Medicare needs your authorization before recognizing someone as your representative. So don't forget to complete the Appointment of Representative form and attach it to the completed Request for Reconsideration form.

That's it. Now you separate the form into its two parts: The blue page will go to the Medicare intermediary. To this sheet, attach a copy of the denial notice and, if applicable, any additional evidence, and the Appointment of Representative Form (if needed). The white page is for you to keep in your appeals file.

DEPARTMENT OF HEALTH AND HUMAN SERVICES
HEALTH CARE FINANCING ADMINISTRATION

Form Approved.
OMB No. 0938–0045

REQUEST FOR RECONSIDERATION OF PART A HEALTH INSURANCE BENEFITS

INSTRUCTIONS: *Please type or print firmly.* Leave the block empty if you cannot answer it. Take or mail the WHOLE form to your Social Security office which will be glad to help you. Please read the statement on the reverse side of page 2.

1. BENEFICIARY'S NAME

2. HEALTH INSURANCE CLAIM NUMBER

3. REPRESENTATIVE'S NAME, IF APPLICABLE

(☐ RELATIVE   ☐ ATTORNEY   ☐ OTHER PERSON)   ☐ PROVIDER FILING

4. PLEASE ATTACH A COPY OF THE NOTICE(S) YOU RECEIVED ABOUT YOUR CLAIM TO THIS FORM.

5. THIS CLAIM IS FOR

☐ INPATIENT HOSPITAL
☐ EMERGENCY HOSPITAL

☐ SKILLED NURSING FACILITY (SNF)
☐ HOME HEALTH AGENCY (HHA)

☐ HEALTH MAINTENANCE ORGANIZATION (HMO)

6. NAME AND ADDRESS OF PROVIDER *(Hospital, SNF, HHA, HMO)* | CITY AND STATE | PROVIDER NUMBER

7. NAME OF INTERMEDIARY | CITY AND STATE | INTERMEDIARY NUMBER

8. DATE OF ADMISSION OR START OF SERVICES | 9. DATE(S) OF THE NOTICE(S) YOU RECEIVED

10. I DO NOT AGREE WITH THE DETERMINATION ON MY CLAIM. PLEASE RECONSIDER MY CLAIM BECAUSE

11. YOU MUST OBTAIN ANY EVIDENCE *(For example, a letter from a doctor)* YOU WISH TO SUBMIT.

☐ I HAVE ATTACHED THE FOLLOWING EVIDENCE:

☐ I WILL SEND THIS EVIDENCE WITHIN 10 DAYS:

☐ I HAVE NO ADDITIONAL EVIDENCE OR OTHER INFORMATION TO SUBMIT WITH MY CLAIM.

13. ONLY ONE SIGNATURE IS NEEDED. THIS FORM IS SIGNED BY:

☐ BENEFICIARY   ☐ REPRESENTATIVE   ☐ PROVIDER REP.

SIGN HERE ▶

14. STREET ADDRESS

12. IS THIS REQUEST FILED WITHIN 60 DAYS OF THE DATE OF YOUR NOTICE?

☐ YES   ☐ NO

IF YOU CHECKED "NO" ATTACH AN EXPLANATION OF THE REASON FOR THE DELAY TO THIS FORM.

CITY, STATE, ZIP CODE

TELEPHONE | DATE

15. If this request is signed by mark (X), TWO WITNESSES who know the person requesting reconsideration must sign in the space provided on the reverse side of this page of the form.

DO NOT FILL IN BELOW THIS LINE — FOR SOCIAL SECURITY USE — THANK YOU

16. ROUTING

☐ INTERMEDIARY

☐ HCFA, RO-MEDICARE

☐ BSS, ODR

18. SSA OR INTERMEDIARY DATE STAMP

17. ADDITIONAL INFORMATION

FORM **HCFA-2649** (8–79) (FORMERLY SSA-2649)
DESTROY PRIOR EDITIONS

✦ APPENDIX 14 ✦

Form for Request for
Review of Part B Medicare Claim

DEPARTMENT OF HEALTH AND HUMAN SERVICES
HEALTH CARE FINANCING ADMINISTRATION

Form Approved
OMB No. 0938-0033

REQUEST FOR REVIEW OF PART B MEDICARE CLAIM
Medical Insurance Benefits - Social Security Act

NOTICE—Anyone who misrepresents or falsifies essential information requested by this form may upon conviction be subject to fine and imprisonment under Federal Law.

1 Carrier's Name and Address

2 Name of Patient

3 Health Insurance Claim Number

4 I do not agree with the determination you made on my claim as described on my Explanation of Medicare Benefits dated:

5 MY REASONS ARE: (Attach a copy of the Explanation of Medicare Benefits, or describe the service, date of service, and physician's name—NOTE.—If the date on the Notice of Benefits mentioned in item 3 is more than six months ago, include your reason for not making this request earlier.)

6 Describe Illness or Injury:

7 ☐ I have additional evidence to submit. (Attach such evidence to this form.)

☐ I do not have additional evidence.

COMPLETE ALL OF THE INFORMATION REQUESTED. SIGN AND RETURN THE FIRST COPY AND ANY ATTACHMENTS TO THE CARRIER NAMED ABOVE. IF YOU NEED HELP, TAKE THIS AND YOUR NOTICE FROM THE CARRIER TO A SOCIAL SECURITY OFFICE, OR TO THE CARRIER. KEEP THE DUPLICATE COPY OF THIS FORM FOR YOUR RECORDS.

8 SIGNATURE OF **EITHER** THE CLAIMENT **OR** HIS REPRESENTATIVE

Representative	Claimant	
Address	Address	
City, State, and ZIP Code	City, State, and ZIP Code	
Telephone Number	Date	Telephone Number	Date

Form HCFA-1964 (8-85)

Form for Appointment of Representative

DEPARTMENT OF
HEALTH AND HUMAN SERVICES
SOCIAL SECURITY ADMINISTRATION

NAME (Claimant) (Print or Type)	SOCIAL SECURITY NUMBER
WAGE EARNER (If different)	SOCIAL SECURITY NUMBER

Section I   **APPOINTMENT OF REPRESENTATIVE**

I appoint this individual _____
(Name and Address)

to act as my representative in connection with my claim or asserted right under:

☐ Title II (RSDI)   ☐ Title XVI (SSI)   ☐ Title IV FMSHA (Black Lung)   ☐ Title XVIII (Medicare Coverage)

I authorize this individual to make or give any request or notice; to present or elicit evidence; to obtain information; and to receive any notice in connection with my pending claim or asserted right wholly in my stead.

SIGNATURE (Claimant)	ADDRESS
TELEPHONE NUMBER (Area Code)	DATE

Section II   **ACCEPTANCE OF APPOINTMENT**

I, _____ , hereby accept the above appointment. I certify that I have not been suspended or prohibited from practice before the Social Security Administration; that I am not, as a current or former officer or employee of the United States, disqualified from acting as the claimant's representative; and that I will not charge or receive any fee for the representation unless it has been authorized in accordance with the laws and regulations referred to on the reverse side hereof. In the event that I decide not to charge or collect a fee for the representation, I will notify the Social Security Administration. (Completion of Section III satisfies this requirement.)

I am a / an _____
(Attorney, union representative, relative, law student, etc.)

SIGNATURE (Representative)	ADDRESS
TELEPHONE NUMBER (Area code)	DATE

Section III (Optional)   **WAIVER OF FEE**

I waive my right to charge and collect a fee under Section 206 of the Social Security Act, and I release my client (the claimant) from any obligations, contractual or otherwise, which may be owed to me for services I have performed in connection with my client's claim or asserted right.

SIGNATURE (Representative)	DATE

WAIVER OF DIRECT PAYMENT

I ONLY waive my right to direct certification of a fee from the withheld past-due benefits of my client (the claimant). I do NOT, however, waive my right to petition for and be authorized to charge and collect a fee directly from my client.

SIGNATURE (Representative)	DATE

Form SSA-1696-U4 (3-88)
Detroy prior editions

✦ APPENDIX 16 ✦

Health Insurance Claims Activity Log

Medicare Coverage					Medigap Coverage			Coverage Gap		Appeal Filed	
Date of Service	Doctor Supplier Provider	Amount Charged	Amount Approved	Amount Medicare Paid	Assignment Yes/No	Date Claim Sent	Amount Medigap Paid	Amount I Must Pay	Date Paid (Check #)	Part A (Dates & Steps)	Part B (Dates & Steps)

✦ APPENDIX 17 ✦

List of Medicare Carriers

Carriers can answer questions about Medical Insurance (Part B)

Note: 1. **The toll-free or 800 numbers listed below can be used only in the states where the carriers are located.**
Also listed are the local commercial numbers for the carriers. Out-of-state callers must use the commercial numbers.
2. These carrier toll-free numbers are for beneficiaries to use and should not be used by doctors and suppliers.
3. Many carriers have installed an automated telephone answering system. If you have a touch-tone telephone, you can follow the system instructions to find out about your latest claims and get other information. If you do not have a touch-tone telephone, stay on the line and someone will help you.

Alabama
Medicare/Blue Cross-Blue Shield of
Alabama
P.O. Box 830-140
Birmingham, Alabama 35283-0140
1-800-292-8855
205-988-2244

Alaska
Medicare/Aetna Life & Casualty
200 S.W. Market Street
P.O. Box 1997
Portland, Oregon 97207-1997
1-800-547-6333
503-222-6831 (customer service site actually in Oregon)

Arizona
Medicare/Aetna Life & Casualty
P.O. Box 37200
Phoenix, Arizona 85069
1-800-352-0411
602-861-1968

Arkansas
Medicare/Arkansas Blue Cross and
Blue Shield
A Mutual Insurance Company
P.O. Box 1418
Little Rock, Arkansas 72203-1418
1-800-482-5525
501-378-2320

California

Counties of: Los Angeles, Orange,
San Diego, Ventura, Imperial, San Luis
Obispo, Santa Barbara
Medicare/Transamerica Occidental Life
Insurance Co.
Box 50061
Upland, California 91785-5061
1-800-675-2266
213-748-2311
Rest of State: Medicare Claims Dept.
Blue Shield of California
Chico, California 95976
(In area codes 209, 408, 415, 707, 916)
1-800-952-8627
916-743-1587
(In the following area codes—**other than
Los Angeles, Orange, San Diego,
Ventura, Imperial, San Luis Obispo, and
Santa Barbara counties**—213, 619, 714,
805, 818)
1-800-848-7713
714-824-0900

Colorado

Medicare/Blue Cross and Blue Shield of
Colorado
Claims:
P.O. Box 173560
Denver, Colorado 80217
Correspondence/Appeals:
P.O. Box 173500
Denver, Colorado 80217
(Metro Denver) 303-831-2661
(In Colorado, outside of metro area)
1-800-332-6681

Connecticut

Medicare/The Travelers Ins. Co.
538 Preston Avenue
P.O. Box 9000
Meriden, Connecticut 06454-9000
1-800-982-6819
(In Hartford) 203-728-6783
(In the Meriden area) 203-237-8592

Delaware

Medicare/Pennsylvania Blue Shield
P.O. Box 890200
Camp Hill, Pennsylvania 17089-0200
1-800-851-3535

District of Columbia

Medicare/Pennsylvania Blue Shield
P.O. Box 890100
Camp Hill, Pennsylvania 17089-0100
1-800-233-1124

Florida

Medicare/Blue Shield of Florida, Inc.
P.O. Box 2525
Jacksonville, Florida 32231
For fast service on simple inquiries
including requests for copies of Explanation of Medicare Benefits notices,
requests for Medpard directories, brief
claims inquiries (status or verification of
receipt), and address changes:
1-800-666-7586
For all your other Medicare needs:
1-800-333-7586
904-355-3680

Georgia

Medicare/Aetna Life & Casualty
P.O. Box 3018
Savannah, Georgia 31402-3018
1-800-727-0827
912-920-2412

Hawaii

Medicare/Aetna Life & Casualty
P.O. Box 3947
Honolulu, Hawaii 96812
1-800-272-5242
808-524-1240

Idaho
Connecticut General Life Insurance
Company
3150 N. Lakeharbor Lane, Suite 254
P.O. Box 8048
Boise, Idaho 83707-6219
1-800-627-2782
208-342-7763

Illinois
Medicare Claims/Blue Cross & Blue
Shield of Illinois
P.O. Box 4422
Marion, Illinois 62959
1-800-642-6930
312-938-8000

Indiana
Medicare Part B/Associated Ins.
Companies, Inc.
P.O. Box 7073
Indianapolis, Indiana 46207
1-800-622-4792
317-842-4151

Iowa
Medicare/IASD Health Services Inc.
(d/b/a Blue Cross & Blue Shield
of Iowa)
636 Grand
Des Moines, Iowa 50309
1-800-532-1285
515-245-4785

Kansas
Counties of: Johnson, Wyandotte
Medicare/Blue Shield of Kansas City
P.O. Box 419840
Kansas City, Missouri 64141-6840
1-800-892-5900
816-561-0900
Rest of State: Medicare/Blue Cross and
Blue Shield of Kansas
P.O. Box 239

Topeka, Kansas 66601
1-800-432-3531
913-232-3773

Kentucky
Medicare-Part B/Blue Cross & Blue
Shield of Kentucky
100 East Vine Street
Lexington, Kentucky 40507
1-800-999-7608
606-233-1441

Louisiana
Arkansas Blue Cross & Blue Shield
Medicare Administration
P.O. Box 95024
Baton Rouge, Louisiana 70895-9024
1-800-462-9666
(In New Orleans) 504-529-1494
(In Baton Rouge) 504-927-3490

Maine
Medicare/Blue Shield of Massachusetts/
Tri-State
P.O. Box 1010
Biddeford, Maine 04005
1-800-492-0919
207-282-5689

Maryland
Counties of: Montgomery, Prince
Georges
Medicare/Pennsylvania Blue Shield
P.O. Box 890100
Camp Hill, Pennsylvania 17089-0100
1-800-233-1124
Rest of State: Maryland Blue Shield, Inc.
1946 Greenspring Drive
Timonium, Maryland 21093
1-800-492-4795
301-561-4160

Massachusetts
Medicare/Blue Shield of
Massachusetts, Inc.
1022 Hingham Street
Rockland, Massachusetts 02371
1-800-882-1228
617-956-3994

Michigan
Medicare Part B/Michigan Blue Cross
& Blue Shield
P.O. Box 2201
Detroit, Michigan 48231-2201
(In area code 313) 1-800-482-4045
(In area code 517) 1-800-322-0607
(In area code 616) 1-800-442-8020
(In area code 906) 1-800-562-7802
(In Detroit) 313-225-8200

Minnesota
Counties of: Anoka, Dakota, Fillmore,
Goodhue, Hennepin, Houston,
Olmstead, Ramsey, Wabasha,
Washington, Winona
Medicare/The Travelers Ins. Co.
8120 Penn Avenue South
Bloomington, Minnesota 55431
1-800-352-2762
612-884-7171
Rest of State: Medicare
Blue Shield of Minnesota
P.O. Box 64357
St. Paul, Minnesota 55164
1-800-392-0343
612-456-5070

Mississippi
Medicare/The Travelers Ins. Co.
P.O. Box 22545
Jackson, Mississippi 39225-2545
(In Mississippi) 1-800-682-5417
(Outside of Mississippi) 1-800-227-2349
601-956-0372

Missouri
Counties of: Andrew, Atchison, Bates,
Benton, Buchanan, Caldwell, Carroll,
Cass, Clay, Clinton, Daviess, DeKalb,
Gentry, Grundy, Harrison, Henry, Holt,
Jackson, Johnson, Lafayette, Livingston,
Mercer, Nodaway, Pettis, Platte, Ray,
St. Clair, Saline, Vernon, Worth
Medicare/Blue Shield of Kansas City
P.O. Box 419840
Kansas City, Missouri 64141-6840
1-800-892-5900
816-561-0900
Rest of State: Medicare/General
American Life Insurance Co.
P.O. Box 505
St. Louis, Missouri 63166
1-800-392-3070
314-843-8880

Montana
Medicare/Blue Cross and Blue Shield
of Montana
2501 Beltview
P.O. Box 4310
Helena, Montana 59604
1-800-332-6146
406-444-8350

Nebraska
The carrier for Nebraska is Blue Shield
of Kansas. Claims should be sent to:
Medicare Part B/Blue Cross/Blue Shield
of Nebraska
P.O. Box 3106
Omaha, Nebraska 68103-0106
1-800-633-1113
913-232-3773 (customer service site in
Kansas)

Nevada
Medicare/Aetna Life and Casualty
P.O. Box 37230
Phoenix, Arizona 85069
1-800-528-0311
602-861-1968

New Hampshire
Medicare
Blue Shield of Massachusetts/Tri-State
P.O. Box 1010
Biddeford, Maine 04005
1-800-447-1142
207-282-5689

New Jersey
Medicare/Pennsylvania Blue Shield
P.O. Box 400010
Harrisburg, Pennsylvania 17140-0010
1-800-462-9306
717-763-3601

New Mexico
Medicare/Aetna Life and Casualty
P.O. Box 25500
Oklahoma City, Oklahoma 73125-0500
1-800-423-2925
(In Albuquerque) 505-843-7771

New York
Counties of: Bronx, Kings, New York,
Richmond
Medicare B/Empire Blue Cross and Blue
Shield
P.O. Box 2280
Peekskill, New York 10566
516-244-5100
Counties of: Columbia, Delaware,
Dutchess, Greene, Nassau, Orange,
Putnam, Rockland, Suffolk, Sullivan,
Ulster, Westchester
Medicare B/Empire Blue Cross and Blue
Shield
P.O. Box 2280
Peekskill, New York 10566

1-800-442-8430
516-244-5100
County of: Queens
Medicare/Group Health, Inc.
P.O. Box 1608, Ansonia Station
New York, New York 10023
212-721-1770
Rest of State: Medicare
Blue Shield of Western New York
7-9 Court Street
Binghamton, New York 13901-3197
607-772-6906
1-800-252-6550

North Carolina
Connecticut General Life Insurance
Company
P.O. Box 671
Nashville, Tennessee 37202
1-800-672-3071
919-665-0348

North Dakota
Medicare/Blue Shield of North Dakota
4510 13th Avenue, S.W.
Fargo, North Dakota 58121-0001
1-800-247-2267
701-282-0691

Ohio
Medicare/Nationwide Mutual Ins. Co.
P.O. Box 57
Columbus, Ohio 43216
1-800-282-0530
614-249-7157

Oklahoma
Medicare/Aetna Life and Casualty
701 N.W. 63rd Street
Oklahoma City, Oklahoma 73116-7693
1-800-522-9079
405-848-7711

Oregon
Medicare/Aetna Life and Casualty
200 S.W. Market Street
P.O. Box 1997
Portland, Oregon 97207-1997
1-800-452-0125
503-222-6831

Pennsylvania
Medicare/Pennsylvania Blue Shield
P.O. Box 890065
Camp Hill, Pennsylvania 17089-0065
1-800-382-1274

Rhode Island
Medicare/Blue Shield of Rhode Island
444 Westminster Street
Providence, Rhode Island 02901
1-800-662-5170
401-861-2273

South Carolina
Medicare Part B/Blue Cross and Blue
Shield of South Carolina
Fontaine Road Business Center
300 Arbor Lake Drive, Suite 1300
Columbia, South Carolina 29223
1-800-868-2522
803-754-0639

South Dakota
Medicare Part B/Blue Shield of North
Dakota
4510 13th Avenue, S.W.
Fargo, North Dakota 58121-0001
1-800-437-4762
701-282-0691

Tennessee
Connecticut General Life Insurance
Company
P.O. Box 1465
Nashville, Tennessee 37202
1-800-342-8900
615-244-5650

Texas
Medicare/Blue Cross & Blue Shield of
Texas, Inc.
P.O. Box 660031
Dallas, Texas 75266-0031
1-800-442-2620
214-235-3433

Utah
Medicare/Blue Shield of Utah
P.O. Box 30269
Salt Lake City, Utah 84130-0269
1-800-426-3477
801-481-6196

Vermont
Medicare
Blue Shield of Massachusetts/Tri-State
P.O. Box 1010
Biddeford, Maine 04005
1-800-447-1142
207-282-5689

Virginia
Counties of: Arlington, Fairfax;
Cities of: Alexandria, Falls Church,
Fairfax
Medicare/Pennsylvania Blue Shield
P.O. Box 890100
Camp Hill, Pennsylvania 17089-0100
1-800-233-1124
Rest of State: Medicare/The Travelers
Ins. Co.
P.O. Box 26463
Richmond, Virginia 23261
1-800-552-3423
804-254-4130

Washington
Medicare
Mail to your local Medical Service
Bureau.
If you do not know which bureau han-
dles your claim, mail to: King County
Medical Blue Shield

P.O. Box 21248
Seattle, Washington 98111-3248
(In King County) 1-800-422-4087
206-464-3711
(In Spokane) 1-800-572-5256
509-536-4550
(In Kitsap) 1-800-552-7114
206-377-5576
(In Pierce) 206-597-6530
(In Thurston) 206-352-2269
Others: Collect if out of call area.

West Virginia
Medicare/Nationwide Mutual
Insurance Co.
P.O. Box 57
Columbus, Ohio 43216
1-800-848-0106
614-249-7157

Wisconsin
Medicare/WPS
Box 1787
Madison, Wisconsin 53701
1-800-362-7221
(In Madison) 608-221-3330
(In Milwaukee) 414-931-1071

Wyoming
Blue Cross/Blue Shield of Wyoming
P.O. Box 628
Cheyenne, Wyoming 82003
1-800-442-2371
307-632-9381

American Samoa
Medicare/Hawaii Medical Services Assn.
P.O. Box 860
Honolulu, Hawaii 96808
808-944-2247

Guam
Medicare/Aetna Life and Casualty
P.O. Box 3947
Honolulu, Hawaii 96812
808-524-1240

Northern Mariana Islands
Medicare/Aetna Life & Casualty
P.O. Box 3947
Honolulu, Hawaii 96812
808-524-1240

Puerto Rico
Medicare/Seguros De Servicio De
Salud De Puerto Rico
Call Box 71391
San Juan, Puerto Rico 00936
(In Puerto Rico) 1-800-462-7015
(In U.S. Virgin Islands) 1-800-474-7448
(In Puerto Rico metro area)
809-749-4900

Virgin Islands
Medicare/Seguros De Servicio De
Salud De Puerto Rico
Call Box 71391
San Juan, Puerto Rico 00936
(In U.S. Virgin Islands) 1-800-474-7448

Medicare Peer Review Organizations (PROs)

PROs can answer questions about hospital stays and other Hospital Insurance (Part A) services. Do not call the PRO with questions about Medicare Medical Insurance (Part B).

Alabama
Alabama Quality Assurance Foundation
Suite 600
600 Beacon Parkway West
Birmingham, AL 35209-3154
1-800-288-4992
205-942-0785

Alaska
Professional Review Organization for
Washington
(PRO for Alaska)
Suite 300
10700 Meridian Avenue, North
Seattle, WA 98133-9008
1-800-445-6941
206-364-9700
(in Anchorage dial 562-2252)

American Samoa/Guam and Hawaii
Hawaii Medical Service Association
(PRO for American Samoa/Guam and
Hawaii)

818 Keeaumoku Street
P.O. Box 860
Honolulu, HI 96808
808-944-3581

Arizona
Health Services Advisory Group, Inc.
301 East Bethany Home Road
Suite B-157
P.O. Box 16731
Phoenix, AZ 85012
1-800-626-1577
(in Arizona dial 1-800-359-9909)
602-264-6382

Arkansas
Arkansas Foundation for
Medical Care, Inc.
P.O. Box 2424
809 Garrison Avenue
Fort Smith, AR 72902
1-800-824-7586
(in Arkansas dial 1-800-272-5528)
501-785-2471

California
California Medical Review Inc.
Suite 500
60 Spear Street
San Francisco, CA 94105
1-800-841-1602 (in-state only)
1-415-882-5800*

Colorado
Colorado Foundation for Medical Care
1260 South Parker Road
P.O. Box 17300
Denver, CO 80217-0300
1-800-727-7086 (in-state only)
1-303-695-3333*

Connecticut
Connecticut Peer Review Organization,
Inc.
100 Roscommon Drive, Suite 200
Middletown, CT 06457
1-800-553-7590 (in-state only)
1-203-632-2008*

Delaware
West Virginia Medical Institute, Inc.
(PRO for Delaware)
3412 Chesterfield Avenue S.E.
Charleston, WV 25304
1-800-522-0446
(Delaware, District of Columbia,
Maryland,
Pennsylvania and Virginia)
304-925-0461
(in Wilmington dial 655-3077)

District of Columbia
Delmarva Foundation for Medical
Care, Inc.
(PRO for D.C.)
341 B North Aurora Street
Easton, MD 21601
1-800-645-0011
(in Maryland dial 1-800-492-5811)
301-822-0697

Florida
Professional Foundation for Health
Care, Inc.
Suite 100
2907 Bay to Bay Boulevard
Tampa, FL 33629
1-800-634-6280 (in-state only)
813-831-6273

Georgia
Georgia Medical Care Foundation
Suite 200
57 Executive Park South
Atlanta, GA 30329
1-800-282-2614 (in-state only)
404-982-0411

Hawaii
Hawaii Medical Service Association
(PRO for American Samoa/Guam and
Hawaii)
818 Keeaumoku Street
P.O. Box 860
Honolulu, HI 96808
1-800-944-3586*
808-944-3581

Idaho
Professional Review Organization for
Washington
(PRO for Idaho)
Suite 300
10700 Meridian Avenue, North
Seattle, WA 98133-9008
1-800-445-6941
206-364-9700
1-208-343-4617* (local Boise and collect)

Illinois
Crescent Counties Foundation for
Medical Care
350 Shuman Boulevard, Suite 240
Naperville, IL 60563
1-800-647-8089
708-357-8770

Indiana
Sentinel Medical Review Organization
2901 Ohio Boulevard
P.O. Box 3713
Terre Haute, IN 47803
1-800-288-1499
812-234-1499

Iowa
Iowa Foundation for Medical Care
Colony Park
3737 Woodland Avenue, Suite 500
West Des Moines, IA 50265
1-800-752-7014 (in-state only)
515-223-2900

Kansas
The Kansas Foundation for Medical
Care, Inc.
2947 S.W. Wanamaker Drive
Topeka, KS 66614
1-800-432-0407 (in-state only)
913-273-2552

Kentucky
Sentinel Medical Review Organization
10503 Timberwood Circle, Suite 200
P.O. Box 23540
Louisville, KY 40223
1-800-288-1499
502-339-7442

Louisiana
Louisiana Health Care Review
9357 Interline Avenue, Suite 200
Baton Rouge, LA 70809
1-800-433-4958 (in-state only)
504-926-6353

Maine
Health Care Review, Inc.
(PRO for Maine)
Henry C. Hall Building
345 Blackstone Boulevard
Providence, RI 02906

1-800-541-9888 or
1-800-528-0700 (both numbers in Maine
only)
401-331-6661
1-207-945-0244*

Maryland
Delmarva Foundation for Medical
Care, Inc.
(PRO for Maryland)
341 B North Aurora Street
Easton, MD 21601
1-800-645-0011
(in Maryland dial 1-800-492-5811)
301-822-0697

Massachusetts
Massachusetts Peer Review
Organization, Inc.
300 Bearhill Road
Waltham, MA 02154
1-800-252-5533 (in-state only)
617-890-0011*

Michigan
Michigan Peer Review Organization
40500 Ann Arbor Road, Suite 200
Plymouth, MI 48170
1-800-365-5899
313-459-0900

Minnesota
Foundation for Health Care Evaluation
Suite 400
2901 Metro Drive
Bloomington, MN 55425
1-800-444-3423
612-854-3306

Mississippi
Mississippi Foundation for Medical
Care, Inc.
P.O. Box 4665
735 Riverside Drive
Jackson, MS 39296-4665
1-800-844-0600 (in-state only)
601-948-8894

Missouri
Missouri Patient Care Review Foundation
505 Hobbs Lane, Suite 100
Jefferson City, MO 65109
1-800-347-1016
314-893-7900

Montana
Montana-Wyoming Foundation for
Medical Care
21 North Main
Helena, MT 59601
1-800-332-3411 (in-state only)
1-406-443-4020*

Nebraska
Iowa Foundation for Medical Care
(PRO for Nebraska)
Colony Park, Suite 500
3737 Woodland Avenue
West Des Moines, IA 50265
1-800-247-3004 (in Nebraska only)
515-223-2900

Nevada
Nevada Peer Review
675 East 2100 South, Suite 270
Salt Lake City, UT 84106-1864
1-800-558-0829 (in Nevada only)
801-487-2290
1-702-385-9933*

New Hampshire
New Hampshire Foundation for
Medical Care
110 Locust Street
Dover, NH 03820

1-800-582-7174 (in-state only)
1-603-749-1641*

New Jersey
The Peer Review Organization of New
Jersey, Inc.
Central Division
Brier Hill Court, Building J
East Brunswick, NJ 08816
1-800-624-4557 (in-state only)
1-201-238-5570*

New Mexico
New Mexico Medical Review Association
707 Broadway N.E., Suite 200
P.O. Box 9900
Albuquerque, NM 87119-9900
1-800-432-6824 (in-state only)
505-842-6236

New York
Island Peer Review Organization, Inc.
9525 Queens Blvd.
Rego Park, NY 11374-4511
1-800-331-7767 (in-state only)
1-718-896-7230*
(in metro area and New York City dial
275-9894)

North Carolina
Medical Review of North Carolina
Suite 200
P.O. Box 37309
1011 Schaub Drive
Raleigh, NC 27627
1-800-682-2650 (in-state only)
803-731-8225

North Dakota
North Dakota Health Care Review, Inc.
Suite 301
900 North Broadway
Minot, ND 58701
1-800-472-2902 (in-state only)
1-701-852-4231*

Ohio
Peer Review Systems, Inc.
Suite 250
3700 Corporate Drive
Columbus, OH 43231-4996
1-800-233-7337
614-895-9900

Oklahoma
Oklahoma Foundation for Peer
Review, Inc.
Suite 400 The Paragon Building
5801 Broadway Extension
Oklahoma City, OK 73118-7489
1-800-522-3414 (in-state only)
405-840-2891

Oregon
Oregon Medical Professional Review
Organization
Suite 200
1220 Southwest Morrison
Portland, OR 97205
1-800-344-4354 (in-state only)
503-279-0100*

Pennsylvania
Keystone Peer Review Organization, Inc.
777 East Park Drive
P.O. Box 8310
Harrisburg, PA 17105-8310
1-800-322-1914 (in-state only)
717-564-8288

Puerto Rico
Puerto Rico Foundation for Medical
Care
Suite 605 Mercantile Plaza
Hato Rey, PR 00918
1-809-753-6705* or 1-809-753-6708*

Rhode Island
Health Care Review, Inc.
Henry C. Hall Building
345 Blackstone Boulevard

Providence, RI 02906
1-800-221-1691 (New England-wide)
(in Rhode Island dial 1-800-662-5028)
1-401-331-6661*

South Carolina
Medical Review of North Carolina
(PRO for South Carolina)
P.O. Box 37309
1011 Schaub Drive, Suite 200
Raleigh, NC 27627
1-800-922-3089 (in-state only)
919-851-2955

South Dakota
South Dakota Foundation for Medical
Care
1323 South Minnesota Avenue
Sioux Falls, SD 57105
1-800-658-2285
605-336-3505

Tennessee
Mid-South Foundation for Medical Care
Suite 400
6401 Poplar Avenue
Memphis, TN 38119
1-800-873-2273
901-682-0381

Texas
Texas Medical Foundation
Barton Oaks Plaza Two, Suite 200
901 Mopac Expressway South
Austin, TX 78746
1-800-777-8315 (in-state only)
512-329-6610

Utah
Utah Peer Review Organization
675 East 2100 South
Suite 270
Salt Lake City, UT 84106-1864
1-800-274-2290
801-487-2290

Vermont
New Hampshire Foundation
for Medical Care
(PRO for Vermont)
110 Locust Street
Dover, NH 03820
1-800-642-5066 (in Vermont only)
603-749-1641
1-802-862-6447*

Virgin Islands
Virgin Islands Medical Institute
P.O. Box 1566
Christiansted
St. Croix, U.S.A. VI 00820-1566
1-809-778-6470*

Virginia
Medical Society of Virginia Review
Organization
1606 Santa Rosa Road, Suite 235
P.O. Box K 70
Richmond, VA 23288
1-800-545-3814 (DC, MD and VA)
804-289-5320
(in Richmond, dial 289-5320)

Washington
Professional Review Organization
for Washington
Suite 300

10700 Meridian Avenue, North
Seattle, WA 98133-9008
1-800-445-6941
206-364-9700
(in Seattle, dial 368-8272)

West Virginia
West Virginia Medical Institute, Inc.
3412 Chesterfield Avenue, S.E.
Charleston, WV 25304
1-800-642-8686
304-925-0461
(in Charleston, dial 925-0461)

Wisconsin
Wisconsin Peer Review Organization
2001 W. Beltline Highway
Madison, WI 53713
1-800-362-2320 (in-state only)
608-274-1940

Wyoming
Montana-Wyoming Foundation
for Medical Care
21 North Main
Helena, MT 59601
1-800-826-8978 (in Wyoming only)
1-406-443-4020*

*PRO will accept collect calls from out of state
on this number.

✦ APPENDIX 19 ✦

Health-Care Financing Administration Regional Offices

REGION 1

Connecticut, Maine, Massachusetts, New Hampshire, Rhode Island, Vermont

1309 J. F. Kennedy Federal Building
Boston, Massachusetts 02203
(617) 565-1188

REGION 2

New Jersey, New York, Puerto Rico, Virgin Islands

26 Federal Plaza, Room 3800
New York, New York 10007
(212) 264-8531

REGION 3

Delaware, District of Columbia, Maryland, Pennsylvania, Virginia, West Virginia

3535 Market Street, Room 10200
Philadelphia, Pennsylvania 19101
(215) 596-6861

REGION 4

Alabama, Florida, Georgia, Kentucky, Mississippi, North Carolina, South Carolina, Tennessee

101 Marietta Tower, Suite 701
Atlanta, Georgia 30323
(404) 331-2329

REGION 5

Illinois, Indiana, Michigan, Minnesota, Ohio, Wisconsin

175 West Jackson, Suite A-8-24
Chicago, Illinois 60604
(312) 353-9845

REGION 6

Arkansas, Louisiana, New Mexico, Oklahoma, Texas

1200 Main Tower Building, Room 2000
Dallas, Texas 75202
(214) 767-6441

REGION 7

Iowa, Kansas, Missouri, Nebraska

601 East 12th Street, Room 225
Kansas City, Missouri 64106
(816) 426-5233

REGION 8

Colorado, Montana, North Dakota, South Dakota, Utah, Wyoming

Federal Office Building, Room 1185
19th & Stout Streets
Denver, Colorado 80294
(303) 844-4024

REGION 9

Arizona, California, Guam, Hawaii, Nevada, Trust Territory of the Pacific Islands

100 Van Ness Avenue, 20th Floor
San Francisco, California 94102
(415) 744-3501

REGION 10

Alaska, Idaho, Oregon, Washington

2901 3rd Avenue, M.S. 407
Seattle, Washington 98121
(206) 553-8194

Samples of Form for Tax
on Lump-Sum Distributions

Sample A. $100,000 with five-year averaging

Sample B. $100,000 with ten-year averaging

Sample C. $100,000, of which $20,000 is capital gain, and $80,000 is five-year averaging

Form **4972**	**Tax on Lump-Sum Distributions** (Use This Form Only for Lump-Sum Distributions From Qualified Retirement Plans)	OMB No. 1545-0193 **1991**
Department of the Treasury Internal Revenue Service	▶ Attach to Form 1040 or Form 1041. ▶ See separate instructions.	Attachment Sequence No. **28**

Name of recipient of distribution	Identifying number

Part I	**Complete this part to see if you qualify to use Form 4972.**		Yes	No
1	Did you roll over any part of the distribution? If "Yes," do not complete the rest of this form.	1		X
2	Was the retirement plan participant born before 1936 (and, if deceased, was the participant at least 50 years old at the date of death)? If "No," do not complete the rest of this form	2	X	
3	Was this a lump-sum distribution from a qualified pension, profit-sharing, or stock bonus plan? (See **Distributions That Qualify for the 20% Capital Gain Election or for 5- or 10-Year Averaging** in the instructions.) If "No," do not complete the rest of this form.	3	X	
4	Was the participant in the plan for at least 5 years before the year of the distribution?	4	X	
5	Was this distribution paid to you as a beneficiary of a plan participant who died? If you answered "No" to 4 **and** 5, do not complete the rest of this form.	5		X
6	Was the plan participant:			
a	An employee who received the distribution because he or she quit, retired, was laid off or fired?	6a	X	
b	Self-employed or an owner-employee who became permanently and totally disabled before the distribution?	6b		X
c	Age 59½ or older at the time of the distribution? If you answered "No" to question 5 and **all** parts of question 6, do not complete the rest of this form.	6c	X	
7	Did you use Form 4972 in a prior year for any distribution received after 1986 from a plan for the same plan participant, including you, for whom the 1991 distribution was made? If "Yes," do not complete the rest of this form	7		X

If you qualify to use this form, you may choose to use Part II, Part III, or Part IV; **or** Part II and Part III; **or** Part II and Part IV.

Part II	**Complete this part to choose the 20% capital gain election.** (See instructions.)			
1	Capital gain part from Box 3 of Form 1099-R. (See instructions.)	1		
2	Multiply line 1 by 20% (.20) and enter here. If you do not elect to use Part III or Part IV, also enter the amount on Form 1040, line 39, or Form 1041, Schedule G, line 1b.	2		

Part III	**Complete this part to choose the 5-year averaging method.** (See instructions.)			
1	Ordinary income from Form 1099-R, Box 2a minus Box 3. If you did not make the Schedule D election or complete Part II, enter the taxable amount from Box 2a of Form 1099-R. (See instructions.)	1	100,000	00
2	Death benefit exclusion. (See instructions.)	2		
3	Total taxable amount—Subtract line 2 from line 1	3	100,000	00
4	Current actuarial value of annuity, if applicable (from Form 1099-R, Box 8)	4		
5	Adjusted total taxable amount—Add lines 3 and 4. If this amount is $70,000 or more, skip lines 6 through 9, and enter this amount on line 10	5	100,000	00
6	Multiply line 5 by 50% (.50), but **do not** enter more than $10,000. **6**			
7	Subtract $20,000 from line 5. If line 5 is $20,000 or less, enter -0- **7**			
8	Multiply line 7 by 20% (.20) **8**			
9	Minimum distribution allowance—Subtract line 8 from line 6	9		
10	Subtract line 9 from line 5	10	100,000	00
11	Federal estate tax attributable to lump-sum distribution. Do not deduct on Form 1040 or Form 1041 the amount attributable to the ordinary income entered on line 1. (See instructions.)	11		
12	Subtract line 11 from line 10	12	100,000	00
13	Multiply line 12 by 20% (.20)	13	20,000	00
14	Tax on amount on line 13. See instructions for Tax Rate Schedule	14	3,000	00
15	Multiply line 14 by five (5). If no entry on line 4, skip lines 16 through 21. Enter the amount on line 22	15	15,000	00
16	Divide line 4 by line 5 and enter the result as a decimal. (See instructions.)	16		
17	Multiply line 9 by the decimal amount on line 16	17		
18	Subtract line 17 from line 4	18		
19	Multiply line 18 by 20% (.20)	19		
20	Tax on amount on line 19. See instructions for Tax Rate Schedule	20		
21	Multiply line 20 by five (5)	21		
22	Subtract line 21 from line 15. (Multiple recipients, see instructions.)	22	15,000	00
23	Tax on lump-sum distribution—Add Part II, line 2, and Part III, line 22. Enter on Form 1040, line 39, or Form 1041, Schedule G, line 1b. ▶	23	15,000	00

For Paperwork Reduction Act Notice, see separate instructions.	Cat. No. 13187U	Form **4972** (1991)

Sample A. $100,000 with five-year averaging

Form **4972**	**Tax on Lump-Sum Distributions** (Use This Form Only for Lump-Sum Distributions From Qualified Retirement Plans) ▶ **Attach to Form 1040 or Form 1041.** ▶ **See separate instructions.**	OMB No. 1545-0193 **1991** Attachment Sequence No. **28**
Department of the Treasury Internal Revenue Service		

Name of recipient of distribution	Identifying number

Part I Complete this part to see if you qualify to use Form 4972.

			Yes	No
1	Did you roll over any part of the distribution? If "Yes," do not complete the rest of this form.	1		X
2	Was the retirement plan participant born before 1936 (and, if deceased, was the participant at least 50 years old at the date of death)? If "No," do not complete the rest of this form	2	X	
3	Was this a lump-sum distribution from a qualified pension, profit-sharing, or stock bonus plan? (See **Distributions That Qualify for the 20% Capital Gain Election or for 5- or 10-Year Averaging** in the instructions.) . . . . If "No," do not complete the rest of this form.	3	X	
4	Was the participant in the plan for at least 5 years before the year of the distribution?	4	X	
5	Was this distribution paid to you as a beneficiary of a plan participant who died? . . . . If you answered "No" to 4 **and** 5, do not complete the rest of this form.	5		X
6	Was the plan participant:			
a	An employee who received the distribution because he or she quit, retired, was laid off or fired? . . .	6a	X	
b	Self-employed or an owner-employee who became permanently and totally disabled before the distribution?	6b		X
c	Age 59½ or older at the time of the distribution? . . . . If you answered "No" to question 5 and **all** parts of question 6, do not complete the rest of this form.	6c	X	
7	Did you use Form 4972 in a prior year for any distribution received after 1986 from a plan for the same plan participant, including you, for whom the 1991 distribution was made? If "Yes," do not complete the rest of this form . . .	7		X

If you qualify to use this form, you may choose to use Part II, Part III, or Part IV; **or** Part II and Part III; **or** Part II and Part IV.

Part II Complete this part to choose the 20% capital gain election. (See instructions.)

1	Capital gain part from Box 3 of Form 1099-R. (See instructions.)	1	
2	Multiply line 1 by 20% (.20) and enter here. If you do not elect to use Part III or Part IV, also enter the amount on Form 1040, line 39, or Form 1041, Schedule G, line 1b	2	

Part III Complete this part to choose the 5-year averaging method. (See instructions.)

1	Ordinary income from Form 1099-R, Box 2a minus Box 3. If you did not make the Schedule D election or complete Part II, enter the taxable amount from Box 2a of Form 1099-R. (See instructions.) . .	1	
2	Death benefit exclusion. (See instructions.)	2	
3	Total taxable amount—Subtract line 2 from line 1	3	
4	Current actuarial value of annuity, if applicable (from Form 1099-R, Box 8).	4	
5	Adjusted total taxable amount—Add lines 3 and 4. If this amount is $70,000 or more, skip lines 6 through 9, and enter this amount on line 10	5	
6	Multiply line 5 by 50% (.50), but **do not** enter more than $10,000. 6		
7	Subtract $20,000 from line 5. If line 5 is $20,000 or less, enter -0- 7		
8	Multiply line 7 by 20% (.20) 8		
9	Minimum distribution allowance—Subtract line 8 from line 6	9	
10	Subtract line 9 from line 5	10	
11	Federal estate tax attributable to lump-sum distribution. Do not deduct on Form 1040 or Form 1041 the amount attributable to the ordinary income entered on line 1. (See instructions.) . .	11	
12	Subtract line 11 from line 10	12	
13	Multiply line 12 by 20% (.20)	13	
14	Tax on amount on line 13. See instructions for Tax Rate Schedule	14	
15	Multiply line 14 by five (5). If no entry on line 4, skip lines 16 through 21. Enter the amount on line 22	15	
16	Divide line 4 by line 5 and enter the result as a decimal. (See instructions.)	16	
17	Multiply line 9 by the decimal amount on line 16	17	
18	Subtract line 17 from line 4	18	
19	Multiply line 18 by 20% (.20)	19	
20	Tax on amount on line 19. See instructions for Tax Rate Schedule	20	
21	Multiply line 20 by five (5)	21	
22	Subtract line 21 from line 15. (Multiple recipients, see instructions.)	22	
23	Tax on lump-sum distribution—Add Part II, line 2, and Part III, line 22. Enter on Form 1040, line 39, or Form 1041, Schedule G, line 1b. . . . . ▶	23	

For Paperwork Reduction Act Notice, see separate instructions.	Cat. No. 13187U	Form **4972** (1991)

Sample B. $100,000 with ten-year averaging

Form 4972 (1991)   Page **2**

Part IV   Complete this part to choose the 10-year averaging method. (See instructions.)

1	Ordinary income part from Form 1099-R, Box 2a minus Box 3. If you did not make the Schedule D election or complete Part II, enter the taxable amount from Box 2a of Form 1099-R. (See instructions.)	1	100,000 00
2	Death benefit exclusion. (See instructions.)	2	
3	Total taxable amount—Subtract line 2 from line 1	3	100,000 00
4	Current actuarial value of annuity, if applicable (from Form 1099-R, Box 8)	4	
5	Adjusted total taxable amount—Add lines 3 and 4. If this amount is $70,000 or more, skip lines 6 through 9, and enter this amount on line 10	5	100.000 00
6	Multiply line 5 by 50% (.50), but **do not** enter more than $10,000 ... 6		
7	Subtract $20,000 from line 5. If line 5 is $20,000 or less, enter -0- ... 7		
8	Multiply line 7 by 20% (.20) ... 8		
9	Minimum distribution allowance—Subtract line 8 from line 6	9	
10	Subtract line 9 from line 5	10	100,000 00
11	Federal estate tax attributable to lump-sum distribution. Do not deduct on Form 1040 or Form 1041 the amount attributable to the ordinary income entered on line 1. (See instructions.)	11	
12	Subtract line 11 from line 10	12	100,000 00
13	Multiply line 12 by 10% (.10)	13	10,000 00
14	Tax on amount on line 13. See instructions for Tax Rate Schedule	14	1,447 00
15	Multiply line 14 by ten (10). If no entry on line 4, skip lines 16 through 21. Enter this amount on line 22	15	14,470 00
16	Divide line 4 by line 5 and enter the result as a decimal. (See instructions.)	16	
17	Multiply line 9 by the decimal amount on line 16	17	
18	Subtract line 17 from line 4	18	
19	Multiply line 18 by 10% (.10)	19	
20	Tax on amount on line 19. See instructions for Tax Rate Schedule	20	
21	Multiply line 20 by ten (10)	21	
22	Subtract line 21 from line 15. (Multiple recipients, see instructions.)	22	14,470 00
23	Tax on lump-sum distribution—Add Part II, line 2, and Part IV, line 22. Enter on Form 1040, line 39, or Form 1041, Schedule G, line 1b ▶	23	14,470 00

★U.S.GPO:1991-0-285-350

Form **4972**	**Tax on Lump-Sum Distributions**		OMB No. 1545-0193		
Department of the Treasury Internal Revenue Service	(Use This Form Only for Lump-Sum Distributions From Qualified Retirement Plans) ▶ **Attach to Form 1040 or Form 1041.** ▶ **See separate instructions.**		**1991** Attachment Sequence No. **28**		

Name of recipient of distribution | Identifying number

Part I Complete this part to see if you qualify to use Form 4972.

			Yes	No
1	Did you roll over any part of the distribution? If "Yes," do not complete the rest of this form.	**1**		
2	Was the retirement plan participant born before 1936 (and, if deceased, was the participant at least 50 years old at the date of death)? If "No," do not complete the rest of this form	**2**		
3	Was this a lump-sum distribution from a qualified pension, profit-sharing, or stock bonus plan? (See **Distributions That Qualify for the 20% Capital Gain Election or for 5- or 10-Year Averaging** in the instructions.) If "No," do not complete the rest of this form.	**3**		
4	Was the participant in the plan for at least 5 years before the year of the distribution?	**4**		
5	Was this distribution paid to you as a beneficiary of a plan participant who died? If you answered "No" to 4 **and** 5, do not complete the rest of this form.	**5**		
6	Was the plan participant:			
a	An employee who received the distribution because he or she quit, retired, was laid off or fired?	**6a**		
b	Self-employed or an owner-employee who became permanently and totally disabled before the distribution?	**6b**		
c	Age 59½ or older at the time of the distribution? If you answered "No" to question 5 and **all** parts of question 6, do not complete the rest of this form.	**6c**		
7	Did you use Form 4972 in a prior year for any distribution received after 1986 from a plan for the same plan participant, including you, for whom the 1991 distribution was made? If "Yes," do not complete the rest of this form	**7**		

If you qualify to use this form, you may choose to use Part II, Part III, or Part IV; **or** Part II and Part III; **or** Part II and Part IV.

Part II Complete this part to choose the 20% capital gain election. (See instructions.)

1	Capital gain part from Box 3 of Form 1099-R. (See instructions.)	**1**	20,000	00
2	Multiply line 1 by 20% (.20) and enter here. If you do not elect to use Part III or Part IV, also enter the amount on Form 1040, line 39, or Form 1041, Schedule G, line 1b	**2**	4,000	00

Part III Complete this part to choose the 5-year averaging method. (See instructions.)

1	Ordinary income from Form 1099-R, Box 2a minus Box 3. If you did not make the Schedule D election or complete Part II, enter the taxable amount from Box 2a of Form 1099-R. (See instructions.)	**1**	
2	Death benefit exclusion. (See instructions.)	**2**	
3	Total taxable amount—Subtract line 2 from line 1	**3**	
4	Current actuarial value of annuity, if applicable (from Form 1099-R, Box 8)	**4**	
5	Adjusted total taxable amount—Add lines 3 and 4. If this amount is $70,000 or more, skip lines 6 through 9, and enter this amount on line 10	**5**	
6	Multiply line 5 by 50% (.50), but **do not** enter more than $10,000 **6**		
7	Subtract $20,000 from line 5. If line 5 is $20,000 or less, enter -0- **7**		
8	Multiply line 7 by 20% (.20) **8**		
9	Minimum distribution allowance—Subtract line 8 from line 6	**9**	
10	Subtract line 9 from line 5	**10**	
11	Federal estate tax attributable to lump-sum distribution. Do not deduct on Form 1040 or Form 1041 the amount attributable to the ordinary income entered on line 1. (See instructions.)	**11**	
12	Subtract line 11 from line 10	**12**	
13	Multiply line 12 by 20% (.20)	**13**	
14	Tax on amount on line 13. See instructions for Tax Rate Schedule	**14**	
15	Multiply line 14 by five (5). If no entry on line 4, skip lines 16 through 21. Enter the amount on line 22	**15**	
16	Divide line 4 by line 5 and enter the result as a decimal. (See instructions.)	**16**	
17	Multiply line 9 by the decimal amount on line 16	**17**	
18	Subtract line 17 from line 4	**18**	
19	Multiply line 18 by 20% (.20)	**19**	
20	Tax on amount on line 19. See instructions for Tax Rate Schedule	**20**	
21	Multiply line 20 by five (5)	**21**	
22	Subtract line 21 from line 15. (Multiple recipients, see instructions.)	**22**	
23	Tax on lump-sum distribution—Add Part II, line 2, and Part III, line 22. Enter on Form 1040, line 39, or Form 1041, Schedule G, line 1b. ▶	**23**	

For Paperwork Reduction Act Notice, see separate instructions.   Cat. No. 13187U   Form **4972** (1991)

Sample C. $100,000, of which $20,000 is capital gain, and $80,000 is five-year averaging

Form 4972 (1991)   Page **2**

Part IV   Complete this part to choose the **10-year averaging method.** (See instructions.)

#	Description		Amount	
1	Ordinary income part from Form 1099-R, Box 2a minus Box 3. If you did not make the Schedule D election or complete Part II, enter the taxable amount from Box 2a of Form 1099-R. (See instructions.)	**1**	80,000	00
2	Death benefit exclusion. (See instructions.)	**2**		
3	Total taxable amount—Subtract line 2 from line 1	**3**	80,000	00
4	Current actuarial value of annuity, if applicable (from Form 1099-R, Box 8)	**4**		
5	Adjusted total taxable amount—Add lines 3 and 4. If this amount is $70,000 or more, skip lines 6 through 9, and enter this amount on line 10	**5**	80,000	00
6	Multiply line 5 by 50% (.50), but **do not** enter more than $10,000 . . . **6**			
7	Subtract $20,000 from line 5. If line 5 is $20,000 or less, enter -0- **7**			
8	Multiply line 7 by 20% (.20) **8**			
9	Minimum distribution allowance—Subtract line 8 from line 6	**9**		
10	Subtract line 9 from line 5	**10**	80,000	00
11	Federal estate tax attributable to lump-sum distribution. Do not deduct on Form 1040 or Form 1041 the amount attributable to the ordinary income entered on line 1. (See instructions.) . . .	**11**		
12	Subtract line 11 from line 10	**12**	80,000	00
13	Multiply line 12 by 10% (.10)	**13**	8,000	00
14	Tax on amount on line 13. See instructions for Tax Rate Schedule	**14**	1,111	00
15	Multiply line 14 by ten (10). If no entry on line 4, skip lines 16 through 21. Enter this amount on line 22	**15**	11,110	00
16	Divide line 4 by line 5 and enter the result as a decimal. (See instructions.)	**16**		
17	Multiply line 9 by the decimal amount on line 16	**17**		
18	Subtract line 17 from line 4	**18**		
19	Multiply line 18 by 10% (.10)	**19**		
20	Tax on amount on line 19. See instructions for Tax Rate Schedule	**20**		
21	Multiply line 20 by ten (10)	**21**		
22	Subtract line 21 from line 15. (Multiple recipients, see instructions.)	**22**	11,110	00
23	Tax on lump-sum distribution—Add Part II, line 2, and Part IV, line 22. Enter on Form 1040, line 39, or Form 1041, Schedule G, line 1b . . . . ▶	**23**	15,110	00

★U.S.GPO:1991-0-285-350

✦ APPENDIX 21 ✦

The Credit for Elderly or Disabled

You will use Schedule R to figure your CED benefit, so we've reproduced Schedule R in Appendix 21. (If you file IRS Form 1040A, use Schedule 3 instead of Schedule R.) Don't get scared off by the form—it's really not as bad as it looks.

Start with Part I. Check the *one* box that fits your situation. The Single category includes Head of Household and Qualifying Widow(er), which we've defined on pages 347–348.

If you are claiming the CED based only on age, not disability (so you would have checked box 1, 3, 7, or 8 in Part I), then you don't have to worry about Part II—skip it and go on to Part III. If you or your spouse has a disability, then fill out Part II. We told you about the Physician's Statement on page 368.

If you don't want to do any more, you don't have to. Just attach Schedule R to your tax return and write CED on the dotted line next to Line 42 of your Form 1040—the IRS then will figure your credit.

Unfortunately, the IRS has been known to make a mistake or two. Try to fill out Part III of Schedule R yourself, using our easy-to-follow instructions below; it's really not too tough. You're better off not to rely on the Government.

On line 10, just write in the amount—$5,000, $7,500, or $3,750—that corresponds to the number you checked in Part I.

If you checked box 1, 3, 7, or 8 in Part I, you can skip line 11 and write in the number from line 10 on line 12.

If you checked box 2, 4, 5, 6, or 9 in Part I (because you or your spouse has a disability), then you must also fill in line 11. Here's how to figure the amount to write in on line 11:

- If you checked box 2, 4, or 9 in Part I, write in the amount of your taxable disability income for the year (this is the amount you reported on your IRS Form 1040).

- If you checked box 5 in Part I, write in the amount of your and your spouse's combined taxable disability income.
- If you checked box 6 in Part I, write in the amount of the taxable disability income of the spouse who is under 65, plus $5,000.

After you have put the right number on line 11, compare the amounts on lines 10 and 11—pick the smaller amount and write it on line 12.

So far, so good (we hope!). Now for line 13a, write in the amount of *nontaxable* Social Security benefits (retirement, survivor, or disability) you (and your spouse, if you file a joint return) received. We discussed how to figure the tax on Social Security benefits in Chapter 1. Include the gross amount of benefits, *before* subtracting the amounts withheld to pay premiums on supplementary Medicare insurance and before any reduction for Worker's Compensation benefits.

On line 13b, write in the amount of any nontaxable veterans' pensions and any other pension, annuity, or disability benefits. Ignore any service-connected disability compensation, life insurance proceeds, proceeds from accident or health insurance, and the portion of any pension which is just the return of your investment.

Add the amounts on lines 13a and 13b, and write the total on line 13c.

On line 14, write in the amount of your adjusted gross income. You can get that amount from line 32 of your Form 1040.

Line 15 is easy; just put in the amount that corresponds to the box number you checked in Part I. The amount will be either $7,500, $10,000, or $5,000.

Subtract the amount on line 15 from the amount on line 14, and put the result on line 16.

Divide the amount on line 16 in half, and put that amount on line 17. Don't sweat, you're almost done!

Add the numbers from lines 13c and 17—the total goes on line 18.

Subtract line 18 from line 12. If you get a number, put it on line 19. If the answer is zero or below, take the Schedule R, roll it into a ball, and toss it in the can—you can't get any CED benefit. Chalk the time up to an exercise in mathematical gymnastics.

Line 20 is already done for you. See—Uncle Sam can be a real sport.

Now get out your calculator and multiply lines 19 and 20; put the result on line 21. Take a good look at the number—that's your tax credit. The amount is *money in your pocket!*

Note: In rare cases, the CED tax break may be limited if both:

- You file Schedule C, D, E, or F (to Form 1040).

- The amount on line 23 of your Form 1040 is more than $30,000 if you are single or head of household; $30,000 if married filing jointly or qualifying widow(er); or $20,000 if married filing separately.

Most people don't have to worry about this limit. If you think you do, get IRS Publication 554, "Tax Information for Older Americans," available free from your local IRS office, for more information.

The Schedule R form we have reprinted is filled out to help you follow the instructions.

Schedule R
(Form 1040)

Department of the Treasury
Internal Revenue Service

Credit for the Elderly or the Disabled

▶ Attach to Form 1040.   ▶ See separate instructions for Schedule R.

OMB No. 1545-0074

1991

Attachment
Sequence No. **16**

Name(s) shown on Form 1040

William M. and Helen A. White

Your social security number

222 00 2222

You may be able to use Schedule R to reduce your tax if by the end of 1991:

- You were age 65 or older, **OR** ● You were under age 65, you retired on **permanent and total** disability, and you received taxable disability income.

But you must also meet other tests. See the separate instructions for Schedule R.
Note: *In most cases, the IRS can figure the credit for you. See page 24 of the Form 1040 instructions.*

Part I   Check the Box for Your Filing Status and Age

If your filing status is:	And by the end of 1991:	Check only one box:
Single, Head of household, or Qualifying widow(er) with dependent child	1 You were 65 or older	1 ☐
	2 You were under 65 and you retired on permanent and total disability . . .	2 ☐
Married filing a joint return	3 Both spouses were 65 or older	3 ☐
	4 Both spouses were under 65, but only one spouse retired on permanent and total disability	4 ☐
	5 Both spouses were under 65, and both retired on permanent and total disability	5 ☒
	6 One spouse was 65 or older, and the other spouse was under 65 and retired on permanent and total disability	6 ☐
	7 One spouse was 65 or older, and the other spouse was under 65 and **NOT** retired on permanent and total disability	7 ☐
Married filing a separate return	8 You were 65 or older and you did not live with your spouse at any time in 1991	8 ☐
	9 You were under 65, you retired on permanent and total disability, and you did not live with your spouse at any time in 1991	9 ☐

If you checked Box 1, 3, 7, or 8, skip Part II and complete Part III on the back. All others, complete Parts II and III.

Part II   Statement of Permanent and Total Disability (Complete **only** if you checked Box 2, 4, 5, 6, or 9 above.)

IF: 1 You filed a physician's statement for this disability for 1983 or an earlier year, or you filed a statement for tax years after 1983 and your physician signed line B on the statement, **AND** William

  2 Due to your continued disabled condition, you were unable to engage in any substantial gainful activity in 1991, check this box . . . . ▶ ☒

- If you checked this box, you do not have to file another statement for 1991.
- If you did **not** check this box, have your physician complete the following statement.

Physician's Statement (See instructions at bottom of page 2.)

I certify that   Helen A. White

Name of disabled person

was permanently and totally disabled on January 1, 1976, or January 1, 1977, **OR** was permanently and totally disabled on the date he or she retired. If retired after December 31, 1976, enter the date retired. ▶ *November 2, 1991*

Physician: Sign your name on **either** line A or B below.

A The disability has lasted, or can be expected to last, continuously for at least a year . . . . .

B There is no reasonable probability that the disabled condition will ever improve . . . .

Physician's signature   *John A. Doctor*   Date 2/7/92

Physician's name   *John A. Doctor*

Physician's address   101 Green St, Hometown, Md 2000

For Paperwork Reduction Act Notice, see Form 1040 instructions.   Cat. No. 11359K   Schedule R (Form 1040) 1991

Schedule R (Form 1040) 1991

Page **2**

Part III Figure Your Credit

10	If you checked (in Part I): **Enter:** Box 1, 2, 4, or 7 . . . . $5,000 Box 3, 5, or 6 . . . . $7,500 Box 8 or 9 . . . . $3,750	**10**	7,500	00

Caution: *If you checked Box 2, 4, 5, 6, or 9 in Part I, you* **MUST** *complete line 11 below. Otherwise, skip line 11 and enter the amount from line 10 on line 12.*

11	If you checked Box 6 in Part I, enter on line 11 the taxable disability income of the spouse who was under age 65 **PLUS** $5,000. Otherwise, enter on line 11 your taxable disability income (and also your spouse's if you checked Box 5 in Part I) that you reported on Form 1040. (For more details on what to include, see the instructions.)	**11**	7,000	00
12	If you completed line 11 above, compare lines 10 and 11, and enter the **smaller** of the two amounts here. Otherwise, enter the amount from line 10	**12**	7,000	00
13	Enter the following pensions, annuities, or disability income that you (and your spouse if you file a joint return) received in 1991 (see instructions):			

a	Nontaxable part of social security benefits, and Nontaxable part of railroad retirement benefits treated as social security.	**13a**	3,000	00
b	Nontaxable veterans' pensions, and Any other pension, annuity, or disability benefit that is excluded from income under any other provision of law.	**13b**		
c	Add lines 13a and 13b. (Even though these income items are not taxable, they **must** be included here to figure your credit.) If you did not receive any of the types of nontaxable income listed on line 13a or 13b, enter -0- on line 13c	**13c**	3,000	00

14	Enter the amount from Form 1040, line 32	**14**	16,200	00
15	If you checked (in Part I): **Enter:** Box 1 or 2 . . . . . . $7,500 Box 3, 4, 5, 6, or 7 . . . $10,000 Box 8 or 9 . . . . . . $5,000	**15**	10,000	00
16	Subtract line 15 from line 14. If line 15 is more than line 14, enter -0-	**16**	6,200	00
17	Divide line 16 above by 2	**17**	3,100	00

18	Add lines 13c and 17	**18**	6,100	00
19	Subtract line 18 from line 12. If the result is zero or less, stop here; you **cannot** take the credit. Otherwise, go to line 21	**19**	900	00
20	Decimal amount used to figure the credit	**20**	×.15	
21	Multiply line 19 above by the decimal amount (.15) on line 20. Enter the result here and on Form 1040, line 42. **Caution:** If you file Schedule C, D, E, or F (Form 1040), your credit may be limited. *See the instructions for line 21 for the amount of credit you can claim*	**21**	135	00

Instructions for Physician's Statement

Taxpayer

If you retired after December 31, 1976, enter the date you retired in the space provided in Part II.

Physician

A person is permanently and totally disabled if **both** of the following apply:

1. He or she cannot engage in any substantial gainful activity because of a physical or mental condition, and

2. A physician determines that the disability has lasted, or can be expected to last, continuously for at least a year, or can lead to death.

✦ APPENDIX 22 ✦

Earned Income Credit Table

TABLE A—Basic Credit

1991 Earned Income Credit

Caution: This is **not** a tax table.

To find your basic credit: First, read down the "At least — But less than" columns and find the line that includes the amount you entered on line 7 or line 9 of Schedule EIC. Next, read across to the column that includes the number of qualifying children you listed on Schedule EIC. Then, enter the credit from that column on Schedule EIC, line 8 or line 10, whichever applies.

If the amount on Schedule EIC, line 7 or line 9, is— At least	But less than	And you listed— One child	Two children
$1	$50	$4	$4
50	100	13	13
100	150	21	22
150	200	29	30
200	250	38	39
250	300	46	48
300	350	54	56
350	400	63	65
400	450	71	74
450	500	79	82
500	550	88	91
550	600	96	99
600	650	104	108
650	700	113	117
700	750	121	125
750	800	129	134
800	850	138	143
850	900	146	151
900	950	154	160
950	1,000	163	169
1,000	1,050	171	177
1,050	1,100	180	186
1,100	1,150	188	195
1,150	1,200	196	203
1,200	1,250	205	212
1,250	1,300	213	221
1,300	1,350	221	229
1,350	1,400	230	238
1,400	1,450	238	247
1,450	1,500	246	255
1,500	1,550	255	264
1,550	1,600	263	272
1,600	1,650	271	281
1,650	1,700	280	290
1,700	1,750	288	298
1,750	1,800	296	307
1,800	1,850	305	316
1,850	1,900	313	324
1,900	1,950	321	333
1,950	2,000	330	342
2,000	2,050	338	350
2,050	2,100	347	359
2,100	2,150	355	368
2,150	2,200	363	376
2,200	2,250	372	385
2,250	2,300	380	394
2,300	2,350	388	402
2,350	2,400	397	411
2,400	2,450	405	420
2,450	2,500	413	428
2,500	2,550	422	437
2,550	2,600	430	445
2,600	2,650	438	454
2,650	2,700	447	463
2,700	2,750	455	471
2,750	2,800	463	480

If the amount on Schedule EIC, line 7 or line 9, is— At least	But less than	And you listed— One child	Two children
$2,800	$2,850	$472	$489
2,850	2,900	480	497
2,900	2,950	488	506
2,950	3,000	497	515
3,000	3,050	505	523
3,050	3,100	514	532
3,100	3,150	522	541
3,150	3,200	530	549
3,200	3,250	539	558
3,250	3,300	547	567
3,300	3,350	555	575
3,350	3,400	564	584
3,400	3,450	572	593
3,450	3,500	580	601
3,500	3,550	589	610
3,550	3,600	597	618
3,600	3,650	605	627
3,650	3,700	614	636
3,700	3,750	622	644
3,750	3,800	630	653
3,800	3,850	639	662
3,850	3,900	647	670
3,900	3,950	655	679
3,950	4,000	664	688
4,000	4,050	672	696
4,050	4,100	681	705
4,100	4,150	689	714
4,150	4,200	697	722
4,200	4,250	706	731
4,250	4,300	714	740
4,300	4,350	722	748
4,350	4,400	731	757
4,400	4,450	739	766
4,450	4,500	747	774
4,500	4,550	756	783
4,550	4,600	764	791
4,600	4,650	772	800
4,650	4,700	781	809
4,700	4,750	789	817
4,750	4,800	797	826
4,800	4,850	806	835
4,850	4,900	814	843
4,900	4,950	822	852
4,950	5,000	831	861
5,000	5,050	839	869
5,050	5,100	848	878
5,100	5,150	856	887
5,150	5,200	864	895
5,200	5,250	873	904
5,250	5,300	881	913
5,300	5,350	889	921
5,350	5,400	898	930
5,400	5,450	906	939
5,450	5,500	914	947
5,500	5,550	923	956
5,550	5,600	931	964

If the amount on Schedule EIC, line 7 or line 9, is— At least	But less than	And you listed— One child	Two children
$5,600	$5,650	$939	$973
5,650	5,700	948	982
5,700	5,750	956	990
5,750	5,800	964	999
5,800	5,850	973	1,008
5,850	5,900	981	1,016
5,900	5,950	989	1,025
5,950	6,000	998	1,034
6,000	6,050	1,006	1,042
6,050	6,100	1,015	1,051
6,100	6,150	1,023	1,060
6,150	6,200	1,031	1,068
6,200	6,250	1,040	1,077
6,250	6,300	1,048	1,086
6,300	6,350	1,056	1,094
6,350	6,400	1,065	1,103
6,400	6,450	1,073	1,112
6,450	6,500	1,081	1,120
6,500	6,550	1,090	1,129
6,550	6,600	1,098	1,137
6,600	6,650	1,106	1,146
6,650	6,700	1,115	1,155
6,700	6,750	1,123	1,163
6,750	6,800	1,131	1,172
6,800	6,850	1,140	1,181
6,850	6,900	1,148	1,189
6,900	6,950	1,156	1,198
6,950	7,000	1,165	1,207
7,000	7,050	1,173	1,215
7,050	7,100	1,182	1,224
7,100	11,250	1,192	1,235
11,250	11,300	1,189	1,232
11,300	11,350	1,183	1,226
11,350	11,400	1,177	1,220
11,400	11,450	1,172	1,214
11,450	11,500	1,166	1,207
11,500	11,550	1,160	1,201
11,550	11,600	1,154	1,195
11,600	11,650	1,148	1,189
11,650	11,700	1,142	1,183
11,700	11,750	1,136	1,177
11,750	11,800	1,130	1,170
11,800	11,850	1,124	1,164
11,850	11,900	1,118	1,158
11,900	11,950	1,112	1,152
11,950	12,000	1,106	1,146
12,000	12,050	1,100	1,139
12,050	12,100	1,094	1,133
12,100	12,150	1,088	1,127
12,150	12,200	1,082	1,121
12,200	12,250	1,076	1,115
12,250	12,300	1,070	1,109
12,300	12,350	1,064	1,102
12,350	12,400	1,058	1,096
12,400	12,450	1,052	1,090
12,450	12,500	1,046	1,084

If the amount on Schedule EIC, line 7 or line 9, is— At least	But less than	And you listed— One child	Two children
$12,500	$12,550	$1,040	$1,078
12,550	12,600	1,034	1,071
12,600	12,650	1,028	1,065
12,650	12,700	1,022	1,059
12,700	12,750	1,016	1,053
12,750	12,800	1,010	1,047
12,800	12,850	1,004	1,041
12,850	12,900	999	1,034
12,900	12,950	993	1,028
12,950	13,000	987	1,022
13,000	13,050	981	1,016
13,050	13,100	975	1,010
13,100	13,150	969	1,003
13,150	13,200	963	997
13,200	13,250	957	991
13,250	13,300	951	985
13,300	13,350	945	979
13,350	13,400	939	973
13,400	13,450	933	966
13,450	13,500	927	960
13,500	13,550	921	954
13,550	13,600	915	948
13,600	13,650	909	942
13,650	13,700	903	935
13,700	13,750	897	929
13,750	13,800	891	923
13,800	13,850	885	917
13,850	13,900	879	911
13,900	13,950	873	905
13,950	14,000	867	898
14,000	14,050	861	892
14,050	14,100	855	886
14,100	14,150	849	880
14,150	14,200	843	874
14,200	14,250	837	868
14,250	14,300	831	861
14,300	14,350	826	855
14,350	14,400	820	849
14,400	14,450	814	843
14,450	14,500	808	837
14,500	14,550	802	830
14,550	14,600	796	824
14,600	14,650	790	818
14,650	14,700	784	812
14,700	14,750	778	806
14,750	14,800	772	800
14,800	14,850	766	793
14,850	14,900	760	787
14,900	14,950	754	781
14,950	15,000	748	775
15,000	15,050	742	769
15,050	15,100	736	762
15,100	15,150	730	756
15,150	15,200	724	750
15,200	15,250	718	744
15,250	15,300	712	738

1991 Earned Income Credit TABLE A—Basic Credit *Continued*

If the amount on Schedule EIC, line 7 or line 9, is—		And you listed—		If the amount on Schedule EIC, line 7 or line 9, is—		And you listed—	
		One child	Two children			One child	Two children
At least	But less than	Your basic credit is—		At least	But less than	Your basic credit is—	
$15,300	$15,350	$706	$732	$18,500	$18,550	$324	$336
15,350	15,400	700	725	18,550	18,600	319	330
15,400	15,450	694	719	18,600	18,650	313	324
15,450	15,500	688	713	18,650	18,700	307	317
15,500	15,550	682	707	18,700	18,750	301	311
15,550	15,600	676	701	18,750	18,800	295	305
15,600	15,650	670	694	18,800	18,850	289	299
15,650	15,700	664	688	18,850	18,900	283	293
15,700	15,750	659	682	18,900	18,950	277	287
15,750	15,800	653	676	18,950	19,000	271	280
15,800	15,850	647	670	19,000	19,050	265	274
15,850	15,900	641	664	19,050	19,100	259	268
15,900	15,950	635	657	19,100	19,150	253	262
15,950	16,000	629	651	19,150	19,200	247	256
16,000	16,050	623	645	19,200	19,250	241	250
16,050	16,100	617	639	19,250	19,300	235	243
16,100	16,150	611	633	19,300	19,350	229	237
16,150	16,200	605	626	19,350	19,400	223	231
16,200	16,250	599	620	19,400	19,450	217	225
16,250	16,300	593	614	19,450	19,500	211	219
16,300	16,350	587	608	19,500	19,550	205	212
16,350	16,400	581	602	19,550	19,600	199	206
16,400	16,450	575	596	19,600	19,650	193	200
16,450	16,500	569	589	19,650	19,700	187	194
16,500	16,550	563	583	19,700	19,750	181	188
16,550	16,600	557	577	19,750	19,800	175	182
16,600	16,650	551	571	19,800	19,850	169	175
16,650	16,700	545	565	19,850	19,900	163	169
16,700	16,750	539	559	19,900	19,950	157	163
16,750	16,800	533	552	19,950	20,000	151	157
16,800	16,850	527	546	20,000	20,050	146	151
16,850	16,900	521	540	20,050	20,100	140	144
16,900	16,950	515	534	20,100	20,150	134	138
16,950	17,000	509	528	20,150	20,200	128	132
17,000	17,050	503	521	20,200	20,250	122	126
17,050	17,100	497	515	20,250	20,300	116	120
17,100	17,150	491	509	20,300	20,350	110	114
17,150	17,200	486	503	20,350	20,400	104	107
17,200	17,250	480	497	20,400	20,450	98	101
17,250	17,300	474	491	20,450	20,500	92	95
17,300	17,350	468	484	20,500	20,550	86	89
17,350	17,400	462	478	20,550	20,600	80	83
17,400	17,450	456	472	20,600	20,650	74	76
17,450	17,500	450	466	20,650	20,700	68	70
17,500	17,550	444	460	20,700	20,750	62	64
17,550	17,600	438	453	20,750	20,800	56	58
17,600	17,650	432	447	20,800	20,850	50	52
17,650	17,700	426	441	20,850	20,900	44	46
17,700	17,750	420	435	20,900	20,950	38	39
17,750	17,800	414	429	20,950	21,000	32	33
17,800	17,850	408	423	21,000	21,050	26	27
17,850	17,900	402	416	21,050	21,100	20	21
17,900	17,950	396	410	21,100	21,150	14	15
17,950	18,000	390	404	21,150	21,200	8	8
18,000	18,050	384	398	21,200	21,250	2	2
18,050	18,100	378	392				
18,100	18,150	372	385	**$21,250 or more**—you may not take the credit			
18,150	18,200	366	379				
18,200	18,250	360	373				
18,250	18,300	354	367				
18,300	18,350	348	361				
18,350	18,400	342	355				
18,400	18,450	336	348				
18,450	18,500	330	342				

✦ APPENDIX 23 ✦

Application for Hospital Insurance

DEPARTMENT OF HEALTH AND HUMAN SERVICES
HEALTH CARE FINANCING ADMINISTRATION

Form Approved
OMB No. 0938-0251

(Do Not Write in this space)

APPLICATION FOR HOSPITAL INSURANCE

(This application form may also be used to
enroll in Supplementary Medical Insurance)

I apply for entitlement to Medicare's hospital insurance under part A of title XVIII of the Social Security Act, as presently amended, and for any cash benefits to which I may be entitled under title II of that Act.

1.	(a) Print your name⟶	(First name, middle initial, last name)
	(b) Enter your name at birth if different from 1 (a) ⟶	
	(c) Enter your sex (check one) ⟶	☐ Male ☐ Female
2.	Enter your Social Security Number ⟶	_ _ _ / _ _ / _ _ _ _
3.	(a) Enter your date of birth (Month, day, year) ⟶	
	(b) Enter name of State or foreign country where you were born⟶	
	If you have already submitted a public or religious record of your birth made before you were age 5, go on to item 4)	
	(c) Was a public record of your birth made before you were age 5?	☐ Yes ☐ No ☐ Unknown
	(d) Was a religious record of your birth made before you were age 5?	☐ Yes ☐ No ☐ Unknown
4.	(a) Have you (or has someone on your behalf) ever filed an application for social security benefits, a period of disability under social security, supplemental security income, or hospital or medical insurance under Medicare? ⟶	☐ Yes ☐ No *If "Yes" answer (b) and (c).)* *(If "No," go on to item 5.)*
	(b) Enter name of person on whose social security record you filed other application ⟶	
	(c) Enter Social Security Number of person named in (b), *(If unknown, so indicate)* ⟶	_ _ _ / _ _ / _ _ _ _
5.	(a) Were you in the active military or naval service (including Reserve or National Guard *active* duty or active duty for training) after September 7, 1939? ⟶	☐ Yes ☐ No *If "Yes" answer (b) and (c).)* *(If "No," go on to item 6.)*
	(b) Enter dates of service ⟶	From: (Month, year) To: (Month, year)
	(c) Have you *ever* been (or will you be) eligible for a monthly benefit from a military or civilian Federal agency? (Include Veterans Administration benefits *only* if you waived military retirement pay) ⟶	☐ Yes ☐ No
6.	Did you work in the railroad industry any time on or after January 1, 1937? ⟶	☐ Yes ☐ No

Form HCFA-18 F5 (10-84) Page 1

| 7. | (a) Have you ever engaged in work that was covered under the social security system of a country other than the United States? ➡ | ☐ Yes ☐ No |
| | (b) If "Yes," list the country(ies). ➡ | |

| 8. | (a) How much were your total earnings last year ➡
 (If none, write "None") | Earnings
 $ |
| | (b) How much do you expect your total earnings to be this year? ➡
 (If none, write "None") | Earnings
 $ |

| 9. | Are you a resident of the United States? ➡
 (To reside in a place means to make a home there.) | ☐ Yes ☐ No |

| 10. | (a) Are you a citizen of the United States? ➡
 (If "Yes," go on to item 11.) (if "No" answer (b) and (c) below.) | ☐ Yes ☐ No |
| | (b) Are you lawfully admitted for permanent residence in the United States? ➡ | ☐ Yes ☐ No |

(c) Enter below the information requested about your place of residence in the last 5 years:

ADDRESS AT WHICH YOU RESIDED IN THE LAST 5 YEARS (Begin with the most recent address. Show actual date residence began even if that is prior to the last 5 years)	DATE RESIDENCE BEGAN			DATE RESIDENCE ENDED		
	Month	Day	Year	Month	Day	Year

(If you need more space, use the "Remarks" space on the third page or another sheet of paper)

11. YOUR CURRENT MARRIAGE	Are you currently married? ➡	☐ Yes ☐ No
	(If "Yes," give the following information about your current marriage.) (If "No" go on to item 12.)	
	To whom married (Enter your wife's maiden name or your husband's name)	When (Month, day, year)
	Spouse's date of birth (or age)	Spouse's Social Security Number *(If none or unknown, so indicate)* __ __ __ / __ __ / __ __ __ __

12. YOUR PREVIOUS MARRIAGE	If you had a previous marriage and your spouse died, OR if you had a previous marriage which lasted 10 or more years, give the following information. *(If you had no previous marriage (s), enter "NONE.")*	
	To whom married *(Enter your wife's maiden name or your husband's name).*	When (Month, day, year)
	Spouse's date of birth (or age)	Spouse's Social Security Number *(If none of unknown, so indicate)* __ __ __ / __ __ / __ __ __ __
	If spouse deceased, give date of death ➡	

(Use "Remarks" space on page 3 for information about any other marriages.)

Form HCFA-18 F5 (10-84) Page 2

13.	Is or was your spouse a railroad worker, railroad retirement pensioner, or a railroad retirement annuitant? ⟶	☐ Yes	☐ No
14.	(a) Were you or your spouse a civilian employee of the Federal Government after June 1960? ⟶ (If "Yes," answer (b).) (If "No," omit (b), (c), and (d).)	☐ Yes	☐ No
	(b) Are you or your spouse now covered under a medical insurance plan provided by the Federal Employees Health Benefits Act of 1959? (If "Yes," omit (c) and (d).) (If "No," answer (c).)	☐ Yes	☐ No
	(c) Are you **and** your spouse barred from coverage under the above Act because your Federal employment, or your spouse's was not long enough? ⟶ If "Yes," omit (d) and explain in "Remarks" below.) (If "No," answer (d).)	☐ Yes	☐ No
	(d) Were either you or your spouse an employee of the Federal Government after February 15, 1965? ⟶	☐ Yes	☐ No

Remarks:

_____

_____

_____

_____

_____

_____

_____

| 15. | If you are found to be otherwise ineligible for hospital insurance under Medicare, do you wish to enroll for hospital insurance on a monthly premium basis (in addition to the monthly premium for supplementary medical insurance)? ⟶ (If "Yes," you MUST also sign up for medical insurance.) | ☐ Yes | ☐ No |

INFORMATION ON MEDICAL INSURANCE UNDER MEDICARE

Medical insurance under Medicare helps pay your doctor bills. It also helps pay for a number of other medical items and services not covered under the hospital insurance part of Medicare.

If you sign up for medical insurance, you must pay a premium for each month you have this protection. If you get monthly social security, railroad retirement, or civil service benefits, your premium will be deducted from your benefit check, if you get none of these benefits, you will be notified how to pay your premium.

The Federal Government contributes to the cost of your insurance. The amount of your premium and the Government's payment are based on the cost of services covered by medical insurance. The Government also makes additional payments when necessary to meet the full cost of the program. (Currently, the Government pays about two-thirds of the cost of this program.) You will get advance notice if there is any change in your premium amount.

If you have questions or would like a leaflet on medical insurance, call any Social Security office.

SEE OTHER SIDE TO SIGN UP FOR MEDICAL INSURANCE

If you become entitled to hospital insurance as a result of this application, you will be enrolled for medical insurance automatically unless you indicate below that you do not want this protection. If you decline to enroll now, you can get medical insurance protection later only if you sign up for it during specified enrollment periods. Your protection may then be delayed and you may have to pay a higher premium when you decide to sign up.

The date your medical insurance begins and the amount of the premium you must pay depend on the month you file this application with the Social Security Administration. Any social security office will be glad to explain the rules regarding enrollment to you.

16.	**DO YOU WISH TO ENROLL FOR SUPPLEMENTARY MEDICAL INSURANCE?** ⟶	☐ Yes ☐ No
	(If "Yes," answer question 17.)	
	(Enrollees for premium hospital insurance must simultaneously enroll for medical insurance.)	☐ Currently Enrolled
17.	Are you or your spouse receiving an annuity under the Federal Civil Service Retirement Act or other law administered by the Office of Personnel Management? ⟶	☐ Yes ☐ No
	(If "Yes," enter Civil Service annuity number here. Include the prefix "CSA" for annuitant, "CSF" for survivor.)	Your No. ⎯⎯⎯ Spouse's No.
	If you entered your spouse's number, is he (she) enrolled for supplementary medical insurance under social security? ⟶	☐ Yes ☐ No

I know that anyone who makes or causes to be made a false statement or representation of material fact in an application or for use in determining a right to payment under the Social Security Act commits a crime punishable under Federal law by fine, imprisonment or both. I affirm that all information I have given in this document is true.

SIGNATURE OF APPLICANT	Date *(Month, day, year)*
Signature *(First name, middle initial, last name) (Write in Ink)* **SIGN HERE** ▶	Telephone Number(s) at which you may be contacted during the day

Mailing address *(Number and street, Apt. No., P.O. Box, or Rural Route)*

City and State	ZIP Code	Enter Name of County (If any) in which you now live

Witnesses are required ONLY if this application has been signed by mark (X) above. If signed by mark (X), two witnesses to the signing who know the applicant must sign below, giving their full addresses.

1. Signature of Witness	2. Signature of Witness
Address *(Number and street, City, State, and ZIP Code)*	Address *(Number and street, City, State, and ZIP Code)*

Form HCFA-18 F5 (10-84) Page 4

A REMINDER TO APPLICANTS FOR THE SOCIAL SECURITY HOSPITAL INSURANCE

NAME OF PERSON TO CONTACT ABOUT YOUR CLAIM	SSA OFFICE	DATE
TELEPHONE NO.		

RECEIPT FOR YOUR CLAIM

Your application for the hospital insurance has been received and will be processed as quickly as possible.

You should hear from us within _____ days after you have given us all the information we requested. Some claims may take longer if additional information is needed.

In the meantime, if you change your mailing address, you should report the change.

Always give us your claim number when writing or telephoning about your claim.

If you have any questions about your claim, we will be glad to help you.

CLAIMANT	SOCIAL SECURITY CLAIM NUMBER

COLLECTION AND USE OF INFORMATION FROM YOUR APPLICATION — PRIVACY ACT NOTICE

PRIVACY ACT NOTICE: The Social Security Administration (SSA) is authorized to collect the information on this form under sections 226 and 1818 of the Social Security Act, as amended (42 U.S.C. 426 and 1395-17) and section 103 of Public Law 89-97. The information on this form is needed to enable social security and the Health Care Financing Administration (HCFA) to determine if you and your dependents may be entitled to hospital and/or medical insurance coverage and/or monthly benefits. While you do not have to furnish the information requested on this form to social security, no benefits or hospital or medical insurance can be provided until an application has been received by a social security office. Failure to provide all or part of the information requested could prevent an accurate and timely decision on your claim or your dependent's claim, and could result in the loss of some benefits of hospital or medical insurance. Although the information you furnish on this form is almost never used for any other purpose than stated above, there is a possibility that for the administration of social security or HCFA programs or for the administration of programs requiring coordination with SSA or HCFA, information may be disclosed to another person or to another governmental agency as follows: 1) to enable a third party or an agency to assist social security or HCFA in establishing rights to social security benefits and/or hospital or medical insurance coverage; 2) to comply with Federal laws requiring the release of information from social security and HCFA records (e.g., to the General Accounting Office and the Veterans Administration); and 3) to facilitate statistical research and audit activities necessary to assure the integrity and improvement of the social security and HCFA programs (e.g., to the Bureau of the Census and private concerns under contract to social security and HCFA).

Form HCFA-18 F5 (10-84) Page 5

Index